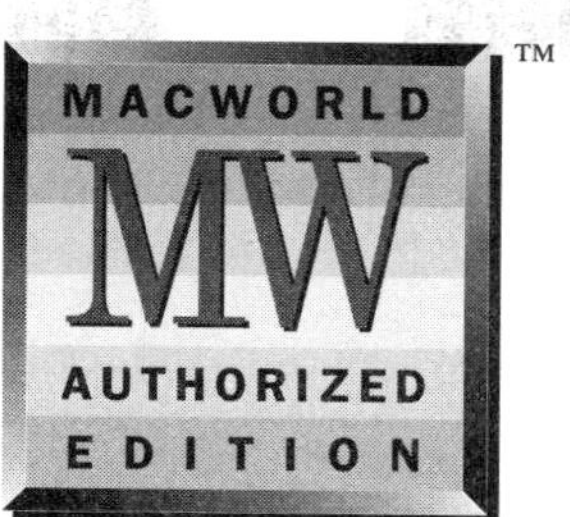


# Macworld Mac OS 7.6 Bible

# Macworld Mac OS 7.6 Bible

**Lon Poole**

*Macworld*
"Quick Tips" columnist

IDG Books Worldwide, Inc.
An International Data Group Company

Foster City, CA ✦ Chicago, IL ✦ Indianapolis, IN ✦ Southlake, TX

**Macworld® Mac OS 7.6 Bible**

Published by
**IDG Books Worldwide, Inc.**
An International Data Group Company
919 E. Hillsdale Blvd.
Suite 400
Foster City, CA 94404
`http://www.idgbooks.com` (IDG Books Worldwide Web Site)



Library of Congress Catalog Card No.: 96-79768

ISBN: 0-7645-4014-9

Printed in the United States of America

10 9 8 7 6 5 4 3 2 1

4B/QV/QS/ZX/FC

Distributed in the United States by IDG Books Worldwide, Inc.

Distributed by Macmillan Canada for Canada; by Contemporanea de Ediciones for Venezuela; by Distribuidora Cuspide for Argentina; by CITEC for Brazil; by Ediciones ZETA S.C.R. Ltda. for Peru; by Editorial Limusa SA for Mexico; by Transworld Publishers Limited in the United Kingdom and Europe; by Academic Bookshop for Egypt; by Levant Distributors S.A.R.L. for Lebanon; by Al Jassim for Saudi Arabia; by Simron Pty. Ltd. for South Africa; by Pustak Mahal for India; by The Computer Bookshop for India; by Toppan Company Ltd. for Japan; by Addison Wesley Publishing Company for Korea; by Longman Singapore Publishers Ltd. for Singapore, Malaysia, Thailand, and Indonesia; by Unalis Corporation for Taiwan; by WS Computer Publishing Company, Inc. for the Philippines; by WoodsLane Pty. Ltd. for Australia; by WoodsLane Enterprises Ltd. for New Zealand. Authorized Sales Agent: Anthony Rudkin Associates for the Middle East and North Africa.

For general information on IDG Books Worldwide's books in the U.S., please call our Consumer Customer Service department at 800-762-2974. For reseller information, including discounts and premium sales, please call our Reseller Customer Service department at 800-434-3422.

For information on where to purchase IDG Books Worldwide's books outside the U.S., please contact our International Sales department at 415-655-3023 or fax 415-655-3299.

For information on foreign language translations, please contact our Foreign & Subsidiary Rights department at 415-655-3021 or fax 415-655-3281.

For sales inquiries and special prices for bulk quantities, please contact our Sales department at 415-655-3200 or write to the address above.

For information on using IDG Books Worldwide's books in the classroom or for ordering examination copies, please contact our Educational Sales department at 800-434-2086 or fax 817-251-8174.

For press review copies, author interviews, or other publicity information, please contact our Public Relations department at 415-655-3000 or fax 415-655-3299.

For authorization to photocopy items for corporate, personal, or educational use, please contact Copyright Clearance Center, 222 Rosewood Drive, Danvers, MA 01923, or fax 508-750-4470.

# ABOUT IDG BOOKS WORLDWIDE

Welcome to the world of IDG Books Worldwide.

IDG Books Worldwide, Inc., is a subsidiary of International Data Group, the world's largest publisher of computer-related information and the leading global provider of information services on information technology. IDG was founded more than 25 years ago and now employs more than 8,500 people worldwide. IDG publishes more than 275 computer publications in over 75 countries (see listing below). More than 60 million people read one or more IDG publications each month.

Launched in 1990, IDG Books Worldwide is today the #1 publisher of best-selling computer books in the United States. We are proud to have received eight awards from the Computer Press Association in recognition of editorial excellence and three from *Computer Currents*' First Annual Readers' Choice Awards. Our best-selling *...For Dummies*® series has more than 30 million copies in print with translations in 30 languages. IDG Books Worldwide, through a joint venture with IDG's Hi-Tech Beijing, became the first U.S. publisher to publish a computer book in the People's Republic of China. In record time, IDG Books Worldwide has become the first choice for millions of readers around the world who want to learn how to better manage their businesses.

Our mission is simple: Every one of our books is designed to bring extra value and skill-building instructions to the reader. Our books are written by experts who understand and care about our readers. The knowledge base of our editorial staff comes from years of experience in publishing, education, and journalism — experience we use to produce books for the '90s. In short, we care about books, so we attract the best people. We devote special attention to details such as audience, interior design, use of icons, and illustrations. And because we use an efficient process of authoring, editing, and desktop publishing our books electronically, we can spend more time ensuring superior content and spend less time on the technicalities of making books.

You can count on our commitment to deliver high-quality books at competitive prices on topics you want to read about. At IDG Books Worldwide, we continue in the IDG tradition of delivering quality for more than 25 years. You'll find no better book on a subject than one from IDG Books Worldwide.

John Kilcullen
President and CEO
IDG Books Worldwide, Inc.

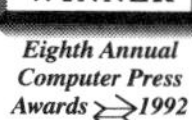

*Eighth Annual Computer Press Awards 1992*

*Ninth Annual Computer Press Awards 1993*

*Tenth Annual Computer Press Awards 1994*

*Eleventh Annual Computer Press Awards 1995*

IDG Books Worldwide, Inc., is a subsidiary of International Data Group, the world's largest publisher of computer-related information and the leading global provider of information services on information technology. International Data Group publishes over 275 computer publications in over 75 countries. Sixty million people read one or more International Data Group publications each month. International Data Group's publications include: **ARGENTINA:** Buyer's Guide, Computerworld Argentina, PC World Argentina; **AUSTRALIA:** Australian Macworld, Australian PC World, Australian Reseller News, Computerworld, IT Casebook, Network World, Publish, Webmaster; **AUSTRIA:** Computerwelt Osterreich, Networks Austria, PC Tip Austria; **BANGLADESH:** PC World Bangladesh; **BELARUS:** PC World Belarus; **BELGIUM:** Data News; **BRAZIL:** Annuário de Informática, Computerworld, Connections, Macworld, PC Player, PC World, Publish, Reseller News, Supergamepower; **BULGARIA:** Computerworld Bulgaria, Network World Bulgaria, PC & MacWorld Bulgaria; **CANADA:** CIO Canada, Client/Server World, ComputerWorld Canada, InfoWorld Canada, NetworkWorld Canada, WebWorld; **CHILE:** Computerworld Chile, PC World Chile; **COLOMBIA:** Computerworld Colombia, PC World Colombia; **COSTA RICA:** PC World Centro America; **THE CZECH AND SLOVAK REPUBLICS:** Computerworld Czechoslovakia, Macworld Czech Republic, PC World Czechoslovakia; **DENMARK:** Communications World Danmark, Computerworld Danmark, Macworld Danmark, PC World Danmark, Techworld Denmark; **DOMINICAN REPUBLIC:** PC World Republica Dominicana; **ECUADOR:** PC World Ecuador; **EGYPT:** Computerworld Middle East, PC World Middle East; **EL SALVADOR:** PC World Centro America; **FINLAND:** MikroPC, Tietoverkko, Tietoviikko; **FRANCE:** Distributique, Hebdo, Info PC, Le Monde Informatique, Macworld, Reseaux & Telecoms, WebMaster France; **GERMANY:** Computer Partner, Computerwoche, Computerwoche Extra, Computerwoche FOCUS, Global Online, Macwelt, PC Welt; **GREECE:** Amiga Computing, GamePro Greece, Multimedia World; **GUATEMALA:** PC World Centro America; **HONDURAS:** PC World Centro America; **HONG KONG:** Computerworld Hong Kong, PC World Hong Kong, Publish in Asia; **HUNGARY:** ABCD CD-ROM, Computerworld Szamitastechnika, Internetto online Magazine, PC World Hungary, PC-X Magazin Hungary; **ICELAND:** Tolvuheimur PC World Island; **INDIA:** Information Communications World, Information Systems Computerworld, PC World India, Publish in Asia; **INDONESIA:** InfoKomputer PC World, Komputek Computerworld, Publish in Asia; **IRELAND:** ComputerScope, PC Live!; **ISRAEL:** Macworld Israel, People & Computers/Computerworld; **ITALY:** Computerworld Italia, Macworld Italia, Networking Italia, PC World Italia; **JAPAN:** DTP World, Macworld Japan, Nikkei Personal Computing, OS/2 World Japan, SunWorld Japan, Windows NT World, Windows World Japan; **KENYA:** PC World East African; **KOREA:** Hi-Tech Information, Macworld Korea, PC World Korea; **MACEDONIA:** PC World Macedonia; **MALAYSIA:** Computerworld Malaysia, PC World Malaysia, Publish in Asia; **MALTA:** PC World Malta; **MEXICO:** Computerworld Mexico, PC World Mexico; **MYANMAR:** PC World Myanmar; **NETHERLANDS:** Computer! Totaal, LAN Internetworking Magazine, LAN World Buyers Guide, Macworld Netherlands, Net, WebWereld; **NEW ZEALAND:** Absolute Beginners Guide and Plain & Simple Series, Computer Buyer, Computer Industry Directory, Computerworld New Zealand, MTB, Network World, PC World New Zealand; **NICARAGUA:** PC World Centro America; **NORWAY:** Computerworld Norge, CW Rapport, Datamagasinet, Financial Rapport, Kursguide Norge, Macworld Norge, Multimediaworld Norge, PC World Ekspress Norge, PC World Nettverk, PC World Norge, PC World ProduktGuide Norge; **PAKISTAN:** Computerworld Pakistan; **PANAMA:** PC World Panama; **PEOPLE'S REPUBLIC OF CHINA:** China Computer Users, China Computerworld, China InfoWorld, China Telecom World Weekly, Computer & Communication, Electronic Design China, Electronics Today, Electronics Weekly, Game Software, PC World China, Popular Computer Week, Software Weekly, Software World, Telecom World; **PERU:** Computerworld Peru, PC World Profesional Peru, PC World SoHo Peru; **PHILIPPINES:** Click!, Computerworld Philippines, PC World Philippines, Publish in Asia; **POLAND:** Computerworld Poland, Computerworld Special Report Poland, Cyber, Macworld Poland, Networld Poland, PC World Komputer; **PORTUGAL:** Cerebro/PC World, Computerworld/Correio Informático, Dealer World Portugal, Mac*In/PC*In Portugal, Multimedia World; **PUERTO RICO:** PC World Puerto Rico; **ROMANIA:** Computerworld Romania, PC World Romania, Telecom Romania; **RUSSIA:** Computerworld Russia, Mir PK, Publish, Seti; **SINGAPORE:** Computerworld Singapore, PC World Singapore, Publish in Asia; **SLOVENIA:** Monitor; **SOUTH AFRICA:** Computing SA, Network World SA, Software World SA; **SPAIN:** Communicaciones World España, Computerworld España, Dealer World España, Macworld España, PC World España; **SRI LANKA:** Infolink PC World; **SWEDEN:** CAP&Design, Computer Sweden, Corporate Computing Sweden, Internetworld Sweden, it.branschen, Macworld Sweden, MaxiData Sweden, MikroDatorn, Nätverk & Kommunikation, PC World Sweden, PCaktiv, Windows World Sweden; **SWITZERLAND:** Computerworld Schweiz, Macworld Schweiz, PCtip; **TAIWAN:** Computerworld Taiwan, Macworld Taiwan, NEW ViSiON/Publish, PC World Taiwan, Windows World Taiwan; **THAILAND:** Publish in Asia, Thai Computerworld; **TURKEY:** Computerworld Turkiye, Macworld Turkiye, Network World Turkiye, PC World Turkiye; **UKRAINE:** Computerworld Kiev, Multimedia World Ukraine, PC World Ukraine; **UNITED KINGDOM:** Acorn User UK, Amiga Action UK, Amiga Computing UK, Apple Talk UK, Computing, Macworld, Parents and Computers UK, PC Advisor, PC Home, PSX Pro, The WEB; **UNITED STATES:** Cable in the Classroom, CIO Magazine, Computerworld, DOS World, Federal Computer Week, GamePro Magazine, InfoWorld, I-Way, Macworld, Network World, PC Games, PC World, Publish, Video Event, THE WEB Magazine, and WebMaster; online webzines: JavaWorld, NetscapeWorld, and SunWorld Online; **URUGUAY:** InfoWorld Uruguay; **VENEZUELA:** Computerworld Venezuela, PC World Venezuela; and **VIETNAM:** PC World Vietnam.

10/22/96

# Foreword

If you are like a great many Mac users, you understand the critical importance of your system software. After all, it's the first thing that's loaded or preloaded in your Mac. Plus, you're constantly being told to place new items in the system folders or find things within those folders. And, when you find yourself troubleshooting, you're often digging around in the system software.

But, alas, many people who use a Macintosh aren't sure why the system software works the way it does. Yet having an understanding of the system software and how to work with it efficiently is one of the greatest boons to anyone's computing productivity. Since the system software underlies every application program you use, its mastery can augment nearly every aspect of your work.

Now, thanks to the expertise of Lon Poole and his creation of the *Macworld Mac OS 7.6 Bible*, our path to a productive Mac life is made easier. Lon has created the most thorough, accurate, and useful guide to the many incarnations of System 7. I can personally and professionally attest to the Mac wizardry of Lon Poole. Lon writes the highly-read "Quick Tips" column for *Macworld.* As an editor, I appreciate Lon's attention to detail, devotion to technical accuracy, and focus on providing Mac users with the most helpful tips and guidance. He accomplishes all of this in an entertaining and readable manner, belying the wealth of technical information contained within the text.

Lon is well-equipped to provide comprehensive coverage of System 7.0, System 7.1, System 7 Pro, System 7.1.2, System 7.5, and Mac OS 7.6 (and more!). Lon has been a devotee of Apple and contributor to *Macworld* from the very beginning. He helped found the magazine way back in 1983 and continues to be one of the key reasons *Macworld* is recognized as the Macintosh authority. Lon's own authority is well-established in volumes of issues and books in which he provides highly specific and truly useful guidance that addresses a wide range of Macintosh computing solutions — making Lon one of the most knowledgeable Mac experts around.

Enjoy this excursion through the system software tour. Lon will tell you which system version is best for your needs, and he will tell you how to use your system software in order to work faster, smarter, and more efficiently.

— Adrian Mello
Editor-in-Chief
*Macworld*

# Preface

When it comes to working on a personal computer, nothing quite equals working on an Apple Macintosh or Mac-compatible computer. What creates this unique working environment is the Macintosh system software, now known as the Mac OS (Operating System) as well as System 7, System 6, and so on.

The Mac OS displays the windows, icons, menus, pointer, and other elements of the graphical user interface (GUI, pronounced "gooey"), and the Mac OS responds to your input through the keyboard and mouse. And that's just the beginning. The Mac OS provides a raft of other services; the following is a partial list:

- ❖ Filing electronic documents and software items
- ❖ Opening application programs and documents and saving document changes
- ❖ Implementing basic text editing (inserting, deleting, replacing, and so on)
- ❖ Drawing two- and three-dimensional graphics on screen
- ❖ Composing text in a variety of typefaces, styles, and sizes

- ❖ Printing graphics and typeset text
- ❖ Managing the computer's memory
- ❖ Participating in a network of computers
- ❖ Accessing the Internet
- ❖ Working with documents from the MS DOS and Windows operating systems
- ❖ Displaying movies and 360-degree panoramas
- ❖ Playing sounds and music
- ❖ Synthesizing and recognizing speech
- ❖ Handling text in dozens of languages and writing systems
- ❖ Facilitating data exchange and communication among application programs
- ❖ Automating tasks with scripts

No matter how much or how little experience you have with the Mac OS, this book can show you something useful about it that you don't already know. The book describes both basic and advanced Mac OS features, and explains how you can use them to make working with your Mac more productive and fun.

Sure, you can discover a lot about the Mac OS by exploring it on your own, but your exploration will go faster and you'll find more with this book as your guide. The Mac OS is not nearly as simple today as it was when Apple released the first Mac system software in 1984. Over the years Apple has added many improvements: a better filing system in 1985, color in 1987, and multitasking in 1988 to name a few. The system software entered a new realm of complexity in 1990 with the release of System 7.0, which is the earliest version discussed in this book. Apple continues to revise the system software, adding more features and capabilities with each new version. System 7.5, introduced in late summer 1994, has more than 50 features not found in its predecessor, System 7.1. Some of System 7.5's new features are simple, such as a digital clock in the menu bar, and some are sophisticated, such as the advanced typography of QuickDraw GX. In the two years after releasing System 7.5, Apple made some new technologies available as add-ons that work with several Mac OS versions. For instance, the OpenDoc plug-in software infrastructure can be used with System 7.1.1 or later. Mac OS 7.6, released in January 1997, integrates OpenDoc and other software that was available separately (and in some cases still is) together with some software updates that are not available separately.

Read this book to learn more about the system software version you're using — 7.6, 7.5.x, 7.1.x, or 7.0.x. (If you have System 6.0.8 or earlier, read this book to find out what you're missing and why you should upgrade.) You can stick to the basics that apply to all versions if you're new to the Mac OS. When you're ready to go beyond the basics, you can learn how to take advantage of the power in your version of System 7, including Mac OS 7.6 and the special versions of System 7.0 and 7.1 made for Macintosh Performa computers. You can also learn what you gain by using related Apple software such as At Ease, Apple Remote Access, AppleShare, Macintosh PC Exchange, QuickTime, PowerTalk, and AppleScript.

# Who This Book Is For

This book is aimed at people who already know Mac OS fundamentals such as choosing commands from menus, opening programs and documents, rearranging the contents of folders and disks, and copying text or graphics from one place and pasting it in another place. If you have spent more than a few days with any Mac OS computer, you know how to do these things and are ready for what's inside this book.

# What's Inside

*Macworld Mac OS 7.6 Bible* covers Mac OS 7.6 and earlier versions progressively in six parts. Here's an overview of each part:

❖ **Part I** takes a quick look at the features of System 7. Use it to get started right away or to get the big picture. This part also sorts through the different System 7 versions from 7.0 to 7.5 so you can decide whether to stick with the system version you have or upgrade.

❖ **Part II** describes in depth what you'll encounter when you first start using System 7. Windows, icons, and menus are in your face from the moment you start up a Mac OS computer, but look closely and you may find some new and useful aspects of them. To get beyond looking around the desktop, you must open programs and open and save documents. After doing a bit of work, you accumulate document files, which you must organize in folders on disks. Part of this housekeeping is sure to involve the special System Folder and its contents. You'll want to fine tune how the system works by adjusting a multitude of settings in software control panels, and you'll also find that the accessory programs that come with System 7 come in handy on occasion.

❖ **Part III** tells you how to use some important System 7 capabilities. You learn how to set up a simple network of computers, share your files with others on the network, and use their shared files. You discover how handy aliases can be. You learn to deal with fonts and typography, and to get printing under control. You also get comfortable with managing your Mac's memory (though you never truly enjoy doing it).

- **Part IV** takes you beyond System 7 basics — way beyond. You learn to create compound documents with drag-and-drop editing or publish and subscribe. You come to realize that the network you used for file sharing and printing back in Part III has other uses: collaborating with others through electronic mail (e-mail), creating and using information catalogs, and more. You find out QuickTime does more than make movies on your Mac. In this part of the book you also get to know how any Mac can speak and some can listen, and how System 7 works with multiple languages.
- **Part V** presents many ways to make the most of System 7. This part of the book introduces AppleScript, and walks you through using it to automate repetitive tasks. A whole chapter is devoted to describing over 100 low-cost software utilities you can use to enhance System 7. Another chapter reveals over 100 System 7 tips and secrets.
- **Part VI** covers the changes made to the system software from System 7.5 to Mac OS 7.6. Be sure to read this part of the book if you've just upgraded or are thinking of upgrading to System 7.5.3, System 7.5.5, or Mac OS 7.6. This part of the book also details how to update or install System 7, including how to install a clean copy.

If you read this book from front to back, you will find that some information appears in more than one place. In particular, everything that Part I covers in summary appears again elsewhere in the book in more detail. Also, the tips and secrets that appear in the midst of relevant subject matter throughout the book appear again, together with additional tips and secrets, in Part V. This duplication is intentional and is meant to be for your benefit.

# How This Book Can Help You

According to popular legend, a Mac OS computer is so easy to use you don't need to read books about it. Alas, if only that were true. In fact, discovering all the power that even the original version of System 7 gives your Macintosh — let alone later versions — would take months of exploring and experimenting. Yes, exploring and experimenting can be fun; you should do some of it. But do you really have months to devote to your computer's operating system? No! Save your time for having fun with games and multimedia, exploring the Internet, or maybe getting some work done. Benefit from the experience of others (in this case the author and his collaborators). Read this book so you can put the full power of the Mac OS to work for you without a lot of poking around the Mac desktop.

Maybe you think you don't need this book because you have Apple's manuals and on-screen help. It's true these are good sources of information. But the *Macworld Mac OS 7.6 Bible* contains a great deal of information you won't find in the manuals or help screens. This book also provides a different perspective on subjects you may not quite understand after reading the manuals. And because this book describes the Mac OS completely, you can use it instead of Apple's manuals if you don't happen to have them.

# Conventions Used in This Book

This book makes use of established conventions in an effort to help guide you through the material.

## System 7 version references

As you may have realized from reading this introduction, this book uses the terms Mac OS and system software to include all versions of the Macintosh system software unless a specific version number is stated, such as Mac OS 7.6. This book also uses terms such as System 7.6 to refer to specific versions of the Mac OS, and uses the term System 7 in an inclusive sense. References to System 7 (without a decimal point or decimal digits) refer to all versions of system software from 7.0 to 7.6. A reference such as System 7.5.x refers to System 7.5 (that is, 7.5.0), System 7.5.1, System 7.5.2, and so on. References to specific versions apply only to the version number cited, such as 7.5.3. In general, this book refers to versions of system software prior to 7.6 as "System" and to versions 7.6 and after as "Mac OS" because that's the terminology that Apple uses.

## Sidebars

Certain discussions in this book are expanded with sidebars. These are shaded boxes that contain background information, expert tips and advice, areas where caution is needed, and other helpful information.

All sidebars feature an icon, or symbol, that categorizes the information contained in the sidebar. These icons are designed to alert you to the type of information you will find. Here's what to look for:

The information in a **Backgrounder** sidebar provides background detail about the issue under discussion.

The information in a **Quick Tips** sidebar points out a useful tip (or tips) that can save you a great deal of time and trouble.

The information in a **Caution** sidebar alerts you to potential problems with an issue under discussion. Solutions and ways to avoid the scary situations are also included.

An **Undocumented** sidebar includes concepts and ideas not found in Apple's documentation for Mac OS users. The information is the result of countless hours of tinkering, troubleshooting, and asking questions of expert sources.

A **Step-By-Step** sidebar provides detailed instructions that show how to perform tasks with the Mac OS. Many issues in the Mac OS can be complex, but these sidebars help break the desired goal into manageable components.

## Concepts and Terms

Each chapter in the book concludes with a helpful concepts and terms section.

**INTRODUCTION CONCEPTS AND TERMS**

- The ***concepts*** section summarizes the major topics discussed in the chapter.
- Several bulleted items provide a concise review of the major points.

**Terms Section**
The Terms section lists and defines the important terminology introduced in the chapter. All terms are listed in alphabetical order and each has an expanded definition.

**More Detailed Definition**
If you come across a new term in the chapter, and the brief definition there doesn't satisfy you, turn to the Concepts and Terms section for a more detailed explanation.

# Feedback, Please

The author and publisher appreciate your feedback on this book. Please feel free to contact us in care of IDG Books Worldwide with questions or comments. You can send e-mail to the *Macworld Mac OS 7.6 Bible* team at *feedback@www.idgbooks.com*.

# Acknowledgments

Once upon a time, when computer technology was so much simpler than it is today, I actually managed to write a couple of books on my own. Well, those days are gone for this carbon-based word processor. Several people have made major contributions to earlier editions of this book, and their work lives on in this edition.

David Angell and Brent Heslop researched and wrote first drafts of three chapters that initially appeared in the first edition and are now Chapters 9, 10, and 14 in this edition. They deserve the credit for those three chapters, and I most gratefully acknowledge their contribution.

Nancy Dunn and Rita Lewis helped reorganize and update much of the book for the third edition, and much of their work survives in this edition. Nancy worked on Chapters 4 through 11, 13, 14, and 16. Rita worked on Chapters 1, 2, 3, 12, 15, 17, and 19.

Derrick Schneider applied his AppleScript expertise to Chapter 18 and deserves recognition for his fine work.

I also want to thank the editorial and production team at IDG Books Worldwide, especially Amy Thomas, the editor for this edition, whose diligence made all the difference.

I reserve my greatest thanks for my wife Karin, and sons Ethan and Adam, without whose love and support this work would have been impossible and pointless.

(The publisher would like to give special thanks to Patrick J. McGovern, without whom this book would not have been possible.)

# Contents at a Glance

# Table of Contents

CHAPTER 5



CHAPTER 6

# Part 3: At Work with System 7 .................. 243

CHAPTER 9

## Sharing Files .......................................................245

xxix

xxxv

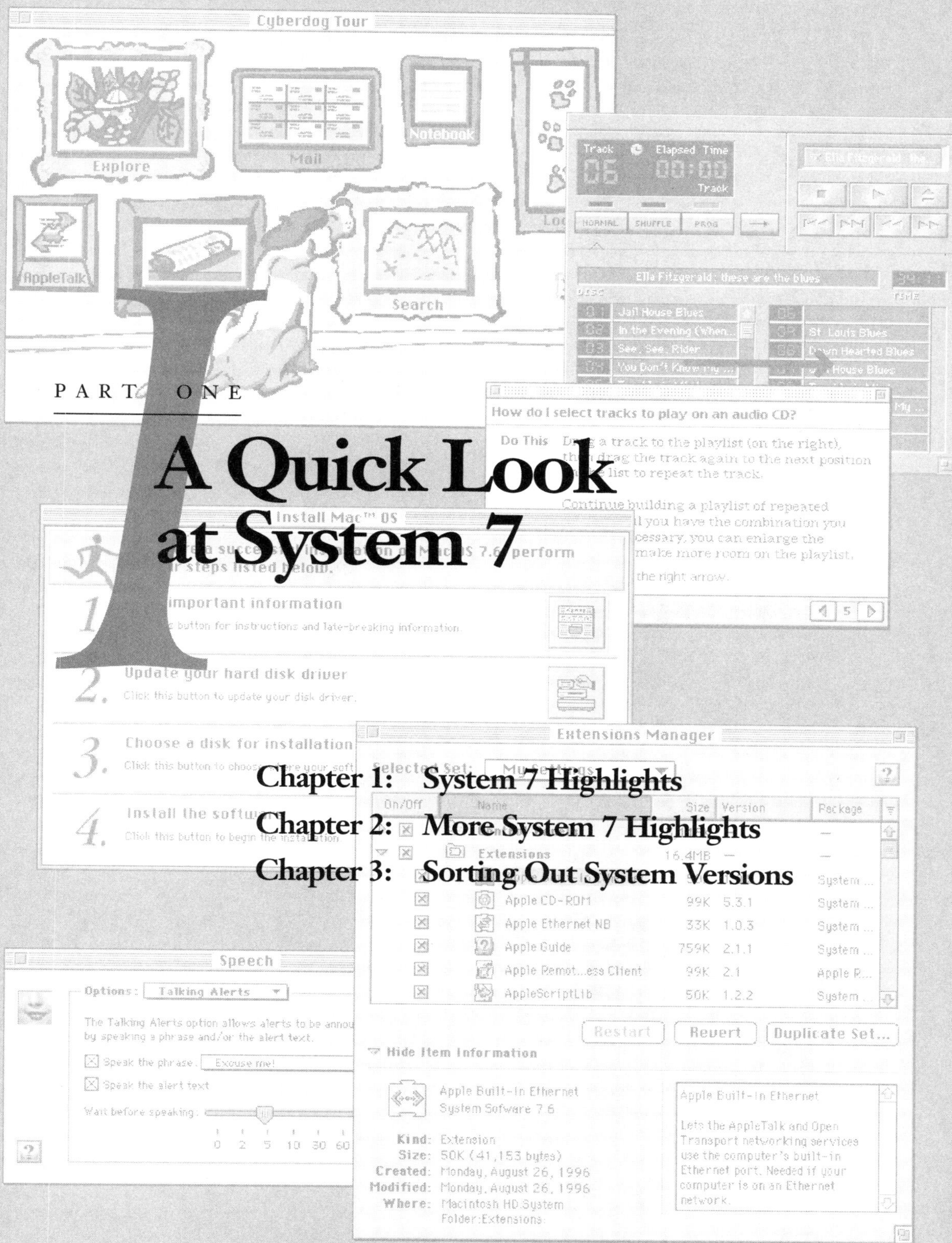


PART ONE

# I

# A Quick Look at System 7

CHAPTER ONE

# System 7 Highlights

- Using features such as balloon help, Apple Guide, the Apple menu, and the Application menu to find your way around the colorful desktop
- Working with directory dialog boxes, aliases, and folder path menus to speed up access to files
- Editing icon names, customizing icons, and using item labels
- Saving time with stationery pads, the Find command, and keyboard shortcuts

System 7 has many capabilities that set it apart from earlier versions of system software. This chapter previews 18 of the most basic, most obvious, and most often used System 7 features. It also points out the most significant differences between System 7 and previous system software versions.

## Revealing a Colorful Desktop

On a Mac with a color monitor you can see that System 7 windows, unlike the windows of previous system software, have three-dimensional (3-D) color shading. Muted colors and shades of gray accent the window components under your control: title bar, close box, zoom box, size box, and scroll bars, as shown in Figure 1-1. Some of the colorized components even look like they work in three dimensions when you use them. For example, clicking the close box makes it look pressed down.

Only the active window has 3-D shading. It stands out from inactive windows behind it because System 7 displays inactive windows with gray borders and a gray title. Of course the contents of inactive windows are never dimmed so that you can see the contents easily.

Icons also can be in color on a System 7 desktop. For the most part, Apple has taken the same low-key approach with its icons as it has taken with windows, using gray shades and subdued colors to make them look three-dimensional. Bright colors are used mainly for highlights.

Most small icons used in menus and Finder windows look better in System 7, where any program developer (indeed, any Mac enthusiast) can design separate small icons. Prior to System 7, the small icons were merely shrunken versions of full-size icons.

Desktop patterns are larger and more colorful with System 7.5 than with earlier versions of System 7, as shown in Figure 1-2. System 7.5 desktop patterns are composed of large tiles, 64 by 64 pixels (dots) each, compared to the small 8 by 8 pixel tiles used previously. (The special versions of System 7 that come with Macintosh Performa computers have always had large, color desktop patterns, but not as large and numerous as System 7.5).

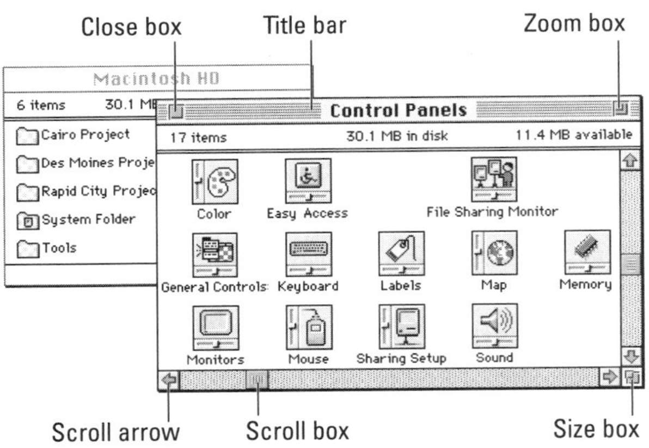


**Figure 1-1: Colorized window controls and icons (shown here in shades of gray).**

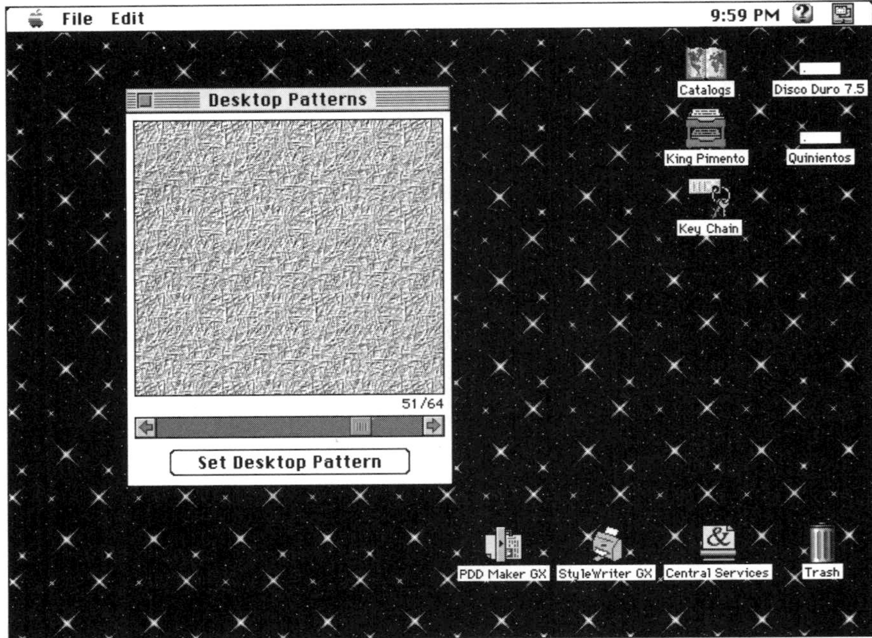


**Figure 1-2: System 7.5 comes with dozens of large, colorful desktop patterns not previously available.**

# Getting On-Screen Help

Although the Mac's graphical interface is easier to learn and remember than a bunch of cryptic command words, it's hard to remember what every icon and graphical doodad means. System 7's optional balloon help can assist your memory. Here's how it works: You choose Show Balloons from the Guide menu (called the Help menu prior to System 7.5), which is always located near the right end of the menu bar. This action turns on balloon help, which works from any application, not just the Finder. Then you use the mouse to point to something — an icon, menu, part of a window, or some other object. A cartoon-style balloon pops up next to the object, as shown in Figure 1-3. Words inside the balloon describe the object to which the balloon points. The message usually tells you what the object is, what it does, or what happens when you click it.

To learn more about what balloons tell you and what it's like to work with balloon help on, see "Guide Menu" in Chapter 4.

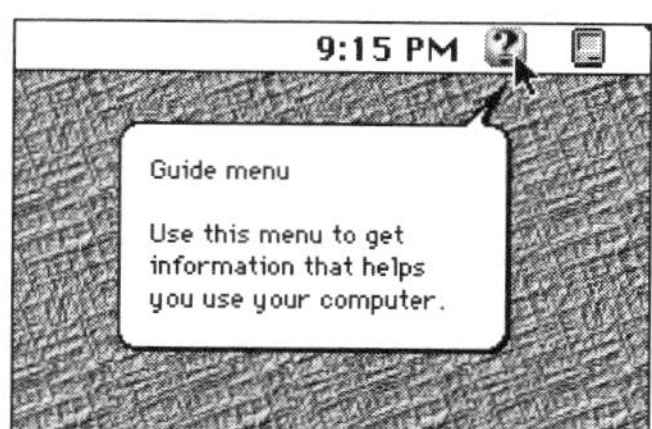


**Figure 1-3: A help balloon describes an object and how it's used.**

System 7.5 includes an interactive help system, called *Apple Guide*, that shows and tells you how to get things done while you actually do them. Step-by-step instructions appear in a guide window, which floats above all other windows, as shown in Figure 1-4. As you move from step to step, the guide may coach you by marking an object on-screen with a circle, arrow, or underline.

Apple Guide watches what you do and can adjust its steps if you work ahead or make a mistake. It can even perform a step for you, such as opening a control panel.

For more information on balloon help and Apple Guide, see "Guide Menu" in Chapter 4.

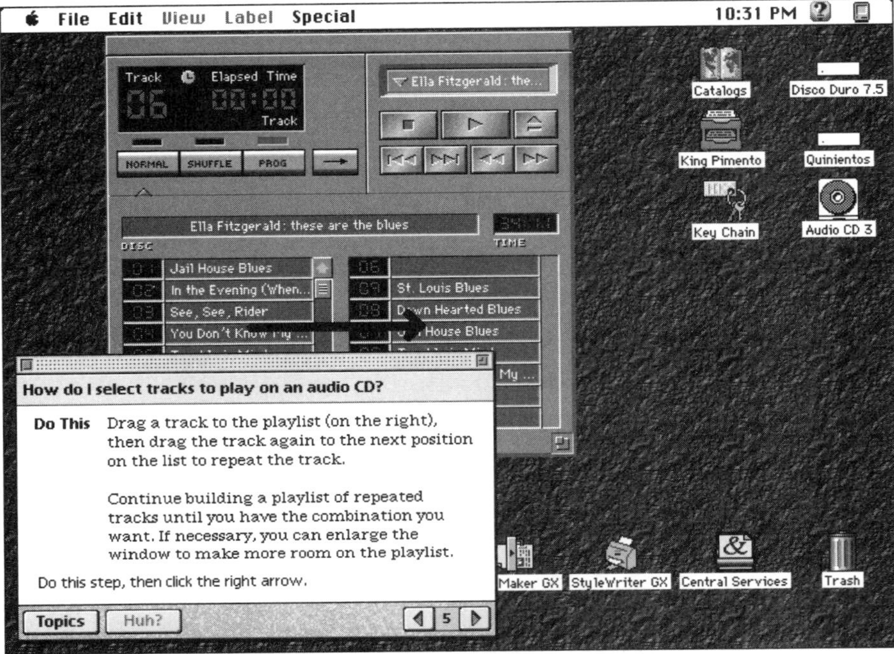


**Figure 1-4: Apple Guide displays step-by-step instructions in a floating window and points out objects on-screen.**

# Tooling Around with the Apple Menu

The Apple menu is like the tool belt a carpenter wears. It doesn't hold all of his tools and equipment, but it holds the things he needs most often and special things for the work he's currently doing. With System 7, you can customize the Apple menu so that it gives you immediate access to programs, documents, folders, and anything else you use frequently or need for a current job. When you choose an item from the Apple menu, it opens right away. You don't have to root around a cluttered desktop or scrounge through folders with the Finder. The Apple menu is available in almost every program. It lists items conveniently in alphabetical order and even shows their icons.

You put an item in the Apple menu by dragging its icon into the Apple Menu Items folder in the System Folder, as shown in Figure 1-5. The item becomes instantly available in the Apple menu — there is no need to restart your Macintosh. To remove an item from the Apple menu, drag its icon out of the Apple Menu Items folder.

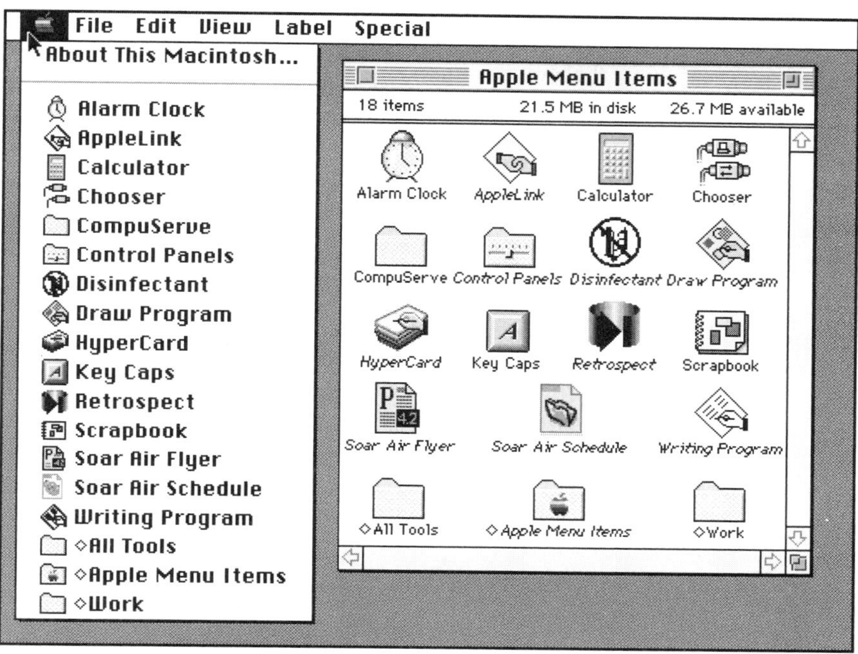


**Figure 1-5: An Apple menu and its Apple Menu Items folder.**

For more information, see "Opening with the Apple Menu" in Chapter 5 and "Apple Menu Items Folder" in Chapter 7.

# Multitasking with the Application Menu

Ever since the introduction of System 6.0 for the Mac, you have been able to keep more than one program open at a time and switch between the open programs. This capability, known as *multitasking*, is optional in System 6 but is fully integrated (not optional) in System 7. You can have as many programs open simultaneously as fit in your computer's memory, as shown in Figure 1-6. You can copy and paste among documents of open programs without closing documents and quitting programs. Also, you can switch to the Finder without quitting programs. From the Finder you can open other programs, find documents, organize folders and disks, and so on.

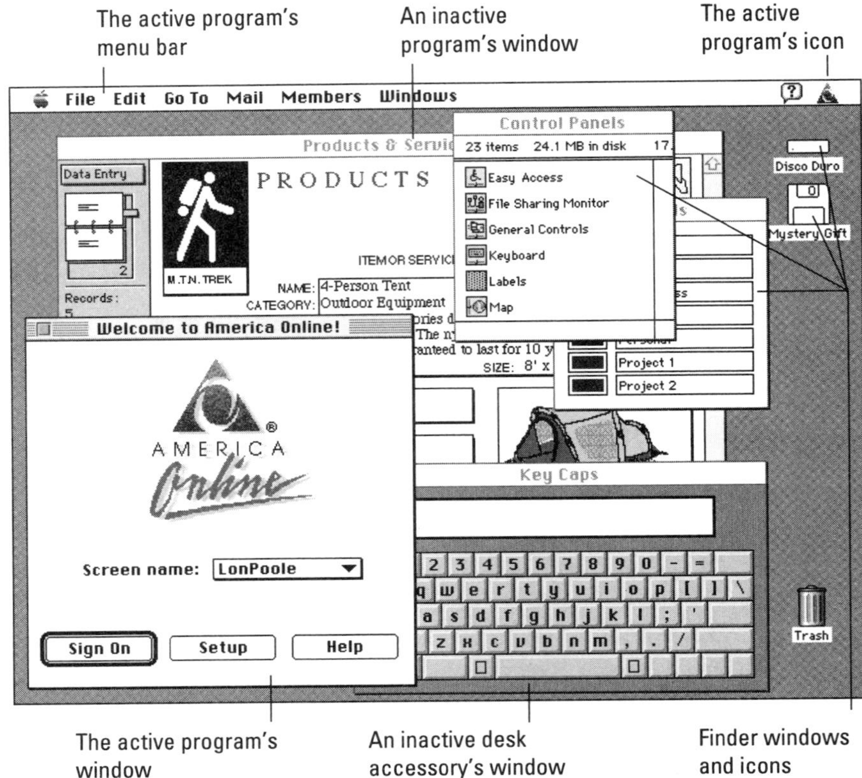


**Figure 1-6: Multiple programs open.**

Multitasking's valuable benefits can have disorienting side effects. For instance, you may think that the program you're using has unexpectedly quit when actually you switched to another open program. You must condition yourself to look at the menu bar when you need to know which open program is currently active.

The active program's icon appears at the right end of the menu bar. Clicking that icon reveals the Application menu, which lists the programs that are open, as shown in Figure 1-7. Choosing a listed program makes it the active program. You can also make a program active by clicking in any of its windows or by opening (double-clicking) its icon or any of its documents' icons in the Finder.

Some programs can use System 7's multitasking capabilities to operate in the background while you work with another program. *Background programs* operate during the intervals — only split seconds long — when the active program isn't using the computer.

**Figure 1-7: The Application menu lists open programs; choosing one makes it active.**

Background programs can't use the menu bar or interact directly with you in any way. They can, however, perform the following tasks:

- ❖ Recalculate spreadsheets
- ❖ Make backup copies of disks
- ❖ Print documents
- ❖ Sort databases
- ❖ Copy items in the Finder
- ❖ Send and receive electronic mail

Having multiple programs open leads to a confusion of windows. You can eliminate window clutter by using Application menu commands to hide windows temporarily, as shown in Figure 1-8.

For more information about multitasking, background operations, and hiding windows, see "Opening Multiple Programs" in Chapter 5.

**Figure 1-8: Use the commands in the Application menu to manage window clutter.**

# Checking the Menu-Bar Clock

With System 7.5, you have the option of adding a digital clock to the menu bar. It appears at the left of the Guide menu, and clicking it alternates between a display of the time and the date. You set the format of this clock with the Date & Time control panel, as shown in Figure 1-9, and can set the clock to chime on the hour, at quarter past, at half past, and at quarter 'til. On a battery-powered Mac, you can have the clock show the battery level. You can hide the clock by pressing Option while clicking it. For more information on the clock, see "Date & Time" in Chapter 8.

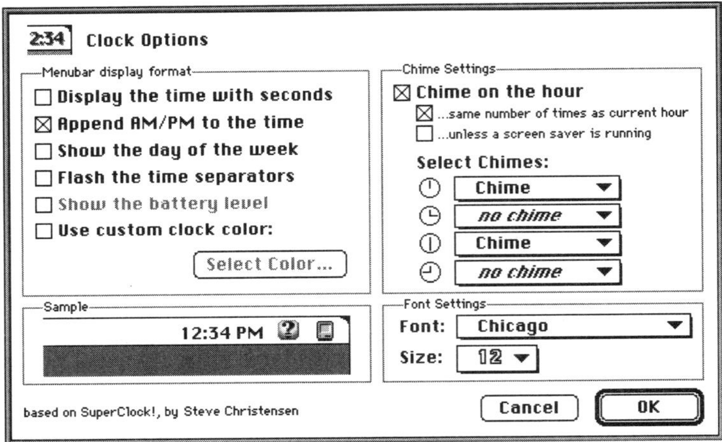


**Figure 1-9: System 7.5's optional menu-bar clock displays the time and more.**

# Opening and Saving

You don't always want to use the Finder to open folders and documents, and you never use the Finder to save documents. When you're working in an application program, use its Open, Save, and Save As commands to open and save documents. Those commands all have similar dialog boxes, which are called *directory dialog boxes* because they show a directory of your disks and folders. The directory dialog boxes you get when you use the Open and Save As commands work like one-window Finders in System 7. A single directory window lists the contents of one folder or disk at a time, alphabetically by name. The System 7 directory window uses compressed-style text for names longer than 25 characters.

## Navigating by mouse

You *navigate* through your folders with buttons and pop-up menus. Selecting a listed folder and clicking the Open button opens the folder and lists its contents in the directory window. To move back to the folder that contains the open folder, use the pop-up menu above the directory window. That pop-up menu can take you all the way back to the desktop, as shown in Figure 1-10. Clicking the Desktop button also takes you to the desktop level. At the desktop level you see the names of all disks and can select and open any of them. In fact, you switch disk drives by opening a disk at the desktop level.

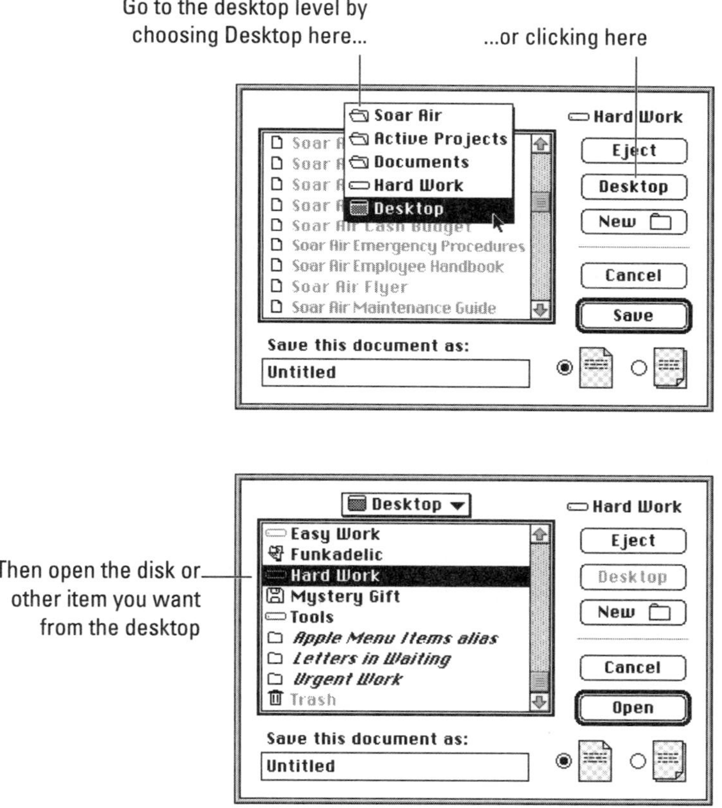


**Figure 1-10: Seeing items on the desktop from a directory dialog box.**

# Navigating by keyboard

You can open items and move through folders in any directory dialog box by using the keyboard as well as the mouse. For example, pressing *k* selects the first item that begins with the letter *K* or *k*. This technique works in any directory dialog box. Thus there are two possible uses of the keyboard in a Save or Save As dialog box: selecting an item in the open folder or entering a name for the file you're saving. Pressing the Tab key alternates between the folder contents area and the name entry area. A heavy black border indicates the current keyboard target, as shown in Figure 1-11. More keyboard shortcuts for System 7 directory dialog boxes are tabulated under "Navigating by Keyboard" in Chapter 5 and on the Quick Reference Card.

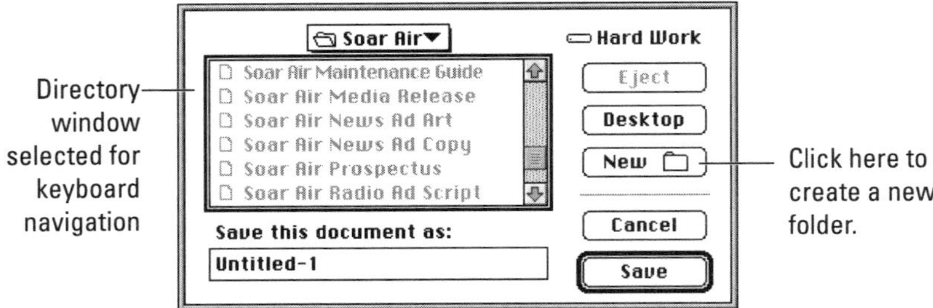


**Figure 1-11: Moving around by keyboard.**

## Creating folders

The Save and Save As dialog boxes in a few programs include a button you can click to create a new folder. However, the New Folder button is absent in the Save and Save As dialog boxes of most programs that have not been updated for System 7.

For more information, see "Directory Dialog Boxes" in Chapter 5.

# Using Aliases

You can't be in two places at once, but your documents, applications, and folders can be in many places at one time. System 7's aliases make this virtual omnipresence possible. An *alias* is a small file (1K to 20K, depending on total disk capacity) that points to another file. When you open an alias, the item it points to opens automatically. When you drag an item to the alias of a folder, the item you drag goes into the folder to which the alias points. You can put aliases anywhere — on the desktop, in the Apple menu, or in other accessible places — and leave the original items buried deep within nested folders.

Aliases have a variety of uses, which include the following:

- ❖ Opening frequently used programs, documents, and folders from the desktop while the real items remain buried in nested folders.
- ❖ Adding items to the Apple menu without moving the original items from their folders.
- ❖ Organizing documents and folders according to multiple filing schemes without duplicating items. For example, you can file documents by project, addressee, date, and topic.
- ❖ Simplifying access to file servers and individual items on servers. Opening an alias of an item on a server makes an automatic connection with the server (except for providing the password, which you must type unless you gained access to the original item as a guest).
- ❖ Getting nearly automatic access to your Mac's hard disks by using a floppy disk in any other Mac on the same network.

An alias looks exactly like the original item except that its name is in italics, and it initially has the word *alias* as a suffix, as shown in Figure 1-12. To learn how to set up aliases and discover more strategies for their use, see Chapter 10.

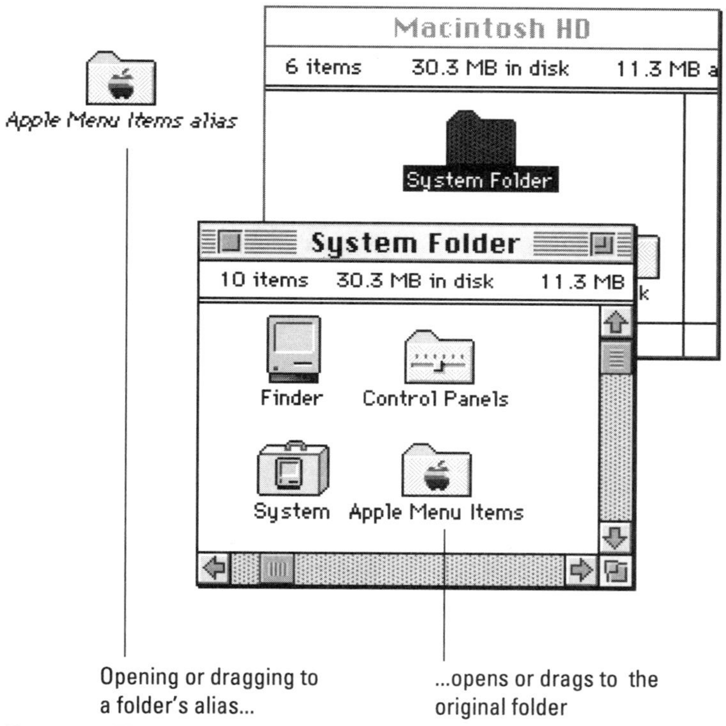


**Figure 1-12: Things you do to an alias happen to its original item.**

# Sharing Files

If your Macintosh has System 7 installed and is connected to other Macs in a network, you can share hard disks, folders, and the files in them with other network users. You can access folders and disks others have made available to you. You can also make your folders and disks available to others on the network, including those using System 6 with AppleShare client software.

## Using someone else's folders

To use another Mac's folder or disk, open the Chooser desk accessory. It lists as AppleShare *file servers* the names of all computers that are sharing their folders and disks. After you choose one, the Chooser asks you to connect as a guest or registered user and then presents a list of items you may share, as shown in Figure 1-13.

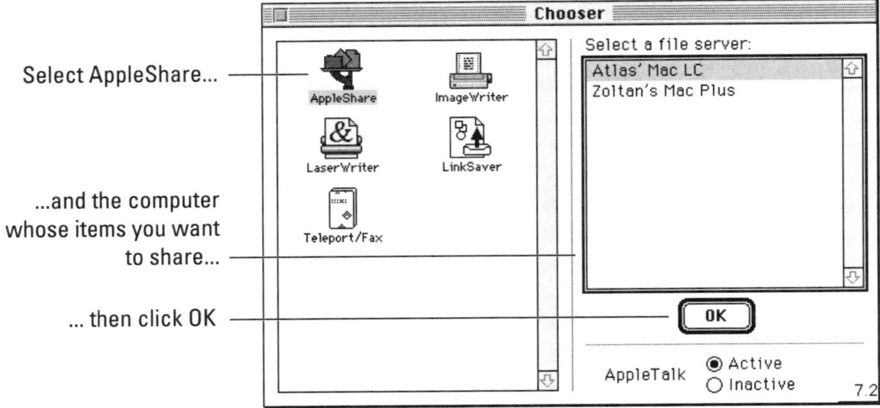


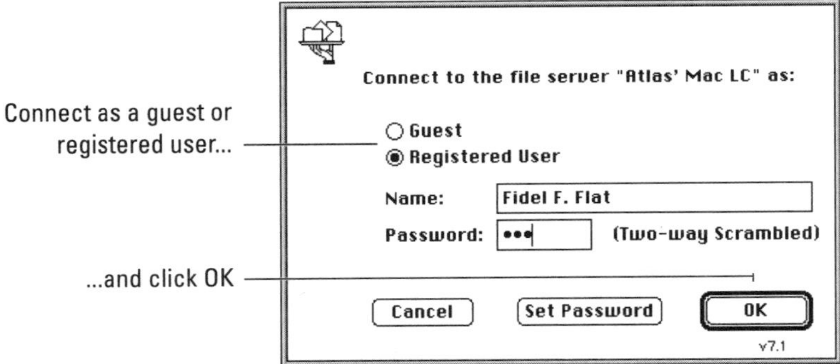


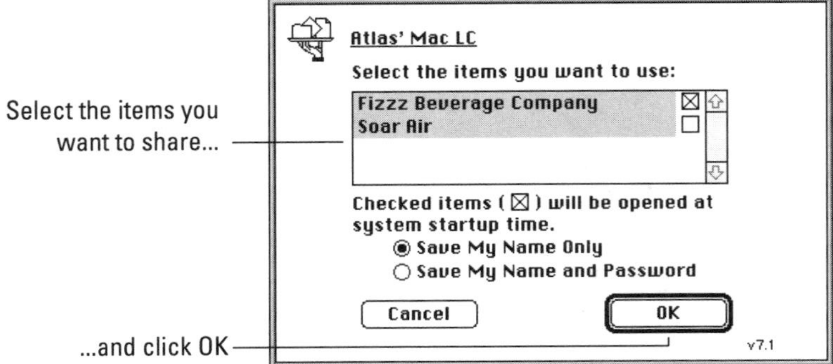


**Figure 1-13: Selecting folders to share.**

Accessing someone else's folders or disks is considerably slower than accessing your own. Also, your computer's performance declines markedly while others share your folders or disks. For better performance, especially in networks that include more than ten active users, everyone can put folders to be shared on the hard disk of a Macintosh dedicated to sharing its files (a dedicated file server). For best results in large networks, you need a dedicated file server, such as Apple's AppleShare 4.0 or AppleShare Pro.

## Sharing your folders with others

Before you can share your disks or folders, you must configure your Macintosh as an AppleShare-compatible file server with the Sharing Setup control panel, as shown in Figure 1-14. Your Mac then shows up as an AppleShare file server in the Choosers of other network users who have System 7 file-sharing software installed. It also shows up as an AppleShare server in the Choosers of System 6 computers that have AppleShare client software installed.

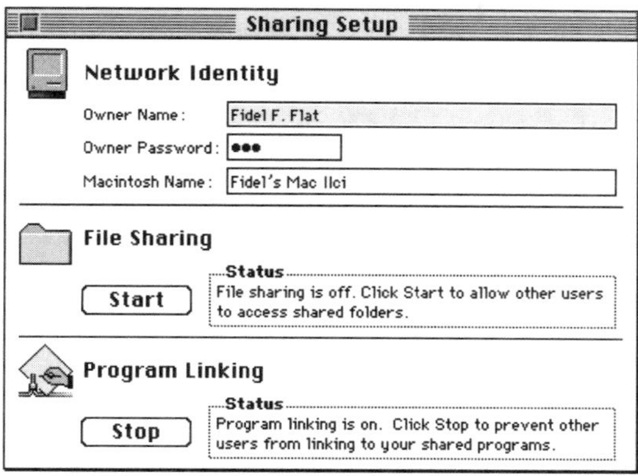


**Figure 1-14: Set up file sharing in the Sharing Setup control panel.**

To share one of your disks or folders with others, select it and then use the Finder's Sharing command to display the item's access privileges window, as shown in Figure 1-15. There you specify who can see the item's folders, view its files, and make changes to them. You can grant different access privileges to the owner of the item (usually you), to one other registered user, to a group of registered users you designate, and to everyone else.

Active Projects

Where: Macintosh HD : Work :

☒ Share this item and its contents

| | | See Folders | See Files | Make Changes |
|---|---|---|---|---|
| Owner: | Atlas Fang | ☒ | ☒ | ☒ |
| User/Group: | Honchos | ☒ | ☒ | ☒ |
| | Everyone | ☒ | ☒ | ☐ |

☐ Make all currently enclosed folders like this one

☒ Can't be moved, renamed or deleted

**Figure 1-15: Use the Sharing command to share an item and set its access privileges.**

You identify registered users, set their passwords, and create groups of users with the Users & Groups control panel, shown in Figure 1-16. Another control panel, File Sharing Monitor, enables you to see who is sharing what and how busy they're keeping your Macintosh. You can also use that control panel to disconnect individual users who are sharing your folders and disks.

To learn more about using file sharing, see Chapter 9.

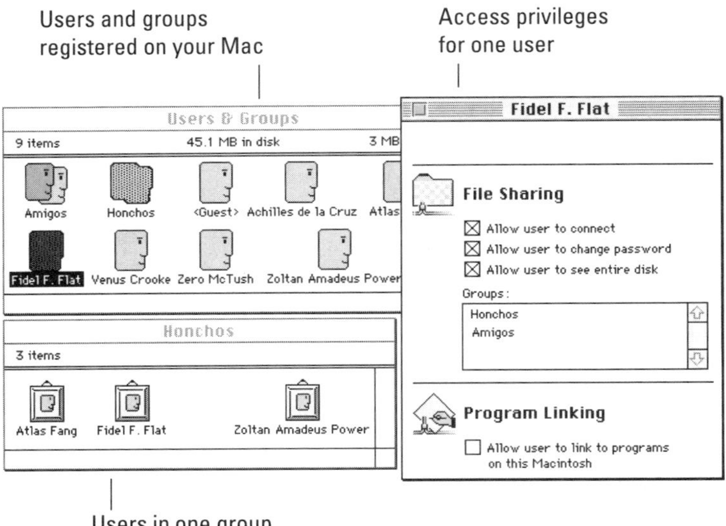


**Figure 1-16: Identify who can use your shared items with the Users & Groups control panel.**

# Dragging to Open

When you double-click a document, the Finder figures out which application you used to create the document and opens the document with that application. With System 7, you can drag a document to any application capable of opening the document (not necessarily the application that created the document), and the Finder has that application open the document. For example, you can drag a diverse collection of documents to an application that compresses them so that they consume less disk space. This drag-and-drop capability speeds up access to your work and works with aliases of documents and applications as well as the actual items. For more information, check out "Drag and Drop Opening" in Chapter 5.

# Outlining in Finder Windows

All versions of the Finder can display a window's contents as icons or as a list of names, sizes, kinds, and other attributes. System 7's Finder can present its list views in an indented outline format. You can see folders and their contents in the same window so that you can select and reorganize items from different folders in the same window. The levels of indentation in the outline clearly diagram the structure of your nested folders. You can expand or collapse any level in the outline to show or hide the corresponding folder's contents by clicking the triangle next to the folder's icon, as shown in Figure 1-17. For more information, see "Viewing Folder Contents" in Chapter 6.

## Folder Path Menus

The title of a Finder window appears to be static, but when you press ⌘ while clicking the window title, a folder path menu pops up, as shown in the figure. The pop-up folder menu reveals the path through your folder structure from the active window to the disk containing it. You can open any folder along the path by choosing the folder from the pop-up menu. To close the active window while opening a folder along the path, press Option while choosing the folder from the pop-up menu.

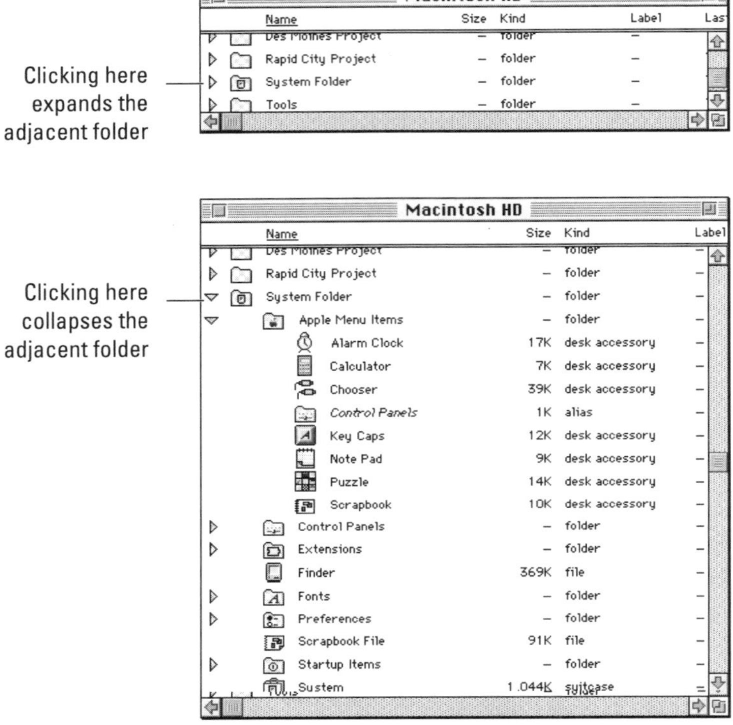


**Figure 1-17: Expanding and collapsing folder outlines in Finder windows.**

# Editing Icon Names

Before you can edit the name of a disk, folder, program, document, or other item in System 7's Finder, you must carefully select the name. When the name is selected for editing, it has a box around it in addition to being highlighted, as shown in Figure 1-18. Clicking the icon itself (not its name) does not select the name for editing as it does with older versions of the Mac's system software. The good news is that you can no longer accidentally and perhaps unknowingly rename a selected document or folder by bumping the keyboard; the bad news is that if you are accustomed to an old version of system software, you have to relearn how to change icon names.

**Figure 1-18: An icon name selected for editing.**

To select the name of an icon, you either click the icon and then press Return or Enter, or you click the name itself. After selecting the name, wait until a box appears around the name. You don't have to wait if you move the mouse slightly after clicking the name or if you move the insertion point by pressing the arrow keys. Pressing the up-arrow key moves the insertion point to the beginning of the name, pressing the down-arrow key moves it to the end, pressing the left-arrow key moves it to the left, and pressing the right-arrow key moves it to the right. Then you can click again to select an insertion point, double-click to select a word, or drag to select a range of text. If you click again before a box appears around the name, the Finder thinks that you're double-clicking the icon and opens the file.

To learn more about how to rename your documents, volumes, disks, folders, and applications, refer to "Renaming Icons" in Chapter 4.

# Creating Custom Icons

Tired of the same old icons? You can replace individual full-size icons with your own designs, as shown in Figure 1-19. First, create a new icon design in color, gray scale, or black and white with a paint program. Copy the new icon to the Clipboard. In the Finder, select the icon you want to customize, choose Get Info from the File menu, select the icon in the Info window, and then paste.

The picture you had copied to the Clipboard replaces the current icon. If your picture is bigger than a standard icon (32 x 32 dots), it is scaled down to fit the icon space. Note that you can replace the icon of any unlocked file, folder, or disk. You cannot replace system software icons, such as the System Folder, Finder, Control Panels folder, or Trash. For more information, see "Custom Icons" in Chapter 4.

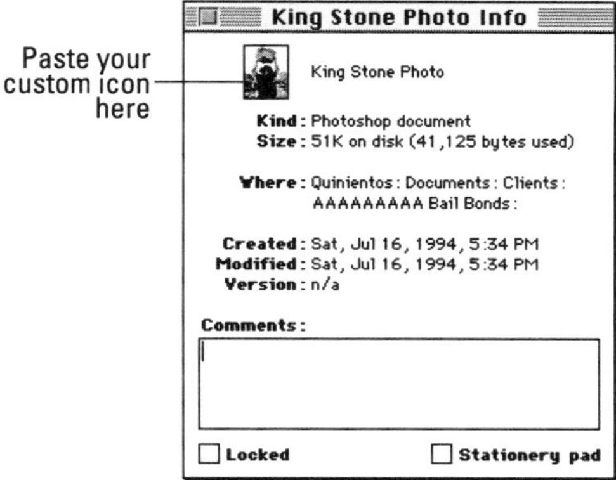


**Figure 1-19: Customizing an icon.**

# Saving Time with Stationery Pads

If you regularly create new documents with common formatting, contents, and so on, you can save time with System 7's stationery pad documents. Opening a stationery pad is like tearing off a page from a pad of preprinted forms — you get a new document with all common elements preset. Stationery pads have a distinctive icon that looks like a stack of document icons, as shown in Figure 1-20. Stationery pads work with most software but work best with software that has been updated to take advantage of them. The Finder uses a generic, blank-looking stationery pad icon when the program that handles that type of document doesn't know about System 7's stationery.

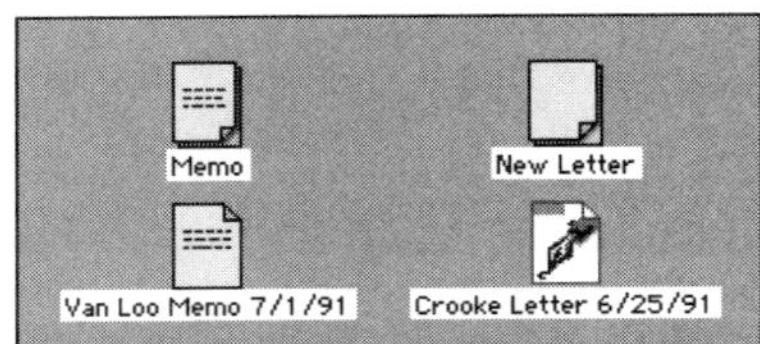


**Figure 1-20: Stationery pad icons and ordinary icons.**

You can make any document a stationery pad by setting the Stationery Pad option in its Info window, as shown in Figure 1-21.

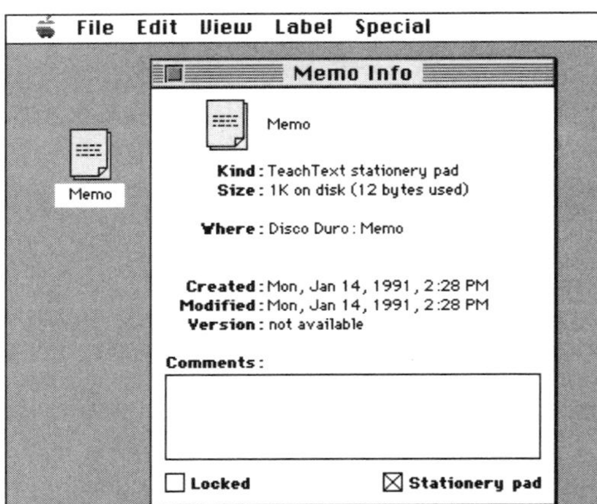


**Figure 1-21: Making a stationery pad with the Finder's Get Info command.**

Some programs enable you to save a document as a stationery pad directly by setting a Stationery Pad option in their Save and Save As dialog boxes, as shown in Figure 1-22. These programs have been upgraded specifically to work with System 7's stationery pads.

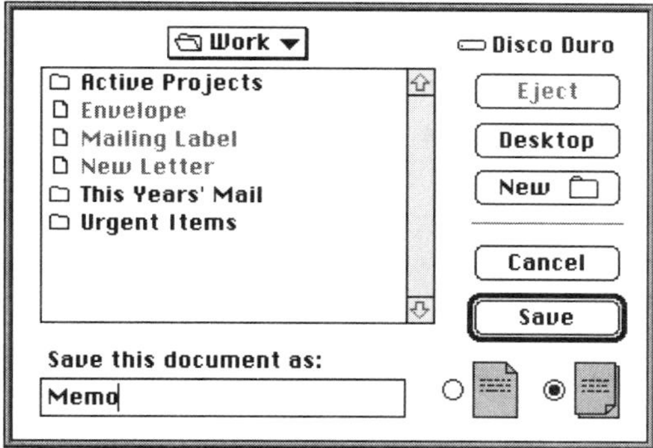


Figure 1-22: Saving a stationery pad within an application.

For more details about making and using stationery pads, see "Stationery Pads" in Chapter 5.

# Finding Files Fast

No more hunting through folders and disks for lost items — a chore even with outline views. System 7's Find command finds and fetches lost items for you quickly. Choosing Find from the Finder's File menu in System 7.5 opens the Find File window. The simplest form of the Find File window, shown in Figure 1-23, allows you to specify where you want to search and one attribute you want to match. It is preset to look on all disks for items whose names contain the text you specify. You can change where Find File looks for items and specify that it look at an attribute other than the item's name. You can also add more search criteria to the Find File window by clicking the More Choices button.

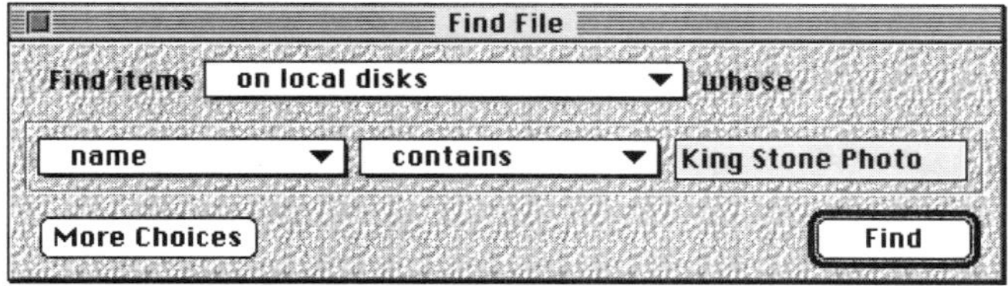


Figure 1-23: Finding items that match one criterion in System 7.5

Clicking the Find button starts the search. When the search ends, Find File displays all the found items in the Find File Results window, as shown in Figure 1-24. Selecting an item (by clicking it) in the list of found items at the top of the Find File Results window displays the item's folder location at the bottom of the window. You can open an item in the Find File Results window by double-clicking it.

You can open a selected item's enclosing folder with a menu command. You can also drag found items from the top of the Find File Results window to the desktop or to any folder or disk visible in the Finder. In addition, you can print found documents and use the Get Info and Sharing commands on found items.

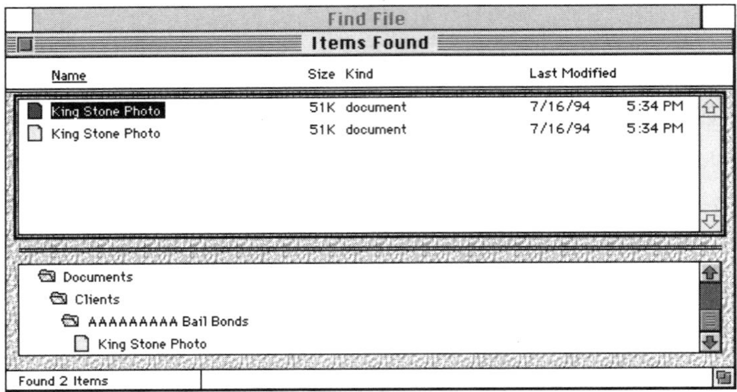


**Figure 1-24: System 7.5's Find File lists all items that matched your search criteria.**

The Find command is different in System 7 prior to System 7.5. You'll find a full description of the Find command in System 7.5 and in prior versions of System 7 under "Finding Items" in Chapter 6.

# Customizing Finder Views

System 7's Finder gives you control over the format and content of its windows. You select options by using the Views control panel (see Figure 1-25), and your settings immediately affect all windows. You can set the following:

- ❖ Font and size of text used for item names and window headings in all views
- ❖ Alignment method in icon and small icon views
- ❖ Content of and icon size in list views

For a complete description of all options, see "Custom List Views" in Chapter 6.

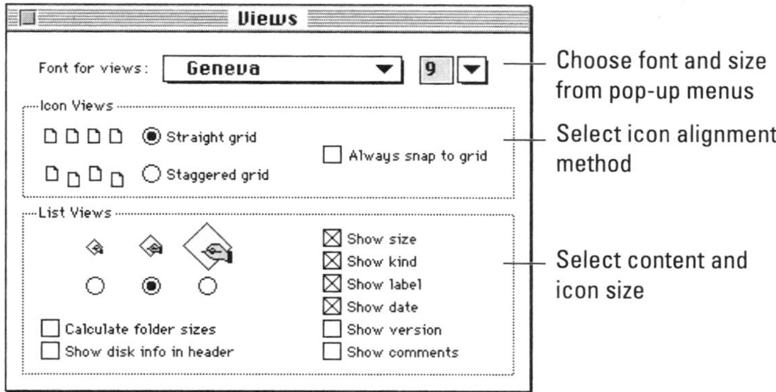


**Figure 1-25: Change the look and contents of Finder windows with the Views control panel.**

# Categorizing with Item Labels

Just as people use colored file folder labels to categorize folders of paper documents, System 7's Finder can categorize folders or other items with color. Colors don't show up on black-and-white screens, however, so each color has an associated text label. You assign an item a color and a label with the Finder's Label menu, as shown in Figure 1-26. After labeling items, you can view the Finder window's contents arranged by label, as shown in Figure 1-27. You can also search for items by label with the Finder's Find command, as shown in Figure 1-28. Label colors and text are not fixed; you can change them by using the Labels control panel, as shown in Figure 1-29.

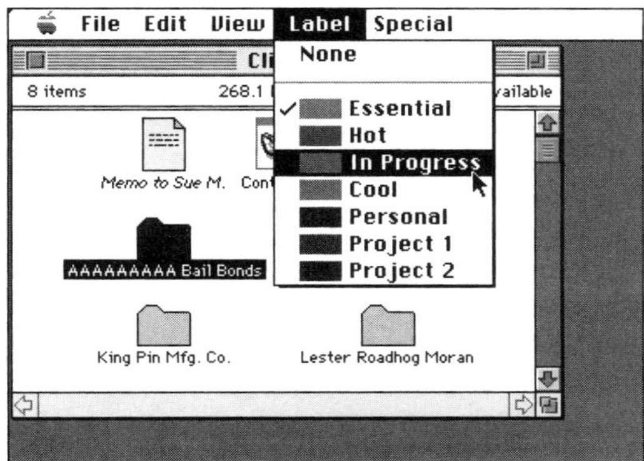


**Figure 1-26: Setting an item's label.**

◇All Tools

| Name | Size | Label | Last Modified |
|---|---|---|---|
| ◇Utilities (Verbal Tools) | 22K | Essential | Tue, Mar 19, 1991, 10:29 AM |
| ◇Communications | 9K | Hot | Tue, Mar 19, 1991, 8:29 AM |
| ◇Graphics | 13K | In Progress | Sat, Mar 2, 1991, 1:47 PM |
| ◇Numbers & Charts | 6K | Cool | Thu, Feb 28, 1991, 5:40 PM |
| ◇Publishing & Presentat... | 5K | Personal | Thu, Feb 28, 1991, 5:40 PM |
| ◇Word Processing | 10K | Project 1 | Fri, Mar 1, 1991, 3:53 PM |
| ◇Info Management | 10K | Project 2 | Thu, Feb 28, 1991, 5:40 PM |
| *MacProject II* | 1K | – | Mon, Dec 31, 1990, 3:33 PM |
| *Microsoft Works* | 1K | – | Mon, Dec 31, 1990, 3:34 PM |

**Figure 1-27: Viewing a Finder window by label.**

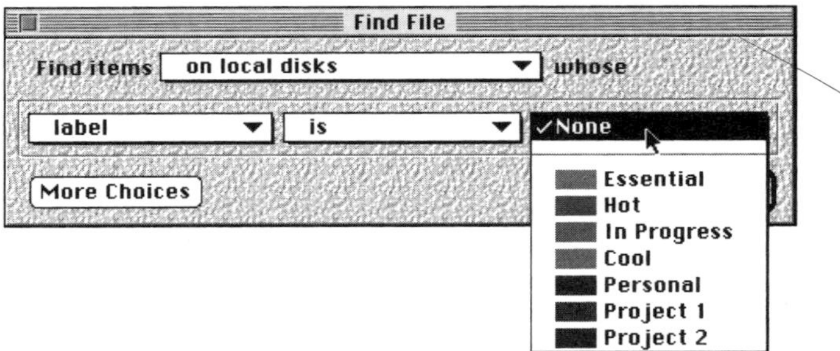


**Figure 1-28: Finding by label.**

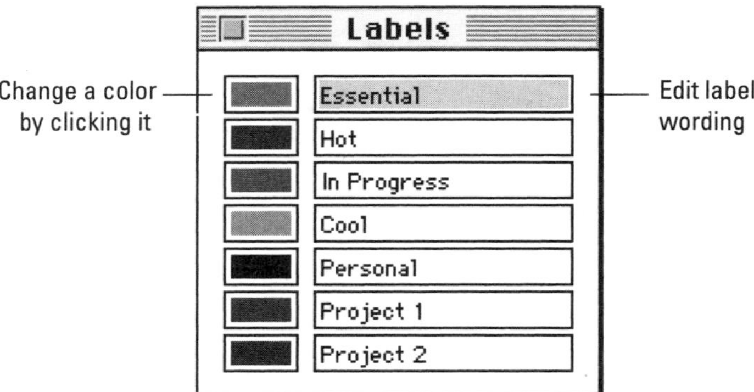


**Figure 1-29: Change label text and color with the Labels control panel.**

For a complete explanation of using and changing labels, see "Labeling Items" in Chapter 6.

Table 1-1
**Finder Keyboard Shortcuts**

| ***Objective*** | ***Action*** |
|---|---|
| Select an item by name | Type the item's full or partial name |
| Select the next item alphabetically | Tab |
| Select the previous item alphabetically | Shift-Tab |
| Select next item up, down, left, or right | Up arrow, down arrow, left arrow, or right arrow |
| Select the startup disk's icon | ⌘-Shift-up arrow |
| Open the selected item | ⌘-O or ⌘-down arrow |
| Open the selected item and close the active window | ⌘-Option-O or ⌘-Option-down arrow |
| Open the parent folder, disk, or volume | ⌘-up arrow |
| Open the parent folder, disk, or volume and close the active window | ⌘-Option-up arrow |
| Make the desktop active | ⌘-Shift-up arrow |
| Begin editing the selected item's name | Return or Enter |
| Expand the selected folder | ⌘-right arrow |
| Expand the selected folder and its nested folders | ⌘-Option-right arrow |
| Collapse the selected folder | ⌘-left arrow |
| Collapse the selected folder and its nested folders | ⌘-Option-left arrow |
| Skip installing all system extensions during one startup | Hold down Shift during startup |

## Keyboard Shortcuts

Much of what you do with the mouse on a Mac you can do with keyboard shortcuts instead. For instance, you can select an item in the active Finder window (or the desktop, if no window is active) without using the mouse by typing the item's name or the first part of its name. Other keystrokes select an item near the currently selected item, open the item, and so on. Table 1-1 gives the details. For more Finder shortcuts, refer to the Quick Reference card.

# CHAPTER 1 CONCEPTS AND TERMS

- System 7 displays color windows and icons, and System 7.5 has large colorful desktop patterns.
- Open frequently used items with the Apple menu, switch among open programs with the Applications menu, and get on-screen help with the Help menu. Check the time and date with System 7.5's menu-bar clock.
- Use aliases to give yourself access to an item from any number of places.
- Share your files with other Macs on a network and access their shared files.
- Open documents by dragging them to any compatible application.
- See outlines of folders in any list view, and use the folder pop-up menu to open the folder that contains an open folder.
- Change the name of a file, folder, or disk by clicking its name (not its icon). Paste a custom icon in the item's Info window.
- Create template documents as stationery pads.
- Find any item quickly with the Find command.
- Customize Finder views with the Views control panel.
- Control many Finder functions with keyboard shortcuts rather than the mouse.

**alias**
A small file that refers to another file, folder, or disk. You can put aliases anywhere, leaving the original items in their original locations, which gives you easy access to the original items without having to move them. An alias does not duplicate the original item's contents, it points to it.

**Apple menu**
The permanent menu at the left end of the menu bar, which you use to open any item. You can easily add and remove documents, folders, aliases, programs, or any other item.

**Application menu**
The permanent menu at the right end of the menu bar that lists the programs that are open. Choosing a listed program makes it active (brings it to the front).

**background program**
A program that operates during the split-second intervals in which the active program isn't using the computer. Background programs cannot interact directly with you in any way and cannot use the menu bar.

**balloon help**
An optional help system in which you point at an item on-screen to reveal a cartoon-style balloon that describes that item.

**directory dialog box**
What you see when you use an Open, Save, or other disk-related command. This dialog box shows a list view of your filing system, one window at a time.

**file server**
A computer whose disks are available for use by other computers over a network.

**folder path menu**
A menu you access by pressing ⌘ while clicking the the title of a Finder window. The menu shows the path through your folder structure from the active window to the disk containing it.

**multitasking**
Being able to keep more than one program open at a time, switch between open programs, and have programs keep working in the background.

**navigate**
To open or close folders until you have the one open that contains the item you want.

**pixel**
One dot on a display screen.

CHAPTER TWO

# More System 7 Highlights

- Organizing the System Folder, using controls panels and desk accessories, emptying the Trash, shrinking windows with WindowShade, posting screen notes with Stickies, and simplifying access to files with At Ease, the Launcher, Easy Open, and PC Exchange
- Working with smooth TrueType fonts and with QuickDraw GX's printing improvements, advanced typography, and WYSIWYG color
- Watching QuickTime movies, collaborating through PowerTalk e-mail and other services, and automating tasks with AppleScript
- Editing text or graphics by dragging it within or between windows, making compound documents with Publish and Subscribe, and working in multiple languages
- Listening to any Mac speak, and speaking to any Mac that can listen

System 7 contains too many features to preview in one chapter. The preceding chapter began an overview of System 7 capabilities, and this chapter concludes the executive summary.

## Organizing the System Folder

The Macintosh System Folder is crowded with all kinds of files — system extensions, control panels, fonts, application preference files, and many more. Prior to System 7, scores of these items floated around loose in the System Folder, making the folder a real mess. System 7 cleans up the mess with a half dozen special folders inside the System Folder. There's a Control Panels folder, a Preferences Folder, an Extensions folder, a Fonts folder, and so on. Each special folder has a distinctive icon, as shown in Figure 2-1. Moreover, the System 7 Finder knows in which special folder to put many items that you drag to the System Folder icon.

To learn more about the System Folder's special folders, see Chapter 7.

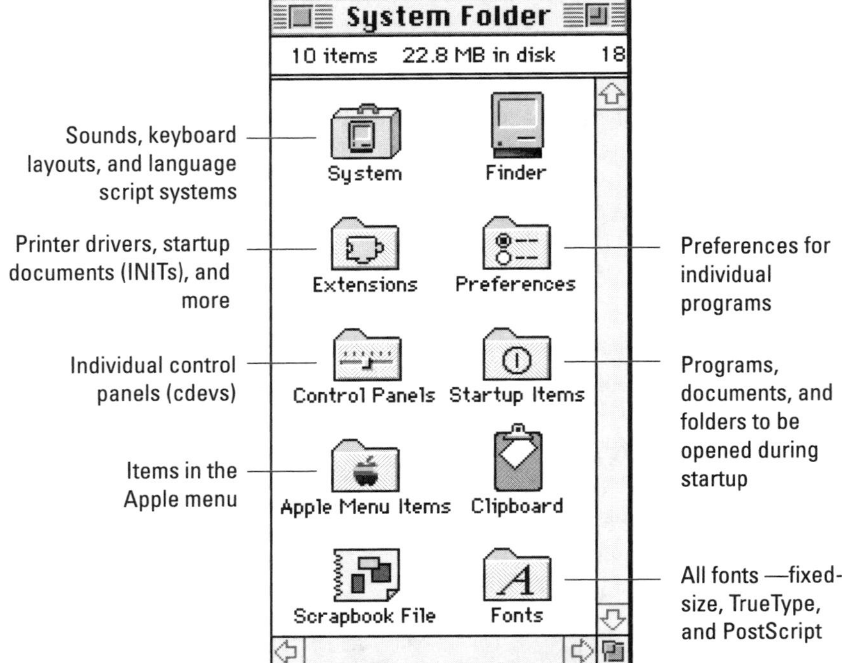


**Figure 2-1: Special folders subdivide the System Folder.**

# Fine Tuning with Control Panels

System 7 encourages fine tuning system appearance and behavior with control panels to an extent not possible in earlier versions of system software. The Macintosh originally had one control panel. Later, it got a modular one-window control panel in which you click the icon of the module whose settings you want to see or change. System 7 comes with 20 or so control panels, and you can add many more from innumerable sources. Each System 7 control panel opens in its own window, as shown in Figure 2-2.

System 7 keeps your collection of these valuable little programs in a special Control Panels folder inside the System Folder. For convenience, the Control Panels folder appears in the Apple menu so that you can open the folder easily. With the Control Panels folder open, you can rearrange the individual control panels in it by using the View menu or by dragging icons.

Some control panel documents (also called *cdevs*) work properly only if you put them in the System Folder itself, not in the Control Panels folder.

For more information, see "Control Panels Folder" in Chapter 7 and "Control Panels" in Chapter 8.

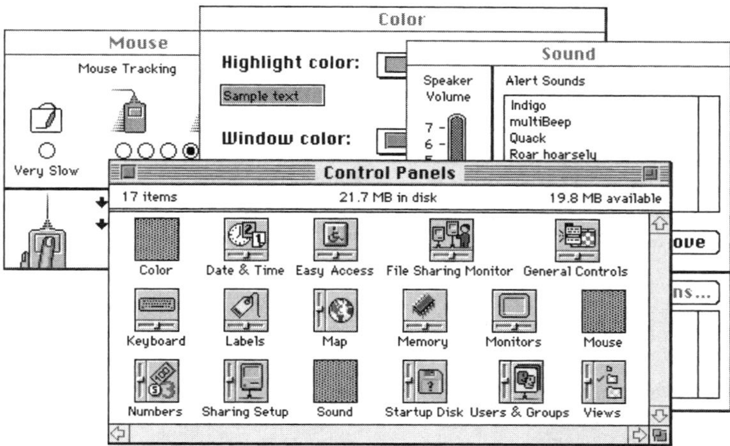


Figure 2-2: Each System 7 control panel opens in its own window.

## Trash Behavior

Items you drag to the Trash remain there indefinitely. You must empty the Trash manually by using the Finder's Empty Trash command found in the Special menu. When you do, the System 7 Finder tells you how many items the Trash contains and how much disk space they occupy, as shown in the following figure. You decide whether to discard them all or cancel the operation. To bypass this notice, press Option while choosing the Empty Trash command.

When you drag locked items to the Trash, the System 7 Finder does not display a warning as older Finders do. Instead, the warning appears when you choose the Empty Trash command with any of the locked items in the Trash. And, unlike older Finders, Finder 7 does not confirm whether you want to discard application programs and system files when you drag them to the Trash. For more information, see "Deleting Items" in Chapter 6.

# Liberating Desk Accessories

Desk accessories once always appeared in the Apple menu, but System 7 removes that restriction. Each desk accessory can have its own icon, which you can put in any folder or on the desktop, as shown in Figure 2-3. You open desk accessories like regular application programs: by double-clicking their icons, for example. You have the option of installing desk accessories in the Apple menu by dragging their icons or aliases of them to the Apple Menu Items folder within the System Folder.

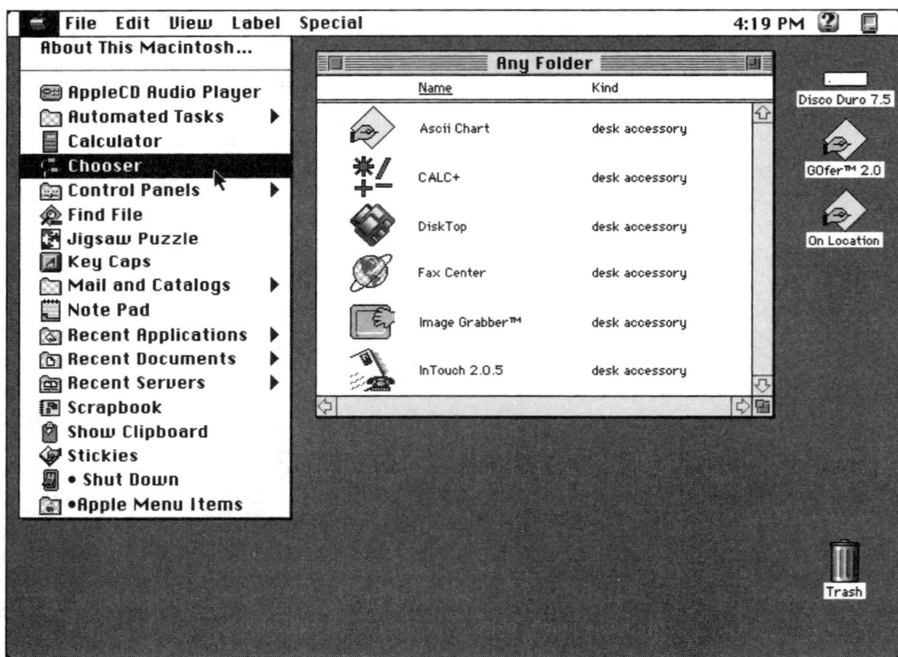


**Figure 2-3: Desk accessories have their own icons and you can put them anywhere.**

For more information about opening and using desk accessories, plus descriptions of the desk accessories that come with System 7, see "Desk Accessories" in Chapter 8.

# Posting Notes on Screen with Stickies

System 7.5 and Mac OS 7.6 come with a utility program, Stickies, that displays notes similar to Post-it Notes on your screen, as shown in Figure 2-4. You can set the color and the text font, size, and style for each note. Stickies windows have no scroll bars, but you can scroll by pressing the arrow keys or by dragging in the note. For more information, see "Stickies" in Chapter 8.

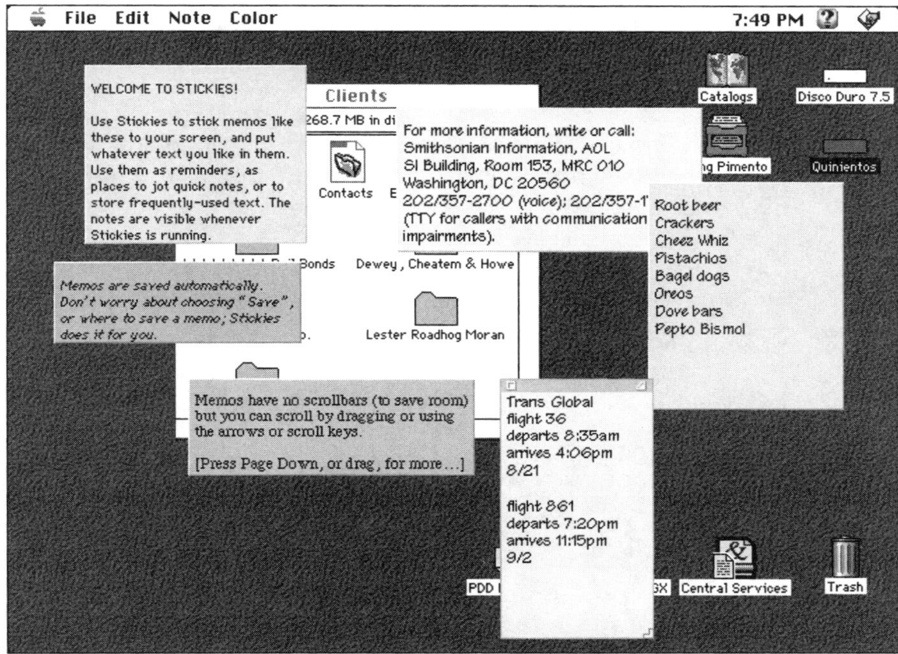


**Figure 2-4: System 7.5's Stickies program displays notes.**

# Opening Items Quickly from the Launcher

If you have trouble finding applications, documents, and other items that you use often, you can put aliases of them in the Launcher control panel that comes with some versions of System 7. The Launcher displays a window that contains large buttons for opening programs, documents, and folders, as shown in Figure 2-5. You open any item in the Launcher window by clicking its button. The Launcher comes with all Macintosh Performa computers and with System 7.5. You'll find the complete story on the Launcher under "Launcher" in Chapter 8.

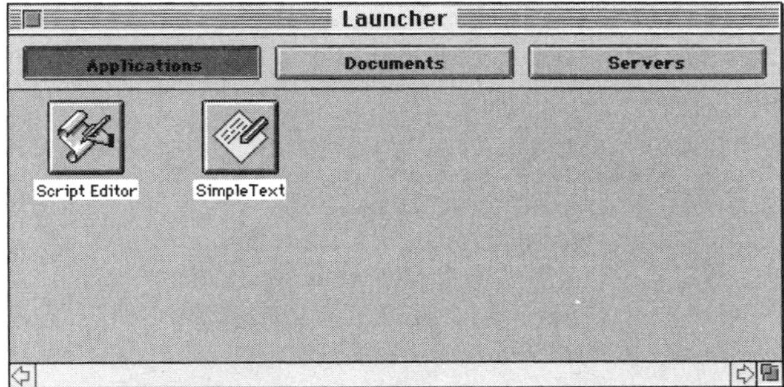


**Figure 2-5: Open items displayed in the Launcher window with one click.**

# Simplifying the Finder with At Ease

As an alternative to the Finder's standard desktop, Apple's At Ease software provides a simplified view of the Macintosh environment, as shown in Figure 2-6. When you install At Ease on a Mac, you determine which programs and documents the users of that computer can access. Each available program and document has a large button on the At Ease desktop, and clicking a button once opens the item (unlike Finder icons, which require double-clicking to open). You can also prevent users from saving documents on the hard disk and can set a password to restrict access to items not on the At Ease desktop or in the Apple menu.

At Ease is not included with System 7. It comes with Performa Macs, and you can also purchase and install it separately on any Mac. For more information, see "At Ease" in Chapter 5.

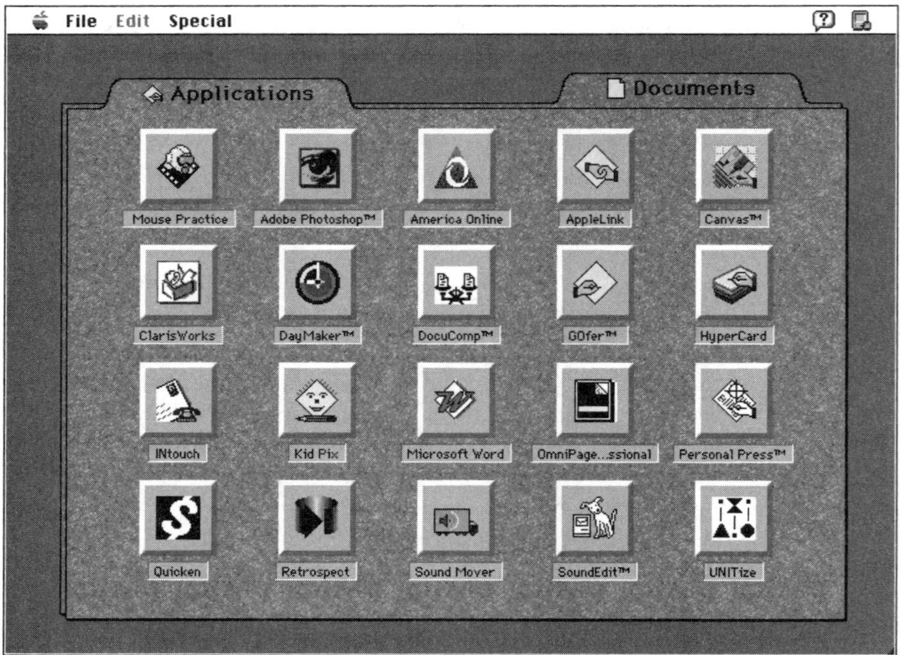


**Figure 2-6: At Ease simplifies the desktop.**

# Opening Strange Items with Easy Open

The Easy Open software relieves your frustration in trying to open a document when you don't have the application that created it. Instead of seeing a message that the document can't be opened, you see a list of applications that can open that kind of document either with or without file translation. Figure 2-7 shows a sample Easy Open list. Easy Open knows which file translators you have installed on your Mac and which kinds of documents your applications can open. Easy Open works with third-party translation software, such as DataViz's MacLink Translators, or with application programs that perform file translation to recognize alien documents and correctly translate them.

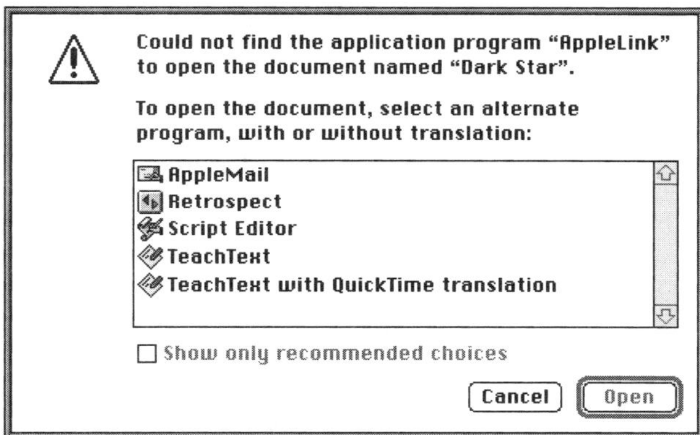
Could not find the application program "AppleLink" to open the document named "Dark Star".
To open the document, select an alternate program, with or without translation:
AppleMail
Retrospect
Script Editor
TeachText
TeachText with QuickTime translation
Show only recommended choices
Cancel
Open

**Figure 2-7: Easy Open offers alternatives for opening unrecognizable documents.**

An Easy Open accessory program, Document Converter, creates document converter icons that can be used to perform file conversions without opening another application. You simply drop your document onto the appropriate converter icon and the translation is performed.

Easy Open comes with System 7.5. It is also included with most file translator software you purchase separately. To learn more about how Macintosh Easy Open works, see Chapter 5.

# Using DOS Disks with PC Exchange

A Mac can access floppy disks from Windows, OS/2, or DOS computers if the PC Exchange control panel is installed. The foreign disk's icon appears on the desktop, and you can open it to see its contents. You can even open document files if you have compatible Mac programs.

# Improving Fonts and Typography

Text fonts look better and are easier to manage in System 7 than in earlier system software. System 7 includes Apple's variable-size font technology, TrueType, for better looking text. Advanced typography is part of the QuickDraw GX technology that comes with System 7.5. And in System 7 you install and remove fonts not by toiling with the Font/DA Mover utility program, as in earlier system software, but by simply dragging icons in the Finder.

## TrueType fonts

Thanks to the TrueType font technology built into System 7, text looks smooth at any size on-screen or on any printing device. *TrueType fonts* are variable-size outline fonts similar to the PostScript fonts that look so sharp on LaserWriters. System 7 smoothly scales TrueType fonts to any size, as shown in Figure 2-8. Old-style fonts still work; they look good at their prescribed sizes and appear lumpy when scaled to other sizes. TrueType fonts work with almost all Macintosh software, but some old programs only provide a limited list of font sizes and must be upgraded to provide a method for accommodating any font size.

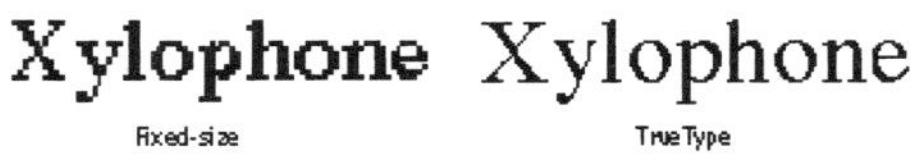

Xylophone Xylophone

Fixed-size TrueType

**Figure 2-8: 36-point Times as a fixed-size and TrueType font.**

You install a variable-size font by dragging it to the System Folder icon. A typical variable-size TrueType font takes up 10K to 20K more disk space than a set of corresponding fixed-size fonts in sizes 9, 10, 12, 14, 18, and 24. However, TrueType fonts save disk space if you use large sizes or if your printing device uses screen fonts. With TrueType, ink jet printers, fax modems, and laser printers without PostScript don't need the double, triple, or quadruple fixed sizes that take up a lot of disk space.

## QuickDraw GX fonts

System 7.5 is the first version of Macintosh system software to include the advanced font technology of QuickDraw GX. In application programs that take advantage of GX fonts, you can stretch, rotate, skew, and manipulate text around objects. In addition, you can manage such type controls as line weights, tracking, and kerning for your fonts — just like a professional typographer. With GX fonts, QuickDraw GX automatically substitutes ligatures by merging two characters into one, such as a and e into æ, as you enter text normally. In addition, QuickDraw GX can automatically form rational fractions like ⁷⁄₈.

### Printed text

LaserWriters and other PostScript devices use PostScript fonts instead of equivalent TrueType fonts. If a document contains a TrueType font that has no PostScript equivalent, System 7 scales the TrueType font to the resolution of the output device. Non-PostScript printers, such as ink jet printers and dot matrix printers, let the Mac scale TrueType fonts to the resolution they require to print cleanly.

With QuickDraw GX installed, text can be automatically kerned and scaled properly to meet the requirements of each printer. QuickDraw GX enables sharing and background printing with non-networked printers such as StyleWriters and ImageWriters. With QuickDraw GX, you can drag a document and drop it on a printer icon on your desktop to get instant printing without using the Chooser. In application programs that take advantage of GX printing, you can also print each page of a document on a different paper size, add watermarks, and customize your printing in many other ways.

For more information about using fixed-size, TrueType, PostScript, and QuickDraw GX fonts, see Chapter 11.

## Printing the QuickDraw GX Way

The printing process remained the same on the Macintosh for more than 10 years, until the arrival of QuickDraw GX with System 7.5. QuickDraw GX both simplifies printing and makes it more flexible. You no longer use the Chooser whenever you need to change printers. Instead, you use the Chooser to create desktop printer icons for every printer, fax modem, or other output device you use. After creating desktop printer icons, you use the Printing menu that QuickDraw GX adds to the Finder to designate a default printer.

Opening a desktop printer icon displays a list of documents waiting to be printed in the background, as shown in Figure 2-9. You can drag the waiting documents to rearrange the printing order, or you can drag waiting documents to another desktop printer icon to redirect printing.

You can print by dragging documents directly to any desktop printer icon. You can also print with the usual Page Setup and Print commands (located in most applications' File menus).

In applications that have been revised to take full advantage of QuickDraw GX printing, the Print and Page Setup commands have simplified dialog boxes in which you can choose a printer from a pop-up menu, as shown in Figure 2-10. The simple dialog boxes expand when you click the More Choices button to offer more options — options such as selecting a paper tray or setting a print time — as shown in Figure 2-11. You can extend the Print and Page Setup options by adding GX printing extensions to your Extensions folder.

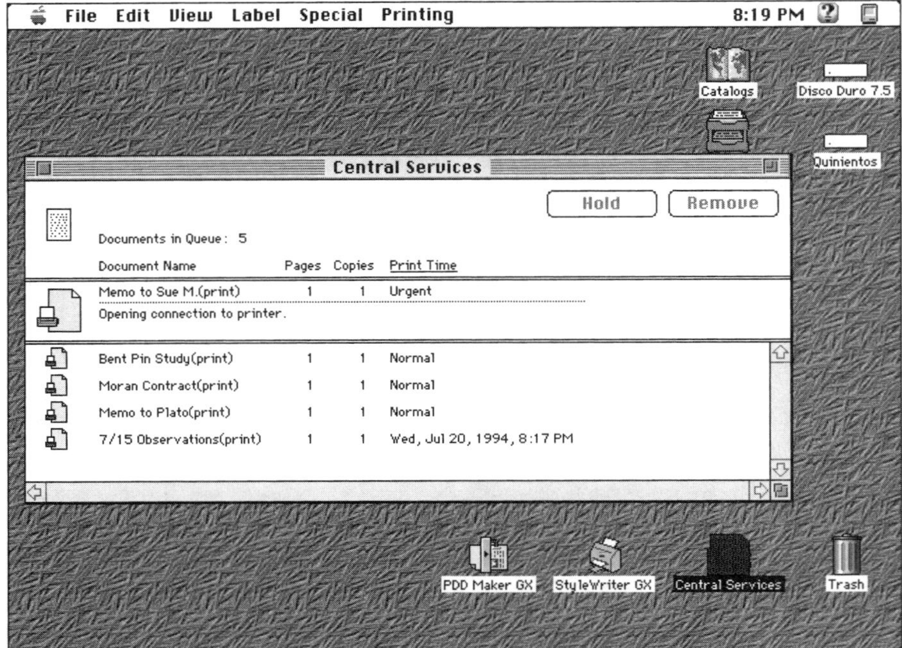


**Figure 2-9: Opening a desktop printer icon lets you see and reschedule documents awaiting printing.**

Instead of printing a document on paper, you can save it as a *Portable Digital Document (PDD)* file. PDDs allow QuickDraw GX users to view and print (on paper) fully formatted on-screen documents without the applications or fonts used to create them.

To create a desktop printer icon for a printer, fax modem, or other output device, you must have GX printer driver software for it. You can still use old printing methods with output devices for which you have no GX printer driver software.

For more information on printing with and without QuickDraw GX, see Chapter 12.

# Extending Memory

Application programs are becoming more memory hungry all the time, and System 7 has a large appetite itself. Seems like a computer can never have too much memory. System 7 includes several memory management capabilities not found in earlier system software, including 32-Bit Addressing and virtual memory. These features and more are described in depth in Chapter 13.

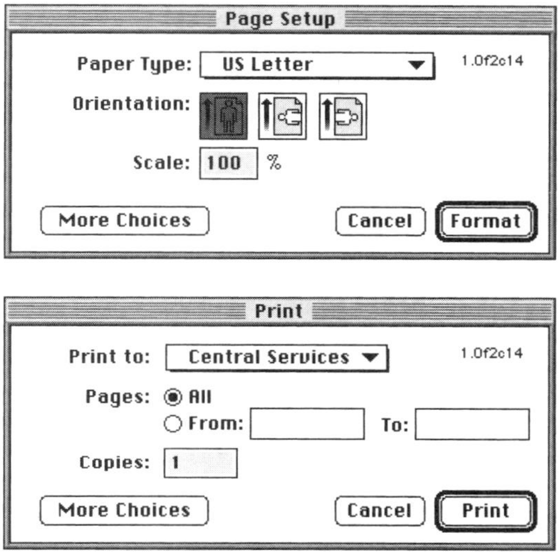

Figure 2-10: Simple Page Setup and Print dialog boxes in an application that has adopted QuickDraw GX printing.

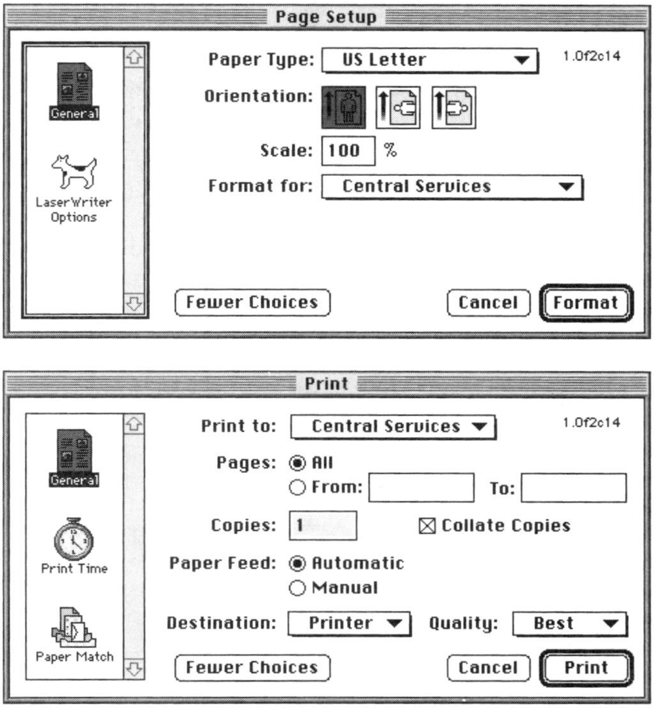

Figure 2-11: Expanded Page Setup and Print dialog boxes in an application that has adopted QuickDraw GX printing.

## 32-Bit Addressing

Most Macintosh models can access more than 8MB of random-access memory (RAM) by using System 7's 32-Bit Addressing capability. With maximum RAM installed, for example, turning on 32-Bit Addressing enables you to use 10MB of RAM on a Mac LC II or Performa 410; 14MB on a PowerBook 160 or 180; 17MB on a IIsi; 36MB on an LC III, Performa 460, or Quadra 605; 68MB on a Quadra 610; 128MB on a Quadra 840AV; 132MB on a Quadra 650; 136MB on a Quadra 800; and a whopping 264MB on a Power Mac 8100/80. If 32-Bit Addressing is turned off, you can only use 8MB of RAM regardless of the amount installed.

The 32-Bit Addressing feature doesn't work on a Mac Plus, SE, or Portable. To use 32-Bit Addressing on a Mac IIcx, IIx, II, or SE/30, you must install the 32-Bit Enabler or Connectix's MODE32 system extension, both of which Apple distributes free through dealers, user groups, and on-line information services. Unfortunately, these software fixes don't work with System 7.5 and later. Also, very old application programs, desk accessories, system extensions, control panels, and hard disk software may not work when 32-Bit Addressing is activated.

## Virtual memory

You may be able to increase the amount of memory available on your Macintosh without installing more RAM. System 7 can use part of a hard disk transparently as additional memory. This extra memory, called *virtual memory*, enables you to keep more programs open simultaneously and increase the amount of memory each program gets when you open it, as shown in Figure 2-12. Given more memory, many programs allow you to open additional or larger documents. You can get by with less RAM by using virtual memory. You buy only as much as you need for average, not peak, use.

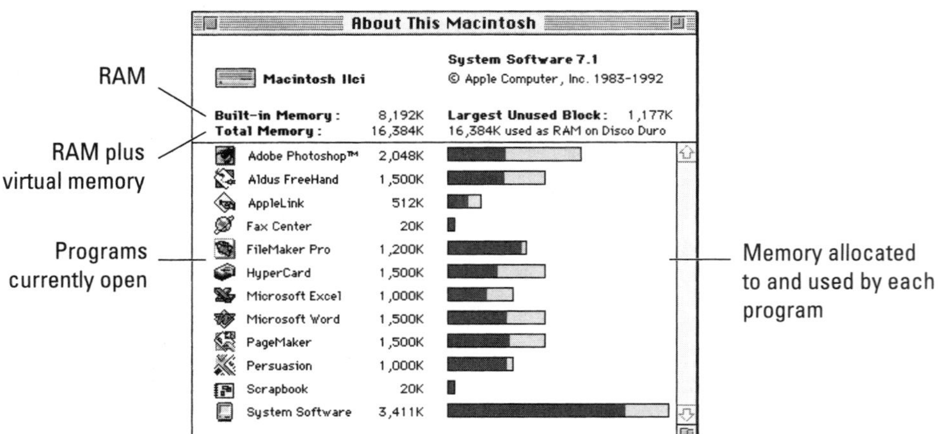


**Figure 2-12: Virtual memory uses disk space to increase the amount of memory available for opening programs.**

Virtual memory only works on a Macintosh equipped with a memory-management unit (MMU). The MMU is a chip, or part of a chip, that knows how much memory is available, what type it is, where to find it, and how to organize it into usable chunks. All of the currently available Performas, LCs, Quadras, PowerBooks, and Power Macs have MMUs. A Mac II can be retrofitted with a MMU; however, a Mac Plus, SE, Classic, or Portable cannot use System 7's virtual memory even if it has such an accelerator. The ROMs in these models lack information that System 7 needs to implement virtual memory.

# Watching QuickTime Movies

A system extension called QuickTime, introduced in 1992, extends the standard Macintosh system software so that you can incorporate movies into documents you create with mainstream application programs. After installing QuickTime, you can copy and paste movies as easily as you copy and paste individual graphics. Quick-Time can also compress individual graphics, and when you open a compressed graphic, QuickTime automatically decompresses it.

Applications use two methods for controlling movie playback. They can display a standard VCR-like controller just below the movie, as shown in Figure 2-13. You use this play bar to play, stop, browse, or step through the movie and adjust its sound level.

**Figure 2-13: A QuickTime movie with a playback controller.**

Applications can also display movies without controllers. In this case, a badge in the lower-left corner of the movie distinguishes it from a still graphic. To play a movie that has a badge and no controller, you double-click the movie. Clicking a playing movie stops it.

Apple began including the QuickTime system extension and a new QuickTime-capable Scrapbook with its System 7.1 products.

For more information about QuickTime and other multimedia topics, refer to Chapter 16.

# Collaborating through PowerTalk Services

With System 7 Pro and System 7.5, Apple includes a number of communication services to the Macintosh desktop. The Finder and system extensions that provide these services are collectively called PowerTalk; they are not compatible with Mac OS 7.6 and later. PowerTalk places a series of icons on your desktop, as shown in Figure 2-14, that provide easy access to e-mail, contact information, and other collaboration services.

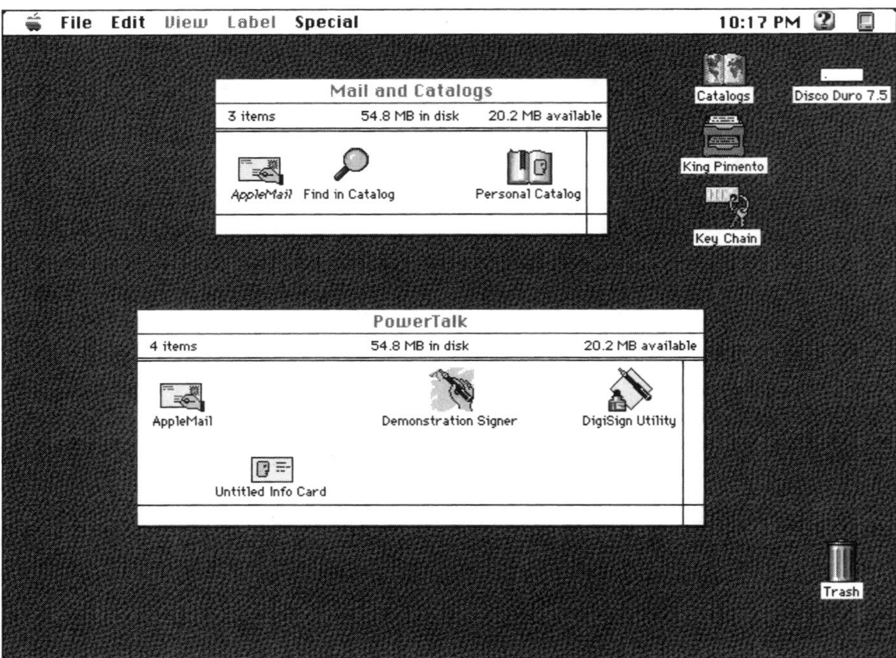


**Figure 2-14: PowerTalk provides many collaboration services.**

PowerTalk consists of the following six services:

❖ **Catalogs** provide quick access to information about people with whom you communicate and network services you use. They include names, phone and fax numbers, postal addresses, electronic addresses, personal notes, and more.

- **Desktop Mailbox** is a personal in-basket and out-basket for retaining e-mail messages, faxes, voice mail messages, and bulletin board information.
- **Key Chain** is an integrated system for accessing network services, such as file servers, by using a single dialog box and password.
- **DigiSign Utility** is a security system that applies your digital signature to messages, guaranteeing that the message is really from you and has not been tampered with.
- **AppleMail** is an application program you use to create and send e-mail.
- **Mailers** let any application program that incorporates PowerTalk technology send a document as e-mail.

PowerTalk uses the Apple Open Collaboration Environment (AOCE) protocol to provide these collaboration services. Most services are available when you install PowerTalk, but application programs must be revised to take advantage of Mailers.

To learn how to use PowerTalk and its related PowerShare file server system, see Chapter 15.

# Listening and Talking through PlainTalk

The very first Macintosh could speak in 1984 — at its debut it thanked Steve Jobs for being "like a father to me." Its voice, created by the MacinTalk system extension, had a heavy robot accent. Today, Apple's PlainTalk technology gives Macs a clearer voice. In addition, the most powerful Macs can use PlainTalk to recognize spoken commands.

PlainTalk synthesizes a variety of voices, male and female, with good inflection. It is quite accurate and can correctly pronounce most words and punctuation — even abbreviations. PlainTalk works on any Mac Plus or newer model, although it requires a 68020 processor or better to generate high-quality voices and up to 6MB of disk space for voice samples and system extensions.

PlainTalk also offers a major advance in speech recognition. With no advance training, it can recognize voice commands of most North American English speakers. This capability requires powerful hardware, starting with 16-bit sound input to digitize spoken commands. To compare the digitized sound with its database of almost 1,000 voice samples, PlainTalk requires either the 68040 processor and a DSP coprocessor of the Centris and Quadra AV models or the PowerPC processor of the Power Macs.

PlainTalk voice recognition doesn't work on older Macs that have been upgraded with PowerPC accelerator cards, such as Apple's PowerPC Upgrade card, because they lack the required 16-bit sound input. The Speech Setup control panel device shown in Figure 2-15 activates and manages speech recognition.

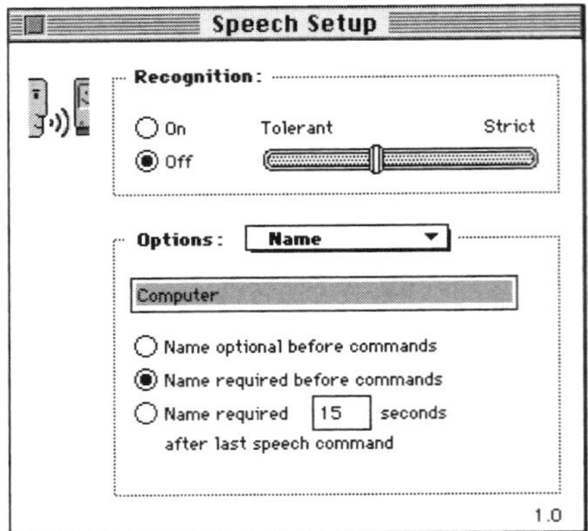


**Figure 2-15: The Speech Setup control panel.**

# Matching Colors with ColorSync

Apple has developed a color management system called ColorSync that minimizes the problem of mismatched color input and output. It ensures that color input from scanners and graphics programs matches color output on monitors, printers, and plotters. ColorSync is part of QuickDraw GX, which is included with System 7.5, and is also included as a separate system extension with the Apple OneScanner and Apple Color Printer. ColorSync works with color management systems, such as Efi Color and the Kodak Color Management System, so applications that depend upon these proprietary systems are compatible with the new architecture.

# Using Foreign Languages with WorldScript

System 7.1 was the first Macintosh system software capable of handling multiple languages without modification. You can install resources called *script systems* in the System file for languages that do not use the Roman alphabet. Each script system supplies fonts, keyboard layouts, rules for text sorting and word breaks, and rules for formatting dates, times, and numbers. Some script systems handle very large character sets and bi-directional or contextual text. Two system extensions, WorldScript I and WorldScript II, process language script systems.

With multiple script systems installed in your System file, a Keyboard menu appears between the Guide menu and the Application menu (see Figure 2-16). You can use it to switch languages and keyboards.

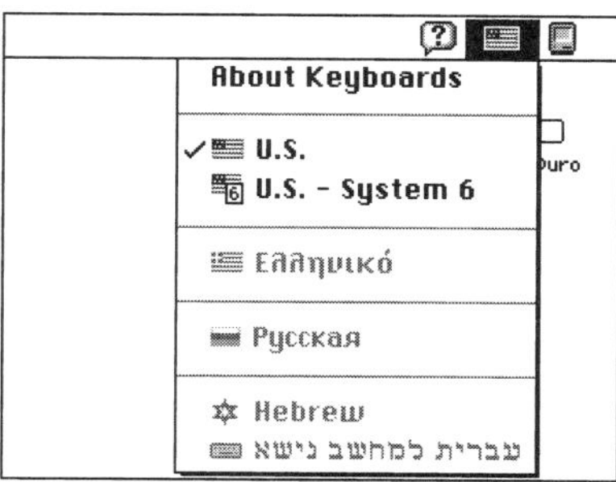


**Figure 2-16: The Keyboard menu appears when multiple language script systems are installed.**

WorldScript I and WorldScript II work on any Macintosh with System 7.1 or later installed. Many programs require no modification to work with simple alphabets (Roman and Cyrillic) and with bi-directional and contextual languages (Hebrew, Arabic, Greek, and Thai). Old programs require updating to use languages with large alphabets, such as Chinese and Japanese, and to take full advantage of WorldScript capabilities. For more information, see Chapter 17.

# Scripting across the System

With the AppleScript extension to System 7, you can automate multistep tasks involving one or many applications, such as renaming a batch of documents in the Finder or pasting graphics from a batch of graphics files into a page layout document. You can create a *script*, or a set of instructions, by performing the task once manually while the AppleScript system watches and records your actions. Then you modify the script with a script editing program, as shown in Figure 2-17.

AppleScript relies on System 7's framework for information interchange, called Apple events. It enables any program to send messages to other programs. System 7 stores Apple events messages sent to a closed program and forwards the messages when the program is next opened. It also dispatches messages across a network to programs on other Macs. Older programs must be upgraded to support Apple events, AppleScript, and script recording.

To learn the basics of creating scripts with AppleScript, see Chapter 18.

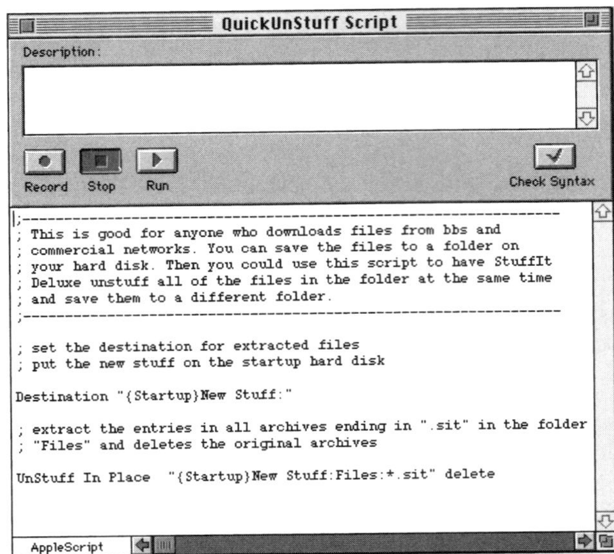


**Figure 2-17: The AppleScript Editor for recording and editing scripts.**

# Publish and Subscribe

System 7 enables you to share information dynamically from one document to other documents. Because the sharing is dynamic, changes made to the original information are automatically reflected in copies of it, wherever they are. Think of it as live copy and paste. The automatic updating extends to computers interconnected on a network, so a document on your computer can dynamically share information from a document on another networked Macintosh. By contrast, copying and pasting shares information statically and only one Mac is involved.

You make a live copy of information by *publishing* an *edition* of it. You include copies of the information in a document by *subscribing* to the edition, as shown in Figure 2-18. Publishing material from a document creates a live copy of the material in an edition file on disk. Any number of other documents (on your Mac or others networked to your Mac) include live copies of the material by subscribing to the edition. When you change the original material and save the document that contains it, the edition is automatically updated. Each subscribing document learns of the update the next time it is opened.

Information can only be shared dynamically among documents created by programs that include Edit menu commands for publishing and subscribing, as shown in Figure 2-19. You don't find these commands in old programs that haven't been upgraded to include publishing and subscribing commands.

To learn how to create and use compound documents, see Chapter 14.

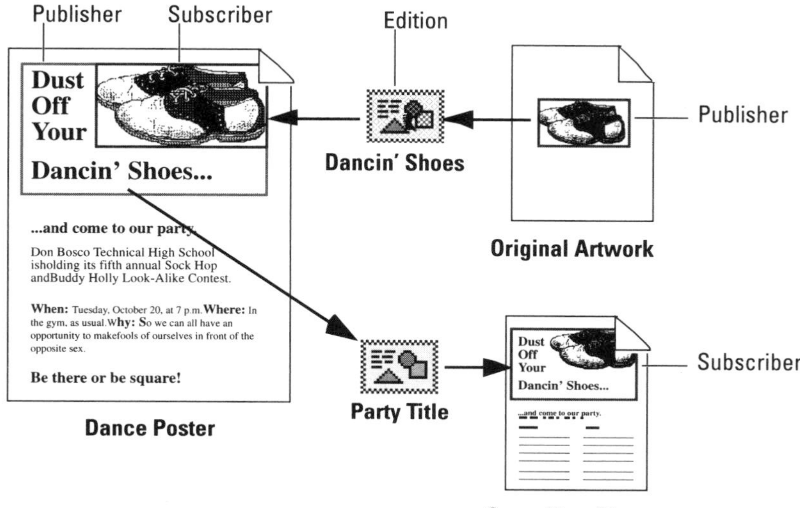


**Figure 2-18: Publishing and subscribing.**

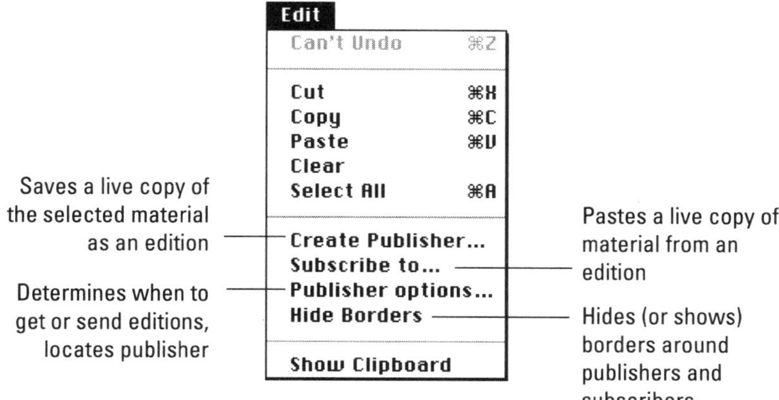


**Figure 2-19: Commands for publishing and subscribing.**

# Editing by Mouse Alone

System 7.5 provides a way to drag text, graphics, or other material from one document window to another, altogether bypassing the Cut, Copy, and Paste commands. You can drag within a document, between documents, and between applications, as shown in Figure 2-20. You can drag material from a document to a Finder window or the desktop and it becomes a clipping file. Conversely, you can drag a clipping file to a document window. This capability, called *drag-and-drop editing*, works only with applications that are designed to take advantage of it. For more information, see "Drag-and-Drop Editing" in Chapter 14.

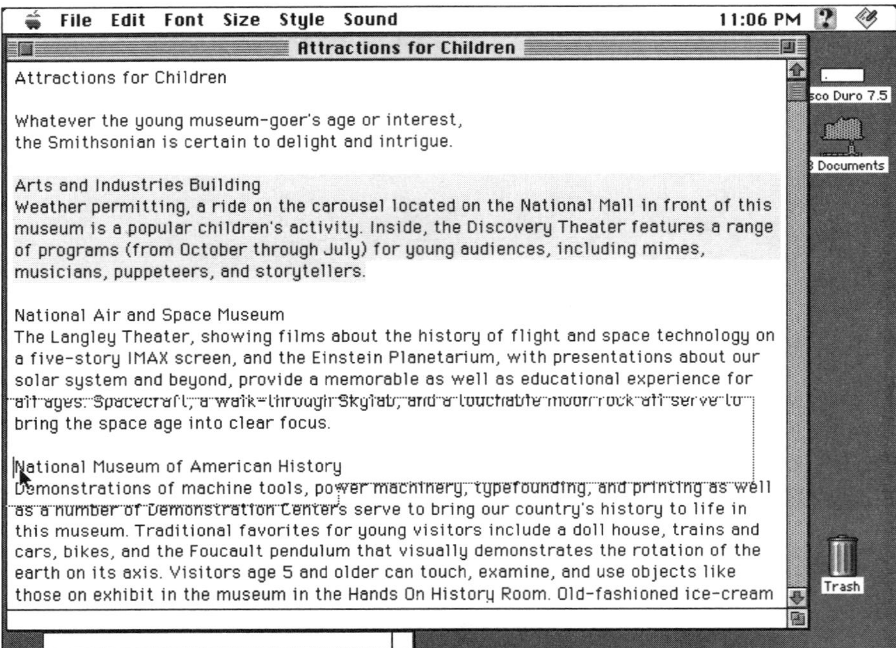


**Figure 2-20: Dragging text from place to place within a document.**

# Making Compound Documents

A new way of working with documents is coming to the Macintosh and other computers. Instead of creating a different kind of document for each kind of content — words, spreadsheets, graphics, movies, and so on — you create one document that can contain any kind of content. To create these compound documents, you don't use large, monolithic application programs, each taking up many megabytes of disk space. Instead, you use specialized software components. Each software component manipulates one kind of content.

Here's how you work with compound documents on the Mac. You click the content you want to work on. That region of the document becomes active, a visible border appears around it, and the software tool that manipulates that kind of content takes over the menu bar. Drag-and-drop editing makes it easy to move content between documents and applications.

# CHAPTER  CONCEPTS AND TERMS

- The System Folder contains separate folders for Apple menu items, control panels, extensions, fonts, preferences, and startup items. Each control panel opens in its own window.
- Desk accessories are not bound to the Apple menu but can be kept in and opened from any folder.
- System 7.5 and Mac OS 7.6 include the Stickies program for posting small notes on the screen, and the Launcher control panel for easy access to items you open regularly.
- The Trash only empties itself when you choose the Empty Trash command.
- For a simplified alternative to the regular Finder, you can install At Ease (not included with System 7).
- When you want to open a document but don't have the application that created it, the Easy Open control panel suggests compatible alternatives. The PC Exchange control panel lets you work with DOS and Windows disks as if they were Mac disks.
- Variable-size TrueType fonts, which are outline fonts similar to PostScript fonts, enable you to see sharp text at any size on any screen, printer, or other output device. QuickDraw GX (part of System 7.5) provides advanced typographical control, such as swash capitals, ligatures, and lowercase numbers for fractions.
- QuickDraw GX simplifies printing with desktop printers and adds more power with GX printing extensions and Portable Digital Documents (PDDs). Revised Print and Page Setup commands offer simpler yet more flexible control in applications that fully adopt GX printing.
- Virtual memory allows you to use disk space as if it were memory for opening programs and documents. 32-Bit Addressing makes it possible to use more than 8MB of RAM.
- Installing the QuickTime system extension allows you to include movies in your documents.
- PowerTalk puts e-mail and other collaboration services on System 7 Pro and System 7.5 desktops.
- PlainTalk gives most Macs the capability to speak any text and gives powerful Macs the ability to recognize voice commands.
- ColorSync improves color consistency in documents by matching scanner color to video monitor and printer color.
- WorldScript handles multiple languages in System 7.1 and later.
- AppleScript brings system-wide scripting to the Macintosh. You can record and write scripts that automate repetitive tasks.
- The Publish and Subscribe commands create links between documents for dynamic updating of shared data, in effect giving you live copy and paste.

**32-Bit Addressing**
Enables you to use an extended amount of memory on certain Mac models.

**Apple events**
System 7's framework for information exchange, which enables any program to send messages to other programs.

**At Ease**
Software that provides a simplified view of the Mac environment and gives you control over which programs and documents users can access.

**control panel**
Located in the System Folder, these programs adjust things such as sound, color, and mouse control.

**desk accessory**
A small program, once only accessible from the Apple menu, but with System 7 can be placed in any folder or on the desktop.

**fixed-size font**
A font which looks best at certain prescribed sizes.

**ligature**
A character created by merging two others, for example merging a and e to get æ.

**PlainTalk**
Speaks text in male and female voices with good inflection, and can also recognize voice commands of most North American English speakers.

**PowerTalk**
The collective name for the new system extensions and utility programs that provide powerful communication services by placing a series of icons on your desktop that provide easy access to e-mail directories and other collaboration services. Consists of Catalogs, Mailbox, KeyChain, DigiSign Utility, AppleMail, and Mailers.

**publish**
To make a live copy of information.

*(continued on next page)*

*(continued from previous page)*

**QuickDraw GX**
Included with System 7.5 and later, provides simplified printing, advanced typography, improved graphics, and color matching.

**QuickTime**
Enables you to incorporate movies into documents that you create with mainstream application programs.

**script**
A set of instructions.

**subscribe**
To include copies of live information in a document.

**System Folder**
The folder that contains system extensions, control panels, fonts, application preference files, and more, subdivided into six more folders.

**TrueType**
Apple's variable-size font technology that makes text look smooth at any size.

**variable-size font**
A font that can be scaled to look good printed in any point size, and on any output device.

**virtual memory**
The transparent use of part of a hard disk as extra memory.

CHAPTER THREE

# Sorting Out System Versions

- The major features and benefits of each system software version
- Which system version makes sense for you
- How to use two versions of system software on one Mac, and what happens when Macs on a network have different versions of the system software
- How much memory and disk space System 7 requires
- Where to get System 7

If you're using an old version of the Mac OS, should you upgrade to the latest? To answer that question, this chapter explains the key features of various System 7 versions and of System 6. If you want to upgrade but have applications that require an older version of system software, this chapter explains how you can switch between the two versions of system software on one Mac. This chapter also describes what happens if you mix different versions of system software on a network. Finally, the chapter details the hardware requirements for using System 7 and where you can get System 7.

## System Versions

More than 90 percent of all Macintosh computers use System 7.0 or later, and over 40 percent use System 7.5 or later. Many Mac OS users got some version of System 7 with their computers. Apple began shipping System 7.0 on all new Macs in the middle of 1991, changed to System 7.1 in October 1992, upgraded System 7.5 in November 1994, and moved to Mac OS 7.6 in the beginning of 1997. During those years millions of people upgraded older Macs from System 6 to System 7 on their own. If you use System 7 but acquired it some time ago, you may be wondering how it compares with newer versions and whether you should upgrade. If you're still using System 6 on a Mac Plus or newer Mac made in the late 1980s or early 1990s, you should seriously consider moving up to the stability and power of System 7.

## System 6

System 6, the immediate predecessor of System 7, still is a viable option for owners of older Mac models. System 6 operates faster than System 7 on slower Macs, and it requires less memory and disk space. Perhaps the greatest advantage of System 6 is its compatibility with old software. If you have an old program that isn't compatible with System 7, you need to have System 6 around.

A few of the features normally associated with System 7 also work with System 6. One such feature is *cooperative multitasking*, which allows you to keep more than one program open if your Mac has enough memory. This capability, provided by the MultiFinder software that comes with all versions of System 6, can be turned on and off in System 6. When MultiFinder is on, you can switch among open applications by clicking an icon in the menu bar. Turning MultiFinder off frees 1MB of memory for opening a large application that you might not be able to open otherwise.

Another feature that System 6 can borrow from System 7 is *TrueType* font technology. Although TrueType has never been included with System 6, a TrueType extension and TrueType fonts are available for System 6.0.7 and 6.0.8. When the TrueType extension and TrueType Fonts are in the System Folder, those versions of System 6 can smoothly scale text at any size on-screen, on any printer, or on any other output device.

A third System 7 feature that System 6 can acquire is QuickTime. Adding the QuickTime extension to the System Folder gives System 6.0.7 or 6.0.8 the capability to play QuickTime movies.

## System 7.0

In the middle of 1991, Apple introduced System 7.0 and changed the way users worked on their Macs. System 7.0 brings colored icons and windows to the Mac environment, opens the Apple menu, and makes fonts easier to manage. Multitasking is no longer optional, but integrated into the Finder. Aliases of files, folders, and disks also appear for the first time in the System 7.0 Finder.

System 7.0 organizes the System Folder with separate folders for system extensions, control panels, Apple Menu items, and files of preference settings saved by individual applications. The capability to open documents by dragging them to a compatible application is another new feature of System 7.0.

System 7.0 was the first system software to come with TrueType, the variable-size-font technology. TrueType fonts display and print smoothly at any size on any printer or screen.

Earlier system software allows users to access files on a network file server, but System 7.0's file sharing allows users to share their own disks, folders, and files directly with other people on the same network. This feature gives small workgroups another use for a network that previously allowed only workgroup members to share a networked LaserWriter.

System 7.0 was the first Mac system software that permitted 32-Bit Addressing, enabling Macs to use more than 8MB of RAM for opening programs. Virtual memory, another System 7.0 first, increases available memory by using hard-disk storage as though it were RAM.

Buried in System 7.0 is the capability to "paste" a live copy of material into another document. This capability, called *publish and subscribe*, is based on Apple's interapplication communications (IAC) technology, known as Apple events. Apple events also makes it possible for programs to link and share functions, although software developers have been slow to take advantage of Apple events.

## System 7.0.1

System 7.0.1 replaced System 7.0 in October 1991 and is still available (as described in "Where to Get System 7" later in this chapter). The new version takes advantage of hardware features in the Quadra and PowerBook models. System 7.0.1 also fixes a few bugs in System 7.0.

## System 7.0.1P

System 7.0.1P has all the capabilities of System 7.0.1 but is designed to appear less complex to the mass-market consumer who got it with a Macintosh Performa 200 or 400. The Performas are, in general, identical to certain Mac models sold in computer specialty stores. Yet, Performas are different because they are meant to be consumer products — easy to assemble and use.

System 7.0.1P comes with extra system components not included with System 7.0.1. The Launcher control panel displays a window of large buttons that permit one-click opening of documents and applications. When a program is opened, the Finder's Desktop is hidden automatically to prevent the user from accidentally switching to the Finder by clicking the desktop. The desktop patterns are more colorful as well.

Changes to the Save command tend to keep documents together in a Documents folder rather than in the folders of the applications that create them; users can override the default setting, however, and save individual documents in any folder.

System 7.0.1P also comes with At Ease version 1, which can be used to restrict access to sensitive parts of the system, such as the System Folder.

## System 7 Tune-Up

System 7.0 is designed to be easy to update and augment via system extensions. One important early system extension is the System 7.1.1 Tune-Up extension.

Tune-Up 7.1.1 is designed for two purposes: to fix a major bug that caused files and folders to disappear from the desktop and to increase the performance of the operating system when it runs in low memory configurations.

If you use System 7.0 or 7.0.1, by all means install Apple's System 7 Tune-Up version 7.1.1. It is available free or for a small charge from Apple dealers, user groups, and on-line services. Do not install earlier versions of the Tune-Up, which you may find available from sources. Earlier versions do not fully fix the problems that the Tune-Up is meant to correct.

## System 7.1

System 7.1 accompanied the Macintosh models introduced in October 1992. This version incorporates the improvements made by System 7 Tune-Up 7.1.1. System 7.1 also has WorldScript technology, which makes it easy to use foreign-language applications, including Asian languages with large alphabets. In addition, System 7.1 is the earliest version extensible with system enabler files (see "System Enablers" later in this chapter).

Several control panels new in System 7.1 make it possible to change the formats for dates, times, numbers, and text behavior (such as sorting). System 7.1 further organizes the System Folder by adding a Fonts folder to contain all types of fonts.

## System 7.1P

System 7.1P is a Performa version of System 7.1. It has all the capabilities of System 7.1, but like System 7.0.1P, it is designed for the mass-market consumer.

The Launcher control panel displays one-click buttons for opening applications and documents. The Finder's desktop is hidden automatically when another program is active. The Performa desktop patterns are more colorful than the regular Mac patterns. The documents that you save go into a Documents folder unless you take the trouble to switch folders when you save them. If other people use your Mac, you can use At Ease version 2 to deny them the use of the Finder, restrict access to the System Folder, and so on.

Apple bundled its Macintosh PC Exchange software with System 7.1P. It lets Performas use disks created on Apple II, DOS, and Windows computers.

## System 7.1.1 and System 7 Pro

System 7 Pro includes all the features of System 7.1, plus PowerTalk and AppleScript. PowerTalk collaboration services include e-mail, catalogs of the people and network devices you work with, simplified connection to file servers, and digital signatures, as described in Chapter 15. You use AppleScript to automate tasks that involve one application or multiple applications, as described in Chapter 18.

System 7.1.1 is a subset of System 7 Pro made for PowerBook 150, 280, 280c, 520, 520c, 540, and 540c computers.

## System 7.1.2

System 7.1.2, a minor variant of System 7.1, is made for Power Macintosh computers. It works only on a Mac that has a PowerPC central processor. In addition to Power Mac enablers, System 7.1.2 has Macintosh PC Exchange to mount DOS and Windows disks, AppleScript to create application scripts, and a new Graphing Calculator to perform complex scientific calculations and display the results.

## System 7.5

System 7.5 simplifies printing and delivers major upgrades of typography, graphics primitives, and color matching. Most of these advanced features require software developers to revise applications.

The major new technology in System 7.5 is QuickDraw GX, the long-awaited successor to the QuickDraw graphics and printing component of the Mac system. QuickDraw GX gives you new printing options right away, as well as the potential for more flexible printing, color matching, typefaces with 65,000 characters, extensive ligature and fraction substitution, and more when developers revise applications.

You have to pull down the Guide menu to see another significant addition: Apple Guide. This new type of help system leads you through tasks step by step, with written instructions and graphical cues.

System 7.5 also incorporates PowerTalk and AppleScript from System 7 Pro, as well as a host of lesser improvements, many of which have been available for years as commercial and shareware utilities. Two of the numerous utilities in System 7.5, Macintosh Easy Open and PC Exchange, help you find translators for documents created by applications that you don't have. These utilities also allow you to work with disks from DOS and Windows computers.

System 7.5 also increases the maximum size of a hard drive to 4063MB (about 4GB). The limit with earlier versions of System 7 is 2GB.

## System 7.5.1

In System 7.5.1, an improved Launcher control panel lets you drag-and-drop to add, remove, and reorganize items. You can turn off the computer by pressing the Power key on the keyboard. The General Controls control panel has a new option for saving documents. With file sharing on, you can eject removable disks and CD-ROMs without turning off file sharing, and a removable disk or CD-ROM is shared automatically when you insert it. If a file server (including a shared disk or folder) disconnects unexpectedly and you have documents open from it, you can usually save them.

## System 7.5.2

System 7.5.2 works only on the following models: the Power Mac 7200/75, 7200/90, 7500/100, 8500/120, 9500/120, and 9500/132; and the PowerBook 190, 2300, and 5300. Other Mac OS computers use System 7.5.3 to get everything System 7.5.2 has to offer and more. In addition, System 7.5.3 is more reliable, so System 7.5.2 users should upgrade to it.

## System 7.5.3

System 7.5.3 includes all the improvements of System 7.5.1 and 7.5.2. In addition, the Finder turns an icon translucent when you drag it on a PowerPC computer, displays long item names better, copies small files faster, and generally retains Get Info comments when rebuilding the desktop. The Close View control panel has new keyboard shortcuts, Find File has a new preference for displaying the kinds of found items, and Memory has a larger standard Disk Cache size. System 7.5.3 also improves performance and fixes countless problems.

Open Transport 1.1, the first reliable version of Apple's modern networking software, comes with System 7.5.3. So does QuickTime 2.1 and English Text-to-speech software. You have the option of installing Desktop Printing 1.0.3 and the digital signatures portion of PowerTalk by itself. The System 7.5.3 CD-ROM includes several bonus items: Mexican Spanish text-to-speech, QuickDraw 3D 1.0.3, and OpenDoc 1.0.4.

See Chapter 21 for more information on the improvements in System 7.5.3.

## System 7.5.4

Apple never distributed System 7.5.4 widely. After distributing it to a small number of software developers, a problem was discovered in System 7.5.4. The fixed version was named System 7.5.5.

## System 7.5.5

System 7.5.5 doesn't add any new features. It simply upgrades system software version 7.5.3 or 7.5.4 to improve reliability and performance. In particular, System 7.5.5 is faster than earlier versions of system software when virtual memory is turned on.

## Mac OS 7.6

Mac OS 7.6 delivers a few minor improvements, fixes some problems, and incorporates a number of system software add-ons that were (and still are) available separately. The core Mac OS 7.6 includes QuickTime 2.5,

LaserWriter 8.4.2, Open Transport 1.1.1, multiprocessor support, Desktop Printing 2.0.2, ColorSync 2.1.1, Extensions Manager 7.6, and additional screen capture options. You also get the performance increases and bug fixes first made in System 7.5.5, 7.5.3, and earlier versions of the system software.

The Mac OS 7.6 installation software makes it easy to add more items in a standard installation, including OpenDoc 1.1.2, OpenDoc Essentials Kit 1.0.1, QuickDraw 3D 1.0.6, MacLinkPlus 8.1, Apple Remote Access Client 2.1, Cyberdog 1.2, Open Transport PPP 1.0, English Text-to-Speech 1.5, and QuickDraw GX 1.1.5.

Some Macs can't use everything that comes with Mac OS 7.6, and some can't use Mac OS 7.6 at all. You can only install QuickDraw 3D on a PowerPC computer. OpenDoc, OpenDoc Essentials, Cyberdog, and LaserWriter 8.4.2 also require a PowerPC processor until Apple fixes the CFM 68K Runtime Enabler problem, which prevents using them on computers with 68030 and 68040 processors (for details, see "Installing Mac OS 7.6 — Compatibility" in Chapter 22). The following Macs can't use Mac OS 7.6: Plus, SE, SE/30, II, IIx, IIcx, Portable, PowerBook 100, original Classic, and original LC.

See Chapter 21 for more information about what's new in Mac OS 7.6.

## System enablers

Prior to System 7.1, Apple brought out a new version of system software to accommodate each new batch of Macintosh models. Now Apple supports a new model or a new series with a plug-in software component called a *system enabler*. A system enabler contains software that modifies the system software to work with a particular kind of Macintosh. The enabler for a particular Mac model must be in the System Folder or the computer will not start up. For example, a PowerBook 160, 165, or 165c requires System Enabler 131 to start up with System 7.1 or System 7 Pro.

Periodically Apple eliminates the need for any of the existing system enablers by combining them all together with other system improvements in a new version of the system software. All the Mac models then in existence when a new system software version comes out don't need enablers if they use that new system software version (though they still need enablers if they use the older system version). For example, a PowerBook 160, 165, or 165c can use System 7.5 or later without a system enabler. Macs introduced later will need system enablers until Apple rolls them into the next new system software version. For example, a Power Mac 6100/66, 7100/80, 8100/100, or 8100/110 requires the PowerPC Enabler with System 7.5.1, but doesn't need an enabler with System 7.5.3 and later.

Table 3-1 lists the Mac models, the system enabler each model requires, the earliest system software version the enabler can be used with, and the earliest system software version that eliminates the need for the enabler.

Table 3-1
**System Enablers**

| *Macintosh Model* | *Enabler Name and Version* | *Use Enabler only with System* | *Enabler not needed with System* |
|---|---|---|---|
| Centris 610, 650 | System Enabler 040 v. 1.1 | 7.1 | 7.5 |
| Centris 660AV | System Enabler 088 v. 1.2 | 7.1 | 7.5 |
| Classic, Classic II | none required | | 7.0 |
| Color Classic | System Enabler 401 v. 1.0.5 | 7.1 | 7.5 |
| II, IIx, IIcx, IIsi, IIci, IIfx | none required | | 7.0 |
| IIvi, IIvx | System Enabler 001 v. 1.0.1 | 7.1 | 7.5 |
| LC, LC II | none required | | 7.0 |
| LC III | System Enabler 003 v. 1.1 | 7.1 | 7.5 |
| LC 475 | System Enabler 065 v. 1.2 | 7.1 | 7.5 |
| LC 520, 550 | System Enabler 403 v. 1.0.2 | 7.1 | 7.5 |
| LC 575 | System Enabler 065 v. 1.2 | 7.1 | 7.5 |
| LC 580 | none required | | 7.0 |
| LC 630 | System Enabler 405 v. 1.0 | 7.1.2P | 7.5 |
| Macintosh TV | System Enabler 404 v. 1.0 | 7.1 | 7.5 |
| Performa 200, 400, 405, 410, 430 | none required | | 7.0 |
| Performa 450,460-467 | System Enabler 308 v. 1.0 | 7.1P6 | 7.5 |
| Performa 475, 476,575-578 | System Enabler 364 v. 1.1 | 7.1P6 | 7.5 |
| Performa 550, 560 | System Enabler 332 v. 1.1 | 7.1P6 | 7.5 |
| Performa 580, 640 | none required | | 7.0 |
| Performa 600 | System Enabler 304 v. 1.0.1 | 7.1P6 | 7.5 |
| Performa 630-638 | System Enabler 405 v. 1.0 | 7.1.2P | 7.5 |
| Performa 6110 series | none required | requires System 7.5 or later | 7.5 |
| Performa 5200, 5300, 6200, 6300 | System Enabler 406 v. 1.0 | 7.5.1 | 7.5.3 |

*(continued on next page)*

Table 3-1 *(continued)*

| ***Macintosh Model*** | ***Enabler Name and Version*** | ***Use Enabler only with System*** | ***Enabler not needed with System*** |
|---|---|---|---|
| Performa 5400, 6400 | System Enabler 410 v. 1.1 | 7.5.3 | 7.5.5 |
| Plus | none required | | 7.0 |
| Portable | none required | | 7.0 |
| Power Mac 5200/75, 5300/100 LC | System Enabler 406 v. 1.0 | 7.5.1 | 7.5.3 |
| Power Mac 6100/60, 7100/66, 8100/80 | PowerPC Enabler v. 1.0.2 | 7.1.2 | 7.5 |
| Power Mac 6100/66, 7100/80, 8100/100, 8100/110 | PowerPC Enabler v. 1.1.1 | 7.5.1 | 7.5.3 |
| Power Mac 7200/75, 7200/90, 7500/100, 8500/120, 9500/120, 9500/132 | System Enabler 701 v. 1.1 | 7.5.2 | 7.5.3 |
| Power Macintosh Upgrade | PowerPC Upgrade Cd Enabler v. 1.0.1 | 7.1.2 | 7.5 |
| PowerBook 100, 140, 145, 145B | none required | | 7.0 |
| PowerBook 150 | PowerBook 150 Enabler v. 1.1 | 7.1.1 | 7.5 |
| PowerBook 160, 165, 165c | System Enabler 131* v. 1.0.3 | 7.1 | 7.5 |
| PowerBook 170 | none required | | 7.0 |
| PowerBook 180, 180c | System Enabler 131* v. 1.0.3 | 7.1 | 7.5 |
| PowerBook 190 | PowerBook 5300/2300/190 Enabler v. 1.2.4 | 7.5.2 | 7.5.3 |
| PowerBook 210, 230, 250** | PowerBook Duo Enabler v. 2.0 | 7.1 | 7.5 |
| PowerBook 270c | PowerBook Duo Enabler v. 2.0 | 7.1 | 7.5 |
| PowerBook 280, 280c | PowerBook Duo Enabler v. 2.0 | 7.1.1 | 7.5 |
| PowerBook 500 Series | PowerBook 500 Series Enabler 1.0 v. 1.0.2 | 7.1.1 | 7.5 |
| PowerBook 2300, 5300 | PowerBook 5300/2300/190 Enabler v. 1.2.1 | 7.5.2 | 7.5.3 |
| Quadra 605 | System Enabler 065 v. 1.2 | 7.1 | 7.5 |

*(continued on next page)*

| Table 3-1 *(continued)* | | | |
|---|---|---|---|
| ***Macintosh Model*** | ***Enabler Name and Version*** | ***Use Enabler only with System*** | ***Enabler not needed with System*** |
| Quadra 610, 650 | System Enabler 040 v. 1.1 | 7.1 | 7.5 |
| Quadra 630 | System Enabler 405 v. 1.0 | 7.1.2P | 7.5 |
| Quadra 660AV | System Enabler 088 v. 1.2 | 7.1 | 7.5 |
| Quadra 700, 900, 950 | none required | | 7.0 |
| Quadra 800 | System Enabler 040 v. 1.1 | 7.1 | 7.5 |
| Quadra 840AV | System Enabler 088 v. 1.2 | 7.1 | 7.5 |
| SE, SE/30 | none required | | 7.0 |

* System Enabler 131 replaces System Enabler 111 and System Enabler 121

** Express Modem users should also install the Duo Battery Patch extension.

## System updates

In the fine tradition of System 7 Tune-Up 1.1.1 (described earlier in this chapter), Apple periodically releases system-software updates to fix bugs and improve performance. The updates that apply to various system software versions include the following:

- **System 7.1 through 7.1.2.** Use System Update 3.0 (which incorporates all improvements from the previous updates: System Update 2.0.1, Hardware System Update 2.0, and Hardware System Update 1.0).
- **System 7.5.** Use System 7.5 Update 2.0 or System 7.5 Version 7.5.3 (which incorporate System 7.5 Update 1.0) and then use System 7.5.5 Update (which incorporates System 7.5.3 Revision 2).
- **System 7.5.3** Use System 7.5.5 Update (which incorporates System 7.5.3 Revision 2).
- **System 7.5.5** The only update is Mac OS 7.6.

## Systems at a glance

Table 3-2 compares System 6.0.8 features with the various versions of System 7.

**Table 3-2**
**Macintosh Systems at a Glance**

| ***Feature*** | ***6.0.x*** | ***7.0.1*** | ***7.1*** | ***7 Pro*** | ***7.1.2*** | ***7.5*** | ***7.5.3*** | ***7.6*** |
|---|---|---|---|---|---|---|---|---|
| Specialized folders | ○ | ● | ● | ● | ● | ● | ● | ● |
| Fonts folder | ○ | ○ | ● | ● | ● | ● | ● | ● |
| Virtual memory | ○ * | ● | ● | ● | ● | ● | ● | ● |
| Can use more than 8MB of memory | ○ * | ● | ● | ● | ● | ● | ● | ● |
| Finds files quickly | ○ * | ● | ● | ● | ● | ● | ● | ● |
| Lists found files | ● | ○ | ○ | ○ | ○ | ● | ● | ● |
| Aliases | ○ | ● | ● | ● | ● | ● | ● | ● |
| Stationery | ○ | ● | ● | ● | ● | ● | ● | ● |
| Publish and subscribe | ○ | ● | ● | ● | ● | ● | ● | ● |
| Customizable icons | ○ | ● | ● | ● | ● | ● | ● | ● |
| Colorized windows and icons | ○ * | ● | ● | ● | ● | ● | ● | ● |
| Cooperative multitasking | ● | ● | ● | ● | ● | ● | ● | ● |
| Subfolders in Finder windows | ○ | ● | ● | ● | ● | ● | ● | ● |
| Icon labels | ○ | ● | ● | ● | ● | ● | ● | ● |
| Drag to open | ○ | ● | ● | ● | ● | ● | ● | ● |
| File sharing | ○ | ● | ● | ● | ● | ● | ● | ● |
| PowerTalk | ○ | ○ | ○ | ● | ○ * | ● | ● | ○ |
| Simple macros | ● | ○ * | ○ * | ● | ● | ● | ● | ● |
| AppleScript | ○ | ○ | ○ * | ● | ● | ● | ● | ● |
| Scriptable Finder | ○ | ○ | ○ | ○ * | ○ * | ● | ● | ● |
| Balloon Help | ○ | ● | ● | ● | ● | ● | ● | ● |
| Apple Guide | ○ | ○ | ○ | ○ | ○ | ● | ● | ● |
| Hierarchical directory dialog boxes | ○ | ● | ● | ● | ● | ● | ● | ● |

*(continued on next page)*

| Table 3-1 *(continued)* | | | | | | | | |
|---|---|---|---|---|---|---|---|---|
| ***Feature*** | ***6.0.x*** | ***7.0.1*** | ***7.1*** | ***7 Pro*** | ***7.1.2*** | ***7.5*** | ***7.5.3*** | ***7.6*** |
| TrueType | ○ * | ● | ● | ● | ● | ● | ● | ● |
| QuickTime | ○ * | ○ * | ● | ● | ● | ● | ● | ● |
| Macintosh PC Exchange | ○ | ○ * | ○ * | ○ * ^ | ● | ● | ● | ● |
| Easy Open | ○ | ○ * | ○ * | ○ * | ○ * | ● | ● | ● |
| Colorful desktop patterns | ○ | ○ * | ○ * | ○ * | ○ * | ● | ● | ● |
| Documents folder | ○ | ○ | ○ | ○ | ○ | ● | ● | ● |
| Finder hiding | ○ | ○ | ○ | ○ | ○ | ● | ● | ● |
| Apple-menu submenus | ○ | ○ * | ○ * | ○ * | ○ * | ● | ● | ● |
| Launcher | ○ | ○ | ○ | ○ | ○ | ● | ● | ● |
| Drag-and-drop editing | ○ | ○ | ○ * | ○ * | ○ * | ● | ● | ● |
| MacTCP | ○ * | ○ * | ○ * | ○ * | ○ * | ● | ● | ● |
| Control Strip | ○ | ○ | ○ | ○ ^ | ○ | ● | ● | ● |
| QuickDraw GX | ○ | ○ | ○ | ○ | ○ | ● | ● | ● |
| Stickies | ○ | ○ * | ○ * | ○ * | ○ * | ● | ● | ● |
| Menu-bar clock | ○ * | ○ * | ○ * | ○ * | ○ * | ● | ● | ● |
| Roll-up windows | ○ | ○ * | ○ * | ○ * | ○ * | ● | ● | ● |
| Improved Scrapbook and Note Pad | ○ | ○ | ○ | ○ | ○ | ● | ● | ● |
| Power key turns off | ○ | ○ | ○ | ○ | ○ | ○ | ● | ● |
| Smarter file sharing | ○ | ○ | ○ | ○ | ○ | ○ | ● | ● |
| Open Transport | ○ | ○ | ○ * | ○ * | ○ * | ○ * | ● | ● |
| Desktop PrintMonitor | ○ | ○ | ○ * | ○ * | ○ * | ○ * | ● | ● |
| Text-to-speech | ○ * | ○ * | ○ * | ○ * | ○ * | ● | ● | ● |
| Translucent drag | ○ | ○ | ○ | ○ | ○ | ○ | ● | ● |
| Multi-processing | ○ | ○ | ○ | ○ | ○ * | ○ * | ○ * | ● |
| ColorSync | ○ | ○ | ○ | ○ * | ○ * | ○ * | ○ * | ● |

*(continued on next page)*

| Table 3-1 *(continued)* | | | | | | | | |
|---|---|---|---|---|---|---|---|---|
| ***Feature*** | ***6.0.x*** | ***7.0.1*** | ***7.1*** | ***7 Pro*** | ***7.1.2*** | ***7.5*** | ***7.5.3*** | ***7.6*** |
| OpenDoc | ○ | ○ | ○ * | ○ * | ○ * | ○ * | ○ * | ● |
| Cyberdog | ○ | ○ | ○ | ○ | ○ | ○ | ○ * | ● |
| QuickDraw 3D | ○ | ○ | ○ | ○ | ○ * | ○ * | ○ * | ● |
| Remote Access | ○ | ○ | ○ * | ○ * | ○ * | ○ * | ○ * | ● |

*The feature is not included with this version of system software, but is available from Apple or an independent software developer (see Chapter 19).

^The feature is not included with this version of system software except on certain Mac models (such as 660AV and 840AV models and PowerBooks).

# Which System Version to Use

Compared with System 6 and earlier versions of system software, System 7 delivers a substantially improved Finder, virtual memory (on most Mac models), file sharing, cooperative multitasking, outline fonts, and other cosmetic improvements. With a growing number of applications, System 7 also delivers 32-Bit Addressing, Balloon Help, publish and subscribe, and user scripting.

Detracting from these benefits are System 7's cost, memory and disk consumption; here-and-there slowness; and complexity. Any of these drawbacks may dissuade you from using System 7 for a while. But as more applications exploit System 7, and as Apple fixes its problems, you'll find saying no harder to do. The Macintosh community is not going back to System 6.

## Who should use System 6

You probably should stick with System 6.0.8 (without MultiFinder) for its lower memory demands if you have a Mac Plus, SE, Classic, Portable, or PowerBook 100 with 1MB or 2MB of RAM. System 7's Finder is noticeably slow on those models, particularly on the Plus. (Apple does recommend System 7 for the PowerBook 100, but the PowerBook 100 works very well with System 6.0.8. All other PowerBooks require System 7.) Of course, you can use System 7 on these models if you need its capabilities — for example, file sharing on a network — or if you want to use application programs that require System 7.

You can continue using System 6 on a Mac SE/30, LC, II, IIx, IIsi, IIcx, IIci, or IIfx if you have application programs that won't work with System 7. Most of the programs that you already have will work with System 7, but there are exceptions.

## Who should use System 7

With any Mac except a Plus, SE, Classic, Portable, or PowerBook 100, System 7 should be your first choice. System 7 is your *only* choice if you have a Mac Classic II; a Color Classic; any LC except the original LC and the LC II, IIvi, and IIvx; any PowerBook except the 100; any Centris; any Quadra; any Power Mac; any Performa, or any Mac OS computer not made by Apple.

If you have a system software version earlier than 7.5, you should consider upgrading to 7.5.1, 7.5.3, 7.5.5, or 7.6. The newer system versions certainly have enough benefits to make upgrading worthwhile, but you do have to be willing to spend some time learning how to use the new benefits. Fortunately, Apple designs system software so that you can learn over a period of time. You don't have to come up to speed in one afternoon. If your computer has enough memory (RAM) to handle a newer version of system software (as detailed later in this chapter in "Memory Requirements"), make the upgrade and take your time getting to know it.

# Mixing Systems

Like many Macintosh users, you may use more than one Macintosh, or your Macintosh may be connected to a network of other Macintoshes. In either scenario, some computers may use System 7 while others use older system software, such as System 6. You may notice some strange behavior if you mix systems. Networked printers may restart themselves. Extra folders may mysteriously appear and desktop items seemingly disappear. None of this is cause for panic. You just need to understand what's going on.

## Mixed networks

All computers on a network must use compatible versions of LaserWriter software; otherwise, the printer must be reinitialized whenever someone uses it with a version of LaserWriter software that is incompatible with the preceding user's version. Before System 7, this situation meant that all computers on a network had to upgrade to a new version of system software at the same time. Not so with System 7.

System 7 and System 6 can coexist on the same network if all System 6 users install LaserWriter software version 6.1, 7.0, or later. LaserWriter 6.1 comes with System 6.0.8 (in fact, the only difference between System 6.0.7 and 6.0.8 is the version of LaserWriter software), and LaserWriter 7 comes with System 7.

### Extra folders and missing items

When you use disks with System 6 after using them with System 7, icons that you saw on the desktop may seem to have mysteriously vanished. Those icons, however, have only been moved to the Desktop folder. In System 7, the Desktop folder is always open and its contents are displayed on the desktop, but the folder itself is invisible. In System 6, the Desktop folder from System 7 becomes visible, but its contents are concealed inside it instead of being on the desktop.

System 7's Trash folder also becomes visible when you use older system software. This folder contains items that you dragged to the Trash and left there (by virtue of not using the Empty Trash command) in System 7. If you were using System 7's virtual memory and restarted with System 6, a file named VM Storage shows up on the hard disk that you designated (in the Memory control panel) for virtual-memory storage.

### Desk accessories and fonts

Older system software sees individual desk accessories and fonts as being meaningless documents with blank icons. To use fonts and desk accessories from System 7 with older system software, you must place them in suitcase files. Then you must install the suitcase files, using the Font/DA Mover program or utility software such as Suitcase II or Master Juggler.

### Automatic rebuilding

When you restart your Macintosh with System 7 after using an earlier version of system software, the Finder may automatically rebuild its desktop database on the startup hard disk. In the process, you lose all comments from Info windows.

## Switching Systems

You can switch between two version of system software if necessary, even if you have only one hard disk. To install a second System Folder on a disk, use the Installer program's Clean Install option (see "Performing a Clean Installation" in Chapter 22). Alternatively, you can drag the System file from the existing System Folder to the Startup Items folder, and rename that System Folder. If you don't remove the System file, the Installer program updates the existing System Folder instead of creating a new System Folder. After installation, move the old System file back to its previous location, either by dragging it there or by selecting it and then choosing the Put Away command. Leave the older System Folder renamed. A System Folder can have any name; having a System file and a Finder together in the same folder qualifies that folder as being a System Folder, regardless of its name.

Apple ordinarily advises against installing two System Folders on the same disk, claiming you can't be sure which System Folder will be used during startup and become the active (or *blessed*) System Folder. Although multiple System Folders can lead to confusion, they don't have to lead to disaster. You can designate which System Folder will be the blessed one during the next startup or restart by using utility software such as System Picker (described in the "System management" section of Chapter 19).

# Equipment Requirements

All Macintosh models except the three oldest can use System 7. Only the original Mac 128K, the Mac 512K, and the Mac XL lack the necessary software in their *ROM* (read-only memory). All other models can use System 7 if they have sufficient *RAM* (random-access memory) and disk space.

You can't use Mac OS 7.6 on a Mac Plus, SE, SE/30, II, IIx, IIcx, Portable, PowerBook 100, original Classic, or original LC. System 7.5.5 is the latest version those models can use.

System 7 requires more memory and more disk space than System 6, and the later versions of System 7 require more memory and disk space than the earlier versions. Heavy memory and disk space consumers include QuickTime (when in use), AppleScript, PowerTalk, and QuickDraw GX.

## Memory requirements

To use System 7 versions 7.1 and earlier, your Macintosh must have at least 2MB of RAM and a hard disk. You'll need more than the minimum 2MB of RAM if you use large or complex application programs; if you want to open several programs at the same time; or if you want to use the file-sharing capability and open any but the smallest program as well. As a rule of thumb, you'll need 1MB more than you use with older system software. You'll enjoy System 7.1 (and earlier versions) more if your Macintosh has 6MB to 8MB of RAM.

For System 7 Pro, Apple recommends that you have at least 4MB of RAM and a hard disk. Figure on needing at least 8MB of RAM if you want to have PowerTalk installed and to keep more than one application open at the same time.

To use System 7.5, you need 4MB of RAM for the core features and 8MB for everything; double these sizes on a Power Mac. You'll need more RAM if you plan to install many extra System extensions or to keep multiple applications open with System 7.5.

System 7.5.3 generally increases the amount of memory used by the system software. The amount of system software memory varies greatly depending on the type of computer, the amount of RAM installed, settings in the Memory control panel, and which system software add-ons are installed. A number of the system components that System 7.5.3 updates must be copied completely into memory; they can't remain partially on the hard disk. Most of the revised components that require more memory affect only PowerPC computers. According to tests conducted by Apple, the system software memory requirement on 680x0 Macs is about 100K higher with System 7.5.3 than with System 7.5.1. On PowerPC computers, System 7.5.3 requires 300K to 850K more than System 7.5.1. Your results may vary.

You can tell how much RAM your Macintosh has by choosing About This Macintosh or About This Computer from the Finder's Apple menu. This command brings up a window like the one shown in Figure 3-1. In this window, the Total Memory is the amount of RAM installed, reported in K instead of MB. To convert to MB, divide the number of K by 1,024 (for example, 2048K ÷ 1024 = 2MB).

Each Macintosh model has specific memory-configuration rules. You can install RAM modules called *SIMMs* (single in-line memory modules) only in certain combinations on each model. Table 3-3 shows the basic rules; dealers and companies that sell SIMMs have complete details.

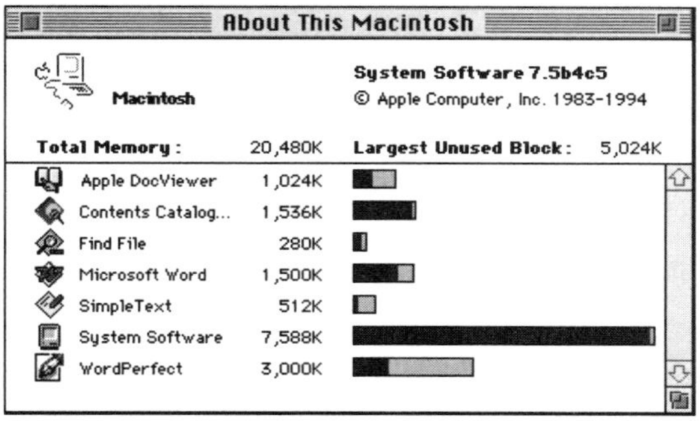

**Figure 3-1: Checking available memory by choosing About This Macintosh from the Apple menu.**

If your Mac needs more RAM, you can have it upgraded by a trained technician, or you can upgrade it yourself. Upgrading involves opening the Macintosh (tricky on a Plus, SE, SE/30, Classic, Classic II, and all PowerBooks except the 500 and 1400 series) and either installing or replacing some small circuit boards. You also must cut a resistor on a Mac Plus or an older SE and move a jumper on a newer SE. Complete instructions come with the SIMMs, which you can order by mail from a plethora of companies that advertise in *Macworld*, *MacUser*, and *MacWeek* magazines. If you don't want to perform the upgrade yourself and you live in a metropolitan area, use the telephone book to shop for the best deal. Memory prices are highly competitive.

Table 3-3
**Macintosh Memory Configurations**

| *Model(s)* | *Permanent RAM (MB)* | *Expansion slots* | *Min. RAM speed* | *Expansion card sizes* | *Total RAM (MB)* |
|---|---|---|---|---|---|
| Plus<br>SE | 0 | 4 30-pin | 150 ns | 256K, 1MB | 1, 2, 2.5, 4 |
| Classic | 1 | 1 Classic | 120 ns | 1, 1.5, or 3MB | 1, 2, 2.5, 4 |
| Classic II<br>Performa 200 | 2 | 2 30-pin | 100 ns | 1, 2, or 4MB | 2, 4, 6, 10 |
| Color Classic | 4 | 2 30-pin | 100 ns | 1, 2, or 4MB | 4, 6, 8, 10 |
| SE/30<br>II, IIx, IIcx | 0 | 8 30-pin | 120 ns | 256K; 1, 4, 8, or 16MB | 1, 2, 3, 4, 5, 6, 8, 9*, 10*, 12*, 16*, 17*, 18*, 20*, 24*, 32*, 64*, 65*, 66*, 68*, 80*, 128* |
| IIsi | 1 | 4 30-pin | 100 ns | 256K, 512K; 1, 2, 4 or 16MB | 2, 3, 5, 9, 17 65 |
| IIci | 0 | 8 30-pin | 80 ns | 256K; 512K; 1, 2, 4, 8, or 16MB | 1, 2, 3, 4, 5, 6, 8, 9, 10, 12, 16, 17, 18, 20, 24, 32, 33, 34, 36, 40, 48, 64, 65, 66, 68, 72, 80, 96, 128 |
| IIfx | 0 | 8 64-pin | 80 ns | 1, 4, 8, or 16MB | 4, 8, 16, 20, 32, 36, 48, 64, 68, 80, 96, 128 |

*(continued on next page)*

Table 3-3 *(continued)*

| ***Model(s)*** | ***Permanent RAM (MB)*** | ***Expansion slots*** | ***Min. RAM speed*** | ***Expansion card sizes*** | ***Total RAM (MB)*** |
|---|---|---|---|---|---|
| LC, LC II<br>Performa 400, 405, 410, 430 | 4 | 2 30-pin | 100 ns | 256K;<br>512K;<br>1, 2, or 4MB | 2, 3, 4, 6, 10 |
| LC III<br>LC 475, 520, 550, 575<br>Performa 450, 460, 466, 467, 475, 476, 550, 560<br>Quadra 605 | 4 | 1 72-pin | 80 ns | 1, 2, 4, 8, 16, or 32MB | 4, 5, 6, 8, 12, 20, 36 |
| IIvx<br>Performa 600 | 4 | 4 30-pin | 80 ns | 256K;<br>1, 2, 4, 8, or 16MB | 4, 5, 8, 16, 20, 36, 68 |
| Quadra 610<br>Centris 610 | 4 | 2 72-pin | 80 ns | 4, 8, 16, or 32MB | 4, 8, 12, 16, 20, 24, 36, 40, 44, 52, 68 |
| Quadra 650<br>Centris 650 | 8 | 4 72-pin | 80 ns | 4, 8, 16, or 32MB | 8, 12, 16, 20, 24, 28, 32, 36, 40, 44, 48, 52, 56, 60, 64, 68, 72, 76, 80, 84, 88, 92, 96, 104, 108, 112, 120, 136 |
| Quadra 660AV<br>Centris 660AV | 4 | 2 72-pin | 70 ns | 4, 8, 16, or 32MB | 4, 8, 12, 16, 20, 24, 28, 36, 40, 44, 52, 68 |
| Quadra 700 | 4 | 4 30-pin | 80 ns | 1, 4, 8, or 16MB | 4, 8, 20, 36, 68 |

*(continued on next page)*

| Table 3-3 *(continued)* | | | | | |
|---|---|---|---|---|---|
| ***Model(s)*** | ***Permanent RAM (MB)*** | ***Expansion slots*** | ***Min. RAM speed*** | ***Expansion card sizes*** | ***Total RAM (MB)*** |
| Quadra 840AV Centris 840AV | 0 | 4 72-pin | 60 ns | 4, 8, 16, or 32MB | 4, 8, 12, 16, 20, 24, 28, 32, 36, 40, 44, 48, 52, 56, 60, 64, 68, 72, 76, 80, 84, 88, 96, 100, 104, 112, 128 |
| Quadra 800 | 8 | 4 72-pin | 60 ns | 4, 8, 16, or 32MB | 8, 12, 16, 20, 24, 28, 32, 36, 40, 44, 48, 52, 56, 60, 64, 68, 72, 76, 80, 84, 88, 92, 96, 104, 108, 112, 120, 136 |
| Quadra 900 | 0 | 16 30-pin | 80 ns | 1, 4, 8, or 16MB | 4, 8, 12, 16, 20, 24, 28, 32, 36, 40, 44, 48, 52, 56, 64 |
| Quadra 950 | 0 | 16 30-pin | 80 ns | 1, 4, 8, or 16MB | 4, 8, 12, 16, 20, 24, 28, 32, 36, 40, 44, 48, 52, 56, 64, 68, 72, 76, 80, 84, 88, 96, 100, 104, 112, 128, 132, 144, 148, 160, 164, 176, 192, 196, 208, 224, 256 |
| Power Mac 6100/60, 6100/60AV | 8 | 2 72-pin | 80 ns | 2, 4, 8, 16, or 32MB | 8, 12, 16, 24, 40, 72 |

*(continued on next page)*

| Table 3-3 *(continued)* | | | | | |
|---|---|---|---|---|---|
| ***Model(s)*** | ***Permanent RAM (MB)*** | ***Expansion slots*** | ***Min. RAM speed*** | ***Expansion card sizes*** | ***Total RAM (MB)*** |
| Power Mac 7100/66, 7100/66AV | 8 | 4 72-pin | 80 ns | 2, 4, 8, 16, or 32MB | 8, 12, 16, 20, 24, 28, 32, 36, 40, 44, 48, 52, 56, 60, 64, 68, 72, 76, 80, 84, 88, 92, 96, 100, 104, 108, 112, 116, 120, 124, 128, 136 |
| Power Mac 8100/80, 8100/80AV | 8 | 8 72-pin | 80 ns | 2, 4, 8, 16, or 32MB | 8, 12, 16, 20, 24, 28, 32, 36, 40, 44, 48, 52, 56, 60, 64, 68, 72, 76, 80, 84, 88, 92, 96, 100, 104, 108, 112, 116, 120, 124, 128, 136, 140, 144, 148, 152, 156, 160, 168, 172, 176, 184, 200, 204, 208, 216, 232, 264 |
| PowerBook 100, 140, 145, 170 | 2 | 1 | 100 ns | 2, 4, or 6MB | 2, 4, 6, 8 |
| PowerBook 145b, 165 | 4 | 1 | 100 ns | 2 or 4MB | 4, 6, 8 |
| PowerBook 160, 165c, 180, 180c | 4 | 1 | 85 ns | 2, 4, or 10MB | 4, 6, 8, 14 |

*(continued on next page)*

Table 3-3 *(continued)*

| ***Model(s)*** | ***Permanent RAM (MB)*** | ***Expansion slots*** | ***Min. RAM speed*** | ***Expansion card sizes*** | ***Total RAM (MB)*** |
|---|---|---|---|---|---|
| PowerBook 520, 520c, 540, 540c | 4 | 1 | 85 ns | 2, 4, 10, or 32MB | 4, 6, 8, 14, 36 |
| PowerBook Duo 210, 230 | 4 | 1 | 85 ns | 4, 8, or 20MB | 4, 12, 24 |
| PowerBook Duo 270c | 4 | 1 | 85 ns | 4, 8, 20, or 28MB | 4, 12, 24, 32 |
| PowerBook Duo 280, 280c | 4 | 1 | 85 ns | 4, 8, 20, or 36MB | 4, 12, 24, 40 |

*The SE/30, II, IIx, and IIcx cannot use 32-Bit Addressing, and these models require either Apple's 32-bit enabler (if running System 7.1 or later) or the MODE32 software (free from Apple dealers) to make use of more than 8MB total RAM for opening programs. The Mac II and IIx require special 4MB SIMMs. Specify your Mac model when ordering. The Mac II cannot use SIMMs larger than 1MB in bank A unless it has the SuperDrive upgrade.

## Disk requirements

Not only do you need plenty of memory, but you also need a hard disk to make practical use of System 7. A standard installation of System 7.0.1 with software and fonts for LaserWriter printing occupies about 4MB of disk space. A standard installation of System 7.5 without PowerTalk or QuickDraw GX uses more than 13MB. Add another 7MB for PowerTalk and QuickDraw GX. Additional control panels, desk accessories, fonts, sounds, and extensions increase the size. A typical installation of Mac OS 7.6 requires 50MB to 70MB of disk space.

You can install a stripped-down System 7 on a 1.4MB high-density floppy disk, but you can't do much with it. Worse, System 7 on a floppy disk is poky.

A hard disk is easy for anyone to plug into the back of a Macintosh. Like memory prices, hard-disk prices are competitive. You can buy a good-quality new 1 gigabyte (1024MB) hard disk for a few hundred dollars.

# Where to Get System 7

If System 7 didn't come with your Macintosh, you once could get the latest version at low cost from user groups or for the cost of downloading from on-line information services. Now only System 7.0.1 is available from those sources. You cannot legally copy system software version 7.1 or later from a friend or co-worker, although it is possible to do so successfully.

The latest Mac OS is available commercially in several forms:

- ❖ Retail package containing floppy disks for a single user
- ❖ Retail package containing a CD-ROM for a single user
- ❖ Multi-user and site licenses through Claris
- ❖ Upgrade for owners of some older Mac OS versions
- ❖ Bundled with Mac OS computers

The Mac OS retail packages are distributed worldwide by Claris Corp. and are sold by computer retailers such as CompUSA, software retailers such as Egghead, mail order merchants such as MacConnection (800-800-6821) and corporate resellers such as Software Spectrum. Upgrades to the latest release are available through the Apple Order Center (800-293-6617). Older versions of the Mac OS, such as the original System 7.5 and System 7.5 Version 7.5.3, are sometimes available from liquidators like Shreve Systems (800-227-3971, *http://www.shrevesystems.com*).

# CHAPTER 3 CONCEPTS AND TERMS

- Each system software version brought numerous features and developments to the Macintosh world.
- The system version you use depends on your needs and equipment. But unless you have an older Mac like a Plus, you should use a version of System 7 since it incorporates many features which are standard in Mac usage.
- System 7 will work on all but the very oldest of Macs. You will need at least 4MB of RAM to work with the basics of System 7.5; more RAM is needed to use the sophisticated features of Mac OS 7.6.
- While you can obtain System 7.0.1 from user groups, you now must legally purchase the latest Mac OS from Apple or an official reseller.

**blessed System Folder**
The active System Folder on a disk that has more than one System Folder. The blessed System Folder is used during startup, and can be designated with the System Picker program.

**cooperative multitasking**
The ability to keep more than one program open at the same time (if your Mac has enough memory). The open programs must cooperate by releasing control of the system when they're not doing anything so other open programs get a chance to work (perhaps in the background).

**publish and subscribe**
A System 7 feature that enables you to place a live copy of material from one document in another document.

**RAM**
Random-access memory. Contains some system software, programs that are open, and data of documents that are open.

**ROM**
Read-only memory. Contains much of the system software.

**SIMMs**
Stands for *s*ingle *in*-line *m*emory *mod*-ules, which are small circuit boards containing RAM chips. You can install SIMMs in your computer to expand its memory.

**System enabler**
A system-software module, introduced with System 7.1, that enables the system software to work with particular Macintosh models.

**TrueType**
A variable-size-font technology that scales text smoothly on any printer or screen.

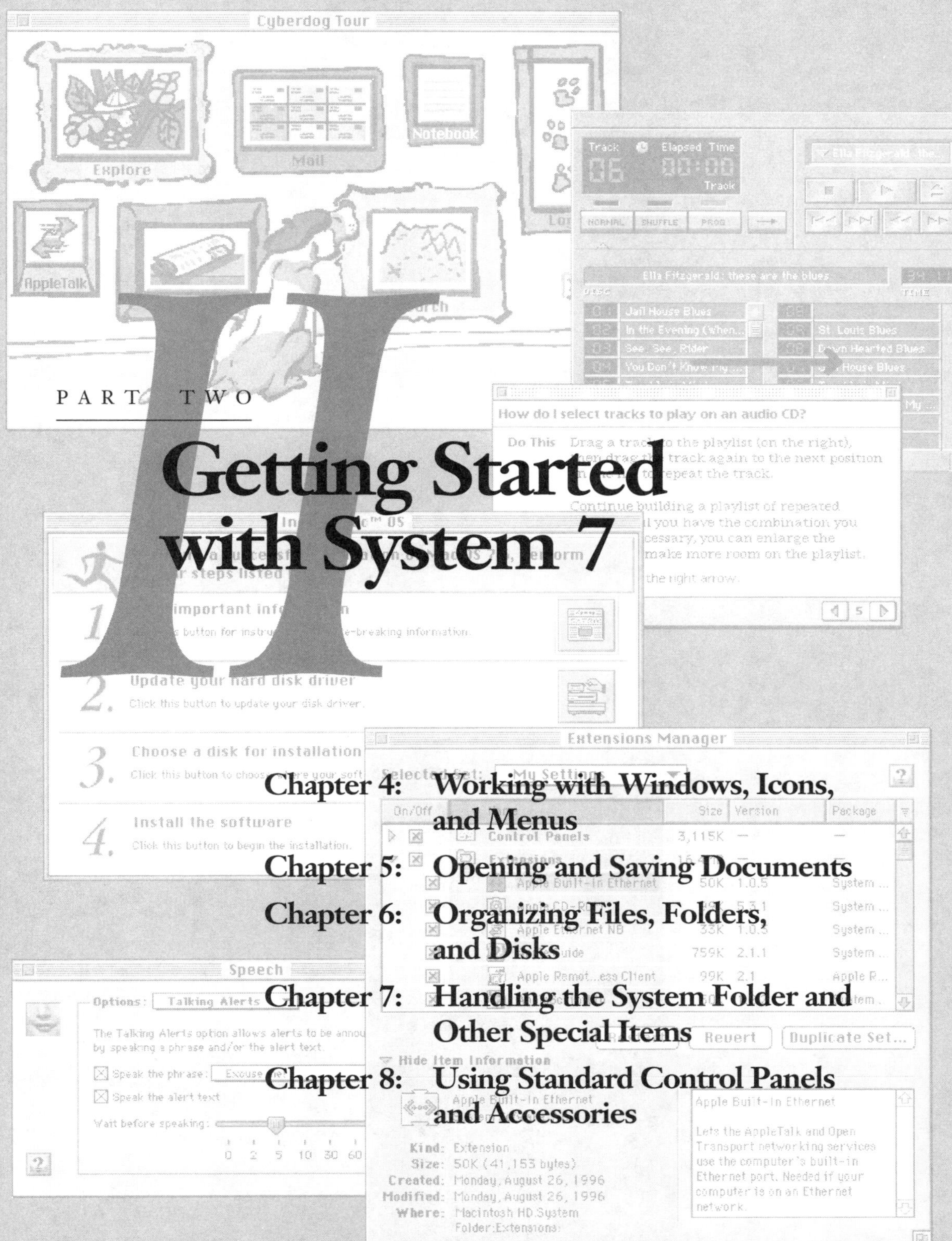

PART TWO

# Getting Started with System 7

CHAPTER FOUR

# Working with Windows, Icons, and Menus

- Adjusting keyboard and mouse settings
- Selecting and customizing your desktop pattern
- Looking into the windows of System 7
- Identifying and using icon variations
- Using balloon help: how the Mac can explain itself
- Getting step-by-step help on-screen from Apple Guide

The desktop, with its windows, icons, and menu bar, serves as a home base for everything you do with your Macintosh. Because you see so much of it, how it looks and operates is important. The system software makes it easy to personalize the desktop, its windows, and its icons and make them more convenient to use.

On color Macs, System 7 subtly enhances the desktop with color and shades of gray. Some of the subtleties are also visible on systems that display true grays but not color. On a basic black-and-white screen (with no colors or gray shades), however, the desktop looks the same as it does with older system software.

Color isn't the only way in which System 7 allows you to tailor the look of your desktop: you can also change the views in windows or easily substitute custom icons for the standard ones. In addition, System 7 has two menus not present in earlier system software: the Application menu for program switching and the Guide menu for controlling on-screen help. The Guide and Application menus, like the Apple menu, have small icons instead of words as titles in the menu bar. Those and other small icons no longer look like mutated standard-size icons.

This chapter describes and illustrates the basics of the Mac *interface* and how to adjust them. Be sure to see the remaining chapters in Part II for detailed information about other aspects of System 7, such as the Finder and the System Folder.

## Keyboard and Mouse Adjustments

Like many aspects of the Mac, the mouse and keyboard settings are adjustable to allow for differences among users. If you find yourself becoming frustrated or impatient as you use the mouse, you may be able to solve the problem by changing the mouse settings. Similarly, if you type a character repeatedly when you mean to type it only once, you can adjust the keyboard sensitivity.

## Setting mouse sensitivity

You can change the way the mouse interprets your actions by adjusting the settings on the Mouse control panel, shown in Figure 4-1. There, you can change the *tracking speed* — how fast the pointer moves as you glide the mouse. This setting is a matter of personal taste. If you feel that the pointer doesn't keep up, try a faster setting. If you often lose track of the pointer as you move it, try a slower one. Often, when you switch from a small monitor to a large one, you need to switch to a faster tracking speed because the pointer has a longer distance to travel from the menu bar to the Trash.

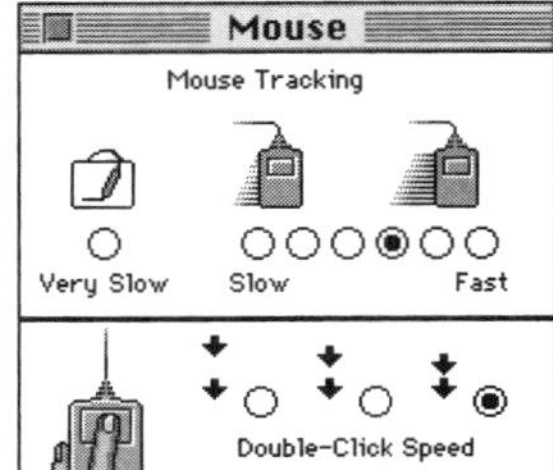


**Figure 4-1: The Mouse control panel.**

The Double-Click Speed option determines how quickly you must double-click for the Mac to perceive your two clicks as one double-click rather than two separate, unrelated clicks. When you select a double-click speed, the button of the mouse illustration demonstrates the double-click interval you've selected.

## Setting keyboard sensitivity

When you press almost any key on the keyboard and hold it down, the Mac types that character repeatedly as long as you keep the key down. (The ⌘, Option, Control, Caps Lock, and Esc keys don't repeat.) On the Keyboard control panel (see Figure 4-2), you can change how quickly the characters repeat and how long you must hold down a key before the repeat feature kicks in. If you find repeating keys annoying rather than handy, you can disable the repeat by selecting Off in the Delay Until Repeat section of the control panel. (The Easy Access control panel gives you some other ways to customize your keyboard; see Control Panels in Chapter 8 for details.)

# Desktop

Look closely at the standard gray desktop on a basic black-and-white screen, and you see a checkerboard pattern of little black and white dots, as shown in Figure 4-3. On a Mac that displays colors or gray shades, however, the standard desktop pattern is made up of two gray shades, as shown in Figure 4-4. The overall effect is a smooth, continuous tone.

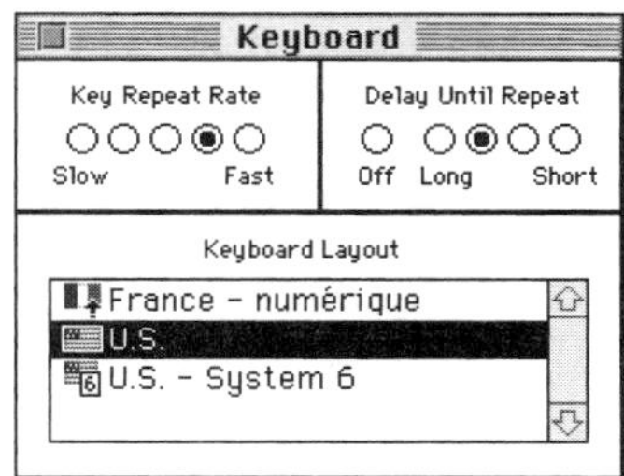


**Figure 4-2: The Keyboard control panel.**

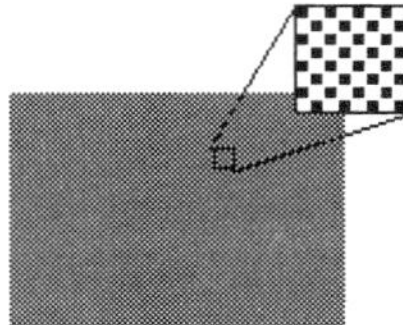

**Figure 4-3: Gray desktop (black-and-white screen).**

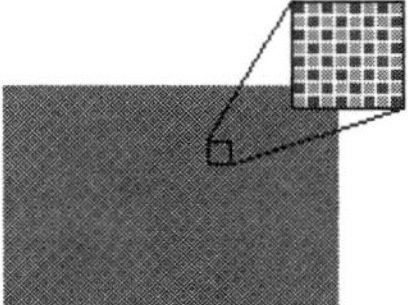

**Figure 4-4: Gray desktop (256-color screen).**

## Desktop patterns

You aren't stuck with the ordinary gray desktop pattern. You can select a different desktop pattern or create your own. With System 7.5, you use the Desktop Patterns program (normally located in the Control Panels folder). With earlier versions of System 7, you use the General Controls control panel. The General Controls panel that comes with Macintosh Performa computers works differently and offers different pattern choices than the one that comes with other Macs.

### Desktop patterns with System 7.5

System 7.5's Desktop Patterns program displays one desktop pattern at a time from the set of available patterns, as shown in Figure 4-5. Two numbers below the large sample of the pattern tell you which of the total number of available patterns you are seeing. You page through the available patterns by clicking the scroll arrows. When you see a pattern you want to use, click the Set Desktop Pattern button at the bottom of the window.

You can remove patterns from the set of available patterns with the Cut command. After cutting (or copying) a pattern, you can use the Paste command to store it in the Scrapbook.

To create a new desktop pattern, use a graphics program, a scanner, or another graphics source. Select the image you want to use as a desktop pattern and copy it by choosing Copy from the Edit menu. Open the Desktop Patterns program and paste the copied image by choosing Paste from the Edit menu. This action adds the copied pattern to the set of available desktop patterns.

With System 7.5's Desktop Patterns program you can also change the pattern that appears in the background of System 7.5 utility windows such as Find File, Calculator, and Scrapbook. Here's how: Open the Desktop Patterns control panel, and scroll to find a pattern you like. Press option to change the Set Desktop Pattern button to Set Utilities Pattern, and click the button. Whatever pattern you set will be the same for all the utility windows; you can't set a different pattern for each utility.

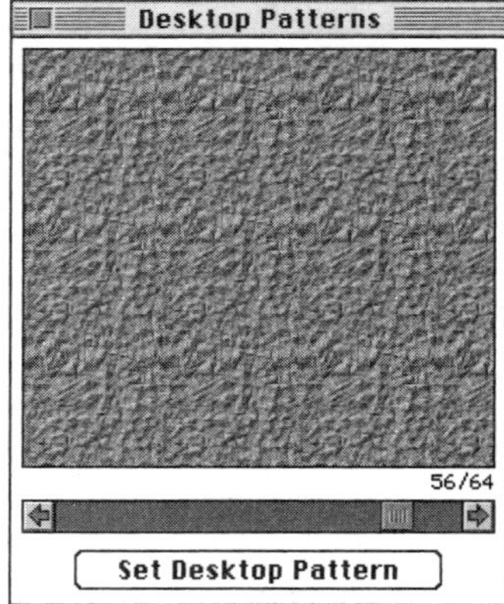


**Figure 4-5: Use the Desktop Patterns program to select a pattern in System 7.5.**

## Desktop patterns with System 7.1.2 and earlier versions

With System 7.1.2 and earlier versions (including System 7 Pro), you use the General Controls control panel to select a desktop pattern. You can also use General Controls to create your own pattern. The Desktop Pattern section of General Controls shows two views of the current desktop pattern.

In a miniature image of the desktop, you see the current pattern in its actual size, and next to it you see an enlargement of the current pattern, as shown in Figure 4-6.

To change the desktop pattern, scroll through the available standard patterns by clicking the miniature menu bar in the Desktop Pattern section. As you scroll, the pattern below the miniature menu bar changes. System 7 comes with 11 color desktop patterns, plus the standard gray, as shown in Figure 4-7. When you see a pattern you like, click it to make it the desktop pattern.

## Editing Desktop Patterns Made Easy

In System 7.5 and later, you can edit an existing desktop pattern with a color painting program.

1. Begin by opening the Desktop Patterns program, bringing the pattern you want to change into view.
2. Scroll the pattern you want to edit into view.
3. Choose Copy from the Edit menu.
4. Now open the color painting program and paste the copied pattern into a new document.
5. Change the pattern as you wish, copy the changed pattern, and paste it into the Desktop Patterns program.

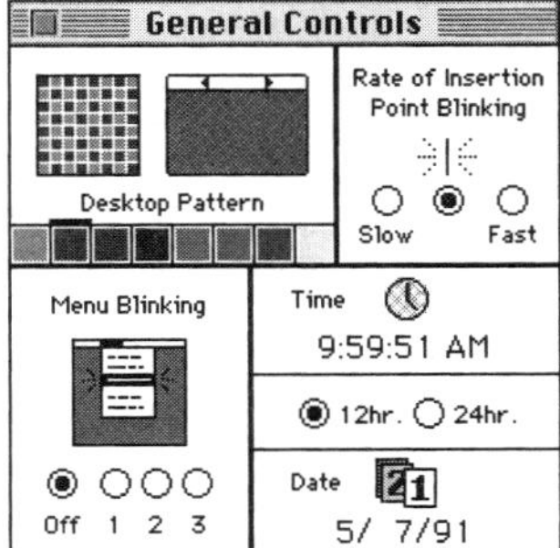


**Figure 4-6: Use the General Controls panel to select or edit a pattern in System 7.0, 7.0.1, 7.1, 7.1.1, or 7.1.2.**

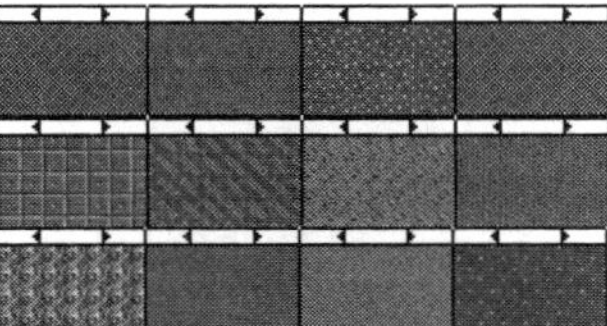

**Figure 4-7: The standard desktop patterns.**

Your Mac does not have the standard patterns if you installed System 7 on a disk that contains custom desktop patterns (created as described in the next paragraph). You can get the new patterns by dragging the System file out of the System Folder before installing System 7. If you do so, any other nonstandard resources that have been installed, such as extra fonts, are not included automatically when you install System 7.

In System 7.1.2 and earlier, you can create a custom pattern by changing the magnified view of a standard pattern in the General Controls control panel. Select a color from the eight-color palette in the Desktop Pattern section of the control panel and click a square in the magnified view, as shown in Figure 4-8.

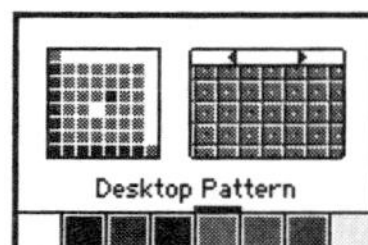

**Figure 4-8: Editing a desktop pattern.**

To change a color in the palette, double-click it. A dialog box opens in which you can pick another color by clicking a color wheel or by typing values for red, green, and blue or hue, saturation, and brightness, as shown in Figure 4-9. When you've created the pattern you want, click below the miniature menu bar to make it the desktop pattern.

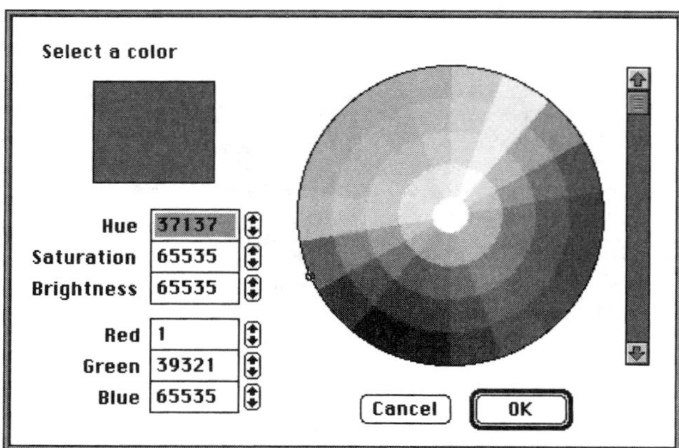

**Figure 4-9: Picking a color for a desktop pattern.**

Changes you make to a desktop pattern persist until you select a different pattern. To make a custom pattern revert to its standard configuration, scroll through all available patterns in the General Controls control panel until you see the standard pattern you want, and then select it.

In System 7.1.2 and earlier (except Performa versions), the desktop pattern is ordinarily made from tiles measuring 8 square pixels (dots). However, you can decorate your desktop with a custom pattern made from much larger tiles. And instead of a desktop pattern, you can display a desktop picture. For complete details on getting bigger desktop patterns or a desktop picture, see "Desktop pattern" in Chapter 20.

## Desktop patterns on Performas

With System 7.1P and 7.0.1P, which are normally installed on Macintosh Performa computers, you can change the desktop pattern with the General Controls control panel. The method of changing the desktop pattern is slightly different in the two versions of Performa system software.

In System 7.1P's General Controls, you click the Change Pattern button to display a dialog box containing samples of all the available patterns, as shown in Figure 4-10. You change the desktop pattern by clicking one of the available patterns to select it and then clicking the OK button.

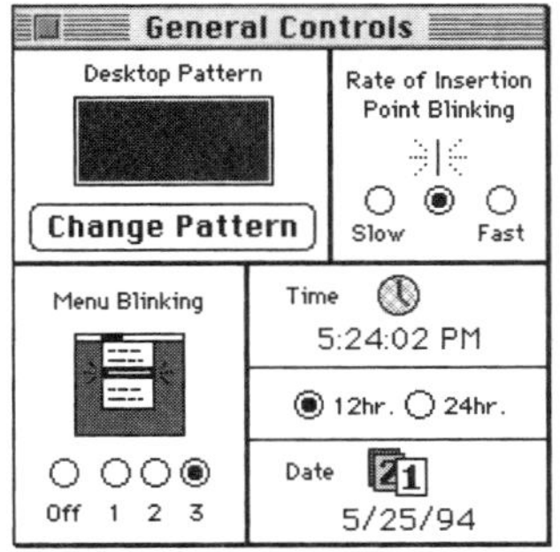


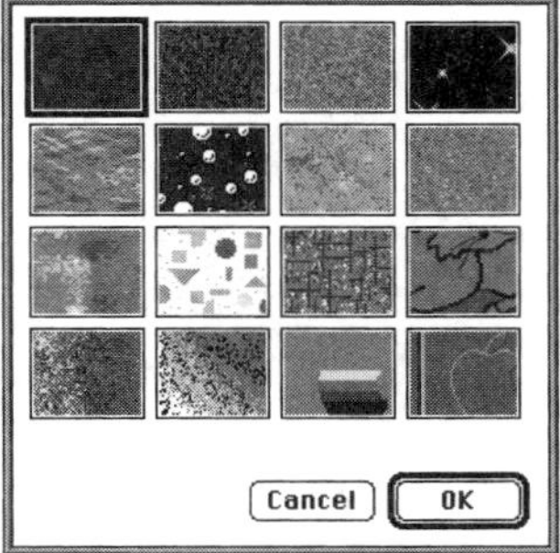


**Figure 4-10: Use the General Controls control panel to select a pattern in System 7.1P (on a Macintosh Performa computer).**

In System 7.0.1P, the General Controls control panel displays the available patterns in a pop-up menu, as shown in Figure 4-11. You select a desktop pattern by choosing from the pop-up menu.

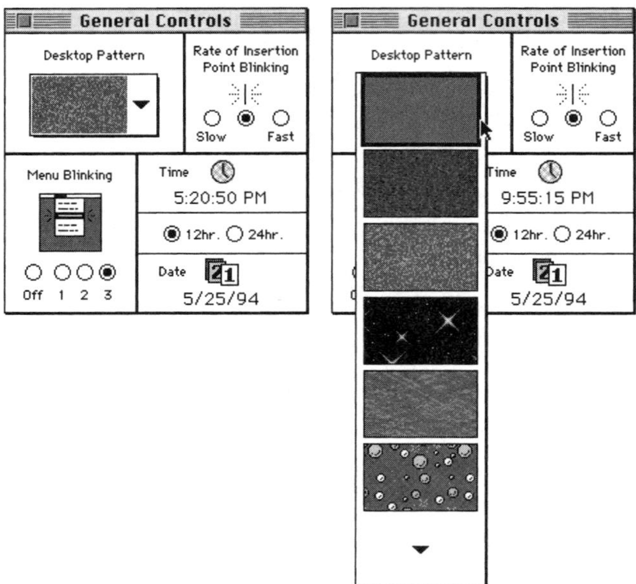


**Figure 4-11: Use the General Controls control panel to select a pattern in System 7.0.1P (on a Macintosh Performa computer).**

# Windows

System 7 updates the vintage 1984 Macintosh windows with trendy 3-D shading on monitors that display colors or gray shades.

## Window controls

Muted colors and shades of gray accent the window components you can manipulate, such as the title bar, scroll arrows, scroll boxes, close box, zoom box, and size box, as shown in Figure 4-12. Subtle colors emphasize the window controls without jerking your attention away from your work as bright colors do.

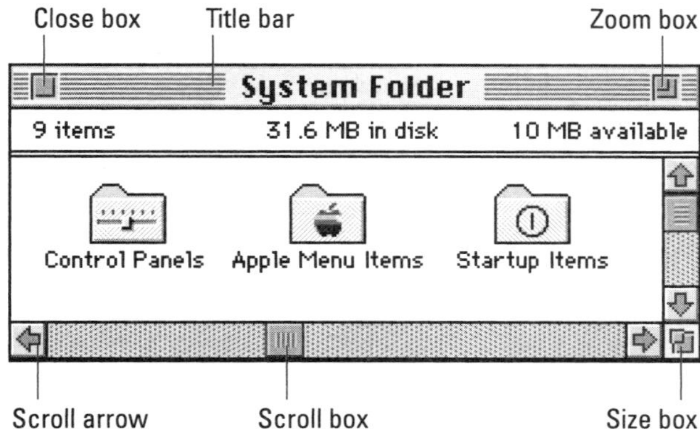

**Figure 4-12: Colors emphasize window controls.**

Clicking a window's close box makes the window go away. Clicking a scroll arrow, clicking in the gray area of a scroll bar, or dragging a scroll box brings other parts of the window's contents into view (if there are other parts to see).

You can move a window by dragging its title bar.

Clicking the zoom box expands the window to be as large as it needs to be, up to the size of the screen. Clicking again makes the window resume its previous size and location. You can adjust the size of a window manually by dragging the window's size box.

With System 7.5 and later, you have the option of hiding all of a window except its title bar. To set up this option, use the WindowShade control panel, shown in Figure 4-13.

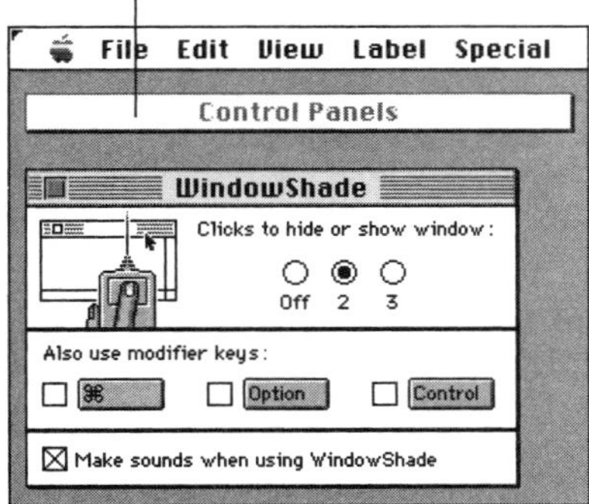

**Figure 4-13: Set up window hiding with System 7.5's WindowShade control panel.**

In this control panel, you can set the number of times you must click a window's title bar to hide the window (or show the window if it is already hidden). You can designate one or more keys that you must press while clicking a window's title bar for WindowShade to do its work. You can also turn sound effects on or off.

## 3-D motion

Shading tricks also make some of the colorized components seem to work in three dimensions when you use them. Clicking a close box or zoom box, for example, makes it look pressed down, as shown in Figure 4-14. (The close box and zoom box also flash when you click them.) The title bar, scroll arrows, and size box do not simulate 3-D motion.

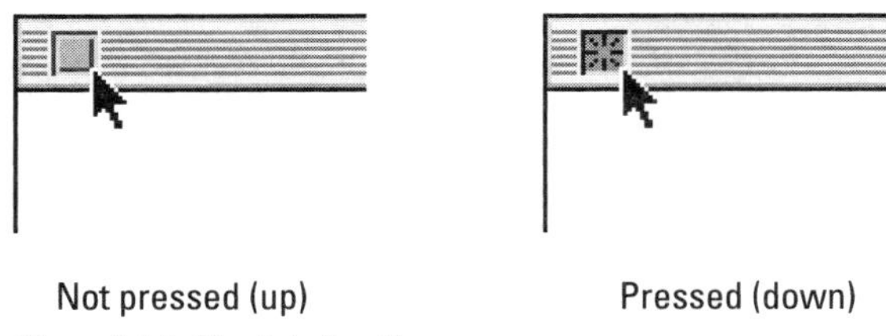

Not pressed (up) Pressed (down)

**Figure 4-14: Simulated motion.**

## Inactive window paling

Only the active window has 3-D shading. It stands out from the inactive windows behind it because System 7 displays inactive windows with gray borders and a gray title, as shown in Figure 4-15. The contents of inactive windows are never dimmed, so you can see the contents easily. Older system software displays black borders and titles for inactive windows.

If the active window is large enough to show the full width or height of its contents without scrolling, System 7 shades its scroll bars light gray.

## Dialog box shading

Three-dimensional shading carries over to standard dialog boxes. System 7 surrounds movable and fixed dialog boxes with a narrow half-round molding, as shown in Figure 4-16. (Movable dialog boxes have a title bar but no close box or size box.)

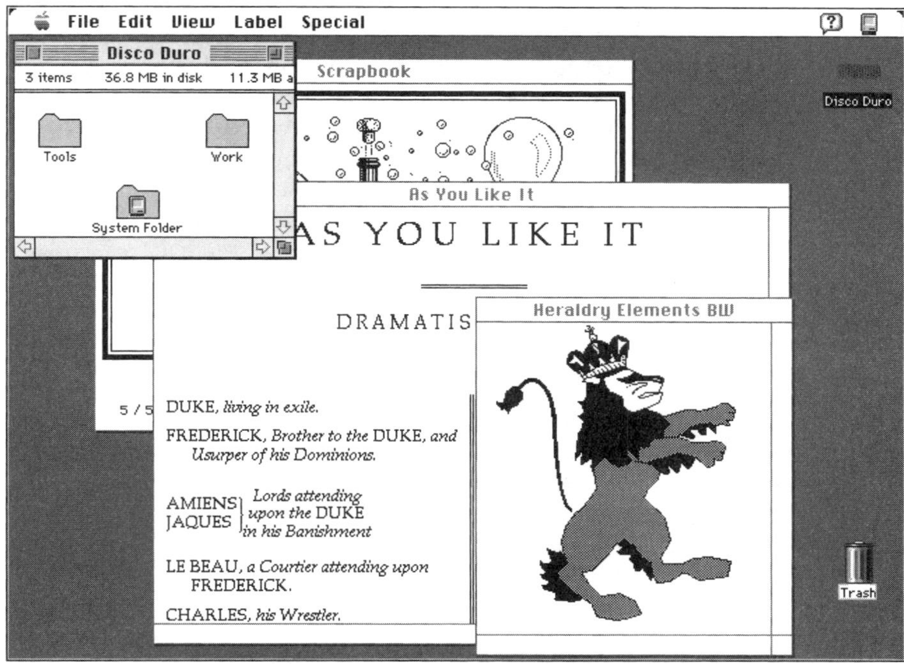


**Figure 4-15: Detail in the title bar and scroll bars helps the frontmost window stand out.**

Immovable dialog box

LaserWriter Page Setup 7.1.2
OK
Cancel
Options
Paper: US Letter, A4 Letter, US Legal, B5 Letter, Tabloid
Reduce or Enlarge: 100 %
Orientation
Printer Effects:
Font Substitution?
Text Smoothing?
Graphics Smoothing?
Faster Bitmap Printing?

Movable dialog box

Find
Find and select items whose
name contains
Search on all disks
all at once
Fewer Choices
Cancel
Find

**Figure 4-16: Dialog box shading.**

## Choosing a window color

The standard color for shading window controls is light purple. You can select any of seven other colors or black and white as the shading color for window control areas by using the Color control panel, as shown in Figure 4-17. Your choice of window tint affects all windows immediately, but the Color control panel doesn't save its settings to disk until you close it. The window tint you choose does not apply to tool palettes and special-purpose windows created by some application programs. You cannot create your own window-shading color by using the Color control panel.

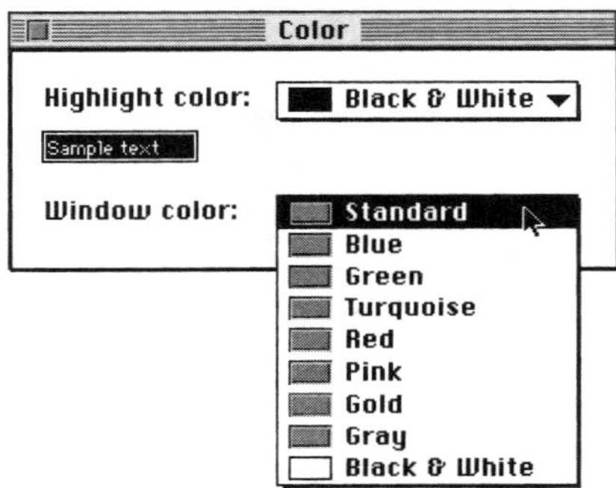


**Figure 4-17: The window color pop-up menu.**

To see colorized windows and shaded dialog boxes on your Mac, you must set your Monitors control panel for at least 16 grays or 256 colors, as shown in Figure 4-18. If it's set at a lower number — or if your Mac has only a black-and-white monitor — your windows and dialog boxes look like pre-System 7 windows, which lack 3-D shading.

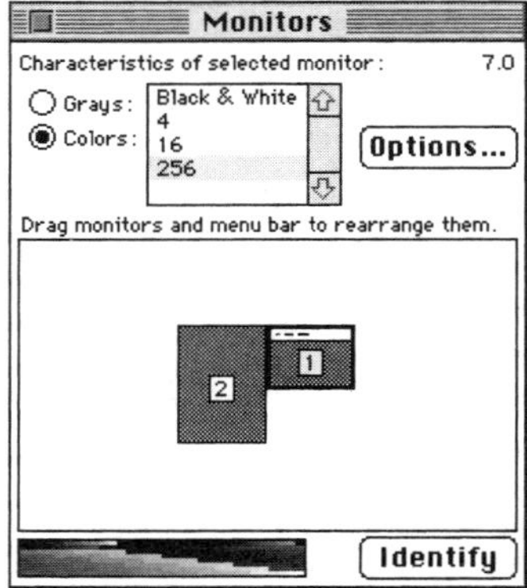


**Figure 4-18: The Monitors control panel set for 256 colors.**

Color windows have a disadvantage: they're slower than black-and-white windows. For best display speed, set the number of colors in the Monitors control panel to 16 or less.

# Icons

Windows aren't the only colorful part of System 7. On color or gray-scale monitors, you see colored or shaded icons for folders, the Finder, the System file, items in the System Folder, Apple utility programs, other Apple software, and generic applications, desk accessories, and documents.

## Icon colors

Most new icons are shaded with a color similar to the standard purple window color to achieve a 3-D effect. Bright colors are used mainly for highlights, as shown in Figure 4-19.

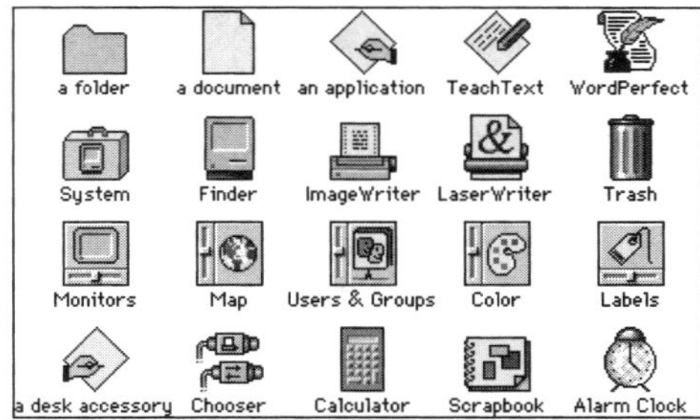


**Figure 4-19: Some full-size color icons (represented by shades of gray).**

The new icons have three separate color schemes. One color scheme is optimized for monitors set to display 256 or more colors or grays. Another color scheme looks best on monitors set to display 16 colors or grays. The third color scheme is used on monitors that display black-and-white or four colors or grays, as shown in Figure 4-20.

You can alter an icon's natural color by selecting it and choosing a label from the Finder's Label menu. The Finder blends the label color with the icon colors. It looks like you covered the icon with a piece of acetate that is the same color as the label. Using the Color control panel to select an alternate window color does not affect the color of any icons. You can make labels colorless by following the procedure described in "Transparent Labels" in Chapter 6.

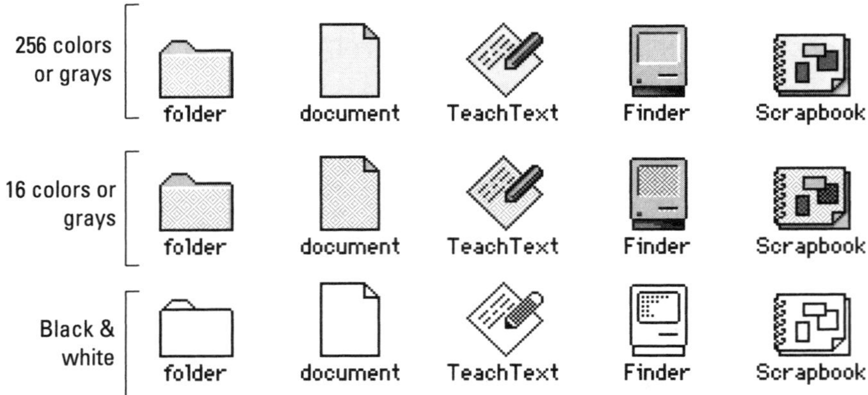


**Figure 4-20: How icons look on monitors displaying different levels of color.**

## Icon sizes

Each color scheme has two icon designs, one large and one small, as shown in Figure 4-21. Large icons appear on the desktop and in the Finder's By Icon view of disk and folder windows. Small icons appear in menus and in the Finder's Small Icon view of disk and folder windows.

Prior to System 7, the small icons were mechanically shrunken from full-size icons. Now any program developer can design separate, better-looking, small icons.

**Figure 4-21: Large and small icons.**

## Icon highlighting

Regardless of icon size and color, System 7 highlights selected icons on monitors displaying 16 or more colors or grays by darkening the icons, as shown in Figure 4-22. On a monitor displaying fewer than 16 colors or grays, System 7 highlights selected icons by inverting the colors; white becomes black and black becomes white.

Many programs have only some of the possible combinations of icon colors and sizes. For example, some programs use the same icons whether the number of colors in the Monitors control panel is set to 256 or 16.

## Updating Old Icons

When you install an updated program that includes redesigned icons on your disk, you usually have to rebuild the disk's desktop to see the new icons for that program and its documents. To rebuild the desktop of any disk whose icon normally appears on the desktop after startup, press ⌘-Option while starting your Macintosh. For each disk in turn, the Finder asks whether you want the disk's desktop rebuilt. To rebuild the desktop of a floppy disk or other removable disk whose icon is not on the desktop, press ⌘-Option while inserting the disk. For more information on desktop rebuilding, see "Desktop Database" in Chapter 7.

***Warning:*** Rebuilding the desktop erases anything you have typed into the Comments box of an icon's Info window (which you access with the Finder's Get Info command). See Chapter 18 for a description of utility software that preserves Get Info comments during desktop rebuilding.

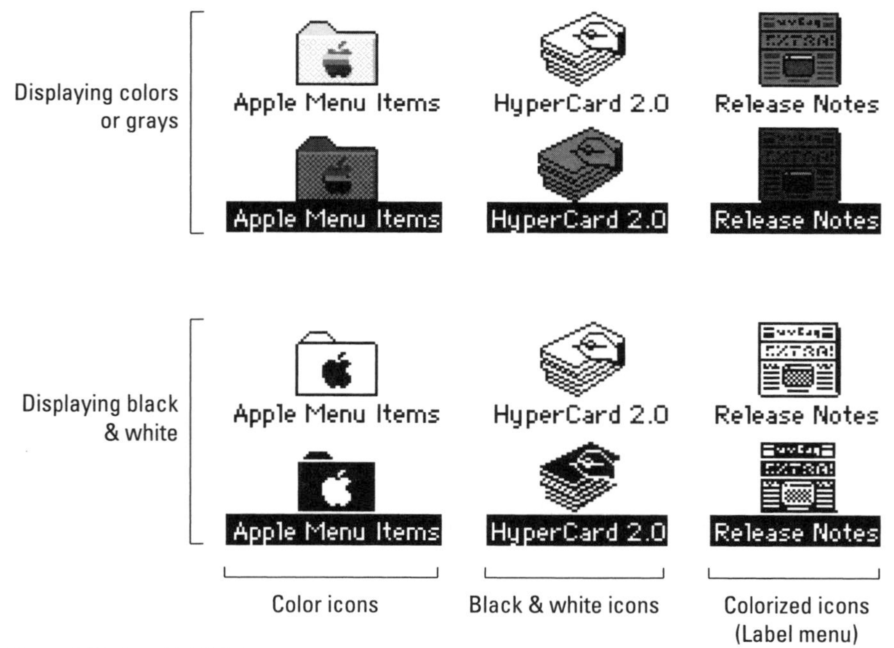


**Figure 4-22: Icon highlighting.**

# Selecting Icons

Everyone who uses a Mac quickly learns how to select items by clicking, but even some seasoned veterans don't know that in windows and on the desktop you can select more than one item at a time. In addition, you can select icons individually by typing instead of clicking.

## Multiple selection by Shift-clicking

Ordinarily, clicking an icon selects it (highlights it) and deselects the icon that was highlighted. You can select a group of icons in the same window or a group of icons on the desktop by pressing the Shift key while clicking each icon in turn. At any time, you can deselect a selected icon by pressing the Shift key and clicking it again.

## Multiple selection by dragging

In addition to Shift-clicking to select multiple icons, you can select adjacent icons by dragging a *selection rectangle* (which looks to some people like marching ants), across them. The Finder in System 7 allows this type of selection in any window, as shown in Figure 4-23.

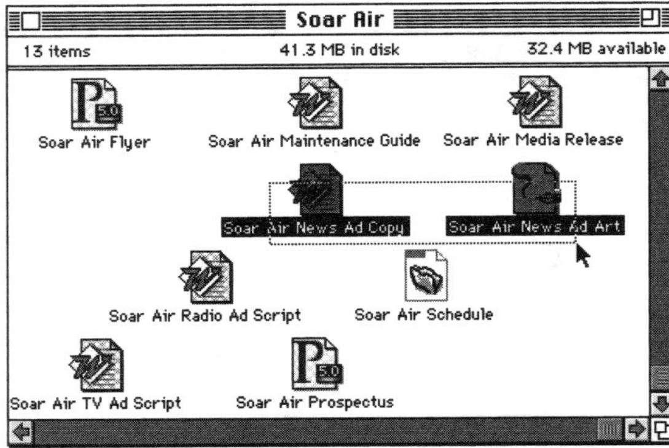


**Figure 4-23: Selecting adjacent items.**

The selection rectangle selects every item whose icon or icon name it touches. All items must be on the desktop or in a single window. Items are highlighted one-by-one as you drag over them, not en masse after you stop dragging.

You can combine dragging with the Shift key. Pressing Shift while dragging a selection rectangle across unselected icons adds the enclosed icons to the current selection. Conversely, pressing Shift while dragging a selection rectangle across selected icons deselects the enclosed group without deselecting other icons (if any).

## Selection by typing

When you know the name of an icon you want to select but aren't sure where it is in a window, you can select it more quickly by typing than by clicking. Typing also may be faster than clicking if the icon you want to select requires lots of scrolling to bring into view.

To select an icon by typing, simply type the first part of its name. You need to type only enough of the name to uniquely identify the icon you want. In a window in which every icon has a completely different name, for example, you need to type only the first letter of a name to select an icon. By contrast, in a folder where every icon begins with *Power*, you have to type those five letters plus enough additional letters to single out the icon you want. When selecting by typing, uppercase and lowercase letters are interchangeable.

While typing, you can select the next item alphabetically by pressing Tab or the previous item alphabetically by pressing Shift-Tab. Pressing an arrow key selects the icon nearest the currently selected icon in the direction that the arrow key points. To select the icon of the startup disk, press ⌘-Shift-up arrow. Table 4-1 summarizes keyboard selection techniques.

Table 4-1
**Selecting Icons by Typing**

| *To Select This* | *Do This* |
|---|---|
| An icon | Type the icon's partial or full name |
| Next icon alphabetically | Press Tab |
| Previous icon alphabetically | Press Shift-Tab |
| Next icon up | Press up arrow |
| Next icon down | Press down arrow |
| Next icon left | Press left arrow |
| Next icon right | Press right arrow |
| Startup disk icon | Press ⌘-Shift-up arrow |
| Multiple icons | Press Shift while clicking each icon or while dragging to enclose them |

# Renaming Icons

Clicking an icon highlights the icon and its name but does not select the icon name for editing. This limitation protects your icons from being accidentally renamed by your cat walking across your keyboard (which has actually happened to people using system software older than System 7). In addition, you can open an icon by double-clicking its name. When you select an icon and begin typing, expecting your typing to rename the selected icon (as happens with system software older than System 7), your typing selects another icon instead (as described in the preceding section).

To rename a disk, folder, program, document, or other item, you must explicitly select its name. Either click the name directly, or click the item's icon and then press Return or Enter. An icon whose name is selected for editing has a distinctive look: the icon is highlighted as usual, and the name has a box around it, as shown in Figure 4-24. The box does not appear when you just click the icon.

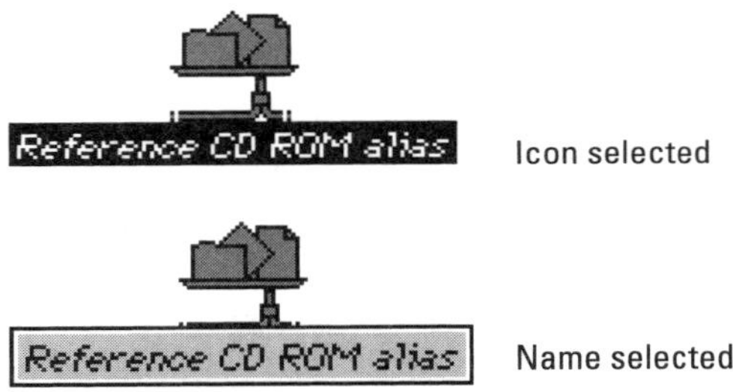


**Figure 4-24: Selecting an icon name.**

***Tip:*** For an additional visual cue that you have selected a name on a color or gray-scale monitor, use the Colors control panel to set the text highlight color to something other than black and white. Then you know that a name highlighted in color (or gray) is ready for editing, whereas a name highlighted in black and white is not.

After selecting a name, you can replace it completely by typing a new name. If instead you want to select an insertion point, word, or range of text, don't click, double-click, or drag right away. Wait until a box appears around the name. If you click again too soon, the Finder thinks that you're double-clicking the icon and opens it.

### Stop Waiting for the Editing Box

After clicking an icon name to edit it, you have to wait and wait for the editing box to appear around the name. To cut the wait short, just twitch the mouse and the name is highlighted for editing. You don't have to wait after clicking an icon's name if you immediately move the pointer. Another way to avoid waiting after clicking an icon's name is to move the insertion point by pressing the arrow keys. Click the name and immediately press the up arrow or the left arrow to move the insertion point to the beginning of the name, or immediately press the down arrow or the right arrow to move the selection point to the end. Once the selection point is established, pressing the left arrow moves it left and pressing the right arrow moves it right.

The length of time you must wait for the editing box to appear around an icon name you clicked depends on the duration of a double-click interval — approximately 1.9 seconds, 1.3 seconds, or 0.9 second, as set in the Mouse control panel. If you have trouble editing icon names without opening the item, try setting a briefer double-click speed with the Mouse control panel.

While editing a name, you can use the Undo, Cut, Copy, and Paste commands in the Edit menu. Use the same methods for editing an icon name as you use to edit text in a word processing program.

Besides selecting all or part of a name and copying it, you can also copy the entire name of any item by selecting its icon and using the Copy command (in the Edit menu). This capability comes in handy when you're copying a disk and want to give the copy the same name as the original.

You can copy the names of multiple icons by selecting the icons and using the Copy command. If the total length of all selected icon names exceeds 256 characters, the Finder copies only the first 256 characters to the Clipboard.

The Undo command works only as long as the icon name remains selected for editing. You cannot undo your changes to a name after you finish editing it. If you change your mind while editing a name and want to revert to the name the icon had before you began editing, simply delete the entire name and press Enter or Return. If an icon has no name when you press Enter or Return (ending the editing of the name), the Finder uses the icon's former name.

You can't change the name of a locked item. (Unlock an item with the Get Info command, or if it's on a disk, by sliding the disk's locking tab.) However, you can copy its entire name as just described.

# Custom Icons

Would you like to see dinosaurs or hummingbirds on your desktop instead of ordinary icons? Finder 7 enables you to replace the icons of individual documents, programs, folders, and disks with your own pictures, as shown in Figure 4-25.

**Figure 4-25: Icons your way.**

The color, gray-scale, or black-and-white picture you use for an icon can come from any of the following sources:

❖ Clip-art disk

❖ Photo or drawing on paper converted to an electronic image with a scanner

❖ Video image captured with special hardware accessories

❖ A picture you made with a painting or drawing program

## Making a custom icon

To replace an icon with your icon, first select the picture and copy it with the Copy command (Edit menu). Then go to the Finder and find the icon you want to replace. Select the icon (click it once) and choose Get Info from the Finder's File menu. In the Info window, click the icon to select it and use the Paste command (in the Edit menu) to replace it with the picture you just copied, as shown in Figure 4-26. You can also copy an icon from an Info window and paste it into a different Info window.

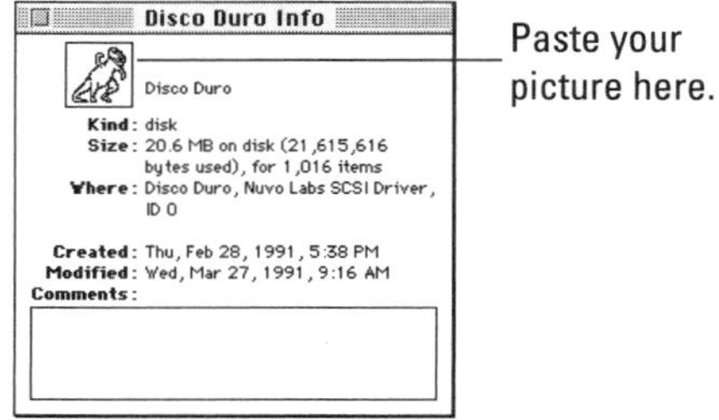


**Figure 4-26: Customizing an icon.**

For best results, your picture should measure 32 by 32 pixels (dots). Multiples of this size, such as 64 by 64, 128 by 128, or 256 by 256, may also yield acceptable results. If your picture is larger than 32 by 32, the Finder reduces it proportionally to fit that amount of space when you replace an icon with it. Reducing a picture distorts it, especially if the original size is an odd or fractional multiple of the final size. If your picture is smaller than 32 by 32, the Finder centers it on a white 32 by 32 square.

When an item with a custom icon appears as a small icon, such as in the Apple menu or in the Application menu, the Finder reduces the standard-size icon by half, as shown in Figure 4-27. If you duplicate or make an alias of an item with a custom icon, the duplicate or alias inherits the custom icon. (To learn about making an alias, see Chapter 10.)

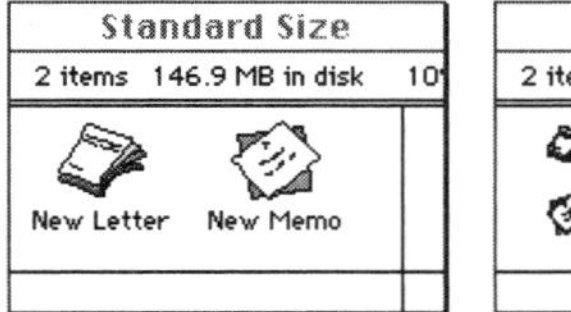


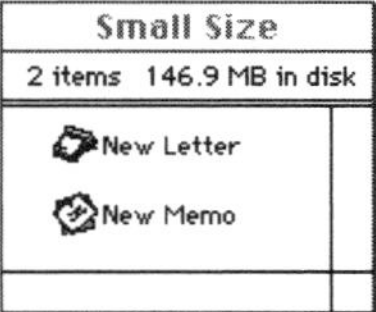


**Figure 4-27: Custom icons in standard and small sizes.**

You cannot replace the icon of a locked item, open document, or open program. Nor can you replace system software icons such as the System Folder, Finder, Control Panels Folder, and Trash. (You can replace individual control panel icons, however.)

When you paste a color picture into an item's Info window, you don't always get the custom icon you expect. The Finder is partly color blind; it sees light colors like yellow or orange at the picture's edge as transparent parts of the icon and omits them from the mask it makes for the custom icon. The defective mask punches an incomplete hole in the desktop for the icon to show through. For instructions on how to fix a defective icon mask, see Chapter 20.

## Reverting to a standard icon

To revert to an item's standard icon, select the item, choose Get Info from the Finder's File menu, select the icon in the Info window, and choose Clear or Cut from the Edit menu.

## Custom Folder Icons

If too many boring, look-alike folders clutter your desktop, you can liven them up by superimposing a relevant application icon. Follow these steps:

1. Copy a folder icon from its Info window.
2. Paste the copied icon into a color paint program.
3. Open the folder that contains the application whose icon you want to use, and choose by Small Icon from the View menu.
4. Take a screen snapshot by pressing ⌘-Shift-3.
5. Open the screen snapshot file (named Picture 1 on your startup disk) with the color paint program, with SimpleText, or with TeachText.
6. Copy the small application icon from the snapshot and paste it over the pasted folder icon.
7. Copy the composite icon from the paint program, paste it into the folder's Info window, and close the Info window.

When selecting the custom icon in the painting application, you must take care to select a rectangular area no larger than 32 by 32 pixels (the maximum size of an icon). If you select a larger area and include lots of white space around your custom icon, for example, the Finder shrinks the selection to 32 by 32 when you paste it into the folder's Info window and your custom icon ends up shrunken. If you select an area smaller than 32 by 32, the Finder centers the selection in the folder's icon space and the custom icon does not line up horizontally with a plain folder icon, which is flush with the bottom of its icon space.

You can create a custom folder icon more simply with the free utility program Folder Icon Maker by Gregory M. Robbins. You just drag a great-looking application or document icon to Icon Maker, and presto, it creates a new folder with a small icon superimposed on it. You can get Icon Maker from user groups such as BCS • Mac (617-864-1700) and from on-line information services.

# Menus

System 7 uses color and true grays to enhance menu looks, as shown in Figure 4-28. The small icons in the Help and Application menu bars appear in color or shades of gray on a monitor displaying at least 16 colors or gray shades. In addition, small icons in menus such as the Apple and Application menus appear in color or shades of gray.

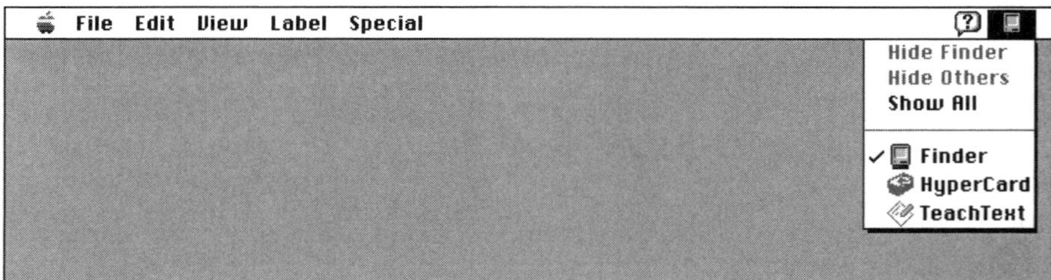


**Figure 4-28: Color in menus.**

### Broken Icons

System 7 keeps a file's custom icon in the file itself. It keeps the custom icon for a folder or disk in an invisible file that it creates automatically inside the folder or disk. The name of this file consists of the word Icon plus a return character. If you manage to delete one of these invisible files, you can no longer cut, clear, or paste the icon in the Info window of the file or folder. When you try, the Mac displays the informative message "The command could not be completed because it cannot be found."

You can work around a broken folder icon by moving the contents of the broken folder to a new folder and discarding the broken folder, but this technique doesn't work for disks. You can fix broken icons with the shareware utility called Custom Killer by Robert Gibson (available from user groups such as BMUG, 800-776-2684 or 510-549-2684, and from on-line information services such as America Online). It's designed to remove custom icons from files, folders, and disks, and it also fixes screwed-up folder and disk icons. You get quicker removal of custom icons by dragging an item or multiple items to the Custom Killer icon than by using the Finder's Get Info command.

On monitors displaying at least four grays or 16 colors, System 7 uses true gray text to display inactive menu titles, inactive menu items, and the gray lines that divide sections of menus. In a program with color menus, System 7 displays inactive items in a blend of the menu item color and the menu background color. On a monitor displaying less than 16 colors, System 7 simulates gray text by alternating black and white dots. Older system software simulates gray text at all color or gray levels and does not display color icons in menus or the menu bar (except for the Apple icon).

Menu enhancement works automatically for most existing application programs. However, programs that don't use standard menu-management software may not display true gray text and dividing lines in menus.

When you use a keyboard shortcut for a command in a menu, the title of the menu flashes briefly to signal that the command has been executed. You can change how many times the title flashes or turn off the signal altogether in the Menu Blinking section of the General Controls control panel.

# Guide Menu

If you're not sure how to proceed, the Mac itself provides a source of advice close at hand: the Guide menu (called the Help menu prior to System 7.5). This menu is labeled with the question mark near the right end of the menu bar, as shown in Figure 4-29. It contains commands for turning on brief messages, called *balloon help*, that explain how to use buttons, commands, windows, or other on-screen elements. Plus, if the program includes a help system of its own, the Guide menu includes a command for reaching that more extensive information.

With System 7.5 and later, the Guide menu also includes access to interactive, step-by-step help called *Apple guide.*

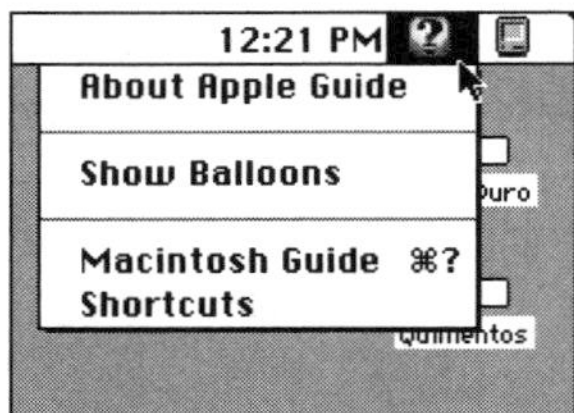


**Figure 4-29: The Guide menu in System 7.5.**

In System 7.1.2 and earlier the Help menu icon looks a little different, but it's located at the same place on the menu bar as System 7.5's Guide menu.

## Balloon help

When you need immediate information about objects you see on-screen, you can turn on System 7's optional balloon help. With balloon help on, you place the pointer over an object and a concise description of it appears in a cartoon-style balloon, as shown in Figure 4-30. The balloon points to the object and tells you what the object is, what it does, what happens when you click it, or some portion of this information. You do not have to press any keys or click anything to make help balloons appear.

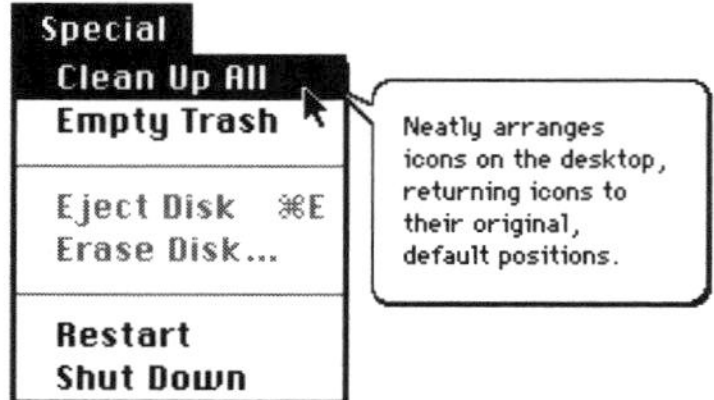


**Figure 4-30: A help balloon.**

### Turning balloon help on and off

You turn on balloon help by choosing Show Balloons from the Guide menu. That command then changes to Hide Balloons, and choosing it again turns off balloon help.

## Working with balloon help on

Everything works normally when balloon help is on. Using balloon help does not put the Macintosh into help-only mode. It's like someone is standing over your shoulder and describing on-screen objects to you.

Help balloons appear whether or not you press the mouse button. You click, double-click, and otherwise use programs normally, except you perceive a slight delay as help balloons come and go when you move the pointer slowly across items that have balloon help descriptions.

The object that a help balloon describes may be large or small and individual or collective, as shown in Figure 4-31. For example, the Close box in the active window's title bar has its own help balloon. In contrast, an inactive window has one balloon for the whole window. Sometimes a help balloon describes a whole group, as in the Mouse control panel, where one balloon tells you about the seven settings for the Mouse Tracking option.

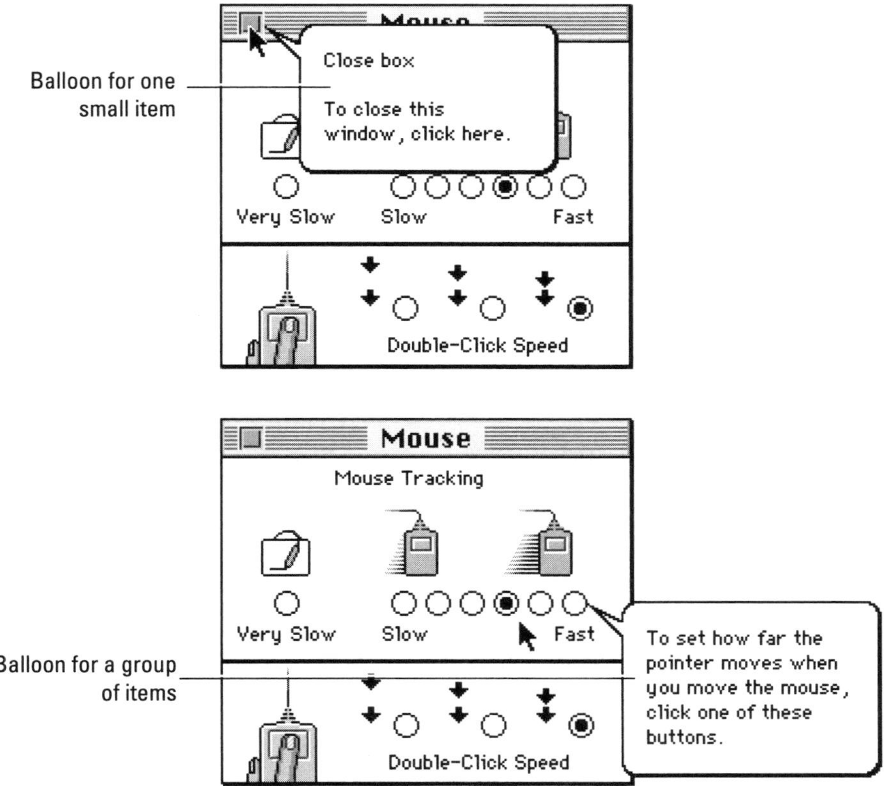


**Figure 4-31: Help balloons vary in scope.**

Moving the pointer slowly over several objects that have help balloons opens and closes balloons in sequence. To prevent excessive flashing of help balloons, they do not appear when you move the pointer quickly. For a help balloon to appear, the pointer must be in the same area for about one-tenth of a second or longer. You cannot change this timing.

### What balloon help knows

Balloon help knows about all standard objects in the Macintosh interface. They include windows in general, system software icons, the Apple menu, the Guide menu, the Application menu (described in "Opening Multiple Programs" in Chapter 5), standard parts of directory dialog boxes (described in "Directory Dialog Boxes" in Chapter 5), the Page Setup dialog box (described in Chapter 12), and the Print dialog box (described in Chapter 12). Balloon help cannot describe a specific program's menu commands, window contents, dialog boxes, and so on unless its developer or publisher has included the necessary information. For example, Apple has provided complete balloon help for the Finder, TeachText, SimpleText, standard control panels, and standard desk accessories.

## Apple Guide

System 7.5 includes a help system that goes far beyond balloon help's answers to your "What is this?" questions. Called *Apple Guide*, this help system answers your "How do I . . . ?" and "Why can't I . . . ?" questions. It shows and tells you how to get things done while you actually do them. Step-by-step instructions appear in a guide window, which floats above all other windows, as shown in Figure 4-32. As you move from step to step, Apple Guide may coach you by marking an object on-screen with a circle, arrow, or underline.

Apple Guide watches what you do and can adjust its steps if you work ahead or make a mistake. The Guide window can include buttons you click to have the guide actually perform a step for you.

### Bringing up and putting away Apple Guide

You bring up Apple Guide by choosing a command from the Guide menu, such as Macintosh Guide or PowerTalk Guide. After a brief pause, the main Guide window shown in Figure 4-33 appears.

You can shrink the Guide window by clicking the Zoom box at the upper-right corner of the window. To enlarge a shrunken Guide window to its full size, click the Zoom box again.

When you are finished with Apple Guide, you put it away by closing the Guide window.

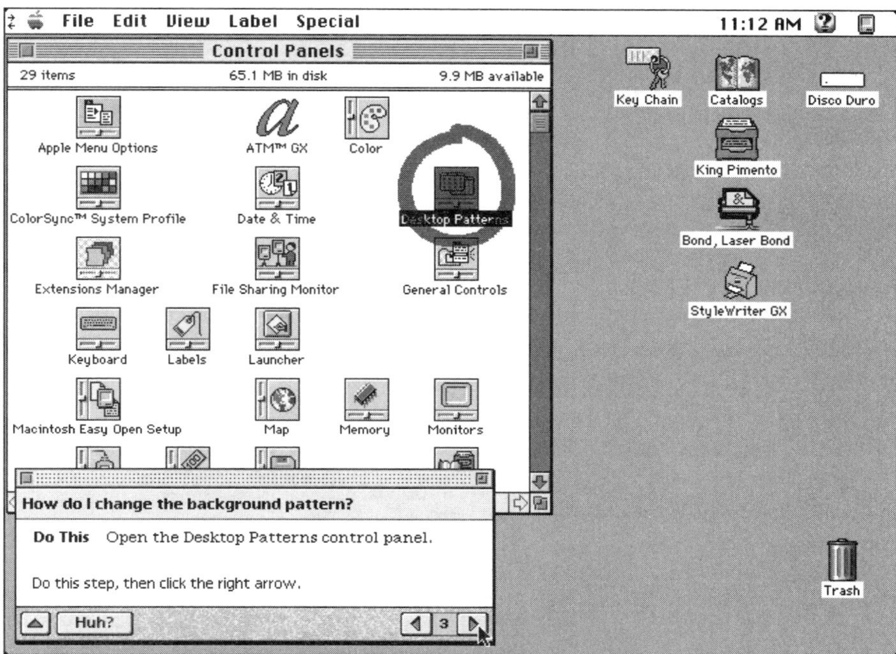


**Figure 4-32: Apple Guide displays step-by-step instructions in a floating window and draws coaching marks to point out objects on-screen.**

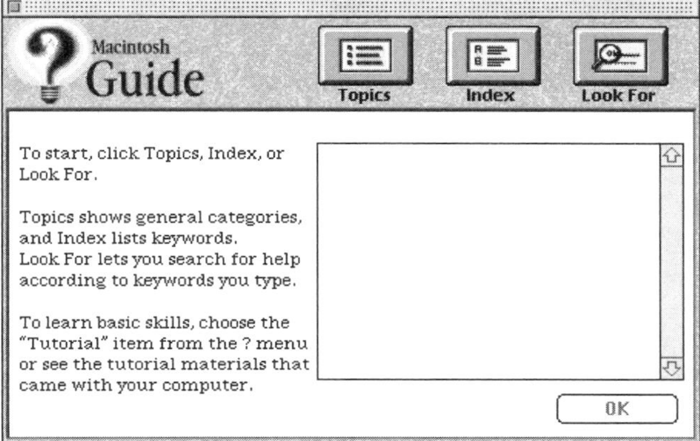


**Figure 4-33: You decide how to find help in the main Guide window.**

### Finding help for a task or term

In the main Guide window, you can choose how you want to find help on a task or a term: by selecting from a list of topics, by browsing an index, or by looking for words in the guide. One of the three methods probably suits you better than the others, but try them all if you have trouble finding a task or term by using your favorite method.

To see a list of help topics, click the Topics button. Clicking a topic on the left side of the main Guide window displays a list of specific tasks and terms on the right side, as shown in Figure 4-34.

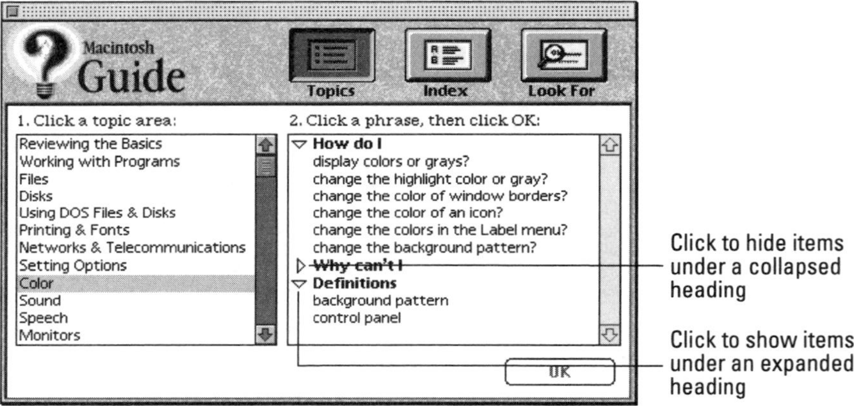


**Figure 4-34: Scanning the list of topics in Apple Guide.**

To browse the index, click the Index button in the main Guide window. Apple Guide displays an alphabetical list of key terms used in the guide. You can scroll through the index with the scroll bar. You can type the first part of a term you want to look up in the index, and the index instantly scrolls to the index entry that most closely matches what you typed. You can also scroll the index to entries starting with a particular letter of the alphabet by dragging the pointer at the top of the index list to that letter or by simply clicking that letter. You can't see all 26 letters of the alphabet at the top of the index list, but you can see more by clicking and dragging the pointer slightly past the last letter you can see. Clicking an entry in the index displays a list of tasks in which that entry appears, as shown in Figure 4-35.

To have Apple Guide look for words you specify, click the Look For button in the main Guide window. Click the arrow button and in the adjacent text entry box that appears on the left side of the window, type words you think are in the step-by-step instructions you want to see. When you click the Search button (or press Enter or Return), a list of relevant tasks appears, as shown in Figure 4-36.

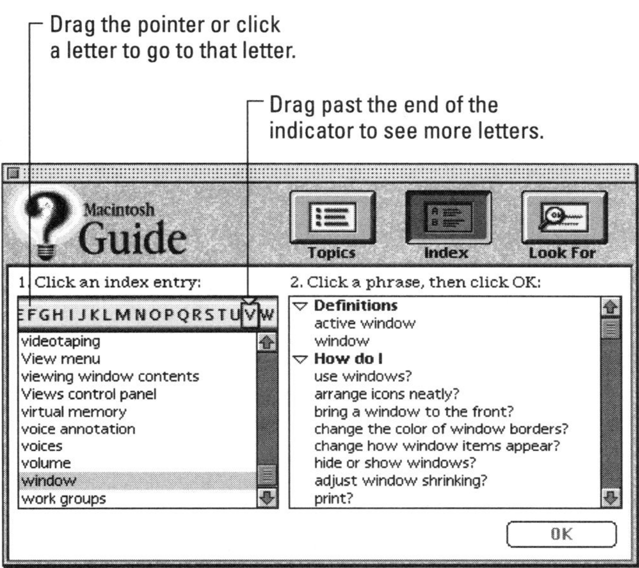


**Figure 4-35: Browsing the index in Apple Guide.**

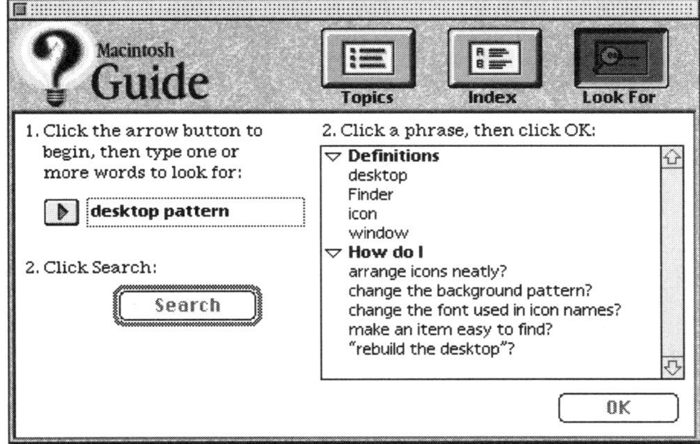


**Figure 4-36: Looking for specific words in Apple Guide.**

## Following step-by-step instructions

When you double-click a task at the right side of the main Guide window (or select the task and click OK), the main Guide window goes away. After a brief pause, another window appears with an introduction to the task or a definition of the term you selected in the main Guide window, as shown in Figure 4-37.

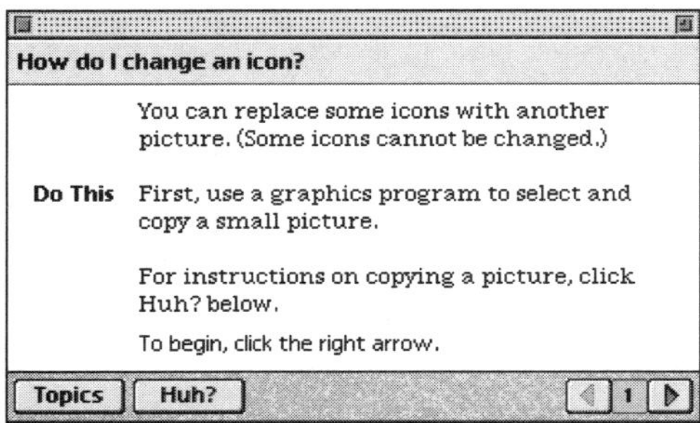

How do I change an icon?
You can replace some icons with another picture. (Some icons cannot be changed.)
Do This
First, use a graphics program to select and copy a small picture.
For instructions on copying a picture, click Huh? below.
To begin, click the right arrow.
Topics
Huh?
1


**Figure 4-37: The first step describes the task or defines the term.**

Read the information in the Guide window and follow any instructions it gives you. To go to the next step in a multiple-step task, click the right-pointing arrow at the bottom right of the Guide window. To back up one step, click the left-pointing arrow.

If you decide that you have selected the wrong task or term, click the up-pointing arrow at the bottom right of the Guide window. The Guide window goes away, and the main Apple Guide window appears after a brief pause. You can also put away Apple Guide altogether by closing all guide windows.

At each new step, the guide may draw a circle, line, or arrow on-screen to point out a menu title or other object you must use to complete the step. These coaching marks appear in red or another color on a color monitor. If the step calls for you to choose from a menu, Apple Guide displays the menu item you should choose in color as well. On a black-and-white screen, it marks the menu choice with an underline.

If the Guide window mentions something you don't understand, try clicking the Huh? button in the window for clarification. Clicking Huh? brings up another window that may contain a definition of a term or begin step-by-step instructions for accomplishing a task related to the task you initially chose. For example, clicking Huh? in step 3 of the task "How do I turn off the computer?" brings up the task "How do I turn off the computer automatically?"

If you work ahead of the step currently displayed in the Guide window, Apple Guide can adjust itself to catch up. When you click the right-pointing arrow to go to the next step, Apple Guide skips ahead to the next step that matches your location in the task.

While you're following the steps in Apple Guide, you can still use your computer normally. If the Guide window is in your way, you can drag it somewhere else or click its zoom box to make it smaller; click again to make it larger. In System 7.5 and later, you can hide all of a Guide window except its title bar by clicking the title bar according to the setup in the WindowShade control panel (described in "Window Controls" earlier in this chapter).

If you have not properly completed a step when you click the right-pointing arrow at the bottom of the Guide window, Apple Guide explains what you need to do to get back on track.

### What Apple Guide knows

System 7.5 and later comes with step-by-step help for system-level tasks such as printing, file sharing, control panel use, and troubleshooting. Developers and system administrators can create additional help, which can cover tasks that involve multiple applications. Apple Guide's usefulness depends greatly on how well crafted the help procedures for individual tasks are. Apple has set a good example with its system-level help procedures.

## Other help

Many programs add how-to help, on-screen references, or other items to the Guide menu. In System 7.1.2 and earlier, for example, the Finder has a Finder Shortcuts item (see Figure 4-38) that displays a dialog box containing tricks for using the Finder.

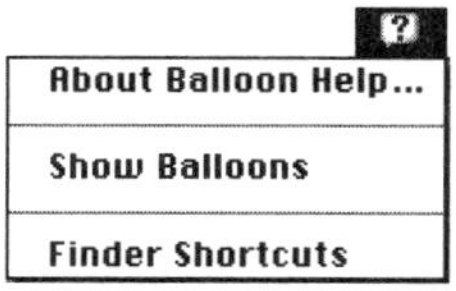

About Balloon Help...
Show Balloons
Finder Shortcuts

**Figure 4-38: The Finder's Help menu in Systems 7.1.2 and earlier.**

## CHAPTER 4 CONCEPTS AND TERMS

- On a Mac that displays colors or gray shades, the standard desktop pattern in System 7 is made up of two gray shades, which results in a smooth, continuous tone.
- The windows in System 7 include 3-D motion and window controls, as well as the capability to select shading color for window control areas.
- In System 7's windows and on the desktop, you can select more than one icon with the selection rectangle, no matter the view.
- System 7's icons come in two sizes to allow for better-looking small icons.
- Balloon help consists of cartoonlike balloons that appear when you place the pointer over any standard object in the Mac's interface. The balloons point to the object and tell you what the object is, what it does, what happens when you click it, or some portion of this information. System 7.5 and later also offers Apple Guide, which gives you step-by-step instructions for completing certain tasks.

**Apple Guide**
In System 7.5, a help system that provides step-by-step instructions for completing certain tasks.

**balloon help**
A help system that makes a cartoonlike balloon appear when you drag the mouse slowly over a standard object in the Mac's interface. The balloon may tell you what the object is, what it does, or what happens when you click it.

**double-click speed**
The rate at which you have to click so that the Mac perceives two clicks in a row as a single click.

**insertion point**
A blinking vertical bar that indicates where text will be inserted if you start typing.

**selection rectangle**
A dotted line box that you drag around items to select them all.

**Shift-click**
Holding down the Shift key while clicking the mouse to select multiple items or a range of items.

**tracking speed**
The rate at which the pointer moves as you drag the mouse.

CHAPTER FIVE

# Opening and Saving Documents

- Using the Apple menu to quickly open items you use frequently
- Working with multiple open programs
- Using directory dialog boxes to reach everything in the Finder
- Making and using stationery pads
- Opening documents with the drag-and-drop shortcut
- Converting unopenable Mac and PC files to a readable format
- Simplifying and controlling the desktop with At Ease

The Macintosh operating system provides several ways to open, close, and save items. You can double-click icons or select an item on the desktop and then select the relevant command from the Finder's File menu.

## Opening with the Apple Menu

Under System 7, the Apple menu expedites opening items you use frequently. Anything you can double-click in the Finder, including documents, application programs, desk accessories, folders, control panels, and even fonts and sounds, you can also put in the Apple menu and open by choosing it there (see Figure 5-1).

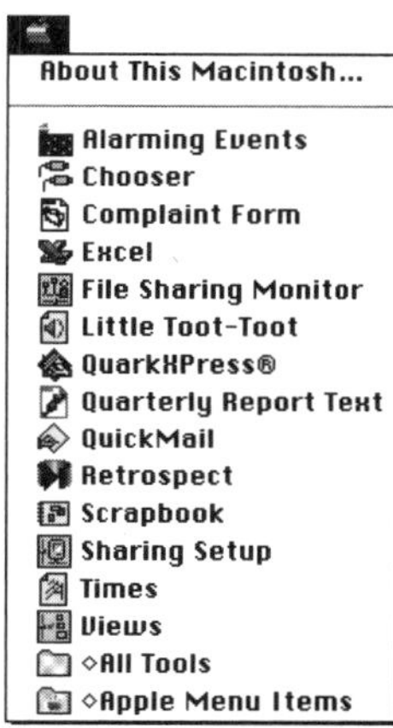


**Figure 5-1: An Apple menu.**

## Adding and removing Apple menu items

You put an item in the Apple menu by dragging it into the Apple Menu Items folder, which is inside the System Folder, as shown in Figure 5-2. The item becomes instantly available in the Apple menu (no need to restart your Macintosh).

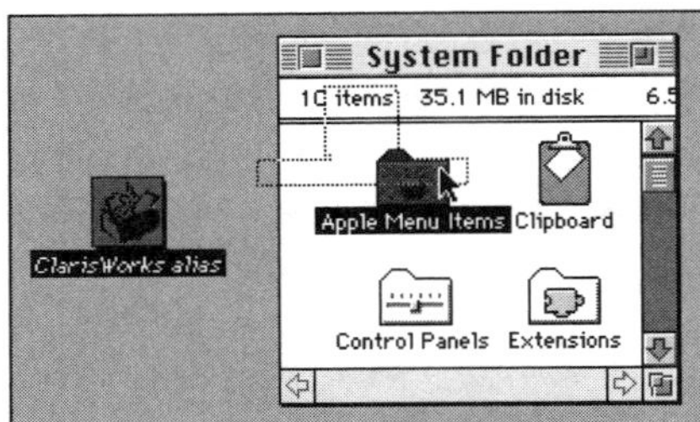


**Figure 5-2: Adding an item to the Apple menu.**

To remove an item from the Apple menu, drag its icon or alias out of the Apple Menu Items folder onto the desktop or into another folder.

## Organizing the Apple menu

The Apple menu always lists items alphabetically in plain Chicago 12-point text. Names of aliases are not italicized in the menu even though they are italicized in the Apple Menu Items folder (for the complete story on aliases, see Chapter 10). You don't affect the Apple menu when you rearrange the contents of the Apple Menu Items folder by dragging icons in its window, clicking column headings in a list view, or using the Finder's View menu.

You can make an item appear at the top of the Apple menu by prefixing its name with a blank space. Prefixing a name with an Apple logo or solid diamond (♦) symbol makes the name appear below names prefixed with a space but above names without prefixes. To prefix a name with an Apple logo or solid diamond, open the Key Caps desk accessory and set it to the Chicago font. Press Control-T for the Apple logo or Control-S for the solid diamond, and use the Copy command to put the symbol on the Clipboard. Switch to the Finder, select an insertion point at the beginning of the item name, and paste. The Apple logo and the solid diamond look like boxes in the Apple Menu Items window because they're not part of the Geneva font, which the Finder uses for text in windows unless you specify another font with the Views control panel. They look right in the Apple menu, however, which uses the Chicago font.

To make items appear at the bottom of the Apple menu, prefix with a hollow diamond (◊) or a bullet (•). Press Shift-Option-V for the hollow diamond or Option-8 for the bullet.

### Forcing Order Invisibly

Forcibly reordering items in the Apple menu by putting spaces or special symbols at the beginning of the items' names has side effects you may dislike. The spaces or symbols visibly alter the names and conspicuously shift the names to the right. Here's how to invisibly force the order you want:

1. Open the Note Pad or a new document in TeachText, SimpleText, or any word processor.
2. Press Return to create a blank line, select the blank line, and copy it to the Clipboard.
3. Switch to the Finder. In the Apple Menu Items folder, click the name of an item that you want to appear at the top of the Apple menu to select the name for editing.
4. Press the up-arrow key to move the insertion point to the beginning of the selected name and paste. The whole name goes blank, but don't fret.
5. Press Enter or click outside the name, and the name springs back into view.

   The renamed item jumps to the top of the window if you're viewing by name. To increase an item's alphabetic buoyancy, paste the blank line two or more times at the beginning of the item's name. Some applications don't work properly with files or folders whose names contain blank lines (blank spaces are okay). If you encounter problems after pasting blank lines at the beginning of file or folder names, you'll have to use blank spaces instead.

## Grouping and separating items

You can group different types of items by prefixing different numbers of blank spaces to their names. The more blank spaces, the higher on the Apple menu the item appears, as shown in Figure 5-3. For example, you can prefix three blank spaces to control panel names, two blanks to desk accessory names, one blank to application programs, and none to other items.

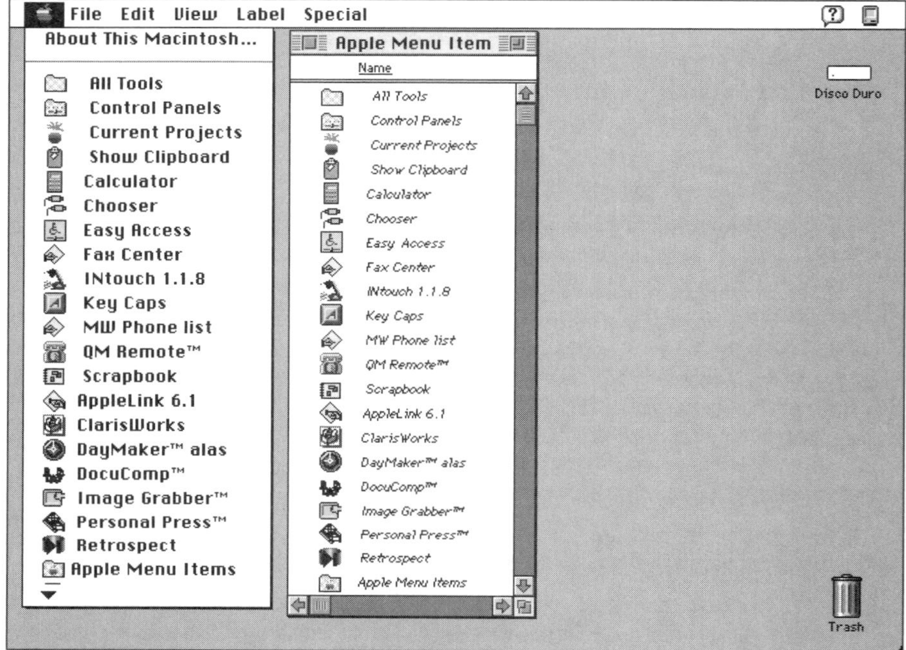


**Figure 5-3: Grouping Apple menu items.**

## Making submenus in the Apple menu

If your Apple menu has so many items that you must scroll to see them all, consider consolidating the less-used items in a folder or two within the Apple Menu Items folder. In System 7.5 and later, you can make the contents of folders within the Apple Menu Items folder appear as submenus of the Apple menu by using the Apple Menu Options control panel (see Figure 5-4). You can also use this control panel to create submenus that list the items you have used recently.

QUICK TIPS

## Dividing Apple Menu Items

A giant list arranged by type can be difficult to scan quickly. It helps to visually separate the different types of items. You can make separators by naming empty folders with hyphens and prefixing the right number of blank spaces to the names so that each one appears between two different types of items.

Instead of using ordinary empty folders to make separators in the Apple menu, you can use aliases. Aliases of the Finder work well as separators because opening one (by accidentally choosing it from the Apple menu) results in a message saying that the item can't be opened. Another possible separator is a sound or alias of a sound. Choosing a separator that's based on a sound file simply plays the sound.

To further refine your Apple menu, you can hide the icons of the separators you make, as shown in the accompanying figure. First, you copy some white space in a painting program. (If you don't have a painting program, open an empty folder in the Finder and press ⌘-Shift-3 to make a screen shot of the empty folder. Open the screen shot in TeachText or SimpleText and copy some white space there.) With white space copied, select a separator item's icon and use the Finder's Get Info command to display the item's Info window. Then select the icon in that window and paste the white space over it.

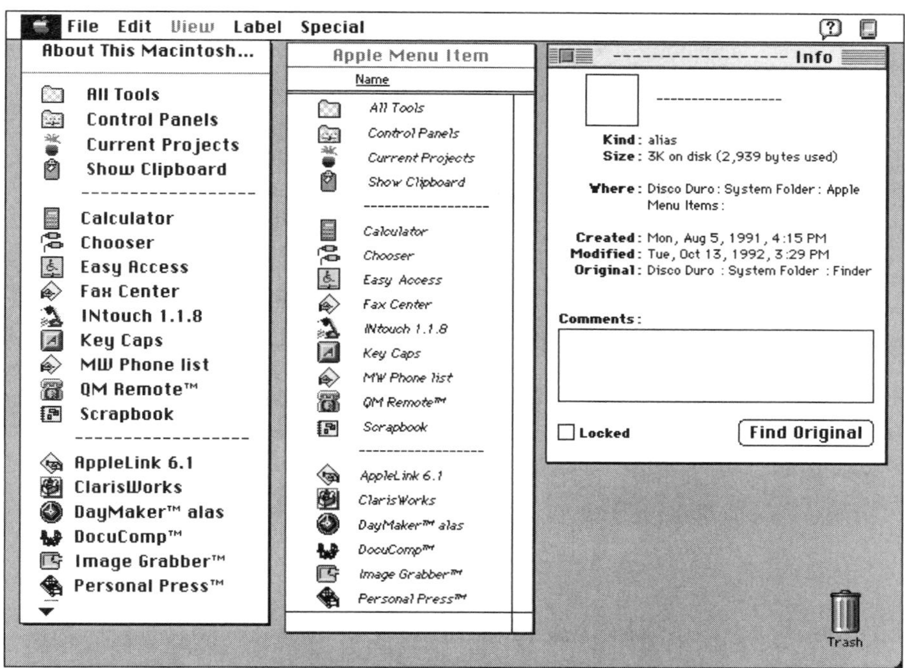

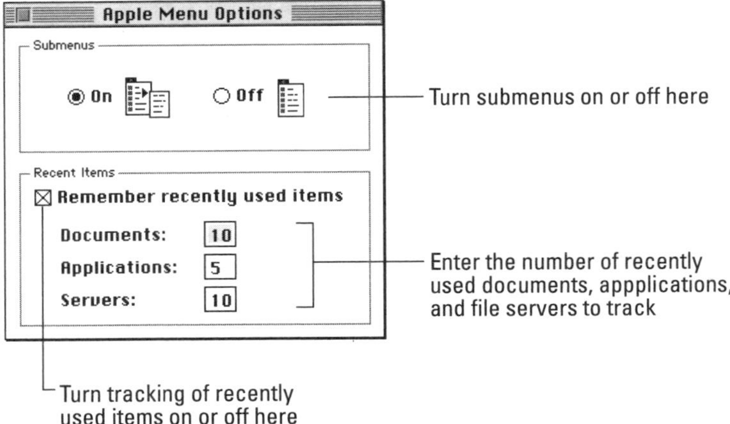


**Figure 5-4: System 7.5's Apple Menu Options control panel can add submenus to the Apple menu and track recently used items.**

If you use a version of System 7 earlier than 7.5, you can get submenus in the Apple menu by installing a control panel such as KiwiPowerMenus from Kiwi Software, HAM from Microseeds, or Now Utilities from Now Software.

# Opening Multiple Programs

With System 7, you can have more than one program open at a time. When you open a program, the Finder remains open in the background. You can switch to the Finder without quitting the program you just opened. If your Mac has enough RAM, you can open additional programs without quitting. You can have as many programs open simultaneously as fit in your computer's memory, as shown in Figure 5-5.

The capability to have multiple programs open simultaneously, called *multitasking*, can be very convenient. For example, you can copy and paste among documents of open programs without closing documents and quitting programs.

Multitasking's convenience has disorienting side effects. For example, a stray mouse click may make another open application active, bringing its windows to the front and covering the windows of the program you were using. If this happens unexpectedly, you may think that the program you're using has crashed when it is actually open and well in the background.

You must get used to having multiple layers of open programs like piles of paper on a desk. Unlike the multitasking provided by MultiFinder in older system software, System 7's multitasking cannot be turned off.

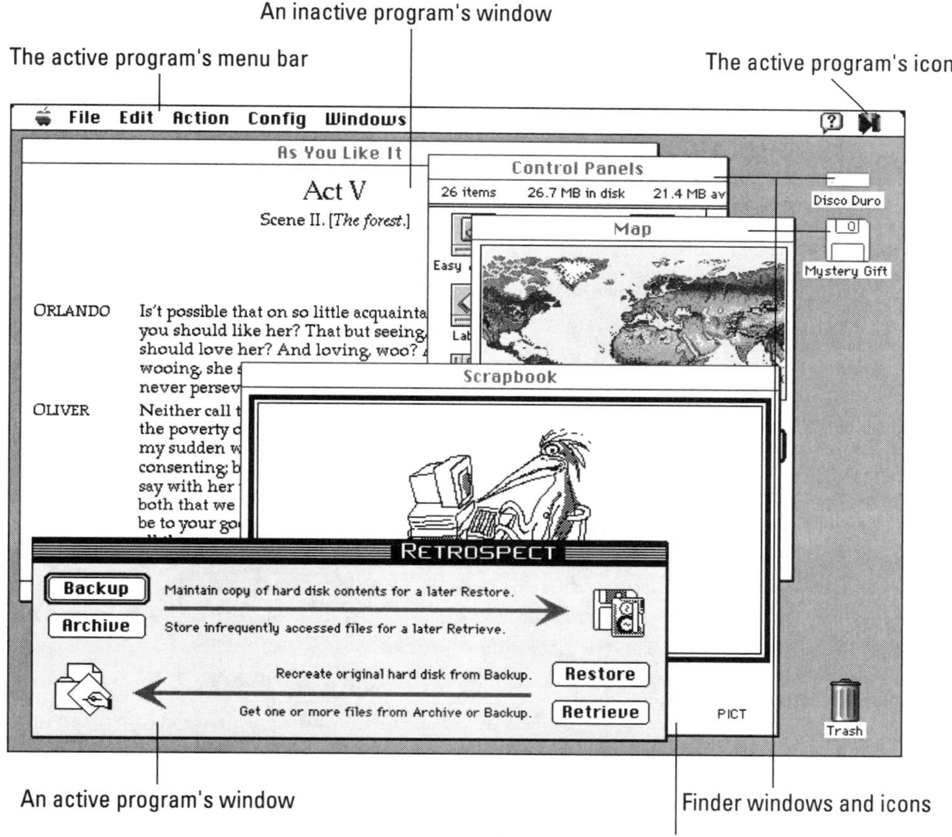


**Figure 5-5: Multiple programs open.**

Regardless of how many programs you have open, only one has control of the menu bar. The program currently in control is called the active program, and its icon appears at the right end of the menu bar. You can tell which open program is currently active by looking at the application icon at the right end of the menu bar. The application icon looks similar to the MultiFinder icon in system software older than System 7, but the icon has a different use.

## Switching programs

Not only does the icon at the right end of the menu bar tell you which application is active, but it also marks the Application menu, as shown in Figure 5-6. You use the Application menu to switch from one open program to another. The Application menu lists all open programs by name and small icon.

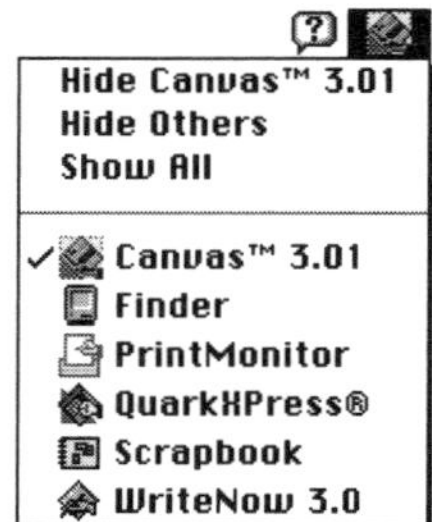


**Figure 5-6: The Application menu.**

To make a program in the Application menu the active program, choose it from the menu. When you do, that program takes over the menu bar and the program's windows come to the front. The program that was active becomes inactive. Its windows drop back but remain visible except for the parts covered by other open programs' windows. You can also make a program the active program by opening its icon or any of its document icons in the Finder or by clicking in any of its windows. Clicking the desktop or a Finder icon makes the Finder active. On one hand, being able to bring the Finder to the front with a single mouse click can be very handy. On the other hand, it can be disorienting to have the application you're using suddenly disappear behind the Finder's windows due to a misplaced click.

You can keep the Finder's desktop hidden while you are working in another program if you use System 7.5 or later or have a Performa. With the Finder's desktop hidden, you can't accidentally activate the Finder by clicking the desktop. To keep the Finder hidden in System 7.5 and later, turn off the "Show Desktop when in background" option in the General Controls control panel, as shown in Figure 5-7. On a Performa, the Finder is always hidden when it is in the background unless you drag the Launcher out of the Control Panels folder (which is inside the System Folder) and restart.

## Reducing window clutter

With many programs open, the desktop quickly becomes a visual Tower of Babel. You can eliminate the clutter by choosing the Application menu's Hide Others command, as shown in Figure 5-8. It hides the windows of all programs except the currently active one. The icons of hidden programs are dimmed in the Application menu. To make the windows of all programs visible, choose Show All from the Application menu.

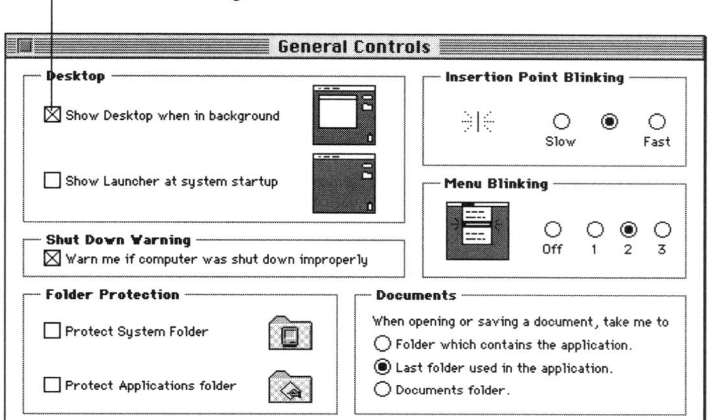


**Figure 5-7: System 7.5's General Controls control panel determines whether the Finder is hidden when it is not the active program.**

You can hide the active program's windows and simultaneously switch to the most recently active program by choosing the first command from the Application menu. The command's name begins with the word Hide and ends with the name of the currently active program.

To hide the active program's windows as you switch to a particular program, press Option while choosing the other program from the Application menu. Or press Option while clicking another program's window. You hide windows and switch to the Finder by pressing Option while clicking the desktop, a Finder icon, or a Finder window. Of course, those methods of switching to the Finder don't work if you set System 7.5 or later to keep the Finder hidden or if you use a Performa, which always keeps the Finder hidden, as described in the preceding section.

# Memory partitions

Every application program and desk accessory you open has its own layer on the desktop and its own part of memory in System 7. (Older system software lumps all open desk accessories together in a single layer and a single memory partition when MultiFinder is active, or includes them with the open application program when MultiFinder is inactive.) You can see how your computer's memory is partitioned at any time by choosing About This Macintosh from the Apple menu when the Finder is active, as shown in Figure 5-9.

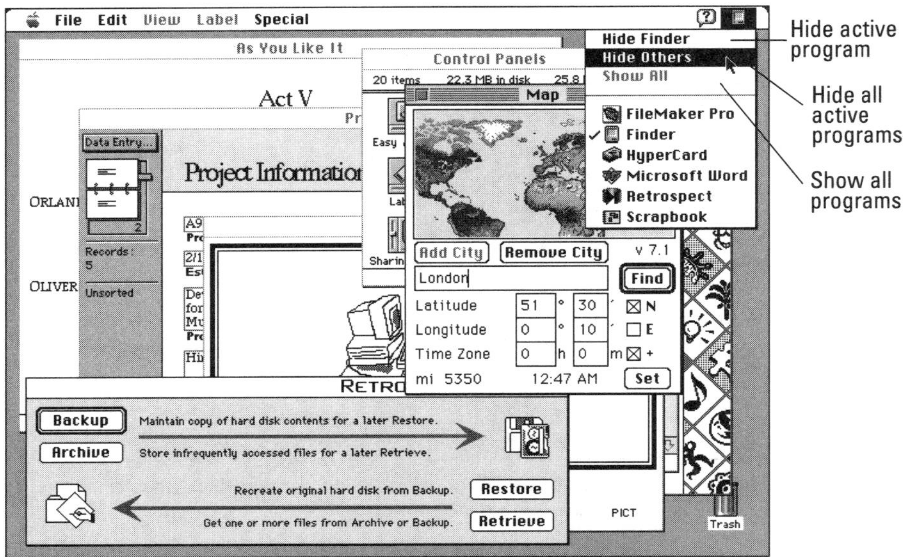


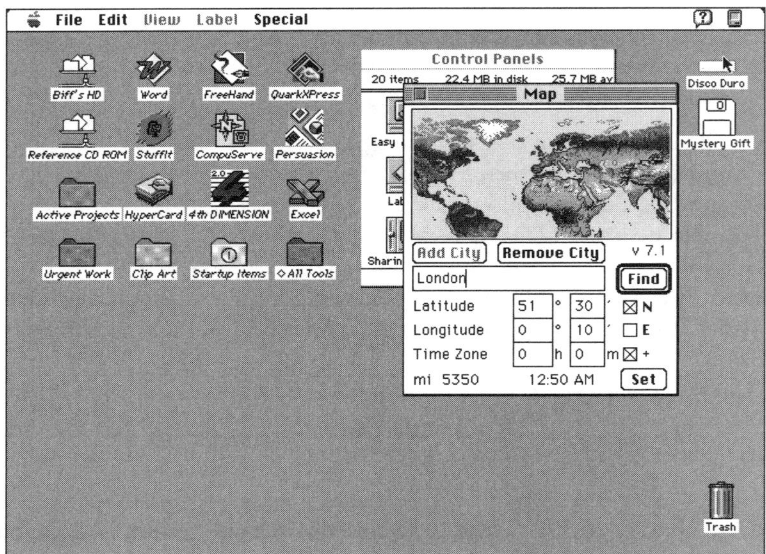


**Figure 5-8: Hiding inactive programs.**

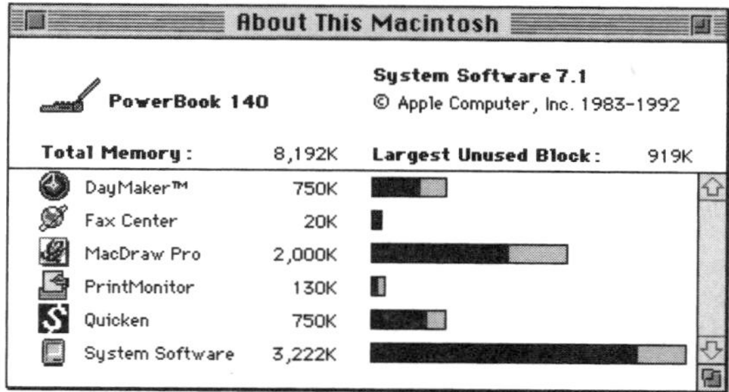


**Figure 5-9: Checking memory use.**

## Background operations

Some programs can operate in the background by using System 7's multitasking capabilities. Background programs run during the intervals, typically less than 1/8 of a second long, when the active program isn't using the computer. They usually work while the active program waits for you to do something.

### Interacting with Background Programs

A background program can't use the menu bar or interact directly with you in any way. It can, however, ask you to activate it by some or all of the following means:

- ❖ Displaying a diamond symbol next to its name in the Application menu
- ❖ Flashing its icon on top of the Application menu's icon or the Apple menu's icon
- ❖ Playing a sound (commonly a beep)
- ❖ Displaying a brief alert message which you must dismiss before continuing

In addition, a program in the background can interact with other open programs by sending them Apple events messages, which are described in Chapter 18.

# Directory Dialog Boxes

In addition to opening items in the Finder, you can also open them with the Open command in most applications. Choosing the Open command from any program's File menu (except the Finder's) displays a directory dialog box, as in Figure 5-10. A directory dialog box in System 7 works like a one-window Finder. (Directory dialog boxes in older system software look similar but work differently.)

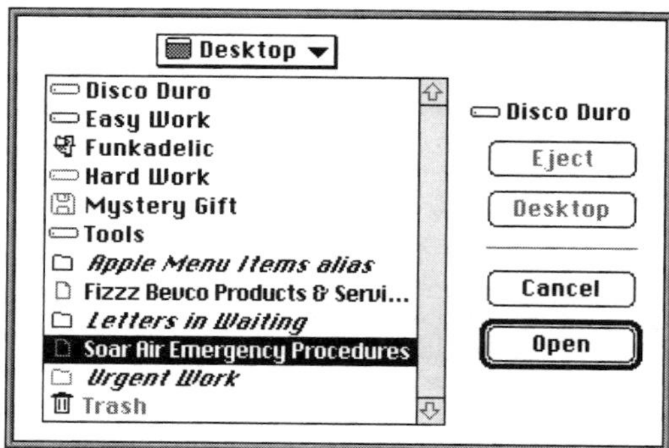


**Figure 5-10: An Open command's dialog box.**

The Save, Save As, and other disk-related commands use directory boxes similar to the Open command's directory dialog box. The Save and Save As directory dialog boxes always include a place to enter the name of the file you're saving, something an Open directory dialog box doesn't need.

All directory dialog boxes have a single directory window, in which you locate an item you want to open or a folder in which you want to save an item. The directory window lists the names of items from one folder or disk at a time, always alphabetically by name. System 7 displays longer names by using compressed-style text for names that exceed 25 characters.

Above the directory window is the name of the folder or disk whose contents are currently listed in the directory window. The folder or disk name is part of a pop-up menu that shows the hierarchy of folders from the currently listed folder, through the folders that contain it (if any), to the desktop. Choosing an item from the pop-up menu takes you to that item, displaying its contents in the directory window. As a shortcut, you can move up one folder in the hierarchy to the folder that contains the currently listed folder by clicking the name of the disk where it is displayed above the Eject button in the directory dialog box.

System 7's directory dialog boxes show the names of items that it can't open (such as the names of files in a Save dialog box) by using true gray text. Also, they can display icons in the seven colors assigned by the Finder's Label menu. Your Monitors control panel must be set for at least 16 colors or four grays. Some programs must be upgraded to show icons in color and text in true gray.

## The desktop

System 7's directory dialog boxes provide a view of the desktop and enable you to open the disks and other items on it. By clicking the Desktop button, you can go to the desktop level and open the disk whose contents you want to see, as shown in Figure 5-11. You can also go to the desktop by choosing it from the pop-up menu above the directory window. (Instead of a Desktop button, directory dialog boxes in system software older than System 7 have a Drive button. Clicking it switches to the next disk whose icon is on the desktop, a more cumbersome procedure for switching among more than two disks.)

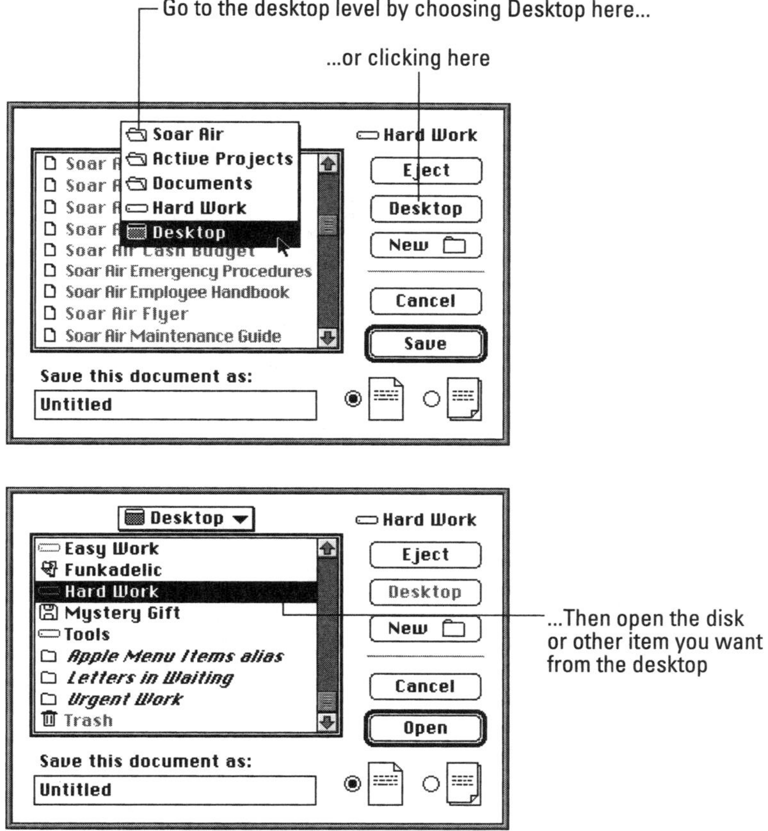


**Figure 5-11: Switching disks at the desktop level.**

# Navigating by keyboard

You can move through folders and open items by using the keyboard as well as the mouse. In an Open dialog box, typing an item's full name or the first part of it selects the item in the directory window. For example, pressing *m* selects the first item that begins with the letter *M* or *m*. Typing several letters quickly specifies a longer name to be selected in the directory window, but pausing between keys starts selecting over. The Key Repeat Rate setting in the Keyboard control panel determines how long you must pause to make a fresh start. After you have selected an item in a directory window (by any means), pressing Return or Enter opens the item.

These keyboard navigation techniques also work in Save and Save As dialog boxes. You can also use the keyboard in these dialog boxes to enter a name for the item you're saving. System 7 lets you know when your typing affects a Save or Save As dialog box's directory window by outlining the window with a heavy black border. A flashing insertion point or highlighted text in the text entry box indicates that your typing goes there, as shown in Figure 5-12. In older system software, you cannot use the keyboard for navigating Save and Save As dialog boxes.

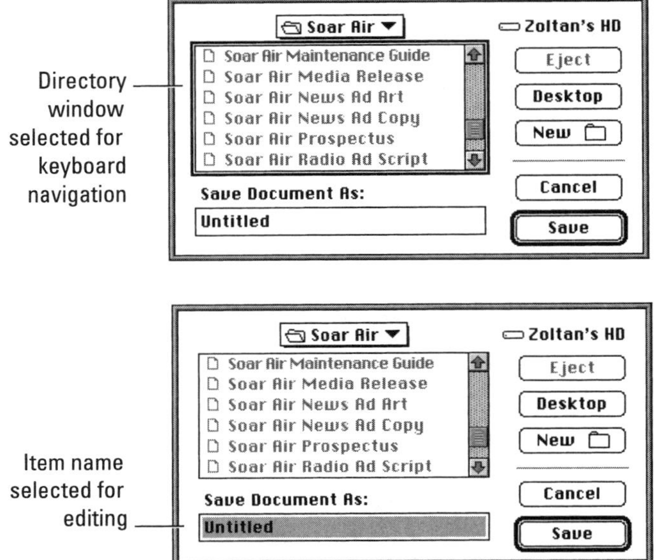


**Figure 5-12: The keyboard's two uses in a Save or Save As dialog box.**

You select the directory window or the text entry box by clicking or dragging in the one you want. You can also alternate between them by pressing Tab. Prior to System 7, pressing Tab in an Open, Save, or Save As dialog box switched you to the next disk. (You can do so in System 7 by pressing ⌘-right arrow or ⌘-left arrow.)

A subtle change occurs in Save and Save As dialog boxes when you select a folder in the directory window. The Save button becomes an Open button, as shown in Figure 5-13. Clicking it opens the selected folder. Prior to System 7, the button works the same way, but it's always named Save (even when clicking it opens a selected folder).

The System 7 directory dialog boxes recognize many keyboard equivalents. Table 5-1 has the details.

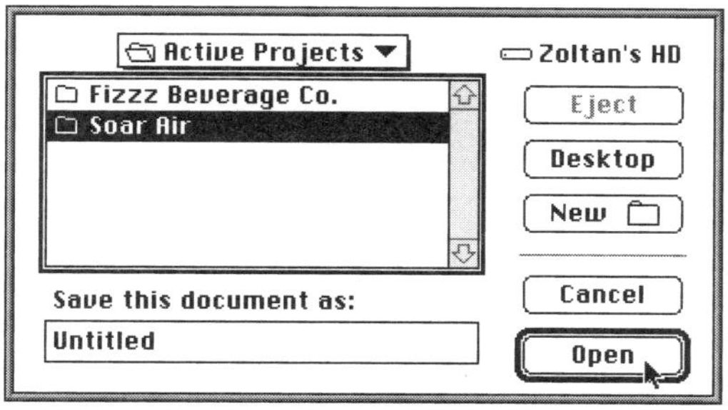

Figure 5-13: Opening a folder while saving.

Table 5-1
**Directory Dialog Box Keyboard Equivalents**

| *Objective* | *Keystroke* |
|---|---|
| Select an item in the directory window | Type the item's full or partial name |
| Scroll up in the directory window | Up arrow |
| Scroll down in the directory window | Down arrow |
| Open the selected item | Return, Enter, ⌘-down arrow, or ⌘-O |
| Open the parent folder, disk, or volume | ⌘-up arrow |
| Go to the previous disk or volume | ⌘-left arrow |
| Go to the next disk or volume | ⌘-right arrow |
| Go to the desktop | ⌘-Shift-up arrow or ⌘-D |
| Eject the current disk | ⌘-E |
| Eject the disk in drive 1 | ⌘-Shift-1 |
| Eject the disk in drive 2 | ⌘-Shift-2 |
| Switch keyboard between the text entry box and the directory window | Tab |
| Click the default button (usually Open or Save) | Return or Enter |
| Cancel the directory dialog | Escape or ⌘-period (.) |
| Make a new folder (in Save dialog boxes only; doesn't work with all programs) | ⌘-N |
| Select the original of the selected alias (instead of opening it) | Option-⌘-O, Option-double-click, or Option-click Open |

### Naming the Item You're Saving

While you are editing the name of the item you're saving, the Cut, Copy, and Paste commands are available from the Edit menu. You can now cut and paste names. When pasting, only the first 31 characters are used; the rest are omitted. In some programs, you must use the keyboard equivalents: ⌘-X for Cut, ⌘-C for Copy, and ⌘-V for Paste.

## Creating a new folder

The System 7 Save and Save As dialog boxes include a button you can click to create a new folder, as shown in Figure 5-14. However, the button is missing from the Save and Save As dialog boxes of most programs that have not been updated for System 7, as well as from many programs that *have* been updated for System 7.

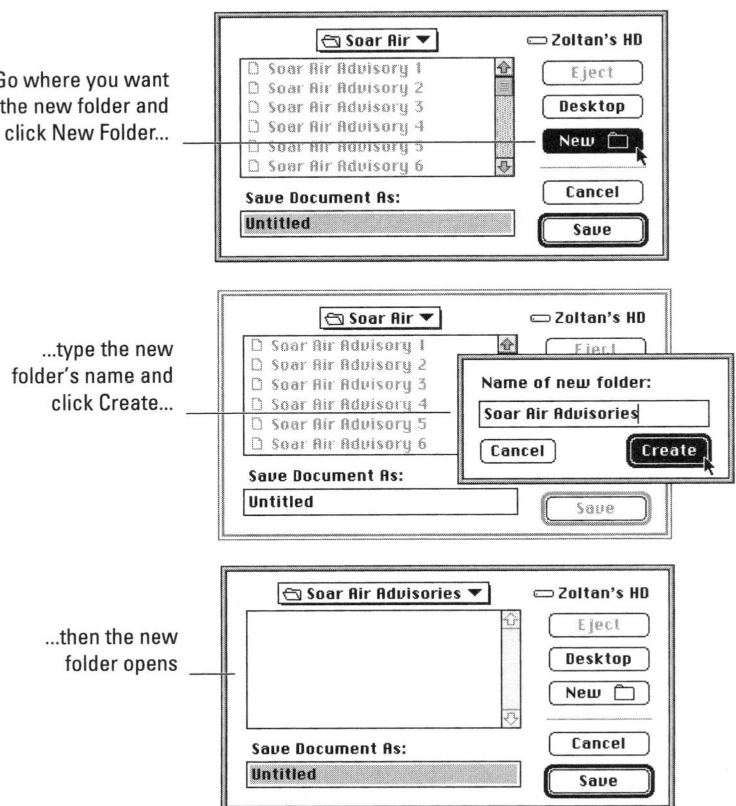


**Figure 5-14: Making a folder while saving.**

### Double-Clicking the Wrong Item

As usual, you can open an item in a directory window by double-clicking it. If you double-click the wrong item and realize it before you release the mouse button, continue pressing the mouse button and drag the pointer to the item you want to open. When you release the mouse button, the currently selected item opens. In older system software, dragging on the second click of a double-click cancels the double-click and opens nothing. To cancel a double-click in a System 7 directory dialog box, hold down the mouse button on the second click and drag the pointer outside the dialog box before releasing the mouse button.

# Stationery Pads

Rather than copy a document for its format and content, you can make it a stationery pad. Opening a stationery pad with the Finder is like tearing a page from a pad of preprinted forms. You get a new document with preset format and contents.

Stationery pad documents have a distinctive icon that looks like a stack of document icons, as shown in Figure 5-15. The Finder uses a generic stationery pad icon if the program that handles that type of document doesn't know about System 7's stationery.

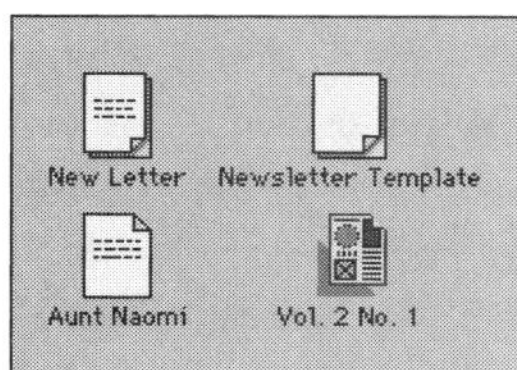


**Figure 5-15: Stationery pad icons (top) and ordinary icons (bottom).**

## Making stationery pads

You can make any document a stationery pad by selecting it in the Finder, choosing the Get Info command, and setting the Stationery Pad option in the Info window, as shown in Figure 5-16. Some programs enable you to directly save a document as a stationery pad by setting a Stationery Pad option when you save the document by using the Save or Save As commands (see Figure 5-17). These programs have been designed specifically to work with System 7's stationery pads.

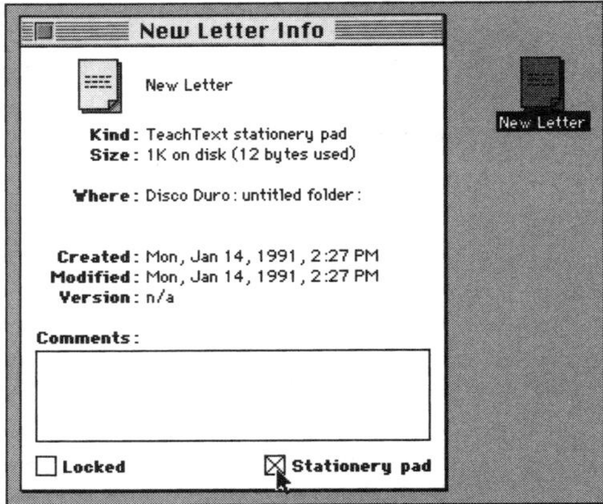


**Figure 5-16: Making a stationery pad with the Finder's Get Info command.**

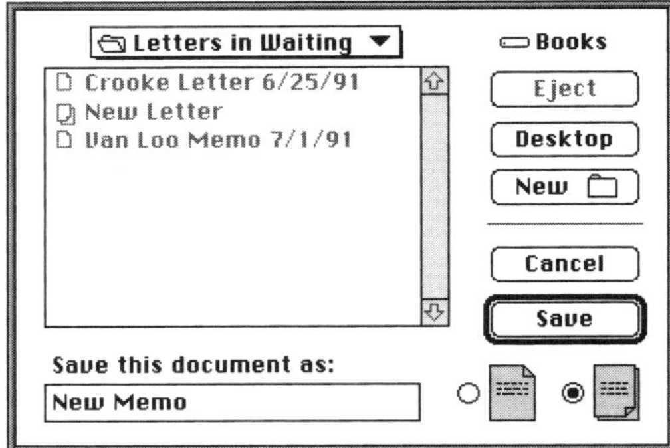


**Figure 5-17: Saving a stationery pad within an application.**

# Using stationery pads

Programs that know about stationery pads open an untitled document with the format and content of the stationery pad. In programs that don't understand stationery pads, the Finder automatically creates a new document by making a copy of the stationery pad, asking you to name it, and having the program open the copy. However, opening a stationery pad from within a program that doesn't know about them (as opposed to opening from the Finder) opens the stationery pad itself, not a copy. A message warns you that you are opening a master stationery pad, as shown in Figure 5-18.

QUICK TIPS

### When Locks Are Better Than Stationery

Opening a stationery document always creates a new document. If you don't want to make a new file every time you open a template, don't make the template a stationery pad. Instead, make the template an ordinary document, but lock it by using the Finder's Get Info command. You may want to use this method with templates for single envelopes and mailing labels, for example. Then you can open the locked template, type or paste the recipient's address, print, and close without saving.

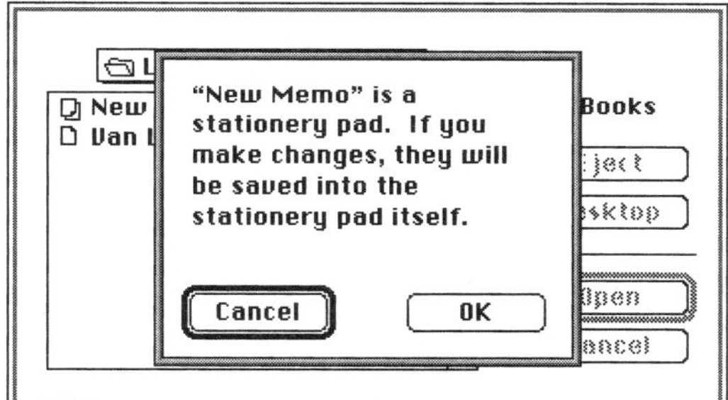


**Figure 5-18: Opening stationery within a program.**

# Drag-and-Drop Opening

You can open a document from the Finder by dragging its icon to the icon of any application program that can open it. The program need not have created the document, but it must be compatible with it. For example, most ReadMe documents are plain text documents that any word processor can open. Dragging a document over a compatible program without releasing the mouse button highlights the program's icon, as if you had dragged the document over a folder (see Figure 5-19). Releasing the mouse button removes the highlighting, opens the program (unless it's already open), and opens the document. If a program can't open a document you drag to it, nothing happens — no highlighting, no opening.

**Figure 5-19: Dragging a document to open it.**

### Polite Drag

When you move or copy an item by dragging it from one window to a folder in an overlapping window, Finder 7 keeps the target window in front of the source window so the destination folder is always in view, as shown in the figure. Older Finders rudely bring the source window in front of an overlapping target window as soon as you begin dragging, sometimes covering the destination folder. In other words, Finder 7 brings a window to the front only if the pointer is in it when you release the mouse. In contrast, older Finders bring a window to the front if the pointer is in it when you press the mouse button.

If you want to drag more than one item at a time to an overlapping window, start by selecting the items in the source window. Next, activate the destination window by clicking along its right edge or its bottom edge (where its scroll bars would be if it were active). You can also click just below the title bar, where the column headings or disk information appears. But don't click anywhere inside the destination window or in its title bar, or you will deselect the items in the source window. Finally, drag the selected items from the now-inactive source window to the now-active destination window. You can drag the whole group of selected items by dragging any one of them, even if they aren't all visible in the inactive source window.

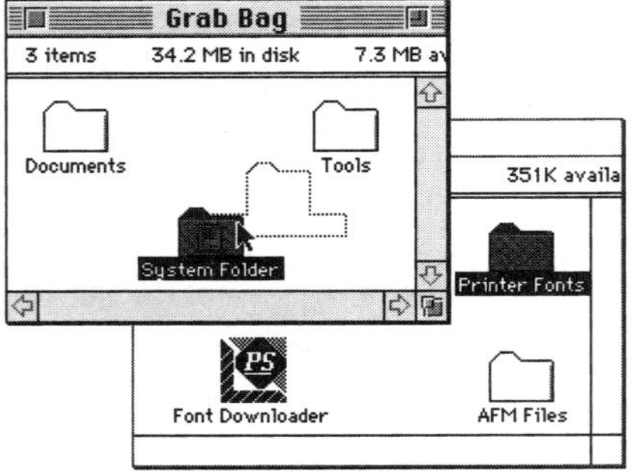


# Macintosh Easy Open

As the Mac operating system has evolved, it has gradually simplified the process of opening documents created with programs that aren't currently installed on your Mac's hard disk. In System 6, when you double-click the icon for a file whose creator program isn't available, you see a message that merely advises that you can't open the document because the application is "busy or missing." (You see the same message when the program is available but already open and when the file has by accident lost its identity and the Finder can't tell which program created it.)

In System 7, when you double-click a file created by a missing program, you may see a similar message saying that the program isn't available. When you try to open a plain text or picture document whose creator application you don't have, System 7's Finder asks whether you want SimpleText (or TeachText) to try to open the document.

System 7.5 includes Macintosh Easy Open software to further simplify opening documents whose creator programs you don't have. Easy Open recognizes many different file types and uses built-in translators to help convert files and open them in an appropriate application that you do happen to have on your Mac. Easy Open is also available separately from Apple for use with System 7.0.1 or later. You can buy more translators to augment the ones that come with System 7.5 from DataViz (800-733-0030 or 203-268-0030).

Easy Open translates Macintosh files for programs you don't have, and it translates files created by many popular MS-DOS and Windows programs. When you double-click file icons or drag and drop icons over the program icon of your choice, Easy Open helps you translate and open those files in the Finder. Easy Open can translate documents when you use a program's Open command as well.

What's more, Easy Open enhances the directory dialog boxes of most Open, Save, Save As, and other disk-related commands. It replaces the tiny generic icons — document, application, folder, and disk — with the small color icons that you see when you view a folder window by small icon in the Finder. These icons indicate the kind of document, application, or disk an item is.

## Easy opening by double-clicking

When you double-click the icon of a file that lacks a corresponding application, Easy Open displays a dialog box that lists translation options, as shown in Figure 5-20. It suggests the translations that would be most apt, based on its translators and the programs it finds on your disks that can open the translated file. You decide which option looks most promising (ideally a translation for a closely related program) and double-click it, and the translated file opens in the program you selected.

The results of recommended options vary, as you can see in Figure 5-21, which shows what happens when a document created by Microsoft Word for Windows is translated by Microsoft Word for the Mac and Microsoft Excel for the Mac.

If you want more choices, you can see a list of all the programs you have that can conceivably open the file, as shown in Figure 5-22. (If your Mac is linked to a network and you want even more choices, you can open the Easy Open control panel and check the "Include Choices from Servers" box.) If you choose an option that's not on the short recommended list, the file probably won't translate fluently. For example, America Online 2.1 (an on-line communications service program) can open a Word for Windows document, but the document comes across as unformatted text with a bunch of extraneous box characters, as shown in Figure 5-23. Some of the programs in Easy Open's long list won't even open the file, so in general you save time when you stick with the recommended translations.

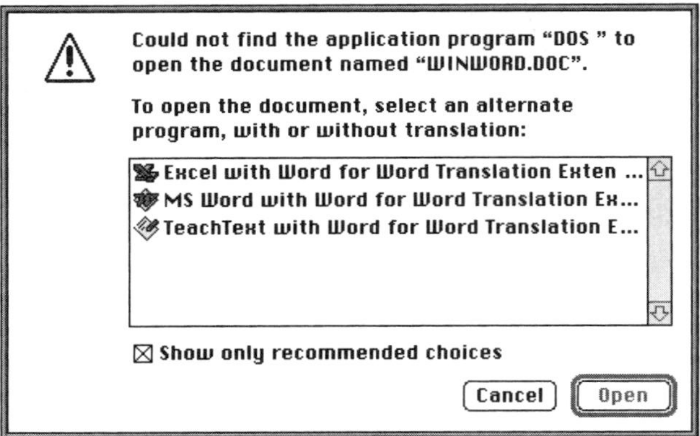


Figure 5-20: Easy Open lists available file translators in its translation dialog box.

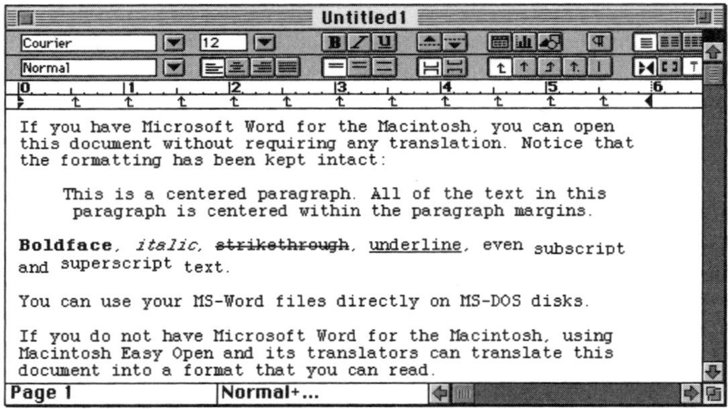


If you have Microsoft Word for the Macintosh, you can open this document without requiring any translation. Notice that the formatting has been kept intact:

This is a centered paragraph. All of the text in this paragraph is centered within the paragraph margins.

**Boldface**, *italic*, ~~strikethrough~~, underline, even subscript and superscript text.

You can use your MS-Word files directly on MS-DOS disks.

If you do not have Microsoft Word for the Macintosh, using Macintosh Easy Open and its translators can translate this document into a format that you can read.

WINWORD.DOC (Converted 3)1

| | A | B | C | D | E | F | G | H | I | J | K | L | M |
|---|---|---|---|---|---|---|---|---|---|---|---|---|---|
| 1 | **If you** | **have Microsoft Word for the** | | | | | | **Macintosh,** | | **you** | **can open this** | | |
| 2 | document without requiring any translation. Notice that the | | | | | | | | | | | | |
| 3 | formatting has | | been | kept | intact: | | | | | | | | |
| 4 | | | | | | | | | | | | | |
| 5 | This | is a | centered paragraph. | | | | All of the text in this paragraph | | | | | | |
| 6 | is centered within the paragraph margins. | | | | | | | | | | | | |
| 7 | | | | | | | | | | | | | |
| 8 | **Boldface** | , | *italic* | | | , strikethrough, | | | | underline | | , even subscript | |
| 9 | and superscript text. | | | | | | | | | | | | |
| 10 | | | | | | | | | | | | | |
| 11 | You can use your MS-Word files | | | | | | | directly on MS- | | | DOS disks. | | |
| 12 | | | | | | | | | | | | | |
| 13 | If you do | | not have Microsoft Word for the Macintosh, using | | | | | | | | | | |
| 14 | Macintosh | | Easy | Open | and its translators | | | | | | | | |
| 15 | can translate this document | | | | | | | | | | | into | a |
| 16 | format that you can read. | | | | | | | | | | | | |
| 17 | | | | | | | | | | | | | |
| 18 | | | | | | | | | | | | | |

Figure 5-21: Results of two recommended Easy Open translations.

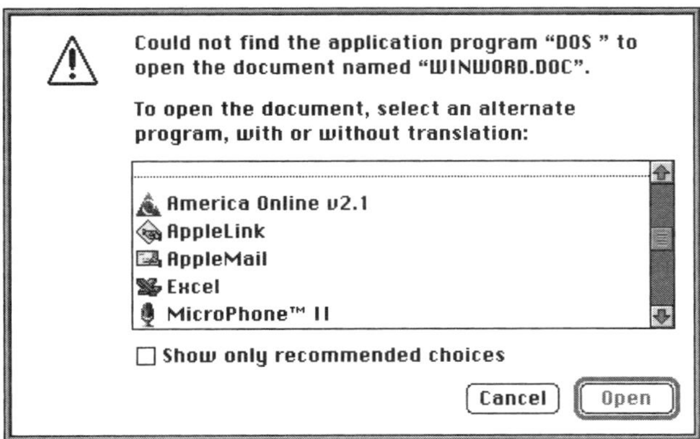


**Figure 5-22: Turning off "Show only recommended choices" may list more translator choices.**

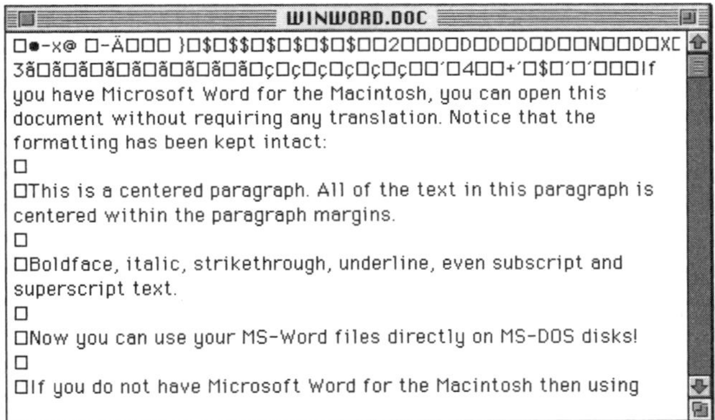


**Figure 5-23: Results of an Easy Open conversion using a program that wasn't recommended.**

## Your translator preferences

The first time you select a translator for a particular kind of file, Easy Open keeps track of your selection. From then on, Easy Open automatically selects the same translator when it presents its list of available translators in its translation dialog box. If you want, you can select a different translator from the list before clicking the Open button.

If you prefer that Easy Open does not have you confirm your preferred translator in this manner, you can turn off the "Always show dialog box" option in the Macintosh Easy Open control panel, which is shown in Figure 5-24. With this option turned off, Easy Open simply opens a file by using the translator you previously selected for that kind of file. You still get the translation dialog box when you open a kind of file that you have never opened.

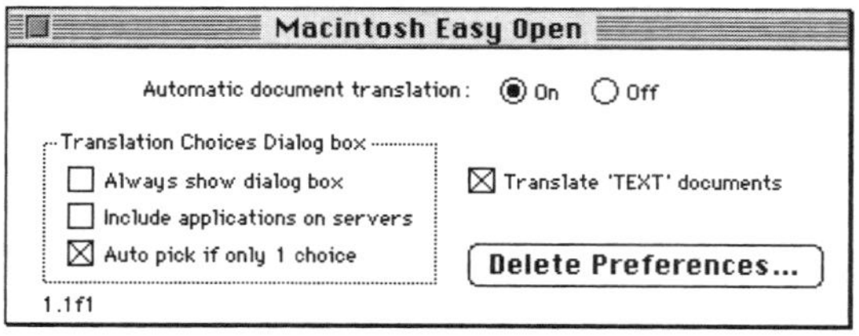

**Figure 5-24: The Macintosh Easy Open control panel.**

To have Easy Open erase its record of your translator preferences, click the Delete Preferences button in the Macintosh Easy Open control panel.

## Easy drag-and-drop opening

If you already know which program you want to have open an alien file and have the program's icon (or an alias) handy in the Finder, you can perform the Easy Open translation simply by dragging the file icon to the program icon. If an appropriate translator is available, the program icon highlights and the translation dialog box appears. Click Open or double-click the name of translation you want. The Mac converts the file and opens it.

## Translating within a program

If Easy Open has a suitable translator and your program has the Mac's standard Open dialog box, you can start translating an alien file by choosing Open from your program's File menu. If the document you select needs translation, the translation dialog box appears; there, you choose the translator you want to try and then click Open to convert and open the file.

## Translating without opening

To translate a document without opening it, you can use the Document Converter software. Document Converter is included if you buy Easy Open separately, and comes with Mac OS 7.6 but not with System 7.5.

You use Document Converter to make a separate converter for each type of conversion you want to have on tap. Once you have the right converter, you can drag and drop files onto it to translate them in one step. When you drag a file to a converter, it automatically adds the word *converted* to the name of the translated file.

To make a converter, first locate the Document Converter and make a duplicate of it. Double-click the duplicate to see a long list of translation options. Figure 5-25 shows a few of the dozens of choices. Scroll through the list to look for the name of the program you want to read your files. After you find the right translator, click Set or double-click the translator's name. Doing so creates a customized converter, renamed to indicate which file format it translates to, as shown in Figure 5-26.

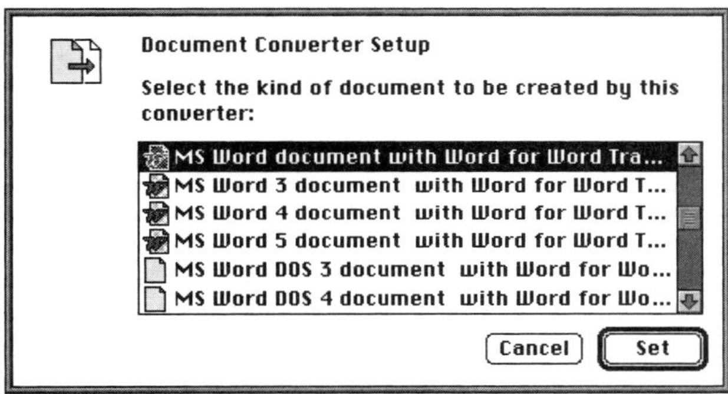


**Figure 5-25: Setting up a document converter.**

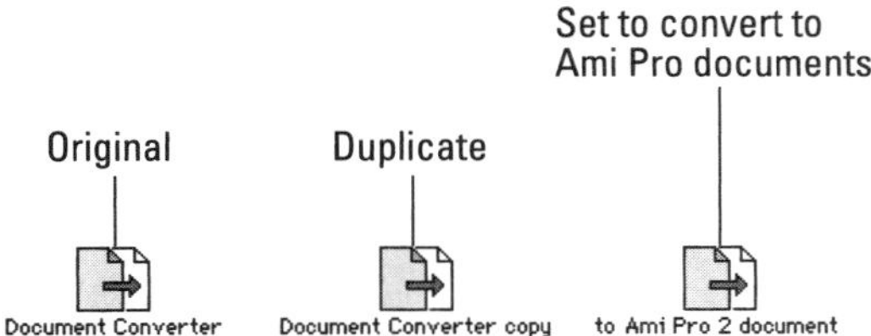


**Figure 5-26: Three stages in the life of a document converter.**

# At Ease

In some situations, the Finder offers too much power, flexibility, and access to items on the hard disk, which can confuse novice Macintosh users. Combine the Finder's flexibility and power with the full access it provides to the hard disk, put that in a setting where several people share the same Mac, and you have a recipe for chaos. For example, everyone has a different idea about how the Finder's desktop ought to be arranged.

As an alternative to the Finder's standard desktop, Apple's At Ease system extension provides a simplified view of the Mac environment with restricted access to programs and documents on the hard disk. At Ease is not included with System 7 except with Macintosh Performa models; you can purchase and install it separately.

At Ease 2.0 closes a security loophole in the original At Ease 1.0, and its desktop, menus, and dialog boxes look different. The At Ease 2.0 desktop has two panels that look like tabbed file folders, as shown in Figure 5-27. One panel, called At Ease Items, has buttons for programs and documents; the other panel shows the current user's name and holds buttons that represent items that the user has saved while working within At Ease. At Ease 1.0 looks a little bit different, as shown in Figure 5-28. One panel has buttons for programs, and the other has buttons for documents.

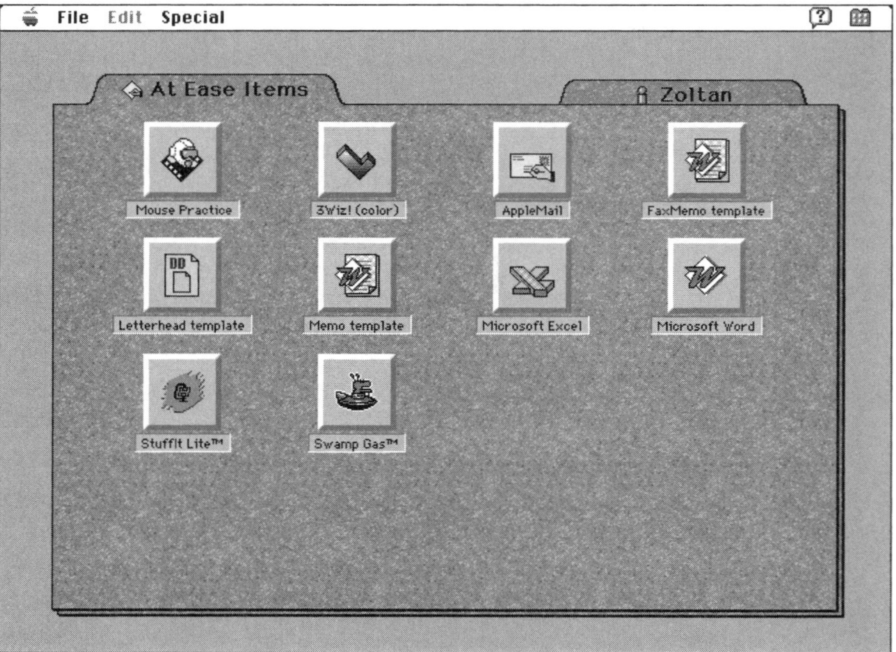


**Figure 5-27: The At Ease 2.0 desktop.**

**Figure 5-28: The At Ease 1.0 desktop.**

# Using At Ease

Each At Ease panel can display 12 or more large buttons at a time and can have multiple pages for additional buttons. The number of buttons per page depends on the screen size. If there are additional pages, the lower corners of the panel turn up to reveal arrow-shaped buttons you click to move from page to page. You can also switch pages by pressing the right-arrow and left-arrow keys.

You click an At Ease button only once to open the item it represents. As in the Finder, At Ease includes balloon help to guide you when you're not sure how to proceed. Also like the Finder, At Ease can open more than one program, and you switch among them with the Application menu. At Ease shows only the active program on-screen, which prevents you from accidentally switching to another open program by unintentionally clicking a window or desktop fragment in the background.

When you set up At Ease 2.0, you decide which items go on the At Ease Items panel for each user. You also decide which users have access to only the most basic menu commands, like Close, Restart, and Shut Down — excluding Finder commands such as Control Panels, Get Info, and Find and At Ease menu items such as Delete and Copy to Floppy. During setup, you can assign passwords to users and give them access to the Finder if necessary. You can also set up At Ease to automatically take certain users to the Finder instead of to the giant At Ease file folder panels.

There's no Trash in At Ease, so inexperienced users can't throw away files or applications by mistake. You can't throw anything away unless you've been given access to the Finder or the Delete command.

If access to menu items is restricted, the Apple menu shows only About This Macintosh and About the active application, as shown in Figure 5-29. If menu access is not restricted, the Apple menu looks more familiar, but it still doesn't show any folders except the Control Panels folder. If you select Control Panels from the unrestricted Apple menu, Control Panels opens and covers the At Ease Items panel, displaying an array of buttons, one for each item in the Control Panels folder. To put away Control Panels, select Close from the File menu or click the square close box in the panel's tab, as shown in Figure 5-30.

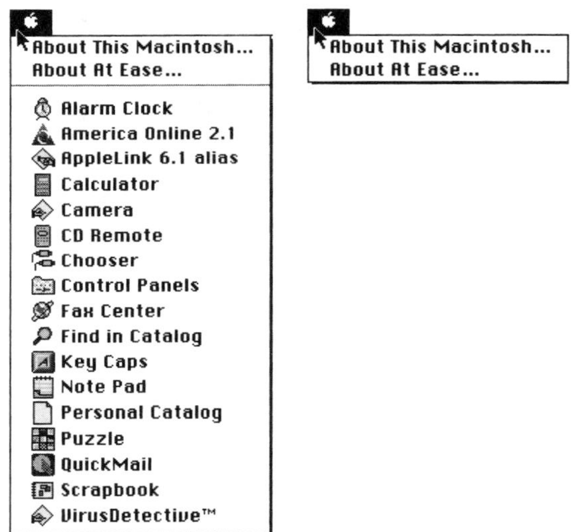


**Figure 5-29: Unrestricted and restricted Apple menus in At Ease 2.0.**

At Ease's File and Special menus are simplified versions of the Finder's menus, as shown in Figures 5-31 and 5-32. The File menu's Quit command ends the current user's work session. It puts away the At Ease panels and displays a dialog box that lists everyone who is set up as an At Ease user on that Mac. A user on the list can start using the Mac by double-clicking his or her name and typing a password (if required).

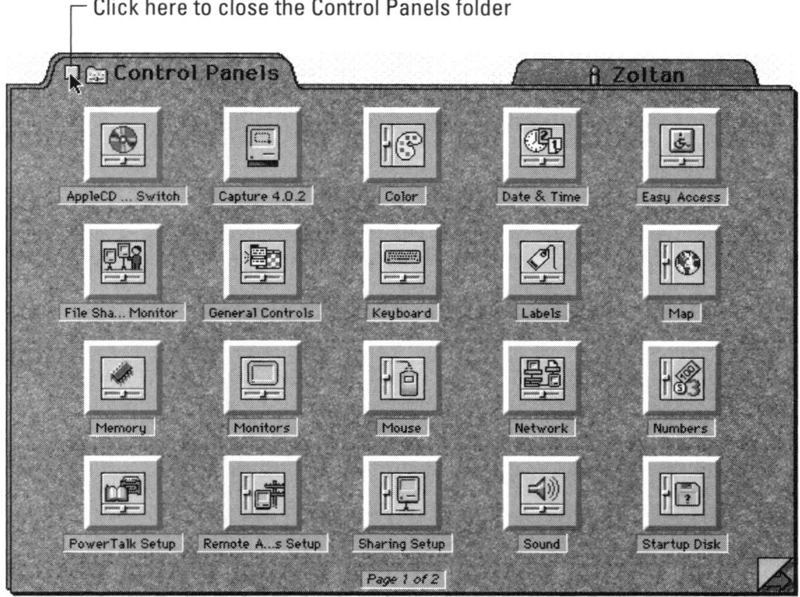


**Figure 5-30: Closing the Control Panels folder.**

**Figure 5-31: At Ease 2.0's unrestricted and restricted File menus.**

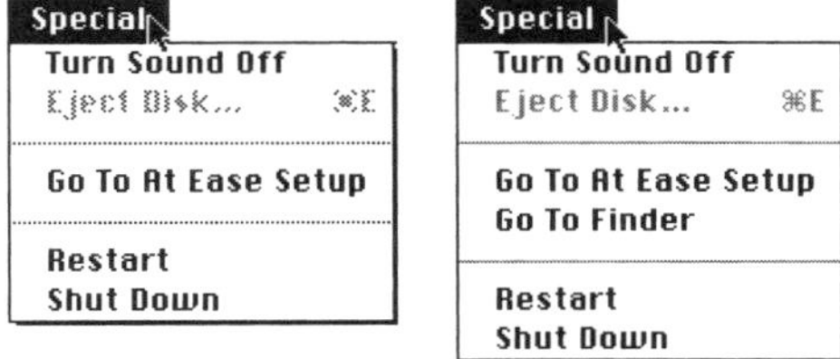


**Figure 5-32: At Ease 2.0's unrestricted and restricted Special menus.**

In the At Ease Special menu, the Turn Sound Off command quiets the sound effects that otherwise accompany actions such as clicking a button on an At Ease panel. Choosing the Turn Sound Off command changes the command to Turn Sound On.

The At Ease Edit menu is dimmed for a user who has been assigned restricted menus because that user cannot edit anything. Someone who has access to unrestricted menus can use the Edit menu commands to rename items on the At Ease panels.

If you have access to unrestricted menus in At Ease 2.0, you have a View menu that works a lot like the Finder's View menu to organize the items on your desktop panels (see Figure 5-33).

View
✓by Name
by Size
by Kind
by Date

**Figure 5-33: At Ease 2.0's optional View menu.**

## Switching between At Ease and the Finder

Users who have the privilege of switching from At Ease to the Finder do so by choosing Go To Finder from the At Ease Special menu.

There are two ways to switch back to At Ease from the Finder. The best method is to choose Go To At Ease from the Finder's File menu. Doing so quits the Finder, eliminating the possibility of accidentally switching back to the Finder by clicking the desktop. You can also switch to At Ease by choosing it from the Application menu.

## Setting Up At Ease

You (or someone else in your group) can set up At Ease with the At Ease Setup program (see Figure 5-34). Open it by choosing Go To At Ease Setup from the At Ease Special menu or from the Finder if you have access to it.

The opening window of At Ease 2.0 Setup has controls for turning At Ease on and off and for configuring each user's access to the system. To add a new user, click New. To change the setup of an existing user, select the user's name and click Open (or double-click the name). Then set up the new or existing user's access by filling out the series of dialog boxes. The first dialog box names the user, optionally assigns the user a password, and determines whether the Mac stays in At Ease or switches automatically to the Finder after startup. The second dialog box lists the programs and documents already installed as buttons on the user's At Ease panels and has buttons you click to add more items. The third user-setup dialog box determines which At Ease menus the user sees and whether At Ease speaks the names of buttons on the user's At Ease panels as the user passes the pointer across them. The fourth and final dialog box sets the location to which the user may open and save documents and determines whether the user has access to the Finder. It takes only a few minutes to set up each new user, the actual time depending upon how many documents you add to each user's At Ease Items panel.

The part of Setup that will most likely be confusing is the process of adding document buttons to a user's At Ease Items panel. You do so by clicking Find Items in the third At Ease 2.0 Setup dialog box, shown in Figure 5-35. That action leads you to a dialog box where you search for the files by name or partial name, as shown in Figure 5-36. When the file you want appears in the list of found items on the left, double-click the file name to add the document to the Items for This User list on the right. After you've added all the documents you want, click OK and continue through the dialog boxes until you reach the last one. Then click Done and either start the process again for another user or select Quit from the setup program's File menu.

If *you* are setting up At Ease, make sure to add yourself as a user and give yourself access to the Finder. If someone else has set up At Ease for you, you may have been given access to At Ease Setup, so you can add items to your At Ease desktop. The Special menu's Go To At Ease Setup command leads to a dialog box where you can select the name of the user whose setup you want to change. You must know a user's password (if one is required) to change the user's At Ease setup. You can learn how to fill in the Setup dialog boxes by turning on balloon help.

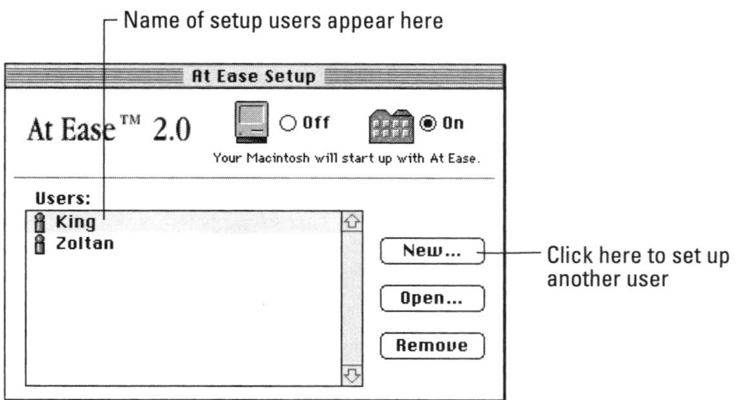


**Figure 5-34: The opening dialog box for the At Ease 2.0 Setup program.**

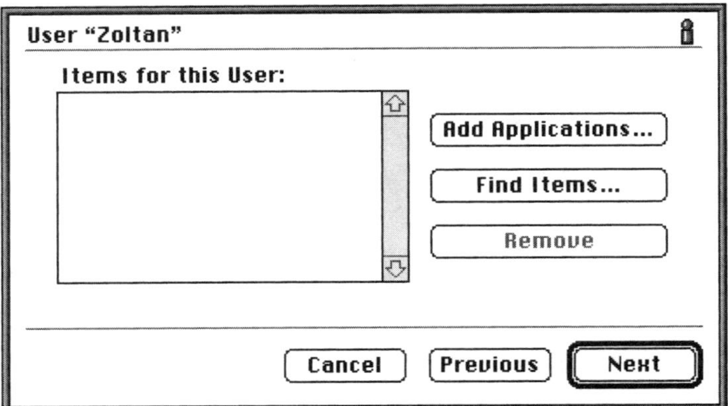


**Figure 5-35: Begin adding document or application buttons for an At Ease user here.**

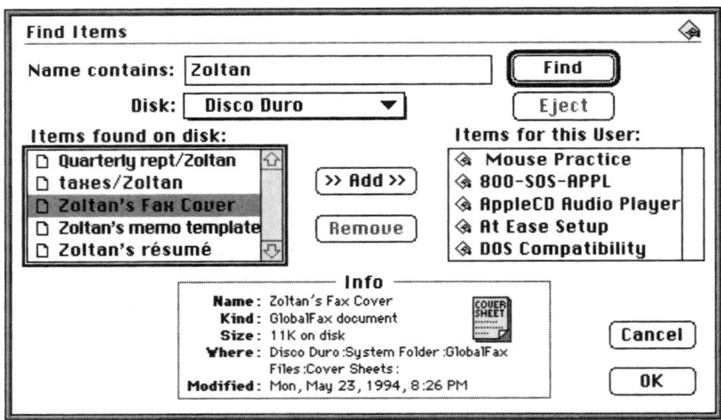


**Figure 5-36: Adding document buttons to an At Ease 2.0 setup.**

## At Ease Items Folder

All items displayed as At Ease buttons are stored as aliases in the special folder called At Ease Items, which is inside the System Folder. You can rename At Ease buttons by changing the names of the corresponding aliases in the At Ease Items folder. (You can also use the Rename command on the unrestricted form of the At Ease File menu.) You can add At Ease buttons by adding aliases to that folder and remove At Ease buttons by removing aliases from that folder. You can add a button for the Finder by putting an alias of the Finder in the At Ease Items folder. For more information about making aliases, see Chapter 10.

## Disabling or removing At Ease

You can turn off At Ease 2.0 if you have access to the At Ease Setup program. Open At Ease Setup, click the Off button, and select Quit from the program's File menu. The next time you restart the Mac, it opens the Finder instead of At Ease.

If you want to permanently remove At Ease 2.0 from a Macintosh, the At Ease installation disk helps you remove everything at once. You start by turning off At Ease through At Ease Setup. Then insert the At Ease 2.0 Install 1 disk, double-click Installer, click the Customize button, select At Ease in the list of items to install, hold down the Option key (which changes the Install button to the Remove button), and click Remove.

If you can't find the installation disk, turn off At Ease in the At Ease Setup program, drag the four At Ease items from your disk to the Trash, and empty the Trash. You need to throw away the At Ease Setup program (found in your startup hard disk's window), the At Ease file and At Ease Items folder in the System Folder, and the At Ease Startup extension in the Extensions folder of the System Folder. You don't have to delete the file called Mouse Practice; it just helps beginners learn how to use the mouse and doesn't include parts of At Ease.

If you try to remove At Ease while it is still turned on, you may make it impossible to start up the Mac from the hard disk, so be sure to turn off At Ease before you attempt to get rid of it.

Temporarily disabling At Ease 1.0 is simple even if you can't open the At Ease Setup control panel to turn it off. You restart the Mac and hold down the Shift key until you see the Welcome to Macintosh box that displays the message "Extensions off." You permanently remove At Ease 1.0 the same way as At Ease 2.0 — by turning off At Ease and then removing it with the installer disk. If you can't find the disk named At Ease Install 1, drag these files to the Trash: At Ease Setup (from the Control Panels folder of the System Folder), At Ease and At Ease Items (from the System Folder), and Control Panel Handler (from the Extensions folder within the System Folder).

# CHAPTER 5 CONCEPTS AND TERMS

- Adding items to the Apple menu by putting them in the Apple Menu Items folder lets you open the items by choosing them from the menu.
- System 7 enables you to have multiple programs open simultaneously. You use the Application menu to switch from one program to another as well as to hide the windows of all programs except the active one.
- Stationery pads provide a way to create templates that contain formats and contents you use routinely. Opening a stationery pad gives you an untitled document that you can modify and save without making changes to the master template.
- A quick way to open documents in the Finder is to drag them to the icon (or alias) of a program that can open them.
- Directory dialog boxes in System 7 enable you to open disks from the desktop without having to use the Drive button from older versions; move through folders and open items by using the keyboard; and edit the name of an item to be saved by using the Cut, Copy, and Paste commands from the Edit menu.
- Easy Open makes it possible to translate and open files created by popular Mac, Windows, or MS-DOS programs that you don't have installed.
- At Ease provides a simpler alternative to the Finder's desktop and lets you restrict access to specific programs and documents.

**active program**
The program whose menus are currently displayed in the menu bar.

**At Ease**
A system extension that provides a simplified view of the Mac environment with restricted access to programs and documents on the hard disk. At Ease is not included with System 7 except on Macintosh Performa models; you can purchase and install it separately.

**background program**
A program that runs during the intervals, typically less than 1/8 of a second long, when the active program isn't using the computer. It usually works while the active program waits for you to do something.

**drag-and-drop open**
To place the mouse pointer over an object (such as a document icon), hold down the mouse button, and move the mouse until the pointer is over another object that can open the first object (such as a compatible application). The pointer drags the first object along, and the second item becomes highlighted when the pointer is on it. Releasing the mouse button drops the first object onto the second object, which opens the first object.

**Easy Open**
A program that further simplifies opening documents whose creator programs you don't have. Recognizes many different file types and uses built-in translators to help convert files and open them in an appropriate application that you do happen to have on your Mac. Comes with System 7.5 and later and works with System 7.0.1 and later.

**multitasking**
The capability to have multiple programs open simultaneously.

**navigate**
To go open (or close) folders until you have the one open that contains the item you need.

**stationery pad**
A template document that contains preset format and contents.

**submenu**
A secondary menu that pops out from the side of another menu. A submenu appears when you place the pointer on a menu item that has an arrowhead at the right side of the menu.

**translator**
A program that translates your documents from one file format, such as Word for the Mac, to another, such as Word for Windows.

CHAPTER SIX

# Organizing Files, Folders, and Disks

IN THIS CHAPTER

- Selecting, scrolling, and zooming with the Finder's smart windows
- Cleaning up, arranging, and customizing list views
- Fetching items quickly by using simple or complex search criteria
- Labeling, copying, and deleting items

Ask 100 Macintosh users to name the application program they use most often, and only a few would come up with the correct answer: the Finder. People don't think of the Finder as a program they use or need to learn to use. In fact, it is a very rich application program that is included with the system software for managing your disks and their contents.

The Finder that comes with System 7 has capabilities that help you organize your disks more effectively and find items more quickly than in older Finders. You use all of System 7's Finder features often, because they're never more than a mouse click away. This chapter details many of these capabilities.

Some aspects of the Finder are covered in other chapters. The preceding chapter discusses opening and saving programs and documents, and the following chapter describes the organization of the System Folder. Aliases are covered in Chapter 10 and file sharing in Chapter 9. Apple PowerBook File Assistant, which helps PowerBook users manage their files, is described in Chapter 19.

## Viewing Folder Contents

You can open folders to see what's inside, but if you layer lots of folders within folders, windows clutter your screen by the time you reach the innermost folder. There is a faster and easier way. The Finder displays list views (name, size, kind, and so on) in an indented outline format, as shown in Figure 6-1. The levels of indentation in the outline show how your folders are nested. The indented outline provides a graphical representation of a disk's organization. You can look through and reorganize folders without opening additional windows.

Documents

| Name | Size | Kind | Label |
|---|---|---|---|
| Urgent Work | – | folder | Essential |
| Letters in Waiting | – | folder | Hot |
| Active Projects | – | folder | In Progress |
| Fizzz Beverage Company | – | folder | Project 1 |
| Soar Air | – | folder | Project 2 |
| Soar Air Schedule | 41K | FileMaker Pro docu... | Essential |
| Soar Air Advisories | – | folder | Hot |
| Soar Air Financial | – | folder | Hot |
| Soar Air Manuals | – | folder | In Progress |
| Soar Air Emergency Pro... | 2K | Microsoft Word do... | Project 2 |
| Soar Air Employee Hand... | 2K | Microsoft Word do... | Project 2 |
| Soar Air Maintenance Gu... | 2K | Microsoft Word do... | Project 2 |
| Stationery | – | folder | Cool |
| Soar Air Marketing | – | folder | Project 2 |
| Clip Art | – | folder | Cool |
| This Year's Mail by Date | – | folder | Cool |

**Figure 6-1: Expanded and collapsed folders.**

Triangles next to folder names tell you whether the folders are expanded or collapsed. If a triangle points to the right, the folder next to it is collapsed and you cannot see its contents. If the triangle points down, the folder is expanded and you can see a list of the items in the folder indented below the folder name.

## Expanding and collapsing folders

To collapse a folder, click the triangle to the left of the folder's icon, as shown in Figure 6-2. To expand a folder, click the triangle to the left of the folder's icon, as shown in Figure 6-3.

When you expand a folder, the Finder remembers whether folders nested within it were previously expanded or collapsed and restores each to its former state.

***Tip:*** To collapse a folder and all the folders nested within it, press Option while clicking the triangle of the outer folder. To expand a folder and all the folders nested within it, press Option while you click.

## Selecting from multiple folders

The Finder's outline views enable you to select multiple items from any number of folders, as shown in Figure 6-4. All folders must be on one disk.

To select an additional item, expand the folder that contains it and press Shift while clicking the item. You can also select consecutive items by pressing Shift while dragging a selection rectangle around them. If you need to deselect a few items, Shift-click each item or Shift-drag across consecutive items.

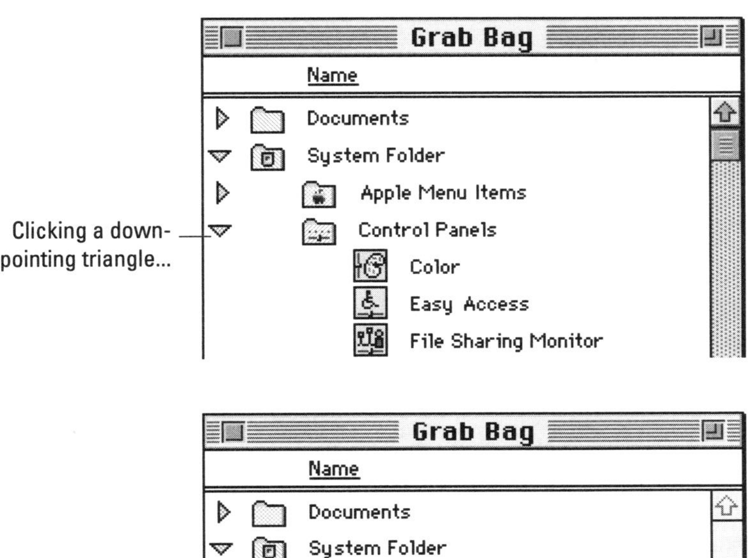


**Figure 6-2: Collapsing a folder.**

## Locking Folders

You may know how to lock a file with the Finder's Get Info command, but how do you lock a folder? System 7 makes it easy. Just select the folder you want to lock, choose Sharing from the Finder's File menu to bring up the folder's file-sharing privileges window, and in it check the box labeled "Can't be moved, renamed or deleted." You don't have to actually share the folder or change any other settings in the privileges window. For this trick to work, System 7's file sharing must be on; the Sharing command tells you to turn it on with the Sharing Setup control panel, if necessary.

In case you've never locked a file, here's the procedure. First you select the file and choose Get Info from the Finder's File menu to bring up the file's Info window. Then you turn on the Locked option in the Info window and close the Info window.

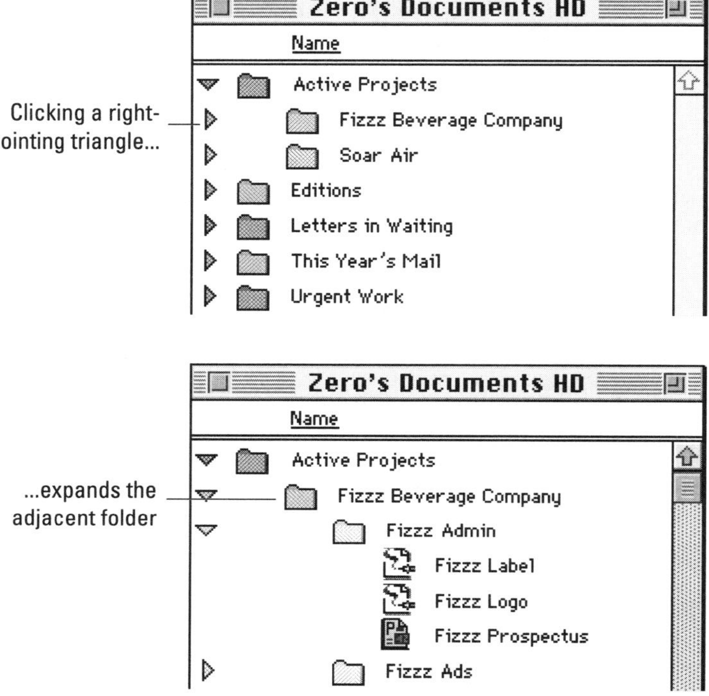


**Figure 6-3: Expanding a folder.**

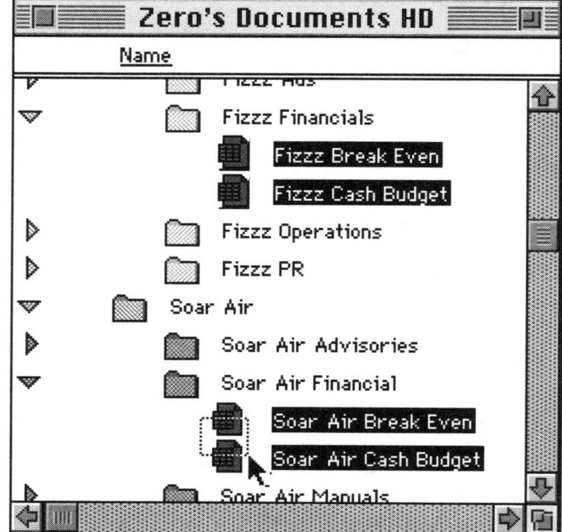


**Figure 6-4: Items selected from multiple folders.**

## Horizontal scrolling

All the information you request for each item with the Views control panel in a list view may not fit across a window even at its maximum width. If a window contains more columns out of view on the right or left, System 7's Finder activates the window's horizontal scroll bar, as shown in Figure 6-5. You can use it to read all of a wide listing. Older Finders never activate the horizontal scroll bar in a list view.

This Years' Mail

| ne | Size | Kind | Label |
|---|---|---|---|
| Person & Date | – | folder | – |
| Power 3/14/92 | 1K | AppleLink 6.1 docu... | Hot |
| Flat 3/8/92 | 2K | AppleLink 6.1 docu... | Cool |
| Power 1/17/92 | 1K | AppleLink 6.1 docu... | Cool |
| Power 2/6/92 | 3K | AppleLink 6.1 docu... | Cool |
| Hashimoto 1/3/92 | 1K | AppleLink 6.1 docu... | Personal |
| de la Cruz 3/26/92 | 2K | AppleLink 6.1 docu... | Project 1 |
| Fang 2/26/92 | 2K | AppleLink 6.1 docu... | Project 1 |
| Flat 1/24/92 | 2K | AppleLink 6.1 docu... | Project 1 |
| de la Cruz 1/7/92 | 1K | AppleLink 6.1 docu... | Project 2 |
| Fang 1/29/92 | 3K | AppleLink 6.1 docu... | Project 2 |
| Subject & Date | – | folder | – |

Scroll to see more

**Figure 6-5: Scrolling from side to side.**

## Smart zooming

After expanding and collapsing folders in outline view, you may want to make a window just large enough to show all the items currently listed in it. To do so, simply click the zoom box, as shown in Figure 6-6.

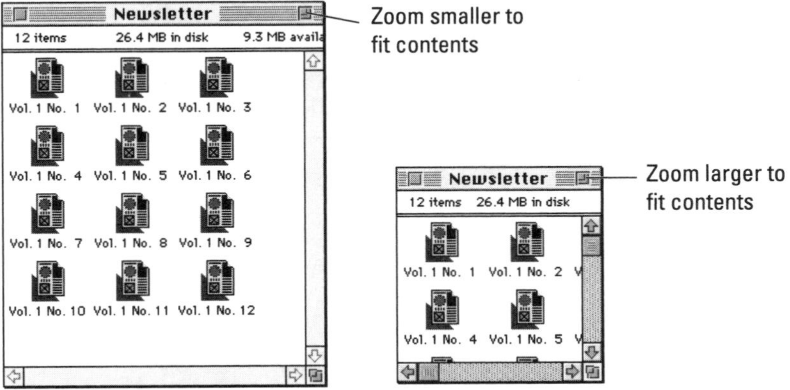


**Figure 6-6: Zoom to fit.**

## Autoscrolling

You can scroll a window in the Finder without using the scroll bars. Simply place the pointer in the window, press the mouse button, and drag toward the area you want to view, as shown in the figure. Drag the pointer up, down, left, or right past the window's active area to begin scrolling. Dragging past a window corner scrolls diagonally.

As you drag, you can vary the scrolling speed. To scroll slowly, drag just to the window's edge (and continue pressing the mouse button). Increase scrolling speed by dragging beyond the window's edge.

You can use this scrolling technique, known as *autoscrolling,* while performing the following operations:

- ❖ Moving an icon or group of icons to a new place in the same window (icon or small-icon view)
- ❖ Moving an item or group of items into a folder in the same window (any view)
- ❖ Dragging a selection rectangle around adjacent items in the same window to select them all (any view)

Be careful when autoscrolling while dragging a selected item or items, especially when autoscrolling to the left. If you accidentally move the pointer completely out of the window and release the mouse button, the Finder places the selected items on the desktop. You can return items from the desktop to their original folder by selecting them and using the Finder's Put Away command.

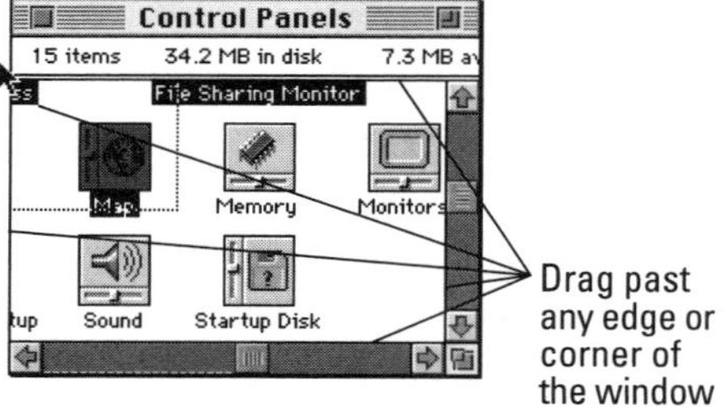


Older Finders always zoom up to full-screen size, but System 7's Finder zooms up or down to fit a window's contents. The window covers the whole screen only if it contains enough items to fill a screen-size window. This smart zooming helps you make best use of your screen real estate after changing views, adding or removing items, rearranging icons, and so on.

***Tip:*** If you do want to zoom a window to fill the screen, press Option while clicking the zoom box.

## Clean-up options

In System 7, the Finder's Clean Up command helps keep your icons organized. As in older Finders, choosing Clean Up from the Special menu aligns the active window's icons (or the desktop icons, if no window is active) in neat rows and columns. But System 7's Finder doesn't move icons into positions that make their names unreadable. If aligning an icon would make its name overlap a neighboring icon's name, the Finder moves it somewhere nearby where the names don't collide.

You can also use the Finder's Clean Up command to align only the icons you select in a window or on the desktop. Pressing Shift changes Clean Up to Clean Up Selection.

## Arranging list views

You can change a window from one list view to any other available list view directly in the window without using the Finder's View menu, as shown in Figure 6-7. Simply click the column heading that corresponds to the view you want. The Finder immediately sorts all the items in the window according to the column you clicked. You can tell the current sort order by looking for the underlined column heading.

### Sorting Icons by Name, Size, Kind, Label, or Date

When the Finder cleans up your icons, you can have it sort them by any of the choices in the View menu. Follow these steps:

1. Choose the sort order you want from the View menu (temporarily changing the view).
2. Use the View menu again to choose By Icon or By Small Icon.
3. Press Option while you choose the Clean Up command. The Finder rearranges all icons in the window, putting the one lowest in the sort order in the upper-left corner and then filling the window from left to right and top to bottom.

If you press Option while cleaning up the desktop (instead of a window), the Finder aligns all desktop icons in a standard configuration. It moves the startup disk's icon to the upper-right corner of the desktop, lines up other disk icons below it, puts the Trash in the lower-right corner, and arranges all other desktop icons in rows and columns next to the disk icons.

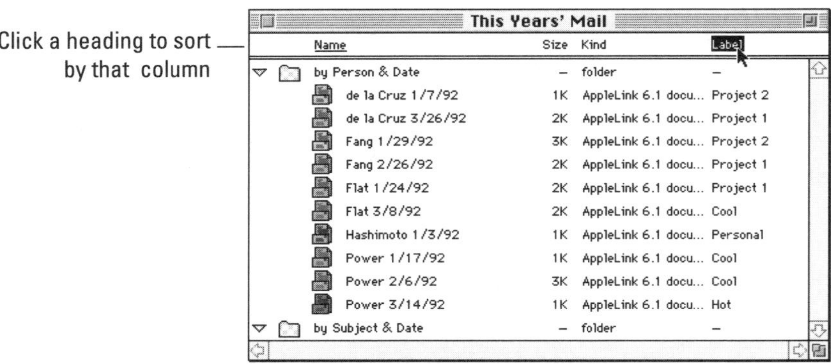


The underline marks the current sort order

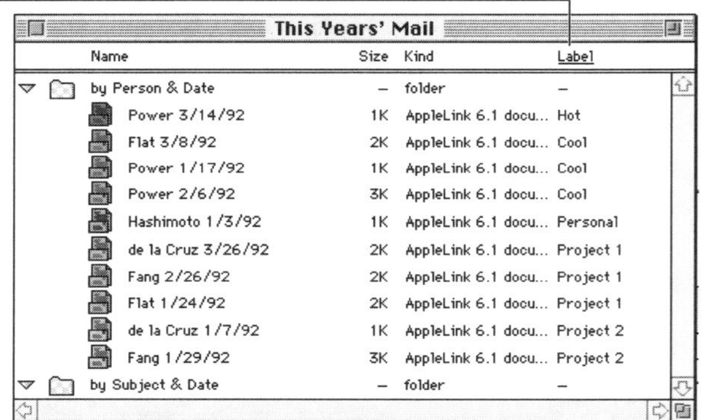


**Figure 6-7: Sorting a list view.**

## Viewing Desktop Items by Name

If you keep lots of items on the desktop, you may want to use the View menu to arrange items on the desktop by name. Unfortunately, the View menu works only in Finder windows, not on the desktop. You can get the same effect with System 7's custom icon capabilities. Do the following:

1. Open a painting program.
2. Select some blank white space and copy it.
3. Using the Finder's Get Info command for each desktop item you want to view by name, paste the white space over the icon in each item's Info window.

Pasting the white space leaves only the item names visible. Six items without icons fit in the space previously occupied by two items with icons.

## Custom list views

In System 7 you can change the format and content of the Finder's windows with the Views control panel, as shown in Figure 6-8. Control panel settings affect all Finder windows and the desktop; you can't format each window separately. After changing settings in the Views control panel, you can resize windows to fit the new format by clicking their zoom boxes.

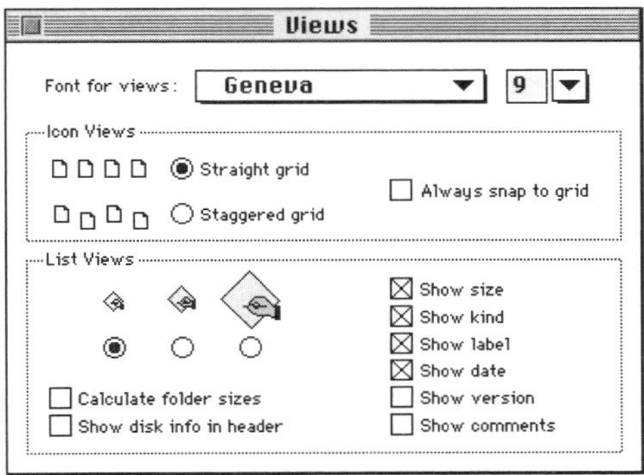


**Figure 6-8: The Views control panel.**

### Setting the text font and size

Choose a text font and a text size for icon names and all the text in list views from the pop-up menus at the top of the Views control panel, as shown in Figure 6-9. If the text size you want isn't listed, you can enter any size between 6 and 36.

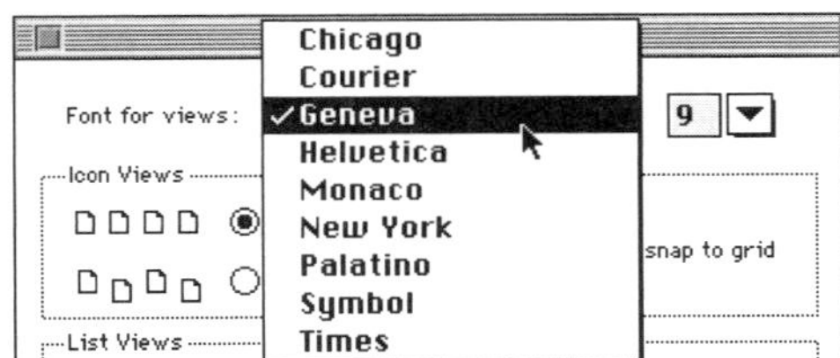


**Figure 6-9: Finder text format options (Views control panel).**

The Finder uses the font and size settings for icon names, the disk information header (number of items, disk space used, and disk space available), and all the text in list views. Your font and size settings affect all windows and icons.

After making the size much larger or smaller, you may want to use the Clean Up command (Special menu) to adjust the spacing of icons on the desktop and in windows. You must clean up each window separately.

## Setting icon alignment

Other settings in the Views control panel determine how the Finder aligns icons, as shown in Figure 6-10. The settings affect icons on the desktop and in all windows with icon or small-icon views. You can set the type of grid the Clean Up command uses and decide whether icons automatically align with that grid when you drag them.

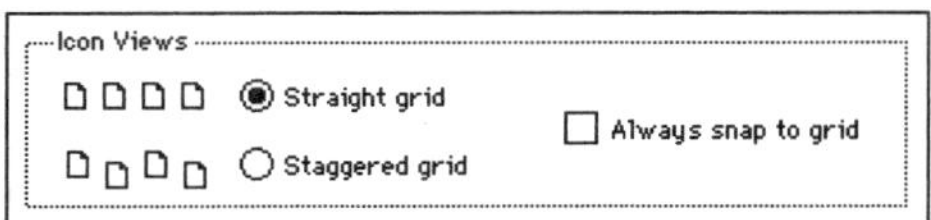


**Figure 6-10: Finder icon alignment options (Views control panel).**

The Staggered Grid option makes it possible to arrange icons close together without their names overlapping. Turning on the Always Snap To Grid option makes icons you have dragged align to the Clean Up command's grid. You can temporarily reverse the Always Snap To Grid setting by pressing ⌘ while dragging.

## Determining list view contents

To determine how much information the Finder shows in all windows with list views (name, size, kind, and so on), you set numerous options at the bottom of the Views control panel, as shown in Figure 6-11.

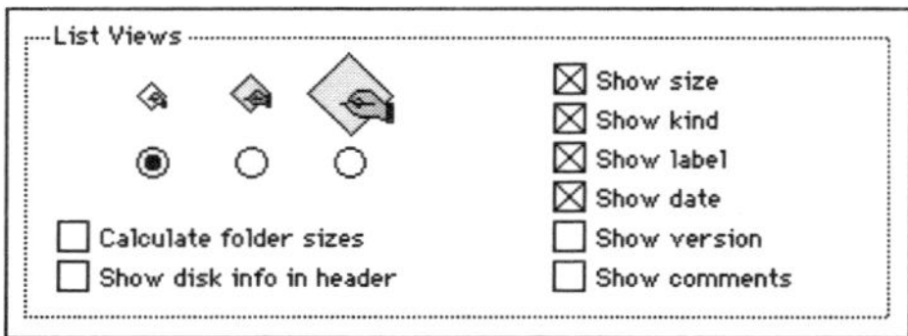


**Figure 6-11: Finder list view options (Views control panel).**

List views always include an icon and name for every item in the window. In addition, you select which of six other columns of information to include: size, kind, label, date, version, and comments. Your selections appear as choices in the Finder's Views menu. You cannot change the order of the columns or their widths, only whether each appears or not. The version and comments, which you otherwise see with the Get Info command (File menu), do not appear in system software older than System 7. Only the first 25 characters of an item's comments are shown in a list view.

Judicious setting of list view options keeps your list view windows as small as possible. You can make a list view window narrower by reducing the number of items checked in the Views control panel and then clicking the window's zoom box.

The Finder in System 7, unlike older Finders, enables you to pick the size of icons it displays in all list views. Tiny icons are like the icons in list views of older Finders. Small icons are like the icons in small-icon view. Standard icons are like desktop icons.

You can also set an option to have the Finder calculate and display folder sizes. Adding up the sizes of items in a large folder can take quite a while. Fortunately, the Finder only calculates sizes of folders you can see and does this work in the background so that you can get on with other tasks.

Another list view option has the Finder show disk information in the header of all list view windows. The disk information includes the number of items in the window, the amount of disk space in use, and the amount of disk space available. This information is standard in icon and small-icon views.

## Finding enclosing folders

In all versions of System 7, you can quickly find and open the folder that encloses any open folder. First, make the open folder's window active by clicking it. Then press ⌘ while clicking the active window's title. A menu pops up showing the path from the window's folder through your nested folder structure to the disk that contains the folder, as shown in Figure 6-12. You can use the menu to open the folder that contains, or *encloses*, the open folder whose window is active. The enclosing folder is sometimes called the *parent folder*. You can also use the pop-up menu to open the other folders along the path or the disk at the root of the path.

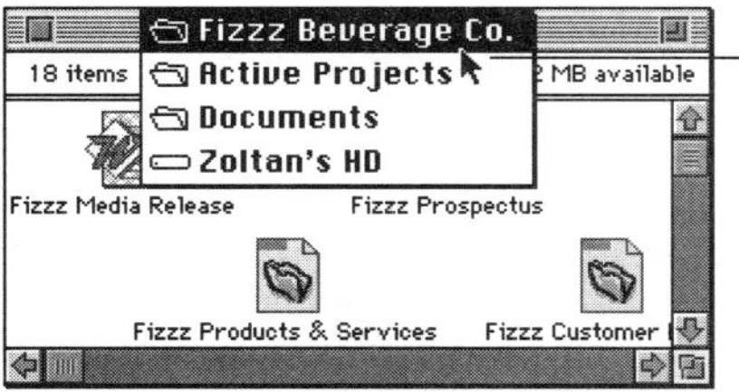


**Figure 6-12: Moving through folders to the disk.**

You can close an open folder's window while opening an enclosing folder. Simply hold down Option and ⌘, click the window title to pop up the menu of enclosing folders, and choose the folder you want to open. You must press Option and ⌘ before clicking the window title. If you press ⌘ alone while popping up the menu of enclosing folders and then press Option, the active window does not close when you choose it from the pop-up menu.

# Finding Items

Outline view helps you hunt through folders and disks for items, but the Finder's Find command fetches lost items with less effort. The Find command works somewhat differently in System 7.5 than in earlier versions of System 7. The following two sections describe its two methods.

## Finding items in System 7.1.2 and earlier

In System 7.1.2 and earlier versions (including System 7 Pro), choosing Find from the Finder's File menu brings up a dialog box in which you specify what you want to find. The Find dialog box has a simple form and an expanded form.

### A simple Find

The simple form of the Find dialog box, shown in Figure 6-13, sets up a search for items whose names contain the text you specify. The Finder searches all disks whose icons are on the desktop and displays the first item it finds, opening the folder that contains the item to show the item in its native surroundings.

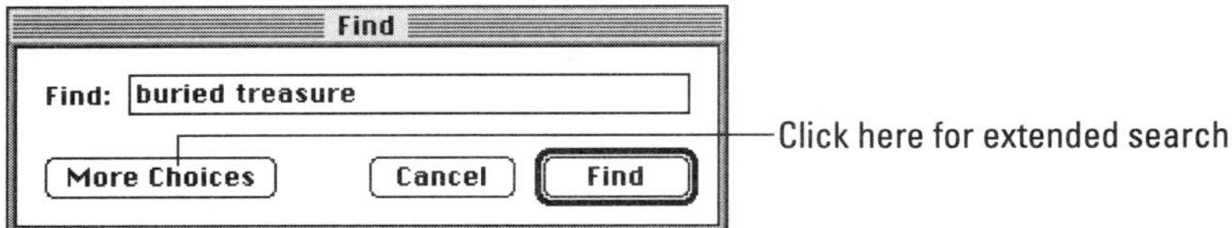


**Figure 6-13: A simple find.**

### An expanded Find

The Find command has an expanded form as well. Clicking the More Choices button in the Find dialog box extends your search options, as shown in Figure 6-14.

You choose the type of search — by name, size, kind, label, date created, date modified, version, comments, or lock status — from a pop-up menu. You also specify exactly what you want to match and how you want it matched. Table 6-1 enumerates the possible criteria combinations. For all combinations, you can restrict the search to a single disk, the active window, or a group of items you select in the active window (or on the desktop) before choosing the Find command. If you restrict the search, you can also have the Finder select all the items it finds at once in an outline view.

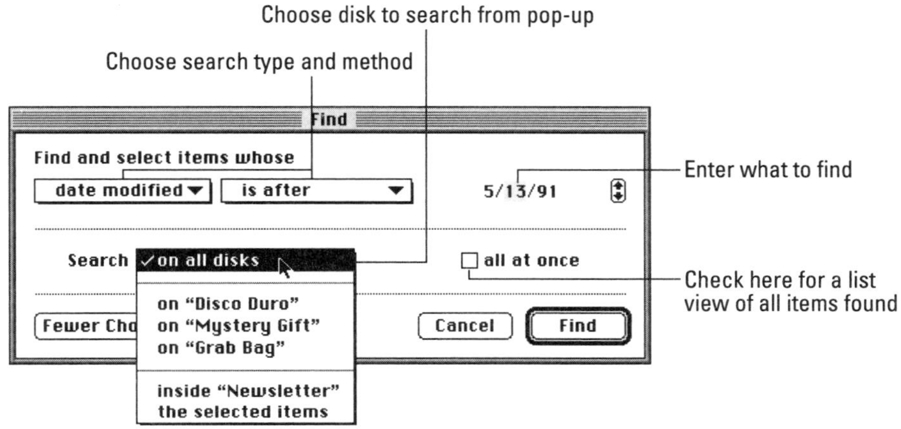


**Figure 6-14: An extended find.**

Table 6-1
**Complex Find Criteria**

| *Search by* | *Search how* | *Search for* |
|---|---|---|
| Name | Contains/starts with/ends with/ is/is not/doesn't contain | Text you enter |
| Size | Is less than/is greater than | Amount you enter, in kilobytes |
| Kind | Contains/doesn't contain | Alias/application/document/folder/ stationery/text you enter |
| Label | Is/is not | Label you choose from pop-up menu |
| Date created | Is/is before/is after/is not | Date you specify |
| Date modified | Is/is before/is after/is not | Date you specify |
| Version | Is/is before/is after/is not | Text you enter |
| Comments | Contain/do not contain | Text you enter |
| Lock | Is | Locked/unlocked |

The Find command does not look inside the System file or suitcase files for fonts, sounds, or desk accessories. It can find those kinds of items in folders and on the desktop, though.

To return to the simple Find dialog box, click the Fewer Choices button. To end searching, click the Cancel button. The Finder remembers whether you were using the simple or the expanded Find dialog box and gives you the same one the next time you use the Find command.

### Find Again

After the Finder finds one item that matches your simple or complex search criterion, you can find additional matching items with the Find Again command in the File menu. The Finder first searches the active window for another item that matches the search criterion. If the active window contains another matching item, the Finder selects it and scrolls it into view. If the active window doesn't contain any more matches to the Find criterion, the Find looks in other folders and disks. If it finds another match, it closes the active window (unless it was already open) and looks for a match in another folder.

***Tip:*** If you know that the active window contains several matches to the Find criterion but know that none of them is the one you want, you can skip to the next folder by closing the active window before using the Find Again command.

## Finding items in System 7.5

In System 7.5, choosing Find or Find Again from the Finder's File menu opens a utility program named Find File. You can use it to search for items that match a single criterion or up to eight criteria.

### Setting up a search

The simplest form of the Find File window allows you to specify where you want to search and one attribute you want to match, as shown in Figure 6-15. It is preset to look on all disks for items whose names contain the text you specify. You can change where Find File looks for items and specify that it look at an attribute other than the item's name.

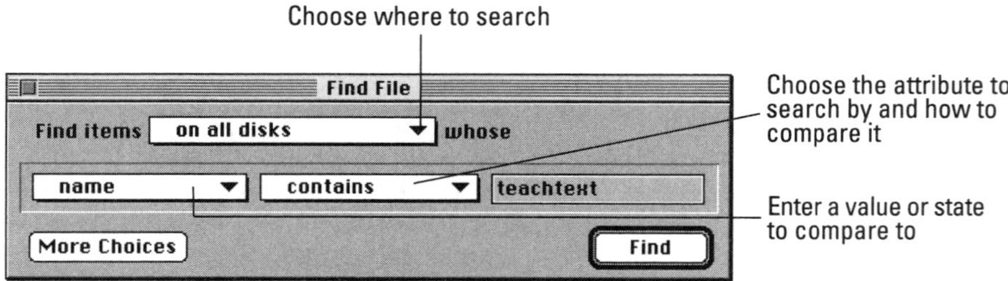


**Figure 6-15: Setting up a simple search in System 7.5's Find File window.**

You use the pop-up menus in the Find File window to specify which attribute you want Find File to look at and how you want Find File to compare that attribute to a value or a state you specify. Table 6-2 lists the possible combinations.

You can have Find File look in the following places: on all disks, on all local disks (not including file servers), on mounted servers (whose icons appear on the desktop), or on a specific disk by name. Unlike the Find command, you cannot restrict the search to the active window or to the items currently selected.

Find File can search for items based on any of 16 attributes, four of which are ordinarily hidden. The 12 attributes you can always see are name, size, kind, label, date created, date modified, version, comments, lock attribute, folder attribute, file type, and creator. The other four attributes are contents, name/icon lock, custom icon, and visibility. To see the extra four attributes, you press the Option key when you first click the left-most pop-up menu in the Find File window.

Table 6-2
**System 7.5's Find File Criteria**

| ***Search by*** | ***Search how*** | ***Search for*** |
|---|---|---|
| Name | Contains/starts with/ends with/ is/is not/doesn't contain | Text you enter |
| Size | Is less than/is greater than | Amount you enter, in kilobytes |
| Kind | Is/is not | Alias/application/clipping file/ document/folder/letter/sound/stationery |
| Label | Is/is not | Label you choose from pop-up menu |
| Date created | Is/is before/is after/is not, is within 1/2/3 days of, is within 1/2/3 weeks of, or is within 1/2/3/6 months of | Date you specify |
| Date modified | Is/is before/is after/is not, is within 1/2/3 days of, is within 1/2/3 weeks of, or is within 1/2/3/6 months of | Date you specify |
| Version | Is/is not | Text you enter |
| Comments | Contain/do not contain | Text you enter |
| Lock attribute | Is | Locked/unlocked |

*(continued on the next page)*

| Table 6-2 *(continued)* | | |
|---|---|---|
| ***Search by*** | ***Search how*** | ***Search for*** |
| Folder attribute | Is/is not | Empty/shared/mounted |
| File type | Is/is not | Text you enter |
| Creator | Is/is not | Text you enter |
| Contents | Contain/do not contain | Text you enter |
| Name/icon lock | is | Locked/unlocked |
| Custom icon | is | Present/not present |
| Visibility | is | Invisible/visible |

You can add more search criteria to the Find File window, as shown in Figure 6-16. Clicking the More Choices button adds a criterion at the bottom of the window. Clicking the Fewer Choices button removes a criterion. Alternatively, you can use the More Choices and Fewer Choices commands in Find File's File menu.

## Find and Find Again in System 7.5

Although the Find command ordinarily opens the Find File utility in System 7.5, you can have it bring up the Find dialog box of earlier System 7 versions instead. To use the old Find command, press Shift while choosing the Find command. After the Finder finds the first item, you can use the Find Again command to have it find the next item. For information about using the Find and Find Again commands, see the preceding section, "Finding items in System 7.1.2 and earlier."

The old Find and Find Again commands can find by the following criteria not available in the Find File utility:

- ❖ A kind that contains or doesn't contain the text you enter
- ❖ A version number that is less than or greater than the text you enter
- ❖ Comments that contain or do not contain the text you enter

In addition, you can restrict Find and Find Again to searching just the active window or selected items.

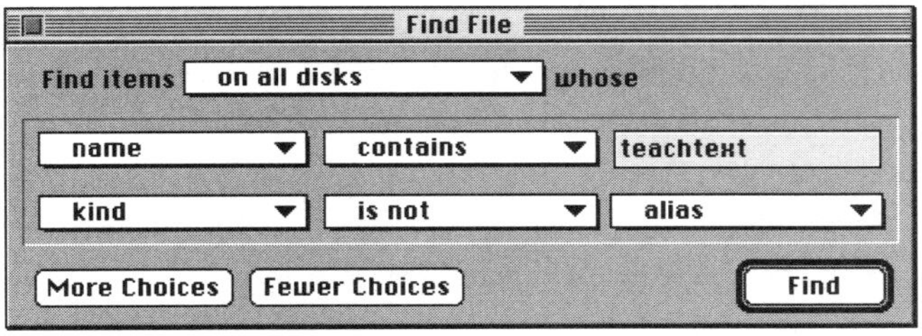

**Figure 6-16: Setting up a complex search in System 7.5's Find File window.**

## Using search results

System 7.5's Find File utility begins searching when you click the Find button in the Find File window. While the search progresses, a count of the number of items found appears in the window. When the search ends, Find File displays all the found items in the Find File Results window, as shown in Figure 6-17.

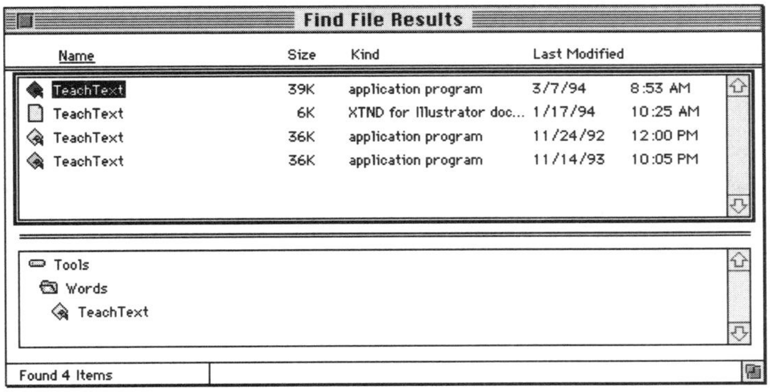

**Figure 6-17: The results of a Find File search.**

You can view the list of found items, which appears at the top of the Find File Results window, by name, size, kind, or modification date. To change the order, use the View menu in the Find File program or click the column heading in the Find File Results window.

Selecting an item (by clicking it) in the list of found items at the top of the Find File Results window displays the item's folder location at the bottom of the window. You can select multiple items in the list of found items as you do in the Finder: by Shift-clicking or dragging a selection rectangle across them. To select all items, use the Select All command in Find File's Edit menu. When you select multiple items at the top of the Find File Results window, no folder location is displayed at the bottom of the window.

You can open an item in the Find File Results window by double-clicking it. If more than one item is selected, double-clicking any of them opens them all. In addition, you can open selected items by choosing Open from Find File's File menu.

To open a selected item's enclosing folder, use the Open Enclosing Folder command. The Finder automatically becomes active, the folder opens, and the Finder scrolls to and selects the item in the folder window.

In addition to opening found items and their enclosing folders, you can also drag found items from the top of the Find File Results window to the desktop or to any folder or disk visible in the Finder. If the destination is on the same disk as the found item you drag, the found item moves to the destination. If the destination is on a different disk, the found item is copied to it.

Besides opening and dragging found items, you can use other commands in Find File's File menu as follows:

- **Print Item** prints selected documents just as the Finder's Print command does.
- **Get Info** displays the Info windows of selected items.
- **Sharing** allows you to share selected folders (as described in Chapter 9) and applications (as described in Chapter 19).

With one item selected at the top of the Find File Results window, you can also select one item at the bottom of the window. Menu commands affect either one item or the other, but not both. The affected item is the one in the section of the window that is surrounded by a thick black rectangle. You can alternate this rectangle between sections of the window by pressing Tab.

# Labeling Items

System 7's Finder enables you to classify folders, programs, and documents by labeling them with a word or phrase. On monitors displaying at least 16 colors, labeling an item also colorizes it.

## Using labels

To label an item, select it and choose a label from the Finder's Label menu, as shown in Figure 6-18. If the icon is a color icon, the Finder blends the label color as if you covered the icon with a piece of acetate that is the same color as the label. To label an item without colorizing it, change the label color to solid black, as described in the next section.

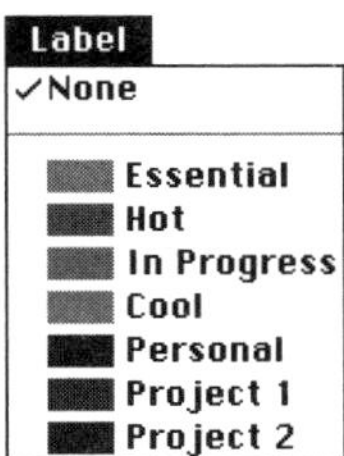


**Figure 6-18: The Label menu.**

After labeling items, you can view Finder window contents arranged by label, as shown in Figure 6-19. You can also search for items by label with the Finder's Find command, as shown in Figure 6-20. Label colors also show up in the Apple menu and in the directory dialog boxes used by many programs' Open and Save commands.

Zero's Documents HD

| Name | Size | Kind | Label | Las |
|---|---|---|---|---|
| Urgent Work | – | folder | Essential | |
| *Van Loo Memo 7/1/91 a...* | 1K | alias | Essential | |
| *ZebraCo Letter* | 1K | alias | Essential | |
| *Crooke Letter 6/25/91 ...* | 1K | alias | Hot | |
| *Newsletter in progress* | 1K | alias | In Progress | |
| *ZebraCo Brochure* | 1K | alias | Project 1 | |
| *ZebraCo Logo* | 1K | alias | Project 1 | |
| Letters in Waiting | – | folder | Hot | |
| Active Projects | – | folder | In Progress | |
| Editions | – | folder | Cool | |
| This Year's Mail | – | folder | Cool | |

**Figure 6-19: Viewing by label.**

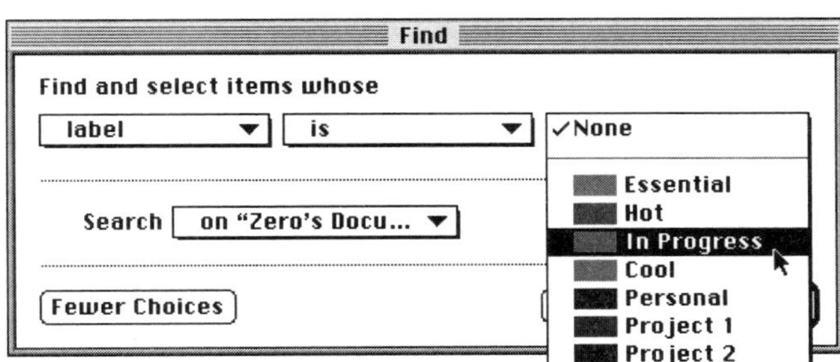


**Figure 6-20: Finding by label.**

## Changing label names and colors

You change the standard label names and colors by using the Labels control panel, as shown in Figure 6-21. If you click a label color to change it, the Finder displays the color picker dialog box shown in Figure 6-22. You pick a new color in it by clicking a color wheel and adjusting the lightness with a slider. You can also specify a color by typing values for hue angle, saturation, and lightness. Hue angle is measured in degrees from 0 to 360, counterclockwise with 0 at the three-o'clock position. Saturation measures the amount of color, from 0 (gray) to 100 (pure color). Lightness varies from 0 to 100 and measures how close the color is to black (0) or white (100). Table 6-3 lists the hue, saturation, and brightness values for the standard colors (in case you want to reset them after experimenting).

To pick a color using a different type of color picker, click the More choices button in the picker dialog box. When you do, the available pickers are listed at the left of the dialog box. The picker shown in Figure 6-22 is the Apple HSL picker, a standard picker included with System 7.5 and later. The Apple RGB picker is another standard picker. With it you use sliders or type numbers to specify the amount of red, green, and blue you want in the color.

Prior to System 7.5, the color picker dialog box looks a bit different. The lightness setting is called brightness and is set with a scroll bar in the color picker window. The hue, saturation, and brightness settings are numbers between 0 and 65535. You can also specify the amount of red, green, and blue instead of hue, saturation, and brightness.

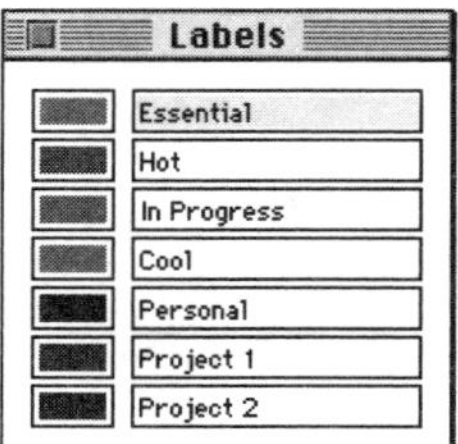


**Figure 6-21: The Labels control panel.**

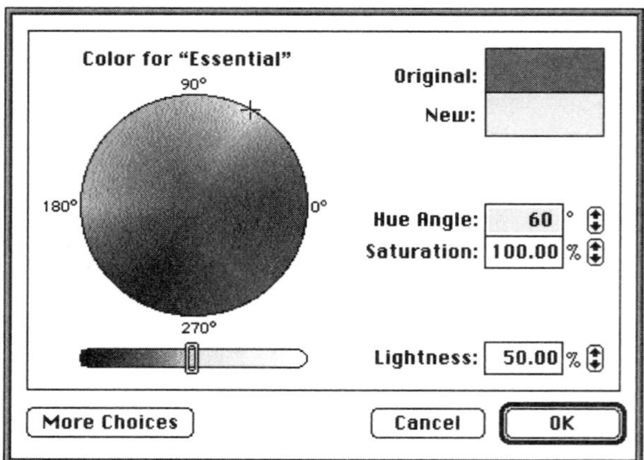


**Figure 6-22: Picking a custom label color in System 7.5.**

Table 6-3
**Values for Standard Label Colors**

| | *System 7.0, 7.0.1, 7.1, 7.1.1, 7.1.2* | | | *System 7.5* | | |
|---|---|---|---|---|---|---|
| ***Label*** | ***Hue*** | ***Saturation*** | ***Brightness*** | ***Hue angle*** | ***Saturation*** | ***Lightness*** |
| Essential | 4223 | 64884 | 65535 | 23° | 100% | 50.5% |
| Hot | 108 | 63573 | 56683 | 1° | 94.18% | 44.54% |
| In Progress | 59733 | 63286 | 62167 | 328° | 93.36% | 49.06% |
| Cool | 35756 | 64907 | 60159 | 196° | 98.1% | 46.34% |
| Personal | 43690 | 65535 | 54272 | 240° | 100% | 41.41% |
| Project 1 | 23764 | 65535 | 25775 | 131° | 100% | 19.66% |
| Project 2 | 5332 | 61619 | 22016 | 29° | 88.72% | 17.8% |

## Transparent Labels

If you've avoided System 7's labels because they discolor your beautiful color icons, wait no longer. You can label a color icon without changing its color — provided the label color is black, white, or any shade of gray. (On a color monitor, icons with white labels are invisible unless they are selected.) You can still view Finder windows by label, find items by label, and so on. To make a label transparent, open the Labels control panel and click the color of a label you want to use. The standard color picker dialog box appears, with its characteristic color wheel. Set the Hue Angle and Saturation to 0, and then set the Brightness to 100 for white, 0 for black, or a number between 0.01 and 99.99 for a shade of gray. You can type the three values in the spaces provided, or you can click the center of the color wheel and adjust the slider. (Prior to System 7.5, you set Hue and Saturation to 65535, and then set Brightness to 65535 for white, 0 for black, or a number between 1 and 65534 for a shade of gray.)

# Copying Items

When you drag items to a folder (or an open folder's window), the Finder figures out whether the destination folder is on the same disk as the source folder. If so, the Finder moves the items you're dragging to the destination folder. If the items you're dragging come from a different disk than the destination folder, the Finder copies the items you're dragging.

***Tip:*** To copy an item from one folder to another folder elsewhere on the same disk, press Option while you drag the item to the destination folder.

When you copy an item to a disk or folder that already contains an item by the same name, System 7's Finder does more than older Finders. It asks whether you want to replace the item at the destination and tells you which item is newer, as shown in Figure 6-23.

The Finder in System 7 is also smart about copying an entire floppy disk to a hard disk. It puts the floppy disk's contents into a new folder on the hard disk and gives the folder the same name as the floppy. You can even copy a floppy to a folder on a hard disk.

## Copy Fitting

When copying batches of files from your hard drive to floppies, you must do heavy mental addition to avoid having the Finder bark, "There is not enough room on the disk...." Have the Finder help you figure out how many files fit on a floppy by following these steps:

1. Create a new folder on the hard drive.

   The new folder must be in a window, not directly on the desktop.

2. Use the Finder's Get Info command to bring up the folder's Info window.
3. Begin dragging files into the folder.

As you drag, the Finder updates the folder's size in its Info window. When the size approaches 1400K for a high-density floppy or 800K for a double-density floppy, you know that you've got enough to fill the disk and no more.

If the Trash is empty, you can collect items in it instead of in a specially created folder. This method has two advantages: you can quickly return all items to their original places with the Put Away command in the File menu, and you don't have to wait for the Finder to make copies of items that come from several disks. (The Finder doesn't copy items to the Trash, but it must copy items you drag from one disk to a folder on another disk.) The Get Info command only reports the size of the Trash to the nearest K, however, whereas it gives you the exact number of bytes in a folder.

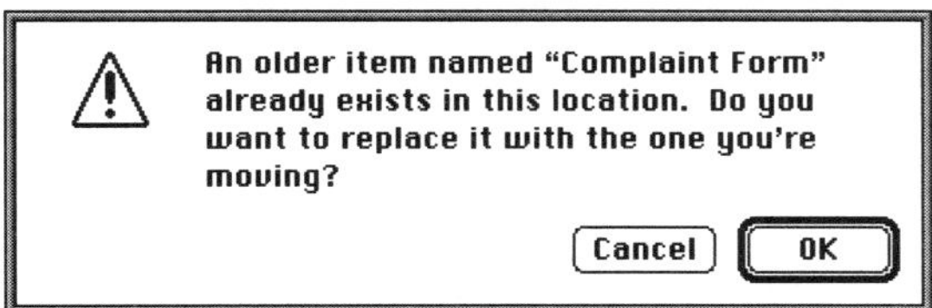


**Figure 6-23: Verifying replacement.**

# Naming Duplicate Items

The Finder constructs the name of a duplicate item you create with the Duplicate command (File menu) by suffixing the name with the word *copy*. Additional copies of the same item also have a serial number suffixed, as shown in Figure 6-24.

**Figure 6-24: Names of duplicate items.**

If any suffixes result in a name longer than 31 characters, the Finder removes characters from the end of the original item's name. For example, duplicating an item named June Income and Expense Report results in an item named June Income and Expense Re copy.

These rules come into play when an item you drag to the Trash has the same name as another item already there. Suppose, for example, that the Trash contains an item named Untitled and you dragged another like-named item there. The Finder renames the item already there to Untitled copy. If you later add another item named Untitled, the Finder changes Untitled copy to Untitled copy 2, changes Untitled to Untitled copy, and leaves the name of the item you just added unchanged. In other words, the item most recently added has the plain name and the next most recently added has the highest number suffix.

The Finder uses similar rules to construct names of aliases. See Chapter 10 for more information.

### Colons Are Special

Icon names can't include colons because programs use colons internally to specify the path through your folder structure to a file. A path name consists of a disk name, a succession of folder names, and a file name, with a colon between each pair of names. For example, the path name "Hard Drive:System Folder:Control Panels:Sound" specifies the location of the Sound control panel on a System 7 startup disk named Hard Drive. Putting a colon in a file name confounds the scheme for specifying paths.

# Deleting Items

The Trash icon looks the same with System 7 as with older system software, but the Trash works differently. In System 7, the Finder does not automatically empty the Trash. You must explicitly remove items from the Trash by choosing Empty Trash from the Finder's Special menu. Until you do, the contents of the Trash remain there even when you open another program, shut down, or restart.

System 7's Finder doesn't allow you to leave items from 400K (single-sided) disks in the Trash, however. When you drag items from a 400K disk to the Trash, a message asks whether you want to delete them immediately or cancel.

## Trash warnings

When you choose the Empty Trash command, the Finder tells you how many items the Trash contains and how much disk space they occupy, as shown in Figure 6-25. Invisible items in the Trash also count toward the total number of items to be permanently removed. (For example, any folder that has a custom icon contains an invisible file named *Icon*, as described in the "Broken Icons" sidebar in Chapter 4.) You decide whether to discard them all or cancel.

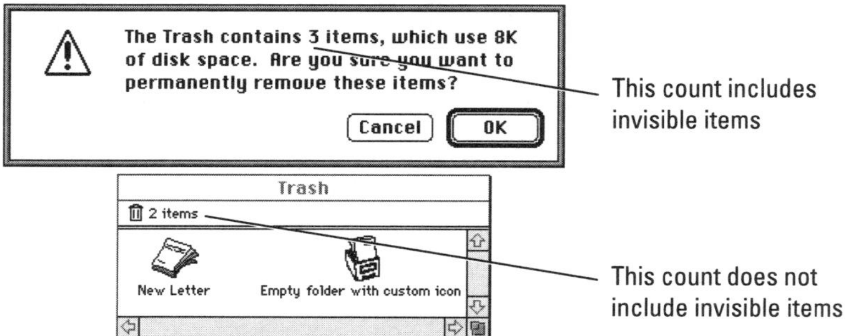


**Figure 6-25: The Trash warning.**

## Trash Pickup

You don't have to drag things to the Trash with the mouse if you have QuicKeys macro software from CE Software (800-523-7638 or 515-224-1995). Use the following steps to define a macro that does it for you. With the macro defined, you can put items in the Trash by selecting them wherever they may be, leaving the pointer over one of them, and pressing the keystroke you designated to activate the macro. Note that this macro puts things in the Trash, but does not empty the Trash.

1. Open the QuicKeys editor and choose Click from QuicKeys' Define menu.
2. When the QuicKeys window disappears and a microphone icon flashes over the Apple menu icon, click the Trash icon on the desktop.
3. In the Click editing window that appears, click the Click button to bring up the Click Location editing window.
4. In the Click Location editing window, select Screen as the Drag Relative To option, and then select Mouse for the Click Relative To option.

   This step instructs QuicKeys to click wherever the pointer is and drag from there to the coordinates of the Trash (which you recorded when you clicked in step 1). Click the OK button to return to the Click editing window.
5. Back in the Click editing window, type a name for the macro and designate a keystroke for activating it (for example, ⌘-T).
6. Click OK to dismiss the Click editing window and OK again to dismiss QuicKeys.

***Tip:*** You can disable the Trash warning by pressing Option while choosing the Empty Trash command. To muzzle the warnings more permanently, select the Trash icon, choose the Get Info command, and turn off the appropriate option, as shown in Figure 6-26.

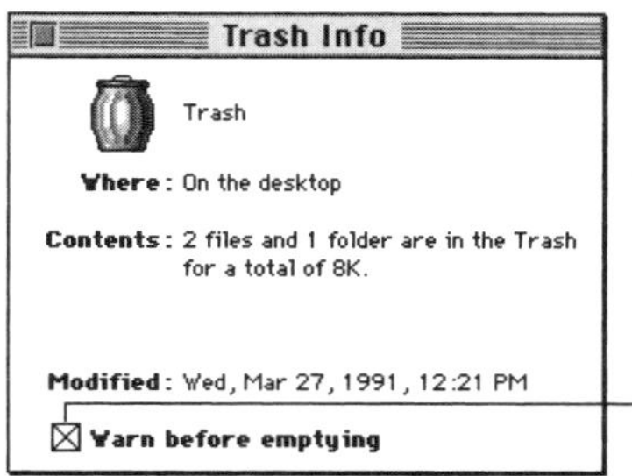


**Figure 6-26: Get Info for the Trash.**

Unlike older Finders, System 7's Finder does not display a warning when you drag locked items, application programs, or system software items to the Trash. However, the Finder does not remove locked items. It advises you that the Trash contains locked items and asks whether you want to remove the other items or cancel. To get rid of locked items in the Trash, press Option while choosing the Empty Trash command.

## Trash retrieval

To put items now in the Trash back where they came from, open the Trash, select the items, and choose Put Away from the Finder's File menu. The Finder returns each selected item to its original folder, though not necessarily to the same place in the folder window.

## Trash contents

The Trash contains all the items that you have dragged to it from all the disks whose icons are on the desktop. The Empty Trash command removes the items from all disks involved. To remove items from only one disk, first put away the icons of the disks whose trash you don't want affected (either drag the disk icons to the Trash or select the icons and choose Put Away from the File menu). The Empty Trash command doesn't affect disks whose icons are not on the desktop. Alternatively, you can open the Trash and drag the items you don't want removed to the desktop or to another folder. Then use the Empty Trash command.

If you eject a floppy disk (and put away its icon) after dragging items from that disk to the Trash, those items disappear from the Trash, but the Finder does not delete them. They reappear in the Trash the next time you insert that disk. If you insert that floppy disk in another Mac, they appear in its Trash. They appear in a folder named Trash when you use that disk with older system software.

### Shared Trash

If you're sharing someone else's disk or folder over a network and you drag an item from the shared disk to the Trash on your desktop, the item does not go into the Trash on the Mac where the shared disk or folder resides. The item is removed from that disk or folder if you use the Empty Trash command on your Mac. From the opposite viewpoint, you do not know when someone sharing your disk or folder drags items from it to his or her Trash. (The owner of a shared disk or folder can set access privileges to keep unauthorized people from dragging items from it to their Trash. See Chapter 9.)

### Back from the Trash

When you delete files by emptying the Trash, the disk space occupied by deleted files becomes immediately available for other files. The Empty Trash command removes a file's entry from the relevant disk's file directory. It also changes the disk's sector-allocation table to indicate that the disk sectors the file occupied are available for use by another file.

To save time, the command does not erase file contents in the now-available sectors. Until the system allocates some of a deleted file's sectors to a new or expanded file, Norton Utilities for Macintosh (NUM) and similar utility software can resurrect the deleted file from its contents by creating a new directory entry for it and reallocating the sectors it occupies. Any blackguard with disk-utility software can retrieve files you deleted — or view any fragment of deleted files' contents — unless you erased their contents with utility software such as NUM.

***Tip:*** Sometimes the Trash contains a folder named Rescued Items. It contains formerly invisible temporary files found when you started up your Macintosh. The Rescued Items folder appears only after a system crash. You may be able to recreate your work up to the time of the system crash from the contents of the Rescued Items folder.

# Removing Disks

Dragging a disk icon to the Trash does not permanently remove anything from the disk, as you may reasonably fear. Instead, this process, known as *unmounting* a disk, removes the icon from the desktop and makes the disk's contents unavailable. If the disk is a floppy disk or CD-ROM, dragging its icon to the Trash ejects the disk from the disk drive. With other types of removable disks, you may have to push a button on the disk drive to remove the disk.

With System 7's Finder, you can also remove a disk icon by selecting it and choosing Put Away from the File menu, as shown in Figure 6-27. The Put Away command ejects floppy disks and CD-ROMs.

To eject a disk without removing its icon from the desktop, select the icon and choose Eject from the Special menu. The ejected disk's icon becomes gray to show that it is unavailable.

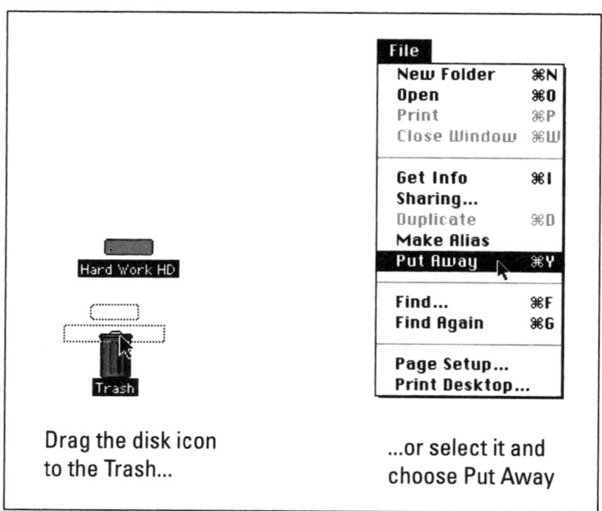


**Figure 6-27: Removing a disk icon.**

# Doing Background Work

Copying files can take a while, but System 7's Finder can do the work in the background while you use another program, as shown in Figure 6-28. Background copying is especially useful during a lengthy copy, such as from or to a shared folder or disk. In addition, the Finder's Duplicate, Empty Trash, and Find commands work in the background. Notice that the dialog boxes of these commands have title bars; you can drag a title bar to move a dialog box.

After starting to empty the Trash or copy, duplicate, or find something, you can switch to another program by clicking in any of its windows or by choosing it from the Application menu or the Apple menu. You can't open a program or document by double-clicking its icon or using the Finder's Open command while the Finder copies, duplicates, empties Trash, or finds, but you can open programs and documents listed in the Apple menu. And after switching from the Finder to another program, you can use that program's Open command to open documents. Control panels are considered part of the Finder, so you can't use them while the Finder performs one of the tasks it can do in the background.

The performance of your Mac suffers while the Finder works on a task in the background. Furthermore, the background task proceeds more slowly than it does in the foreground. The pointer jerks across the screen. The mouse button and keyboard may seem to stop working for a few seconds from time to time. If you type faster than the screen can display the characters, the system remembers the most recent 20 characters you type (about five seconds of typing at 40 words per

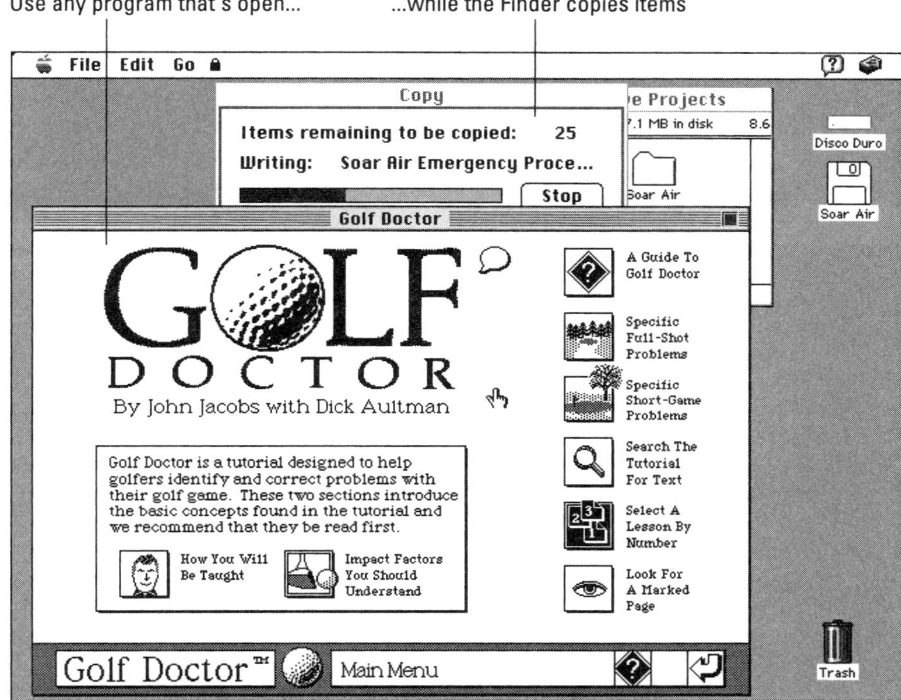


**Figure 6-28: Working while you copy.**

minute). The system can also remember one click or double-click and can catch up with your dragging as long as you don't release the mouse button.

# Partitioning Hard Disks

If you work with lots of small files, you can save a significant amount of disk space by *partitioning* a large hard drive into several smaller volumes. For example, a short memo that takes 4K on a 230MB hard drive takes only 1K on a 60MB partition, saving 3K per small file. If you have lots of small files, the savings can literally add up to megabytes.

Each partitioned volume looks and acts exactly like a hard disk. Every volume has its own disk icon on the desktop, and all volumes appear at the desktop level of directory dialog boxes (which are described in Chapter 5). Think of volumes as individual disks that happen to be stored on the same mechanism.

Partitioning has other advantages besides using disk space more efficiently. Here are three:

- ❖ Items can be easier to find.
- ❖ You can secure an individual volume's contents with a password or lock it against overwriting.
- ❖ Accidental corruption of one volume is unlikely to affect other volumes.

On the down side, partitioning reduces storage flexibility. Each volume has a separate amount of available space. If you fill one volume, you can't store any more on it even though other volumes on the same drive have plenty of space available. Also, making multiple volumes increases the clutter of icons on the desktop. But these disadvantages are minor. Unless most of your files are larger than 3K, it makes sense to partition a hard disk whose capacity is larger than 192MB.

## Partitioning a hard disk

You can partition a hard drive with a disk formatting utility program such as Hard Disk ToolKit from FWB or Drive 7 from Casa Blanca (415-461-2227). Norton Utilities for Macintosh from Symantec (800-441-7234 or 408-253-9600) also includes partitioning capabilities. Apple's disk formatting utility program, HD SC Setup, can create volumes for alternate operating systems such as A/UX but cannot partition a hard drive into multiple volumes for use with System 7. However, you can use one of the other utility programs to install different disk-driver software on the hard disk and then partition the disk into multiple volumes for System 7.

## Optimum volume size

The hardest part about partitioning a hard disk is deciding how many volumes to create and what size to make each one. Generally, you want to make a volume large enough to hold all related items and leave room to add items in the future. For example, you can create one volume to hold all your software — application programs and system software — and another volume to hold all your documents. Unless you create very large documents (in which case you may be better off not partitioning), the volume for applications and the System Folder probably needs to be bigger than the volume for documents.

The size of a volume determines the minimum size of a file on that volume. The smallest amount of space that can be allocated to a file on a volume is called the *allocation block size*. Larger volumes have larger allocation block sizes. For example, a 50-word memo needs only about 300 bytes of storage space, but it uses up to 8K (8192 bytes) on a 500MB volume or 1K (1024 bytes) on a 60MB volume.

Minimum allocation block size grows by 0.5K for every 32MB in volume capacity, as tabulated in Table 6-4. Some documents, and all programs, are allocated two blocks. One of these blocks is for the file's data fork and the other block is for the file's resource fork.

Table 6-4
**Smallest File Sizes for Various Volume Sizes**

| *Volume Size* | *Allocation Block Size* |
|---|---|
| 0 to 31MB | 0.5K |
| 32 to 63MB | 1K |
| 64 to 95MB | 1.5K |
| 96 to 127MB | 2K |
| 128 to 159MB | 2.5K |
| 160 to 191MB | 3K |
| 192 to 223MB | 3.5K |
| 224 to 255MB | 4K |
| 256 to 287MB | 4.5K |
| 288 to 319MB | 5K |
| 320 to 351MB | 5.5K |
| 352 to 383MB | 6K |
| 384 to 415MB | 6.5K |
| 416 to 447MB | 7K |
| 448 to 479MB | 7.5K |
| 480 to 511MB | 8K |
| 512 to 543MB | 8.5K |
| 544 to 575MB | 9K |
| 576 to 607MB | 9.5K |
| 608 to 639MB | 10K |
| 640 to 671MB | 10.5K |
| 672 to 703MB | 11K |
| 704 to 735MB | 11.5K |
| 736 to 767MB | 12K |
| 768 to 799MB | 12.5K |
| 800 to 831MB | 13K |

*(continued on next page)*

Table 6-4 *(continued)*

| ***Volume Size*** | ***Allocation Block Size*** |
|---|---|
| 832 to 863MB | 13.5K |
| 864 to 895MB | 14K |
| 896 to 927MB | 14.5K |
| 928 to 959MB | 15K |
| 960 to 991MB | 15.5K |
| 992 to 1023MB | 16K |
| 1024 to 1055MB | 16.5K |
| 1056 to 1087MB | 17K |
| 1088 to 1119MB | 17.5K |
| 1120 to 1151MB | 18K |
| 1152 to 1183MB | 18.5K |
| 1184 to 1215MB | 19K |
| 1216 to 1247MB | 19.5K |
| 1248 to 1279MB | 20K |

# CHAPTER 6 CONCEPTS AND TERMS

- The Finder windows are smart about zooming, scrolling, and selecting.
- You can see, select, and reorganize items from different folders in one window by using the outline folder structure in list views.
- You can customize the format of Finder windows.
- The versatile Find command locates items in your disks quickly.
- You can classify items in a window or on the desktop by using words and colors.
- The Finder does not automatically empty the Trash; you must explicitly remove items by choosing the Empty Trash command.
- The Finder can copy, find, delete, and duplicate items in the background.

**allocation block size**
The smallest amount of space that can be allocated to a file on a volume. Larger volumes have a larger allocation block size.

**autoscrolling**
Scrolling through a Finder window without using the scroll bars by placing the pointer in the window, pressing the mouse button, and dragging toward the area you want to view.

**color picker**
The dialog box in which you specify a custom color either by clicking a color wheel or by entering color values.

**enclosing folder**
The folder that contains the open folder whose window is active.

**label**
A means of categorizing files, folders, and disks. Each label has its own color and text, and you can change them with the Labels control panel.

**parent folder**
The folder that encloses another folder.

**partition**
To divide a hard drive into several smaller volumes, each of which the computer treats as a separate disk. Also, another name for any of the volumes created by dividing a hard drive.

**unmount**
To drag a disk icon to the Trash. This action removes the icon from the desktop and makes the disk's contents unavailable but does not delete the items in that disk permanently.

**volume**
A disk or a part of a disk that the computer treats as a separate storage device. Each volume has a disk icon on the desktop.

CHAPTER SEVEN

# Handling the System Folder and Other Special Items

- Working with the System file's contents
- Exploring the folders inside the System Folder and removing items from the System Folder
- Dealing with conflicts between system extensions
- Putting control panels, system extensions, fonts, sounds, keyboard layouts, and language scripts where they belong
- Looking at the desktop database and additional special folders outside the System Folder

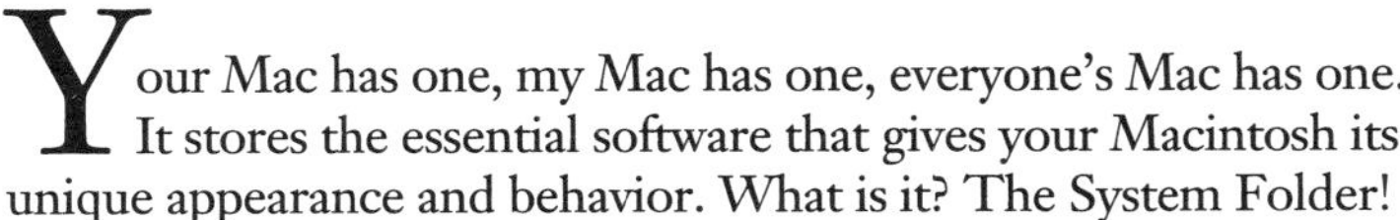

Your Mac has one, my Mac has one, everyone's Mac has one. It stores the essential software that gives your Macintosh its unique appearance and behavior. What is it? The System Folder!

In System 7, items that formerly floated loose in the System Folder go in one of several folders inside it. All the folders have distinctive folder icons, as shown in Figure 7-1. In addition, you can open the System file to view, add, or remove sounds and other resources in it (prior to System 7, you could not open the System file).

Still at large in the System Folder are the Finder, the Scrapbook File, and the Clipboard. Moreover, preferences files and other items crowd the System Folder if you use old application programs and desk accessories. These leftovers gradually find their way into the Preferences folder and other special folders as you upgrade your programs for System 7.

This chapter describes the System file, each standard folder in the System Folder, and other special items outside the System Folder.

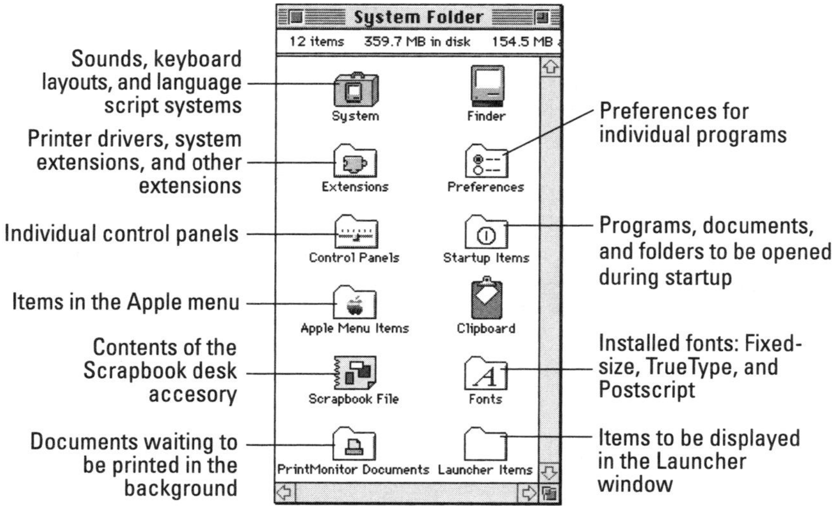


**Figure 7-1: Inside a System Folder.**

# System File

The System file has long been terra incognita to all but the most intrepid resource-hacking Macintosh users. Although a large part of it remains an uncharted wilderness of basic system software, the Finder in System 7 lets everyday Mac users see and work with some of the System file's contents.

## Seeing System file contents

You can open the System file as if it were a folder and see which alert sounds, keyboard layouts, and script systems for foreign languages it contains, as shown in Figure 7-2. Several items do not appear when you open the System file because they are permanently installed in every Mac that can use System 7. They include the simple beep sound, the U.S. keyboard layout, and the Roman script system for Western languages.

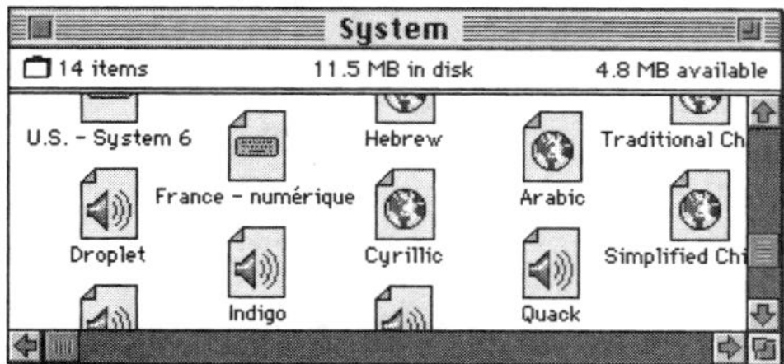


**Figure 7-2: System file contents.**

In Systems 7.0 and 7.0.1, the System file also contains two types of fonts, fixed-size (also called *bitmap*) and TrueType (also called *variable-size* or *outline*). In System 7.1 and later, fonts are kept in a separate folder (see "Fonts Folder" later in this chapter). No version of System 7 keeps desk accessories in the System file, as does older system software. In System 7, desk accessories stand alone in folders or on the desktop like application programs (see "Desk Accessories in System 7" in Chapter 8).

## Working with System file contents

Not only can you see the contents of the System file, you can also drag items in and out of it as if it were a folder. Changes to sounds (and fonts in System 7.0 or 7.0.1) take effect as soon as you close the System file, but changes to other items require restarting your Macintosh first. The Finder doesn't allow you to drag items in or out of the System file when other programs are open. You must quit all open programs, make your changes to the System file contents, and then open the programs again.

Items you drag out of the System file become independent files. You can move them to any folder or the desktop and copy them to other disks. You can rename sounds but not other items in the System file. You can open a sound that's in or out of the System file, which makes the Mac play it.

Installing sounds in the System file makes them available as the system alert sound, which you choose with the Sound control panel. These sounds are not HyperCard sounds. The sounds used in HyperCard don't work properly as system alert sounds.

The keyboard layouts you install appear as choices in the Keyboard control panel. Selecting a different keyboard layout there changes your Mac's arrangement of the keys on your keyboard. Selecting the Español (Spanish) layout, for example, makes the semicolon key on a U.S. keyboard produce an *ñ*. Chapter 17 includes more details about foreign-language keyboard arrangements.

# Fonts Folder

Prior to System 7.1, fonts were kept in the System file and the Extensions folder, both inside the System Folder. System 7.1 simplifies font organization by keeping all fonts — TrueType, fixed-size, and PostScript — in a special Fonts folder inside the System Folder, as shown in Figure 7-3. Installing fonts in the Fonts folder makes them available in programs that let you choose fonts. Newly installed fonts may not be available in programs that are already open until you quit and reopen the programs. A Fonts folder can contain up to 128 items — fonts, suitcases, or a combination. Each suitcase in the Fonts folder can contain any number of fixed-sized and TrueType fonts up to a maximum of 16MB, so if you need room for more than 128 fonts, you can group fonts together in suitcases. (For more information about fonts, see Chapter 11.)

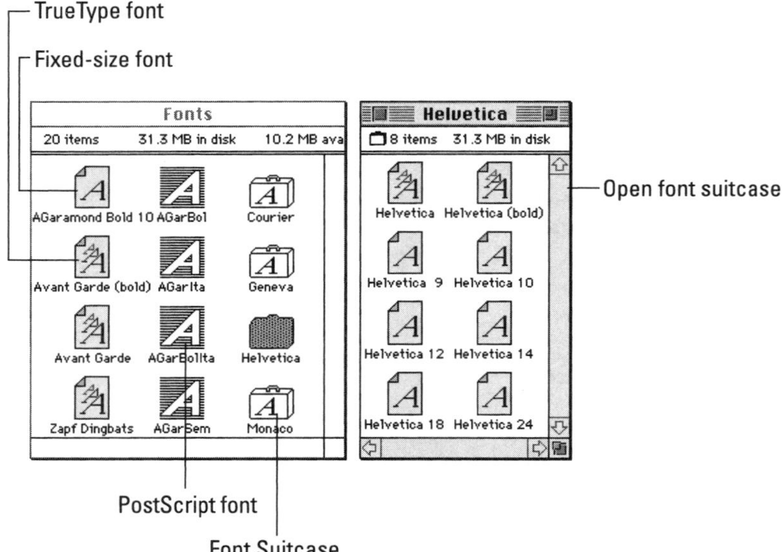


**Figure 7-3: Font files and font suitcase files in the Fonts folder.**

Note that Aldus PageMaker versions 4.01 and earlier and Adobe Type Manager (ATM) versions 2.0 and earlier can find PostScript fonts only in the System Folder. PageMaker 4.2 and ATM 2.0.2 and 2.0.3 also look for PostScript fonts in the Extensions folder, but not in the Fonts folder. If you use these products or if text looks bad on your PostScript printer, you should put PostScript fonts in the Extensions folder or the System Folder itself.

### Exchanging Fonts with Older Systems

With System 7, you can also open font suitcase files and old System files. You can drag items in and out of these files. Old System files contain fonts, sounds, and desk accessories. Font suitcase files contain only fonts. You need font suitcases if you use the Font/DA Mover program to move fonts with older system software. You do not need the Font/DA Mover program with System 7 because System 7 lets you manipulate fonts directly. You can create a new font suitcase file with System 7 by duplicating an existing font suitcase file, opening the duplicate, and dragging its contents to the Trash. You can also create font suitcase files by using version 4.1 of the Font/DA Mover with System 7.

# Apple Menu Items Folder

The Apple Menu Items folder enables you to quickly open anything you use often. All the items in the folder appear on the Apple menu (see Figure 7-4), and choosing an item from the menu has the same effect as opening (double-clicking) the corresponding item in the folder. The Apple menu plays a larger role in System 7 than in older system software because it can do more than open desk accessories. (For more information, see "Opening Multiple Programs" and "Opening with the Apple Menu" in Chapter 5.)

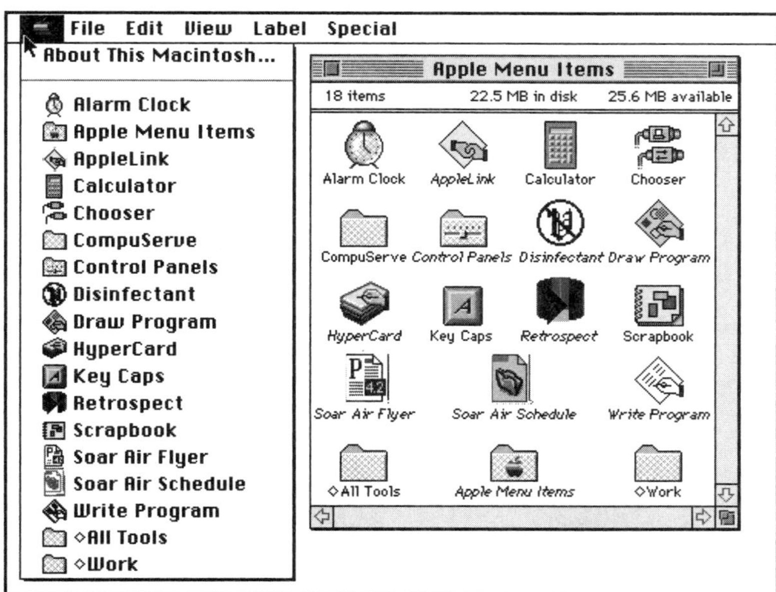


**Figure 7-4: The Apple Menu Items folder and the Apple menu.**

# Startup Items Folder

Everything you put in the Startup Items folder — application programs, desk accessories, documents, control panels, sounds, and so on — gets opened when you start up your Macintosh, as shown in Figure 7-5. Items in the folder are opened in alphabetical order.

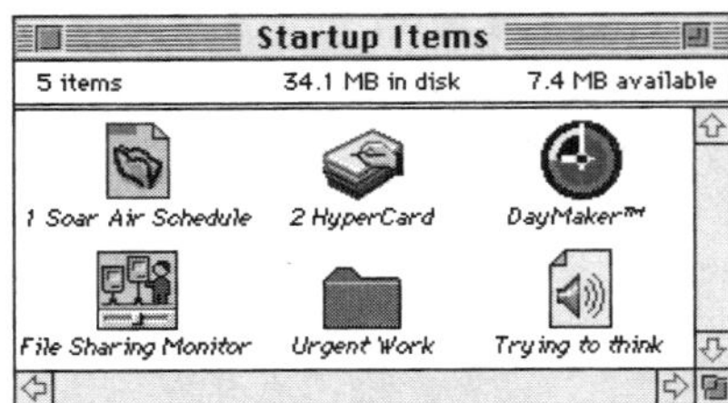


**Figure 7-5: Inside a Startup Items folder.**

To have your Mac open an item at startup time, drag it to the Startup Items folder. Dragging an item out of that folder removes it from the startup sequence. You can avoid dragging programs and other items out of their folders by making aliases of them as described in Chapter 10 and dragging the aliases to the Startup Items folder.

## Arranging Startup Items

If you open several programs during startup, you may have to quit some of them later to free up memory for opening another. Naturally, you'll want to quit the programs least important to you. You'll get maximum benefit from quitting the last items opened during startup. To do so, rename the programs in your Startup Items folder so that the most important comes first alphabetically, the next most important comes second, and so on. You can avoid renaming original programs by putting aliases in the Startup Items folder, as described in Chapter 10.

Don't bother renaming desk accessories, control panels, folders, or aliases of any of those items in the Startup Items folder, however. During startup, the Finder first opens applications alphabetically, next aliases alphabetically, then documents alphabetically, and last, desk accessories, control panels, and folders as a group alphabetically. For example, the Finder opens aliases of MacDraw Pro and QuarkXPress before it opens the Control Panels folder, the File Sharing Monitor control panel, or the Key Caps desk accessory.

QUICK TIPS

### Canceling Startup Items

You can probably imagine times when hearing Darth Vader say, "What is thy bidding, master?" while your Mac starts up would not be politically correct. You can suppress the playing of sounds and opening of all other items in System 7's Startup Items folder by pressing the Shift key when the Finder's menu bar appears. (If you press Shift earlier, you may additionally inhibit the opening of extensions from the Extensions folder, Control Panels folder, and System Folder.)

Once the Mac begins to open startup items, you can cancel the process by pressing ⌘-period (.). The Mac immediately stops playing any sound and skips all startup items it has not already opened. When you press ⌘-period while the Mac is first opening an application, document, or desk accessory from the Startup Items folder, the Mac finishes opening that item and ignores all other startup items.

Canceling the opening of startup programs can be tricky, because the Finder usually does not finish opening one before it starts opening the next. You can see how quickly the Finder goes through the items in the Startup Items folder by restarting your Mac and watching the menu bar closely as the names of startup programs flash by. To cancel the opening of a startup program, you must press ⌘-period before the Finder begins to open it.

Including desk accessories and folders or control panels in the Startup Items folder can disrupt the automatic startup sequence. Whenever a folder or control panel follows a desk accessory alphabetically, the Finder stops opening items and flashes its icon at the right end of the menu bar. You must switch to the Finder (for example, by choosing it from the Application menu), whereupon it opens the folders and control panels that come next alphabetically. For example, if you have both the Alarming Events desk accessory and the Control Panels folder in your Startup Items folder, after the Finder opens Alarming Events you must manually switch to the Finder before it will open the Control Panels folder.

# Control Panels Folder

The items in the Control Panels folder give you control over system appearance and behavior. The folder contains small programs called *control panels*, as shown in Figure 7-6. They are also known as *control panel devices*, *control panel sections*, and *cdevs*. Each affects one aspect of the system. Some control panels also add functions to the basic system software during startup. For information about using individual control panels, see "Control Panels" in Chapter 8.

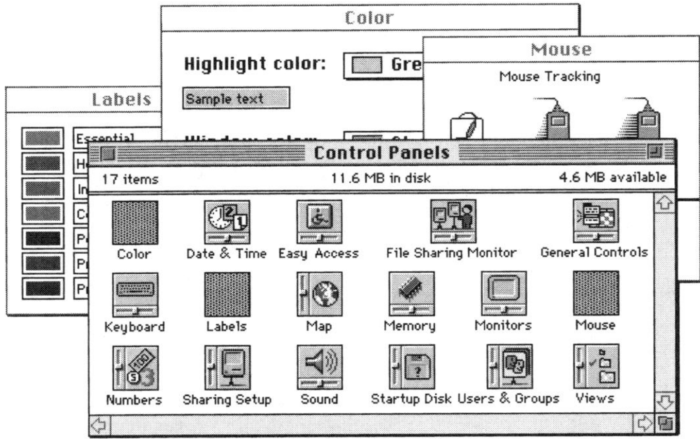


**Figure 7-6: Some control panels.**

# Extensions Folder

The items in the Extensions folder are small software modules called *system extensions*, as shown in Figure 7-7. They customize your Macintosh by extending the services and functions of system software. The version of System 7 and system software options you have installed determine the contents of your Extensions folder. They may include some of the following:

- LaserWriter, StyleWriter, ImageWriter, and other Chooser extensions (also called *printer drivers*) enable your system to print on a specific type of printer, as described in Chapter 12.
- Printer Descriptions contain information about specific printers for use with version 8.0 and later of the LaserWriter extension, as described in Chapter 12.
- Printer Share makes it possible to share more types of printers on a network.
- The PrintMonitor program prints documents in the background while you continue working, as described in Chapter 12.
- Apple CD-ROM, Apple Photo Access, Audio CD Access, Foreign File Access, High Sierra File Access, and ISO 9660 File Access enable the Mac to read CD-ROMs in a variety of formats, including audio CDs and Kodak Photo CDs.
- QuickTime displays movies and decompresses compressed pictures on your Mac, as described in Chapter 16.
- AppleShare, a Chooser extension, enables you to use folders and disks from other computers connected to yours, as described in Chapter 9.

- File Sharing Extension and Network Extension enable you to share your folders and disks with other people in your network, as described in Chapter 9.
- EtherTalk and TokenTalk enable you to connect some Macintosh models to EtherTalk and Token-Ring networks.
- Finder Help provides on-screen help for the Finder, as described in Chapter 4.
- System Update (old versions are called Hardware System Update) fixes bugs and makes minor improvements in the system software, as described in Chapter 3.
- Sound Manager upgrades system software to improve the handling of sound.
- PowerTalk Extension, PowerTalk Manager, Mailbox Extension, Catalogs Extension, Business Card Templates, and AppleTalk Service provide the PowerTalk collaboration services described in Chapter 15 — if you choose to install PowerTalk with System 7.1.1 through 7.5.5.
- AppleScript and Scripting Additions, included with System 7 Pro and later, make it possible to automate tasks in one application or many, as described in Chapter 18.

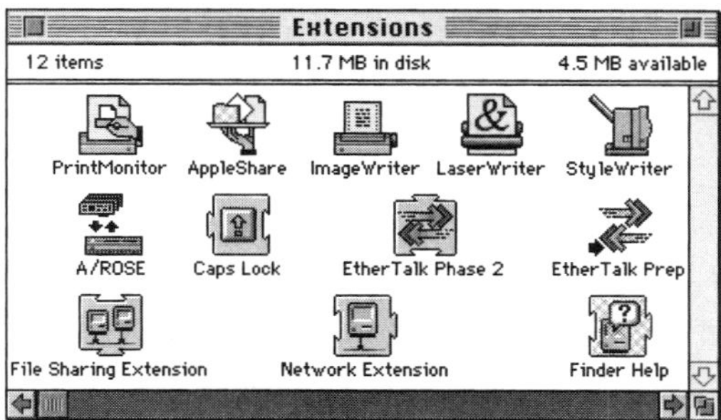


**Figure 7-7: Items inside an Extensions folder.**

System 7.5 and later have still more items in the Extensions folder:

- Apple Guide, About Apple Guide, Macintosh Guide, PowerTalk Guide, and Shortcuts provide step-by-step interactive help for various tasks, as described in Chapter 4
- Finder Scripting Extension enables you to automate Finder tasks with AppleScript, as described in Chapter 18.
- Clipping Extension enables drag-and-drop editing within and between documents and applications, as described in Chapter 14.

- ❖ Color Picker improves the dialog box in which you select a custom color, as described in Chapter 6.
- ❖ Find File Extension assists the Find File program in searching for items on disks, as described in Chapter 6.

If you install QuickDraw GX, the Extensions folder also contains the following:

- ❖ QuickDraw GX provides the advanced typography described in Chapter 11 and the simplified printing described in Chapter 12.
- ❖ LaserWriter GX, StyleWriter GX, ImageWriter GX, PDD Maker GX, and other printer drivers enable QuickDraw GX printing on specific types of printers, as described in Chapter 12.
- ❖ ColorSync ensures that color input from scanners and graphics programs matches color output on monitors, printers, and plotters.
- ❖ QuickDraw GX Helper enables turning off GX desktop printing in individual applications, as described in Chapter 12.

To use a system extension, you simply put it in the Extensions folder and restart your Mac. When you remove a system extension from the Extensions folder, you must again restart for the removal to take effect.

## Finding and Fixing Extension Conflicts

In System 7, extensions may be in the Extensions folder, the Control Panels folder (where they are built into some control panels), or the System Folder itself. During startup, System 7 installs extensions in three groups. First, it goes through the Extensions folder in alphabetical order. Then it installs the extensions that are built into items in the Control Panels folder, again alphabetically. Finally, it checks the System Folder itself and alphabetically installs system extensions it finds there. This installation sequence can cause problems for old system extensions and control panels created before System 7 existed.

Some system extensions and control panels have peculiar names that put the items first or last in the installation sequence, as shown in Figure 7-8. Names of items meant to come first usually begin with blank spaces. Names meant to come last often begin with a tilde (~) or a diamond (◊).

*(continued on next page)*

(continued from previous page)

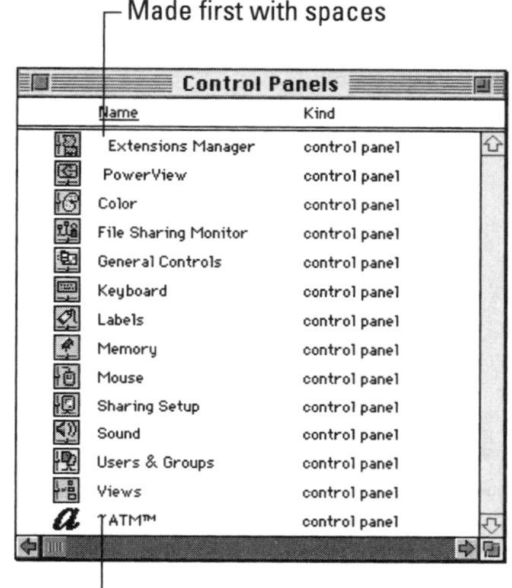


To have control panels whose names begin with blank spaces installed first during startup, put them in the Extensions folder. To have control panels whose names start with tildes or diamonds installed last during startup, put them in the System Folder. For convenient access to the control panels you move out of the Control Panels folder, make aliases for them and put the aliases in the Control Panels folder.

If items you add to the System Folder, Extensions folder, or Control Panels folder don't work, or if your Macintosh refuses to start up, then system extensions in those places may be in conflict during startup. Sometimes changing the order in which the Mac installs system extensions resolves the conflict.

Fixing other conflicts between system extensions and control panels involves experimenting. Start by removing all the items you have added to the System Folder and its inner folders since the trouble began. Then drag half the extensions and control panels to the desktop and restart. If this solves the problem, the offending item is among the half you removed to the desktop; if not, it is among the other half. In either case, leave only half the group containing the offending item (one quarter of all extensions and control panels) on the desktop and restart. If the problem occurs again, the offender is among the group you just put back; if not, it is among the group on the desktop. Continue halving the offending group until you reduce it to a single item (the troublemaker). Instead of dragging control panels and extensions to and from the desktop, you can drag them to and from a new folder you create for that purpose. Alternatively, you can use an extension management utility such as Extension Manager to turn them on and off individually without dragging them in and out of folders (see "Extension Manager" in Chapter 19).

When you find an item that causes a conflict, try renaming it so that it comes before or after other system extensions in the same folder. By experimenting with names, you may find a startup sequence that works.

As a last resort, move all system extensions and control panels to the desktop. Then put them in the System Folder (not the Extensions or Control Panels folders) one at a time, from most important to least. Restart your Mac each time you add another item to the System Folder. When you find an item that causes a conflict, discard it and try the next item you previously moved to the desktop. You may be able to resume using the items you discarded when they are next upgraded.

If a conflict prevents you from starting up from your hard disk, start from a floppy disk with any version of system software. Make a change to the System Folder on the hard disk and try restarting from it.

# Preferences Folder

What you see in your Preferences folder depends on what you have installed on your hard disk. Some programs save preference settings in the Preferences folder. Most programs with commands for publishing and subscribing information also save an alias named Last Edition Used whenever they save an edition, as described in Chapter 14. Also, the system software saves the following items in the Preferences folder (see Figure 7-8):

❖ The File Sharing folder contains file-sharing access privileges for your disks and folders. You don't have this folder if File Sharing has never been turned on.

❖ Finder Preferences contains many of the settings you make with control panels.

❖ Apple Menu Options Prefs, Desktop Pattern Prefs, Extensions Manager Prefs, Find File Preferences, General Controls Prefs, Launcher Preferences, Macintosh Easy Open Preferences, PC Exchange Preferences, and WindowShade Preferences all contain additional settings you make with control panels in System 7.5.

❖ The Users & Groups Data File contains names and privileges for registered users and groups to whom you have given access to your computer.

❖ ColorSync Profiles stores color matching information for specific scanners, monitors, and printers.

❖ AppleMail Letterheads, PowerTalk Setup Preferences, and PowerTalk Startup Preferences contains e-mail forms and control panel settings for PowerTalk — if you install it in System 7 Pro or System 7.5.

❖ AppleCD Audio Player Prefs and CD Remote Programs contain album and song titles that you enter for individual audio CDs together with other settings for the AppleCD Audio Player program.

❖ QuickDraw GX Helper Prefs identifies the applications in which you have turned off GX desktop printing.

❖ Jigsaw Picture contains the picture that the Jigsaw Puzzle program uses to make its puzzles.

❖ Stickies file contains the text of notes you post on your screen with the Stickies program in System 7.5.

Most preference files of old programs are loose in the System Folder, where they must remain until you upgrade the programs to versions that take advantage of System 7. If you drag a preferences file from the System Folder to the Preferences folder, the program that uses it probably won't be able to find it and will use its standard settings by default.

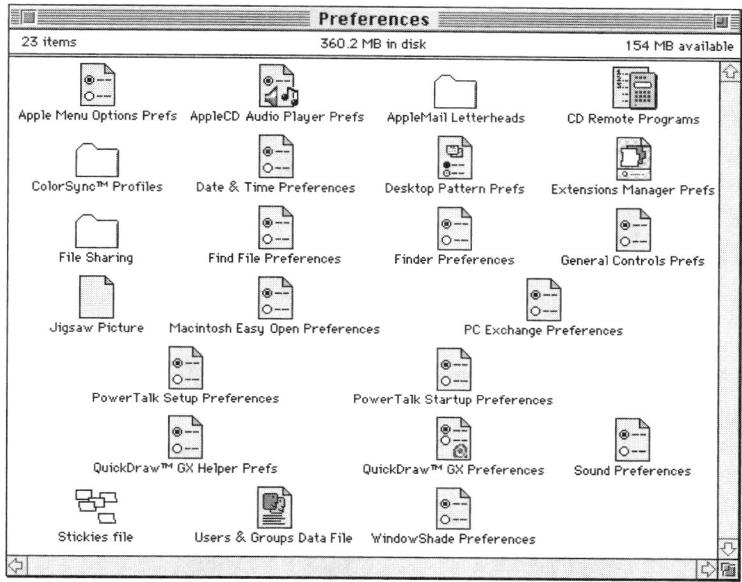


**Figure 7-8: Items inside a Preferences folder.**

# Adding Items to the System Folder

Putting control panels, system extensions, fonts, sounds, keyboard layouts, or language scripts where they belong is just as easy as putting them all in the System Folder. You simply drag the items to the System Folder icon. The Finder recognizes items that go in special folders or the System file and asks whether you want the items put into their proper places, as shown in Figure 7-9.

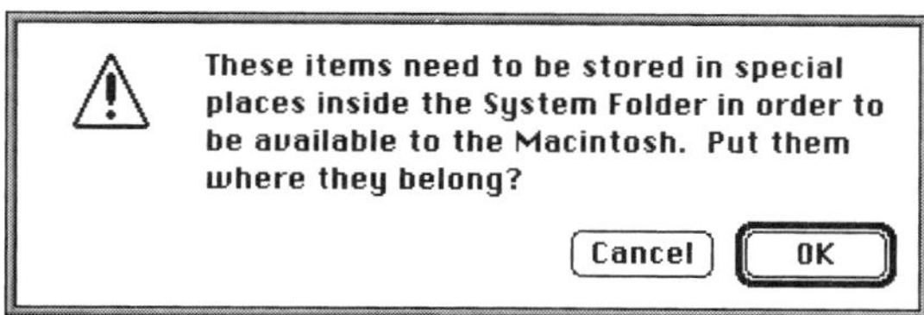


**Figure 7-9: Dragging items to the System Folder helps you put them where they belong.**

If you consent, the Finder distributes items as follows:

❖ Control panels go to the Control Panels folder.

❖ Apple Guide documents, Chooser extensions, communications tools, Modem LinkTools, network extensions, PowerTalk extensions, the PrintMonitor program, and system extensions are placed in the Extensions folder.

❖ Desk accessories go to the Apple Menu Items folder.

❖ TrueType, fixed-size, and PostScript fonts are moved to the Fonts folder (in Systems 7.0 and 7.0.1, the Finder puts TrueType and fixed-size fonts into the System file and puts PostScript fonts into the Extensions folder).

❖ Sounds, keyboard layouts, and language script systems go to the System file.

❖ All other items remain in the System Folder itself.

When you drag folders to the System Folder, the Finder looks inside them and puts items it recognizes in the Control Panels, Extensions, Fonts, or Apple Menu Items folders. If a folder you drag contains items the Finder doesn't recognize, the Finder leaves them in the folder and puts the folder loose in the System Folder. If an item you drag to the System Folder has the same name as an item already there, the Finder not only asks whether you want to replace the latter with the former, but also tells you which is newer.

When the Finder finishes putting items in their places, it tells you how many items of each type it moved, as shown in Figure 7-10. (It counts a folder and its contents as one item no matter how many items it contains.)

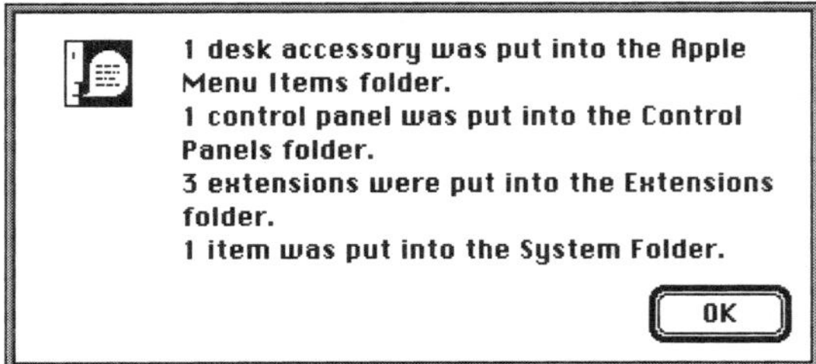


**Figure 7-10: After you drag items to the System Folder, the Finder tells you how many items it moved.**

When you drag items to the System Folder window instead of the System Folder icon, the Finder does not put them in the inner folders for you.

If you happen to discard a special folder, you can make a replacement by using the Finder's New Folder command (in the File menu). After creating a new folder, change its name to that of the special folder you want. Wait a few seconds and you'll see its icon get the distinctive look of the special folder you're creating.

QUICK TIPS

### Overriding the Finder

The Finder sometimes makes mistakes when it puts items in special folders for you. It may put some items in the correct places and incorrectly leave others in the System Folder itself. For example, it may put a control panel in the Control Panels folder but leave that control panel's auxiliary folder in the System Folder. That control panel won't work right because it expects to find its auxiliary folder in the same folder. You must open the System Folder and drag the auxiliary folder to the Control Panels folder yourself, as shown in the figure.

Moreover, the Finder never puts anything you drag to the System Folder icon into the Preferences folder or the Startup Items folder. You must open the System Folder and drag items to those folders directly. Some items from old System Folders don't work right when you put them in the Extensions, Fonts, Control Panel, or Preferences folders. If you have trouble with an item in one of the special folders, try dragging the item from the special folder to the System Folder window.

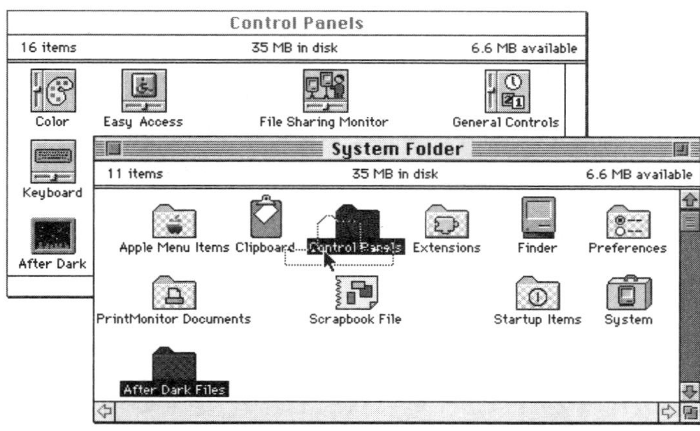


# Removing Items from the System Folder

Before you can remove an item from the System Folder, you must know which inner folder contains it. If you're not sure, use the Finder's Find command to locate the item (see "Finding Items" in Chapter 6). Be sure to drag items from the special folders onto the desktop or into an ordinary folder. Many items you drag out of special folders remain installed if you merely drag them to the System Folder window.

# System Folder Locking

Because so much of your Mac's behavior depends on the contents of the System Folder, you may like to prevent other people who have access to your computer from changing the System Folder's contents. If you have System 7.5 or later, you can protect the System Folder with the General Controls control panel. Simply turn on the Protect System Folder option, as shown in Figure 7-11. With this option turned on, no one can rename or remove items in your System Folder. Keep in mind, though, that anyone who is the least bit savvy can easily turn off this option and go to town on your System Folder.

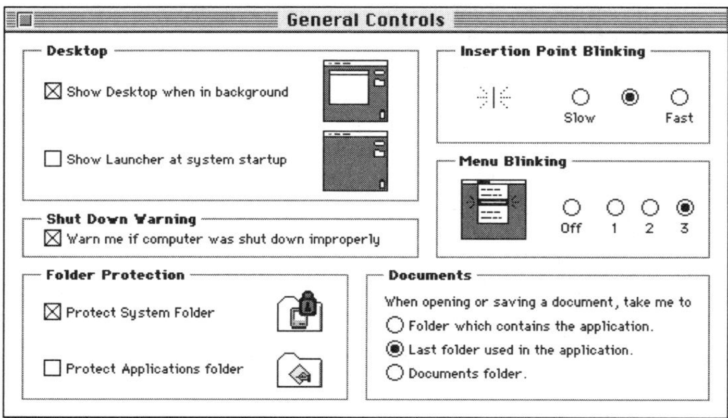


**Figure 7-11: Protecting the System Folder in System 7.5.**

# More Special Folders Outside

System 7 further organizes your disks with additional special folders outside the System Folder. The Finder creates the following special folders as needed on each disk:

- ❖ The invisible Temporary Items folder contains temporary files created by the programs you are using. A program normally deletes its temporary files automatically when you quit it.
- ❖ The Trash folder contains the items you drag from the disk to the Trash icon. Your disks' Trash folders are invisible, but you see their consolidated contents when you open the Trash icon. A visible Trash folder in a shared disk contains items from the disk that are located in the owner's Trash.

- ❖ The Network Trash folder contains items that people who share the disk drag from the shared disk to their Trash icons. Inside this folder are folders named Trash Can #2, Trash Can #3, and so on. They contain items from your shared disk or folder that users have dragged to the Trash — but have not yet permanently removed — on other Macs. These items appear in their Trash folders, not yours.
- ❖ The Rescued Items folder contains items the Finder finds in the Temporary Items folder when you restart after a system crash (or after switching off the power without using the Shut Down command — tsk, tsk!). You may be able to reconstruct your work by opening them. If a Rescued Items folder exists, you can always see it by opening the Trash.
- ❖ The Desktop folder contains items located on the desktop. Although it is invisible on your disks, the Desktop folder of a shared disk is visible to others and contains items from the disk that are on the owner's desktop.

All these special folders become visible when you start up your Mac with system software older than System 7.

# Desktop Database

Something you don't see in the System Folder is the invisible desktop database that the Finder uses to keep track of the following:

- ❖ How icons look (unless you have customized them, as described under "Custom Icons" in Chapter 4)
- ❖ Which kind of file each icon refers to
- ❖ Where programs are
- ❖ What comments you enter with the Finder's Get Info command

The Mac keeps this database hidden so users don't alter it inadvertently, but you can see some of the information the database contains by selecting a file in the Finder and choosing Get Info from the Finder's File menu. System 7's desktop database improves on the previous versions; Finder 7 handles hard disks containing hundreds or thousands of items more efficiently than older Finders.

System 7 creates a new desktop database on every disk larger than 2MB. Each smaller disk has an old-style Desktop file, because you can usually eject those disks and insert them into other systems that use system software older than System 7.

## Cleaning Up Desktop Corruption

A desktop database (or old-style Desktop file) can become corrupt, not through greed or false pride but as a side effect of system crashes or programs quitting unexpectedly. Typical symptoms include blank icons and the Finder being unable to find the program to open a document. These symptoms also occur when the program that created a document is on an ejected disk (or when you don't have the program).

Restarting your Macintosh may eliminate the blank icons. If not, rebuilding the desktop usually does the trick. To rebuild the desktop, simply press ⌘-Option while starting up, and wait for the Finder to inquire whether you indeed wish to rebuild the desktop on the startup disk. If you have multiple hard disks, the Finder asks about rebuilding each one in turn. To rebuild the desktop on a floppy disk, press ⌘-Option while inserting the floppy.

Rebuilding the desktop erases all comments you have entered in Get Info windows for items on the disks involved. See Chapter 19 for a description of Comment Keeper software, which you can use to retain Get Info window comments while rebuilding the desktop.

If rebuilding a desktop database by pressing Command-Option doesn't fix problems, the desktop database may be corrupted. To remove it and replace it with a new one, use the Reset DTDBs software described in Chapter 19.

# CHAPTER 7 CONCEPTS AND TERMS

- Three folders — the Control Panels folder, the Extensions folder, and the Preferences folder — go a long way toward organizing the contents of the System Folder.
- The Fonts folder contains all fonts in System 7.1 and later: TrueType, fixed-size, and PostScript.
- The Apple Menu Items folder lets you decide which items to list on the Apple menu for quick opening.
- The Startup Items folder contains the things you want opened automatically at startup time.
- The System file contains sounds, keyboard layouts, and language system scripts.
- The Finder helps you keep the System Folder organized by putting many of the items you drag to its icon into the proper inner folders.
- The General Controls control panel can lock the System Folder in System 7.5 and later.
- In addition to the special folders found inside the System Folder, there are more special folders — Temporary Items, Trash, Network Trash, Rescued Items, and Desktop — created by the Finder as needed on each disk.
- The invisible desktop database keeps track of each file's icon, its location on disk, the program required to open the file, and other details. If the desktop database becomes damaged, you may have trouble opening files by double-clicking them.

**control panel**
A small program that you use to set the way some part of the system looks and behaves.

**desk accessory**
A type of program that System 7 allows you to open from any folder on the desktop, whereas older system software only allows opening them from the Apple menu.

**desktop database**
Used by the Finder to keep track of the location, icon, and Info window comments for every file, folder, and disk. The Mac keeps it hidden because you don't use it directly.

**Fonts folder**
Located in the System Folder, includes all fixed-size, PostScript, and TrueType fonts in System 7.1 and later.

**Preferences folder**
Holds files that contain the settings you make in control panels and with the Preferences commands of application programs.

**printer driver**
Software that prepares page images for, and communicates with, one type of printer, such as a laser printer with PostScript or a StyleWriter.

**Startup Items folder**
Items you place here are opened automatically in alphabetical order when you start up your Mac.

**system extension**
Customize your Mac by extending the services and functions of system software.

**System file**
Contains sounds, keyboard layouts, and script systems, and also contains fixed-size and TrueType fonts in System 7.0 and 7.0.1.

**System Folder**
Stores the essential software, including the Finder, the Clipboard, and the Startup Items folder, that gives your Mac its unique appearance and behavior.

CHAPTER EIGHT

# Using Standard Control Panels and Accessories

- Individual control panels, which look like independent Finder documents, provide settings for many types of adjustments
- Desk accessories move to the desktop and behave like ordinary application programs
- Control panels, desk accessories, and accessory applications that Apple includes with various versions of System 7 are described

Fitting the Macintosh to your work environment is easier than it once was. System 7 removes the special rules of older system software for installing and using desk accessories and control panels. Now you use these items in a manner more consistent with ordinary programs and documents. System 7.5 and later blur the distinction further by including application programs in the Control Panels and Apple Menu Items folders.

## Control Panels

You use control panels to set a wide variety of options that affect the way your Mac works. Control panels also can enhance System 7. By convention, control panels go into the special Control Panels folder inside the System Folder. When you open the Control Panels folder, its window acts as a master control panel, as shown in Figure 8-1. You can rearrange the individual control panels in this window by using the Finder's View menu or by dragging icons. So that you can open the Control Panels folder easily, it is listed in the Apple menu. (The Apple Menu Items folder contains an alias of the Control Panels icon.)

You open one or more individual control panels as you would open any document — for example, by double-clicking it. Each open control panel appears in its own window. In System 7, control panels come in all sizes and shapes.

The Control Panels folder may contain items that are not, strictly speaking, control panels. For example, System 7.5 and later come with the application program Desktop Patterns in the Control Panels folder. The main difference is that control panels are considered to be part of the Finder. Open control panels aren't listed in the Application menu (at the right end of the menu bar) together with application

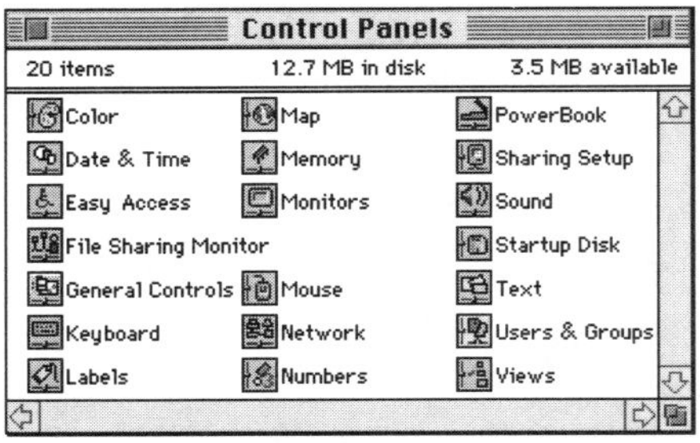

Figure 8-1: An open Control Panels folder.

programs and desk accessories. To use a control panel that's already open, you can switch to the Finder (by choosing it from the Application menu or by clicking the desktop) and find the control panel's window.

Control panels may contain software that extends System 7 during startup, such as the System extensions in the Extensions folder. These control panels won't work unless they're located in the Control Panels folder, the Extensions folder, or the System Folder. During startup, the system looks in those places for system software extensions. To tell whether a control panel extends the system software, watch to see whether its icon appears at the bottom of the screen during startup. A few control panels that extend system software don't display their icons during startup (notably the standard Close View, Easy Access, and in some cases Memory), but most do.

Some old control panels (also called *cdevs*) work properly only if you put them in the System Folder itself, not in the Control Panels folder. You should make an alias of each control panel that you put in the System Folder and then put the alias in the Control Panels folder so that you can open that control panel from the Control Panels window (which you see upon choosing Control Panels from the Apple menu). For details about making and using aliases, see Chapter 10.

The following sections describe the control panels that come with various versions of System 7.

# Apple Menu Options

System 7.5's Apple Menu Options control panel, shown in Figure 8-2, can create submenus in the Apple menu. This control panel also can create folders of recently used documents, applications, and servers. Turning on the Submenus option creates a hierarchy of submenus in the Apple menu. After turning on the Submenus option, you see submenus whenever you highlight a folder listed in the Apple menu. A submenu lists the contents of the highlighted folder. Highlighting a folder listed in a submenu displays another submenu, up to five levels deep.

Turning on the Recent Items option creates folders in the Apple menu for tracking the documents, applications, and servers that you most recently used. You can set

Apple Menu Options
Submenus
On
Off
Recent Items
Remember recently used items
Documents: 10
Applications: 5
Servers: 10

**Figure 8-2: The Apple Menu Options control panel.**

the number of documents, applications, and servers that you want to track. The control panel tracks recent items by creating aliases of those items and placing the aliases in the Recent Applications folder, Recent Documents folder, or Recent Servers folder (where appropriate) in the Apple menu. If you wish to suppress tracking of one type of item, set the number to be remembered to zero and discard the appropriate recent items folder if it exists.

# ATM GX

The Adobe Type Manager GX (ATM GX) control panel controls the smooth scaling of PostScript Type 1 fonts on-screen and on non-PostScript printers, as shown in Figure 8-3. ATM GX is installed when QuickDraw GX is installed (together with System 7.5) on your Mac. It also works without QuickDraw GX, and you can install it separately by using the QuickDraw GX installer's Custom Install option.

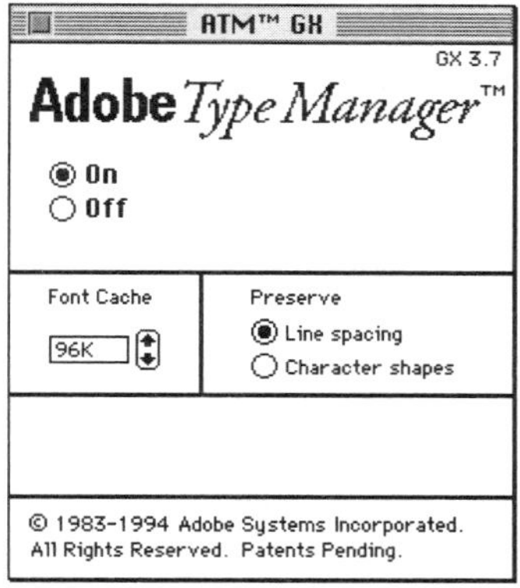


**Figure 8-3: The ATM GX control panel.**

The Font Cache option affects performance. If applications seem to scroll more slowly with ATM GX turned on, try increasing the Font Cache size.

The Preserve option determines whether ATM GX preserves line spacing or character shapes when it scales text. Preserving line spacing keeps line breaks and page breaks from changing with and without ATM, but this setting may clip the bottoms of some letters and vertically compress some accented capital letters. Preserving character shapes reduces the clipping but may change line breaks. The clipping occurs only on-screen and on output devices that don't use PostScript. No clipping occurs on a PostScript printer.

## AutoRemounter

Use the AutoRemounter control panel to determine whether — and when — a PowerBook automatically reconnects to shared disks and folders, as shown in Figure 8-4.

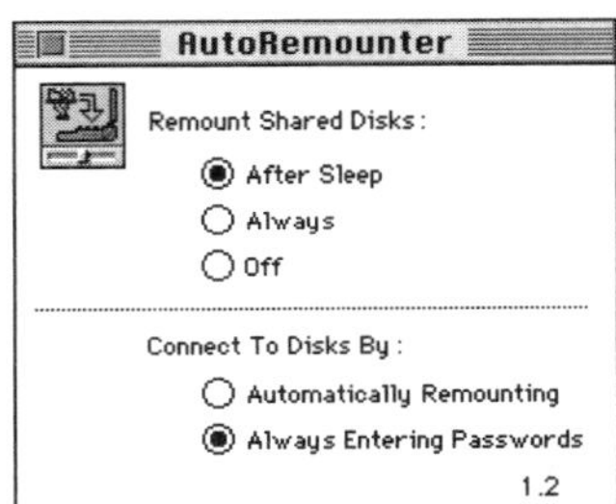


**Figure 8-4: The AutoRemounter control panel.**

Choose the After Sleep option to have the PowerBook reconnect upon waking up. Choose the Always option to have the PowerBook reconnect after sleep and upon restart. Choose the Off option if you don't want the PowerBook to reconnect automatically. If you want the PowerBook to insist that each shared item's password (if any) be entered before reconnecting to the item, choose the Always Entering Passwords option. If you want the PowerBook to reconnect without asking for passwords, choose the Automatically Remounting option.

## Brightness

On some Macintosh models, you adjust the brightness of your monitor by dragging the slide control in the Brightness control panel, as shown in Figure 8-5. If a message advises that you can't use the Brightness control panel when you try to open it, use the brightness knob on the monitor instead.

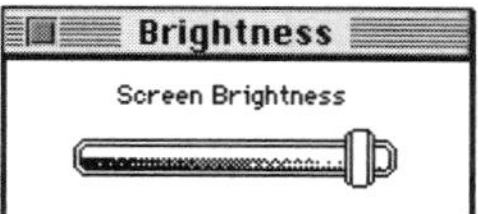


Figure 8-5: The Brightness control panel.

## CloseView

You can use the CloseView control panel to magnify your screen 2 to 16 times and to invert the displayed colors, as shown in Figure 8-6. CloseView is not installed automatically with the rest of the control panels; you must drag it manually from the Apple Extras folder on your startup disk (or the installation disk) to your Control Panels folder.

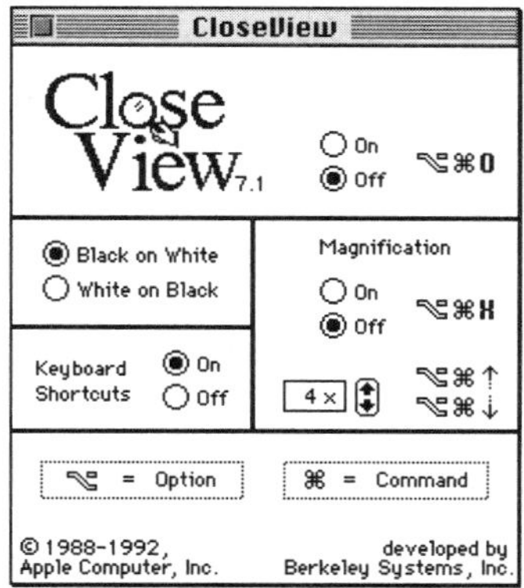


Figure 8-6: The CloseView control panel.

## Color

The Color control panel has settings for text-highlighting color and window-shading color, as shown in Figure 8-7. You choose a tint for window borders from the Window Color pop-up menu (for more information, see "Choosing a window color" in Chapter 4). You choose a color for text highlighting from the Highlight Color pop-up menu.

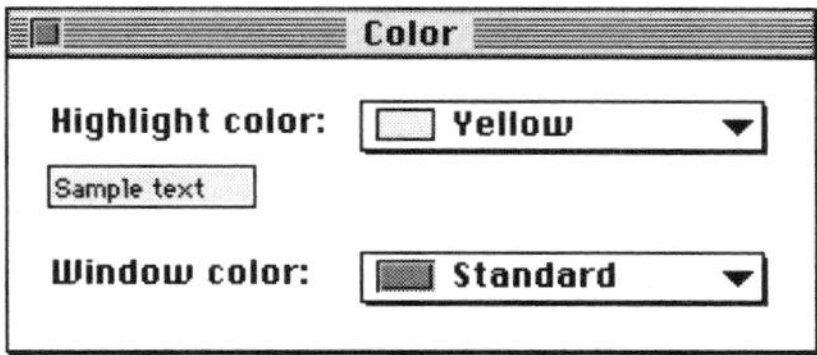


Figure 8-7: The Color control panel.

If you choose Other Color for the highlight color, the standard color-picker dialog box appears, as shown in Figure 8-8.

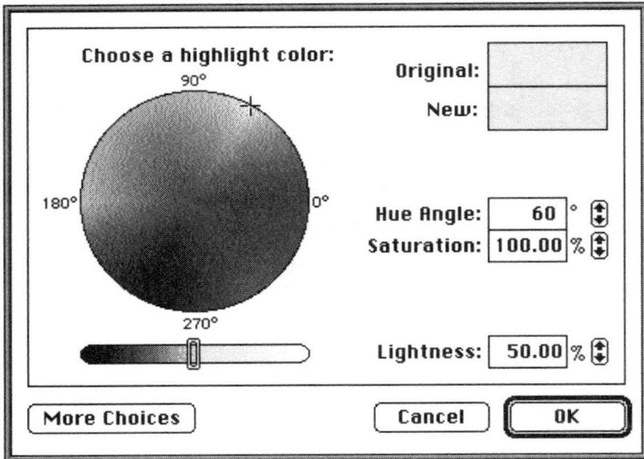


**Figure 8-8: System 7.5's standard color-picker dialog box.**

In this dialog box, you can choose another color by clicking a color wheel and adjusting the lightness with the slider. You also can specify a color by typing values for hue angle, saturation, and lightness. Hue angle is measured in degrees from 0 to 360, counterclockwise with 0 at the three-o'clock position. Saturation measures the amount of color, from 0 (gray) to 100 (pure color). Lightness varies from 0 to 100 and measures how close the color is to black (0) or white (100).

To pick a color with a different type of color picker, click the More Choices button in the picker dialog box. When you do, the available pickers are listed at the left of the dialog box. The picker shown in Figure 8-8 is the Apple HSL picker, a standard picker included with System 7.5. The Apple RGB picker is another standard picker. With the RGB picker, you move sliders or type numbers to specify the amount of red, green, and blue you want in the color.

Prior to System 7.5, the color-picker dialog box looks a bit different. The lightness setting is called brightness and is set with a scroll bar in the color-picker window. The hue, saturation, and brightness settings are numbers between 0 and 65535. You can also specify the amount of red, green, and blue instead of hue, saturation, and brightness.

## ColorSync System Profile

On a Mac with ColorSync, Apple's color-matching software, you use the ColorSync System Profile control panel to specify a color profile for your display screen, as shown in Figure 8-9. The profile specifies the range of colors that a

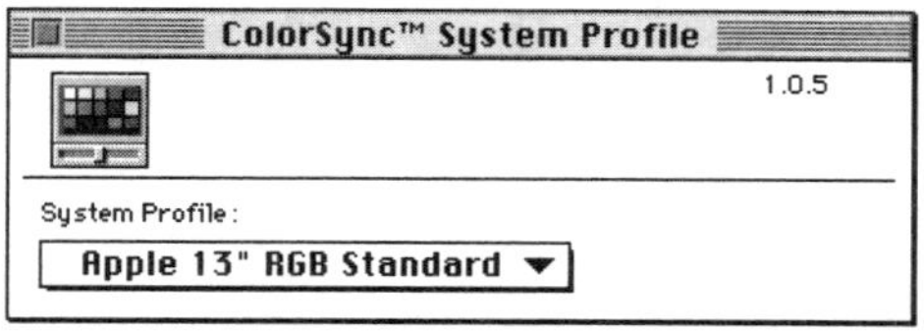

**Figure 8-9: The ColorSync System Profile control panel.**

particular type of monitor can display. Other types of input and output devices, such as scanners and printers, have unique color profiles, and the ColorSync software uses the profiles to shift colors so that they look the same on all compatible devices.

The ColorSync software, including the ColorSync System Profile control panel and profiles for several Apple monitors, is installed when you install Mac OS 7.6 or QuickDraw GX and System 7.5 through 7.5.5. Profiles for other devices come with the devices.

# Control Strip

The modular Control Strip control panel provides quick access to commonly adjusted features that are unique to PowerBooks, as shown in Figure 8-10. Clicking a button in the Control Strip pops up a menu of related settings. Each button in the Control Strip corresponds to a module in the Control Strip Modules folder (inside the System Folder). The modules initially appear in the Control Strip in alphabetical order, from left to right.

**Figure 8-10: The Control Strip control panel.**

The Control Strip comes with the following modules:

- **AppleTalk Switch** shows whether AppleTalk is active (network wires on Mac icon) or inactive (no network wires). You also can use this module to activate and deactivate AppleTalk. (Deactivating AppleTalk conserves battery power.)
- **Battery Monitor** shows the battery level and indicates whether the power adapter is plugged in. You can use this module to hide and show the battery-level indicator.
- **File Sharing** shows the status of file sharing and the identity of connected users (if any). You also can use this module to open the Sharing Setup control panel and to turn file sharing on and off. An icon on the File Sharing module's button indicates whether file sharing is turned on and people are connected (two faces);

file sharing is turned on and no one is connected (a black-tabbed-folder icon with network wires); file sharing is off (a white-tabbed-folder icon with no network wires); or file sharing is starting up (a folder icon with a blinking tab and blinking network wires).

- **HD Spin Down** shows whether the internal hard drive is spinning. You can use this module to spin down and spin up the hard drive.
- **Power Settings** allows you to change the battery-conservation setting or open the PowerBook control panel.
- **Sleep Now** allows you to put the PowerBook to sleep.
- **Sound Volume** allows you to adjust the sound level.
- **Video Mirroring** enables you to set an external monitor to mirror the built-in monitor (available only on PowerBooks with built-in video ports).

The Control Strip floats above all application windows. You can collapse and expand the strip by clicking or dragging the tab at the end nearest the center of the screen. To collapse the strip to its smallest size, click the box at the opposite end. You can move the strip by pressing the Option key and dragging the tab, but the strip must touch the left or right edge of the screen.

# Date & Time

You use the Date & Time control panel, included with System 7 versions 7.1 and later, to set the current date and the current time (like the General Controls control panel, described later in this chapter), as shown in Figure 8-11. Through the Date Formats and Time Formats buttons, this control panel also enables you to set how the date and time are displayed to suit your preference or the language that you're using.

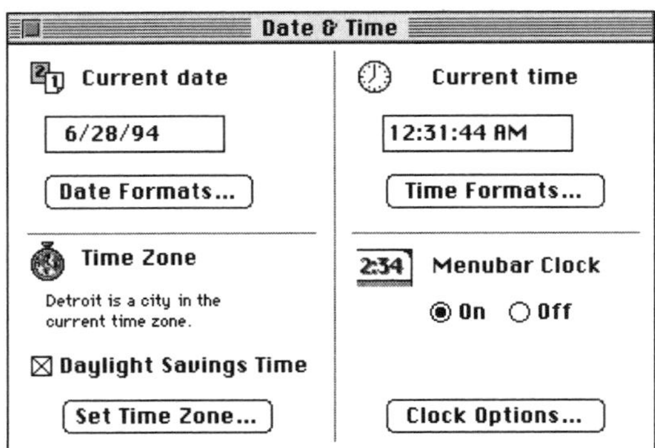


Figure 8-11: System 7.5's Date & Time control panel.

In the Time Zone section of the control panel (not present in System 7.0 and 7.0.1), you can see and set the time zone in which you are using your Mac. You also can adjust the Mac's clock for Daylight Savings Time. Clicking the Set Time Zone button brings up a list of city names; select one in your time zone. (You can find out what time it is in a different zone by selecting a city in that time zone.)

Changing the current time zone in the Date & Time control panel also changes the Mac's location as set in the Map control panel (described later in this chapter). Likewise, setting a new location in the Map control panel may change the time zone reported in the Date & Time control panel. Checking the Daylight Savings Time checkbox sets the Mac's clock ahead one hour; unchecking this checkbox sets the Mac's clock back one hour, returning it to standard time. The first time you set this option, you may have to adjust the hour displayed at the top of the control panel.

In the Menu-bar Clock section (present only in System 7.5 and later), you can turn on and off an optional digital clock next to the Help menu. Clicking the Clock Options button in this section brings up a dialog box in which you can set the display format of the clock and set the clock to chime on the hour, half-hour, and quarter-hour. On a battery-powered Mac, you also can turn on a battery-level indicator, which appears next to the clock.

Clicking the clock in the menu bar shows the date, and clicking again shows the time. Option-clicking hides the clock, or shows the clock if it is hidden. Control-clicking the battery indicator (if present) puts the computer to sleep.

# Desktop Pattern

The Desktop Pattern application sets the desktop pattern in System 7.5, as shown in Figure 8-12. Selecting a desktop pattern and editing patterns are covered in the "Desktop patterns with System 7.5" section of Chapter 4.

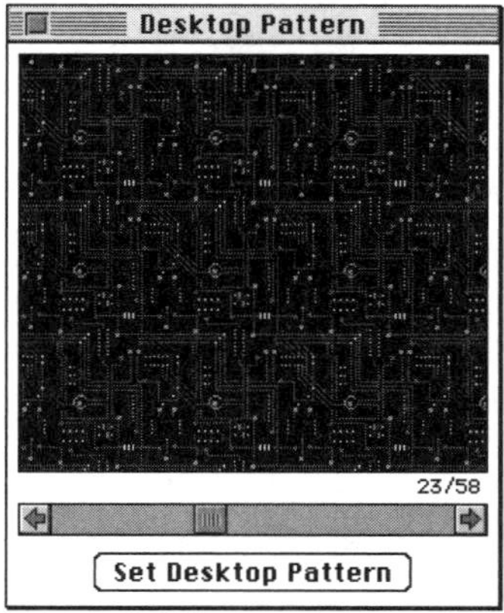


**Figure 8-12: System 7.5's Desktop Pattern utility.**

Notice that although Desktop Pattern appears in the Control Panels folder, it actually is an application program. If you leave Desktop Pattern open, you can switch to it by choosing it from the Application menu.

## Easy Access

The Easy Access control panel sets up three alternative methods of using the keyboard and mouse, as shown in Figure 8-13: Mouse Keys, Slow Keys, and Sticky Keys. In System 7, Easy Access whistles when you turn any of these features on or off. You can silence the whistle by turning off the audio-feedback option at the top of the Easy Access control panel. To work, Easy Access must be in the Control Panels folder at startup time.

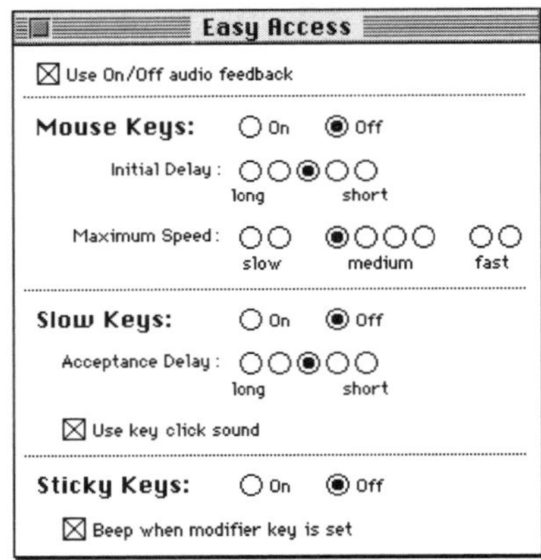


**Figure 8-13: The Easy Access control panel.**

Mouse Keys enables you to click, drag, and move the pointer with the keypad instead of the mouse. Mouse Keys is very handy for moving graphic objects precisely. You can turn on Mouse Keys by pressing ⌘-Shift-Clear instead of using the Easy Access control panel. You also can turn it off by pressing Clear. When Mouse Keys is on, the 5 key in the keypad acts like a mouse button. Press once to click; press twice to double-click; or hold it down. The eight keys around 5 move the pointer left, right, up, down, and diagonally. Pressing 0 locks the mouse button down until you press the period key in the keypad.

Slow Keys makes the Macintosh wait before it accepts a keystroke, thereby filtering out accidental keystrokes. You can turn Slow Keys on or off from the keyboard by holding down the Return key for about 10 seconds. No icon indicates whether Slow Keys is on or off, but about five seconds after you begin holding down the Return key, the Mac makes three short, quiet beeps; about four seconds after that, the Mac whistles to confirm that Slow Keys is being turned on or off. You don't hear these sounds if you use the Easy Access control panel, however, and some applications (such as Microsoft Word) may mute the sounds.

QUICK TIPS

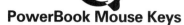

### PowerBook Mouse Keys

You can't use Mouse Keys to point and click on a PowerBook, because PowerBooks have no numeric keypad. The System extension Mouse Keys modifies the Easy Access control panel to recognize different keys instead of the numeric keypad. It substitutes the *K* key and the keys next to it for the 5 key and the keys next to it on the keypad. The Escape key substitutes for the Clear key. Thus, after installing the Mouse Keys extension, you turn on Mouse Keys by pressing ⌘-Shift-Escape, and you turn it off by pressing Escape.

When Mouse Keys is on, the *K* acts like a trackball or trackpad button. Press once to click; press twice to double-click; or hold it down. The eight keys around *K* move the pointer left, right, up, down, and diagonally. Pressing the spacebar locks the mouse button down until you press Enter.

Be careful not to press ⌘-Option-Escape, which, instead of activating Mouse Keys, brings up a dialog box that asks whether you want to force the active program to quit.

Sticky Keys enables you to type combination keystrokes such as ⌘-Shift-3 (which puts a snapshot of your screen in a picture document that most graphics programs can open) one key at a time. Sticky Keys also enables you to lock down any modifier key by pressing it two times in a row. You can turn on Sticky Keys by pressing Shift five times in succession. When Sticky Keys is on, an icon at the right end of the menu bar shows its status (see Figure 8-14). You can turn Sticky Keys off by pressing Shift five times again or by pressing any two modifier keys simultaneously.

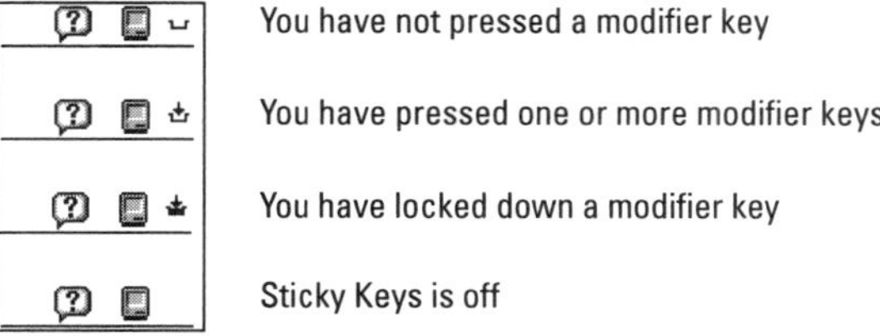
You have not pressed a modifier key
You have pressed one or more modifier keys
You have locked down a modifier key
Sticky Keys is off

**Figure 8-14: Sticky Keys' status.**

# Extensions Manager

The Extensions Manger control panel can individually disable System extensions, control panels that contain System extensions, and Chooser extensions. Disabled startup items don't use RAM and can't conflict with other startup items. A list of the startup items that are present in your System Folder appears in the Extensions Manager window, as shown in Figure 8-15.

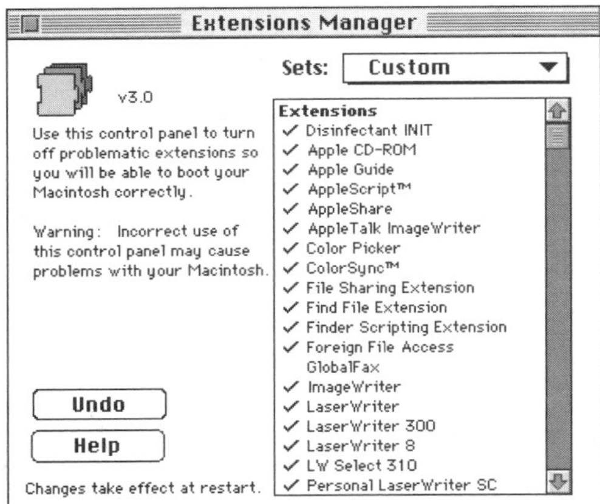


**Figure 8-15: System 7.5's Extensions Manager control panel.**

First in the list are items in the Extensions folder; second are items in the Control Panels folder; and third are items stored loose in the System Folder. A check mark next to an item means that the item is enabled. Items without check marks are disabled and will not be loaded the next time the Mac starts. To change the state of an item — enabled or disabled — you click it. The Undo button in the Extensions Manager window reverts all items to the states they were in when you opened the control panel.

You can save the current state of all items as a set by choosing Save Set from the Sets pop-up menu. After you save a set, it appears in the Sets pop-up menu. Choosing a set from the pop-up menu sets the state of all items to match their state when the set was saved. Choosing All On from the pop-up enables all items, and choosing All Off disables all items. Choosing System 7.5 Only enables only the items that are installed as part of System 7.5.

Extensions Manager puts disabled System extensions in a folder named Extensions (disabled). Disabled control panels are stored in a folder named Control Panels (disabled). Disabled items from the System Folder go into a folder named System Extensions (disabled).

You can bring up the Extensions Manager control panel at the beginning of the startup process by holding down the spacebar. Holding down the shift key at the beginning of the startup process temporarily disables all extensions, without affecting settings in the Extensions Manager control panel.

System 7.5 comes with Extensions Manager 3. Earlier versions of Extensions Manager, which actually have more capabilities, are available as shareware from user groups and on-line information services (as described in Chapter 19).

# File Sharing Monitor

File Sharing Monitor monitors file-sharing activity (see Figure 8-16). This control panel lists the disks and folders that you have made available for others to share, identifies who is connected to your Macintosh, and allows you to disconnect other users individually. File Sharing Monitor also shows how much of your computer's processing time currently is occupied by handling file sharing. (For more information, see "Monitoring File-Sharing Activity" in Chapter 9.)

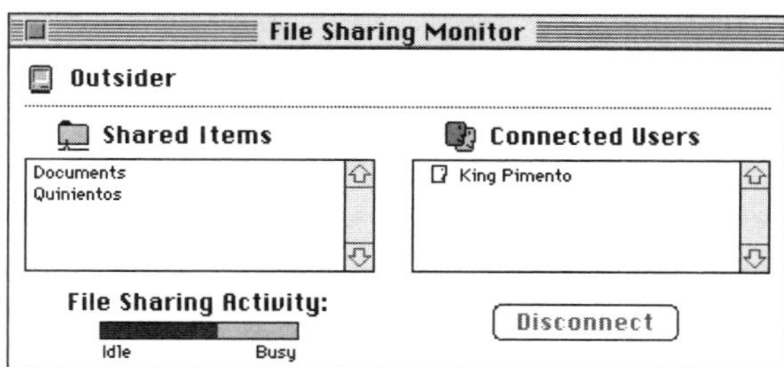


**Figure 8-16: The File Sharing Monitor control panel.**

# General Controls

The General Controls control panel sets a number of system options, as shown in Figures 8-17 and 8-18. The options are different in System 7.5 than in earlier versions of System 7. All versions of General Controls have settings for insertion-point blinking and menu blinking.

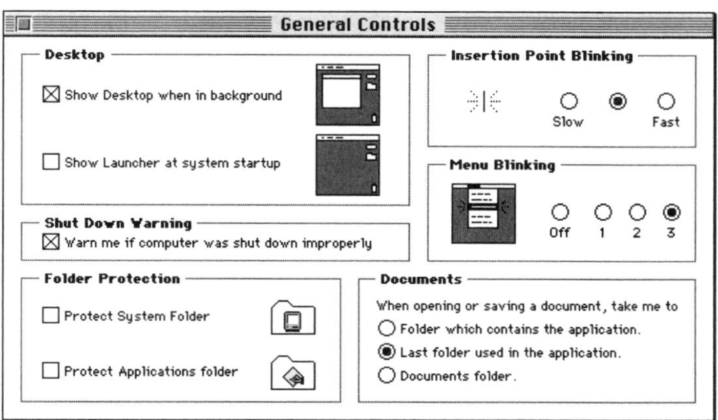


**Figure 8-17: The General Controls control panel in System 7.5.**

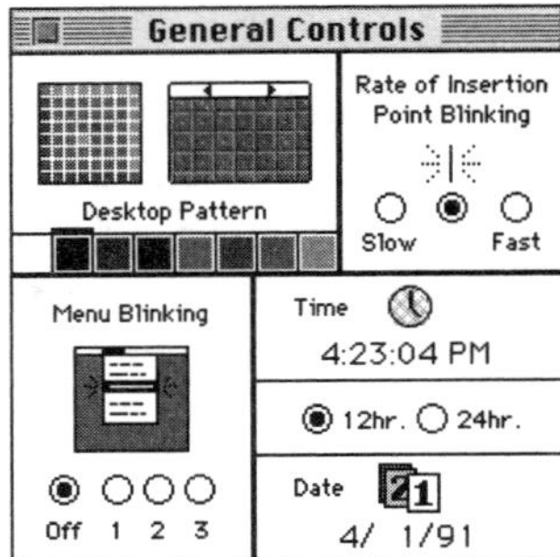


**Figure 8-18: The General Controls control panel before System 7.5.**

In System 7.5, General Controls includes settings for showing or hiding the Finder's desktop when the Finder is not the active application; opening the Launcher control panel during startup (by placing an alias of the Launcher in the Startup Items folder); warning during startup if the computer crashed or was not shut down properly; and individually protecting the System Folder and the Applications folder on the startup disk (preventing items in them from being renamed or removed).

Another setting in System 7.5's General Controls control panel determines which folder you see first in a Save or Open dialog box. One option is the folder that contains the application from which you chose the Save or Open command. A second option is the most recent folder used in the application. The third option is the Documents folder on the startup disk.

In versions of System 7 before 7.5, General Controls includes settings for the desktop pattern, the time, and the date. Selecting a pattern and making a custom pattern are covered in the "Desktop" section of Chapter 4. Menu blinking is covered in "Menus" in Chapter 4.

# Keyboard

The Keyboard control panel sets the key repeat rate and the delay time until key repeating begins, as shown in Figure 8-19. Using the settings is described in the section "Keyboard and Mouse Adjustments" in Chapter 4. If your system has multiple keyboard layouts installed, you can use the Keyboard control panel to select a different layout.

# Labels

The Labels control panel sets the names and colors (on a color or grayscale monitor) of items in the Finder's Labels menu, as shown in Figure 8-20. For more information, see "Changing label names and colors" in Chapter 6.

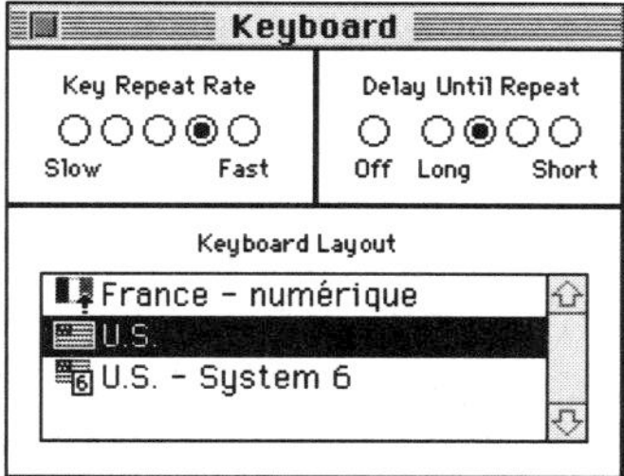


Figure 8-19: The Keyboard control panel.

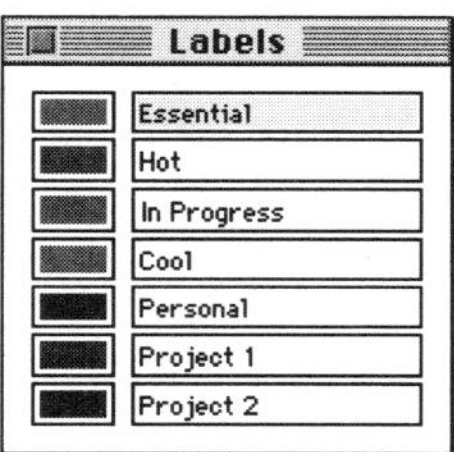


Figure 8-20: The Labels control panel.

# Launcher

The Launcher control panel (see Figure 8-21) displays a window that contains large buttons for opening programs, documents, and folders. You open any item in the Launcher window by clicking its button. The Launcher comes with all Macintosh Performa computers and with System 7.5 and later. With System 7.5.1 and later the Launcher has additional features that are described in Chapter 21.

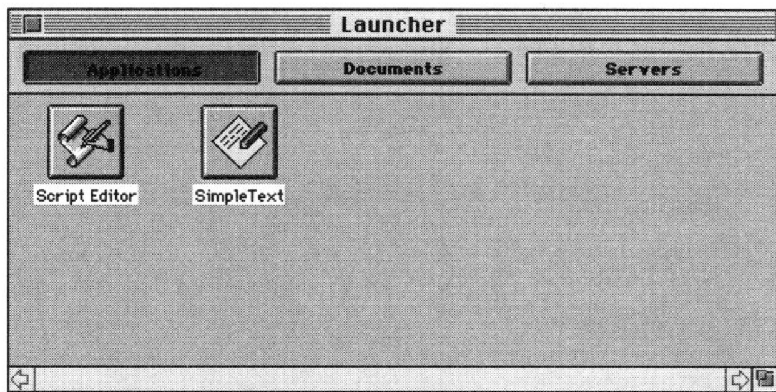


Figure 8-21: The Launcher control panel.

Items in the Launcher window are aliases in the Launcher Items folder inside the System Folder. You can categorize items in the Launcher by placing their aliases in specially named folders within the Launcher Items folder. The name of a category folder must begin with a bullet (press Option-8). The names of up to eight category folders appear as button names in a panel at the top of the Launcher window, and clicking a category button displays the items in the corresponding category folder. Here is a shortcut for opening a category folder: press Option and click the folder's button in the Launcher window. To open the Launcher Items folder itself, Option-click the Applications button in the Launcher window.

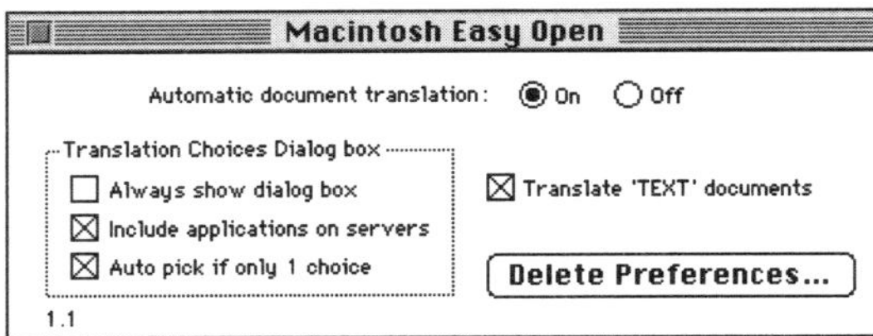


**Figure 8-22: The Macintosh Easy Open control panel.**

# Macintosh Easy Open

The Macintosh Easy Open control panel (see Figure 8-22) sets options that affect the opening of documents created by applications that you do not have.

When you try to open a document created by a program that you don't have, Easy Open displays a dialog box listing programs that may be able to open the document. Easy Open keeps track of the alternative program that you most recently used to open each type of document. If you want Easy Open to display the dialog box only the first time that you open a particular type of document, turn off the "Always show dialog box" option in the control panel. Turn on this option if you want Easy Open to display the list of alternative programs every time you open a document for which you don't have the creator program. Easy Open does not waste your time with the list of alternative programs if there is only one alternative and the "Auto pick if only 1 choice" option is turned on.

If you want the list of alternative programs to include programs from file servers, which operate more slowly than programs on your local disks, turn on the option "Include applications on file servers."

Turning on the "Translate 'TEXT' documents" option tells Easy Open to look at the contents of the text documents you open to see whether those contents can be translated to some type of formatted document. Turning off this option speeds the opening of plain-text documents.

Macintosh Easy Open comes with System 7.5 and later and is available separately for earlier versions of System 7. For more information on opening documents with Easy Open active, see "Macintosh Easy Open" in Chapter 5.

# MacTCP

The MacTCP control panel, shown in Figure 8-23, enables you to connect your Mac to UNIX networks and the Internet. Clicking the More button brings up a large dialog box full of network settings. Configuring this dialog box requires specific information about your network connection, and is best done with the help of the person who administers your UNIX network or Internet connection.

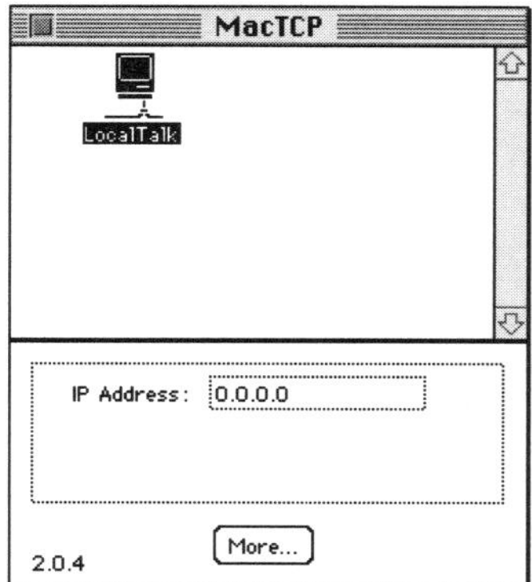


**Figure 8-23: The MacTCP control panel.**

# Map

The Map control panel sets the world location (latitude and longitude) and the time zone of your Macintosh, as shown in Figure 8-24. This control panel also can compute the time difference and distance between any two places. But unless you have a portable Mac and like to keep track of the time difference between where you are and where your home base is, this control panel mainly is a diversion.

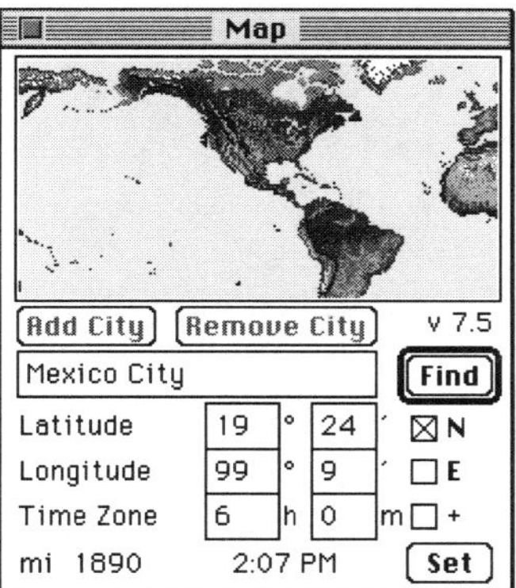


**Figure 8-24: The Map control panel.**

Tiny flashing dots on the map mark known places; the preset locations include an idiosyncratic mix of major cities and obscure locations, among them the Middle of Nowhere. Click a dot or drag across one to see its name. You can type a place name in the space provided and click the Find button, or go through the list of known places alphabetically by pressing Option while clicking Find. The latitude, longitude, and time zone entries pertain to the most recently selected location, which Map marks with a flashing star. The map scrolls if you drag beyond its boundaries.

To add a new place, specify its latitude and longitude by clicking, by dragging, or by typing the coordinates in the spaces provided. Then type the place name and click the Add City button. After adding a new place, verify the estimated time zone and correct it, if necessary.

Map marks the location of your Macintosh with a flashing dark cross. Set this element by finding or adding the proper location and then clicking the Set button, or by choosing a new location for your time zone in the Date & Time control panel (described earlier in this chapter) and then closing and reopening Map. Map automatically adjusts the time and date of your system's clock according to the difference between the old and new locations. Your Macintosh stores its location in battery-powered memory, along with the time of day and other semipermanent settings.

The distance or compass direction from your Macintosh to the place marked with the flashing star appears at the bottom of the control panel, along with the time at the distant place. Change from distance in miles to distance in kilometers or direction in degrees by clicking the unit of measurement in the lower-left corner of the control panel. To see the time difference between that place and your Macintosh, click the words *Time Differ* in the control panel. (If you don't see the words Time Differ, first click the words Time Zone.)

You can enlarge the map by pressing Option while opening the Map control panel. To magnify more, press Shift-Option while opening (choose the Open command from the File menu).

### Color Map

The Map control panel normally displays a black-and-white map of the world, but you can replace it with a color map from the standard System 7 Scrapbook. Simply scroll in the Scrapbook to the color world map, copy it, open the Map control panel, and paste. If you can't find a color map in your Scrapbook, you don't have the standard System 7 Scrapbook file. To get it, temporarily move the Scrapbook file from your System Folder to the desktop. Next, copy the Scrapbook file from the Tidbits installation disk to your System Folder. Copy the color map as described earlier. Finally, select the Scrapbook file on the desktop, choose Put Away from the Finder's File menu, and click OK when the Finder asks whether it's OK to replace the Scrapbook file in the System Folder with the one that you're moving (putting away) from the desktop.

### What's Your Time?

If you deal with people in multiple time zones, you can use the Map control panel to keep track of local times for various people and offices without having to remember the names of their cities. Here's what you do:

1. Open the Map control panel.
2. Have Map locate the person's city by typing the name of the city and clicking the Find button.
3. Type the person's name over the city name, and click the Add City button.

Now you need only type a person's name in Map and click the Find button to determine whether it is a polite time to call.

If you want Map to remember a person whose city isn't on the map, you can substitute a known city in the same time zone or add the unknown city.

Whenever you add a new place or person to Map, verify the time zone and correct it, if necessary. Map estimates the time zone of a new place based on its latitude and longitude, but time-zone boundaries have many irregularities. Also, Map does not know about Daylight Savings Time. If you are on Daylight Savings Time and someone else is not (or vice versa), Map will be off by one hour in computing the other person's local time.

# Memory

The Memory control panel (see Figure 8-25) sets the size of the disk cache, turns virtual memory and 32-Bit Addressing on and off, and also makes it possible to set aside part of memory as a very speedy RAM disk. Some settings are not available on certain Mac models. For detailed information about the settings, see the "Memory Control" section of Chapter 13.

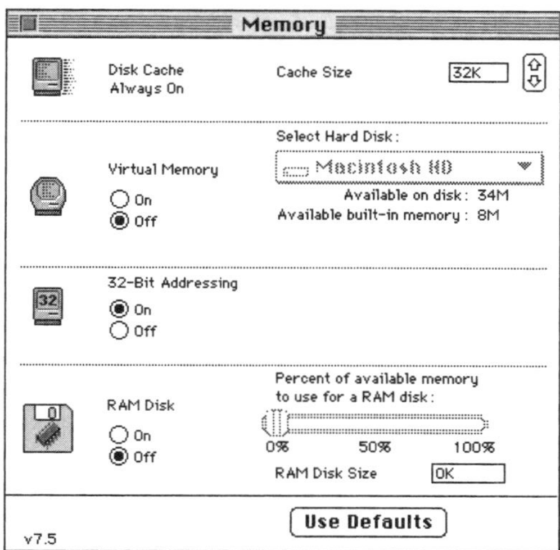


**Figure 8-25: The Memory control panel.**

## Monitors

The Monitors control panel sets the number of colors or grays of one or more monitors, as shown in Figure 8-26. Any changes that you make in these settings take effect immediately.

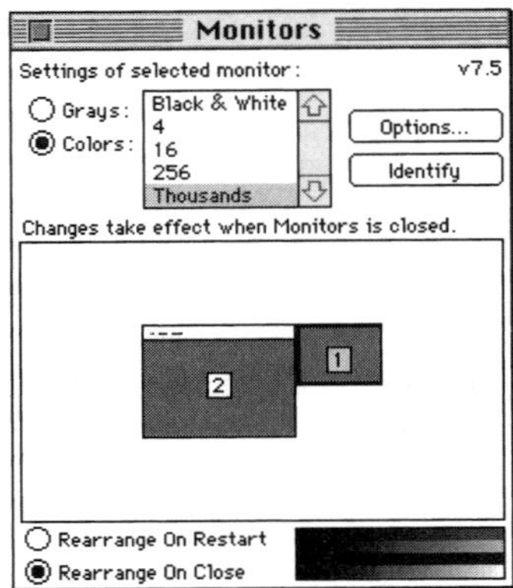


**Figure 8-26: The Monitors control panel in System 7.5.**

If your Macintosh has multiple monitors, you can drag little images of those monitors around the Monitors control panel to determine their relative positions. You can set which monitor has the menu bar by dragging the little menu bar to the appropriate little monitor in the control panel. You also can designate which monitor displays startup messages and icons. Press the Option key to display a tiny Macintosh icon; then drag this icon to the monitor that you want to use during startup.

In System 7.5, you decide when the new position and menu-bar arrangements take effect by choosing the "Rearrange On Restart" option or the "Rearrange On Close" option in the Monitors control panel. When "Rearrange On Close" is selected, you can press the Option key to have changes take effect immediately. In earlier versions of System 7, which do not have these options, changes in monitor positions take effect when you close the Monitors control panel, and settings that affect the menu bar and startup monitor take place the next time you restart your Macintosh.

On some Mac models, you also can use the Monitors control panel to limit the number of colors or grays available with built-in video. The higher the limit, the more memory the built-in video uses. You set the limit in the Monitors Options panel, shown in Figure 8-27. To see it, press Option while clicking the Options button in the Monitors control panel. With a 640-by-480 color monitor, 256 colors require 320K, 16 colors require 160K, four colors require 96K, and black-and-white requires 74K.

## Gamma Options

If you press the Option key while clicking the Options button in the Monitors control panel, you see a dialog box containing gamma options, similar to the one shown in the following figure.

Gamma options provide alternative color balancing for video displays. Color balancing is necessary because the intensity of color on a video display does not correspond uniformly to the intensity of the electron beam that traces the video picture on the phosphor coating inside the video display tube. The computer's video circuitry compensates to provide the most accurate color possible. This compensation commonly is called *gamma correction.*

The built-in video circuitry of color Macs and of Apple video cards provides gamma correction for the phosphor composition of Apple's original 13-inch RGB display, the de facto standard for Mac monitors. In addition, the built-in video on some Macs provides alternative gamma-correction methods for users who prefer nonstandard color correction, perhaps to simulate different degrees of paper whiteness. You select one of the available gamma-correction methods in the Options dialog box of the Monitors control panel. Changing the gamma correction has no effect on video performance, only on color balance.

If a particular brand or model of monitor has a phosphor composition different from the standard, the monitor maker can provide a gamma-correction method specifically for it. The monitor maker also can provide alternative gamma-correction methods for users who prefer nonstandard color correction. The monitor maker supplies its gamma-correction methods in a monitors extension or a special control panel that goes into your Control Panels folder, and the operating system automatically installs the alternative gamma-correction methods as options in the Monitors control panel.

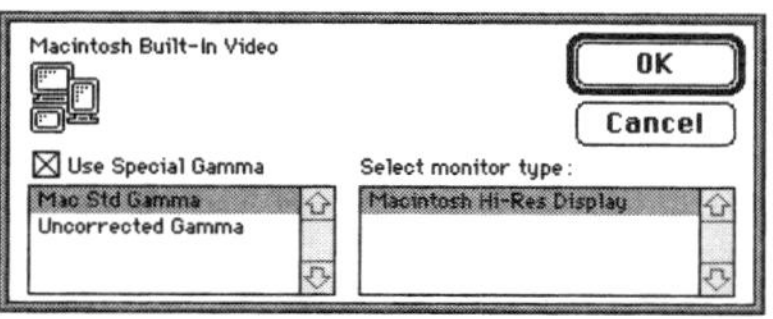


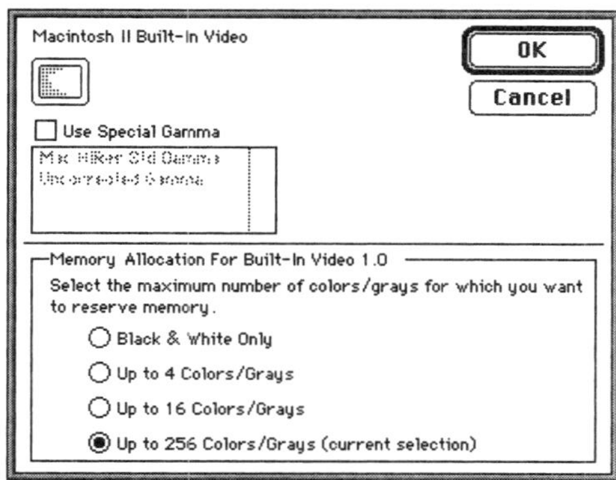


**Figure 8-27: The Monitors Options panel.**

## Mouse

The Mouse control panel, shown in Figure 8-28, sets the mouse-to-pointer (or trackball-to-pointer) tracking speed and the double-click interval. The double-click interval also determines how long you have to wait after selecting an icon name before it is ready for editing (see "Setting mouse sensitivity" and "Renaming Icons" in Chapter 4).

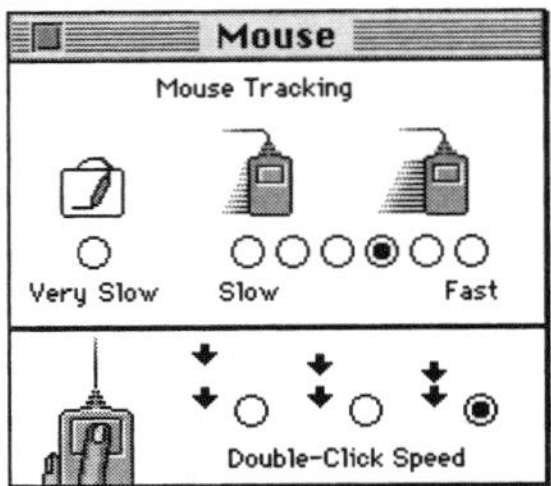


**Figure 8-28: The Mouse control panel.**

## Network

The Network control panel (see Figure 8-29) determines which network connection to use if more than one is available to your Macintosh. For details, see "Selecting Your Network" in Chapter 9.

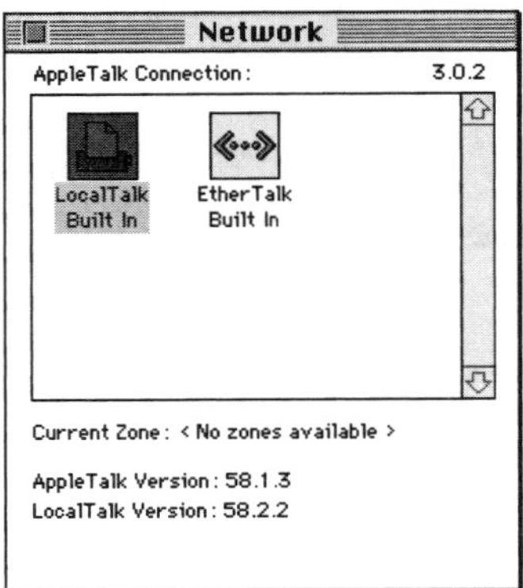


**Figure 8-29: The Network control panel.**

## Numbers

The Numbers control panel (see Figure 8-30) sets the number format — decimal separator, thousand separators, and currency symbol — for a region of the world that you choose from a pop-up menu of the languages installed in the System file. This control panel is not included with System 7.0 or 7.0.1.

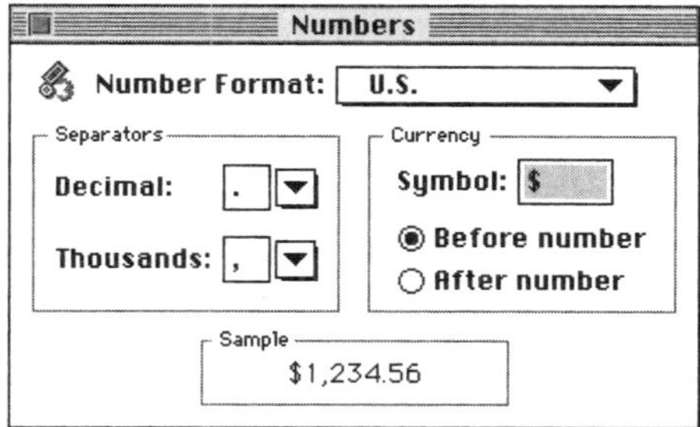


**Figure 8-30: The Numbers control panel.**

# PC Exchange

With the PC Exchange control panel installed, the Mac can access floppy disks from Windows, OS/2, or DOS computers. When you insert a disk from one of those computers into a Mac, the foreign disk's icon appears on the Finder's desktop. You can open the foreign disk and see its files and folders (which are called *subdirectories* in DOS, Windows, and OS/2). You can open folders by double-clicking them, and you can open document files if you have compatible Mac programs.

When you double-click a document file on a foreign disk, the Finder can determine which Mac program to have open the file by looking up the DOS *file-name extension* (the three characters following the period) in PC Exchange, shown in Figure 8-31. PC Exchange contains a list that correlates DOS file-name extensions with Mac programs and document types. A file whose name ends with .TXT, for example, is opened by SimpleText (or TeachText, in older versions of System 7) as a text document.

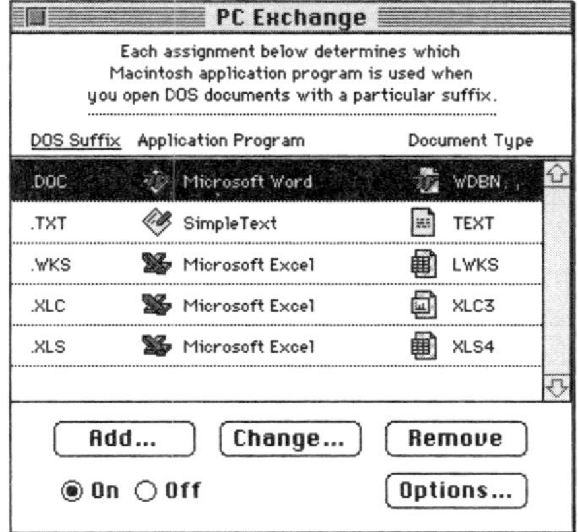


**Figure 8-31: The PC Exchange control panel.**

To change an item in the list, you click the Change button in the PC Exchange control panel. A suffix-assignment dialog box appears, as shown in Figure 8-32. In this dialog box, you can edit the suffix, select a different program from the ones on your disks, and select a document type from the ones that the selected application can open.

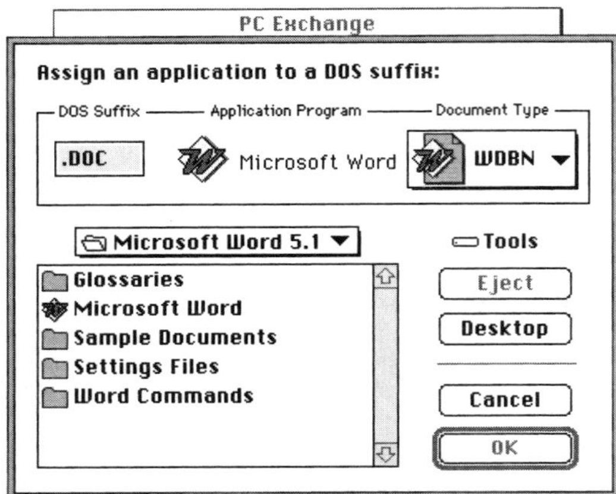


**Figure 8-32: The PC Exchange control panel's suffix-assignment dialog box.**

To add a suffix (and corresponding Mac application and document type), click the Add button in the PC Exchange control panel. This action brings up the suffix-assignment dialog box, in which you type a suffix, select a Mac program, and choose a document type.

Clicking the Remove button in the PC Exchange control panel removes the currently selected item from the list. Before clicking Remove, you can select multiple items in the list by ⌘-clicking them (to select them individually) or Shift-clicking (to select a range).

# Portable

The Portable control panel sets special features of the Macintosh Portable or PowerBook computers that use System 7.0.1. The Portable control panel shown in Figure 8-33 comes with System 7.0.1. This control panel has a slider for setting the minutes of inactivity before the internal hard disk spins down and a second slider for setting the minutes of inactivity before the system goes to sleep. Both sliders are ignored when the "Stay awake when plugged in" option is turned on and the power adapter is plugged into the computer.

When used with a PowerBook that has an internal modem, the Portable control panel includes a section for choosing between the internal modem and a device connected to the modem port. If the internal modem option is selected and the "Wake On Ring" option is turned on, the modem wakes the computer when it detects an incoming call.

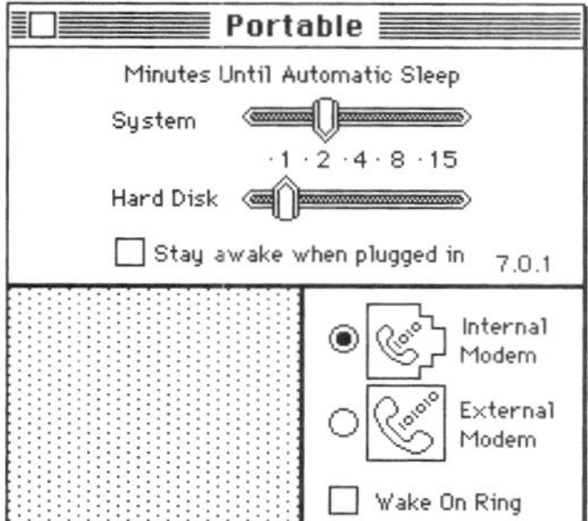


**Figure 8-33: The Portable control panel for System 7.0 and 7.0.1.**

# PowerBook (with System 7.1 and 7.1.1)

The PowerBook control panel sets special features of the Macintosh Portable or PowerBook computers that use System 7 versions 7.1 and later. Two versions of the PowerBook control panel exist. The earlier version, shown in Figure 8-34, comes with System 7.1 and 7.1.1 (System 7 Pro).

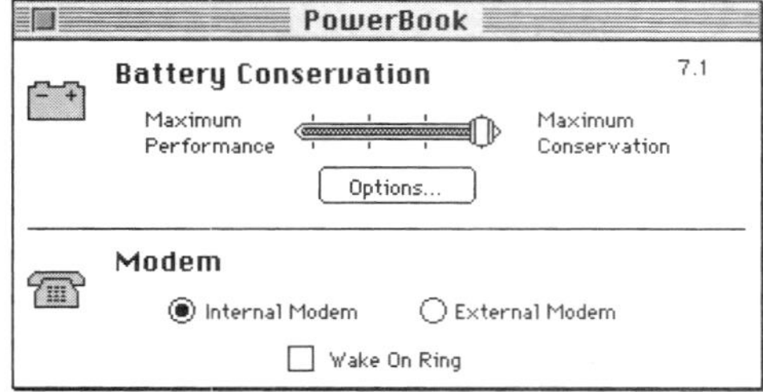


**Figure 8-34: The PowerBook control panel for System 7.1 and 7.1.1.**

Moving the single battery-conservation slider to the right conserves battery power (by reducing the time before hard-disk spindown and system sleep). Moving the slider to the left increases system performance (by allowing more idle time before the PowerBook spins down the hard disk and goes to sleep).

Clicking the Options button in the control panel brings up a dialog box that contains two additional battery-conservation options. If the "Don't sleep when plugged in" option is turned on, the computer and hard disk do not sleep while the power adapter is plugged into the computer. If the Processor Cycling option is set to allow cycling, the processor turns itself off when it is idle. "Allowing processor cycling" saves battery power but may cause some programs to work very slowly.

On a PowerBook equipped with an internal modem, the early version of the PowerBook control panel includes a section for choosing between the internal modem and a device connected to the Modem port. If the internal modem option is selected and the "Wake On Ring" option is turned on, the modem wakes the computer when it detects an incoming call.

## PowerBook (with System 7.5)

The later version of the PowerBook control panel, shown in Figure 8-35, sets battery conservation and system responsiveness for PowerBook computers that use System 7.5. When the PowerBook control panel's Easy/Custom switch is set to Easy, the control panel collapses to show only the single conservation-performance slider. When the switch is set to Custom, the control panel expands to display all its options.

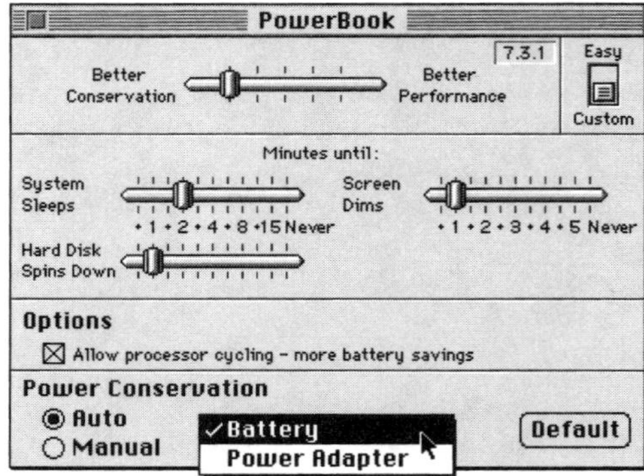


**Figure 8-35: The PowerBook control panel for System 7.5.**

Moving the conservation/performance slider to the left conserves battery power by making the computer sleep, the hard disk spin down, the screen dim, and processor cycling occur after shorter periods of inactivity. Moving the conservation/performance slider to the right increases system responsiveness by lengthening the period of inactivity before the computer sleeps, the hard disk spins down, the screen dims, and the processor cycles.

The extended control panel has three sliders for individually setting the idle time until system sleep, hard-disk spindown, and screen dimming. Also, you can turn processor cycling on or off. You can set the three sliders and the processor-cycling option differently for battery operation than for operation with the power adapter plugged into the computer. You choose the power mode from the pop-up menu in the Power Conservation section of the control panel. The computer determines whether to use the battery settings or the power-adapter settings as long as power conservation is set to Auto. When power conservation is set to Manual, the settings in the expanded section of the control panel stay in effect indefinitely.

# PowerBook Setup

The PowerBook Setup control panel, shown in Figure 8-36, configures the Modem port for a PowerBook that has an internal modem and uses System 7.5. You can set the PowerBook to use the internal modem or a device connected to the external Modem port. When the internal modem is selected, the "Wake On Ring" option determines whether the modem wakes the computer to receive an incoming call.

**Figure 8-36: The PowerBook Setup control panel.**

# PowerTalk Setup

The PowerTalk Setup control panel (see Figure 8-37) has configuration settings for PowerTalk collaboration services that come with System 7 Pro and System 7.5. Besides turning all collaboration services off or on, you can set your PowerTalk Key Chain to lock itself automatically after a period of inactivity whose duration you specify. You also can set PowerTalk to require entry of your Key Chain access code during startup. For details on the Key Chain, access code, and other PowerTalk services, see Chapter 15.

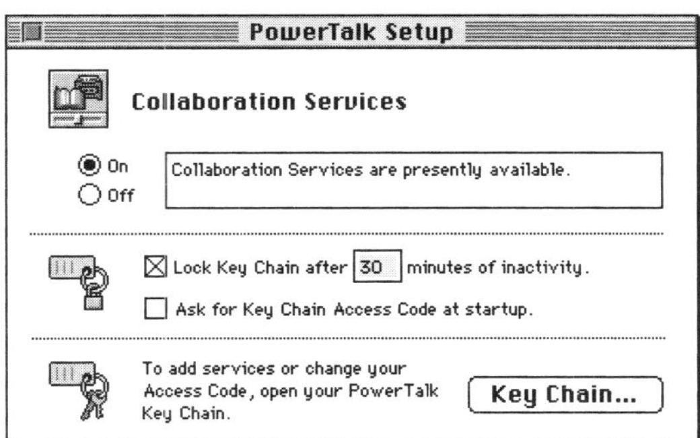


**Figure 8-37: The PowerTalk Setup control panel.**

# Sharing Setup

The Sharing Setup control panel (see Figure 8-38) names your Macintosh and its owner on its network, sets the owner's network password, and starts or stops file sharing and program linking. For complete information on these settings, see "Identifying Your Macintosh" and "Starting and Stopping File Sharing" in Chapter 9, and "Setting up program linking" in Chapter 18.

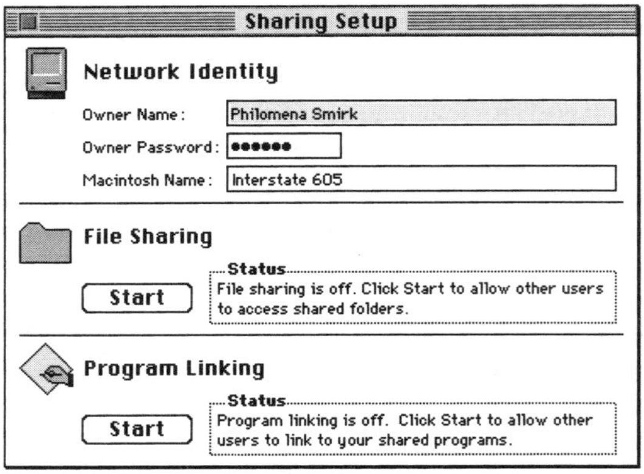

**Figure 8-38: The Sharing Setup control panel.**

# Sound

The Sound control panel configures the sound input and output options, which are not the same on all Macs. Two types of Sound control panels exist. The newer type, shown in Figure 8-39, has separate sections for different types of sound settings. You choose a section from the pop-up menu at the top of the control panel.

This type of Sound control panel is included with System 7.5, System 7 Pro, all Power Macs, and the Centris and Quadra 660AV and 840AV. This type of Sound control panel also is included with several software-update packages from Apple, including Hardware System Update versions 2.0 and 2.0.1, System Update 3, and Sound Manager 3.

In the Sound Out section of the newer Sound control panel, the Rate and Size options affect the fidelity of the Mac's sound output. Many Macs have only one setting for each of these options. On Macs that offer multiple settings, higher numbers yield higher fidelity.

The older type of Sound control panel, shown in Figure 8-40, comes with System 7.0, 7.0.1, and 7.1. This control panel has a section for setting the system alert sound and the speaker volume; it also includes controls for recording new alert sounds if your Macintosh has sound-input equipment.

In all types of Sound control panels, you can add and remove alert sounds by using the Edit menu's Cut, Copy, and Paste commands. For example, the standard System 7 Scrapbook (described earlier in this chapter) contains an extra sound that you can copy from there and paste into the Sound control panel. You also can add and remove alert sounds by dragging them in and out of the System file, as described in the "System File" section of Chapter 7.

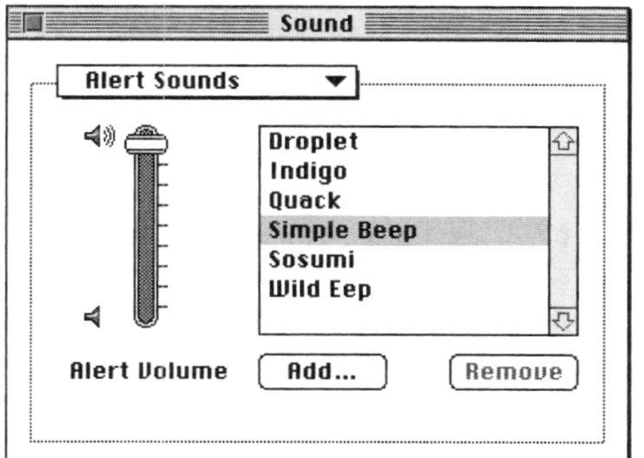


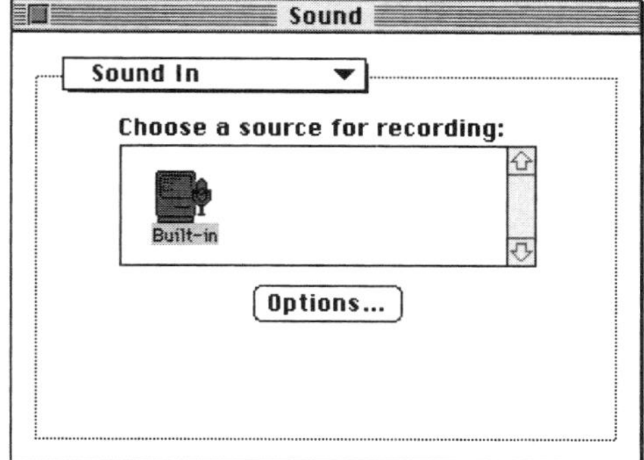


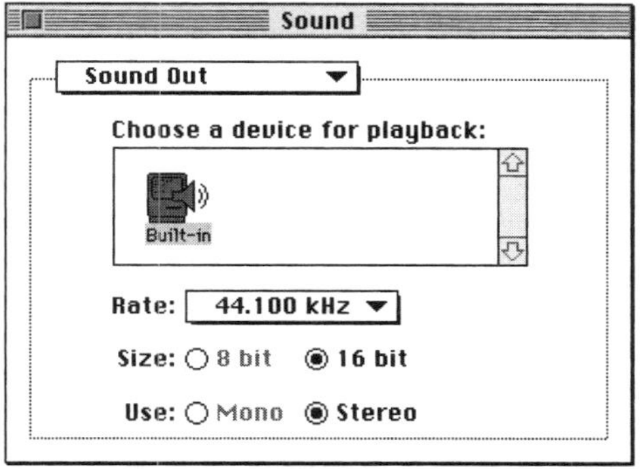


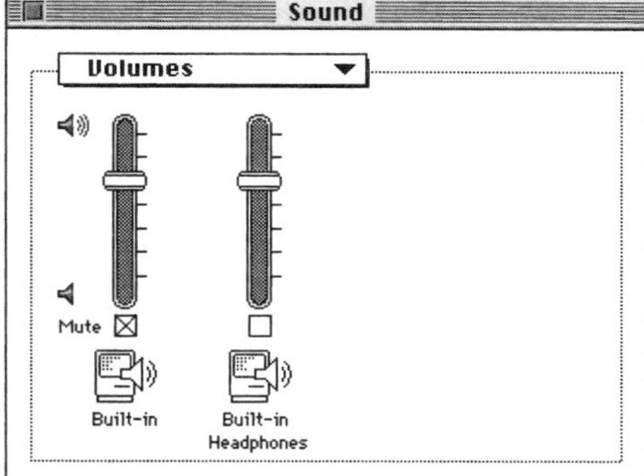


**Figure 8-39: Sections of the Sound control panel (newer type); the exact contents depend on each Mac's sound capabilities.**

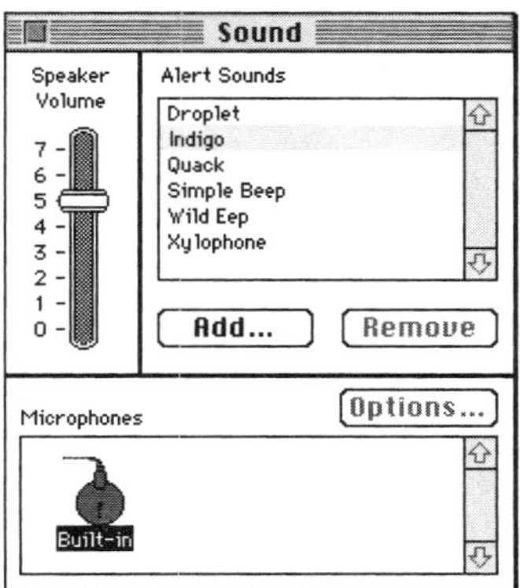


**Figure 8-40: The Sound control panel (older type); the exact contents depend on each Mac's sound capabilities.**

To record a new alert sound (on a Mac that has a microphone or sound input port), click the Add button in the Alert Sounds section of the control panel. This action brings up a dialog box that has buttons for controlling recording and playback, and a gauge that measures the duration of the recorded sound (see Figure 8-41). Click the Record button to record or re-record up to 10 seconds of sound from the Mac's microphone or another audio source connected to the sound port. Click the Play button to hear your recording. When you're satisfied with your recording, click the Save button, and type a name for the new alert sound when you're asked.

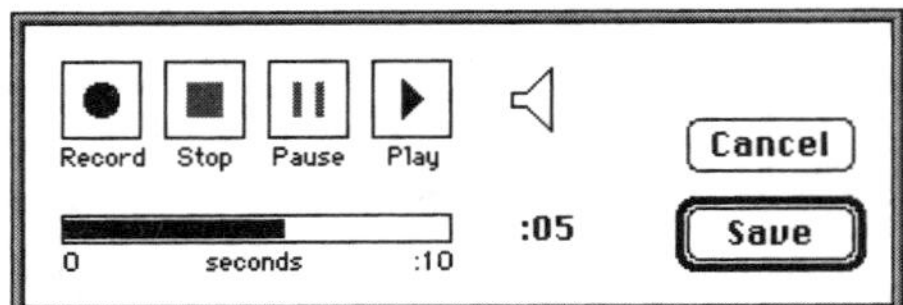


**Figure 8-41: The Sound control panel's buttons for recording an alert sound.**

# Startup Disk

The Startup Disk control panel (see Figure 8-42) sets which hard disk your Macintosh uses the next time it starts. This control panel doesn't work with a Macintosh Plus, and it has no effect unless your Macintosh has more than one hard disk that contains a System Folder. And in most cases, Startup Disk won't enable you to choose among multiple volumes from a single partitioned hard disk. To choose a volume from a partitioned hard disk, use the System Picker program (described in Chapter 19).

**Figure 8-42: The Startup Disk control panel.**

# Text

The Text control panel (see Figure 8-43) enables you to choose among the installed language-script systems, such as Roman, Cyrillic, Arabic, Japanese, and Chinese. For the chosen script system, you also can choose among the installed languages that it supports. For example, the Roman script system is used by these Western European languages: Danish, Dutch, English, Finnish, French, French Canadian, German, Italian, Norwegian, Spanish, and Swedish.

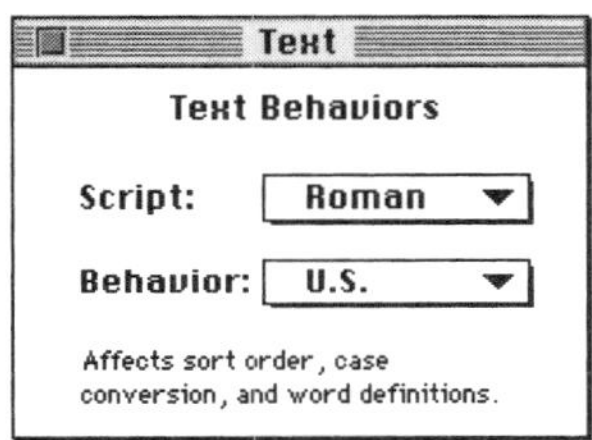


**Figure 8-43: The Text control panel.**

Choosing a language affects the computer's rules for alphabetizing, capitalizing, and distinguishing words. The Text control panel comes with System 7.5 and with other versions of System 7 that have been localized for languages other than English.

# Users & Groups

The Users & Groups control panel, shown in Figure 8-44, identifies people and groups to whom you give specific access privileges for file sharing and program linking. For complete information on this control panel's settings and on other file-sharing topics, see "Identifying Who Can Access Your Shared Items," "Controlling Access to Shared Items," and "Comparing Access-Privilege Scenarios" in Chapter 9.

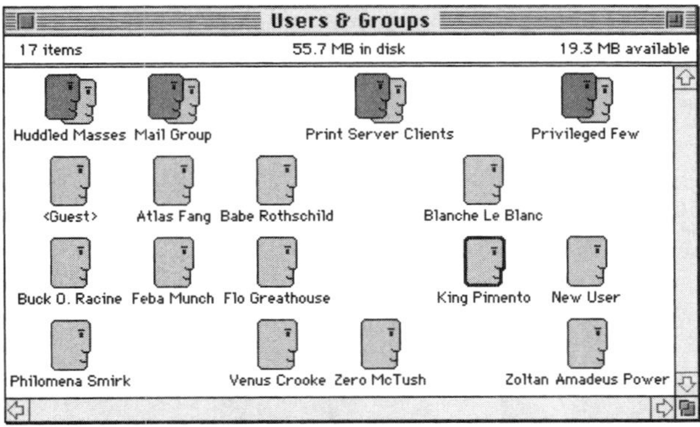


**Figure 8-44: The Users & Groups control panel.**

## Views

The Views control panel, shown in Figure 8-45, sets format and content options for Finder windows. For a detailed description, see "Custom list views" in Chapter 6.

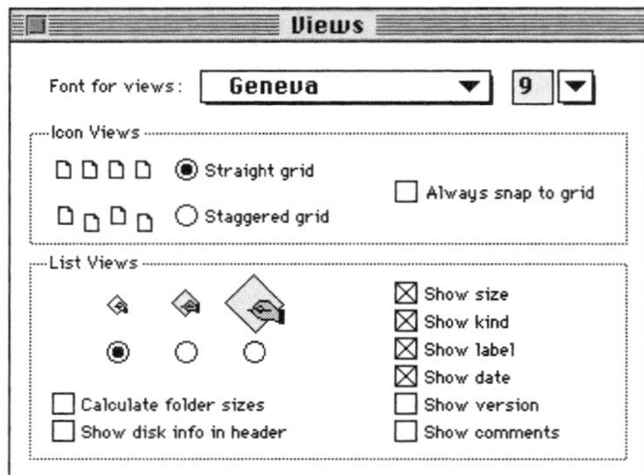


**Figure 8-45: The Views control panel.**

## WindowShade

The WindowShade control panel (see Figure 8-46) gives you the option of collapsing a window into its title bar. The effect, which is like rolling up a window shade, works with all windows and palettes (not just Finder windows).

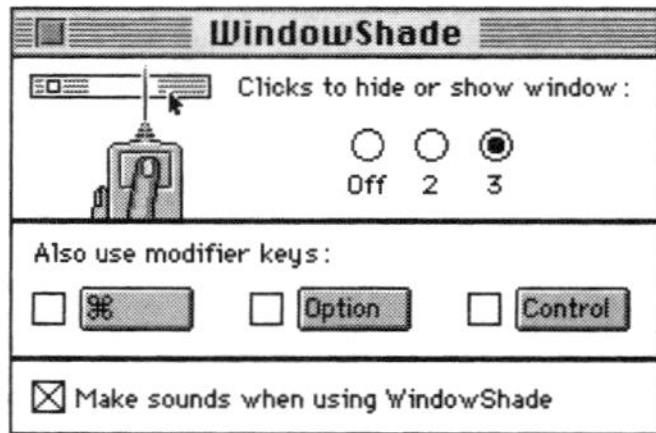


**Figure 8-46: System 7.5's Window-Shade control panel.**

In the control panel, you designate the combination of mouse clicks and modifier keys that trigger window collapsing and expanding. You also can turn roller-shade sound effects on and off. WindowShade comes with System 7.5 and later, and it is available separately from user groups and on-line information services (see Chapter 19).

# Accessory Programs

Apple has always included accessory programs with the Macintosh system software. Prior to System 7 they were all desk accessories, and you opened them from the Apple menu. System 7 allows desk accessories to operate apart from the Apple menu. System 7.5 and later include some accessory programs that are actually applications, not desk accessories.

This section explains how desk accessories work and describes the accessory programs installed in the Apple menu with various versions of System 7. The kind of program is noted for each item.

## Desk accessories in System 7

Very little differentiates desk accessories and application programs in System 7. You can put both types of items in folders, on the desktop, or in the Apple menu, as shown in Figure 8-47. Each desk accessory can have its own family of icons, consisting of small and standard sizes in black-and-white, 16 colors, and 256 colors. Most old desk accessories, however, use the generic desk-accessory icons, which look like generic application icons.

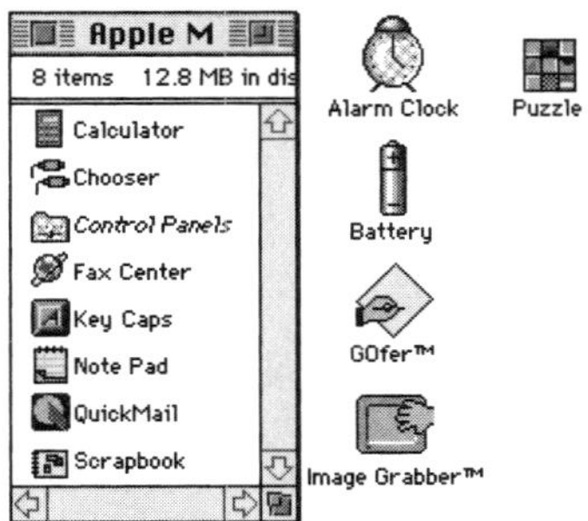


**Figure 8-47: Some desk accessories.**

You move and copy desk accessories by dragging their icons in the Finder, just as you would with any application. If you want to install a desk accessory in the Apple menu, simply drag it to the System Folder icon; you don't have to use the Font/DA Mover utility program. For compatibility with older system software, desk accessories can exist in suitcase files, which the Font/DA Mover program creates. You can use Font/DA Mover version 4.1 (but not earlier versions) with System 7.

### Opening desk accessories

System 7's full-time multitasking always enables you to open any desk accessory or application program without quitting the program that you're using (available memory permitting). You open a desk accessory as you would an application program — by double-clicking it, by selecting it and then choosing the Finder's Open command, or by choosing it from the Apple menu. Unlike an application program, however, you can't open a desk accessory by opening one of its documents. Thus, you can't open a desk accessory by double-clicking one of its documents or by dragging a document to the desk accessory icon. Also, desk accessories in a suitcase file can't be opened. You first must drag them out of the suitcase into a folder or onto the desktop.

### Using desk accessories

System 7 puts each desk accessory that you open in its own memory partition and adds its name to the Application menu. You make a single desk accessory the active program by choosing it from the Application menu or clicking its window, just as you would an application. While a desk accessory is the active program, its About command appears in the Apple menu. (Older system software lumps all open desk accessories together in one partition when MultiFinder is active, or the older system software includes them with the open application when MultiFinder is inactive.)

All desk accessories have a File menu with Close and Quit commands. These commands work differently in System 7 than in older system software. The Close command closes the desk accessory's active window and — in most desk accessories — quits the active desk accessory. The Quit command quits the active desk accessory (not all open desk accessories, as in older system software).

## Alarm Clock

The Alarm Clock desk accessory shows the time of day (see Figure 8-48). It can be expanded to show the date, set the time or date, or set an alarm. When the alarm goes off, you hear the system alert sound (as set in the Sound control panel), and the Alarm Clock icon flashes in front of the Apple Menu icon at the left end of the menu bar. To stop the flashing, you need only open the Alarm Clock desk accessory.

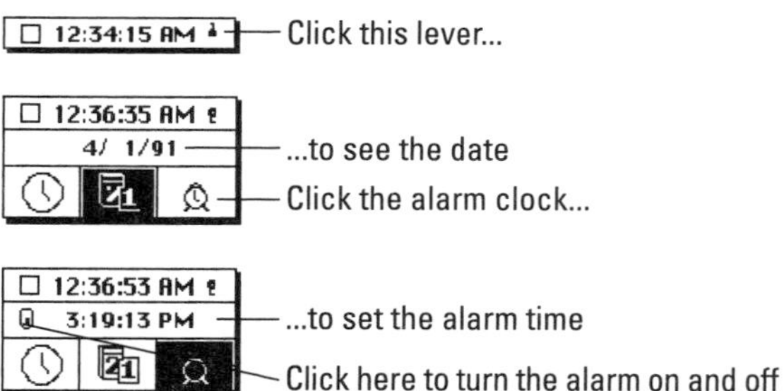


**Figure 8-48: The Alarm Clock desk accessory.**

## AppleCD Audio Player

The AppleCD Audio Player application, shown in Figure 8-49, plays audio CDs in your CD-ROM drive. The program has an Options menu, which you can use to change the window color and the number-display color. You also can use this menu to play back the left channel or right channel only.

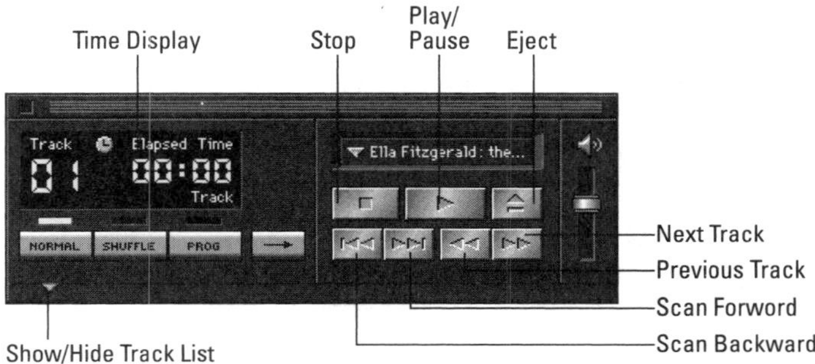


**Figure 8-49: The AppleCD Audio Player program.**

You can play, pause, stop, skip back, skip forward, scan back, and scan forward by clicking the buttons on the right side of the control panel. Clicking the Normal button plays the CD tracks sequentially. Clicking the Shuffle button plays the tracks in random order; each time you click Shuffle, the order changes. Clicking the Prog button plays the tracks in an order that you specify, as described later in this section. Clicking the arrow button next to the Prog button alternates between playing the CD one time or continuously in the mode that you've selected (normal, shuffle, or program).

The small down arrow above the Stop button is a pop-up menu that lists the tracks on the CD. Use this menu to play a specific track.

The clock icon is a pop-up menu. Use this menu to set the display to show elapsed or remaining time on the current track or on the entire disc.

To program the AppleCD Audio Player, click the Prog button. Then click the tiny Edit List button (the down arrow located below the Normal button) to display the track list and play list, as shown in Figure 8-50. The track list, on the right side of the window, lists all tracks sequentially. Build a play list on the right side of the window by dragging tracks from the track list to slots in the play list. If necessary, you can enlarge the window by dragging its size box. To remove a track from the play list, drag it back to the track list.

The AppleCD Audio Player identifies every audio CD generically — as Audio CD with tracks named Track 1, Track 2, and so on — unless you type the CD title and track titles. To enter titles, the Apple CD Audio Player must be in Normal mode or Shuffle mode (not Prog mode). The AppleCD Audio Player stores the titles that

**Figure 8-50: Programming the AppleCD Audio Player.**

you enter for each CD, and the custom play list that you build for it (if any), in the file CD Remote Programs in the Preferences folder inside the System Folder.

You can also operate many of AppleCD Audio Player's controls from the keyboard. Press the left-arrow and right-arrow keys to scan backward or scan forward track by track. Press the space bar or the Enter key to alternately play and pause, and the Delete key or the Clear key to stop playing. To eject the CD, press Command-E. And if the AppleCD Audio Player includes a volume control, you can operate it by pressing the up-arrow and down-arrow keys. (The presence of the volume control depends on the capabilities of the CD-ROM drive.)

## Battery

The Battery desk accessory, shown in Figure 8-51, monitors battery conditions on Portable and PowerBook computers. The gauge measures the remaining battery charge, and a lightning bolt across the battery icon indicates that the Mac is trying to charge the battery. Clicking the lever in the upper-right corner alternately shows and hides the Sleep section of the program. Clicking the Sleep button puts the computer to sleep. In System 7.5, the Date & Time control panel's menu-bar clock options (detailed earlier in this chapter) duplicate the Battery program.

## Calculator

The Calculator desk accessory (see Figure 8-52) adds, subtracts, multiplies, and divides numbers that you enter. You can type numbers and operation symbols or click the keys in the desk accessory. In addition, you can copy the text of a calculation — for example, 69.95+26.98+14.99*.0725 — and paste it into the Calculator.

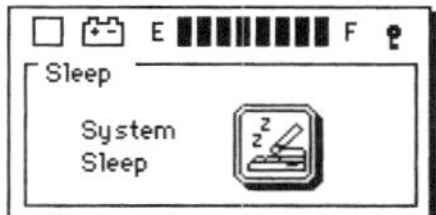


Figure 8-51: The Battery desk accessory.

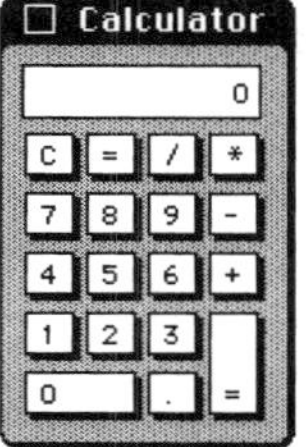


Figure 8-52: The Calculator desk accessory.

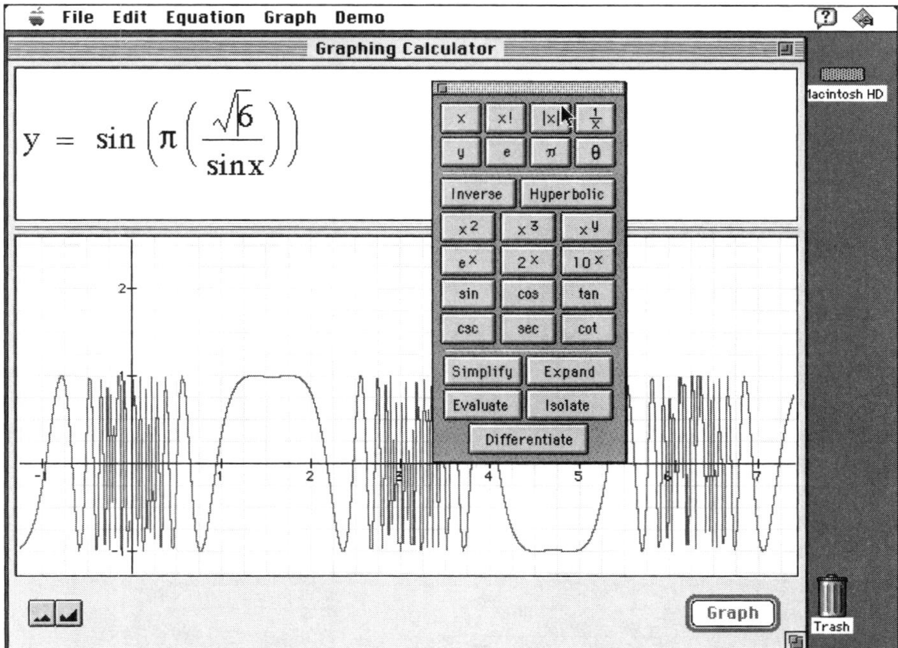


Figure 8-53: The Graphing Calculator program on Power Macs.

Power Mac computers come with a different Calculator program to show off their processing power. The Graphing Calculator, shown in Figure 8-53, can graph an equation in the same time that it takes the ordinary Calculator to perform arithmetic on a lesser Mac.

## Chooser

The Chooser desk accessory (see Figure 8-54) enables you to select a printer or other output device and to make connections with other computers that are networked to your Mac. System 7's Chooser is larger than older versions, to make room for more devices and network zones. Also, you no longer enter the Macintosh owner's name in the Chooser, but in the Sharing Setup control panel (as described in Chapter 9).

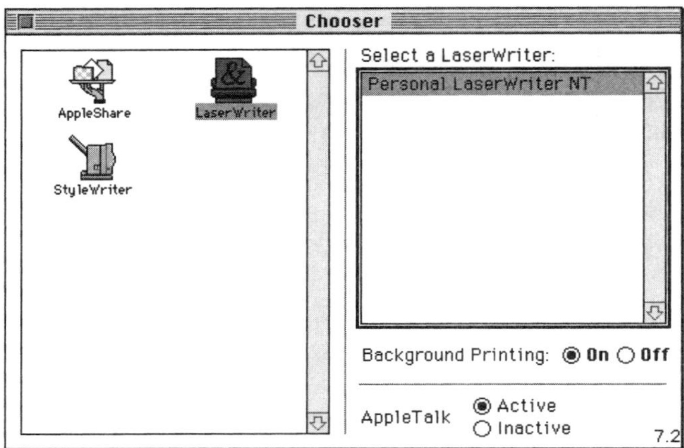


**Figure 8-54: The Chooser desk accessory.**

# Find File

System 7.5's Find File utility program (see Figure 8-55) finds files, folders, and disks that match up to eight criteria. Find File is described fully in the "Finding items in System 7.5" section of Chapter 6.

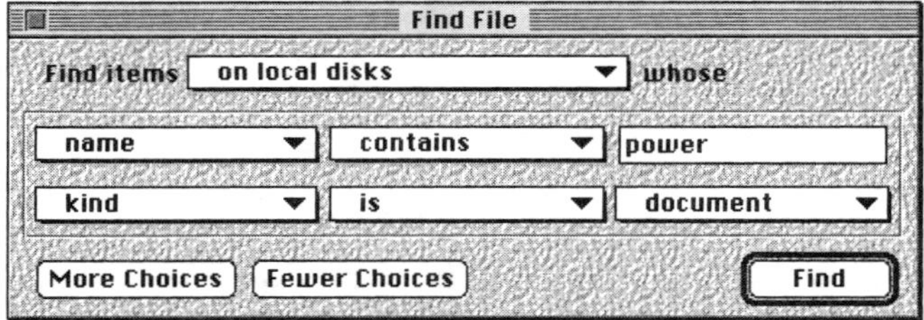


**Figure 8-55: The Find File program in System 7.5.**

# Jigsaw Puzzle

The Jigsaw Puzzle program in System 7.5, shown in Figure 8-56, is a replacement for the Puzzle desk accessory. This desk accessory can create endless numbers of jigsaw puzzles with large, medium, or small pieces from any graphics file that is compatible with SimpleText (that is, in PICT format). You can have the program show the picture on which the puzzle is based (like the box top of a conventional puzzle), and you also can have it solve the puzzle for you.

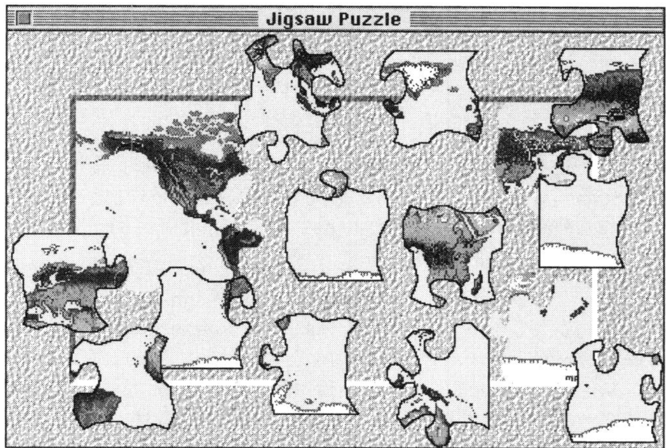


**Figure 8-56: The Jigsaw Puzzle program in System 7.5, with a medium-piece puzzle.**

# Key Caps

The Key Caps desk accessory (see Figure 8-57) shows all the characters that you can type in any font installed in your system. You choose the font from the Key Caps menu, which appears to the right of the Edit menu when the Key Caps desk accessory is active. Key Caps changes to show the effect of pressing Shift, Option, or Control separately or in combination.

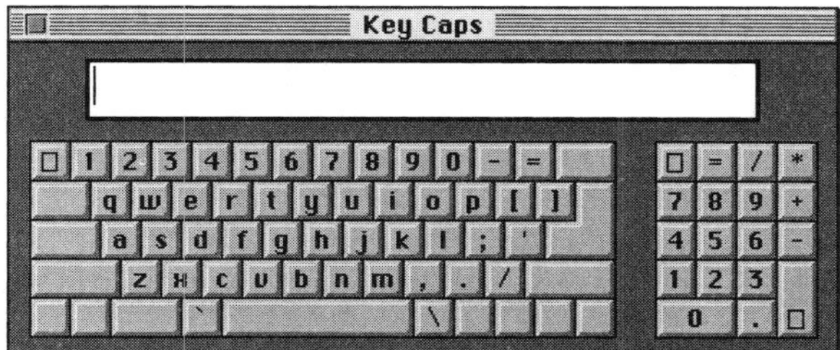


**Figure 8-57: The Key Caps desk accessory.**

In System 7's Key Caps, pressing Option outlines the keys that, when pressed along with Option, don't directly produce a character (see Figure 8-58). Each of those Option-key combinations, called *dead keys*, adds an accent or other diacritic to certain subsequently typed keys. Pressing a dead key — for example, Option-E for an accent — outlines the keys that can have that diacritic added.

### Printing Key Caps

You may want to print Key Caps as a handy reference, but it has no Print command. To work around this situation, take a picture of the screen and print that picture, as follows:

Open Key Caps, choose the font that you want it to show, and press any modifier keys (Shift, Option, Control, or ⌘) that you want to be in effect. Move the mouse pointer to an empty area of the menu bar; hold down the mouse button; temporarily release the modifier keys; press ⌘-Shift-3; again press the modifier keys that you released temporarily; and, finally, release the mouse button. Your gyrations should be rewarded by the sound of a camera shutter as the system snaps a picture of the screen.

Now open your startup disk, and look for a document named Picture 1. Print this document, using TeachText, SimpleText, or any graphics program. Cut out the Key Caps window with scissors after printing, or crop it out with a graphics program before printing. If you take additional snapshots, those snapshots are numbered sequentially.

Pressing Option outline keys can add a diacritic, and pressing one of them while pressing Option ...

outlines the keys that can have that diacritic added

**Figure 8-58: Reviewing dead keys and their effects.**

## Note Pad

The Note Pad records brief messages that you type or paste into it. Two versions of the Note Pad exist. The newer version, shown in Figure 8-59, is an application that comes with System 7.5 and later. You can print notes, go to any note by number, and find text in one note or all notes. Each note can contain up to 32K (about 32,000) characters. You can drag text between the Note Pad and another application that has adopted drag-and-drop editing, such as the Scrapbook and SimpleText (see "Editing the Drag-and-Drop Way" in Chapter 14). You can scroll and resize the Note Pad window. In addition, you can set the font and size of the text in the notes.

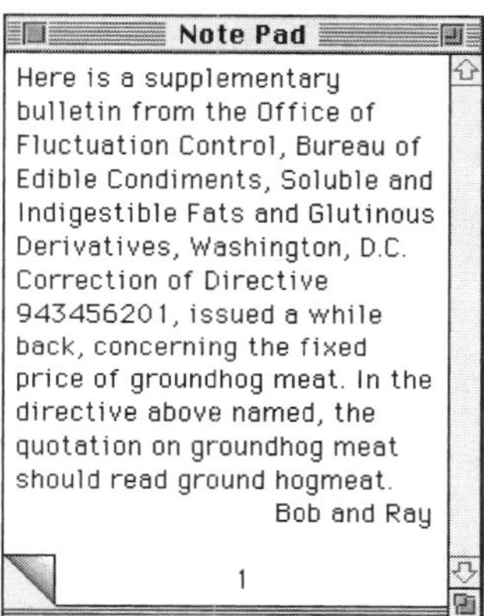


**Figure 8-59: System 7.5's Note Pad program.**

The older version of the Note Pad, shown in Figure 8-60, is a simple desk accessory that comes with System 7 versions older than 7.5. This version cannot print notes. The only way to go through the notes is to click the dog ears in the lower-left corner. The window is fixed in size and has no scroll bars, but you can use the arrow keys to scroll. You have no choice of font or font size.

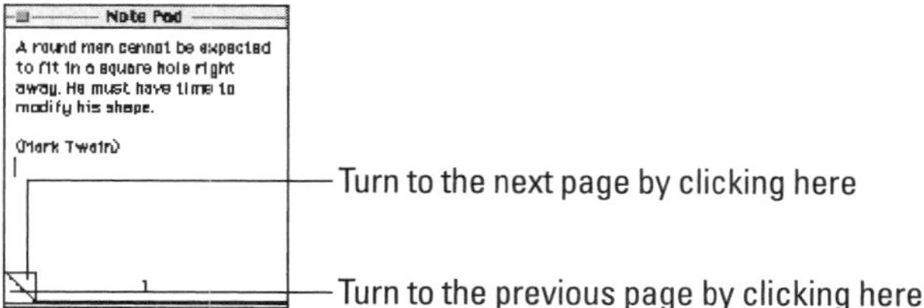


**Figure 8-60: The Note Pad desk accessory before System 7.5.**

# Puzzle

The Puzzle desk accessory (see Figure 8-61) is a game in which you unscramble tiles to make a picture. Push a tile in the same row or column as the vacant space toward the vacant space by clicking the tile. Puzzle has two configurations: one with numbered tiles, and another with a picture of the Apple logo. Choose Clear from the Edit menu to switch between them.

**Figure 8-61: The Puzzle desk accessory.**

You can replace the picture of the Apple logo. Just copy a picture in another program, switch to the Puzzle, and paste. The next-to-last picture in the standard System 7 Scrapbook, for example, provides a challenging puzzle.

# Scrapbook

The Scrapbook stores and retrieves text, pictures, sounds, and other types of information that you paste into it, one item at a time. Several versions of the Scrapbook exist. All versions of the Scrapbook used with System 7 can play sounds as well as display text and pictures. All but the oldest versions also can play QuickTime movies (on a Mac with QuickTime installed, as described in Chapter 16).

The Scrapbook version that comes with System 7.5 (see Figure 8-62) is an application program. You can copy an item to or from this Scrapbook by dragging from or to another application that has adopted drag-and-drop editing, such as SimpleText or the Finder (see "Editing the Drag-and-Drop Way" in Chapter 14 for details).

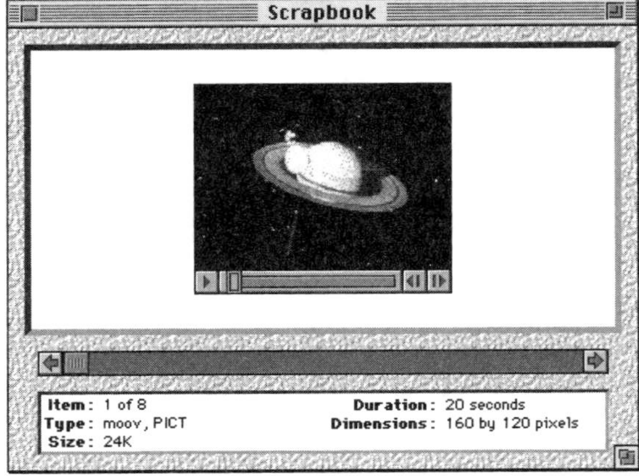


**Figure 8-62: The Scrapbook program in System 7.5.**

You can resize the window of this Scrapbook. As you scroll through items, this Scrapbook reports the number of the item, the type of the item, and its size. For picture items, the Scrapbook also reports the item's dimensions and the amount (if any) by which the item is reduced for display in the Scrapbook. The Scrapbook also

QUICK TIPS

### Relieving Scrapbook Clutter

After extensive use, your Scrapbook may become cluttered with old clippings. If you can't bear to throw them out, make a copy of the Scrapbook file in your System Folder (use the Finder's Duplicate command and store the copy in some other folder) before you start weeding. Later, you can use the old copy that you made by dragging the current Scrapbook file out of the System Folder, dragging the old copy in, and changing its name to Scrapbook file. To get the standard System 7 Scrapbook file, you must install System 7 on a disk that has no Scrapbook file in its System Folder. The Installer does not replace a Scrapbook file that it finds in the System Folder when you install System 7.

Older versions of the Scrapbook are desk accessories with fixed-size windows, as shown in Figure 8-63. These versions report only the item number and type.

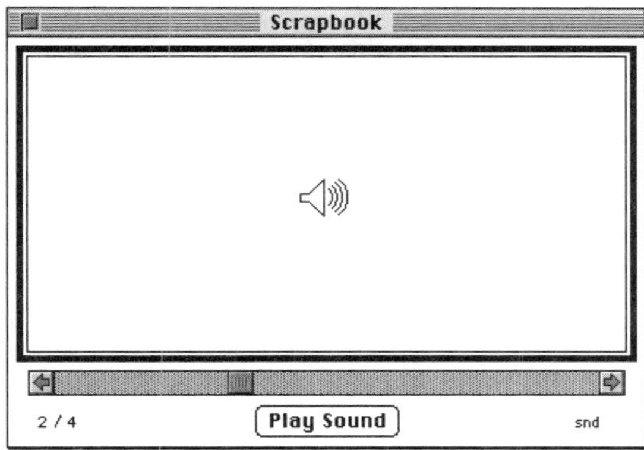


**Figure 8-63: An older version of the Scrapbook desk accessory.**

## Stickies

The Stickies application displays notes similar to Post-it Notes on your screen, as shown in Figure 8-64. You can set the color and the text font, size, and style for each note. You can drag selected text to move it within a note, copy it between notes, or copy it between a note and another application that has adopted drag-and-drop editing, such as SimpleText and the Note Pad. Stickies windows have no scroll bars, but you can scroll by pressing the arrow keys or by dragging in the note.

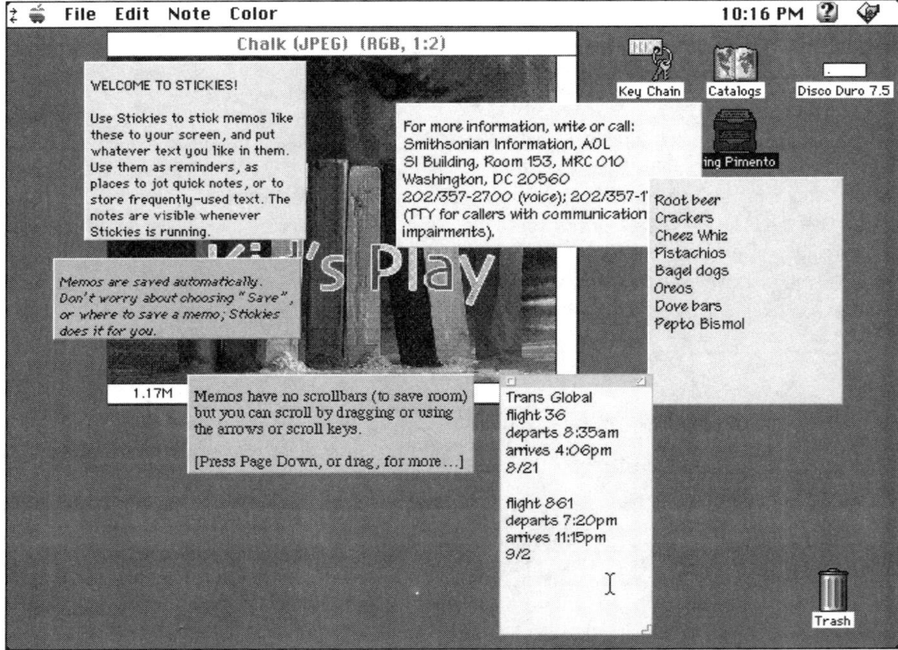


**Figure 8-64: The Stickies program in System 7.5.**

# CHAPTER 8 CONCEPTS AND TERMS

- More than a dozen individual control panels that you open like Finder documents give you settings for controlling many aspects of the Mac.
- Desk accessories work outside the Apple menu, in folders, and on the desktop, and can be used like ordinary application programs.
- System 7 comes with several accessory programs, some desk accessories, and several other applications.

**cdevs**
Another term for control-panel documents. Some old cdevs work properly only if you put them in the System Folder itself, not in the Control Panels folder.

**color picker**
The dialog box in which you specify a custom color either by clicking a color wheel or by entering color values.

**dead keys**
The keys that generate accented characters when typed in combination with the Option key and in proper sequence. For example, typing Option-E followed by O generates ó. In System 7, the Key Caps desk accessory outlines the dead keys when you press the Option key.

**Disk Cache**
Improves System performance by storing recently used information from the disk in a dedicated part of memory. Accessing information in memory is much faster than accessing information on disk.

**extension**
A software module that is loaded during startup and adds features or capabilities to the system software.

**file-name extension**
The three characters following the period in a DOS file name. The file-name extension indicates the kind of file on a DOS or Windows computer.

**file sharing**
The ability to make files (in folders) available to other computers over a network, and to access another computer's files (in folders).

**gamma correction**
A method the computer's video circuitry uses to balance color on a video display. Color balancing is necessary because the intensity of color on a video display does not correspond uniformly to the intensity of the electron beam that traces the video picture on the phosphor coating inside the video display tube.

**the Internet**
A worldwide network that provides e-mail, news, and file storage and retrieval.

**network**
A collection of interconnected, individually controlled computers, printers, and other devices, together with the hardware and software used to connect them. A network allows users to share data and devices, such as printers.

**subdirectories**
The equivalent on Windows, OS/2, and DOS computers to folders on Mac computers. With the PC Exchange control panel installed, the Mac displays subdirectories of DOS disks as folders on the Mac screen.

**RAM disk**
You can use the Memory control panel to set aside RAM to be used as though it were a very fast hard disk. A RAM disk stores items only until the next restart, shutdown, or power outage.

**startup disk**
A disk with the Finder and System files in its System Folder, which allows the computer to begin operation.

**submenu**
A secondary menu that pops out from the side of another menu. A submenu appears when you place the pointer on a menu item that has an arrowhead at the right side of the menu.

**UNIX**
An operating system (system software) popular on computers of the workstation class and larger.

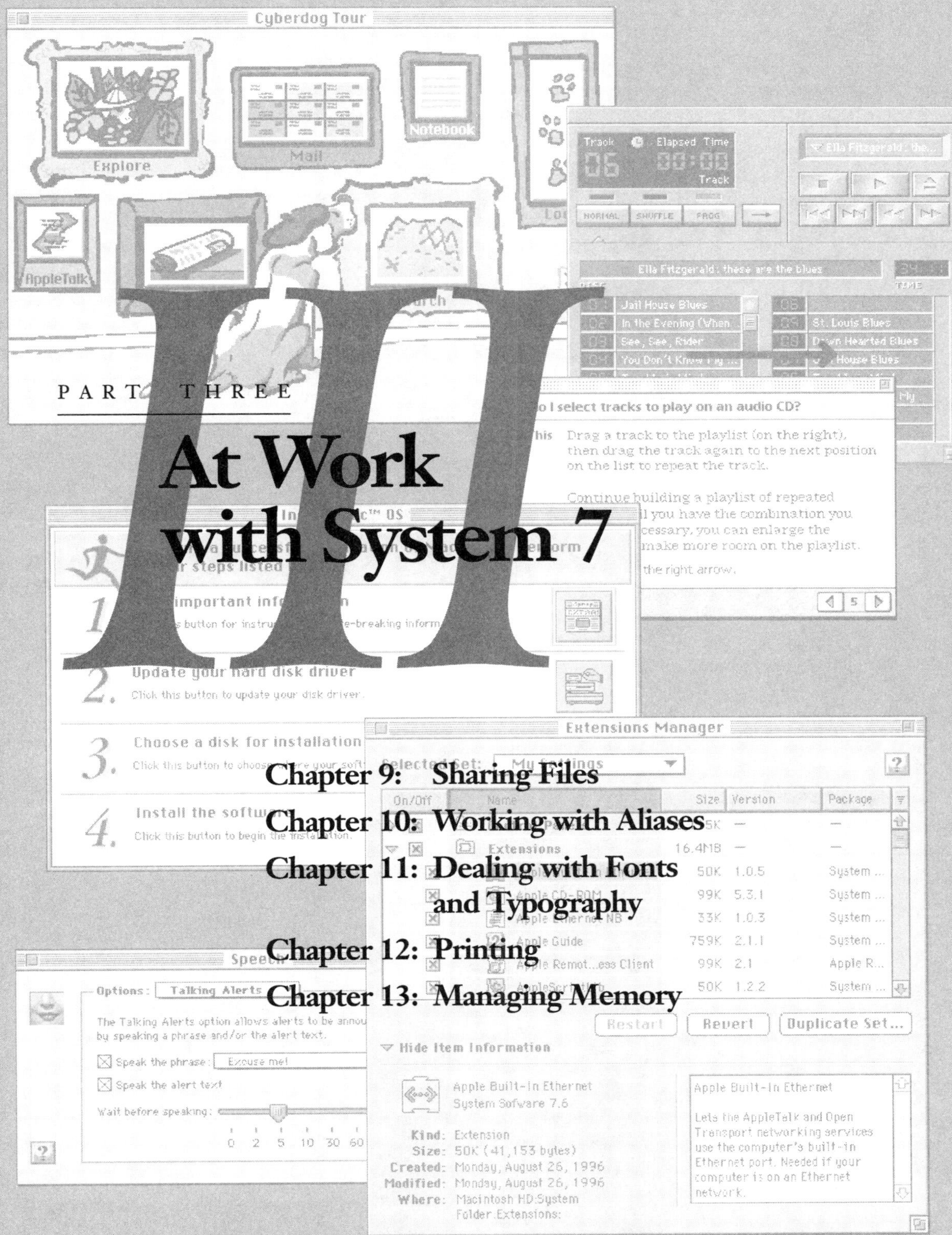


P A R T   T H R E E

# III

# At Work with System 7

CHAPTER NINE

# Sharing Files

- Understanding networks and the services they can provide
- Building a network, identifying your Mac on it, and making your Mac available to others on the network
- Accessing a network over ordinary telephone lines
- Designating which folders and disks you want to share, with guidelines for optimizing sharing and preventing potential problems
- Registering users and groups of users
- Setting access privileges, including making a private in-box folder and a bulletin-board folder
- Seeing which folders and disks you are sharing and who is connected to your computer
- Accessing the folders and disks of another Macintosh on the network

Similar to a library, *file sharing* allows you to share files, folders, and disks with people whose computers are connected to your Macintosh in a network. You can share items from your Macintosh with other users, they can share their items with you, and they can share their items with one another. In effect, these network users become librarians of their shared information, controlling who has access to shared items and determining what a user can do to files.

Your network may consist of two computers in the same room, several computers located near one another, or computers scattered throughout a building. Your computer can even join the network from a distance, by telephone. This chapter explains how to use System 7's file-sharing capabilities to manage the flow of shared information across a network of any complexity.

## Comparing File Sharing to File Servers

System 7's built-in networking capabilities make sharing items across a network surprisingly easy. Previously, to create a network to share items, you needed to purchase additional networking software, such as AppleShare or Sitka's TOPS. With System 7 and LocalTalk or LocalTalk-compatible connectors, you can easily create a ready-to-use network for sharing files, folders, and disks. File sharing is one type of network service; networks also can provide printing services, modem and fax/modem services, and more.

File sharing can be implemented in a distributed or centralized fashion. In a distributed file-sharing network, each Macintosh user makes files, folders, and disks available to other people using the network. While you are sharing your files, you are free to use your Macintosh for normal tasks. By contrast, a centralized file-sharing network enables everyone to share items from a computer that is dedicated to providing file-sharing services. Such a computer is referred to as a *dedicated file server.* Usually, the Macintosh that acts as a dedicated file server needs more than minimal processing capabilities. A Centris, Quadra, or perhaps an old IIfx or IIci can handle network demands. The computer will need one or more large hard disks.

System 7's file-sharing capabilities are designed for distributed file sharing among up to ten users at one time. (More than ten can be connected to the network, but only ten can share files at the same time.) You also can use System 7's file-sharing capabilities on a Macintosh that is dedicated to sharing files. Dedicating an ordinary Macintosh to System 7's file sharing turns the computer into a simple, inexpensive file server for a small work group. Folders or entire hard disks on this file-server Mac can be made available to different network users, who in turn can back up important files of their own to the file server.

The problem with a home-made file server is its performance. System 7's file sharing assumes somebody will use the file-server Mac for more than sharing files, and reserves about 50 percent of the file-server Mac's processing power for the nominal user — who in this case doesn't exist — to run applications. A utility called Nok Nok 2.0 from the AG Group (510-937-7900), which sells for about $50, can adjust the amount of processing power reserved for file sharing, greatly improving file-sharing performance. Apple's AppleShare Server 4.0 software also allocates most of the computer's processing capacity to file sharing, but it costs about $1000. It does more than just optimize file-sharing speed, but for many situations you don't need more.

Many people can access a shared folder or disk at the same time, but only one person can use a shared file at a time unless the application involved is a network version, which enables multiple users to work with the same program or document. For best performance, multiuser application programs and their documents are usually kept on a dedicated file server.

# Connecting Your Network

You establish a LocalTalk network simply by plugging Apple's LocalTalk connectors into the printer ports of two or more Macintosh computers and then connecting the computers with LocalTalk wiring. For a less expensive network that actually performs better, you also can use Farallon Computing's PhoneNet connectors (or the equivalent) and ordinary telephone cables. Either way, you have a basic LocalTalk network.

System 7 includes optional software for connecting your Macintosh to two other types of networks: EtherTalk and TokenTalk. These sophisticated networking

### AppleShare Dedicated File Server

A network with more than ten people actively sharing files needs a dedicated file server administered by software such as Apple's AppleShare Server 3 software. A faster edition, AppleShare Server 4, is available for Macs based on a 68040 CPU; version 4.1 works with Apple workgroup servers that use the PowerPC CPU. The AppleShare Server extends network file-sharing and background-printing services beyond System 7's standard capabilities. Installing AppleShare Server software turns any Macintosh into an efficient centralized file server capable of sharing the files and folders on its hard disk (or disks) among 120 users of Macintosh, Apple II, and MS-DOS computers on an AppleTalk network.

Centralized disk storage reduces the amount of local disk storage required by each networked computer, while providing a way for people who work together to share information. People can store files on the server's disks, where other people can open or copy them. Many people can access the server's disks and folders simultaneously, and new files become available to everyone instantly. Unlike the file sharing provided by System 7, no one uses the server's Macintosh to do personal work because it is dedicated to providing network services. Conversely, your Macintosh is not burdened when someone else on the network accesses one of your shared items on the AppleShare server's disk.

A centralized file server is set up and maintained by a trained person called a *network administrator.* The AppleShare Server software includes organizational, administrative, and security features to manage file access on the network. The network administrator does not control access to folders and files on the server's disks; that is the responsibility of each person who puts items on the disks.

AppleShare's file-sharing capabilities are compatible with those of System 7. You use the same methods (described in this chapter) to share your files with other users, to control access to those files, and to access files that other users have made available to you.

options provide more powerful networking capabilities than LocalTalk, but connectors and wiring cost more. The latest Macs have built-in Ethernet ports, but older Macs need extra-cost internal or external Ethernet adapters. You install EtherTalk or TokenTalk software by using the same Installer program that installs System 7.

# Connecting to a Network by Phone

Your Macintosh can connect to an AppleTalk network through another Macintosh over standard telephone lines. Both computers need compatible modems and copies of Apple's Apple Remote Access software (often called ARA). When connected, you can use System 7's file sharing to access shared files on the computers connected to the network, and you can access other network services as well. Apple Remote Access can call into any type of AppleTalk network: LocalTalk, PhoneNet, EtherTalk, or TokenTalk.

You set up Apple Remote Access with the Remote Access Setup control panel (see Figure 9-1), specifying the type of modem you have and the port to which it's connected.

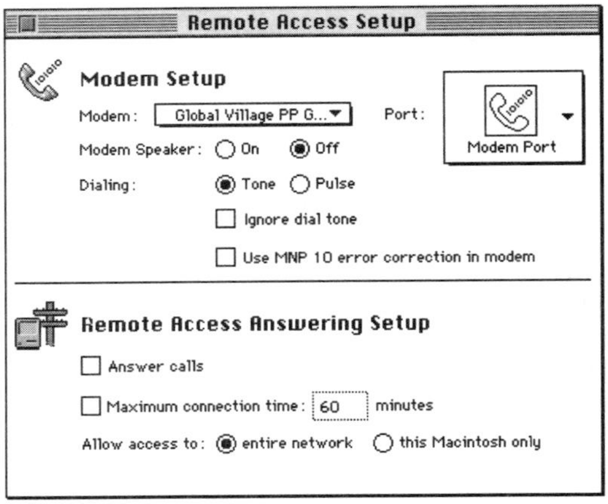

Figure 9-1: The Remote Access Setup control panel.

To connect, you have your copy of Apple Remote Access call Apple Remote Access on the computer whose network you want to access, as shown in Figure 9-2. Data travels over the phone lines as sounds, and the modems convert between the sounds and the computer's digital data. You can't let anyone on the network access your shared files, but you can access files (using the methods described in this chapter) that people on the network have made available for sharing exactly as though you were connected to the network locally.

Apple has improved on the original ARA; version 2 tightens security to make it harder for unauthorized people to connect to a network by dialing in with ARA. Some other details have changed. For example, you now can buy a separate copy of the client software that you need to dial in to the network. This software is a smaller program than the combined client/server ARA 1, which makes the version 2 client attractive for PowerBook users.

Trilobyte Software makes a shareware equivalent to ARA called ARACommander, which offers some features that the Apple version lacks. The product became so popular that the author upgraded it and now also offers ARACommander 2 as a commercial product. The commercial version gives users more options than Apple's own ARA does, and it simplifies the process of automating connections for a certain time each day. ARACommander 2 also makes it easy for network administrators to set up temporary ARA user accounts that self-destruct after a certain date.

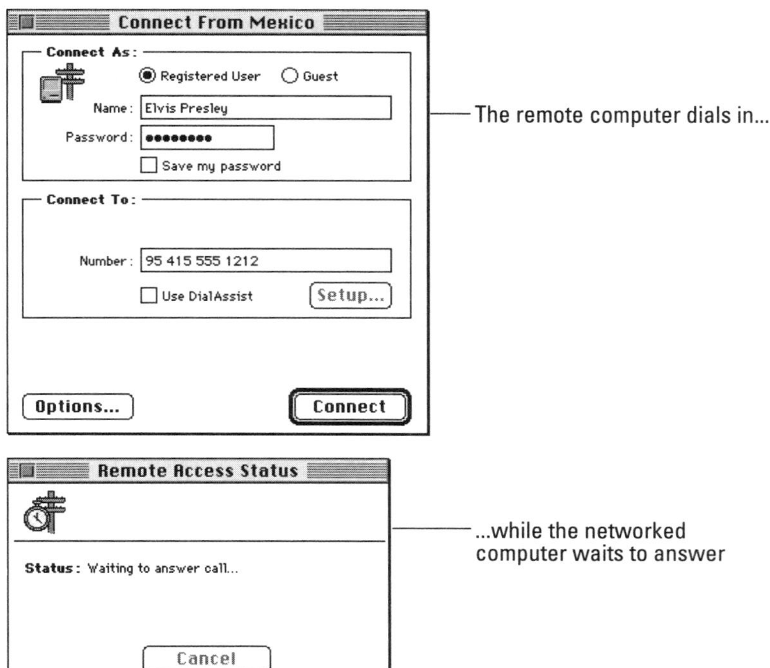


**Figure 9-2: Connecting to a distant network with Apple Remote Access.**

# Selecting Your Network

If your Macintosh has an EtherTalk or TokenTalk network connection, you switch between LocalTalk and the other network or networks by using the Network control panel. If your Macintosh is using Apple Remote Access to connect to a remote network, you can use the Network control panel to disconnect from your local network (if any). You would disconnect if you were unable to access a device on the remote network because it was being masked by a device on your local network, or if you had no local network and needed to use your printer port for a nonnetworked printer (such as a StyleWriter). You usually don't find the Network control panel in your Control Panels folder unless your Macintosh has an Ethernet connector, is directly connected to a network other than LocalTalk (such as EtherTalk), or has Apple Remote Access installed.

The Network control panel displays the network option icons, shown in Figure 9-3. To select a network, click its icon. A message warns that you'll lose any network services that you're using with your current network connection because you can maintain a connection to only one network at a time. When you switch to a different network, you'll no longer be able to access any file servers, printers, or other network services on the original network.

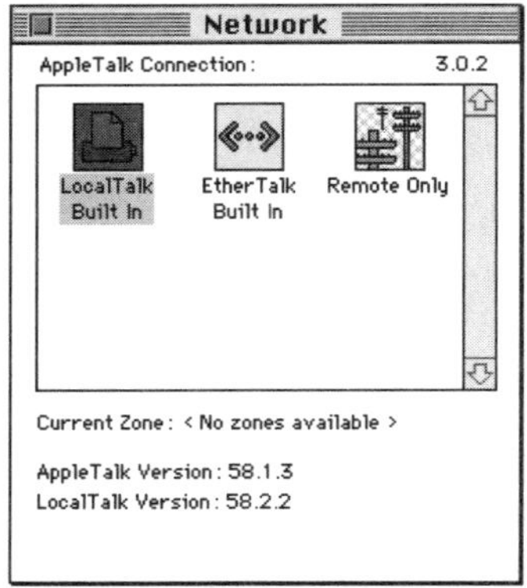


**Figure 9-3: The Network control panel.**

# Turning AppleTalk On and Off

As soon as you connect to a network and turn on your Macintosh, AppleTalk is turned on for you automatically. AppleTalk is the built-in software that enables your Macintosh to communicate with a network. In some cases, you may need to turn off AppleTalk, meaning that you want to disconnect your Macintosh from the network. To turn off AppleTalk, use the Chooser desk accessory, shown in Figure 9-4. Click the Inactive button to turn off AppleTalk.

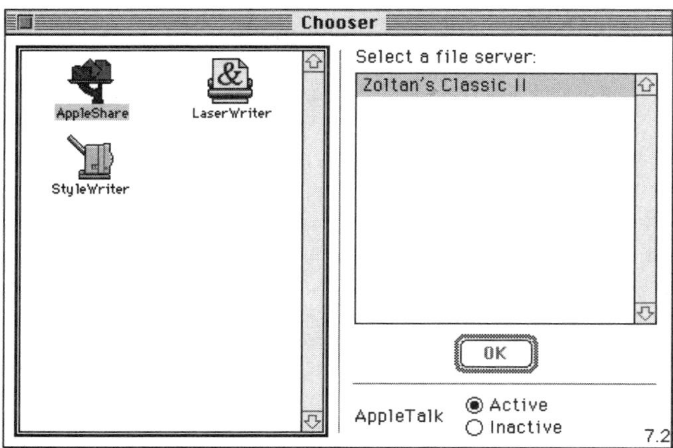


**Figure 9-4: The Chooser desk accessory.**

If you attempt to turn off AppleTalk while you are connected to a network service, such as file sharing, you get a message warning you that these services will be disconnected. In this case, click the Cancel button, close the Chooser, and then close any shared items. Remember that if you turn off AppleTalk, it remains off until you turn it on again by clicking the Active button in the Chooser.

# Identifying Your Macintosh

Before you can begin sharing files, you must identify your Macintosh to the network, using the Sharing Setup control panel (see Figure 9-5). Identifying your Macintosh involves entering the name of its owner, a password to prevent other users from connecting to your Macintosh as its owner, and a name for your Macintosh. Identifying the owner of your Macintosh plays an important role in determining who has access to your shared items. When people on the network want to share items from your Macintosh, they first select your Macintosh by name from a list in their Chooser.

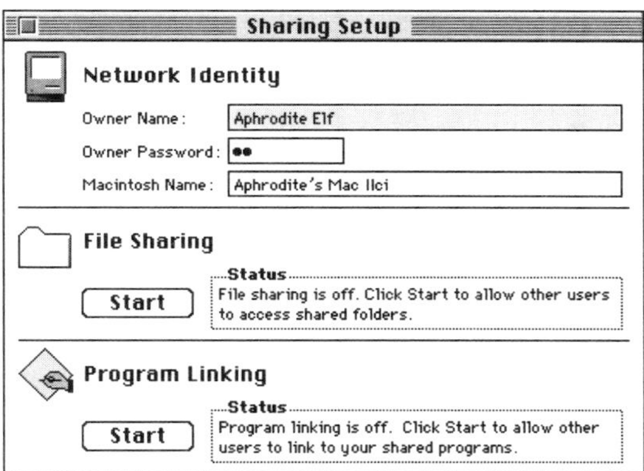


**Figure 9-5: The Sharing Setup control panel.**

The Owner Password can be up to eight characters long. A password is *case-sensitive* meaning that if you create a password that includes uppercase and lowercase letters, you must re-enter that password with the same uppercase and lowercase letters to gain access. Select a password that is easy for you to remember but difficult for others to guess.

***Tip:*** For better security, mix letters with numbers; try replacing the letters *I* and *O* with the numbers 1 and 0, for example. You must know the Owner Password to access your Macintosh from another Macintosh on the network. As you enter your password, the Sharing Setup control panel displays bullets in place of the actual characters to prevent others from seeing the password.

In the Macintosh Name text box, give your Macintosh a name that others will easily recognize when they see it in their Choosers. If a name already appears in the Macintosh Name text box, you can use that name or type a new one. You can change any of these settings later by returning to the Sharing Setup control panel.

# Starting and Stopping File Sharing

You also use the Sharing Setup control panel to start file sharing. Activating file sharing enables the network users to access your computer and its shared items.

To start file sharing, click the Start button in the File Sharing section of the Sharing Setup control panel. The Start button's label changes to Cancel, and the status message next to the button describes what is happening while file sharing is starting. When the status line says "File sharing is now on" and the button's label changes to Stop, your Macintosh is ready to share files. You can close the Sharing Setup control panel anytime after clicking the Start button, but you won't know precisely when file sharing is enabled if you do.

If you shut down or restart your Macintosh while file sharing is on, System 7 automatically starts file sharing the next time the Macintosh is started. In other words, file sharing stays on until you explicitly stop it.

You can stop file sharing so that other users on the network cannot access your computer. Stopping file sharing does not unshare items that you've already designated as shared (as described in the next section), but it denies other users on the network access to any of your shared items until you turn file sharing on again.

To stop file sharing, click the Stop button in the Sharing Setup control panel. The system asks you to enter the number of minutes' warning to be given to anyone who is sharing items from your Macintosh. (Allow enough time for people sharing items from your Macintosh to close any shared items.) Every Macintosh sharing items from your Macintosh sees a message indicating that access to your computer is going to be disconnected at the end of the time you specified, as shown in Figure 9-6. The same message goes out when you shut down or restart your Macintosh with file sharing on.

***Caution:*** People sharing your items receive no notification of impending shutdown if you shut down or restart your Macintosh with At Ease's Special menu instead of the Finder's.

If you plan to share a CD-ROM or a removable hard disk, you must insert the disk before starting file sharing with the Sharing Setup control panel. You can share only disks whose icons are on your desktop when you start file sharing. Conversely, before starting file sharing, you must eject a CD-ROM or removable hard disk that you do not want to share. You cannot eject a CD-ROM or removable hard disk that was mounted when sharing started; you have to turn off sharing before ejecting.

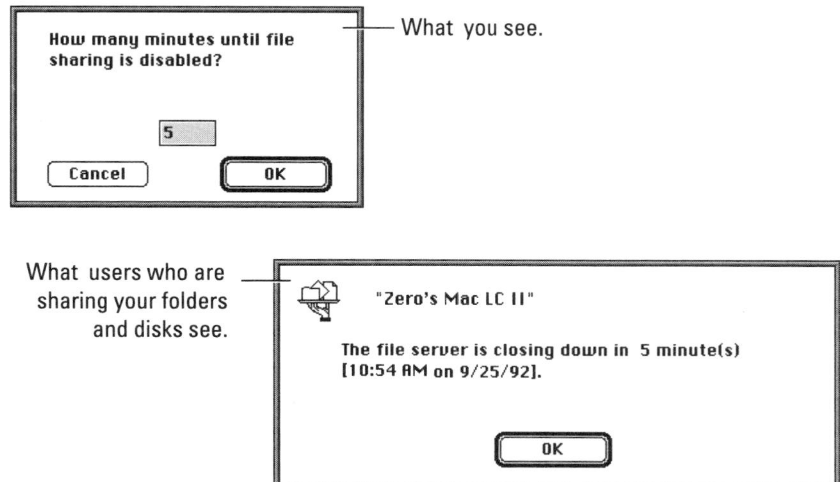


**Figure 9-6: Messages that appear when you stop file sharing.**

# Sharing Your Folders and Hard Disks

After identifying your Macintosh and activating file sharing, you designate the folders and hard disks that you want to share. You can share up to ten folders and hard disks (including CD-ROMs and removable hard disks) at a time. To share just one file, you must drag it into a folder and share the folder.

When you share a folder or hard disk, every item it contains is shared, including enclosed folders. You can't share a document by itself (outside a folder) or an item located on a floppy disk. After you share a folder or hard disk, you can drag unshared items into the shared folder or hard disk to share them.

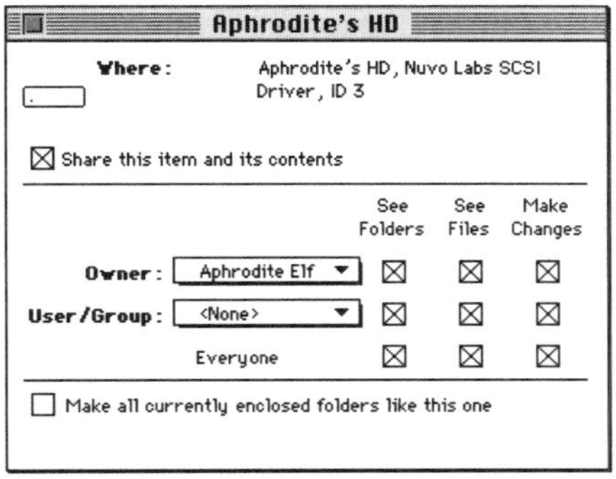

**Figure 9-7: The Sharing info window.**

To make a folder or hard disk available for sharing, select the item and then choose Sharing from the File menu to display the Sharing info window (see Figure 9-7), in which you specify access privileges. Turn on the "Share this item and its contents" option.

The remaining options in the Sharing info window establish which users can access the shared item and what privileges they have, as explained in "Controlling Access to Shared Items" later in this chapter. The initial settings for a shared item enable anyone on the network to access that item and make any changes he or she wants.

When you close the Sharing info window, the system asks whether you want to save the changes to the access privileges that you just specified. If you click the Save button, the item is shared and available to everyone on the network. All items in the selected folder or hard disk also are available.

The settings that you make in an item's Sharing info window persist until you use the Sharing command again to change them. Shutting down or restarting your Macintosh does not affect Sharing info window settings; neither does stopping file sharing with the Sharing Setup control panel.

The icon of a shared folder on your Macintosh appears with network cables and a tabbed folder, indicating its shared status. When people on your network are connected to a shared folder, the folder icon displays faces in the center to indicate that the folder is in use (see Figure 9-8). Notice that shared-hard-disk icons, unlike folders, don't change.

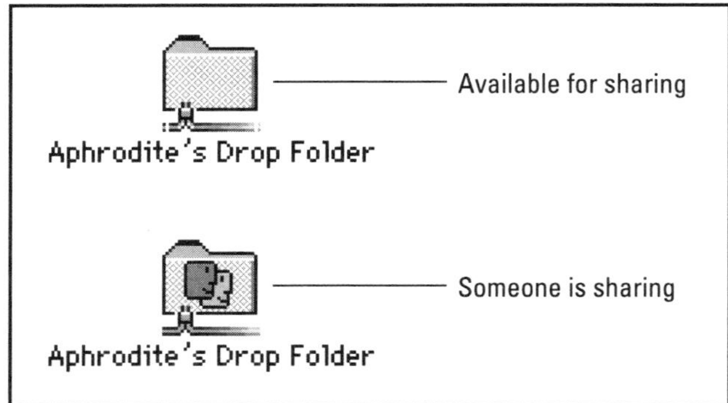


**Figure 9-8: Shared folders on your Macintosh.**

You can use the Views control panel to set icon size so that you'll see the network folder icons. You can move a shared folder anywhere on your Macintosh except to a floppy disk.

### Network Trash

If another user throws away a shared item from your Macintosh, the Finder creates an invisible folder on your Macintosh with the label *Network Trash Folder.* As long as the user doesn't empty the Trash, the items thrown away appear inside the Network Trash Folder in folders labeled *Trash Can #1, Trash Can #2,* and so on — one for each Macintosh with something of yours in its Trash. To restore an item that someone else has trashed, simply drag it out of the *Trash Can #* folder and rename it. You can set access privileges to prevent others from trashing your shared items, as described in "Controlling Access to Shared Items" later in this chapter.

You can't rename a shared folder or disk; nor can you drag it to the Trash. Also, you can't eject and put away a removable hard disk or CD-ROM that you are sharing. To do any of these things, you first must use the Sharing Setup control panel to stop sharing — or unshare the item. You unshare any folder or disk with the Sharing command. In the item's Sharing info window, turn off the "Share this item and its contents" option and close the Sharing info window.

# Guidelines for Sharing Folders and Disks

You can do several things to optimize file sharing and prevent potential problems. The following are some guidelines and tips for sharing folders and disks:

- Share from the highest level of your disk and folder structure. For example, a disk can't be shared if it contains an already-shared folder (no matter how deeply nested in the unshared disk). If you attempt to share a disk or folder that contains an already-shared folder, you get a message telling you that the disk or folder cannot be shared because it contains a shared folder. To work around this situation, use the File Sharing monitor to identify the shared items (as explained in "Monitoring File-Sharing Activity" later in this chapter), unshare it, and then share the enclosing disk or folder.
- Share as few folders as possible. The more shared folders being accessed, the greater the memory demands on your Macintosh. Sharing too many folders can slow your system to a crawl.
- Check any applicable licensing agreements before sharing folders that contain programs, artwork, or sounds. Often, licensing agreements or copyright laws restrict use of these items to a single computer.
- Set up a dedicated Macintosh to act as a centralized file server for the shared information. This method is often the most efficient way to share numerous files or to share folders with several users simultaneously.

# Identifying Who Can Access Your Shared Items

When you initially share a folder or disk with System 7, that folder or disk is made available to every user on the network. Every network user can access the shared items on your Macintosh as a guest, without any restrictions. This arrangement may be fine if you know — and trust absolutely — everyone who might use another network Macintosh to access your shared items. Otherwise, you should take steps to restrict access.

The Users & Groups control panel allows you to specify which users can access the shared folders and disks on your Macintosh (see Figure 9-9).

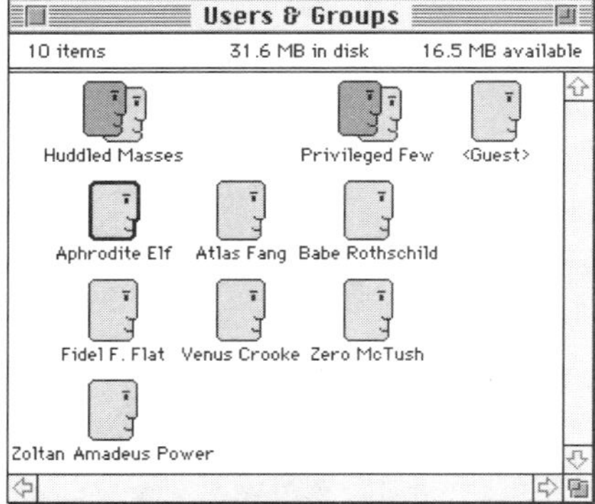


**Figure 9-9: Users & Groups control panel.**

When you first open the Users & Groups control panel, two user icons appear. The one with the dark border is for your Macintosh's owner; the other is for guests (that is, anyone on your network). You create additional icons for registered users to whom you want to grant greater access privileges than guests have. Registered users must enter their names and any passwords you've assigned them before they can access your Macintosh to share information.

After you create your set of registered users, you can use the Sharing command to specify special access privileges that one registered user has to a particular shared item. You also can create groups of registered users and assign to a group (instead of an individual) special access privileges to any item (again using the Sharing command). You can create as many as 100 registered users and groups in the Users & Groups control panel; for optimal performance, however, you shouldn't name more than 50.

## The Owner

The Owner icon, outlined in bold in the Users & Groups control panel, represents the owner of your Macintosh as a registered user. This icon is created automatically when you use the Sharing Setup control panel to identify your Macintosh. The name of the Owner icon comes from the name in the Sharing Setup control panel's Owner Name text box. You have special access rights when you connect to your Macintosh as its owner from any other Macintosh on the network.

Opening the Owner icon displays the owner-privileges window, shown in Figure 9-10.

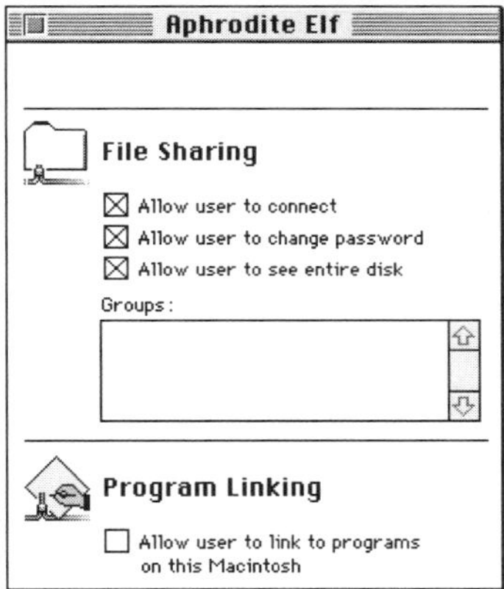


**Figure 9-10: The Owner's access privileges.**

Turning on the "Allow user to connect" option gives you access to your Macintosh from another Macintosh connected to the network. Turning on the "Allow user to change password" option enables you to change your password remotely. The option "Allow user to see entire disk" enables you to see and use any items on any hard disk attached to your Macintosh. This setting gives you access to all shared or unshared disks and folders on your Macintosh (while you are connected to your Mac from another Macintosh), whether or not you're named the owner of a shared folder and regardless of the privileges assigned to your shared disks.

## Guests

The Guest icon in the Users & Groups window enables anyone connected to the network to access your shared information. You can, however, restrict Guest access to your Macintosh. Generally, it's a good idea to prevent unwelcome users from accessing your Macintosh by restricting Guest access and granting specific access privileges to registered users. For directions on restricting access privileges for individual shared items, see "Controlling Access to Shared Items" later in this chapter.

To disable all Guest access, open the Guest icon in the Users & Groups control panel to display the Guest privileges window (see Figure 9-11), and turn off the "Allow guests to connect" option. Now only registered users are allowed to share items on your Macintosh.

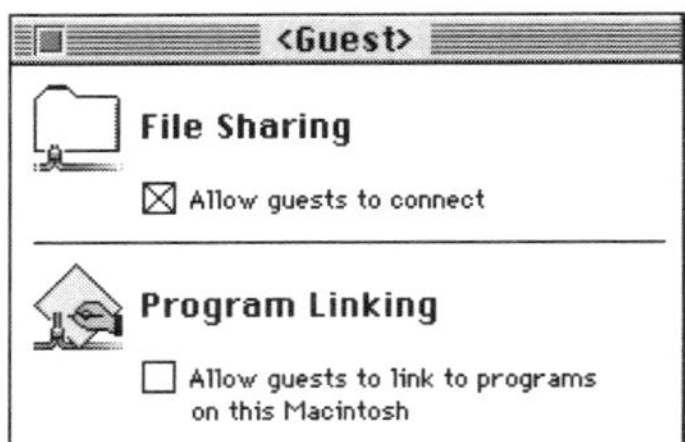


**Figure 9-11: A Guest's access privileges.**

## Registered users

Establishing registered users helps secure your shared items from unauthorized access. To identify a registered user, first open the Users & Groups control panel. Next, choose New User from the File menu to create a New User icon in the Users & Groups control panel, as shown in Figure 9-12. The New User command is available only when the Users & Groups control panel is open.

**Figure 9-12: The icon of a new registered user.**

Replace the name *New User* with the name of the user you want by typing the user's name while the icon name is selected. (Registered user names are not case-sensitive, so it doesn't matter how you mix uppercase and lowercase letters.) You can save the user's time when connecting to your Macintosh if you use the Owner Name from his or her Sharing Setup control panel. Contact the user to get the right name. If you use a different name than the Owner Name, you need to notify the user of the name you enter here, because the user must type the exact name to connect to your Macintosh. The user now is registered on your Macintosh, and you can grant him or her special access privileges to specific shared items on your Macintosh. For information on setting access privileges of your shared items, see "Controlling Access to Shared Items" later in this chapter.

You can add another level of security by assigning to a registered user a password that he or she needs to type to access your shared items. You assign a password by opening the user's icon to display the registered-user privileges window, shown in Figure 9-13. Enter a password up to eight characters long. Keep in mind that the user must type the password exactly as you type it here, including uppercase and lowercase letters.

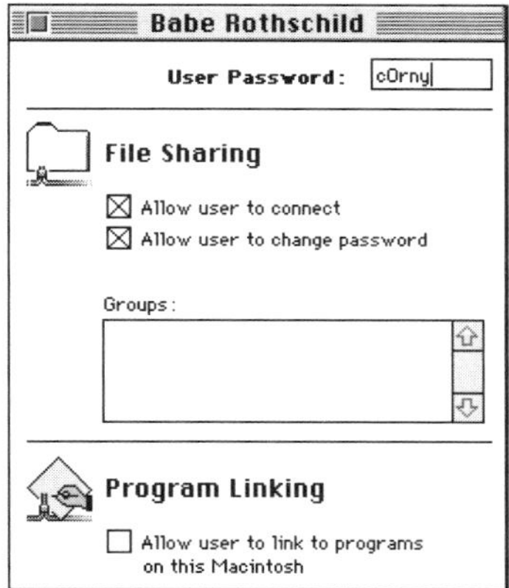


**Figure 9-13: A registered user's access privileges.**

Two additional settings in the registered-user privileges window enable you to specify the user's general access privileges. Turning on the "Allow user to connect" option permits the user to access your Macintosh. If you want to enable this user to change the password you assigned, turn on the "Allow user to change password" option. When you finish setting the registered user's access privileges, close the registered-user privileges window to make your changes take effect.

You can modify a registered user's access privileges or remove the user from your set of registered users at any time. To remove a registered user, drag its icon from the Users & Groups control panel to the Trash.

## Apple Remote Access privileges

If you have installed the Apple Remote Access software, the various user-privileges windows include additional settings, shown in Figure 9-14.

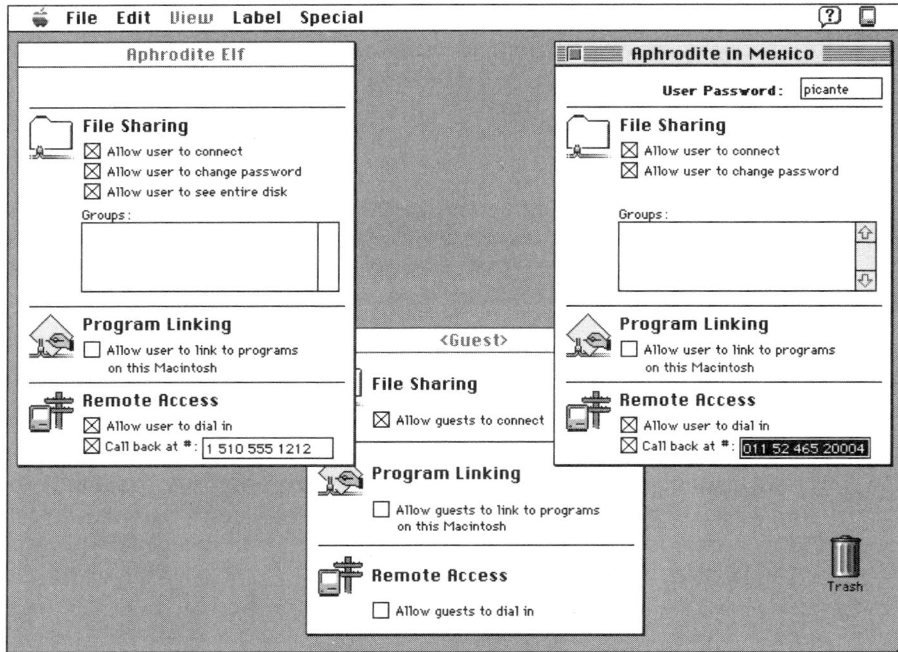


**Figure 9-14: Remote access privileges for owner, guest, and registered users.**

You can allow or deny remote access to the owner, to guests, and to each registered user individually. For the owner and for each registered guest, you can specify a call-back phone number. When Apple Remote Access gets a call from a user who has a call-back number, the program hangs up and calls the user back at the specified number. This procedure prevents an unauthorized person from gaining access to your computer by learning a registered user's password and trying to call from an unauthorized location. When you specify a call-back number, you have to pay the cost of the phone call for the connection, but you know that the person accessing your computer has the correct password and is calling from the user's computer.

## Groups of users

Office or work environments usually consist of groups of people, such as departments or project teams, who need to share certain items. System 7's file sharing enables you to specify special access privileges for groups as well as for individual users. Groups simply are collections of individual registered users, and you can grant specific access privileges for a shared item to a group instead of to a single user.

To establish a group of users, open the Users & Groups control panel and choose New Group from the File menu. A new icon named New Group appears in the Users & Groups control panel, as shown in Figure 9-15. Notice that the group icon is different from the single-user icon. Replace the name *New Group* with your own group name by typing while the icon name is selected.

**Figure 9-15: A new group.**

To add registered users to a group, drag their icons to the group icon. The system displays a message indicating that the user or users are being added to the group. The registered-user icons are copied into the group icon. You also can add a user to a group by dragging the group icon to the user icon. To speed the process of adding users to groups, Shift-click to select all the registered users and then drag them to the group icon. (You don't need to include the Owner icon in groups.)

To see the members of the group, open the group icon. The group window shows a member icon for every user in the group, as shown in Figure 9-16. If you want to see or change information for a registered user, you can open either the user icon or the member icon. You cannot create a new registered user from within the group window, however.

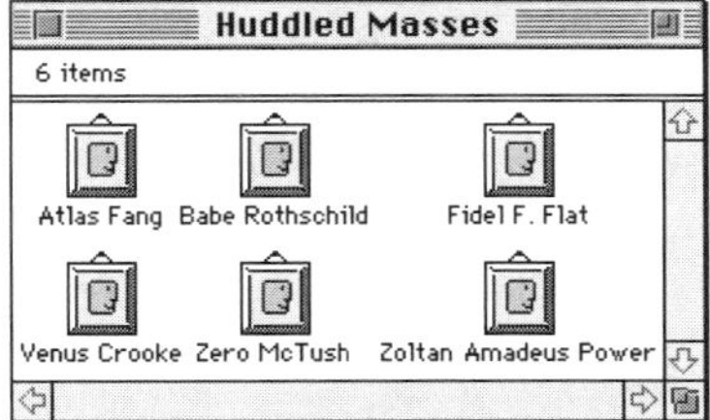


**Figure 9-16: Members of a group.**

To see all the groups to which an individual user belongs, open the registered or member user icon. In both cases, the user's access-privileges window displays a list of groups to which the registered user belongs, as shown in Figure 9-17.

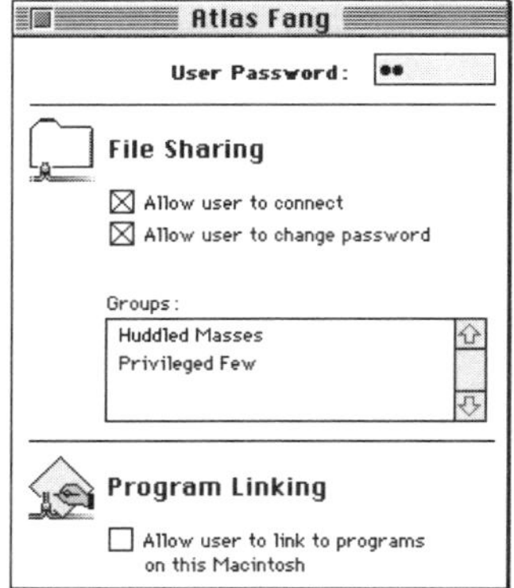


**Figure 9-17: The groups to which a registered user belongs.**

# Controlling Access to Shared Items

Anyone can use and make changes to a shared folder or disk and its contents when you first share the folder or disk. System 7 provides access-privilege settings with which you control who can see and change your shared files, folders, and disks. You specify access privileges for three categories of users: the owner, one user or group, and everyone. For example, you might want to ensure that a user or group of users can access templates on your Macintosh but not modify them. Access privileges also enable you to selectively share confidential documents, such as an employee's performance review.

You set the access privileges of a folder or disk in its Sharing info window, which appears when you select the folder or disk and choose the Sharing command from the File menu, as shown in Figure 9-18. You can't set a file's access privileges directly; instead, you place the file in a shared folder and set the folder's access privileges.

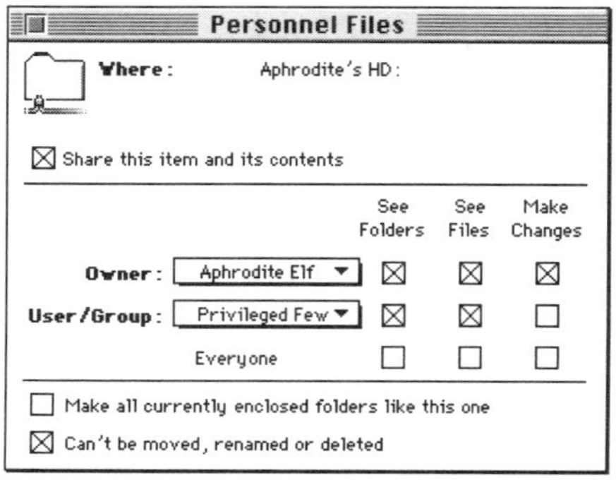

**Figure 9-18: A Sharing info window.**

Table 9-1
**Disk and Folder Access-Privilege Settings**

| ***Privilege*** | ***Purpose*** |
|---|---|
| See Folders | Shows or hides the folders in a shared folder or disk. Users who don't have this privilege can't see the folders in the shared folder or disk. |
| See Files | Shows or hides the files in a shared folder or disk. Users who don't have this privilege can't see files in the shared folder or disk. |
| Make Changes | Allows designated users to make changes to the shared item, including duplicating, deleting, and saving. |

## Setting access privileges

You can grant three types of access privileges for each user category in the Sharing info window. Table 9-1 describes these access-privilege settings.

Additional settings in the Sharing info window provide access-privilege uniformity and greater security for shared items. Turning on the "Make all currently enclosed folders like this one" option for a shared disk or folder assigns its privileges to folders that you recently moved into it and to enclosed folders that previously had different privilege settings. This option makes the privileges of all enclosed folders the same as those of the enclosing folder. When you're sharing a disk or folder for the first time, you don't need to turn on this option, because the shared item's contents, as well as any new folders that you later create in it, automatically are set to the same privileges as the shared item.

To prevent anyone on the network (including yourself) from moving, deleting, or renaming a shared folder, turn on the "Can't be moved, renamed, or deleted" option. This option is always in force for shared disks, so it is not listed for them. You can set different privileges for a folder inside a shared folder or disk by opening its Sharing info window and selecting or deselecting checkboxes, turning off the "Same as enclosing folder" option in the enclosed folder's Sharing info window, as shown in Figure 9-19. (The "Same as enclosing folder" option appears only for folders that are inside a shared folder or shared disk.)

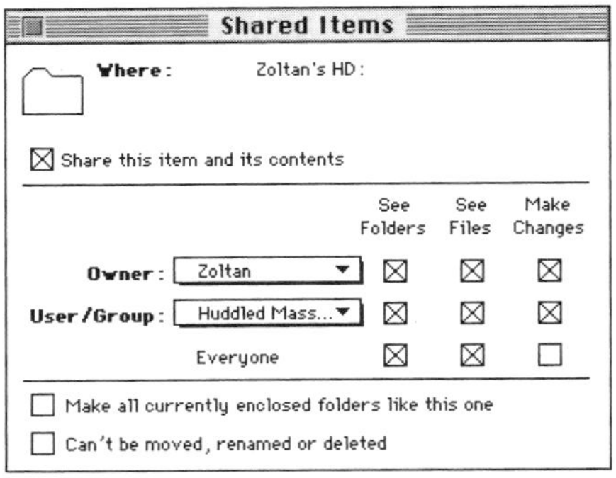

**Figure 9-19: Making an enclosed folder's privileges unique.**

## Specifying who has access privileges

The Sharing info window displays three categories of users to whom you can grant or deny access privileges. The Owner category is the person or group that created the shared folder (not necessarily your Macintosh's owner). The User/Group category refers to one registered user or one group of users. The Everyone category refers to anyone who connects to your Macintosh as a guest. The three categories of users are dimmed if the "Share this item and its contents" option is off or (for enclosed folders) if the "Same as enclosing folder" option is on.

Ownership of a folder or disk gives you the right to modify its access privileges. You can transfer ownership of a folder or disk to a particular registered user, to a group, or to any registered user on the network. To change ownership of a folder or disk located on your Macintosh, use the Owner pop-up menu in the Sharing info window. The Owner pop-up menu lists the registered users and groups to whom you can transfer the ownership of the folder, as shown in Figure 9-20. (If you have added a new user or group that doesn't appear in the pop-up menu, close the Sharing info window and then reopen it.)

You also can change ownership of a folder or disk that you own on someone else's Macintosh. In this case, no Owner pop-up menu appears, so you must type the new owner's name.

Keep in mind that after you transfer ownership of a folder or disk, the new owner can restrict your access to that item and its contents — but only when you try to access the folder from another Mac on your network. Giving away ownership of a folder or disk on your Macintosh doesn't take away your ability to open, use, or modify it from your own Mac. In effect, an item can have dual ownership, giving two users ownership privileges. If you make another user the owner of an item on

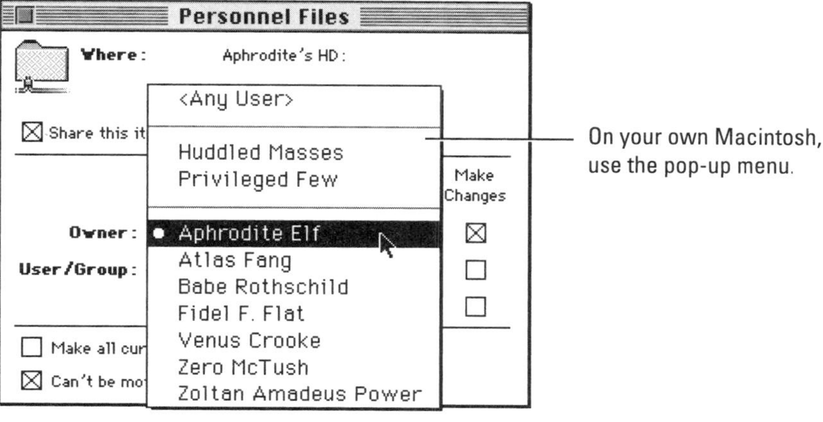


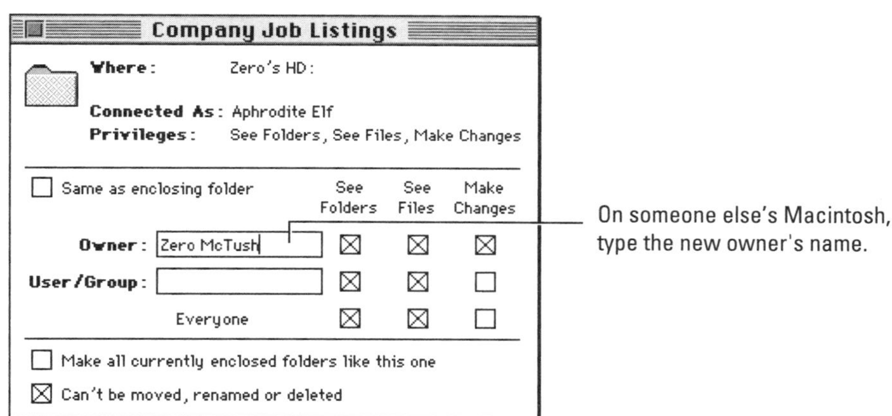


**Figure 9-20: Changing an item's owner.**

your Macintosh, both you and that other user have ownership privileges. You can reclaim sole ownership at any time by making yourself the owner in the item's Sharing info window.

You choose the registered user or a group to which you want to grant specific access privileges by using the User/Group pop-up menu. This menu lists all the registered users and groups in your Users & Groups control panel, as shown in Figure 9-21. You also can change the User/Group setting for an item that you own on another computer (or on your computer, when you're accessing it from another computer on the network). In this case, you must type the name of the registered user or group because the pop-up menu does not appear.

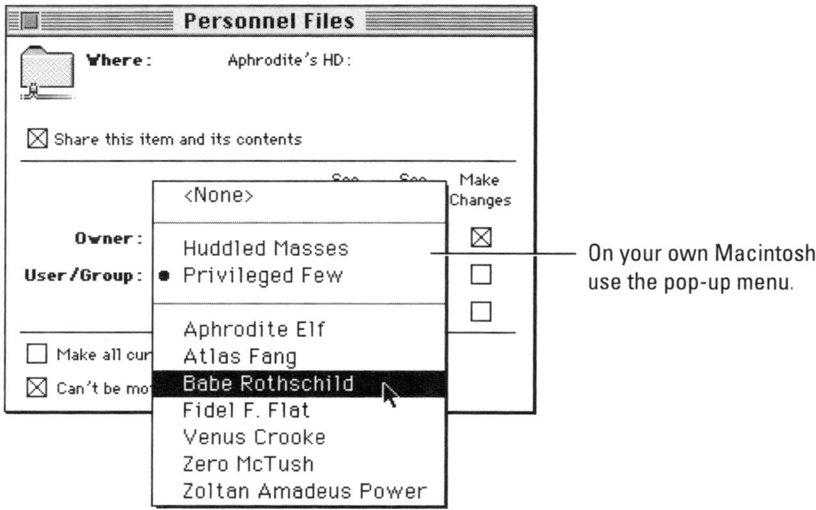


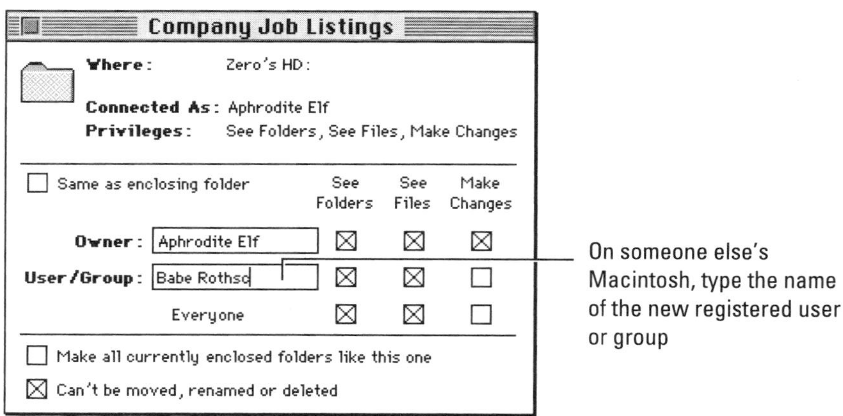


**Figure 9-21: The Remote Access Setup control panel.**

# Recognizing access privileges

People who share your folders can see the privileges you assigned to a folder by looking at its icon, as shown in Figure 9-22. A folder icon with a belt around it indicates that the user doesn't have access privileges. A belt-strapped folder icon with an accompanying down arrow acts like a mailbox; the user can drop items into the folder but cannot open it or use anything inside it. A tabbed folder icon tells the user that he or she is the folder's owner. A plain folder icon means that the user can open and use the folder.

## Giving Rank Its Privileges

It's important to remember to make Everyone's access privileges less than or the same as those of the designated user or group because the Mac does not grant registered users or the owner fewer privileges than are granted to guests. However, you won't see an alert box that tells you so if you happen to assign more privileges to Everyone than to higher-ranking users. Further, you ought to set the User/Group privileges lower than the Owner privileges. For example, granting broad access privileges to the User/Group category is useless if you don't also restrict access privileges in the Everyone category. Just remember: rank hath its privileges.

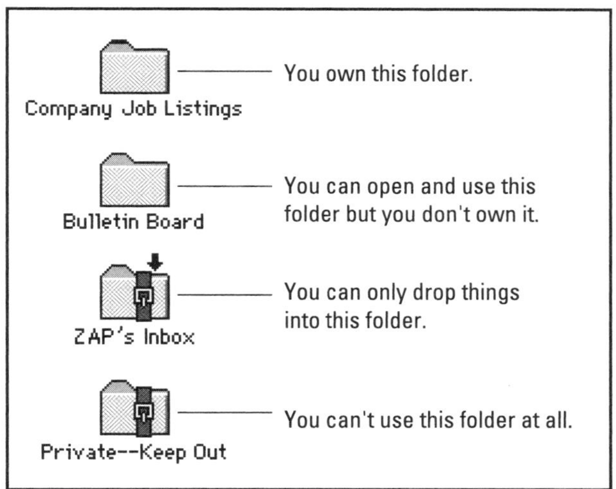


**Figure 9-22: The four shared-folder icons.**

When you open a folder that belongs to someone else, look for one to three icons just below the window's close box. The icons indicate any privileges that the folder's owner has denied you. A pencil with a line through it means that you can't make changes to items in the window. A document with a line through it means that you can't see files in the window. A folder with a line through it means that you can't see folders in the window.

# Comparing Access-Privilege Scenarios

Controlling who can do what with files in shared areas opens new possibilities for working in groups. Using access-privilege settings, you can keep folders private between two users, make the folders accessible to everyone on the network, or assign combinations between these extremes. The following sections explain setting access privileges for five interesting file-sharing scenarios.

## Universal access

Allowing everyone on the network access to a shared item and its contents is easy: just grant the See Files, See Folders, and Make Changes privileges to the Everyone category (see Figure 9-23). It doesn't matter how you set the User/Group and Owner categories.

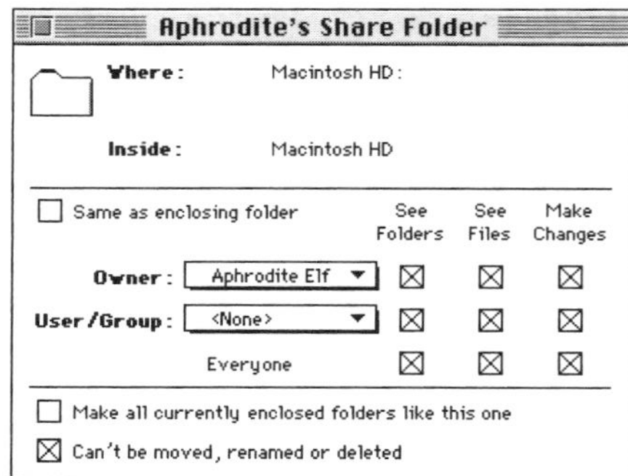


**Figure 9-23: Access privileges for universal access.**

## Restricted access

If you want to give one registered user or one group access to a shared item but deny access to guests, turn on all privileges in the User/Group category, and turn off all privileges in the Everyone category, as shown in Figure 9-24.

## Private access

If you own a folder on someone else's computer, you can keep that folder private by turning off all privileges in the User/Group and Everyone categories, as shown in Figure 9-25. Only you and the user of that Macintosh can access your folder. Anyone who connects to that Macintosh sees a strapped folder without a down arrow, indicating that he or she can't use the folder at all.

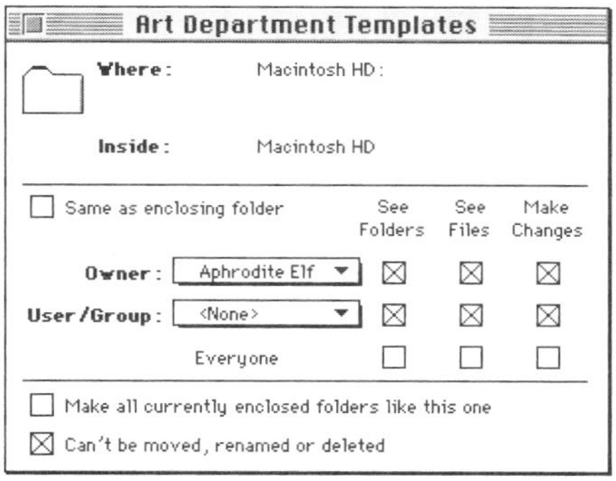

**Figure 9-24: Access privileges for restricted access.**

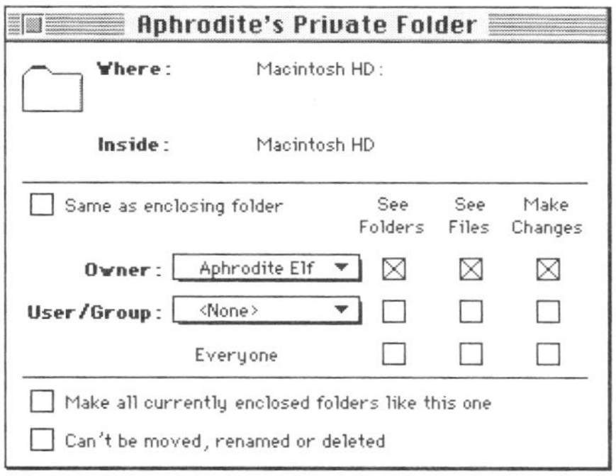

**Figure 9-25: Access privileges for private access.**

To keep a folder or disk on your own computer private, make sure that its "Share this item and its contents" option is off; use the Finder's Sharing command to verify its status.

## A private in-box folder

Setting up a folder to act as an in-box (or in-basket) enables other network users to deposit documents, folders, and other items in that folder. In-box folders sometimes are referred to as *drop folders*, meaning that other users can drop in items, but only you can take those items out.

You prevent all other people from seeing, removing, or changing your folder's contents by denying the User/Group and Everyone access privileges to see folders and files, as shown in Figure 9-26. Anyone connecting to your Macintosh sees a strapped folder accompanied by a down arrow, indicating that they can only add folders and documents to the folder.

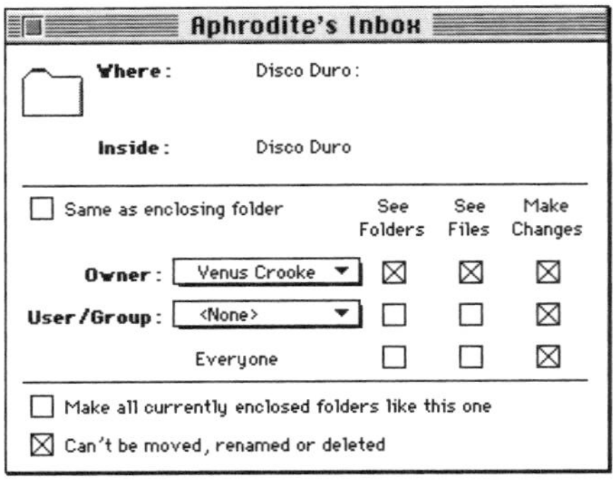

**Figure 9-26: Access privileges for an in-box folder.**

# A user or group bulletin board

Another useful configuration of access privileges is setting up a folder to act as a bulletin board, enabling other users to open and read documents but preventing them from adding or changing documents.

To establish a bulletin-board folder, create and name an empty folder. Select the folder, and choose Sharing from the File menu. If you don't want to share your bulletin-board folder with everyone, select the user or group that you want to give access to the bulletin-board folder, and set their access privileges to see folders and files. Deny privileges to make changes for the User/Group and Everyone categories, as shown in Figure 9-27. If you want a user or group only to access your bulletin-board folder, deny all privileges in the Everyone category.

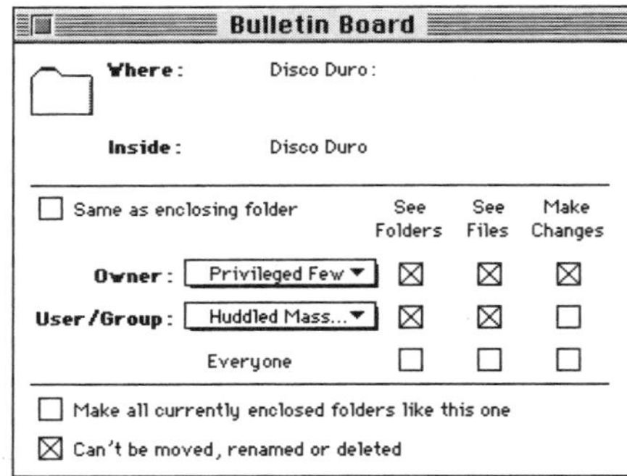


**Figure 9-27: Access privileges for a bulletin-board folder.**

# Monitoring File-Sharing Activity

When file sharing is on, you can view who is connected to your Macintosh and list which of your folders and disks you are sharing. To monitor file-sharing activity, open the File Sharing Monitor control panel, as shown in Figure 9-28.

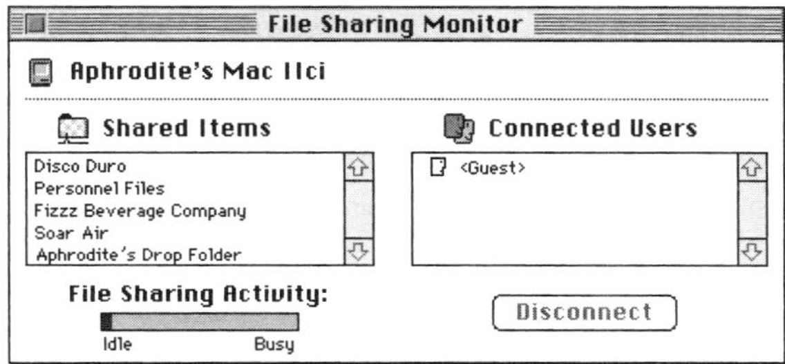


**Figure 9-28: The File Sharing Monitor control panel.**

A list of your shared folders and disks appears on the left side of the File Sharing Monitor control panel. Only the folders and disks that you're sharing (by using the Sharing command) are displayed; all the files and folders contained in those folders and disks also are accessible, although they aren't explicitly listed.

A list of the network computer users currently connected to your Macintosh appears on the right side of the control-panel window. The File Sharing Activity indicator shows how much of your Macintosh's total processing time is being spent handling file sharing.

## Temporarily disconnecting users

The File Sharing Monitor control panel also allows you to disconnect a user who is connected to your Macintosh. This disconnection doesn't turn off file sharing, as the Sharing Setup control panel does, but it temporarily prevents all users (or selected users) from sharing items on your Macintosh.

To disconnect a user, select the user you want to disconnect from the list of connected users in the File Sharing Monitor control panel. To select more than one user, press Shift while clicking the names of the users you want to disconnect. When you click the Disconnect button, the system asks you to specify the number of minutes you want to elapse before the disconnection occurs. It's good networking etiquette to give people enough time to save any changes they have made to the files before you disconnect them. To disconnect a user immediately, specify 0 minutes. Remember that this procedure disconnects the user only temporarily; he or she still can connect again and access your shared folders.

# Sharing Someone Else's Folders and Disks

So far, you have created and set access privileges for items that you're sharing with other network users. Other users on the network who are sharing their items have performed similar tasks to make folders or disks available to you and to other users. Before you can access another user's shared items as a guest, you need to know the name of the Macintosh you want to access. To access the shared items as a registered user, you also must know your registered name and password on the other computer. In addition, if your network has zones, you need to find out the name of the zone in which the other Macintosh is located.

## Connecting as a registered user or guest

To make a connection to another Macintosh, open the Chooser. Make sure that AppleTalk is active (so that you can connect to another Macintosh on the network), and click the AppleShare icon. If your network contains zones, click the zone in which the other Macintosh to which you want to connect resides. The Chooser then displays a list of computers whose folders and disks you can share. From the list, select the name of the Macintosh to which you want to connect; then click the OK button. A dialog box appears, allowing you to identify yourself as a registered user or guest (see Figure 9-29).

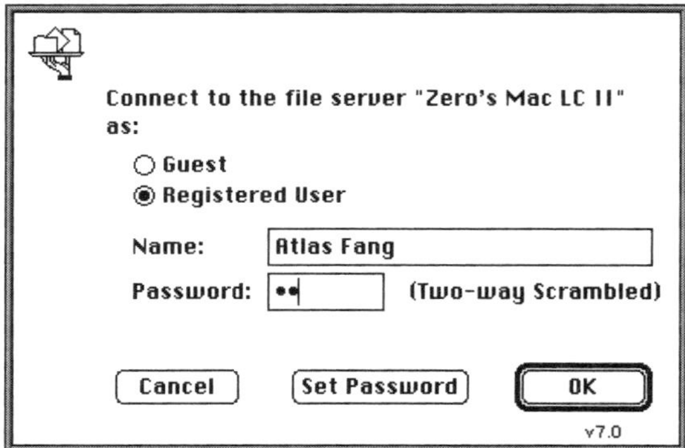


**Figure 9-29: Identifying yourself to another computer.**

To connect as a registered user, click the Registered User button, and enter your registered name and password in the appropriate text boxes. (This name and password must have been assigned by the owner of the Macintosh that you want to access.) Type your password exactly as it was assigned, including uppercase and lowercase letters, and then click the OK button.

If you're not a registered user and the Guest option isn't dimmed, you can access the other Macintosh as a guest. If the Guest option is dimmed, guests are not permitted access to the selected Macintosh. If you're accessing your own Macintosh from another Macintosh, you enter your password (the owner password in the Sharing Setup control panel on your Macintosh). You can connect to another Macintosh on the network automatically by using aliases (see Chapter 10).

You change your password by clicking the Set Password button. A dimmed Set Password button indicates that the owner of the Macintosh to which you want to connect does not allow you to change your password.

# Selecting shared disks and folders

After you connect as a registered user or guest, the Chooser displays a list of the items you can share, as shown in Figure 9-30. A dimmed name indicates either that you're already sharing that folder or disk or that the owner of that folder or disk hasn't granted you access privileges to see it.

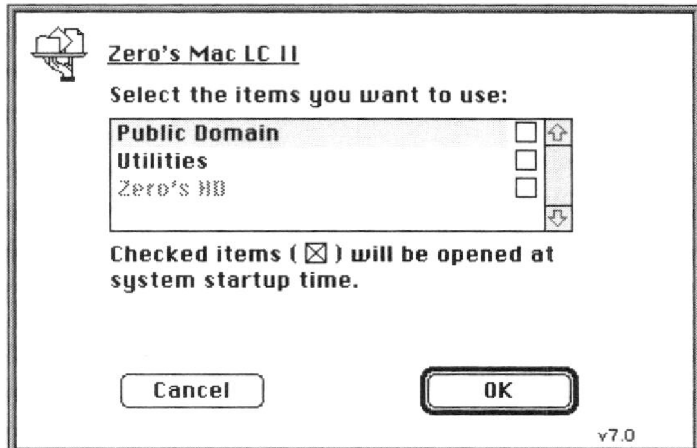


**Figure 9-30: The Chooser's list of items you can access.**

Select the name of the shared folders and disks that you want to use. To select more than one, press Shift while clicking the names of the shared folders or disks you want. (You can scroll through the list or type the first few letters of a shared item's name to find it.)

When you click OK to close the dialog box, a shared-volume icon appears on your Desktop, as shown in Figure 9-31. Your Macintosh treats a shared volume like a disk, no matter whether it's a folder or a disk on the owner's Macintosh.

**Figure 9-31: The icon of a shared disk or folder.**

Table 9-2 shows the access privileges that you need in order to perform common tasks with a shared item.

## Sharing items from another Macintosh automatically

You also use the Chooser's list of shareable items to designate which of them you want System 7 to open automatically at startup time. This feature is a real time saver if you frequently use certain shared folders or disks. Designate the items that you want to be opened automatically by marking the checkbox next to each one.

If you mark a checkbox and are a registered user, two options appear in the dialog box below the list. Select the "Save My Name Only" option if you want the system to ask for your password before opening the shared folder or disk during startup. Use this option to prevent unauthorized people from accessing the shared folder or disk from your Macintosh. If you select the "Save My Name and Password" option, your Macintosh automatically supplies your password when it opens the marked items.

**Table 9-2: Access privileges for common tasks**

| *To do this with a shared folder or disk:* | *You need these privileges:* See Folders | See Files | Make Changes |
|---|---|---|---|
| Open a file from | | ✓ | |
| Save changes to a file in | | ✓ | ✓ |
| Drag something to | | | ✓ |
| Copy a file from | | ✓ | |
| Copy a folder from | ✓ | | |
| Discard a file from | | ✓ | ✓ |
| Discard a folder from | ✓ | | ✓ |
| Create a new folder in | ✓ | | ✓ |

## Working with items shared from another Macintosh

You use the items shared from another Macintosh in the same manner that you use items on your own Macintosh. What you can do with a shared item, of course, depends on the access privileges that its owner has granted you. To see your access privileges, select the shared item, and choose Sharing from the File menu. For an item shared from another Macintosh, the Sharing info window tells where the item is, the name by which you're connected, and your access privileges for that item.

When you open a shared document, the Finder searches your local disks for the program needed to open the document. If the program isn't found, the Finder tries to find it on the Macintosh from which you're sharing the file and to open it across the network. Running programs over a network is considerably slower than running a program on your Macintosh. Whenever you send or receive information across the network by using System 7's file sharing, a double-arrow icon flashes in the upper-left corner of the menu bar.

If you access your own Macintosh remotely (or use another Macintosh as its owner), you can see and use everything on that Macintosh. In other words, you have full access privileges to all items, whether or not they have been designated for sharing (with the Sharing command). This feature is handy if you've forgotten an important file or need to refer to some information on your Macintosh when you're no longer in your office. By connecting to your computer over the network, you can copy those files to the Macintosh at which you're working and then read, change, or print those files. It's possible to deny the owner the ability to see unshared items or to prevent the owner (yourself) from connecting at all. To do so, turn off the "Allow user to see entire disk" setting or the "Allow user to connect" setting in the owner's access-privilege window (refer to Figure 9-10 earlier in this chapter).

## Transferring items between computers

The most common use of sharing folders and disks is to transfer items from one Macintosh to another. For the most part, you transfer items between computers just as you would copy files to a floppy disk. If you try to move a folder or file to the desktop, a message asks whether you want to copy the item to your startup disk. If you click OK, the item appears on your desktop.

## Disconnecting from another Macintosh

You can disconnect from another Macintosh in three ways:

- ❖ You can select the icons of all items that you're sharing from that Macintosh and then choose Put Away from the File menu.
- ❖ You can drag those file-server icons to the Trash.
- ❖ If you're done working on your Macintosh, choose the Shut Down command from the Finder's Special menu; you disconnect from the other Mac while shutting down.

# Coping with Network Insecurity

Can hackers invade your network? System 7's file-sharing capability puts your hard disks at risk if your Mac is connected to a network. The risk of invasion exists even if you normally have file sharing turned off. Someone who spends 40 seconds at your keyboard can open your Sharing Setup control panel, change your owner password (without knowing your current password), start file sharing, and close the control panel, leaving no sign of these activities. Then, at his or her leisure, the hacker can use another Mac on the network to connect to your Mac as its owner and snoop through everything on your hard disks without leaving any electronic footprints.

You eventually would notice if someone changed your files, of course, and you would see that your password had been changed if you tried to connect to your Macintosh from another computer. But a less easily detectable invasion involves altering access privileges with the Users & Groups control panel and the Finder's Sharing command; this procedure takes only five to ten minutes.

Apple could make your system more secure by adding password access to the Sharing Setup and the Users & Groups control panels. In the meantime, you can install and use At Ease to prevent unauthorized access to your Control Panels folder, thereby preventing access to the Sharing Setup and Users & Groups control panels inside it (see "At Ease" in Chapter 5).

On another level, you can password-protect your disks or folders by using software such as Folder Bolt from Kent-Marsh. Otherwise, you must either remove the File Sharing extension from your Extensions folder or trust everyone who has access to a Mac on your network.

# CHAPTER 9 CONCEPTS AND TERMS

- System 7's built-in file sharing makes connecting Macintosh computers and sharing files, folders, and disks easier than ever before.
- Using LocalTalk or PhoneNet connectors to connect two or more Macintosh computers, anyone can create a ready-to-use AppleTalk network to share and transfer files.
- After you install Apple Remote Access, one Macintosh can connect to an AppleTalk network through another Macintosh over standard telephone lines.
- You use the Sharing Setup control panel to start and stop file sharing from your Macintosh.
- In the Users & Groups control panel, you create registered users and groups of users, and assign general access privileges to each.
- You use the Finder's Sharing command to designate which of your disks and folders you want to share with others and what each item's access privileges are for three categories of users: the owner, one registered user or group, and everyone on the network.
- The File Sharing Monitor control panel tells you which items you are sharing with other users and who is currently connected to your Macintosh.
- You get access to other computers (and to the folders and disks on them) by using the Chooser desk accessory. When you have access to a shared item, your Macintosh treats it like a disk.

**AppleTalk**
The networking software and communication protocols built into every Macintosh and most LaserWriters.

**case-sensitive**
Describes a password in which capitilization matters. For instance, capital A is not the same as lower case a.

**drop folders**
A folder in which users may place items, but only the folder's owner can see them.

**dedicated file server**
A computer that is dedicated to providing file-sharing services.

**Ethernet**
A high-speed cabling system built into many newer Mac and LaserWriter models. Its connectors and cabling cost more than LocalTalks

**EtherTalk**
A network connection that uses AppleTalk software and communications protocols over Ethernet cabling

**file sharing**
Allows you to share files, folders, and disks with people whose computers are connected to yours in a network.

**groups**
Collections of individual registered users. You can grant specific access privileges for a shared item to a group instead of to a single user.

**guest**
A network user who has no special access privileges to your shared items.

**hacker**
A computer user who gains unauthorized access to network services by circumventing access privilege restrictions.

**LocalTalk**
Apple's cabling system for connecting computers, printers, and other devices to create an AppleTalk network. LocalTalk uses the built-in printer ports of Macintosh computers and the LocalTalk ports of many LaserWriter printers.

**network administrator**
Someone who sets up and maintains a centralized file server. The network administrator does not control access to folders and files on the server's disks; that is the responsibility of each person who puts items on the disks.

**owner**
A registered user or group that has greater access privileges to a shared folder than all other users and groups. Also, the person who can access all disks and folders (even those not explicitly shared with the Sharing command); this owner's name and password are set in the Sharing Setup control panel.

**password**
A combination of letters, digits, and symbols that must be typed accurately to gain access to shared items on a file server (including another Mac that is sharing its folders).

**PhoneNet**
An inexpensive cabling system for connecting computers, printers, and other devices to an AppleTalk network. PhoneNet uses the built-in printer ports of Macintosh computers and the LocalTalk ports of many LaserWriter printers.

**registered user**
Users to whom you want to grant greater access privileges than guests have. Registered users must enter their names and any passwords you've assigned them before they can access your Macintosh to share information.

CHAPTER TEN

# Working with Aliases

- Using aliases to organize documents and folders in multiple filing schemes without duplicating items
- Adding items to the Apple menu or the Startup Items folder without moving the items from their folders
- Opening any item from the desktop without moving it from its folder
- Cutting laterally across your folder structure in directory dialog boxes
- Getting quick access to selected items in your System Folder
- Opening items on floppy disks and CD-ROMs that are not inserted
- Simplifying networking tasks with aliases

The hierarchical order of the Macintosh universe enables you to organize programs and documents into folders. Nesting folders within folders keeps related items together but can turn your disk into a labyrinth. The Finder's Find command helps you locate items without digging through folders, but it's no substitute for well-organized disks.

Finder *aliases* cut through the organizational red tape. Aliases act like real items when you open them or drag items to them. Think of an alias as a stand-in or an agent for a real program, document, folder, or disk. You can place these agents at your beck and call in any handy location, such as on the desktop or in the Apple menu. When you open aliases or drag items to them, they act like the real items they represent. Aliases even look like the items they represent, except that their names are italicized.

## Understanding Aliases

Like the documents, programs, and other items on your disks, aliases are files that contain information. An alias doesn't contain text or a picture like a file you create, or program instructions like an application file. Rather, an alias contains information that points to a file, a folder, or a disk, as shown in Figure 10-1.

Based on the information in an alias, the system software can locate the alias's *original item* (also known as its *target*). The system software can successfully *resolve* an alias, locating its original item, even if you move or rename the original item or move the original item to a different folder. The only way you can break the connection between an alias and its original item is to drag the original item to the Trash and empty the Trash. The system software cannot successfully resolve an alias whose original item no longer exists.

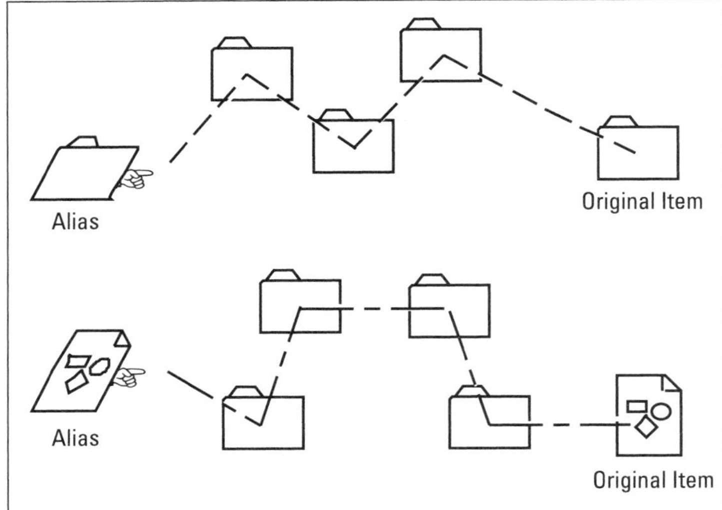


**Figure 10-1: An alias points to its original item.**

When you open an alias, the system software resolves the information in the alias, locates the original item, and opens the original. Dragging an item to the alias of a folder or disk in the Finder has the same effect as dragging it to the original folder or disk — the Finder resolves the information in the alias, locates the original folder or disk, and places the item you dragged there. Likewise, dragging a document to an alias of a compatible program opens the document. You can even drag an alias to an alias; the Finder resolves the information in both aliases and deals with the original items.

Sometimes the Finder treats a file as an alias — italicizing its name — when it isn't an alias. This happens with some old files because the System 7 Finder flags a file as an alias by setting a *bit* (a single binary digit) that older Finders reserved for a disused copy-protection scheme. The Finder detects these problems and fixes them, explaining, "Sorry, this item is not an alias (oops!). The problem has now been corrected. Please try again," or "The alias 'FileName' could not be opened, because this item is really not an alias (oops!). The problem has now been corrected. Please try again."

# Making an Alias

You can make an alias for any item you can open from the Finder. That category includes documents, application programs, desk accessories, folders, disks, control panels, and even fonts and sounds. Making an alias is a simple procedure. In the

Finder, select the item for which you want to create an alias and choose Make Alias from the File menu, as shown in Figure 10-2. A new item with the same icon as the original item, an italicized name that matches that of the original item, and the suffix *alias* appears, as shown in Figure 10-3.

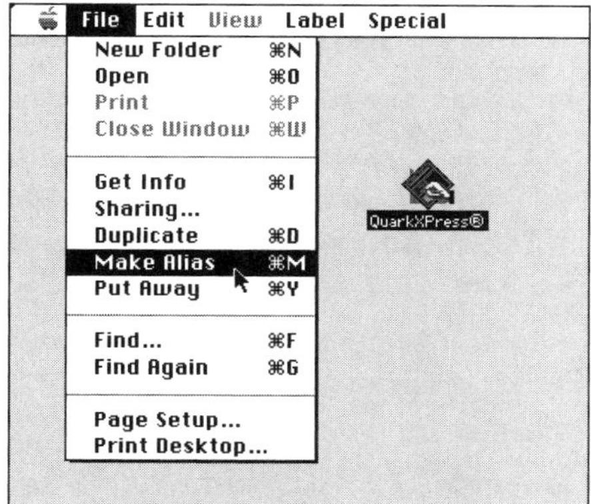


**Figure 10-2: Using the Make Alias command.**

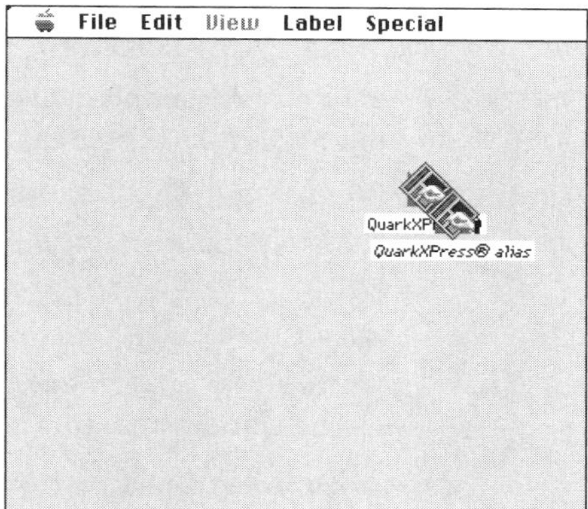


**Figure 10-3: A newly made alias with the original item.**

Immediately after you create an alias, its name is selected for editing. You can change the name by typing a replacement or by using other standard text-editing techniques (see "Renaming Icons" in Chapter 4). To keep the name as is, click anywhere outside the name or press Return or Enter.

## Same Alias, Different Size

Aliases vary in size from 1K to 3K or more, depending on the capacity of the disk they're on. For example, an alias takes up 1K of a floppy disk, 20MB hard disk, or 40MB hard disk. On an 80MB hard disk, an alias takes up 2K, and aliases on CD-ROMs occupy 10K each. If a hard disk is partitioned into multiple volumes (each having its own icon on the desktop), the volume capacity determines the size of the aliases on it. For details on the relationship between partition size and file size, see "Optimizing Disks" in Chapter 6.

# Changing an Alias

After you make an alias, you can manipulate it as you would any other item. Move it to another folder on the same disk or to the desktop; the alias still knows where to find its original item.

Copy an alias by using the Finder's Duplicate command or by dragging the alias to another disk or to a folder on another disk. To copy an alias or other item to another folder on the same disk, press Option while dragging. All copies of the alias point to the same original item.

You rename an alias as you would any other item on the desktop or in a Finder window. If you want an alias to have exactly the same name as its original item, the two cannot be in the same folder. You must move one out.

Like any item, you remove an alias by dragging it to the Trash. Remember, throwing away an alias doesn't affect the original item. You're only throwing away the alias, not the item to which it points.

An alias inherits its icon from the original item. If you subsequently change the original item's icon, the alias icon is updated automatically the next time you double-click it. Like most other icons, you can customize an alias icon in its Info window. You reveal the Info window by using the Finder's Get Info command (see "Custom Icons" in Chapter 4). The alias's custom icon won't be affected by changes to the icon of the original item. You can also type comments about the alias and lock the alias in its Info window. Locking an alias in its Info window prevents changing the name or icon of the alias — the same as locking any file. Locking an alias does not lock its original item.

### Oodles of Aliases

You can create multiple aliases for the same original item so that you can access the original from different locations. Only disk space limits the number of aliases you can create. To make aliases for several items in the same window at once, select them all and use the Make Alias command. An alias appears for every item you selected. All the new aliases are automatically selected so that you can immediately drag them to another place without having to manually select them one by one.

### Removing the Suffix 'Alias'

To quickly remove the word *alias* from the end of an alias's name, click the name once to select it for editing, pause briefly (or avoid the pause by moving the mouse slightly to the right after you click the alias name), double-click the last word of the name, and then press Delete twice (once to delete the selected word alias and a second time to delete the space before that word). If you double-click too soon after selecting the name, the Finder opens the item to which the alias points rather than selecting the last word of the name.

Alternatively, you can select the name for editing, press the down-arrow key or right-arrow key to move the insertion point to the end of the name, and press Delete six times to erase the last word and the space preceding it. To conclude your name editing, click anywhere outside the name or press Return or Enter. If you want the Finder never to add the word *alias* as a suffix, you can modify the Finder as described in "Removing aliases" in Chapter 20.

# Changing an Original Item

Aliases are truly amazing at finding items. Not only can you rename and move an alias's original item, but you also can replace it with another file that has the same name, all without breaking the link to the alias. You may wonder how the system software can find an alias's original item after you rename or move the original item. If the system software cannot find an item that has the same name and folder location as the original, it searches for the original item's unique *file ID number*, which the system software internally assigns to each file. Once the system software finds the item by using this ID number, it updates the alias with the original item's current name and folder location.

You can prevent the system software from updating an alias with the current name and folder location of the alias's original item. To do this, lock the alias by turning on the Locked option in its Info window. Locking an alias does not prevent the system software from finding its original item, only from updating the alias if the original item's name or folder location have changed.

When you copy the original item referenced by an alias, the alias still points to the original item. Sounds reasonable — unless you forget the difference between copying an item and moving it.

In many cases, copying and moving an item feel and look the same. Both involve the same action — dragging an item to another place. If that other place is a folder in the same disk as the item you're dragging, the item is moved and the item's alias knows where to find the moved item. If the other place is a folder in another disk, the item is copied. The alias knows where the original item is, but not the copy. Deleting the original item breaks the alias's link to the item, even though a copy of the item exists on another disk. If you use an alias for which the original item has been deleted, the system software tells you that it can't find the original item, as shown in Figure 10-4.

You can use utility software to connect an orphaned alias to its original file or to a copy of the original (see "Alias Assistance" in Chapter 19). Although an orphaned alias may seem utterly useless, "Confirming Startup Items" later in this chapter proves otherwise.

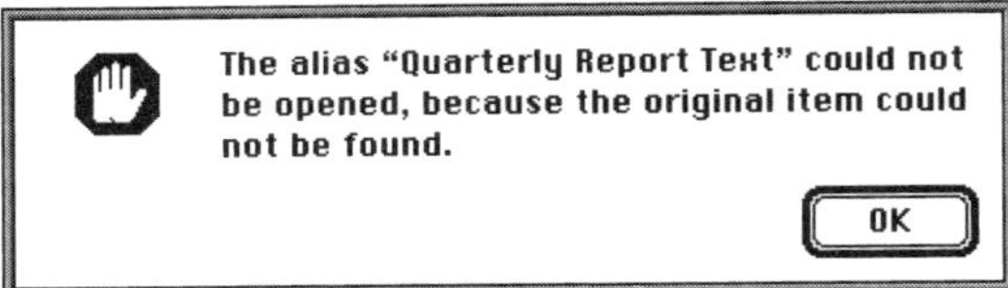


**Figure 10-4: After deleting an original item, you will receive this message.**

# Finding an Original Item

You can find an alias's original item by using the Get Info command to display the alias's Info window, as shown in Figure 10-5. The disk and folder path to the original item appear above the Comments box next to the heading Original. Clicking the Find Original button in the Info window opens the folder that contains the original item and selects the original item.

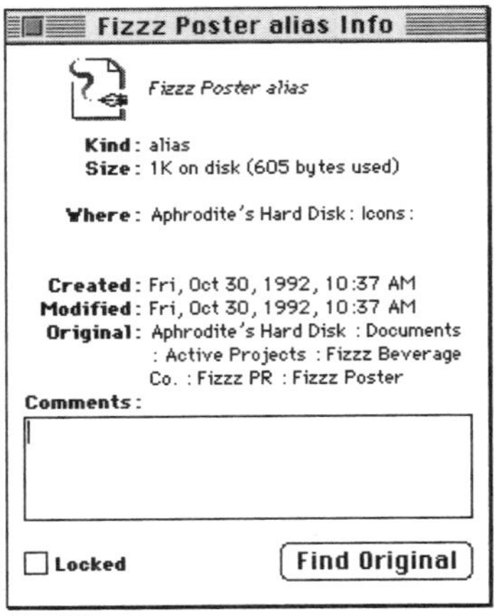

**Figure 10-5: An alias's Info window.**

If the original item is on a disk whose icon is not on the desktop, the Finder asks you to insert that disk. If the missing disk is a removable hard disk cartridge, the Finder is unable to find the original item unless a removable cartridge has appeared on the desktop since you started up or restarted your computer. Also, the needed removable cartridge must have the same hard disk driver software as the first cartridge mounted during or after startup.

# Discovering the Many Uses of Aliases

There are many useful applications for aliases. The most common is quick access to programs and documents you work with frequently. For example, you can make an alias of a spreadsheet you use regularly to update sales figures and place the alias in a convenient location, such as the desktop. Some of the most important uses of aliases include: adding items to the Apple menu or to the list of items opened at startup time; adding desktop convenience for accessing items; accessing archived information from floppy disks; and streamlining access to shared items. The following sections provide a collection of scenarios to leverage the power of aliases, providing express service to a wide range of items.

## Aliases in the Apple menu

With System 7, the most convenient place from which to open application programs, desk accessories, control panels, documents, folders, and other items is the Apple menu. Because the Apple menu is always on the menu bar, items in the Apple menu are never more than a mouse click away. You can add to the Apple menu any item that you can open by using the Finder, including aliases.

Placing an alias in the Apple menu is as easy as dragging the alias icon to the Apple Menu Items folder, which is in the System Folder. The alias and the original item it points to become instantly available. (You don't have to restart your Macintosh for changes to the Apple Menu Items folder to take place.) Items in the Apple menu are displayed alphabetically in plain (not italic) text. You may want to change the name of your alias to adjust its position in the Apple menu.

Items in the Apple menu appear alphabetically by name. You can force an item to the top of the menu by putting a blank space at the beginning of its name or force it to the bottom of the list by beginning its name with a bullet (•). These and other techniques for organizing the Apple menu are described in more detail in "Apple Menu Organization" in Chapter 5.

You can add as many aliases as you want to the Apple Menu Items folder. However, it's a good idea to keep the number within a reasonable range to avoid having to scroll through an extra-long menu. To remove an alias from the Apple menu, drag its icon out of the Apple Menu Items folder.

*Tip:* One of the most useful aliases you can add to the Apple menu is an alias of the Apple Menu Items folder. Adding this alias allows you to open the Apple Menu Items folder quickly and easily customize the Apple menu anywhere, anytime.

## Universal Show Clipboard

Some application programs lack a Show Clipboard command, and others that have one use a private clipboard whose contents may look different when pasted into another program. With a System 7 alias, you can put a Show Clipboard command in your Apple menu for reviewing the standard Clipboard contents from any application program. First, make an alias of the Clipboard file, which is in the System Folder. Then place the alias in the Apple Menu Items folder and rename the alias Show Clipboard. Now, choosing Show Clipboard from the Apple menu switches to the Finder and opens the Clipboard.

## Aliases as startup items

Every time you start up (or restart) your Macintosh with System 7, the Finder automatically opens everything in the Startup Items folder. For example, if you regularly use a particular program, you may want it ready to go immediately after you start up your Macintosh. But some programs must remain in a folder with other auxiliary files, and the programs won't work correctly if you move their icons to the Startup Items folder. Furthermore, returning items to their previous locations when you no longer want them opened at startup time can be a drag.

Moving an alias of a program, document, or other item to the Startup Items folder causes the original item to open during startup. To remove an alias from the startup sequence, drag the alias out of the folder.

Application programs in the Startup Items folder open in alphabetical order, so you can rename the alias of an application program to determine when it starts relative to other application programs in that folder. Aliases of desk accessories, control panels, and folders open alphabetically after all application programs have opened. For more information about the Startup Items folder, see "Startup Items Folder" in Chapter 7.

## Aliases on the desktop

Other than the Apple menu, the desktop is the most accessible place for opening items and the most accessible place for folders to which you want to drag items. Rather than drag frequently used programs, control panels, documents, and folders themselves onto the desktop, make aliases of them and put the aliases on the desktop. Putting aliases of nested items on the desktop gives you quick access to the folders without digging through other folders to find them.

STEP-BY-STEP

## Confirming Startup Items

Here's a trick for System 7 users who sometimes want to open items in the Startup Items folder and sometimes don't:

1. Make a duplicate of an application (such as TeachText).
2. Make an alias of the duplicate.
3. Drag the duplicate application to the Trash.
4. Empty the Trash.
5. Place the alias of the application you just deleted in the Startup Items folder.
6. Give the alias a name that alphabetically precedes all other items in that folder.

When the Finder encounters the alias, it displays an alert telling you that it cannot find the alias's original item, as shown in the figure. Click Stop to cancel opening the startup items, or click Continue to finish opening them.

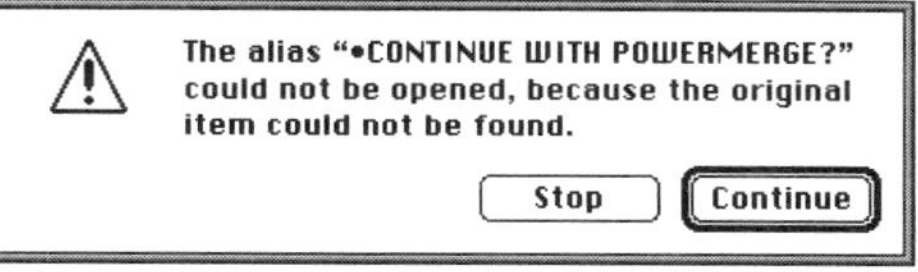
The alias "•CONTINUE WITH POWERMERGE?" could not be opened, because the original item could not be found.
Stop
Continue

Putting aliases of programs on the desktop avoids problems that can occur when you move the programs themselves onto the desktop. Such programs depend on support files being with them in the same folder (or on the desktop). For example, a word processor may also need a dictionary file on the desktop in order to check spelling. Aliases save you the hassle of guessing which support files a program needs in order to run correctly and avoid the mess that may result when you place those support files on the desktop. By creating an alias for an application, the alias accesses the original application in its folder, saving you from moving the application and its supporting files to get full access to the application.

By making aliases of documents and programs you use frequently and putting the aliases on the desktop, you never have to remember where you put the original items. Also, you can open several related items at the same time, even if the original items happen to be in different folders or on different disks, by opening aliases on the desktop.

When windows of open programs obscure desktop aliases, you can hide those windows by choosing Hide Others from the Application menu while the Finder is active. When Finder windows cover desktop aliases, you can close all those windows at once by pressing Option while clicking the Close box of any Finder window. With System 7.5 and later you can shrink windows by using the WindowShade control panel.

If your desktop becomes too cluttered with aliases, you can put related aliases together in folders on the desktop. For example, you can make aliases of the Trash and hard disk, put the aliases in a folder, and put the folder in your Apple menu for instant access. Leave that folder open and its window comes to the front along with the other Finder windows whenever you switch to the Finder. If you want that folder of aliases open all the time, put an alias of the folder in the Startup Items folder (located in the System Folder).

You don't have to create your own special folder for frequently used aliases if you have System 7.5 or later or a Performa with any version of System 7. System 7.5 and later and the Performas have the Launcher control panel, whose window displays the aliases you put in the Launcher Items folder, as described in Chapter 7.

***Tip:*** If you're lucky enough to have a big monitor, put aliases of the Trash in the upper and lower left corners of the desktop. The extra Trash icons expedite discarding items when you're working on the left side of the desktop. Extending this idea, if you have two monitors, put a Trash alias on the desktop of the second monitor. That way, you never have to drag icons across two screens to throw them away.

## Directory shortcuts

Alias names appear in italics in directory dialog boxes, as shown in Figure 10-6. Opening an alias there (by double-clicking it, for instance) opens its original item. Instead of opening an alias's original item, you can quickly select the original item in a directory dialog box by pressing Option while opening the alias. In this case, System 7 opens the folder containing the original item and selects the original item (but does not open the original item).

***Tip:*** To make an alias appear near the top of the list in directory dialog boxes, put a blank space at the beginning of the alias's name. Items having initial blank spaces in their names float alphabetically to the top of the directory dialog box's list. (When you view the desktop level in a directory dialog box, disks always appear at the top of the list above all other items.)

If you don't like how initial spaces look, you can paste a blank line at the beginning of each name that you want to appear at the top of the list. Create the blank line by pressing Return in the Note Pad or any word processor. For step-by-step instructions, see "Forcing Order Invisibly" in Chapter 5.

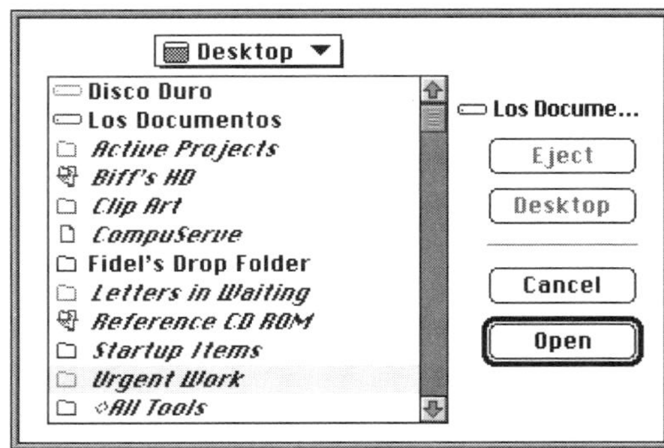


**Figure 10-6: Aliases in a directory dialog box. Names beginning with spaces are listed first after disks.**

## Quick Access to Favorite Folders

For quick access to a favorite folder when you use the directory dialog boxes you get with Open, Save, and other disk-related commands, put an alias of the folder on the desktop. In a directory dialog box, you can quickly get to aliases of favorite folders at the desktop level by clicking the Desktop button. Instead of working your way down through one branch of your folder structure and then working your way up another branch to the folder you want, you zip to the desktop level and there open the alias of the folder you want. It's as if you can jump from one branch of a tree to root level and then jump to a spot on another branch on another tree without having to crawl up the trunk and along the other branch.

Chances are you will only use this folder alias in directory dialog boxes, never in the Finder. The specially named folder alias doesn't have to clutter up your desktop to appear at the desktop level of directory dialog boxes. You can hide the folder alias behind another icon. Follow these steps:

1. Open an empty folder in the Finder, and press Command-Shift-3 to make a screen shot of the empty folder.
2. Open the screen shot in TeachText or SimpleText, select some white space in it, and choose Copy from the Edit menu.
3. Switch to the Finder and select the specially named folder alias on the desktop. Use the Get Info command to bring up the alias's Info window.
4. In the alias's Info window, select the icon image and choose Paste from the Edit menu to replace the alias's icon with white space. Close the alias's Info window.
5. On the desktop, align the icon behind which you want to hide the alias. You can align the icon by holding down the Command key while dragging the icon slightly. Still pressing Command, drag the alias's name (it no longer has a visible icon) near the icon that will cover it. Release the mouse button and the alias's name should snap to the same position as the icon. Abbreviate the alias's name if it is longer than the startup disk's name.
6. Click the desktop anywhere to deselect the alias, and then type the first part of the coverup icon's name to select it and bring it to the front, hiding the alias's name.

## Abridged System Folder

Aliases can help you quickly find folders in the System Folder whose contents you need to get at, such as the Startup Items folder and the folder containing your incoming electronic mail. Here's how you do it: Make aliases for the System Folder items you access often — including the System Folder itself — and put all those aliases in a new folder. You can open and find an item in that new folder faster than in the System Folder. To make the new folder look like a System Folder, copy the icon from the System Folder's Info window and paste it into the new folder's Info window.

## Aliases of items on floppy disks

You can use aliases to keep track of and quickly open items on floppy disks — even floppies that aren't currently inserted in your Macintosh. For example, suppose you're keeping track of your company's bills, and the month of March doesn't balance. You want to close out the quarter and archive the monthly detail files to floppy disk, but you know that you may need to access the March file later. Instead of keeping the monthly detail files on your hard disk, go ahead and copy them all to a floppy that has a unique name, such as First Qtr. Select the March file on the floppy and choose Make Alias from the File menu. Copy the alias to your hard disk. When you need the March file again, open its alias on the hard disk. The system tells you the name of the disk to insert so that it can open the alias's original item, as shown in Figure 10-7. If you change your mind or can't find the needed disk, click the Cancel button.

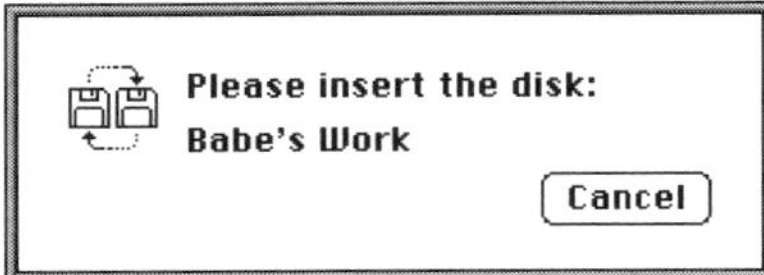
Please insert the disk:
Babe's Work
Cancel

**Figure 10-7: Opening an item archived to a floppy disk.**

Keeping aliases on your hard disk and the original items on floppies saves valuable hard disk space, because aliases almost always take up less space than the original items they represent. Just be sure to make aliases of the archived items *after* copying them to floppies, not before. If you make aliases of the items while they are still on the hard disk, the aliases stop working when you delete the original items from the hard disk after copying them to floppies. (Remember, aliases point to the original items, not to copies of the originals on other disks.)

QUICK TIPS

## Personal Icon Library

A single floppy disk can use aliases to store hundreds of interesting icons for later use as custom icons for any file, folder, or disk. Just make aliases of files, folders, or disks having icons you want to save and copy the aliases to a floppy named Personal Icon Library. Whenever you want to use one of the custom icons from the floppy disk, copy the icon from the alias's Info window and paste it into the Info window of the file, folder, or disk whose icon you want to customize (as described in Chapter 4).

### Aliases and CD-ROM

Slowly wading through folders on a CD-ROM can be a royal pain (unless you can somehow see the experience as stately pomp and circumstance). Cut through the drudgery by making aliases of items inside the CD-ROM folders. Because CD-ROMs are permanently locked, you must put the aliases on your hard disk (or a floppy disk). Opening an alias makes a beeline to the original item on the CD-ROM.

## Aliases of shared items

System 7's file-sharing capabilities enable you to share items from someone else's Macintosh that is connected to the same network. But getting access to shared items involves wading through a fair amount of bureaucracy in the Chooser.

Aliases cut through the red tape. Here's how: You access a shared disk or folder once by using the Chooser (see "Sharing Someone Else's Folders and Disks" in Chapter 9). Next, select the shared item or any folder or file in it and choose Make Alias from the File menu. Finally, copy the alias to your desktop or hard disk, as shown in Figure 10-8. An alias keeps track of its original item even when the original item is on another networked Mac.

**Figure 10-8: Aliases of shared items.**

Once you make an alias of a shared item, you can get to the shared item by opening the alias either from the Finder or from an Open command's directory dialog box. Dragging something to the alias of a shared disk or folder also automatically accesses that shared item. You still must enter a password unless you initially access the original item as a guest. If the shared item is not available — for example, because the Mac in which it resides is turned off — then the Finder tells you that it cannot find the alias on the network.

## Aliases of remote shared items

Not only do aliases work across a local network, they also work across a remote network connection made with Apple Remote Access (ARA, described in Chapter 9). If you create an alias of a remote file, folder, or disk, disconnect the remote network, and then open the alias, the system software tries to make the remote network connection again automatically.

Instead of locating the alias's original item on the remote network as it should, the system software may locate another item that coincidentally has the same name on your local network. Sound far-fetched? Suppose the alias's original item is a shared disk with a common name such as Macintosh HD on a remote Mac with a common name such as Quadra 605. Further suppose your Mac is connected to a local network on which someone is sharing a hard disk named Macintosh HD from a Mac named Quadra 605. If you double-click the alias, the system software will open the Macintosh HD on your local network, not the one on the remote network. A similar situation can occur if you sometimes connect to two remote Macs that are named alike and have shared hard disks with the same names.

Situations like these can develop suddenly when someone changes the name of a Mac or a shared disk; suddenly double-clicking an alias opens the wrong item. What's worse, the system software updates the alias so that the information in it now points to the wrong item. Even after you fix the conflicting aliases by changing one of the original item's names, the alias will continue representing the wrong item.

You can prevent the system software from updating an alias by locking the alias. It's a good idea to lock aliases of items on remote file servers, especially if you use ARA to connect to more than one Mac. A locked alias will start working again when all the file servers you access have unique names. To lock an alias, select it, choose Get Info from the Finder's File menu, and set the Locked option in the alias's Info window.

## Aliases keep shared documents current

Besides providing easy access to shared items from other computers, aliases can help you make sure that others who share your documents have the latest versions.

Suppose, for example, that you create a letter template that you want the rest of your group to use. By making an alias of the template and copying it to a shared folder, other users can copy the alias to their disks and use the alias to open the original template. If you later replace the original template with a version having the same name, the aliases that people already copied open the new version. Users who share the alias always get the newest version of the original item it represents, even when the original frequently changes.

The only drawback to using an alias to share a template is that unless you're using a program that allows more than one person to open the same document, only one person can access the template document at a time. However, anyone who opens the template can quickly and easily save it with a different name and then close it to free it for someone else to open.

## Your Office on Disk

Aliases can give you nearly automatic access to your Macintosh's hard disks by using a floppy disk in any other Macintosh on the same network.To set up access to your office from a floppy disk, follow these steps:

1. Make sure that file sharing is turned on in your Sharing Setup control panel.
2. Select all your hard disk icons and choose Sharing from the File menu, opening a Sharing Info window for each disk.
3. In each window, turn on the Share This Item and Its Contents option and turn off the See Folders, See Files, and Make Changes options for the User/Group and Everyone categories, as shown in the figure.

   These settings restrict access to your disks so that only you can make changes or see files or folders.
4. Make an alias of each hard disk and copy the aliases to a floppy disk.

Disco Duro
Where: Disco Duro, Nuvo Labs SCSI Driver, ID 0
☒ Share this item and its contents
See Folders | See Files | Make Changes
Owner: Fidel F. Flat ☒ ☒ ☒
User/Group: <None> ☐ ☐ ☐
Everyone ☐ ☐ ☐
☐ Make all currently enclosed folders like this one

Now you can use that floppy disk to access your hard disk from any Mac on your network, as long as file sharing is active on your Mac. You simply insert the disk, open the alias for the disk you want to use, and enter your password when asked. Correctly entering your password allows you access to all applications, folders, and documents on your disk from any remote Macintosh. You don't have to bother opening the Chooser, selecting Apple Share, selecting your computer, and typing your name as the registered user.

# ShareMail

Using nothing more than some aliases, System 7 file sharing, and TeachText, a few people on a small network can easily exchange e-mail messages. To do so, follow the steps outlined in the next section.

Rather than go through the rigmarole described in the lengthy steps in "Creating ShareMail System Using Aliases," you can use Apple's PowerTalk technology to send and receive mail, as described in Chapter 15.

## An Alias's Alias

When you move a drive from one AppleShare file server to another, network users have to tediously search all servers (by using the Chooser) for the moved drive unless you inform them of its new location. You may have to move a shared drive from a busy server to an idle server or from a server needing repair to a temporary substitute.

You can solve this problem by creating an alias of an alias of every shared hard disk. Follow these steps:

1. Working from a shared hard disk that is always available to everyone, create an alias of every shared hard disk on the network.
2. Create aliases of those hard-drive aliases and copy the second set of aliases to each user's Mac.

With the double aliases in place, a shared hard disk named Crown Jewels, for example, can be accessed by double-clicking the alias named "Crown Jewels alias alias" on any user's Mac. That alias points to the alias "Crown Jewels alias" on the always-available shared drive, which in turn points to Crown Jewels itself.

Now, if you move Crown Jewels to a different file server, you merely make a new alias to replace the old Crown Jewels alias on the always-available shared drive. You do not have to update users' copies of "Crown Jewels alias alias," and users do not need to know that Crown Jewels has been moved.

This example uses the initial alias names that the Mac generates, but you can rename aliases freely. For example, both the alias and the alias's alias could be named Crown Jewels like the hard disk.

## Creating a ShareMail System Using Aliases

To set up a basic e-mail system based on aliases and file sharing, follow these steps:

1. On each Mac that will receive messages, start file sharing with the Sharing Setup control panel. Then select the startup disk and choose Sharing from the Finder's File menu to display the startup disk's Sharing Info window. Turn on the option "Share this item and its contents" and close the window.
2. On each Mac that will send messages, use the Chooser to access the shared disks of all the networked Macs that will receive messages.
3. Open the shared disk of each receiving Mac and make an alias of the folder named Desktop folder. As you make each alias, change its name to identify the owner of the Mac that contains the alias's original item.
4. Put all these aliases in a new folder on the desktop of each sending Mac (you can name the new folder Mail).
5. You can now select all the shared disk icons and use the Put Away command (or drag them to the Trash) to stop sharing them.

To create an e-mail message, simply use TeachText or any other program the recipient has. You can

*(continued on next page)*

*(continued from previous page)*

create any type of document — text, graphics, spreadsheet, database, and so on — as long as the recipient has a program that can open the document you send.

### Sending a message

To send a message, you can drag its icon to the recipient's alias in your desktop Mail folder. Alternatively, you can send a message from the program in which you created it. Follow these steps:

1. With the message open on your Mac, choose Save As from the File menu. The Save dialog box appears.
2. In the Save dialog box, double-click the recipient's alias, which is in the Mail folder on your desktop. Your Mac automatically connects to the recipient's Mac (asking you for your password on the recipient's Mac, if needed), finds the hard disk, and opens the recipient's desktop in the Save window.
3. Now, name the message file and click the Save button. The message appears on the recipient's desktop.

### Improving security

By sharing your whole hard disk with standard (that is, unrestricted) access privileges, you allow everyone with access to your network to snoop through your folders and files without leaving any electronic footprints.

If you desire to improve security, do the following:

1. Use the Finder's Sharing command to set access privileges for your hard disk as shown in the figure.

   These access-privilege settings allow network users to access a hard disk but not to see its files, and what they can't see they can't open. (If you also deny the See Folders privilege, those users won't be able to access the hard disk at all.) You can always decide later to grant privileges to see files or make changes in specific folders, leaving the remainder restricted.

Disco Duro

Where: Disco Duro, FWB SCSI 2 v10917g

☒ Share this item and its contents

| | | See Folders | See Files | Make Changes |
|---|---|---|---|---|
| Owner: | King Pimento | ☒ | ☒ | ☒ |
| User/Group: | <None> | ☒ | ☐ | ☐ |
| | Everyone | ☒ | ☐ | ☐ |

☒ Make all currently enclosed folders like this one

2. Then create a folder at the root level of your hard disk, give the folder a name that identifies it as your in-box (for example, King's In-box), and set the folder's access privileges as shown in the figure that follows.

   These access-privilege settings set up a drop-box folder that works like the corner mailbox. Network users can deposit files and folders in the drop-box folder but can't see what's inside it.

King's In-box

Where: Disco Duro:

Inside: Disco Duro

| ☐ Same as enclosing folder | | See Folders | See Files | Make Changes |
|---|---|---|---|---|
| Owner: | King Pimento | ☒ | ☒ | ☒ |
| User/Group: | <None> | ☐ | ☐ | ☒ |
| | Everyone | ☐ | ☐ | ☒ |

☐ Make all currently enclosed folders like this one

☒ Can't be moved, renamed or deleted

Network users can make aliases of each other's in-box folders (instead of their Desktop folders) and send messages by dragging files to the in-box aliases. Under this scheme, network users cannot save a message directly in an in-box folder — that's the price of privacy.

*(continued on next page)*

*(continued from previous page)*

This scheme has another peculiarity that you may consider a drawback. If you send a message in haste (by dropping it onto someone's in-box alias), you can't retract it because you don't have privileges to see files in anyone else's in-box folder.

### Retracting messages

To extend the in-box scheme so that people can retract items they have sent, follow these steps:

1. On each receiving Mac, use the Users & Groups control panel to create a mail group and populate it with registered users who may send mail or other files. (You create registered users and the mail group with the Users & Groups control panel, as described in Chapter 9.)
2. Also on each Mac, create an in-box folder and inside it create and name an additional folder for each registered user in the mail group.
3. For the in-box folder, use the Sharing command to designate the mail group as the User/Group and grant all privileges except Make Changes to the Owner and the User/Group, but no privileges to Everyone.
4. For each of folders inside the in-box folder, designate the user for whom the folder is named as the User/Group and grant all privileges to the Owner and the User/Group, but no privileges to Everyone (that is, guests).

To send an item to a user in the mail group, you drop the item on the folder named for you inside the receiver's in-box folder.

To retract an item you've sent, open the folder onto which you dropped it and drag the item to the Trash.

You can simplify accessing your folders inside other people's in-box folders by making aliases of your folders, giving each alias the name of the person on whose Mac the alias's original folder is located, and collecting the aliases in an out-box folder on your Mac. If you want to see at a glance whether you've received something new in any of the folders inside your in-box folder, set your in-box folder for viewing by name and expand all the folders inside it (shortcut: press ⌘-A to select all folders and then press ⌘-right arrow to expand all selected folders).

# CHAPTER  CONCEPTS AND TERMS

- Aliases look and act like the real programs, documents, folders, disks, or other items they represent. But aliases are actually small pointer files.
- You can use aliases to add items to the Apple menu without moving those items from their folders and to increase the flexibility of the Startup Items folder.
- Employ aliases to open frequently used programs, documents, folders, and control panels from the desktop while the real items remain buried in nested folders.
- Aliases speed access to archived items stored on disks that are not inserted and to items buried on CD-ROMs.
- Aliases streamline access to shared items from another Mac on your network and keep items you share with other network users current.
- Use aliases to get nearly automatic access to your Macintosh's hard disks by using a floppy disk in any other Macintosh on the same network.

**alias**
A stand-in or agent for a real program, document, folder, or disk. The alias does not duplicate the item it represents; the alias points to the item it represents.

**file ID number**
The number that the system software uses internally to identify the original item to which an alias is attached even if you have renamed or moved that original item.

**Find Original button**
Located in an alias's Info window, this button tracks down the original item to which the alias is linked and selects it.

**Make Alias command**
Located in the File menu, this command creates a copy of an item with the same icon and same name in italics.

**original item**
A file, folder, or disk to which an alias points. The file, folder, or disk that actually opens when you open its alias. (Same as **target**.)

**orphaned alias**
An alias that has lost its link with its original item. An alias whose original item the system software cannot find.

**resolve an alias**
What the system software does to find the original item represented by an alias.

**target**
A file, folder, or disk to which an alias points. The file, folder, or disk that actually opens when you open its alias. (Same as **original item**.)

**update**
What the system software does to the information in an alias after finding the alias's original item has a new name or folder location.

CHAPTER ELEVEN

# Dealing with Fonts and Typography

- Comparing TrueType, fixed-size, and PostScript font technologies
- Displaying samples of TrueType and fixed-size fonts
- Installing and removing fonts
- Mixing TrueType with fixed-size fonts
- Printing with TrueType, PostScript, and fixed-size fonts
- Understanding how outline fonts work
- Obtaining TrueType and PostScript fonts
- Adding sophisticated typography to compatible programs by installing QuickDraw GX

With old Macintosh font technology, text looks great when displayed or printed as long as you stick to a half-dozen font sizes — usually 9, 10, 12, 14, 18, and 24 points. Apple's TrueType font technology, a standard part of System 7, makes odd sizes and big sizes like 11, 13, 36, 100, and 197 look just as good. The optional QuickDraw GX software provides much more refined control of type, as long as the typefaces and programs that you're using take advantage of the advanced capabilities.

## Comparing Three Font Technologies

Your Macintosh can display and print text in three types of fonts: fixed-size, TrueType, and PostScript. Which looks best depends on the font size and the output device (display screen or type of printer).

### Fixed-size fonts

Before the advent of TrueType fonts, all Macs used fixed-size fonts to display text on-screen and to print on many types of printers. A *fixed-size font* contains exact pictures of every letter, digit, and symbol for one size of a font, as shown in Figure 11-1. Fixed-size fonts often are called *bitmapped fonts* because each picture precisely maps the dots, or *bits*, to be displayed or printed for one character.

Each fixed-size font looks great in one size only, so fixed-size fonts usually are installed in sets. A typical set includes 9-, 10-, 11-, 14-, 18-, and 24-point sizes. If you need text in a size for which no fixed-size font is installed, the system software must scale a fixed-size font's character bit maps up or down to the size you want. The results are lumpy, misshapen, or blocky, as shown in Figure 11-2.

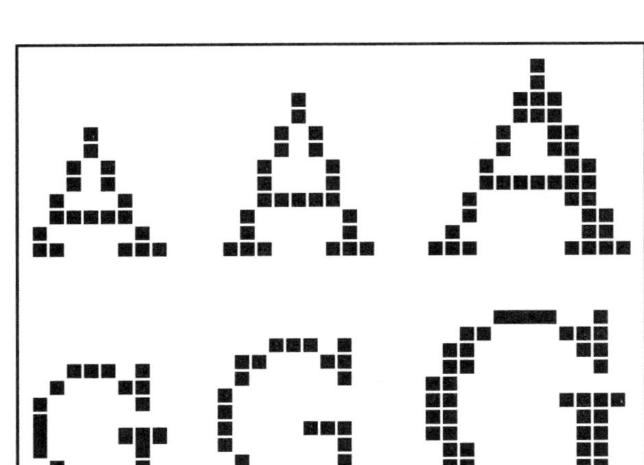

**Figure 11-1: Times capital A and G bit maps in sizes 12, 14, and 18 (enlarged to show detail).**

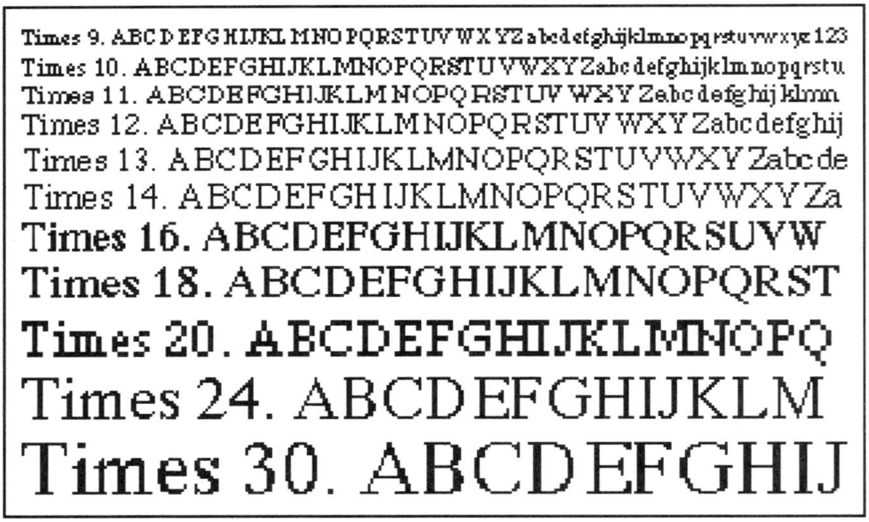

Times 9. ABCDEFGHIJKLMNOPQRSTUVWXYZabcdefghijklmnopqrstuvwxyz123
Times 10. ABCDEFGHIJKLMNOPQRSTUVWXYZabcdefghijklmnopqrstu
Times 11. ABCDEFGHIJKLMNOPQRSTUVWXYZabcdefghijklmn
Times 12. ABCDEFGHIJKLMNOPQRSTUVWXYZabcdefghij
Times 13. ABCDEFGHIJKLMNOPQRSTUVWXYZabcde
Times 14. ABCDEFGHIJKLMNOPQRSTUVWXYZa
Times 16. ABCDEFGHIJKLMNOPQRSUVW
Times 18. ABCDEFGHIJKLMNOPQRST
Times 20. ABCDEFGHIJKLMNOPQ
Times 24. ABCDEFGHIJKLM
Times 30. ABCDEFGHIJ

**Figure 11-2: Fixed-size Times (9-, 10-, 12-, 18-, and 24-point sizes installed).**

## TrueType fonts

TrueType fonts work with the programs you already have. You can mix these fonts with the fixed-size and PostScript fonts you already have. TrueType fonts work with all Macintosh models and all types of printers, including PostScript printers.

*TrueType fonts* don't use fixed bit maps to define characters; instead, they use curves and straight lines to outline each character's shape. Because of this methodology, these fonts sometimes are called *outline fonts* (see Figure 11-3).

**Figure 11-3: Outline for TrueType Times capital G.**

TrueType fonts are variable-size fonts. The Macintosh system software can smoothly scale a single TrueType font's character outlines to any size, large or small, with good results, as shown in Figure 11-4.

Times 9. ABCDEFGHIJKLMNOPQRSTUVWXYZabcdefghijklmnopqrstuvwxyz123
Times 10. ABCDEFGHIJKLMNOPQRSTUVWXYZabcdefghijklmnopqrstu
Times 11. ABCDEFGHIJKLMNOPQRSTUVWXYZabcdefghijklmn
Times 12. ABCDEFGHIJKLMNOPQRSTUVWXYZabcdefghij
Times 13. ABCDEFGHIJKLMNOPQRSTUVWXYZabcde
Times 14. ABCDEFGHIJKLMNOPQRSTUVWXYZa
Times 16. ABCDEFGHIJKLMNOPQRSUVW
Times 18. ABCDEFGHIJKLMNOPQRST
Times 20. ABCDEFGHIJKLMNOPQ
Times 24. ABCDEFGHIJKLM
Times 30. ABCDEFGHIJ

**Figure 11-4: TrueType Times.**

TrueType GX fonts differ from earlier TrueType fonts only in their capability to take advantage of some advanced typography controls available in QuickDraw GX and the programs that take advantage of it (as described in the section "Advancing Typography with QuickDraw GX" later in this chapter).

## PostScript fonts

TrueType fonts look great in any size on-screen or output on any printer, but this is nothing new; Adobe Type Manager (ATM) has done the same with PostScript fonts since 1989. Like TrueType fonts, *PostScript fonts* use outlines to define character shapes; consequently, they look good at any size.

Although PostScript fonts originally were designed for printing on LaserWriters and other PostScript output devices, ATM smoothly scales PostScript fonts to any size for non-PostScript printers and the display screen, just like TrueType. With ATM and PostScript fonts, you don't need a set of fixed-size or TrueType fonts for the screen display.

Many longtime Macintosh users have invested thousands of dollars in PostScript fonts, and for them, it makes sense to stick with PostScript and ATM. Apple teamed up with Adobe and includes ATM with QuickDraw GX. If you don't install QuickDraw GX, you can purchase ATM separately.

If you don't already have a collection of PostScript fonts, you may prefer to go with TrueType instead. More PostScript fonts are available than TrueType, but TrueType fonts sometimes cost less, and some are even free. (For example, TrueType versions of the 11 standard LaserWriter fonts come free with System 7.)

To make use of ATM, you must buy PostScript fonts for your System Folder; fonts built into your printer don't help. Adobe includes the four basic LaserWriter fonts — Times, Helvetica, Courier, and Symbol — with the purchase of ATM. The Adobe Type Basics package includes all 11 standard LaserWriter font families — Avant Garde, Bookman, Courier, Helvetica, Helvetica Narrow, New Century Schoolbook, Palatino, Symbol, Times, Zapf Chancery, and Zapf Dingbats — along with 16 other font families and ATM. Think of TrueType not as a challenger of PostScript fonts but as a replacement for fixed-size (bitmapped) fonts.

## How to recognize the best font sizes

You usually can tell which font sizes will look good on-screen by inspecting the Font menu of a program that you're using. The program highlights the best-looking sizes with outline-style numbers. All sizes of a TrueType font are highlighted (If you have PostScript fonts and ATM installed, all the sizes also look good.) Only the installed sizes of fixed-size fonts are highlighted, as shown in Figure 11-5.

Size
7 pt
9 pt
10 pt
✓12 pt
14 pt
18 pt
24 pt
36 pt
48 pt
60 pt
72 pt
Other... ⇧⌘O

A fixed-size font

Size
7 pt
9 pt
10 pt
✓12 pt
14 pt
18 pt
24 pt
36 pt
48 pt
60 pt
72 pt
Other... ⇧⌘O

A TrueType font

**Figure 11-5: Smooth sizes are outlined.**

# Seeing Font Samples

In System 7, all fonts can exist as individual items, each with its own icon, as shown in Figure 11-6. A single capital *A* appears on the icons of fixed-size fonts. The icons of TrueType fonts have three capital *A*s, each a different size to suggest the variable sizing of the font. The icons of PostScript fonts may look like a generic laser printer, or they may have custom graphics designed by the companies that make the fonts.

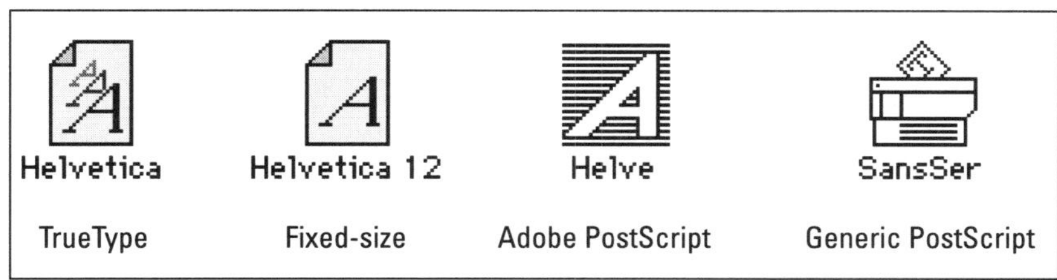


**Figure 11-6: Font icons.**

## About Font Styles

Text varies by style as well as size. The Macintosh system software can display and print four basic styles — plain, bold, italic, and bold italic — and many others (as listed in your friendly Style menu). The system software can derive various styles by modifying the plain style, but you get better-looking results by installing separate styled versions of fonts, as shown in the figure. Many fixed-size, TrueType, and PostScript fonts come in the four basic styles. Some PostScript font families include 20 or more styled versions. Collectively, the styled versions together with the plain version of a font are known as a *font family.*

| Times, Times bold, Times italic, and Times bold italic installed | Only plain Times installed; other styles derived from it |
|---|---|
| Necessity never made a good bargain. | Necessity never made a good bargain. |
| *Three may keep a secret, if two of them are dead.* | *Three may keep a secret, if two of them are dead.* |
| ***Lost time is never found again.*** | ***Lost time is never found again.*** |
| **He that lives upon hope will die fasting.** | **He that lives upon hope will die fasting.** |

You can see a sample of any TrueType or fixed-size font by opening the font from the Finder, as shown in Figure 11-7.

The fonts that you're not using can be kept in any folder or on the desktop. You also can store spare TrueType and fixed-size fonts in *font suitcases*, which are created with the Font/DA Mover program for storing and distributing fonts in older system software. (You do not need the Font/DA Mover program with System 7, which enables you to manipulate fonts directly.) You can create a new font-suitcase file in System 7 by duplicating an existing font-suitcase file, opening the duplicate, and dragging the contents of the duplicate to the Trash. You also can use version 4.1 of the Font/DA Mover with System 7 to create font suitcases.

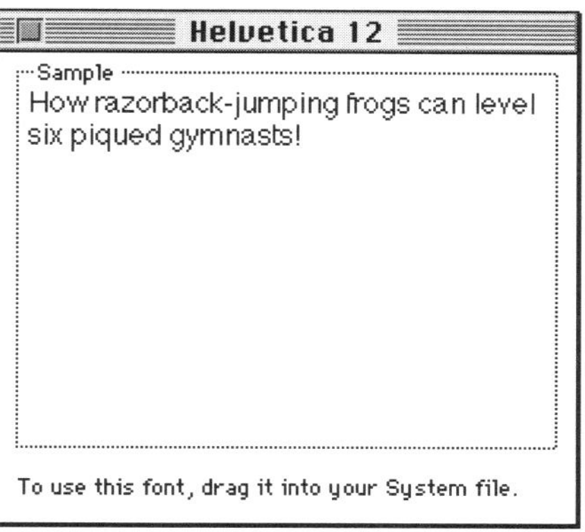


**Figure 11-7: TrueType and fixed-size font samples.**

With System 7.1 and later, the Fonts folder is the place you install the TrueType and fixed-size fonts that you want to list in your Font menus. The Fonts folder is also the preferred location for PostScript fonts that you may have, but you can also put them in the Extensions folder or directly in the System Folder. Prior to System 7.1 your TrueType and fixed-size fonts go in the System file and PostScript fonts go in the Extensions folder (or the System Folder itself if you wish).

Old applications, however, may not look in the right folders. If text prints in the wrong font on a PostScript printer or looks lumpy on-screen, try putting PostScript fonts in the System Folder itself (not the Fonts folder or the Extensions folder). For example, Aldus PageMaker versions 4.01 and earlier and ATM versions 2 and earlier can't find PostScript fonts in the Extensions folder. ATM versions 2.0.2 and 2.0.3 look in the Extensions folder (and the System Folder) but not in the Fonts folder, and ATM versions 3.0 and later look in the Fonts folder (and in the Extensions folder and the System Folder).

# Adding and Removing Fonts

When you install System 7, Apple's Installer program puts a basic set of TrueType fonts and fixed-size fonts in the Fonts folder for you. You can add or remove both types of fonts at any time with the System 7 Finder.

To add more TrueType or fixed-size fonts, you first must quit all programs that are open, except the Finder. Then you drag the additional fonts to the System

Folder icon, as shown in Figure 11-8. You can drag font suitcases, folders containing fonts, or loose fonts to the System Folder icon. You do not use the Font/DA Mover program, as you would in older system software.

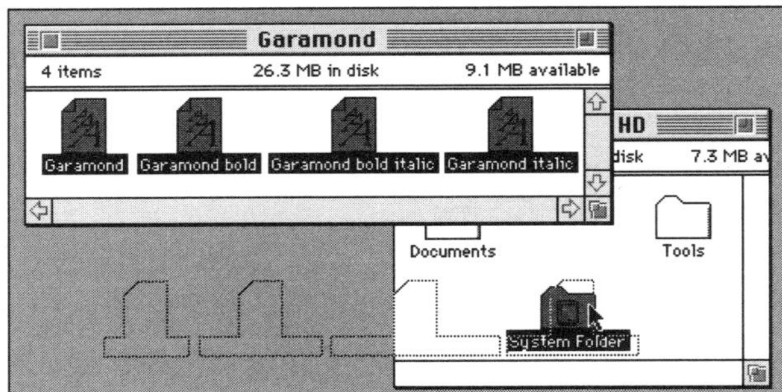


**Figure 11-8: Installing TrueType or fixed-size fonts.**

When you drag fonts to the System Folder icon, the System 7 Finder puts them where they belong (see Figure 11-9). (With System 7.1 and later, the Finder puts them in the Fonts folder.) The Finder automatically extracts fonts and font suitcases from folders that you drag to the System Folder icon. If a folder contains items other than fonts or font suitcases, the Finder puts the other items in the places where they belong (see "Adding Items to the System Folder" in Chapter 7). The Finder does not distribute items for you if you drag them to the System Folder window instead of the System Folder icon.

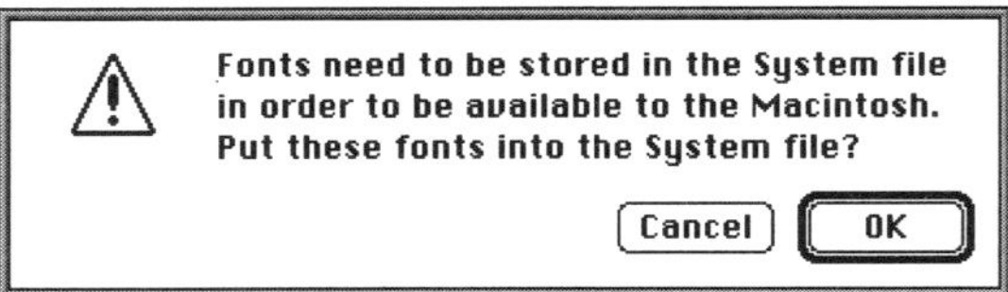


**Figure 11-9: The Finder knows where fonts go.**

If you prefer, you can drag TrueType, PostScript, and fixed-size fonts directly to the Fonts folder icon, as shown in Figure 11-10. You also can open the Fonts folder and drag TrueType, PostScript, and fixed-size fonts to its window.

To remove fonts from your system, open the Fonts folder and drag the fonts or suitcases to another folder, the desktop, or the Trash, as shown in Figure 11-11.

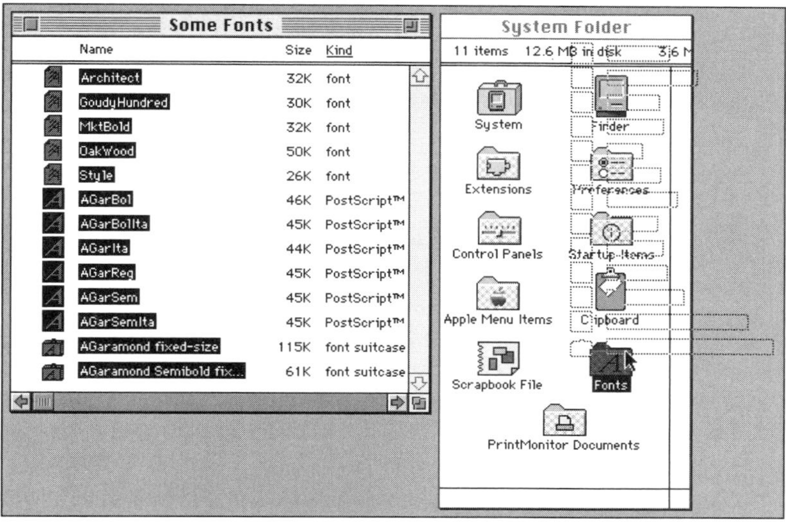


Figure 11-10: Adding fonts to the Fonts folder.

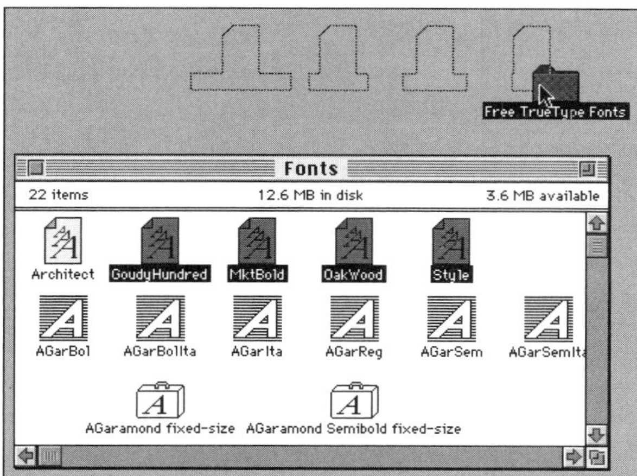


Figure 11-11: Removing fonts from the Fonts folder.

You can add or remove PostScript fonts from the Fonts folder anytime, but you must quit all open programs before adding or removing TrueType or fixed-size fonts. (Inspect the Application menu to see what's open.) Changes take effect immediately; you don't have to restart your Macintosh.

## Combining Fixed-Size and TrueType Fonts

Look closely at some text in a TrueType font and at the same text in an equivalent fixed-size font. You'll see differences in letter shape, width, and height that may affect text spacing, as shown in the figure. The TrueType fonts match the PostScript fonts used in printers better than fixed-size fonts do. Fixed-size fonts display faster, however, and many of them look better on-screen in sizes smaller than 18 points.

| | |
|---|---|
| Today we are on the verge of creating new tools that will empower individuals, unlock worlds of knowledge, and forge a new community of ideas. | TrueType Times 12-point plain |
| Today we are on the verge of creating new tools that will empower individuals, unlock worlds of knowledge, and forge a new community of ideas. | Fixed-size Times |
| ***Today we are on the verge of creating new tools that will empower individuals, unlock worlds of knowledge, and forge a new community of ideas.*** | Fixed-size Times 12-point bold italic |
| ***Today we are on the verge of creating new tools that will empower individuals, unlock worlds of knowledge, and forge a new community of ideas.*** | TrueType Times 12-point bold italic |

You can install TrueType and fixed-size versions of the same font together in the System Folder. For each font and size, the system software's first choice is a fixed-size font with its hand-tuned bit maps. If the system software can't find the right fixed-size font, it scales a TrueType font to the needed size. Notice that when you install both fixed-size and TrueType versions of the same font, System 7 always derives styled fonts from the fixed-size version, even if a styled TrueType version is installed. For example, if you have a fixed-size 11-point Times and a TrueType Times italic installed (but no fixed-size 11-point Times italic), the system software derives an 11-point Times italic by slanting the fixed-size 11-point Times.

*(continued on next page)*

*(continued from previous page)*

Individual programs can tell the system software to ignore fixed-size fonts if a TrueType equivalent is available, and current versions of many popular programs now work this way. You may be able to turn this behavior on and off in some of your programs. Check each program's preference settings for one that tells the program that you prefer outline fonts. A decision to ignore fixed-size fonts in one program does not affect other programs; the general System preference for fixed-size fonts dominates in a program unless you specifically override the preference for that program.

# Printing with TrueType

As much as TrueType fonts improve text displayed on-screen, they improve printed text more. These fonts work directly with printers that don't use PostScript. TrueType fonts also work in conjunction with PostScript fonts on printers that use them.

## TrueType alone

With TrueType fonts in your System file, you're no longer limited to a few font sizes when printing on a StyleWriter, fax/modem, or other non-PostScript output device. You can print any font size that fits on the page at the best resolution the printer can manage, as shown in Figure 11-12.

Without TrueType fonts, printers that don't use PostScript require extra-large fixed-size fonts to achieve their highest resolution. When you select Best quality for an ImageWriter II, for example, the system software prints double-size fonts at a 50 percent reduction to get 144 *dpi* (dots per inch) resolution — twice the screen's 72 dpi resolution. The scarcity of extra-large fixed-size fonts limits the number of font sizes you can print. Moreover, the extra-large fixed-size fonts take up 25K to 50K apiece on your startup disk. After installing System 7, you no longer need these extra-large fixed-size fonts. Remove them to free that disk space.

## TrueType and fixed-size

If you have both fixed-size and TrueType fonts installed, text may not look quite the same on-screen as it does on paper. Character shapes may be different. More important, the spacing of words in the line may not match. When this happens, the system software used a fixed-size font for display (at 72 dpi) and a TrueType font for printing (at a higher resolution). You can fix the problem by removing the fixed-size font from your System file. In some programs, you may also be able to set an option that tells the system software to ignore fixed-size fonts.

## TrueType and PostScript

When System 7 displays TrueType fonts on-screen, LaserWriters and other PostScript devices print PostScript fonts if the system software can find ones that

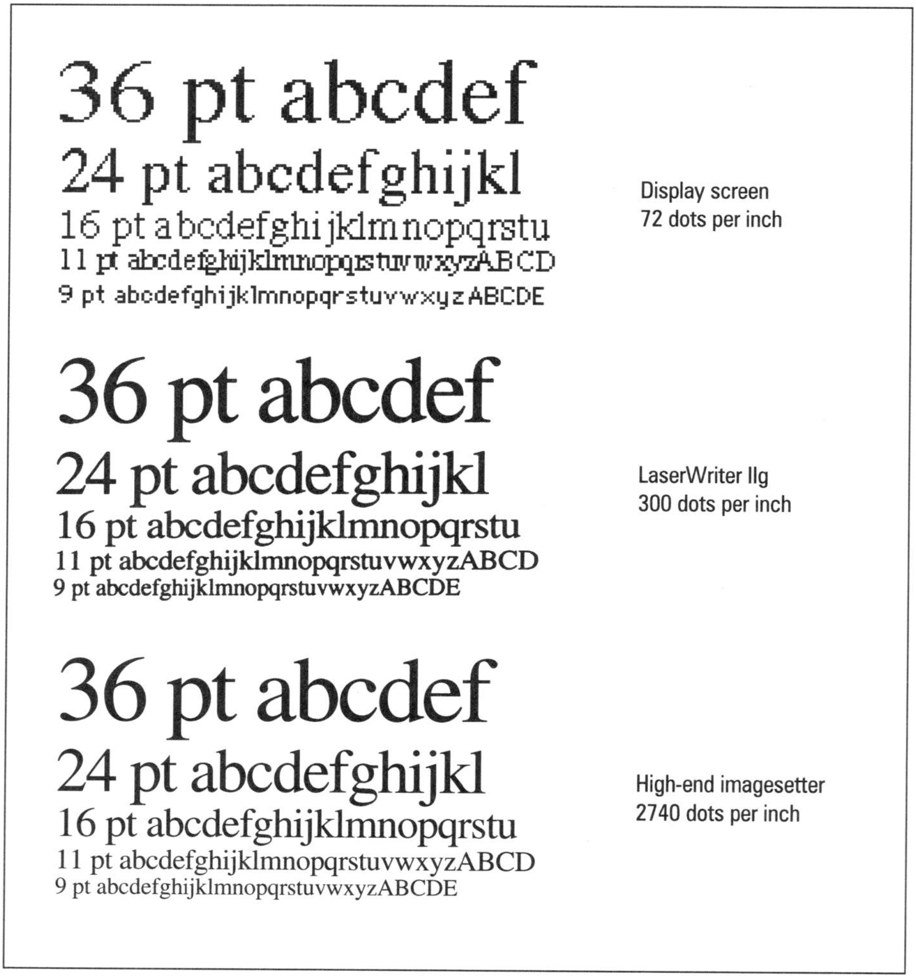

36 pt abcdef
24 pt abcdefghijkl
16 pt abcdefghijklmnopqrstu
11 pt abcdefghijklmnopqrstuvwxyzABCD
9 pt abcdefghijklmnopqrstuvwxyzABCDE

Display screen
72 dots per inch

36 pt abcdef
24 pt abcdefghijkl
16 pt abcdefghijklmnopqrstu
11 pt abcdefghijklmnopqrstuvwxyzABCD
9 pt abcdefghijklmnopqrstuvwxyzABCDE

LaserWriter IIg
300 dots per inch

36 pt abcdef
24 pt abcdefghijkl
16 pt abcdefghijklmnopqrstu
11 pt abcdefghijklmnopqrstuvwxyzABCD
9 pt abcdefghijklmnopqrstuvwxyzABCDE

High-end imagesetter
2740 dots per inch

**Figure 11-12: TrueType on various output devices.**

match the screen fonts. The printer contains a basic set of PostScript fonts in its own permanent memory; you can put others in your System Folder. When used in conjunction with PostScript fonts, smoothly scaled TrueType fonts provide a much better match between the screen and the printed page than fixed-size fonts do.

If the system software can find no PostScript equivalent for a TrueType font, it smoothly scales the TrueType font to the resolution of the printer. The PostScript printer prints the scaled TrueType font at a quality equal to that of a PostScript font.

TrueType fonts do not signal an end to PostScript output devices, however, for a number of reasons. For one, far more PostScript fonts are available than TrueType fonts. For another, PostScript can set text at any angle or along a curve or other nonlinear path, which is possible with TrueType only with QuickDraw GX. Also, PostScript offers more than outline fonts. It precisely specifies the location and other characteristics of every text and graphics item on the page, making it roughly comparable to QuickDraw GX, not just TrueType.

# Understanding Outline Fonts

To understand why TrueType fonts look different from equivalent fixed-size fonts, you need to know how outline-font technology works. Like PostScript fonts and any other outline fonts, a TrueType font defines each character mathematically as a set of points that, when connected, outline the character's shape. The Macintosh system software can vary the font size by moving the points closer together or farther apart and then drawing the character again.

After scaling the outline to the size you want, the system software fills the outline with the dots that make up the text you see on-screen and on paper. The dot size, which is determined by the resolution of the screen or other output device, governs the smoothness of the result at a given size, as shown in Figure 11-13. Devices with more dots per inch produce smoother results, particularly in smaller point sizes.

At small sizes, however, simply scaling the font outlines results in text that has unpleasant problems, such as gaps in diagonal lines or unwanted dots on the edges of curves. These imperfections occur because the outline does not precisely fit the grid in small point sizes, especially if the dots are relatively large, as they are on the Macintosh's 72-dpi screen. On the display screen, the system software must draw a typical 11-point letter in a space eight dots square. At small sizes and relatively low resolutions, deciding which dots to darken is difficult. The system software reduces the character outline, lays it over the grid, and darkens the dots whose center points fall inside the outline, as shown in Figure 11-14.

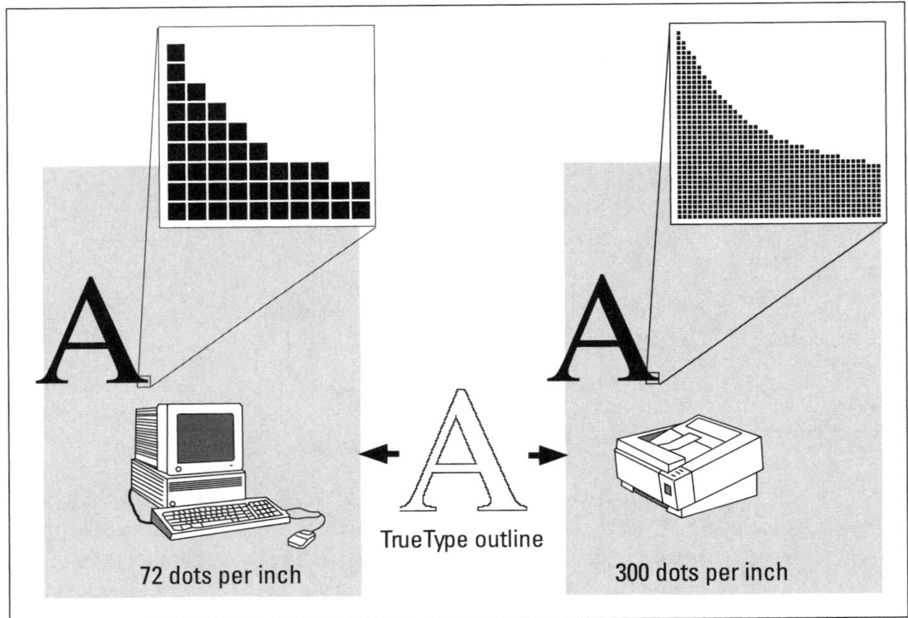


**Figure 11-13: Output device resolution affects smoothness.**

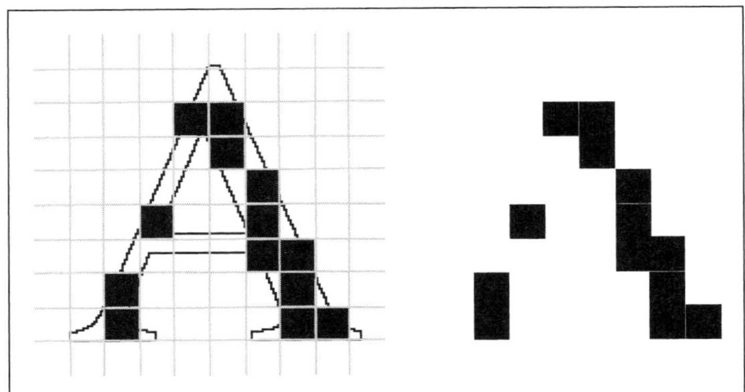

**Figure 11-14: Scaling a font outline to a small size may leave gaps.**

TrueType and PostScript fonts include a mechanism for adjusting the outline at small sizes on low-resolution devices. The font designer provides a set of instructions (also known as *hints*) that tells the system software how to modify character outlines to fit the grid, as shown in Figure 11-15. This process is called *grid fitting*.

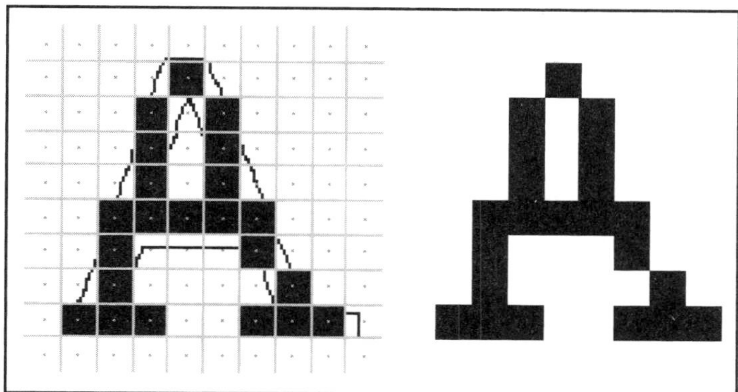

**Figure 11-15: Hints modify outlines at small sizes.**

High-resolution devices such as typesetters and film recorders usually don't need grid-fitting instructions; their grids are so fine that the character outlines don't need adjusting to get filled with dots. A 300-dpi grid is 4 times finer than a 72-dpi grid, and a 1, 270-dpi grid is more than 16 times finer.

Scaling and grid fitting occur so quickly that you may not even notice a delay, especially if you have a fast Macintosh model. TrueType and PostScript fonts are not as fast as fixed-size fonts, however, and the lag often is perceptible on-screen.

# Obtaining Fonts

System 7 comes with a standard set of TrueType fonts. This set includes TrueType versions of the PostScript fonts, Times, Helvetica, Palatino, Courier, and Symbol, as well as the standard Apple fonts, Chicago, Geneva, Monaco, and New York.

You also can get a variety of TrueType and PostScript fonts at nominal cost from user groups and on-line information services. Figure 11-16 illustrates some of the available freeware and shareware TrueType fonts that are available. For more information on obtaining freeware and shareware products, see Chapter 19.

In addition, many type companies make TrueType and PostScript fonts, including the following companies:

Adobe Systems Inc.
1585 Charleston Road
P.O. Box 7900
Mountain View, CA 94039
800-833-6687

Bitstream Inc.
215 First Street
Cambridge, MA 02142-1270
617-497-6222, 800-522-3668

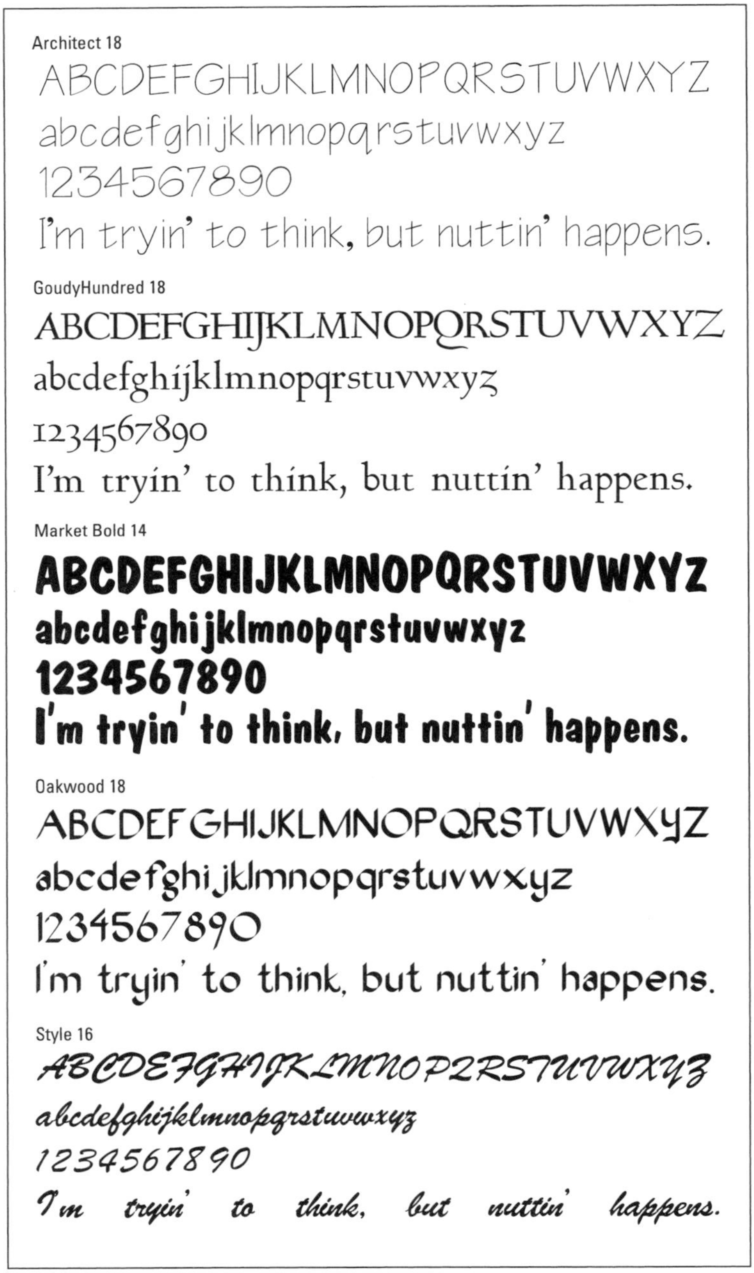

Architect 18

ABCDEFGHIJKLMNOPQRSTUVWXYZ
abcdefghijklmnopqrstuvwxyz
1234567890
I'm tryin' to think, but nuttin' happens.

GoudyHundred 18

ABCDEFGHIJKLMNOPQRSTUVWXYZ
abcdefghijklmnopqrstuvwxyz
1234567890
I'm tryin' to think, but nuttin' happens.

Market Bold 14

ABCDEFGHIJKLMNOPQRSTUVWXYZ
abcdefghijklmnopqrstuvwxyz
1234567890
I'm tryin' to think, but nuttin' happens.

Oakwood 18

ABCDEFGHIJKLMNOPQRSTUVWXYZ
abcdefghijklmnopqrstuvwxyz
1234567890
I'm tryin' to think, but nuttin' happens.

Style 16

ABCDEFGHIJKLMNOPQRSTUVWXYZ
abcdefghijklmnopqrstuvwxyz
1234567890
I'm tryin' to think, but nuttin' happens.

**Figure 11-16: Some freeware and shareware TrueType fonts.**

Casady & Greene Inc.
22734 Portola Drive
Salinas, CA 93908
408-484-9228

Letraset
40 Eisenhower Drive
Paramus, NJ 07653
201-845-6100

Linotype-Hell Co.
425 Oser Avenue
Hauppauge, NY 11788
516-434-2000 (ask for Type Sales)

Miles Inc., Agfa Division
90 Industrial Way
Wilmington, MA 01887
508-658-5600, 800-424-8973

Monotype Typography Inc.
150 South Wacker Drive, Suite 2630
Chicago, IL 60606
800-666-6897

Precision Type
47 Mall Drive
Commack, NY 11725
516-864-0167, 800-248-3668

# Advancing Typography with QuickDraw GX

Changes to the Mac OS in System 7.5 and later, especially the inclusion of QuickDraw GX, make it possible for any compatible program to use some fine-typesetting techniques that previously were available mainly in specialized publishing programs. With a program that's been updated to take advantage of QuickDraw GX typography, and with a font that has the necessary characters, you can choose to automatically insert the following elements:

- ❖ Fancy swashed initial or final characters in words or lines
- ❖ Lowercase (or old-style) numerals
- ❖ *Ligatures* (linked characters)
- ❖ Small caps instead of standard caps

You also can type diagonal fractions from the keyboard and format subscript or superscript in one step. In compatible programs, QuickDraw GX also makes it possible to customize certain fonts, making them bolder, lighter, skinnier, or wider. In any QuickDraw GX-compliant program — not just in high-end page-layout or illustration programs — you easily can control the letter spacing within words. Figure 11-17 shows the pop-up menu from a demonstration program that offers most of the type options (it's a long list).

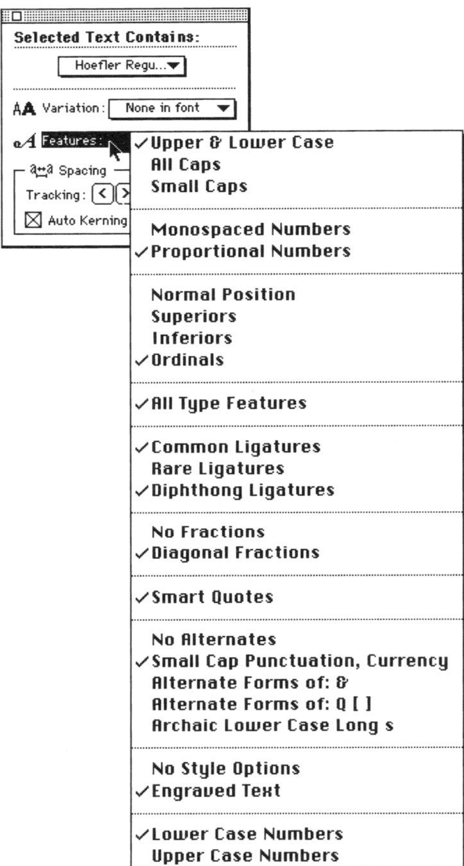


**Figure 11-17: A pop-up menu offers type options in a QuickDraw GX-compliant program.**

QuickDraw GX comes with Adobe Type Manager GX (ATM GX) Version 3.7 or later. Like earlier versions of ATM, the GX version smoothly scales PostScript Type 1 outline fonts so that they look good on-screen — and printed on non-PostScript printers — at any size. Unlike ATM 3.6 (SuperATM), ATM GX 3.7 cannot substitute multiple-master PostScript fonts for missing PostScript fonts. However, ATM 3.8 can substitute fonts, works with QuickDraw GX, and is accelerated for Power Macs.

## How QuickDraw GX Changes PostScript Fonts

Installing QuickDraw GX, an optional part of System 7.5 and Mac OS 7.6, converts the PostScript Type 1 font files in your Fonts folder, Extensions folder, or System Folder to files that look like TrueType font files. A converted PostScript font file has an icon with three capital As, and you can open it to see a sample of the PostScript font. During the installation of QuickDraw GX, the converted PostScript Type 1 font files are put in font suitcases inside the Fonts folder, and your old PostScript font files are put in a folder named Archived Type 1 Fonts (in the System Folder).

Only PostScript Type 1 fonts are converted to GX versions. Most PostScript fonts are Type 1, but any PostScript Type 3 you may have will not be converted to GX versions.

If you have PostScript Type 1 font files outside your System Folder when you install QuickDraw, you convert them separately using the Type 1 Enabler program. To get the Type 1 Enabler program, open the QuickDraw GX installer, and choose Custom Install from the pop-up menu in the Installer window. The Install window displays a list of QuickDraw GX modules you can install. Select the QuickDraw GX Utilities module (by clicking its checkbox) and click the Install button.

Before you can convert old PostScript Type 1 font files with the Type 1 Enabler, each font family to be converted must have a font suitcase that contains only fixed-sized fonts for the family. For example, to convert the Adobe Garamond font family, you must have a font suitcase that contains fixed-size versions of Adobe Garamond but no TrueType versions. (You can create a new, empty font suitcase by duplicating an existing suitcase, renaming the duplicate, and dragging the duplicate's contents to the Trash.)

Create a new folder named Old Fonts (or another name of you like). Move the old PostScript Type 1 font files and the matching font suitcase files (which contain only fixed-size fonts, no TrueType fonts) into the Old Fonts folder.

Open the Type 1 Enabler program, and in the Open dialog box that appears, select the Old Fonts folder and click the Select "Old Fonts" button. The program inspects the fonts and then displays a dialog box in which you select the destination for the converted fonts. Open your Fonts folder and then click the Select "New Fonts" button to select it as the destination, unless you have a reason for selecting a different destination. (If the program finds a problem with the unconverted fonts, it displays a message in its log window.)

The Type 1 Enabler program converts the fonts to GX versions. The log window reports the outcome of the conversion process. When it finishes, you may quit.

If you look in your Fonts folder for the converted fonts, you will see a suitcase with the same name as the one containing the original fixed-size fonts. Inside the new suitcase, you will find copies of the fixed-size font files together with new files for the converted PostScript Type 1 fonts. These files look like TrueType font files, but are actually PostScript Type 1 GX fonts.

Notice that QuickDraw GX is not automatically installed when you install the core System 7.5 or the core Mac OS 7.6. The type features described in the rest of this chapter work only if you've installed QuickDraw GX in addition to the core System 7.5 or Mac OS 7.6.

## TrueType GX

With the introduction of System 7.5, Apple also introduced TrueType GX fonts. They work pretty much the way that older TrueType fonts work — but they include additional typographic information (contained in a resource of type sfnt) that gives QuickDraw GX-compatible programs more convenient access to the fonts' complexity. TrueType GX fonts should work fine on Macs without QuickDraw GX, including Macs with System 7 versions earlier than 7.5. Older TrueType fonts should look fine and print well with QuickDraw GX installed, although application programs will be unable to access special features of the fonts.

## Ligature substitution

Some fonts include linked letter groups as a single character to substitute for individual letters when they fall together in a word — for example, diphthongs such as *ae*, and *ff* or *fi* in words such as *afflicted* and *official.* If you have QuickDraw GX installed, if you're running a program that allows you to turn on automatic substitution of ligatures for the traditionally linked letter groups, and if you are using a font that contains the ligatures, the ligatures appear automatically as you type, as shown in Figure 11-18.

Official spokesperson
Common ligatures turned on

Un œuf, Un œil, Lycænidæ
Ligatures for dipthongs (vowel blends) turned on

**Figure 11-18: With QuickDraw GX and the right program, ligatures automatically appear as you type.**

Without QuickDraw GX and a compatible program, you'd have to type Option-key combinations to access alternative characters in the font. Under older system software, if you type those alternative ligature characters, spelling checkers do not recognize them as the correct letters, and hyphenation routines in programs do not properly divide words in the middle of ligatures. QuickDraw GX corrects those problems. You also can use normal text-editing methods to select and edit the individual letters that make up a ligature.

## Automatic swashes

Some fonts include alternate *glyphs*, or characters, that have fancy tails called *swashes* on some of the strokes, usually on ascenders and descenders. The swashed alternatives are meant to be optional decorative characters, usually for letters that begin or end a line. Programs that take advantage of QuickDraw GX fonts allow you to decide just how swashbuckling you want your type to be (assuming that you have a font that includes alternate swashed glyphs), as shown in Figure 11-19.

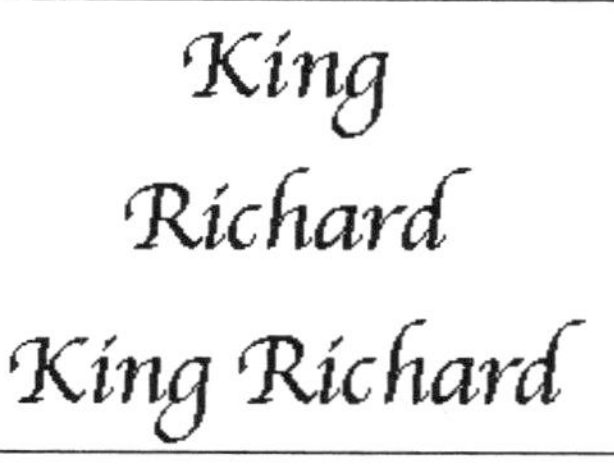

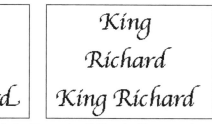

**Figure 11-19: A QuickDraw GX font with swashes (left) and without swashes (right) at the ends of lines.**

## Numeral and fraction options

Some fonts offer more than one set of numerals, perhaps both proportional and monospaced numerals, or both uppercase numerals that stand as tall as capital letters and lowercase (or old-style) numerals that dip below the baseline of the type, as shown in Figure 11-20. Programs that take advantage of QuickDraw GX allow you to choose which of a font's number sets to use.

| 1234567890<br>Proportional numerals | 1234567890<br>Uppercase proportional numerals |
|---|---|
| 1234567890<br>Monospaced numerals | 1234567890<br>Uppercase monospaced numerals |

**Figure 11-20: QuickDraw GX and compatible programs make it easy to choose among a font's numeral sets.**

In addition, because QuickDraw GX provides more control of the vertical and diagonal spacing of characters, compatible programs can let you type professional-looking fractions with either diagonal or horizontal lines. You don't need a specialized fractions font. Also, you don't need to remember arcane keyboard commands to call up special fraction characters.

## Font variations

If you're familiar with Adobe Systems' Multiple Masters line of fonts, you'll immediately understand the font-weight and width-variation controls that QuickDraw GX makes available in applications that take advantage of them. Here's how they work: a type designer can build into a font some leeway to allow the user to change the font's weight (making the characters bolder or lighter) and width (extending or condensing the font characters). A program that includes QuickDraw GX font-variation controls offers a pop-up menu, sliders, or some other simple controls that allow you to modify selected text instantly (see Figure 11-21).

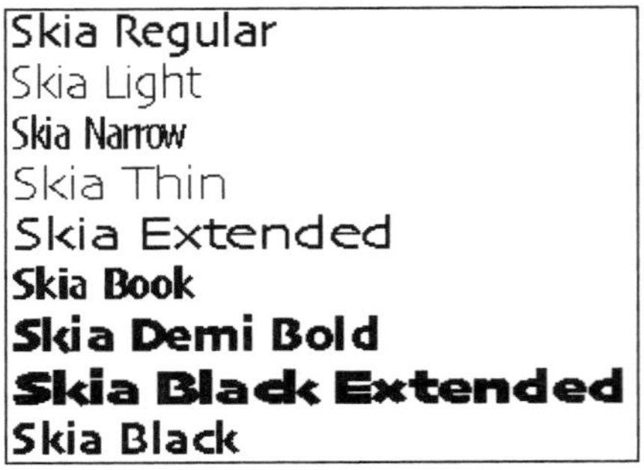

Skia Regular
Skia Light
Skia Narrow
Skia Thin
Skia Extended
Skia Book
Skia Demi Bold
Skia Black Extended
Skia Black

**Figure 11-21: With an application that takes advantage of QuickDraw GX, you can control the weight and width of some QuickDraw GX fonts.**

## Letter-spacing controls

Without QuickDraw GX, only programs for publishing and design specialists include decent tools for moving characters closer together or farther apart. With QuickDraw GX, any compatible program can offer simple letter-spacing controls.

The overall spacing between letters in an entire document or text selection is called *tracking*. Text with loose tracking has extra space between the characters in words. Text with tight tracking has characters squeezed close together, as shown in Figure 11-22 (examples from a QuickDraw GX demonstration program).

Changing tracking can come in handy when you're trying to fit text into a space that's a little too big or too small. You also can adjust tracking to improve the appearance of the text in headlines, script typefaces, or logos or to create arty effects.

Sometimes, particularly in large sizes, letters that are supposed to look like they're part of the same word have too much space between them. A capital *T* at the beginning of a word may not be close enough to the lowercase *r* that follows, making the word harder to read. Correcting the spacing between certain letter pairs is called *kerning*.

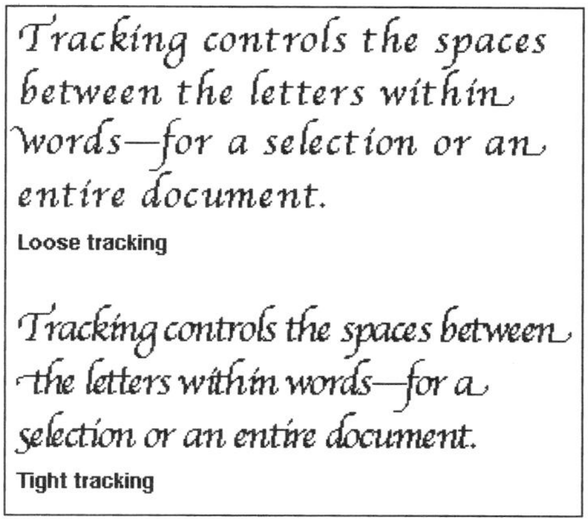

Tracking controls the spaces between the letters within words—for a selection or an entire document.

Loose tracking

Tracking controls the spaces between the letters within words—for a selection or an entire document.

Tight tracking

**Figure 11-22: Tracking controls the spacing between characters in a selection or an entire document.**

Many fonts include kerning information for letter pairs that commonly need closer spacing for legibility, but you may find cases that are not covered by a font's built-in kerning. In QuickDraw GX-compatible programs, you can just select the two letters that need closer spacing and click a control until the spacing satisfies you (see Figure 11-23).

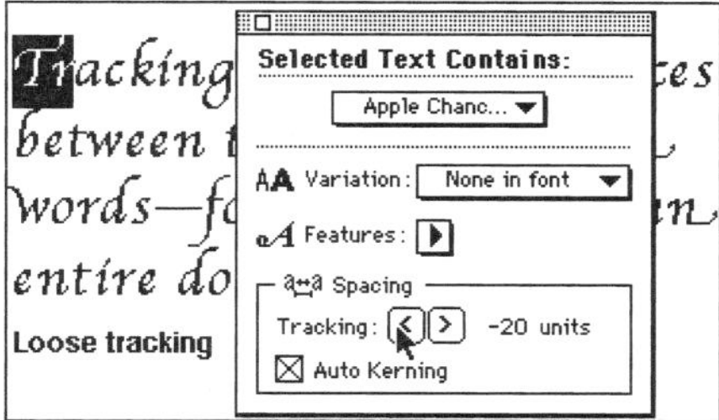


**Figure 11-23: Kerning brings together pairs of letters that are too far apart, such as the *T* and *r* in this figure.**

# Subscript and superscript

Some programs have for years made it possible to insert subscript and superscript numbers and text, such as footnote references in text and elements of formulas. Any program that takes advantage of QuickDraw GX enables you to easily insert subscript or superscript that's properly positioned and in a size that's in scale with the nearby text (see Figure 11-24).

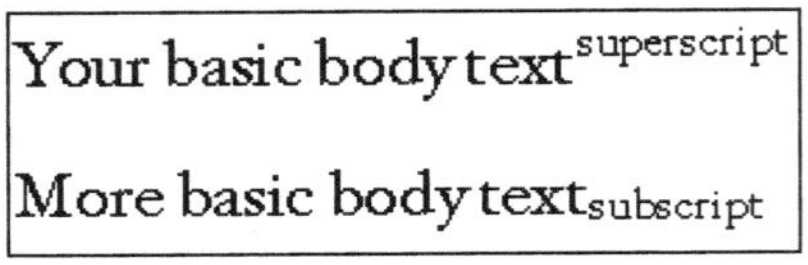

Your basic body text$^{superscript}$

More basic body text$_{subscript}$

**Figure 11-24: With QuickDraw GX and a compliant program, you can format subscripts and superscripts in one step.**

## CHAPTER  CONCEPTS AND TERMS

- Fixed-size fonts look best at their installed sizes; TrueType fonts look good at any size on any screen or printer; and PostScript fonts look good at any size on any PostScript printer.
- With Adobe Type Manager (ATM) software installed, PostScript fonts look good at any size on-screen or output on any printer (not just PostScript printers).
- You can see samples of fixed-size and TrueType fonts by opening them in the Finder.
- You add and remove fonts by dragging icons in the Finder.
- Fixed-size fonts look better on the display screen than many TrueType fonts at sizes smaller than 18 points, but TrueType fonts look better when printed. You can mix both types in the same system.
- The system software chooses the fixed-size version of a font over the TrueType version when both are present.
- When System 7 displays TrueType or fixed-size fonts on-screen, PostScript printers substitute PostScript fonts if the system software can find ones that match the screen fonts.
- QuickDraw GX, which comes with System 7.5 and later, includes typographic refinements that improve the handling of ligatures, alternative number sets, numerical fractions, subscript and superscript, small caps, and swash initials and finale — but only with compliant programs and fonts.

**bitmapped font**
Same as *fixed-size font.*

**character**
A written representation of a letter, digit, or symbol; a basic element of a written language.

**dpi (dots per inch)**
A measure of how fine or coarse the dots are that make up a printed image. More dots per inch mean smaller dots, and smaller dots mean finer (less coarse) printing.

**fixed-size font**
Contains exact pictures of every letter, digit, and symbol for one size of a font. Fixed-size fonts often are called *bitmapped fonts* because each picture precisely maps the dots, or *bits*, to be displayed or printed for one character.

**font**
A set of glyphs having a common and consistent design.

**font family**
A collection of differently styled variations (such as bold, italic, and plain) of a single font. Many fixed-size, TrueType, and PostScript fonts come in the four basic styles. Some PostScript font families include 20 or more styled versions.

**font suitcase**
A folder-like container specifically for fixed-size and TrueType fonts. With QuickDraw GX, font suitcases can also contain GX-enabled PostScript Type 1 fonts. You can create a new font-suitcase file in System 7 by duplicating an existing font-suitcase file, opening the duplicate, and dragging its contents to the Trash. You also can use version 4.1 of the Font/DA Mover with System 7 to create font suitcases.

**glyph**
A distinct visual representation of one character (such as a lowercase z), multiple characters treated as one (such as the ligature æ), or a nonprinting character (such as a space).

**grid fitting**
The process of modifying characters at small point sizes so they fit the grid of dots on the relatively coarse display screen. The font designer provides a set of instructions (also known as *hints*) for a TrueType or PostScript font that tells the system software how to modify character outlines to fit the grid.

**kerning**
Adjusting the space between pairs of letters so the spacing within the word looks consistent.

**ligature**
A glyph composed of two merged characters. For example, f and l can be merged to form ﬂ.

**outline font**
A font whose glyphs are outlined by curves and straight lines that can be smoothly enlarged or reduced to any size and then filled with dots.

**PostScript fonts**
An outline font that conforms to the specifications of the PostScript programming language. They can be smoothly scaled to any size, rotated, and made to follow a curved path. Originally designed for printing on LaserWriters and other PostScript output devices, the ATM software makes PostScript fonts work equally well on-screen and with non-PostScript printers.

**swash**
The fancy tail on an alternate, decorative form of a character, or the character with its fancy tail. To use swashes, you need QuickDraw GX, a GX font that includes swashes, and an application that lets you set the text style to show swashes.

*(continued on next page)*

(continued from previous page)

**tracking**
The overall spacing between letters in an entire document or text selection is called *tracking*. Text with loose tracking has extra space between the characters in words. Text with tight tracking has characters squeezed close together.

**TrueType**
The outline font technology built into System 7 (and available as an add-on to System 6.0.7 and 6.0.8). TrueType fonts can be smoothly scaled to any size on-screen or any type of printer.

**Type 1 font**
A PostScript font that includes instructions for grid fitting so they can be scaled to small sizes with good results. Type 1 fonts come with matching fixed-size fonts for use on-screen. Type 1 fonts need to be enabled for use with QuickDraw GX (using the Installer program or the Type 1 Enabler program that comes with QuickDraw GX).

CHAPTER TWELVE

# Printing

- Installing printer drivers and other printing software for common printers including the differences between the LaserWriter 7 and LaserWriter 8 printer drivers
- Choosing a printer, using the Page Setup and Print commands, managing background printing, and sharing printers without QuickDraw GX
- Choosing a printer, using desktop printers, using the Page Setup and Print commands, managing printing, and sharing printers with QuickDraw GX

On a Macintosh, you always set up and control printing the same basic way, regardless of the application you are using or the type of printer you have. The Macintosh system software enforces this consistency by providing complete printing services to applications. All applications use the same piece of software to prepare the page image for, and communicate with, a particular type of printer. This software, called a *printer driver*, resides in the Extensions folder inside the System Folder. Compare this uniformity to other types of personal computers, on which you often have to install printer-driver software separately for each application, and you see the benefit.

You choose a printer with the standard Chooser desk accessory, which comes with the system software, and that choice persists among all applications and through restarts until you choose again. You control the rest of the printing process with your application's Page Setup and Print commands; the standard options for these commands are the same in all applications. Alternatively, you can select one document or a group of documents (created by one application or several) and then give the command to print the selected documents from the Finder.

You don't have to wait for documents to finish printing before continuing with other work. With many printers System 7 can manage printing in the background, so you can continue working on other tasks.

QuickDraw GX, which comes with System 7.5 and later, improves the administration of background printing and allows you to print documents by dragging their icons to a printer icon on the desktop. QuickDraw GX also allows you to choose a printer with the Print command, bypassing the Chooser and giving you complete control of the printing process without leaving your application.

You can print documents on a Macintosh system without understanding how pages are transformed from what you see on-screen to what you get on a printer. But understanding the printing process will help you cope when what comes out of the printer deviates too much from what is displayed on-screen. All the most common types of printers compose page images of dots on paper, but the dot size and the method used to prepare the page image vary among different types of printers. The dot size and page-preparation method affect the appearance of graphics, patterns, rotated and curved text, and much more.

This chapter describes the system-level software that you need and the methods that you use to print with System 7 on the most common printers used with Macs. Because printing is fundamentally different when QuickDraw GX is installed, the first section of the chapter describes printing without QuickDraw GX, and the second section of the chapter describes printing under QuickDraw GX.

# Printing without QuickDraw GX

This section describes the software you need and the methods you use for printing without QuickDraw GX. If your Mac does not have QuickDraw GX installed, this section is for you. (If your Mac does have QuickDraw GX, see "Printing under QuickDraw GX" later in this chapter.)

Your Mac most likely does not have QuickDraw GX if it uses any version of System 7 before 7.5. (Even if your Mac has System 7.5 or Mac OS 7.6, it may not have QuickDraw GX; although QuickDraw GX comes with System 7.5 and later, its installation is optional.) Theoretically, QuickDraw GX works with System 7.1 and System 7 Pro, but the QuickDraw GX installers that come with System 7.5 and Mac OS 7.6 will not install QuickDraw GX on a version of System 7 older than 7.5.

You can tell whether your Mac has QuickDraw GX by looking for it in the Extensions folder (inside the System Folder of your startup disk). You can use other methods, such as looking for a desktop printer icon, but checking the Extensions folder is foolproof.

## Comparing printer-driver software

To print on a particular type of printer, a Macintosh needs software for that printer in its Extensions folder. That software is called a printer driver. A printer driver prepares a complete description of each page to be printed, in a format that the printer can interpret, and then sends the page descriptions to the printer.

Figure 12-1 displays the icons of the printer drivers that come with System 7 Pro.

Your application prints by sending a description of your document to the printer-driver software in the Extensions folder in the System Folder. The printer software translates the description into data that the printer can use.

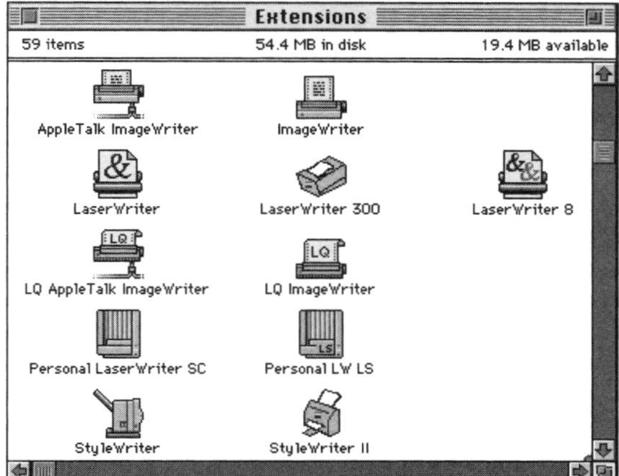


**Figure 12-1: The System 7 Pro printer drivers.**

Many printers work with Macs, and each printer requires its own printer driver software. Apple supplies printer drivers for its printers in several ways: with System 7; with Apple printers; and through Apple dealers and the Apple Order Center (800-293-6617). See "Obtaining Installation Software" in Chapter 22 for more information.

In general, you should use the latest version available. For example, if you buy an Apple printer after installing (or upgrading) System 7, and you find that the printer comes with older driver software than the driver that came with System 7, use the driver that came with System 7.

## PostScript printer drivers

Printers that interpret PostScript commands to create printable images are called *PostScript printers*. Examples include Apple's LaserWriter Plus, II, IINT, IINTX, IIf, and IIg; Personal LaserWriter IINT, IINTR, and 320; LaserWriter Select 360; and LaserWriter Pro 600, 630, and 810.

Almost all Apple LaserWriters with PostScript — and many PostScript printers made by other companies — use Apple's LaserWriter driver software. Examples of other laser printers that can use Apple's LaserWriter drivers are Texas Instruments' MicroLaser Pro and PS35, GCC Technologies' GLP Elite, and NEC's SilentWriter 2/90.

Two major versions of the LaserWriter driver work with all versions of System 7: LaserWriter 7 (which usually is named simply LaserWriter) and LaserWriter 8. To determine which version of the LaserWriter driver you have, select its icon and choose Get Info from the Finder's File menu. You then see the driver's Info window, which reports the version number.

You can use either LaserWriter 7 or LaserWriter 8 with all LaserWriters that have the original version of PostScript, which is called PostScript Level 1. You should use LaserWriter 8 with newer LaserWriters that have the newer version of PostScript, known as PostScript Level 2. Printers that should use LaserWriter 8 include the LaserWriter Select 360, LaserWriter Pro 630 and 810, and Personal LaserWriter 320. All versions of System 7 before 7.5 come with LaserWriter 7 software, but you can use LaserWriter 8 with any version of System 7.

Besides taking advantage of PostScript Level 2, the LaserWriter 8 driver provides other enhancements. With LaserWriter 8, you can print multiple pages per sheet of paper. You also can see the effect of choosing certain page-size and orientation options in a miniature representation of the page as you make those choices.

Apple developed LaserWriter 8 in collaboration with Adobe Systems (creator of PostScript) to take advantage of PostScript Level 2. Adobe distributes the LaserWriter 8 driver under the name PSPrinter. If you buy a non-Apple printer, it may come with the PSPrinter driver. Printers that should use PSPrinter 8 (or LaserWriter 8) include the Texas Instruments MicroLaser and the NEC SilentWriter 640.

Adobe has updated PSPrinter, and Apple has updated both LaserWriter 7 and LaserWriter 8 since their initial release, adding features and fixing bugs. Do not use LaserWriter 8.0 or PSPrinter 8.0; instead, use LaserWriter 8.2, PSPrinter 8.2, or a later version of either. The 8.2 version fixes bugs in the versions.

Some applications (notably, PageMaker 5) require LaserWriter 8 or PSPrinter. However, LaserWriter 8 and PSPrinter do not work well with all applications, particularly older applications. If you experience problems on your Mac or on your LaserWriter when using version 8.2 or a newer version of either LaserWriter 8 or PSPrinter, use LaserWriter 7.

Macs that share a LaserWriter or another PostScript printer on a network need not all have the same version of LaserWriter 7, LaserWriter 8, or PSPrinter software. All versions of LaserWriter 7, LaserWriter 8, and PSPrinter coexist peacefully on a network. Networked Macs using System 6.0.7 and 6.0.8 can use any version of LaserWriter 7 or LaserWriter 8 for compatibility with other Macs on the network. (LaserWriter 7, LaserWriter 8, and PSPrinter do not work with System 6.0.5 and earlier versions.)

If you have installed QuickDraw GX, which comes with system software 7.5, 7.5.3, and 7.6 but is optional, you need a GX version of the LaserWriter driver. For more information, see "Printing under QuickDraw GX" later in this chapter.

### PostScript Printer Description files

The LaserWriter 8 and PSPrinter drivers can take advantage of a particular printer's features, such as its *resolution* (the number of dots it can print per inch) and the size and capacity of its paper trays. These PostScript Level 2 drivers get these details from special files called PostScript Printer Description (PPD) files. A set of PPD files comes with the LaserWriter 8 or PSPrinter driver, and the PPDs reside in a folder named Printer Descriptions inside the Extensions folder (which is in the System Folder). In addition, printer manufacturers include the appropriate PPD with each printer that has PostScript Level 2.

### Other printer drivers

Many printers do not use PostScript to create page images. Examples include Apple's StyleWriter II, ImageWriter II, Personal LaserWriter 300, and LaserWriter Select 300. Non-PostScript printers from other companies include Hewlett-Packard's DeskWriter family and GCC Technologies' PLP II.

Each non-PostScript printer has its own printer-driver software. With few exceptions, your Extensions folder must include a different driver for each non-PostScript printer that you use. A couple of notable exceptions are the Apple StyleWriter, which can (and should) use a StyleWriter II driver; and the Apple Personal LaserWriter LS, which can (and should) use a LaserWriter 300 driver.

Other types of output devices, although not technically printers, also have printer-driver software. These devices include fax/modems, plotters, and portable document makers such as Acrobat and Common Ground. If you have any of these devices, each must have a driver in your Extensions folder.

If you have installed QuickDraw GX, which comes with system software 7.5, 7.5.3, and 7.6 but is optional, you need a GX version of your printer driver. For more information, see "Printing under QuickDraw GX" later in this chapter.

## Using the Chooser

System 7 can print, or otherwise create output, from an application on any printer or other output device for which you have a driver in your Extensions folder. The output device could be a fax/modem, a plotter, a personal printer, a network printer, and so on. You must designate which device you want to use. If you want to send a fax, for example, you have to tell the Mac that your output device is a fax/modem. If your organization has different printers for different types of printing (letterhead, envelopes, plain paper, and so on), you can change printers based on your need.

On a system without QuickDraw GX, you designate an output device by selecting it in the Chooser desk accessory. For some types of printers, you also use the Chooser to turn background printing on and off, and to set up the printer.

## Selecting a printer

To select a printer or other output device (if QuickDraw GX is not installed), choose the Chooser from the Apple menu. Each printer or other output device for which you have a driver in your Extensions folder appears as an icon in the Chooser. In the Chooser window, shown in Figure 12-2, select the icon of the printer or other device that you want to use.

If you select a printer or other device connected to a network, the Chooser lists the names of all printers of that type that currently are available on your network, as shown in Figure 12-3. You select the printer you want by clicking its name. If your network has zones, you see the names of printers in the currently selected zone. You can select a different zone in the lower-left part of the Chooser. The Chooser does not display a list of zones unless your network has more than one zone.

If you select a printer or device that connects directly to your Mac, the Chooser lists the ports to which it could be connected, as shown in Figure 12-4. You click the port to which the printer is connected.

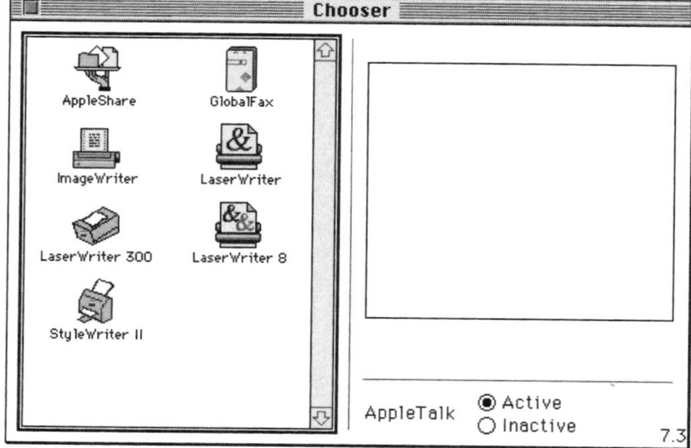


**Figure 12-2: The Chooser shows the icons of available printers and other output devices.**

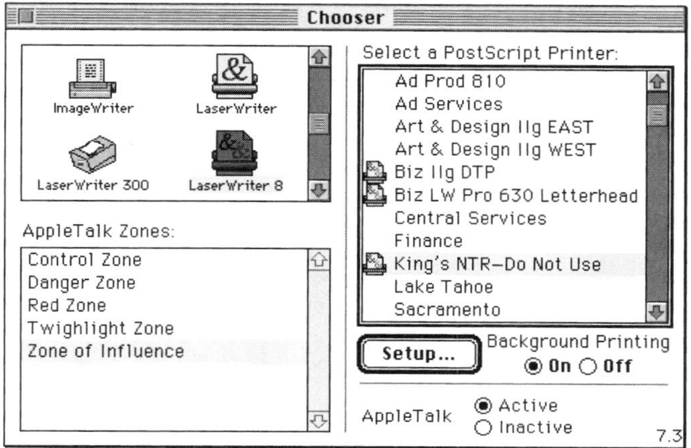


**Figure 12-3: The Chooser lists the available networked printers.**

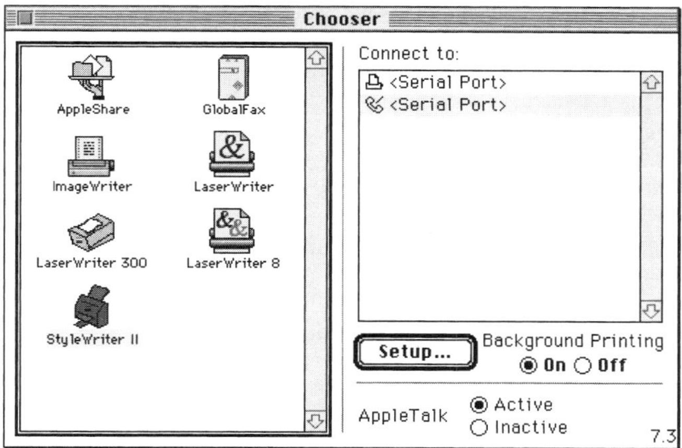


**Figure 12-4: The Chooser lists ports for directly connected printers.**

### Creating a GrayShare StyleWriter or Personal LaserWriter LS

Are you stuck with a StyleWriter and wish that it had the StyleWriter II's GrayShare technology for printing shades of gray and sharing your printer on a network? All you need is the StyleWriter II software, a Mac with Color QuickDraw, and time. Lacking Color QuickDraw, Macs that came with 68000 microprocessors (the Plus, SE, Classic, Portable, and PowerBook 100) can't use the StyleWriter II software to print shades of gray.

Apple has approved version 1.2 of the StyleWriter II driver for both StyleWriter and StyleWriter II printers; the company also has approved the LaserWriter 300 driver for use with Personal LaserWriter LS printers. These drivers are part of an Apple software upgrade kit euphonically titled StyleWriter and Personal LaserWriter LS Printer Driver Upgrade (Apple part number M1900LL/A). These drivers also are available on eWorld.

The StyleWriter II 1.2 driver speeds printing by approximately 50 percent for simple text and by some 2,700 percent for multiple fonts and styles. Grayscale printing looks fabulous, but it takes longer and uses immense amounts of disk space for temporary files on the startup disk. For example, printing a half-page Freehand document (Aldus' sample Medical Illustration) took 19 minutes (35 minutes printing in the background) and 11.5MB of disk space. Your results will vary, depending on the speed of your Mac, the complexity of your documents, and what else you are doing with your Mac at the same time.

If you do get the StyleWriter II software, install it with the Installer program located on the first installation disk. The Installer updates the Chooser to version 7.3 and may update other system software, depending on the model of your Mac and the version of your system software. The StyleWriter II software probably won't work if you merely drag the StyleWriter II icon to your System Folder.

## Turning background printing on and off

Many printer drivers offer the option of printing in the background while you do other work. You turn background printing on or off separately for each type of printer that offers it.

To turn on background printing for a type of printer, select that printer's icon in the Chooser. If background printing is possible on that printer, the Chooser displays On and Off buttons below the words "Background Printing" at the right side of its window. These words and buttons do not appear if the selected printer does not allow background printing.

When you print with the Background Printing option turned on, the printer driver saves the page descriptions that it creates in a file for later automatic printing. This file is called a *spool file*, and the process of saving it is called *spooling*. The

PrintMonitor application (located in the Extensions folder) automatically opens in the background and prints spool files when there are any in the PrintMonitor Documents folder (located in the System Folder). For information on managing background printing with PrintMonitor, see "Managing background printing" later in this chapter.

## Setting up a printer

The Chooser gives you a third function for some printer drivers: the capability to specify what features of your printer you want to use. If, for example, the Extensions folder contains version 7.2 of the LaserWriter driver and you select the LaserWriter icon in the Chooser, a Setup or Review button appears on the right side of the Chooser window. A Setup button also appears if you select LaserWriter 8, LaserWriter 300, PSPrinter, or StyleWriter II.

When LaserWriter (version 7.2) is selected in the Chooser, setup is automatic. After you select a specific printer by name, clicking the Setup button displays the dialog box shown in Figure 12-5. If you click the Setup button in this dialog box, the LaserWriter driver (version 7.2) automatically gets the setup information it needs from the selected printer.

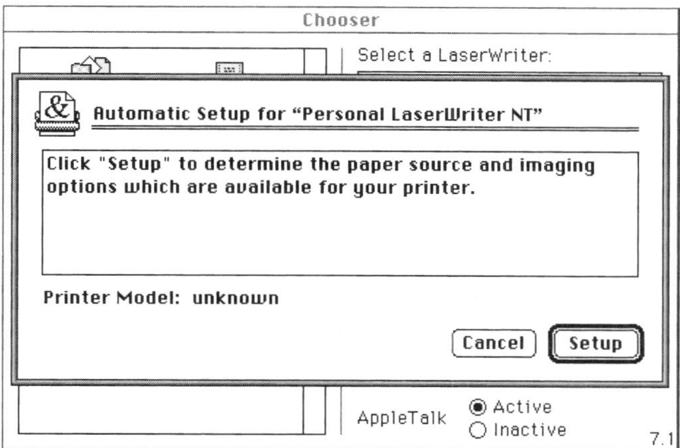


**Figure 12-5: Printer Setup with the LaserWriter driver (version 7.2).**

When LaserWriter 8 or PSPrinter is selected in the Chooser, setup can be automatic or manual. With LaserWriter 8 version 8.2, selecting a printer by name and clicking the Setup button in the Chooser automatically determines the correct PPD file and set paper tray options for the selected printer. To manually select a PPD and paper tray options, click the Setup button a second time. With

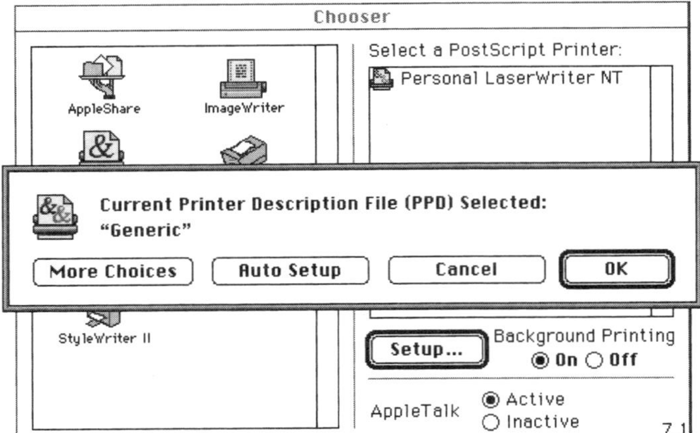


**Figure 12-6: Automatic printer setup with the LaserWriter 8 or PSPrinter driver.**

LaserWriter 8 versions 8.1.1 and earlier, selecting a specific printer by name and clicking the Setup button displays the dialog box shown in Figure 12-6.

For automatic setup, click the Auto Setup button in this dialog box, and wait while the driver gets the setup information that it needs from the selected printer.

For manual setup, click the More Choices button to expand the dialog box, as shown in Figure 12-7. In the expanded dialog box, click the Select PPD button, and then select a PPD from the list of the PPD files in your Printer Descriptions folder (described in "PostScript Printer Description files" earlier in this chapter). Clicking the Configure button in the expanded dialog box allows you to set options that can be installed on the printer, such as paper trays and memory expansion. Clicking the Printer Info button displays the printer name, product name, PostScript level and version, resolution, printer memory statistics, and other information.

When the StyleWriter II or LaserWriter 300 driver is selected in the Chooser, clicking the Setup button allows you to configure the printer for sharing on a network. The process is described fully in "Sharing printers" at the end of this section.

## Using the Page Setup command

After choosing a printer or other device with the Chooser but before printing a document, you need to specify how you want the document pages to be formatted. You need to set the paper size (such as letter or legal size), a page orientation (horizontal or vertical), a reduction or enlargement factor, and other options that affect how the document is arranged on the page. With some printers, you also can turn optional printer effects on and off.

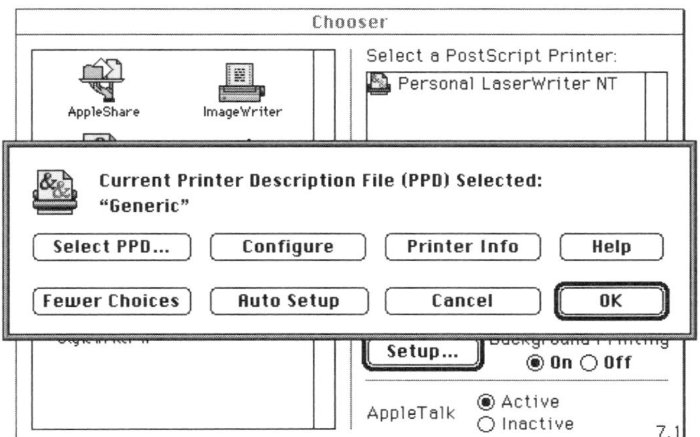


Figure 12-7: Manual printer setup with the LaserWriter 8 or PSPrinter driver.

You set page-formatting and printer-effects options with the Page Setup command, usually located in the application's File menu. The specific options available depend on the type of printer selected in the Chooser, as detailed in the following sections of this chapter:

- ❖ LaserWriter 7 Page Setup
- ❖ LaserWriter 8 Page Setup
- ❖ LaserWriter 300 Page Setup
- ❖ StyleWriter II Page Setup
- ❖ ImageWriter Page Setup

You may notice additional options that are not described in these sections, because some applications add their own options to the Page Setup command. Check the application's documentation for explanations of options not described here.

## LaserWriter 7 Page Setup

When the LaserWriter driver (any revision of version 7) is selected in the Chooser, choosing the Page Setup command displays the dialog box shown in Figure 12-8. In this dialog box, you can set the paper size, reduction or enlargement percentage, page orientation, and printer effects. An Options button gives you access to more printer effects.

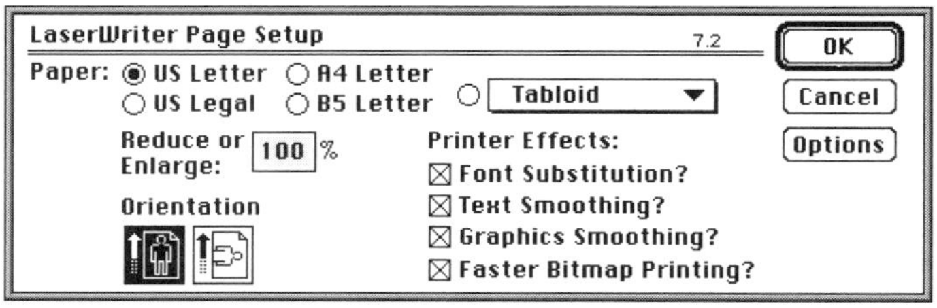

LaserWriter Page Setup 7.2
Paper: US Letter A4 Letter US Legal B5 Letter Tabloid
Reduce or Enlarge: 100 %
Orientation
Printer Effects:
Font Substitution?
Text Smoothing?
Graphics Smoothing?
Faster Bitmap Printing?
OK
Cancel
Options

**Figure 12-8: Page Setup with LaserWriter 7.**

Your paper-size options include US Letter ($8\frac{1}{2}$ by 11 inches), US Legal ($8\frac{1}{2}$ by 14 inches), and A5 and B5 (European standard sizes). You can also choose other paper sizes (such as 11-by-17-inch tabloid) and envelope sizes from the pop-up menu.

The four Printer Effects options, which you can toggle on and off, have the following effects:

❖ **Font Substitution** substitutes PostScript fonts for any fixed-sized screen fonts for which no PostScript or TrueType equivalent is available (as described in Chapter 11). For example, Geneva becomes Helvetica, and New York becomes Times. The one drawback of font substitution is that although the variable-size font is substituted for its fixed-sized cousin, the spacing of letters and words on a line does not change, and the printed results often are remarkably ugly. For best results, do not use fixed-size fonts that lack TrueType or PostScript equivalents (such as Venice or London), and leave the Font Substitution option off.

❖ **Text Smoothing** smoothes the jagged edges of fixed sizes for which there are no matching PostScript fonts or TrueType fonts (such as Venice 14 and London 18). For best results, avoid such fonts, and leave the Text Smoothing option off.

❖ **Graphics Smoothing** smoothes the jagged edges of bit-mapped graphic images created with painting programs such as MacPaint. Smoothing improves some images but blurs the detail out of others. Try printing with Graphics Smoothing set both ways, and go with the one that looks best to you. Notice that this option has no effect on graphics created with drawing programs such as MacDraw, FreeHand, and Illustrator.

❖ **Faster Bitmap Printing** may speed the printing of bit-mapped images, such as those created by a painting program. Paradoxically, setting this option actually slows printing in a few applications. Moreover, most printers made since 1992 are fast enough that you won't notice a difference whether this option is set or not.

Clicking the Options button in the LaserWriter 7 Page Setup dialog box brings up the dialog box shown in Figure 12-9.

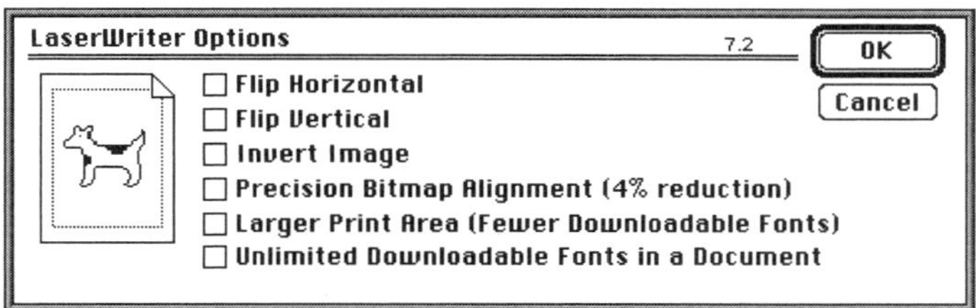


**Figure 12-9: Page Setup options with LaserWriter 7.**

The options in this dialog box have the following effects:

- **Flip Horizontal** and **Flip Vertical** create mirror images of your document. You can see the result in the illustration in the dialog box when you click the checkbox. The Flip Horizontal option flips the image right to left, which is useful if you are creating a film image on a Linotronic imagesetter for a transparency or if the pages have to be emulsion side down. Flipping the image vertically (upside down) has no apparent use because turning the paper around has the same effect.
- **Invert Image** makes all the black parts of a page print white, and vice versa. You probably won't have much use for this parlor trick unless you create film negatives on a slide printer that has no method of its own for creating negative images.
- **Precision Bitmap Alignment** reduces the entire printed image to avoid minor distortions in bit-map graphics. The distortions occur because of the nature of the dot density of bit-map graphics. For example, 72 dpi (dots per inch), which is the standard screen-image size, does not divide evenly into 300 dpi, 400 dpi, or 600 dpi (the dot density of laser printers). When you are printing to a 300-dpi printer, for example, turning on this option reduces page images by 4 percent, effectively printing them at 288 dpi (an even multiple of 72 dpi). The reductions align the bitmaps properly to produce crisper output.
- **Larger Print Area** is one of the reasons to bother with the LaserWriter Options dialog box. Most laser printers place a quarter-inch margin on every printed page, whether you want one or not. Thus, if you are trying to match an image that stretches across two pages, you will run into this vast white space. You can reduce the margin to 1/8 inch by selecting this option. Older printers lack the RAM to support this option and may not print your document. Newer printers that contain more RAM allow this useful option.

❖ **Unlimited Downloadable Fonts** allows you to use more fonts than your printer's memory can hold at one time by removing fonts from the printer's memory after they are used, making way for other fonts. You can use this option in conjunction with the Larger Print Area option. Be aware that the constant downloading and flushing of font files takes time and thus slows printing. EPS (Encapsulated PostScript) graphics that use fonts that are not present elsewhere on the page will not print correctly because the printer will substitute Courier for those orphan fonts. If you see Courier in a graphic where you did not want it, make sure that this option is turned off.

## LaserWriter 8 Page Setup

When LaserWriter 8 is selected in the Chooser, choosing the Page Setup command displays the dialog box shown in Figure 12-10. This dialog box looks substantially different from the one for LaserWriter 7, but it offers similar options. You can choose a paper size from a pop-up menu, enter a reduction or enlargement percentage, and select a page orientation. You can use the Layout pop-up menu to choose the number of page images to be printed per sheet of paper. (LaserWriter 7 does not offer the Layout option.)

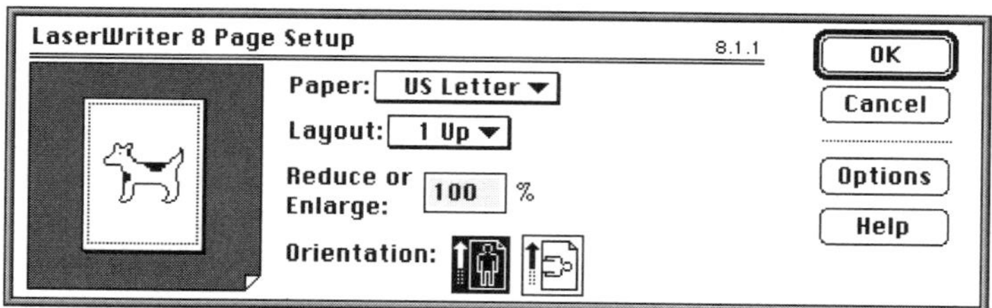


**Figure 12-10: Page Setup with LaserWriter 8.**

LaserWriter 8 relegates all printer options to the secondary dialog box shown in Figure 12-11, which you open by clicking the Options button. All these options are explained fully in the preceding section, "LaserWriter 7 Page Setup."

## LaserWriter 300 Page Setup

When the LaserWriter 300 driver is selected in the Chooser, choosing the Page Setup command displays the dialog box shown in Figure 12-12.

LaserWriter 8 Options 8.1.1
OK
Cancel
Help
Visual Effects:
Flip Horizontal
Flip Vertical
Invert Image
Printer Options:
Substitute Fonts
Smooth Text
Smooth Graphics
Precision Bitmap Alignment
Larger Print Area (Fewer Downloadable Fonts)
Unlimited Downloadable Fonts in a Document

**Figure 12-11: Page Setup options with LaserWriter 8.**

LaserWriter 300 Page Setup 1.2
OK
Cancel
Help
Options
Page Size: US Letter
Scaling (%): 100
Orientation:

**Figure 12-12: Page Setup with LaserWriter 300.**

In this dialog box, you can choose a page size from a pop-up menu. You can enter any reduction or enlargement percentage, or you can choose one of the four optimum reduction factors from the Scaling pop-up menu. Also, you can select vertical or horizontal page orientation. Clicking the Options button displays a secondary dialog box, shown in Figure 12-13. For full descriptions of the two options in this dialog box, refer to "LaserWriter 7 Page Setup" earlier in this chapter.

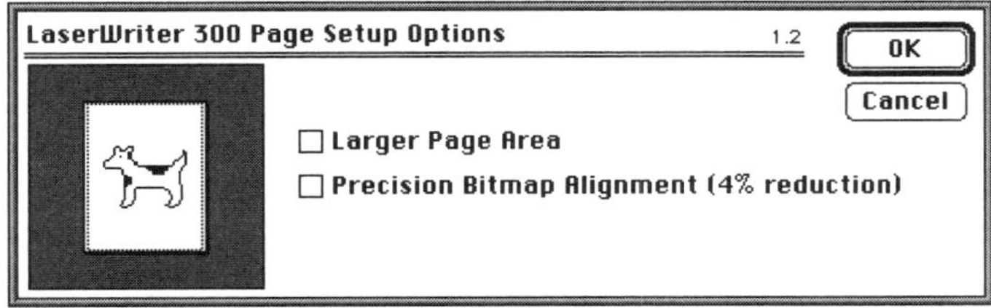


**Figure 12-13: Page Setup options with LaserWriter 300.**

The LaserWriter 300 driver works with the Apple Personal LaserWriter 300 and Personal LaserWriter LS. These printers do not prepare their own page images based on PostScript descriptions sent by the printer driver. Instead, the driver prepares page images based on QuickDraw graphics that are built into every Macintosh.

## StyleWriter II Page Setup

When StyleWriter II is selected in the Chooser (for printing on a StyleWriter II or an original StyleWriter printer), choosing the Page Setup command displays the dialog box shown in Figure 12-14. In this dialog box, you can choose a page size from a pop-up menu; enter any reduction or enlargement percentage or choose an optimum reduction factor from the Scaling pop-up menu; and select the page orientation. The StyleWriters do not have any visual effect or printer options.

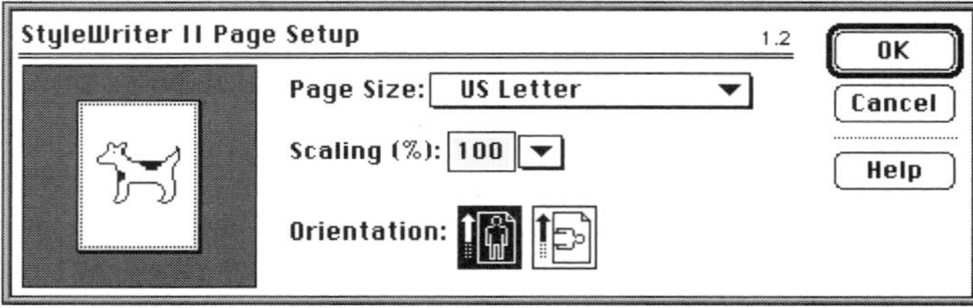


**Figure 12-14: Page Setup with StyleWriter.**

## ImageWriter Page Setup

When the ImageWriter driver is selected in the Chooser, choosing the Page Setup command displays the dialog box shown in Figure 12-15. This dialog box offers a choice of five page sizes, vertical or horizontal page orientation, and a single reduction factor (50 percent).

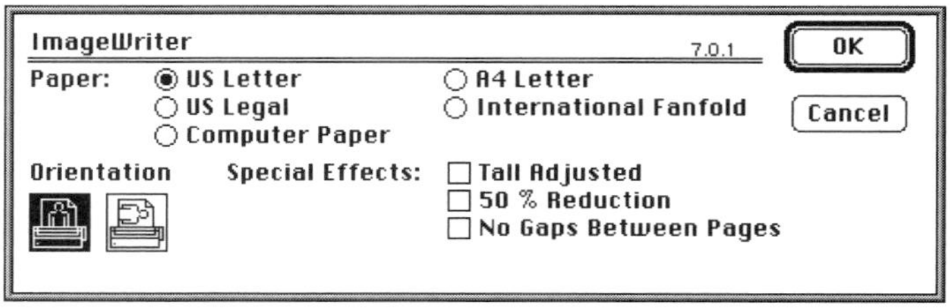

**Figure 12-15: Page Setup with ImageWriter.**

Turning on the Tall Adjusted option makes graphics print with correct proportions but widens individual text characters. Turning off the Tall Adjusted option makes text print with correct proportions but elongates graphics. For example, squares print as tall rectangles when this option is off.

Turning on the No Gaps Between Pages option eliminates top and bottom margins, primarily for printing continuously on fanfold paper.

## Using the Print command

After choosing a printer or other device with the Chooser and setting page-formatting options with the Page Setup command, you can print a document with the Print command (located in the File menu of most applications).

The Print command has several options. You can specify a range of pages, a number of copies, and a paper source. You may have additional options, depending on the type of printer selected in the Chooser, as detailed in the following sections of this chapter:

- ❖ LaserWriter 7 Print
- ❖ LaserWriter 8 Print
- ❖ LaserWriter 300 Print
- ❖ StyleWriter II Print
- ❖ ImageWriter Print

Besides the standard Print options described in these sections, you may notice additional options; some applications add special options to the Print command. Check the application's documentation for explanations of options not described here.

### LaserWriter 7 Print

When LaserWriter driver version 7.2 is selected in the Chooser, choosing the Print command displays the dialog box shown in Figure 12-16. In this dialog box, you can enter the number of copies you want to print, as well as a starting and ending page number.

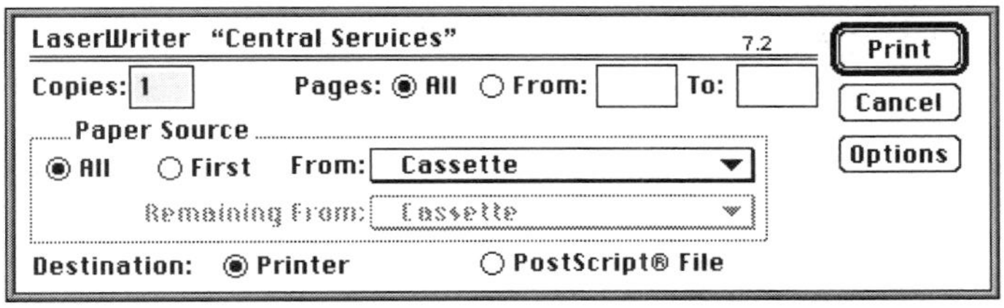

LaserWriter "Central Services" 7.2 Print
Copies: 1 Pages: ◉ All ○ From: To: Cancel
Paper Source Options
◉ All ○ First From: Cassette
Remaining From: Cassette
Destination: ◉ Printer ○ PostScript® File

**Figure 12-16: The LaserWriter 7.2 Print dialog box.**

If your printer has more than one paper source — for example, a multipurpose tray and a paper cassette — you can set all pages to come from one paper source, or you can set the first page (of each copy printed) to come from one source and subsequent pages to come from another source. You choose a paper source from a pop-up menu. The setting of the Destination option determines whether the LaserWriter 7.2 driver sends page images to the printer or saves them as a PostScript file.

If you set the Destination option to PostScript File, the Print button becomes a Save button. Clicking it brings up a Save dialog box, in which you name the PostScript file and select the folder where you want to save the file. Clicking Save in this dialog box creates a file that contains all the PostScript instructions for your document. You then can send the file to a printer by using the LaserWriter Utility. PostScript files are easier to take to service bureaus than actual document files are, because you don't have to worry that the service bureau has the application that created the document.

Clicking the Options button in the Print dialog box displays the secondary dialog box shown in Figure 12-17.

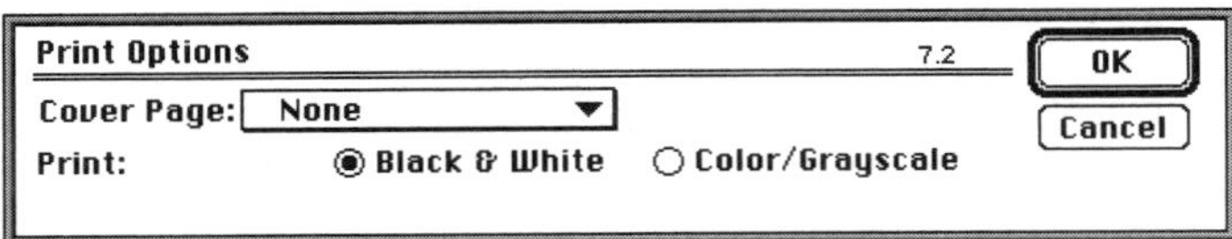


**Figure 12-17: LaserWriter 7.2 Print options.**

The options in this dialog box have the following effects:

- **Cover Page** sets whether to print a cover page before printing the document, after printing the document, or not at all. A cover page reports the document's name, the owner name of the Mac that printed it, and when it was printed.
- **Black & White** prints colors and shades of gray in black and white. A document that contains colors or shades of gray may print faster when this option is set.
- **Color/Grayscale** prints colors in a document in color (on a color PostScript printer) or as shades of gray (on a monochrome PostScript printer).

The Print dialog box for revisions of the LaserWriter 7 driver older than 7.2 contains the same options as the LaserWriter 7.2 dialog box, but it looks different (see Figure 12-18).

LaserWriter "Central Services" 7.1.2
Print
Copies: 1 Pages: All From: To:
Cancel
Cover Page: No First Page Last Page
Paper Source: Paper Cassette Manual Feed
Print: Black & White Color/Grayscale
Destination: Printer PostScript® File

**Figure 12-18: LaserWriter 7 (before revision 7.2) Print options.**

## LaserWriter 8 Print

When LaserWriter 8 is selected in the Chooser, choosing the Print command displays the dialog box shown in Figure 12-19. This dialog box offers options similar to those for the LaserWriter 7.2 driver. You can enter a page range and the number of copies to be printed. You can set all pages to come from one paper source, or you can set the first page (of each copy printed) to come from one source and subsequent pages to come from another source. The Destination option determines whether LaserWriter 8 sends page images to the printer or saves them in a PostScript file.

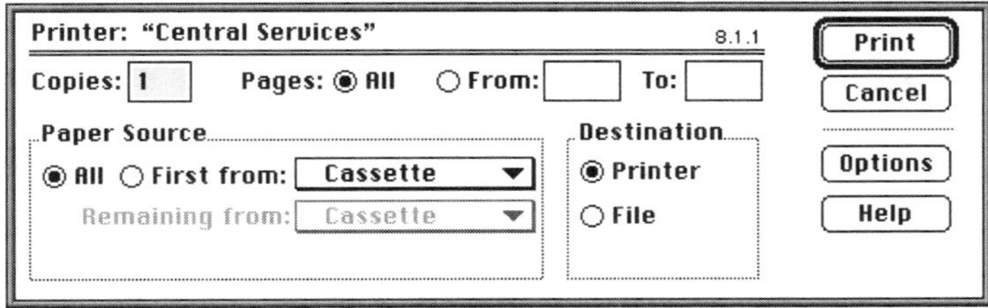


**Figure 12-19: The LaserWriter 8 Print dialog box.**

Clicking the Options button in the Print dialog box brings up the secondary dialog box shown in Figure 12-20.

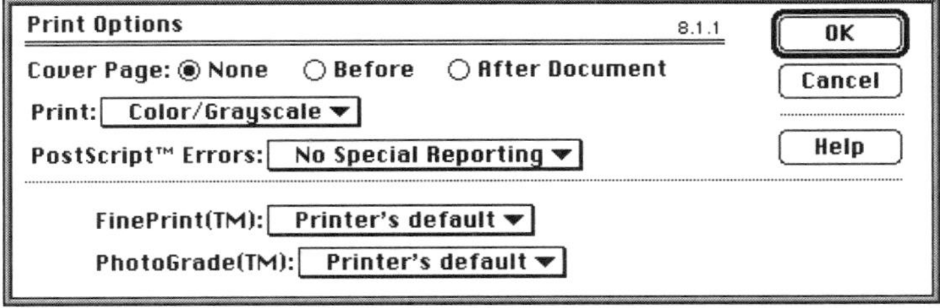


**Figure 12-20: LaserWriter 8 Print options (available options depend on the specific type of printer).**

The contents of the Print Options dialog box depend on the printer model and on how the printer is equipped, but the following options always are available:

- ❖ **Cover Page** specifies whether to print a cover page before printing the document, after printing the document, or not at all. A cover page reports the document's name, the owner name of the Mac that printed it, and when it was printed.
- ❖ **Print** determines how colors and shades of gray are printed. The Black and White setting prints everything in black or white. The Color/Grayscale setting prints grays as grays and colors as colors on a color printer, or colors and grays as shades of gray on monochrome printers. Calibrated Color/Grayscale prints grays as grays and colors as colors, matching printed colors to displayed colors as closely as possible; this setting requires a printer that uses the device-independent color capabilities of PostScript Level 2.
- ❖ **PostScript Errors** sets the desired level of error reporting during printing: no error reporting, errors summarized on-screen, or errors printed on paper.

For some printers, the Print Options dialog box contains other settings. If the printer selected in the Chooser has Apple's FinePrint and PhotoGrade technologies, for example, the Print Options box contains pop-up menus for turning those capabilities on and off.

## LaserWriter 300 Print

When LaserWriter 300 is selected in the Chooser, choosing the Print command displays the dialog box shown in Figure 12-21. Here, as in the dialog boxes for the LaserWriter 8 and LaserWriter 7.2 drivers, you can enter a page range and number of copies to be printed. You can set all pages to come from one paper source — paper cassette or manual-feed tray — or you can set the first page to come from one source and the remaining pages to come from another source. The LaserWriter 300 driver is not for PostScript printers, and it cannot save page images as a PostScript file.

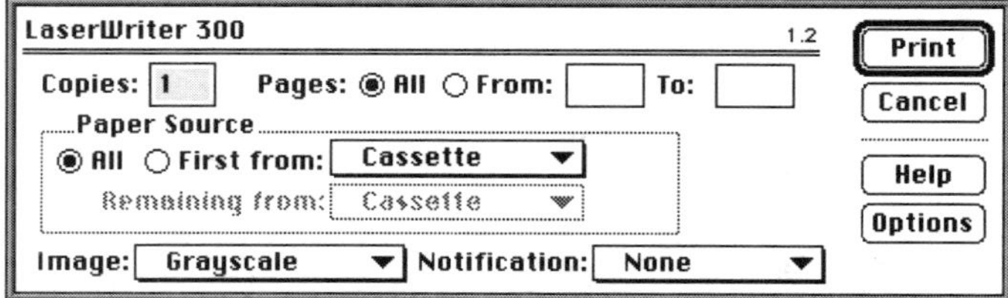


**Figure 12-21: The LaserWriter 300 Print dialog box.**

## Creating an EPS or PostScript file

Instead of printing, the Print command can save a document as a PostScript file for later printing on another system. When LaserWriter 7, LaserWriter 8, or PSPrinter is selected in the Chooser, the Print command also can save one page of a document as a high-quality graphic PostScript file (like the files saved by Adobe Illustrator and Aldus Freehand) for placement in a page-layout program.

To create a PostScript file, set the Print command's Destination option to File. The Print button becomes a Save button, and clicking it brings up a Save dialog box (shown for LaserWriter 8 in this sidebar), in which you select the folder where you want to save the PostScript file, name the file, and set several options. (The options are not available with any revision of LaserWriter 7.)

The Format pop-up menu sets the kind of PostScript file. Choose PostScript Job to create a standard PostScript file for later printing. Choose one of the three EPS (Encapsulated PostScript) formats to create a one-page graphic for placement in another document. The EPS Mac Standard Preview includes a 72-dpi bit-mapped image for previewing on-screen. The EPS Mac Enhanced Preview includes a PICT preview image, which can be smoothly reduced or enlarged on the screen display. The EPS Mac No Preview takes the least amount of disk space because it has no preview image. Without a preview image, you can't see the file on-screen, but this option prints just like the other EPS formats.

Choosing the ASCII option creates a more widely compatible PostScript file than the Binary option, but the Binary option can speed printing on a printer that can handle it.

Choose the Level 1 Compatible option for a file that can be used on a printer with PostScript Level 1 or PostScript Level 2. If you are using only PostScript Level 2 printers, choose the Level 2 Only option to take advantage of the speed and enhanced features of Level 2.

Use the Font Inclusion menu to embed all, some, or none of the fonts from the document in the PostScript file. The None option, which does not embed any fonts, uses the least disk space but prints correctly only on a system that has all needed fonts. The All option, which embeds every font used in the document, may use a great deal of disk space, but all fonts will print from any system. The All But Standard 13 option embeds all the fonts used except the 13 fonts that commonly are factory-installed on PostScript printers.

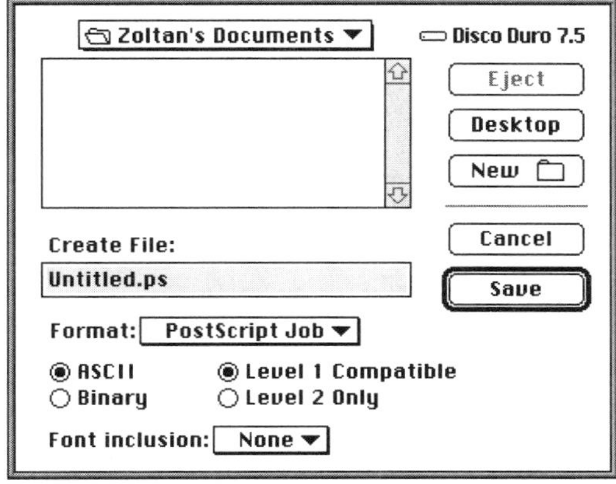

The LaserWriter 300 Print dialog box contains two more options. From the Image pop-up menu, you can choose Grayscale for printing shades of gray or Black & White for fastest printing. You use the Notification menu to choose a sound that indicates that your document is finished printing.

Clicking the Options button in the Print dialog box brings up a dialog box in which you can set the print density (see Figure 12-22). Dragging the slider to the left makes printing lighter, saving toner. Dragging to the right makes printing darker, using extra toner.

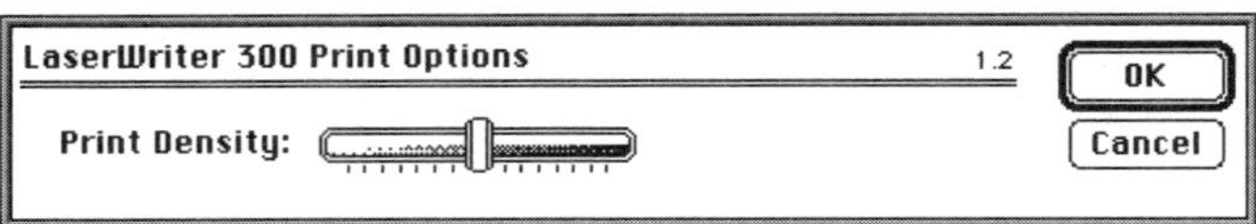


**Figure 12-22: LaserWriter 300 Print options.**

## StyleWriter II Print

When StyleWriter II is selected in the Chooser, choosing the Print command displays the dialog box shown in Figure 12-23. In this dialog box, you can enter the first and last page to be printed, as well as the number of copies to be printed. The dialog box contains three print-quality options, offering a tradeoff between appearance and speed. You can use the Image pop-up menu to choose Grayscale for printing grays or Black & White for faster printing without grays. The Notification pop-up menu sets a sound that indicates that a document is finished printing.

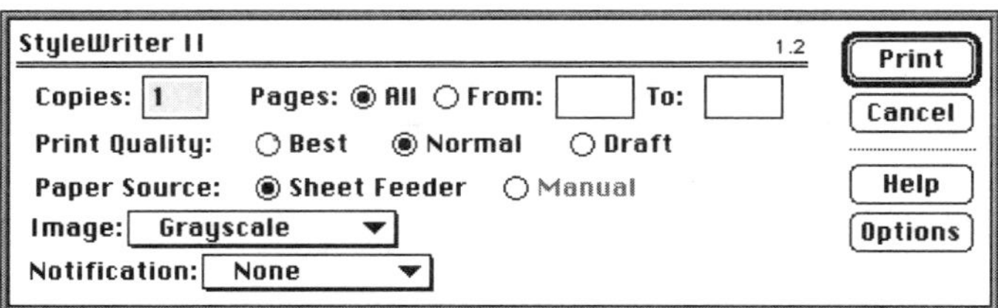


**Figure 12-23: The StyleWriter II Print dialog box.**

Clicking the Options button in the Print dialog box brings up another dialog box, in which you can set an option to have the printer clean its ink cartridge before printing the document automatically (see Figure 12-24). Do not turn on this option if you have an original StyleWriter; only the StyleWriter II can clean its ink cartridge.

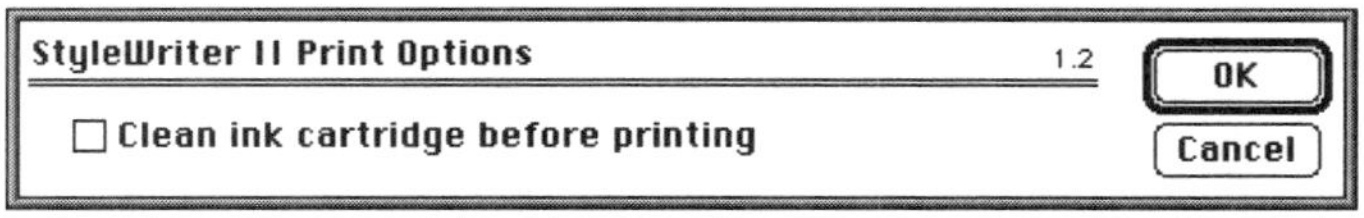

StyleWriter II Print Options 1.2
Clean ink cartridge before printing
OK
Cancel

**Figure 12-24: The StyleWriter II cleans clogged print heads if you check the appropriate box.**

## ImageWriter Print

When ImageWriter is selected in the Chooser, choosing the Print command displays the dialog box shown in Figure 12-25. In this dialog box, you can specify the desired print quality, the number of copies to be printed, which pages to be printed, and a paper source.

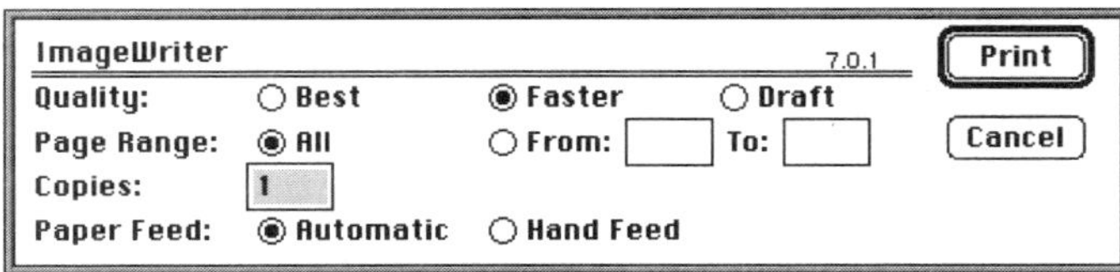


**Figure 12-25: The ImageWriter Print dialog box.**

Choosing the Best quality option prints your document at 144 dpi, which is twice the screen resolution. Best quality is slower than Faster quality, which prints at 72 dpi. Draft quality prints text only (no pictures) with a font built into the printer. The built-in font's spacing matches the spacing of Monaco 10 and other 10-point monospaced fonts. Printing proportionally spaced fonts in Draft quality results in poorly spaced letters and words that may be hard to read.

# Managing background printing

When you click the Print button in the Print dialog box, the printer driver begins creating page descriptions for each page to be printed. If you turned on background printing in the Chooser (as described in "Turning background printing on and off" earlier in this chapter), the driver saves the page images in a file for later background printing. The file also includes information about which printer to use, the number of copies to be printed, the paper source, and so on.

### Hints for Better ImageWriter Printing

If pictures printed on an ImageWriter look vertically stretched, as though El Greco had drawn them, choose the Page Setup command's Tall Adjusted option. This option adjusts the Macintosh output from 72 dpi to the 80-dpi vertical resolution of the printer, thus generating a proportional image.

To avoid the irregular word spacing that occurs in draft mode, change your document's font to a monospaced font, such as Monaco or Courier, for printing out a draft. The fixed-spaced font on the screen then will match the spacing of the printer's internal font, making the draft easier to read. Change your document to a more professional variable-sized font, such as Helvetica or Times, when you are ready to print your final copy.

Always install fonts in groups of twos — 9 point with 18 point, 10 point with 20 point, and so on — so that the Font Manager portion of the system software has the larger font available for scaling in best mode. The best way to avoid spacing problems is to use TrueType fonts and let the Mac do the scaling for you.

A very clear font for use with the ImageWriter family is Boston II, a shareware font that is available from user groups and on-line information services.

Best quality looks clearest with a slightly used printer ribbon, not with a brand-new ribbon, because there is less smudging of characters due to high levels of ink on the ribbon.

Do not stockpile ribbons for an ImageWriter; buy them one or two at a time. The ink in the ribbons dries out over time.

The PrintMonitor program handles printing in the background. This program opens in the background automatically whenever there are files in the PrintMonitor Documents folder (inside the System Folder), deletes each file that it prints, and quits automatically when the PrintMonitor Documents folder is empty.

## Activating and opening PrintMonitor

While PrintMonitor is open in the background, you can make it the active application by choosing it from the Application menu. You also can open it at any time by double-clicking its icon, which is located in the Extensions folder. Making PrintMonitor active or opening it brings up its window, shown in Figure 12-26. The PrintMonitor window identifies the file that it is printing, lists the files waiting to be printed, and displays the status of the current print job.

The PrintMonitor window automatically hides when you switch to another program, but the PrintMonitor program remains open and working in the background.

PrintMonitor

Printing

MS7B fig 12- 4 @ Central Services

Waiting

1 MS7B fig 12- 5 @ Central Services
2 MS7B fig 12- 6 @ Central Services
3 MS7B fig 12- 7 @ Central Services
4 MS7B fig 12- 3 @ Central Services

Cancel Printing | Set Print Time...

Printing Status: MS7B fig 12- 4

One Page To Print
status: preparing data

**Figure 12-26: The PrintMonitor program's window.**

## Handling PrintMonitor notifications

PrintMonitor notifies you if the file that it's printing calls for manually fed paper. The notification takes the form of an alert message and a blinking PrintMonitor icon in the menu bar. You can suppress all notification or suppress only the alert message with PrintMonitor's Preferences. Choosing Preferences from PrintMonitor's File menu displays the dialog box shown in Figure 12-27.

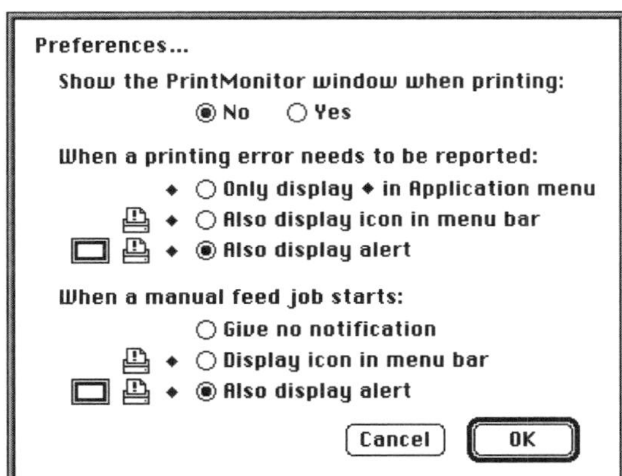


**Figure 12-27: PrintMonitor preferences.**

You also can use the Preferences command to suppress notification of printing errors, such as not being able to locate a printer that is supposed to print a file. Notification of printing errors takes the form of an alert message, a blinking PrintMonitor icon in the menu bar, and a solid diamond next to the PrintMonitor name in the Application menu. You can turn off the alert message or the alert message and the blinking icon.

## Changing the order of printing

PrintMonitor ordinarily prints files in chronological order, oldest first. You can change the order by dragging files in the PrintMonitor window. You drag a file by its icon, not by its name or sequence number. While you drag, an outline of the file follows the mouse pointer, as shown in Figure 12-28.

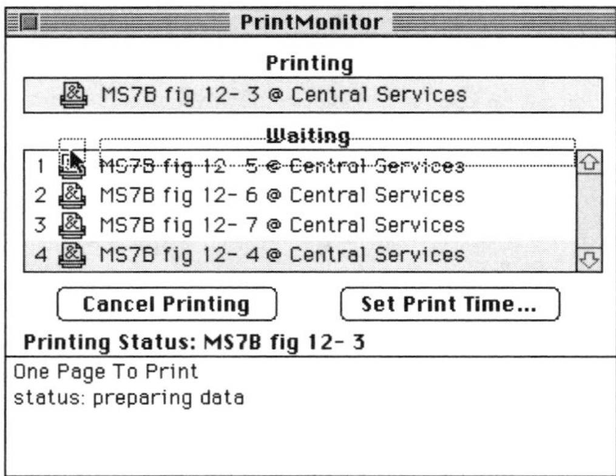


**Figure 12-28: Changing the order of files waiting to be printed.**

## Scheduling printing jobs

You can schedule when PrintMonitor will print a file, or you can postpone printing a file indefinitely. In the PrintMonitor window, you first select the file you want to schedule (by clicking it). You can select the file being printed or any file waiting to be printed. Then click the Set Print Time button. A dialog box appears in which you can set a time and date for printing (see Figure 12-29). If you choose the Postpone Indefinitely option, the file will not be printed until you schedule a print time for it.

A file scheduled for later printing appears in PrintMonitor's waiting list with an alarm-clock icon in place of a sequence number. A file postponed indefinitely appears in the waiting list with a dash in place of a sequence number.

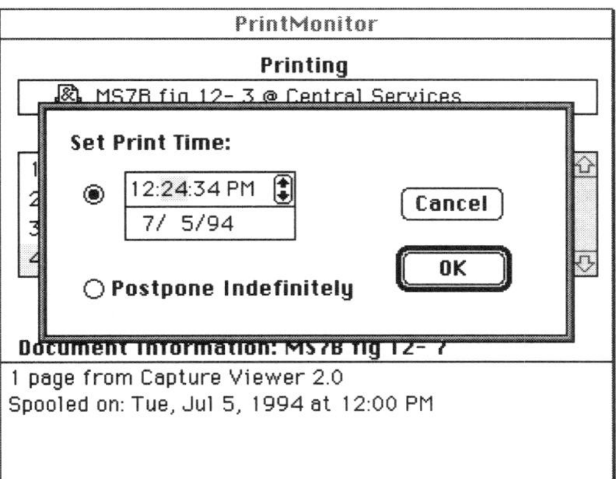


**Figure 12-29: Scheduling a specific time for a print job.**

## Suspending printing

You can suspend all background printing by choosing Stop Printing from PrintMonitor's File menu. Before PrintMonitor stops printing, it finishes the file that it is currently printing. To resume printing, choose Resume Printing from the File menu.

### Print Later

If your Mac is not attached to a printer, but you want to be able to print documents when you finish them, you can delay printing. Turn on background printing in the Chooser and print the desired files. Then open PrintMonitor and use its Stop Printing command to suspend printing. Now any documents that you print wait in PrintMonitor's queue until you connect to a printer and begin printing with PrintMonitor's Resume Printing command. To avoid PrintMonitor's nagging alert messages and blinking icon in the menu bar, use PrintMonitor's Preferences to suppress notification of printing errors.

To shut down your Mac while it is not connected to a printer and background printing is turned on, you must respond correctly to two PrintMonitor alerts that appear during the shutdown process. The first alert tells you that something is being printed and asks whether you want to finish printing or print later; you must click the Print Later button. Then another alert tells you that the printer can't be found; click the Cancel Printing button to conclude the shutdown process without losing any spool files. (If you click Try Again instead, you abort the shutdown process, and PrintMonitor tries again to find the missing printer.) This process is somewhat confusing, because clicking Cancel Printing under other circumstances *does* delete the spool file that is being printed.

## Sharing printers

When Apple introduced the first LaserWriter in 1985, it was the first printer that came ready for sharing. Because all Macs and most LaserWriters contain LocalTalk ports (and some now contain Ethernet ports as well), you can daisy-chain several Macs together with a LaserWriter to create a network. When several people share a printer, it may not always be available when you want to print. You don't have to wait for a shared printer to become available if you turn on background printing with your Chooser. As you continue working, PrintMonitor prints in the background when the shared printer becomes available.

Although PrintMonitor solves the problem of a busy shared printer, it isn't a perfect solution. When PrintMonitor prints in the background, it slows the active application. Also, PrintMonitor doesn't enable sharing printers that lack network ports, such as a StyleWriter or LaserWriter Select 300. To relieve individual Macs of background-printing chores, and to enable sharing of nonnetworked printers, you can dedicate a Mac to managing one or more shared printers. This Mac is called a *print server*. The print server runs special software, such as the AppleShare Print Server (part of the AppleShare package), that manages shared printers.

### Sharing a StyleWriter or Personal LaserWriter

You can share a StyleWriter, StyleWriter II, Personal LaserWriter LS, and LaserWriter Select 300, even though these printers do not have network ports. Apple's GrayShare technology, which is built into version 1.2 and later versions of the StyleWriter II and LaserWriter 300 drivers, makes a print server of the Mac to which the printer is connected.

To make a StyleWriter available to other network Macs, open the Chooser on the Mac to which the printer is connected. In the Chooser, select the StyleWriter II icon and the serial port to which the printer is connected (the modem port, if the printer port is used to connect to the network). Then click the Setup button to bring up the dialog box shown in Figure 12-30.

In this dialog box, turn on the Share this Printer option. If you want, you can enter a distinctive name by which the printer will be known on the network. You also can enter a password that anyone who wants to use the printer will have to enter. You have the option of keeping a log of printer activity. Click OK to dismiss the dialog box and close the Chooser.

To use a StyleWriter that someone has made available for sharing, your Mac must have StyleWriter II driver 1.2 or later and Chooser 7.3 or later. When you open the Chooser on your Mac and select the StyleWriter II icon, the names of the available shared StyleWriters are listed on the right side of the Chooser window (see Figure 12-31). Select the shared StyleWriter that you want to use.

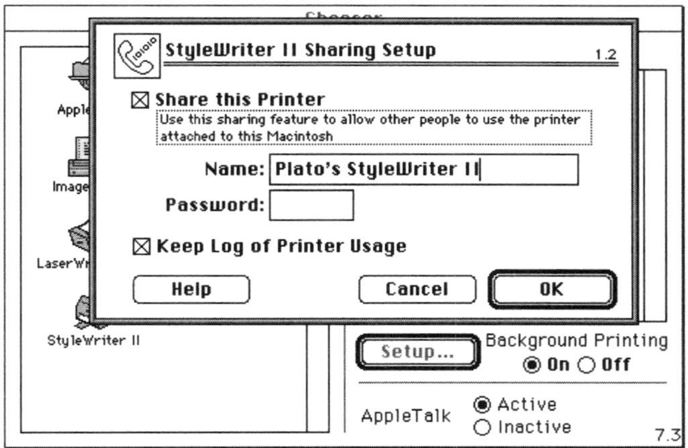


Figure 12-30: Making a StyleWriter available for sharing.

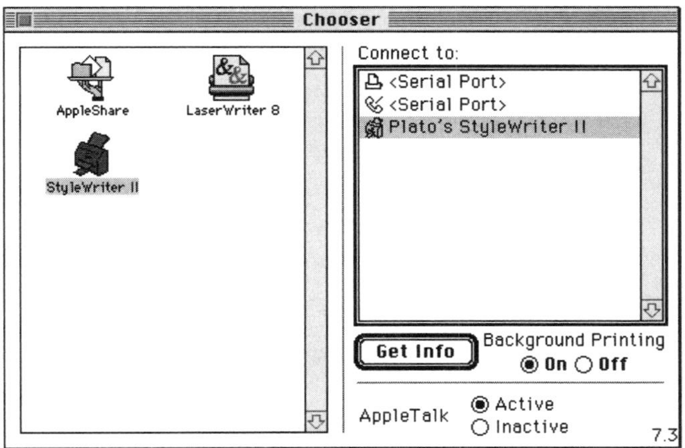


Figure 12-31: Selecting an available shared StyleWriter.

Before closing the Chooser, you can get information about the StyleWriter that you're sharing by clicking the Get Info button in the Chooser. The dialog box that appears reports the System 7 version installed on the StyleWriter's Mac, the name of that Mac, and the fonts installed on your Mac that are missing on the StyleWriter's Mac. Any documents containing fonts that are not installed on the StyleWriter's Mac print slowly or may not print correctly.

To make a LaserWriter Select 300 or a Personal LaserWriter LS available for other network users to share, or to use one of those printers that someone has made available for sharing, use the method just described for StyleWriters, but substitute the LaserWriter 300 driver for the StyleWriter II driver.

## Home-Brew Print Server

When you use a Mac running System 7 file sharing and the LaserWriter 8 printer driver, you can make your Mac a cheap, effective print server within minutes. A print server takes over the burden of background printing from client Macs. Clients get the benefits of background printing without the drag on foreground tasks. The server and all the client Macs must have System 7 installed, must have LaserWriter 8 installed, and must be connected in a network (such as PhoneNet, LocalTalk, or EtherTalk). Unfortunately, the LaserWriter 7 drivers do not work with this technique.

To set up your own print server, follow these steps:

1. On the Mac that is to be the print server, use the Sharing Setup control panel to start file sharing.
2. Open the Users & Groups control panel, and make sure that it contains a user icon for each Mac that will be a client of the print server.

   If necessary, create user icons with the Finder's New User command.
3. Create a new group icon, name it Print Server Clients, and drag the user icons of all client Macs to the new group icon.
4. Open the System Folder, and use the Finder's Sharing command to set access privileges for the PrintMonitor Documents folder.

   For optimum security, turn off all privileges at the Everyone level (thus disallowing guest access); turn on all privileges at the User/Group and the Owner levels; set the User/Group to Print Server Clients; and turn on the option "Can't be moved, renamed or deleted." The following figure shows examples of the Users & Groups control panel and the access privileges window of the PrintMonitor Documents folder.
5. On each client Mac, use the Chooser to access the server's shared PrintMonitor Documents folder or the disk that contains it (whichever is named in the Chooser's list of shareable items).
6. Remove the PrintMonitor Documents folder from the client's System Folder.

   If the client Mac tells you that its PrintMonitor Documents folder is locked when you try to remove it, use the client's Sharing Setup control panel to stop file sharing (you can start it again after removing the PrintMonitor Documents folder).
7. Still on the client Mac, make an alias of the server's PrintMonitor Documents folder, change the alias's name to PrintMonitor Documents, and drag the alias to the client's System Folder.

From now on, the client will forward print jobs to the server automatically.

If the print server is not available (if it is turned off, for example), the client cannot forward print spool files to the server. When the server becomes available, look in the client's System Folder for files with names like PS Spool File 1, and drag these files to the PrintMonitor Documents alias. The Finder copies the files across the network to the server. You then can drag those files to the client's Trash.

To have a client Mac resume handling its own background printing, simply drag the PrintMonitor Documents alias out of its System Folder. The client will create a new PrintMonitor Documents folder automatically the next time it prints.

*(continued on next page)*

*(continued from previous page)*

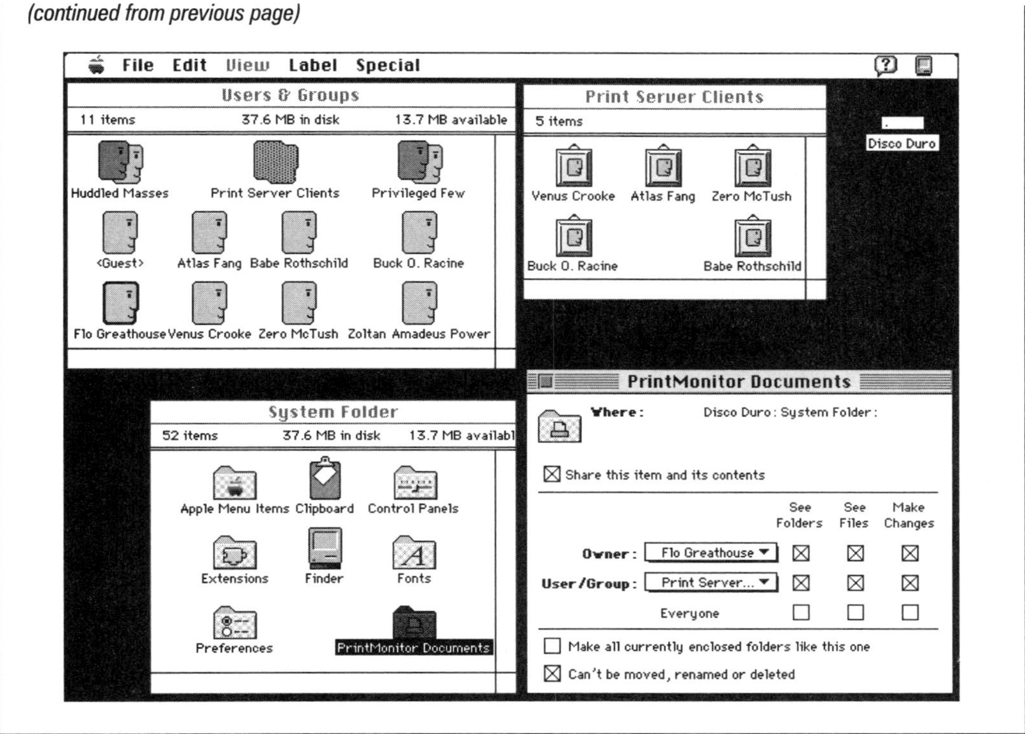


# Printing under QuickDraw GX

System 7.5 and later come with QuickDraw GX, which provides advanced typography (described in Chapter 11) and the following new printing features:

❖ **Desktop printer icons** give you drag-and-drop printing and improved management of background printing, including the ability to redirect a print job from one printer to another.

❖ **Simplified Page Setup and Print commands** offer simple options, or at the click of a button they offer expanded options in participating applications — options such as choosing a printer at print time and combining multiple page sizes and margins in a single document.

❖ **Printer extensions** add special effects such as watermarks and multiple pages per sheet of paper to every participating application.

❖ **Portable Digital Documents** allow you to view and print fully formatted documents without the applications that created them and without the fonts used to create them.

❖ **Printer sharing** enables you to share printers that previously couldn't be shared and (optionally) to secure any shared printer with a password.

This section describes the software you need and the methods you use to print under QuickDraw GX. If your Mac has QuickDraw GX installed, this section is for you. (If your Mac does not have QuickDraw GX, refer to the previous major section of this chapter, "Printing without QuickDraw GX.")

Your Mac may have QuickDraw GX installed if it uses System 7.5 or Mac OS 7.6, but it most likely does not have QuickDraw GX if it uses an earlier version of System 7. QuickDraw GX is included with System 7.5 and later but is not part of the core installation. The QuickDraw GX installers that come with System 7.5 and Mac OS 7.6 will not install QuickDraw GX on a version of System 7 older than 7.5, although in theory, QuickDraw GX works with System 7.1 and System 7 Pro.

If you're not sure whether your Mac has QuickDraw GX, look for it in the Extensions folder (inside the System Folder). The presence of a printer icon on your Mac's desktop suggests that QuickDraw GX is installed, but this test is not foolproof.

To get the most benefit from QuickDraw GX, you need applications that take advantage of it. Most applications are compatible with QuickDraw GX, but compatibility is not enough. Look for upgrades that offer the GX-style Page Setup and Print commands (described later in this section).

## Comparing GX printer-driver software

A standard installation of QuickDraw GX adds several new printer drivers to the Extensions folder, as shown in Figure 12-32.

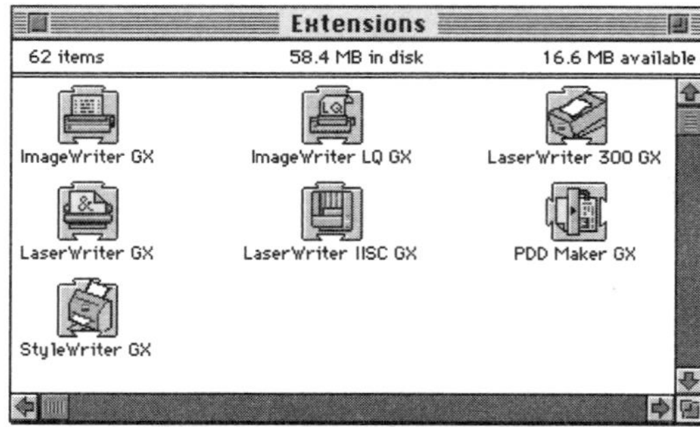


**Figure 12-32: QuickDraw GX printer drivers.**

These options include the following:

- **LaserWriter GX** for printing on PostScript printers, such as Apple's LaserWriter Plus, II, IINT, IINTX, IIf, and IIg; Personal LaserWriter IINT, IINTR, and 320; LaserWriter Select 360; and LaserWriter Pro 600, 630, and 810. LaserWriter GX takes the place of LaserWriter 7, LaserWriter 8, and PSPrinter, but it can coexist on a network with those older drivers. LaserWriter GX does not use PPD files.
- **StyleWriter GX** for printing on a StyleWriter II or the original StyleWriter.
- **LaserWriter 300 GX** for printing on a LaserWriter Select 300 or Personal LaserWriter LS.
- **ImageWriter GX** for printing on an ImageWriter or ImageWriter II.
- **ImageWriter LQ GX** for printing on an ImageWriter LQ.
- **LaserWriter IISC GX** for printing on a LaserWriter IISC.

A GX printer driver prepares an image of each page to be printed in a form that is compatible with many different types of printers. You can preview the page image on-screen before printing. Pre-GX drivers are not removed from the Extensions folder during the installation of QuickDraw GX, but none of those drivers appear in the Chooser when QuickDraw GX is installed. It is possible to print using most older drivers and Apple's GX Helper software (as described in "Bypassing GX printing" later in this chapter), but for best results, you should get GX drivers from the makers of devices such as fax/modems, non-Apple printers, and portable document makers.

## Extending GX printing capabilities

You can add to the basic functions of a printer driver by installing printing-extension software in the Extensions folder. Some printing extensions give you access to a particular printer's features, such as its resolution and the size and capacity of its paper trays. Other printing extensions modify the appearance of a document during the printing process. For example, a printing extension could provide the option of watermarking every page with a light-gray text message (such as *Draft*) or a faint picture (such as a company logo); the ordinary contents of each page would print over this "watermark." Printing extensions are distributed by independent software developers.

## Choosing a GX printer

With QuickDraw GX installed, you do not use the Chooser to choose an output device for printing; instead, you use the Chooser to create desktop printer icons for each printer, fax/modem, or other output device that you use. After creating the desktop printer icons, you use the Finder, not the Chooser, to choose and set up a printer. Background printing is always on for all devices; you cannot turn it off with the Chooser.

### Creating desktop printers

Installing QuickDraw GX creates a desktop printer icon for the printer that was selected in the Chooser before installation. If you use more than one printer, or if you had not selected a printer in the Chooser before installing QuickDraw GX, you use the Chooser to create desktop printer icons. Each printer must have its own icon. If you use three LaserWriters, for example, you need three LaserWriter GX desktop icons. You cannot print to a printer until you create a desktop icon for it.

To create a desktop printer icon for any device, open the Chooser. Each printer or other output device for which there is a GX driver in the Extensions folder appears as an icon in the Chooser. In the Chooser window, shown in Figure 12-33, select the icon of the device that you want to use.

Use the Chooser's Connect Via pop-up menu to choose the type of connection for the device you selected. Choose AppleTalk for a device connected to a LocalTalk or EtherTalk network; choose Servers for a shared device (described in "Sharing printers under QuickDraw GX" later in this chapter); choose Serial for a device connected without a network adapter box to the Mac's modem or printer port; or choose SCSI for a device connected to the Mac's SCSI port. The pop-up menu lists only relevant choices for the selected device; it does not list all choices for all devices. The pop-up menu does not appear for devices that have no connection options.

If you chose AppleTalk as the Connect Via option for the selected printer, you see a list of the names of all printers of that type that currently are available on your network (see Figure 12-34). You select the specific printer that you want by clicking its name. If your network has zones, you see the names of printers in the currently selected zone. You can select a different zone in the lower-left part of the Chooser. The Chooser does not display a list of zones unless your network has more than one zone.

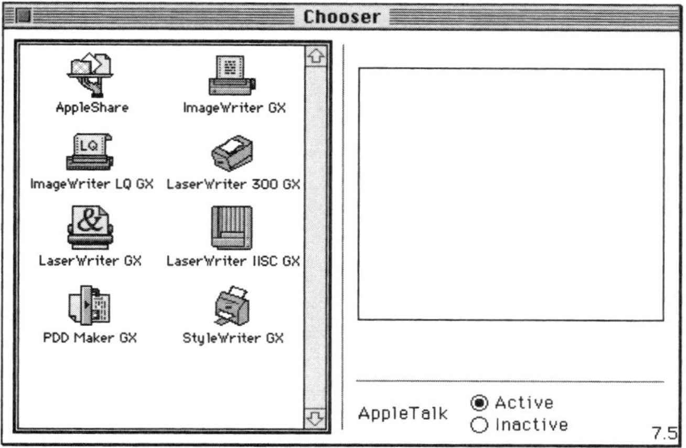


**Figure 12-33: The GX Chooser shows icons of printers and other output devices that have GX drivers.**

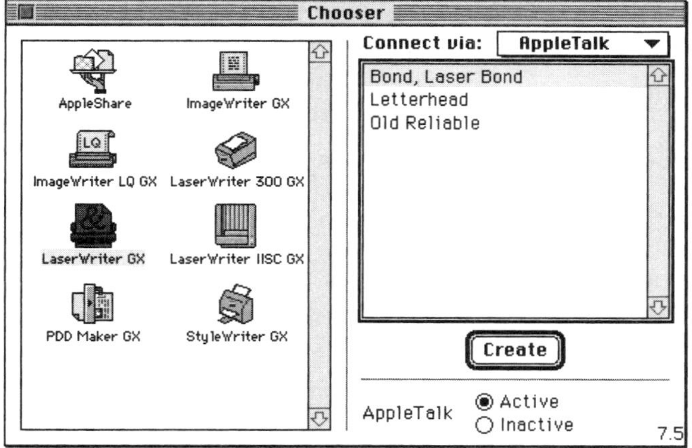


**Figure 12-34: The GX Chooser lists the names of available printers if the Connect Via option is AppleTalk.**

If you choose Serial as the Connect Via option for the selected printer, the Chooser lists the ports to which the printer can be connected (see Figure 12-35). You click the port to which the printer is connected.

After selecting a specific printer or other device (for example, by name or by port), click the Create button to create a desktop icon for that printer or device. This icon refers only to the printer or device that was selected when you clicked the Create button. If you need a desktop icon for another printer or device of the same type, you must select it and click Create again.

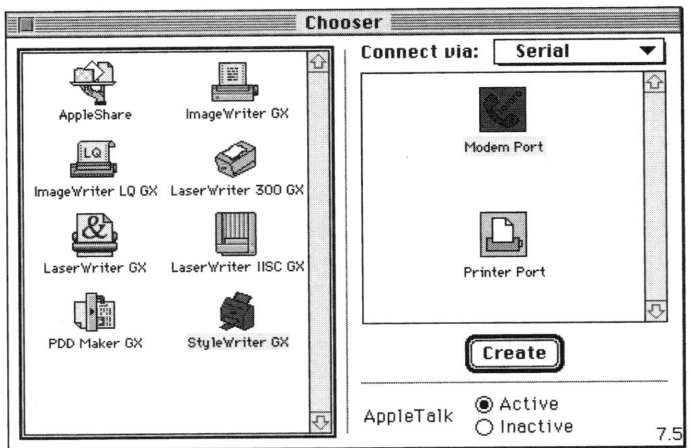


**Figure 12-35: The GX Chooser lists ports if the Connect Via option is Serial.**

## Choosing the default printer

After creating desktop printer icons for all the printers you use, you must designate which one you want to use by default. First, select the printer's desktop icon; a Printing menu appears next to the Finder's Special menu. Choose Set Default Printer from that menu. The Finder indicates the default printer by drawing a heavy black border around its desktop icon, as shown in Figure 12-36.

## Setting up the printer

The Finder's Printing menu contains commands not only for designating the default printer, but also for setting up any printer that has a desktop icon. The Input Trays command specifies the type of paper present in the paper trays of the printer whose desktop icon is selected, as shown in Figure 12-37. This information is used by the Print command of applications that have adopted GX printing (described later in this chapter).

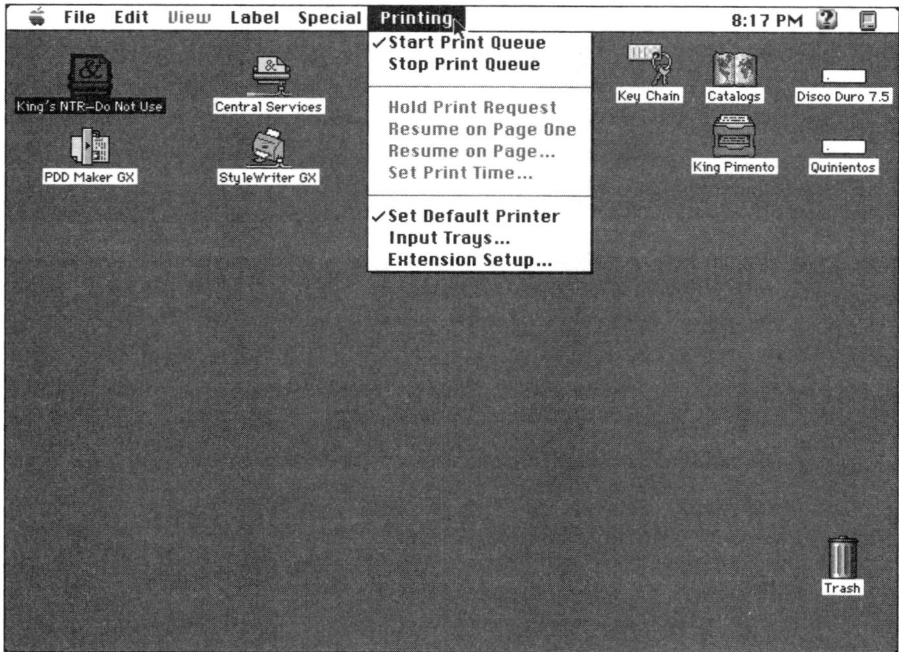


**Figure 12-36: Use the Printing menu to designate the printer you want to use by default.**

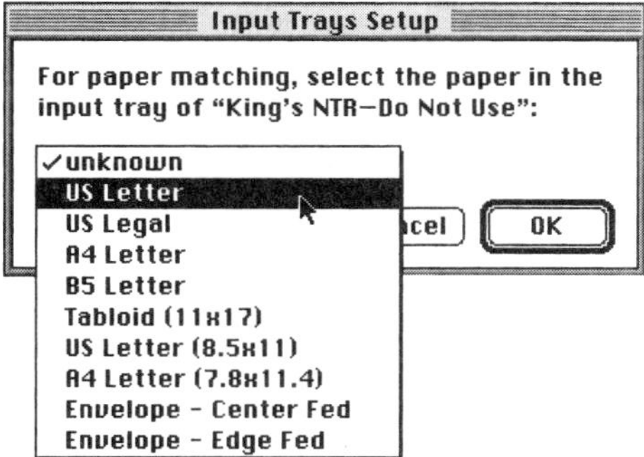


**Figure 12-37: Specifying the type of paper in a printer's input tray or trays.**

The Extension Setup command specifies which of the available GX printing extensions (installed in the Extensions folder) to use with the printer whose desktop icon is selected, as shown in Figure 12-38. The active extensions are applied in the order listed, from top to bottom. You can change the order of printing extensions by dragging them up or down the list in the Extension Setup dialog box.

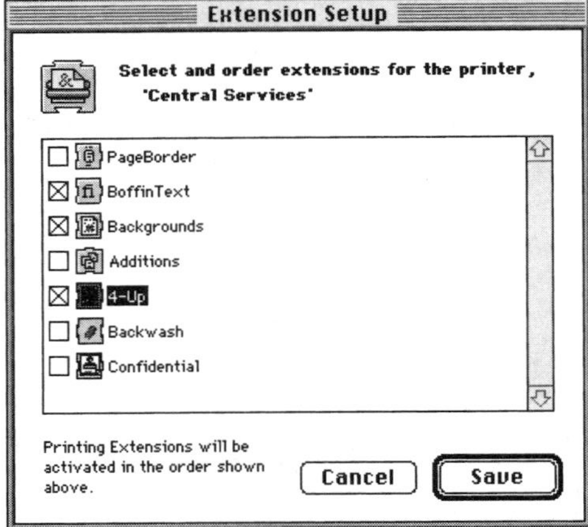


**Figure 12-38: Specifying which GX printing extensions are active for a printer and the order in which they apply.**

The other commands in the Finder's Printing menu are covered in "Managing GX printing" later in this chapter.

# Using the GX Page Setup command

Before printing a document, you need to format the document pages. You must specify the type of paper, page orientation, reduction or enlargement factor, and other formatting options. The exact options available depend on the type of printer you are using and on whether the application in which you choose the Page Setup command (usually from the File menu) has adopted GX printing. The following section describes the GX Page Setup command in applications that have adopted GX printing; the section after that one describes the GX Page Setup command in applications that have not adopted GX printing.

In addition to the options described in these sections, you may encounter options added by printing extensions or by individual application programs. For information on these options, see the documentation for the software that is responsible for them.

## GX Page Setup in participating applications

Applications that take full advantage of GX printing offer the same general Page Setup options for every type of output device. These applications display the simplified Page Setup dialog box shown in Figure 12-39. The title bar at the top of this dialog box means that its location is not fixed; you can drag the Page Setup dialog box by its title bar.

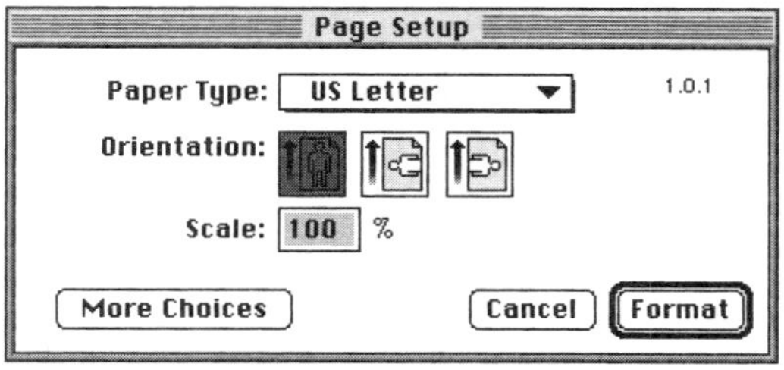

**Figure 12-39: The simplified GX Page Setup dialog box displayed by applications that have adopted GX printing.**

In the GX Page Setup dialog box, the Paper Type pop-up menu lists the paper sizes that are available on the selected printer. (For example, tabloid size — 11 by 17 inches — is available on LaserWriters but not on StyleWriters.) You also can choose one of three page orientations and enter a reduction or enlargement percentage.

Clicking the More Choices button in the simplified Page Setup dialog box expands the dialog box, as shown in Figure 12-40. The expanded Page Setup dialog box includes all the general options of the simplified dialog box. In addition, you can choose a printer from a pop-up menu. The Format For pop-up menu lists every type of printer for which the Extensions folder contains a GX printer driver; the menu also lists the name of every printer with a desktop icon. Choosing a printer from this pop-up menu does not change the default printer; use the Finder's Set Default Printer command for that purpose.

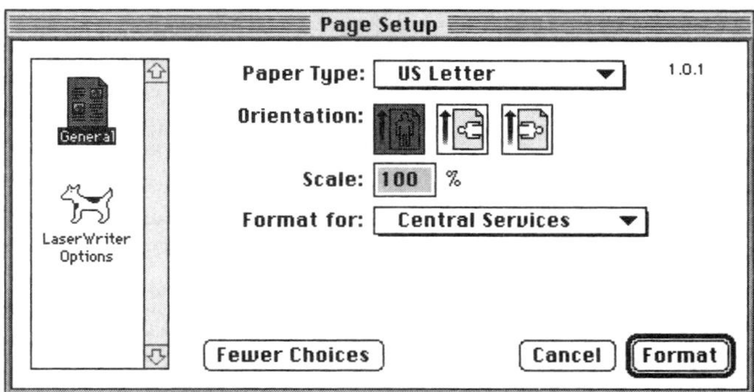


**Figure 12-40: The expanded GX Page Setup dialog box displayed by applications that have adopted GX printing.**

The icons on the left side of the expanded GX Page Setup dialog box represent panels of options. Many printers, including all StyleWriters and ImageWriters, have only the General panel of options.

The LaserWriter GX dialog box contains the options shown in Figure 12-41. LaserWriter GX has far fewer options than LaserWriter 7 or LaserWriter 8 (shown and described in "LaserWriter 7 Page Setup" and "LaserWriter 8 Page Setup" earlier in this chapter). LaserWriter GX sets the missing options automatically for best results.

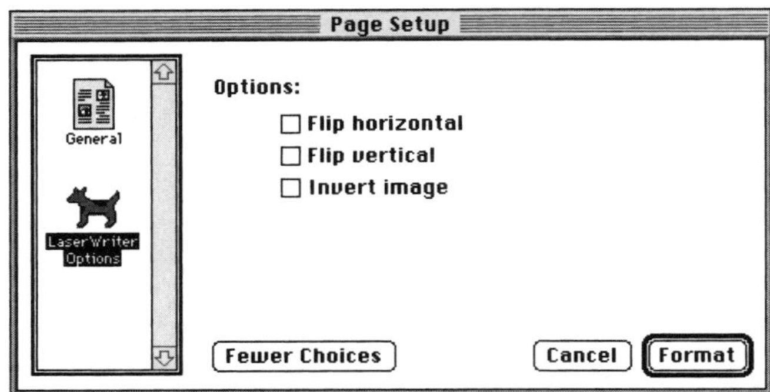


**Figure 12-41: LaserWriter GX Page Setup options displayed by applications that have adopted GX printing.**

## GX Page Setup in nonparticipating applications

When QuickDraw GX printing is active, you still can use the Page Setup command in applications that have not been updated to take full advantage of GX printing. Figures 12-42 through 12-45 show the Page Setup options offered for several common printers. These Page Setup options are similar to the options offered when GX is inactive; for details, refer to "Using the Page Setup command" earlier in this chapter.

Notice that you cannot choose a printer in the Page Setup dialog box of an application that has not been updated for GX printing. Before using the Page Setup command in such an application, you must be sure to choose the printer by selecting its desktop icon and using the Finder's Set Default Printer command (as described in "Choosing a GX printer" earlier in this chapter).

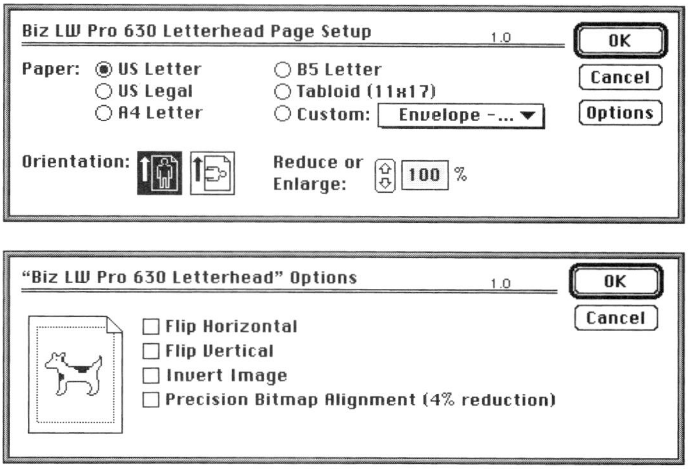

Figure 12-42: LaserWriter GX Page Setup and Page Setup Options displayed by applications that have not adopted GX printing.

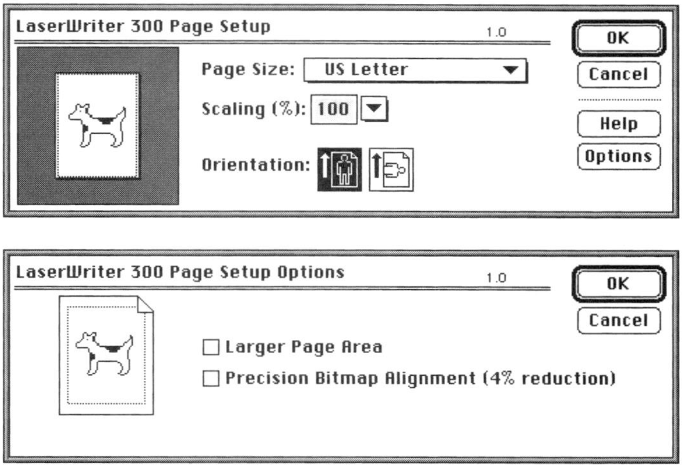

Figure 12-43: LaserWriter 300 GX Page Setup and Page Setup Options displayed by applications that have not adopted GX printing.

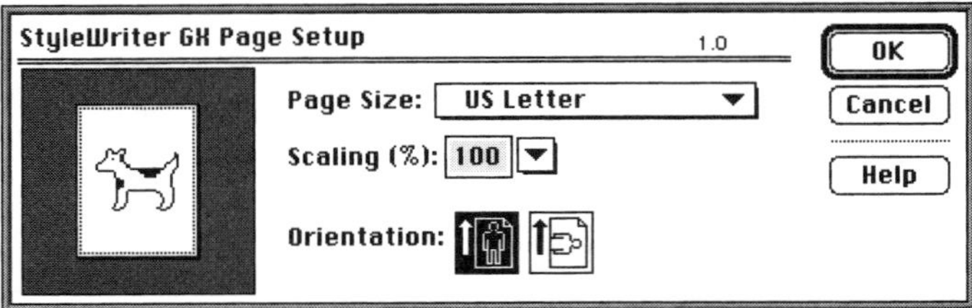


Figure 12-44: StyleWriter GX Page Setup displayed by applications that have not adopted GX printing.

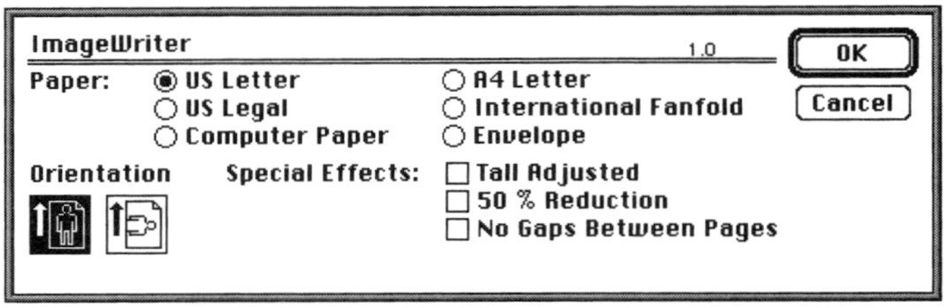

Figure 12-45: ImageWriter GX Page Setup displayed by applications that have not adopted GX printing.

## Using the GX Print command

After setting page-formatting options with the Print command, you can print a document by choosing the Print command (located in the File menu of most applications). In the Print dialog box, you can specify the range of pages, the number of copies, and a paper source. You may have additional options, depending on the type of printer and on whether the application in which you choose the Print command has adopted GX printing. The following section describes the GX Print command in applications that have adopted GX printing; the section after that one describes the GX Print command in applications that have not adopted GX printing.

In addition to the options described in these sections, you may encounter options added by printing extensions or by individual application programs. For information on these options, see the documentation for the software that is responsible for them.

### GX Print in participating applications

Applications that take full advantage of GX printing offer the same general Print options for every type of output device. These applications display the simplified Print dialog box shown in Figure 12-46. The GX Print dialog box is movable; you can drag it by its title bar.

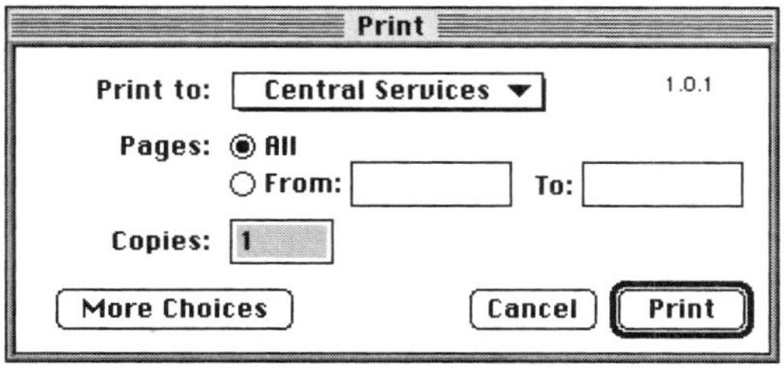

**Figure 12-46: The simplified GX Print dialog box displayed by applications that have adopted GX printing.**

In this dialog box, you can choose the printer you want to use from the Print To pop-up menu. The initial choice for a new document is the default printer (as designated by the Finder's Set Default Printer command), but you can choose any printer that has a desktop icon. You also can specify a range of pages and a number of copies to print.

Clicking the More Choices button in the simplified Print dialog box expands the dialog box, as shown in Figure 12-47. The expanded Print dialog box includes all the general options of the simplified dialog box. You also can specify a paper source — automatic or manual paper feed — and whether multiple copies will be collated as they are printed.

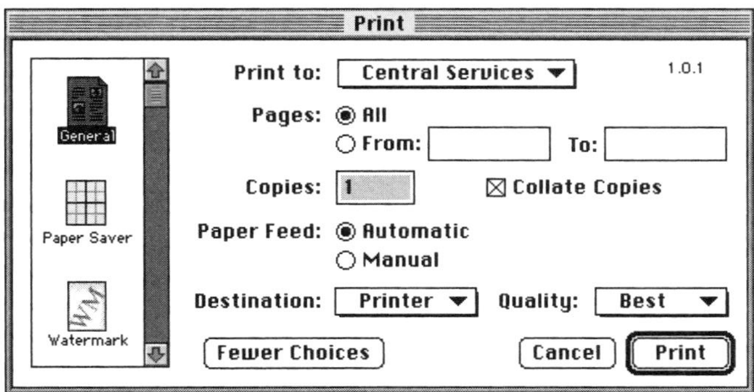


**Figure 12-47: The expanded GX Print dialog box displayed by applications that have adopted GX printing.**

You have additional options with some printers. With PostScript printers, you can choose to have the page images saved as a PostScript file by choosing PostScript from the Destination menu. With a StyleWriter, you can choose one of three print qualities from the Quality menu.

You can access still more Print options by clicking one of the icons on the right side of the Print dialog box. All printers have the General panel of options; most printers have the Print Time and Paper Match options as well. Still more panels of options may be provided by GX printing extensions in the Extensions folder (inside the System Folder).

The Print Time options, shown in Figure 12-48, determine when your document will be printed. You can elect to have the Mac notify you when printing starts, when printing ends, or at both times.

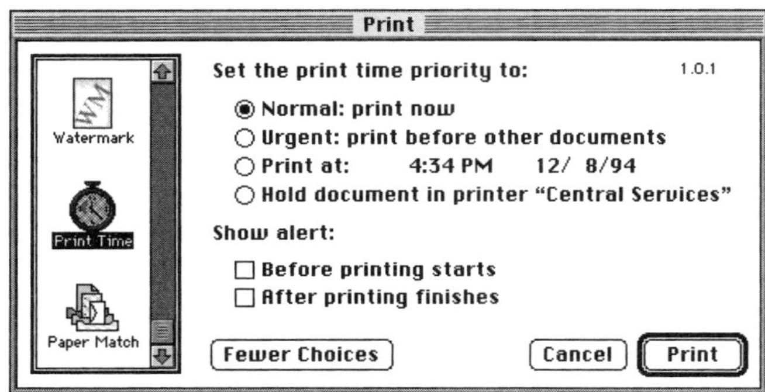


**Figure 12-48: The GX Print Time options.**

The Paper Match options, shown in Figure 12-49, set the type of automatically fed paper and its source. One option is to have the printer driver deduce the type of paper and its source based on the information you specified with the Finder's Input Trays command (described in "Setting up a printer" earlier in this chapter). Alternatively, you can select a different type of paper (which you have put, or intend to put temporarily, in the paper tray). If you select a particular tray or paper, you can specify how you want the printer driver to handle pages that are too large. You can have the excess portion cropped at the left and bottom margins; you can have pieces of the page printed full-size on multiple sheets of paper that you later tape together; or you can have the page scaled to fit the paper.

## GX Print in nonparticipating applications

In an application that has not been updated to take full advantage of QuickDraw GX, choosing the Print command displays a dialog box similar to the one that appears when QuickDraw GX is inactive. Figures 12-50 through 12-53 show the Print options for several common printers. These options are described in "Using the GX Print command" earlier in this chapter.

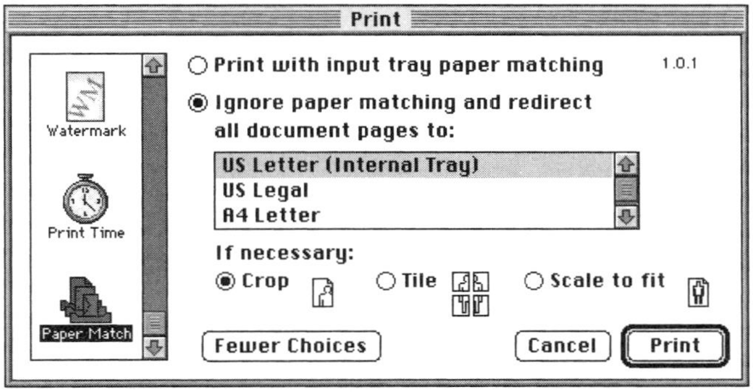

Figure 12-49: The GX Paper Match options.

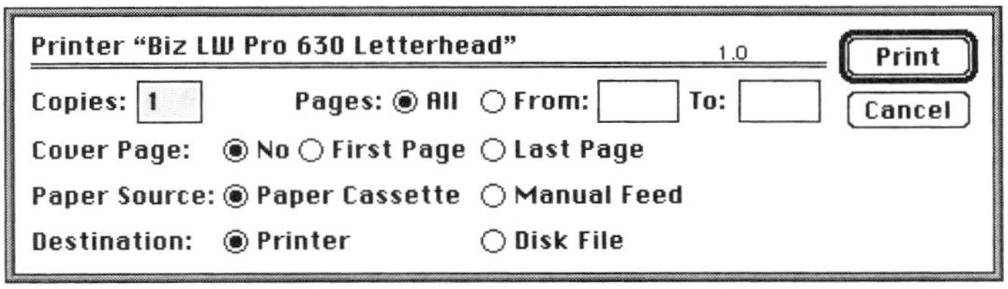

Figure 12-50: LaserWriter GX Print displayed by applications that have not adopted GX printing.

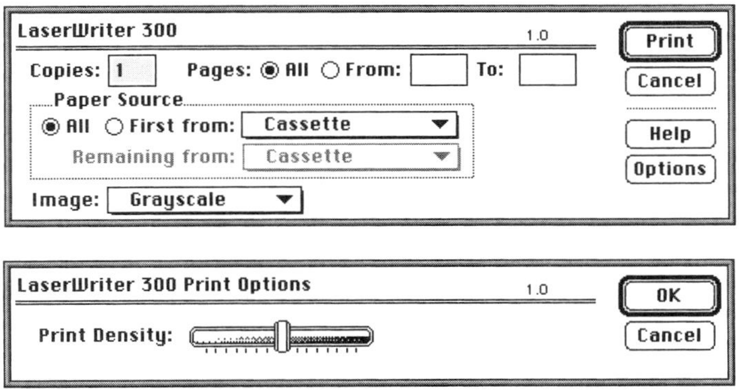

Figure 12-51: LaserWriter 300 GX Print and Print Options displayed by applications that have not adopted GX printing.

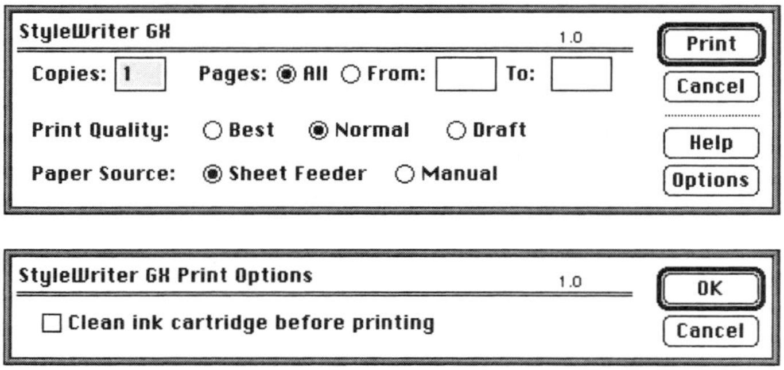

Figure 12-52: StyleWriter GX Print and Print Options displayed by applications that have not adopted GX printing.

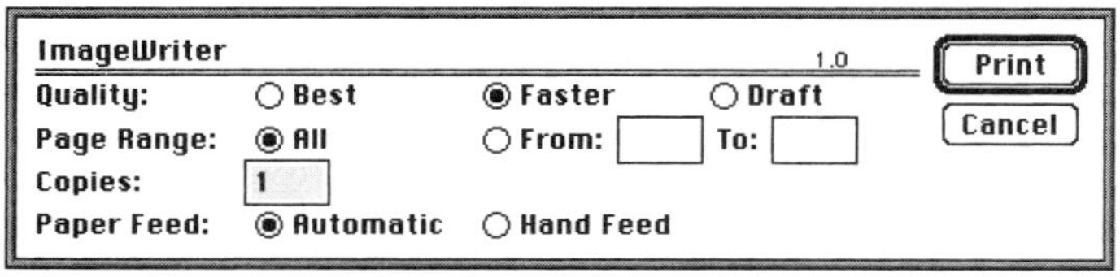

Figure 12-53: ImageWriter GX Print displayed by applications that have not adopted GX printing.

Notice that you cannot choose a printer in the Print dialog box of an application that has not been updated for GX printing. Before using the Print command in such an application, you must be sure to choose the printer by selecting its desktop icon and using the Finder's Set Default Printer command (as described in "Choosing a GX printer" earlier in this chapter).

## Managing GX printing

When you click the Print button in a GX Print dialog box, the GX printer driver and any GX printing extensions create page descriptions for each page to be printed, saving the page images in a file for later printing. Normally, these files are printed in the background automatically, while you continue working. You can view and manage the queue of waiting print files for each printer individually by using the desktop printer icons and the Finder's Printing menu.

The Finder controls background printing for QuickDraw GX. As long as the Finder is open (even in the background), printing proceeds normally. If the Finder is not open, nothing prints. The Finder normally is not open when At Ease (version 2 and earlier) is present. It's best not to use At Ease 2 and earlier versions with QuickDraw GX.

## Viewing a print queue

At any time, you can see the queue of files waiting to be printed on a particular printer by opening that printer's desktop icon in the Finder. Opening a desktop printer icon brings up its window, as shown in Figure 12-54. A desktop printer's window identifies the file that it is printing, reports the status of that print job, and lists the files that are waiting to be printed. You can sort the list of waiting print files by name, number of pages, number of copies, or print time. Choose a sort order from the View menu, or click the column heading in the desktop printer's window.

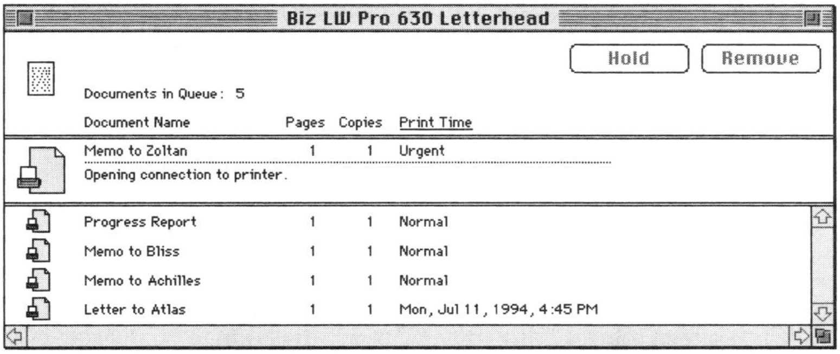

**Figure 12-54: A Desktop printer's window lists files that are waiting to be printed.**

You can preview any print file on-screen by simply double-clicking the file's icon. The SimpleText application opens the file and displays one page. Use the Next Page and Previous Page commands in SimpleText's Edit menu to see other pages.

Redirecting a print file from one printer to another is quite easy. Simply drag the printer file from its current location to the desktop icon or window of another printer.

## Changing the order of printing

Files are printed in the order in which they are listed in the desktop printer's window. Urgent files are listed first, followed by normal files and files with specific print times. You can change the order of urgent files and the order of normal files by dragging them up and down in the window. You cannot drag an urgent file below the first normal file, and you cannot drag a normal file above the lowest urgent file. You can, however, change a normal file to an urgent file (and vice versa) by selecting the file and choosing Set Print Time from the Finder's Printing menu. You also can use the Set Print Time command to schedule a file to print at a specific time and date.

You can postpone printing a file indefinitely. Select the file in the desktop printer's window and click the Hold button or choose Hold Print Request from the Finder's Printing menu.

To resume printing a file that is on hold, select it and then click the Resume button in the desktop printer's window. Clicking this button displays the Resume Print Request window, in which you can specify the page at which you want printing to resume. (Instead of clicking the Resume button, you can choose Resume on Page One or Resume on Page from the Printing menu.)

### Starting and stopping printing

To stop all printing on a particular printer, select its desktop icon and then choose Stop Print Queue from the Printing menu. A small stop sign appears on the printer's desktop icon.

To start printing again, select the printer's desktop icon and then choose Start Print Queue from the Printing menu.

## Sharing printers under QuickDraw GX

Beginning with the first Apple LaserWriter, it's always been possible to share printers that connect directly to a network. QuickDraw GX extends printer sharing in two ways: it enables sharing most printers that connect directly to computers (not to networks), and it can limit access to a networked printer. In both cases, the printer must have a desktop icon (which means that it must have a GX printer driver in the Extensions folder). For details on creating a desktop printer icon, refer to "Creating desktop printers" earlier in this chapter.

To share a directly connected printer or to restrict access to a networked printer, select the printer's desktop icon and then choose Sharing from the Finder's Sharing menu. A printer-sharing window appears, as shown in Figure 12-55.

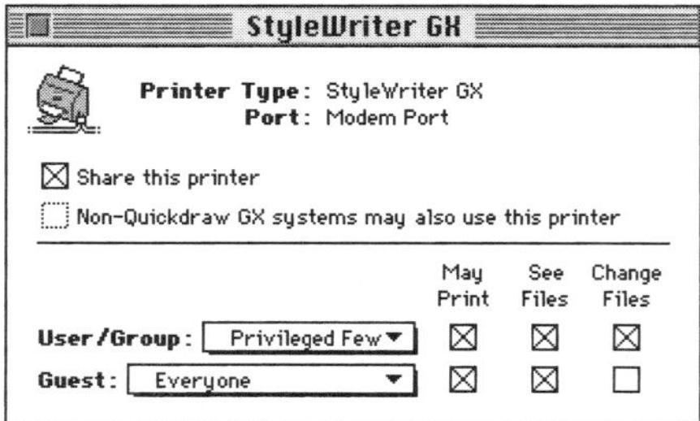


**Figure 12-55: Setting up sharing of a directly connected printer.**

In the printer-sharing window, turn on the "Share this printer" option. If you want people who do not have QuickDraw GX to be able to share this printer, turn on the "Non-QuickDraw GX systems may also use this printer" option. (This option is not available for all types of printers.) From the User/Group pop-up menu, choose a registered user or group to which you want to give special access. Use the Guests pop-up menu to specify whether you want to allow all network users, or only users in your zone, to access the shared printer as guests. Unlike registered users and members of groups, guests do not have to enter a password to access a shared printer. (For information on creating registered users and groups, see "Indentifying Who Can Access Your Shared Items" in Chapter 9.)

Turn on and off the various access privileges for guests and for the designated user or group. The May Print privilege allows printing on the printer. The See Files privilege allows display of all the waiting print files for the shared printer. The Change Files privilege allows changing the sequence of print files and removing print files.

There is a catch to sharing a printer that is directly connected to your Mac: your hard disk must store all the print files waiting to be printed by everyone who's using your printer, and your Mac must print those files in the background. If you continue working while your Mac handles all that background printing, you may notice a performance slowdown.

## Using Portable Digital Documents (PDDs)

QuickDraw GX's print files actually are portable digital documents (PDDs). PDDs are document files that anyone who has QuickDraw GX can view and print without the applications and fonts that were used to create them. One of Apple's GX drivers, PDD Maker GX, facilitates creating PDDs from any application. PDDs can be sent to other QuickDraw GX users for viewing and printing with SimpleText. A PDD retains all its text formatting and graphics.

Creating a PDD is as easy as printing. If you want to "print" a PDD from an application that has not been updated to use QuickDraw GX printing, you must select the PDD Maker GX's desktop icon and then choose Set Default Printer from the Finder's Printing menu. You also can choose PDD Maker Setup from the Printing menu to select a folder in which to save PDDs by default. (You can always select a different folder when you create a PDD.) Then you can switch to the application in which you want to "print" a PDD and use the Page Setup and Print commands as though you were printing to a printer.

The Print dialog box has a Save button instead of the usual Print button. Clicking the Save button brings up an ordinary Save directory dialog box, in which you select a folder and type a name for the PDD file (see Figure 12-56). This Save dialog box also has a pop-up menu from which you choose the fonts that you want to include in the PDD. Your choices are to include all fonts used in the document, all fonts except the standard 13 found on most PostScript printers, or no fonts. Fonts included in a PDD work only with that PDD, and they cannot be extracted and installed in the system.

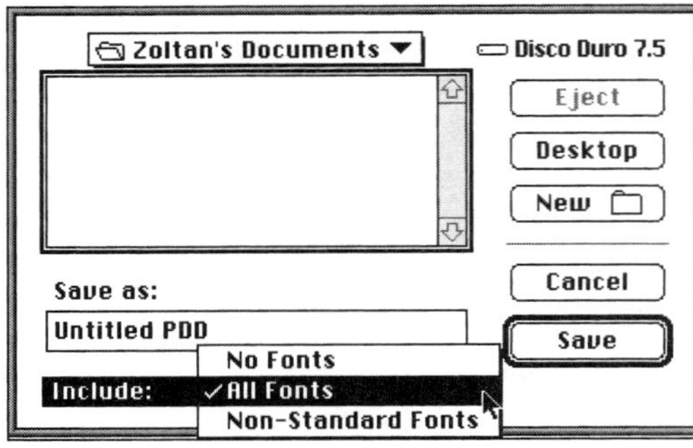


**Figure 12-56: Saving a portable digital document (PDD).**

## Bypassing GX printing

Printing with QuickDraw GX requires a GX driver, but you may be able to bypass QuickDraw GX to use a printer, fax/modem, or other output device that has no GX driver. Installing Apple's QuickDraw GX Helper system extension enables you to turn off GX printing for applications individually. Installing QuickDraw GX Helper in the Extensions folder adds the command Turn Desktop Printing Off near the top of the Apple menu in applications that allow bypassing GX printing.

When you choose Turn Desktop Printing Off from the Apple menu, QuickDraw GX Helper tries to find a non-GX printer driver that is equivalent to the current default desktop printer. For a printer that uses the LaserWriter GX driver, QuickDraw GX Helper substitutes LaserWriter 7.2. For the StyleWriter GX driver, QuickDraw GX Helper substitutes StyleWriter II 1.2. If QuickDraw GX Helper successfully substitutes a non-GX driver for the current default desktop printer, you can use the Page Setup and Print commands as though QuickDraw GX were not installed (as described in "Using the Page Setup command" and "Using the Print command" earlier in this chapter). To choose a different non-GX driver, select an equivalent desktop printer and then choose the Finder's Set Default Printer command.

When GX printing is turned off in one application, you still can use GX printing in other applications.

## Non-GX Drivers Without GX Equivalents

If you want to use a non-GX driver for which no equivalent desktop printer exists, you may have to resort to a bit of chicanery. You will need a copy of Chooser version 7.0 or 7.1, which come with System 7.0.1 and System 7.1, respectively. When you have one of these Choosers, follow these steps:

1. In the Finder, select a LaserWriter desktop printer, and choose Set Default Printer from the Finder's Printing menu.

   If you don't have a LaserWriter desktop printer, use the Chooser to create one.

2. Switch to the application in which you want to use the non-GX driver, and choose Turn off Desktop Printing from the Apple menu.

   A message appears, advising you that QuickDraw GX Helper has selected the (non-GX) LaserWriter driver as a substitute for the current default printer.

3. Click OK to dismiss the message.

4. Open Chooser version 7.0 or 7.1, and select the non-GX driver's icon on the left side of the Chooser window.

   You must use one of these Chooser versions; version 7.3 and later versions do not work.

5. On the right side of the Chooser window, select the port (for nonnetwork devices) or the specific device (for network devices).

6. Click OK to dismiss the Chooser.

7. Use the Page Setup and Print commands to output documents with the selected non-GX driver.

If you use the Finder's Set Default Printer command again, you must repeat steps 4 through 6 to reselect the non-GX driver.

# CHAPTER  CONCEPTS AND TERMS

- On a Macintosh, you always set up and control printing the same basic way, regardless of the application you are using or the type of printer you have. The Macintosh system software enforces this consistency by providing complete printing services to applications.
- To print on a particular type of printer, a Macintosh needs software for that printer in its Extensions folder. That software is called a printer driver. A printer driver prepares a complete description of each page to be printed, in a format that the printer can interpret, and then sends the page descriptions to the printer.
- On a Mac without QuickDraw GX, you use the Chooser to select a printer, an application's Page Setup command to format the printed page, and the application's Print command to print pages. You control background printing with the PrintMonitor application.
- QuickDraw GX changes the printing process. Although QuickDraw GX comes with System 7.5 and later, you must install it separately. Your Mac most likely does not have QuickDraw GX if it uses any version of System 7 before 7.5.
- On a Mac with QuickDraw GX, you use the Chooser to create desktop printer icons and the Finder's Printing command to select a printer. You use an application's Page Setup command to format the printed page, and use the application's Print command to print pages. The Page Setup and Print commands are different in applications that have adopted GX printing than in applications that have not.
- GX printing requires GX printer drivers, but by installing QuickDraw GX Helper, you can bypass GX printing in individual applications.
- Under QuickDraw GX, you merge background printing with desktop printer icons and the Finder's Printing menu.
- QuickDraw GX's print files actually are portable digital documents (PDDs). PDDs are document files that anyone who has QuickDraw GX can view and print without the applications and fonts that were used to create them.

**dpi**
Measures the density of the dots a particular printer uses to print images on a page. More dots per inch mean smaller dots, and smaller dots mean finer (less coarse) printing.

**Portable Digital Document (PDD)**
A document that can be viewed on a computer without the application and fonts used to create the PDD. A PDD made with QuickDraw GX's PDD Maker can be viewed and printed with the SimpleText.

**PostScript printers**
Printers that interpret PostScript commands to create printable images.

**print server**
A Mac that is dedicated to managing one or more shared printers.

**printer driver**
Software that prepares pages for, and communicates with, a particular type of printer. This software resides in the Extensions folder inside the System Folder.

**resolution**
The perceived smoothness of a displayed or printed image. Printed resolution is measured in dots per inch (dpi). A high-resolution printed image has more dots per inch than a low-resolution printed image.

**spooling**
A printer-driver operation in which the driver saves page descriptions in a file (called a *spool file*) for later printing.

CHAPTER THIRTEEN

# Managing Memory

- Looking at how much memory your Mac software uses
- Managing your Mac's memory in the face of increasingly intense memory usage
- Avoiding unnecessary loss of memory capacity due to memory fragmentation
- Using System 7's Memory control panel to allocate the Mac's RAM efficiently
- Opening more programs and bigger documents with virtual memory and 32-Bit Addressing
- Using a portion of your Mac's RAM as a disk
- Using utility software to double the number of programs you can keep open

If you never open more than one program at a time and don't care about your computer's performance or effectiveness (not to mention your own), you can ignore the topic of memory management. But to get the most from your Macintosh, you must pay attention to how you use its memory.

Think of your computer's memory as a pie, as shown in Figure 13-1. You need to know the size of the pie, how much of the pie each open program uses, and how much is unused and available for opening additional programs. You also need to know how big a piece of the memory pie each of the additional programs would need if you opened it.

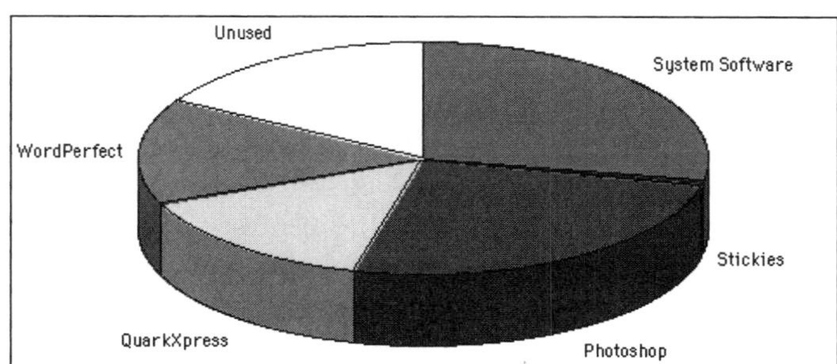


**Figure 13-1: Each open program gets a piece of your Mac's memory pie.**

# Memory Management

For information on the condition of your Macintosh memory pie, switch to the Finder and choose About This Macintosh from the Apple menu. The Finder displays a window that reports the total amount of memory installed in your Macintosh and the largest amount available for opening another program. It also graphs the amount allocated to and currently used by the system software and each open program (see Figure 13-2).

To learn the exact amount the system software or an open program is using at the moment, turn on Balloon Help and point at the item's memory-use bar in the About This Macintosh dialog box.

If you add up the amounts of memory allocated to system software and to each open program, you may come up with a total that's less than the reported amount of total memory. Built-in video uses 40K to 600K on some Mac models and this amount is not reported by About This Macintosh. There may be an additional discrepancy of several K due to rounding errors.

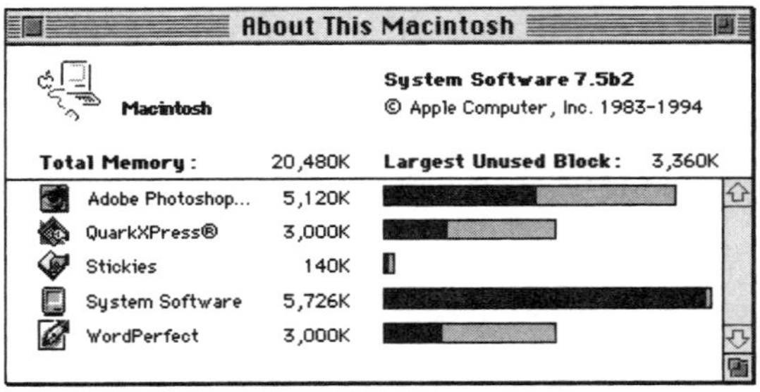

**Figure 13-2: An About This Macintosh window.**

## Adjusting system memory size

As reported by About This Macintosh, the system software (which includes the Finder) takes up a large chunk of memory. You can reduce the system software's memory size to its minimum by pressing Shift while restarting your Macintosh. Look for the message "Extensions Off" during startup. It confirms that you have suppressed loading of all items in the Extensions folder, Control Panels folder, and System Folder that would increase the system software's memory size. You have also bypassed opening items in the Startup Items folder, reduced the disk cache to 16K, forced virtual memory off, and prevented file sharing from starting.

None of these changes persist when you restart without pressing Shift. To make changes stick, you must drag items out of the special folders and change settings in the Memory and File Sharing control panels. The disk cache, virtual memory, and the Memory control panel are described later in this chapter. See Chapter 9 for information on file sharing.

Most items listed as system extensions in a By Kind view of the Extensions folder or System Folder (except PostScript fonts with Systems 7.0 and 7.0.1) increase the system software's memory size during startup. So do some other types of items besides extensions.

But some items in the Extensions folder do not increase memory size. Chooser extensions for printers (LaserWriter, StyleWriter, ImageWriter, and so on), communications tools, MNPLinkTool documents, Finder Help, or the PrintMonitor application fall in this category.

Control panels that display an icon at the bottom of the screen during startup (or offer the option of doing so) have system extensions built in and most of them increase the system software's memory size. Control panels that don't display startup icons generally don't increase system software's memory size, though there are exceptions such as Easy Access.

The amount of memory you recover by removing a particular item from the Extensions folder, Control Panels folder, or System Folder depends partly on what items remain, so you'll have to experiment. On a test system, for example, Adobe Type Manager 3.6 (ATM) added 444K, and Apple's PowerTalk and PowerTalk Manager extensions added 618K. Other items had smaller memory appetites. Easy Access 7.0 added only 12K, for instance.

For big memory savings, turn off file sharing if you're not using it. The same goes for virtual memory: If you're not using it, turn it off with the Memory control panel (see the section "Using virtual memory," later in this chapter). In fact all the settings in the Memory control panel directly affect the system memory size. For details, see the section "Memory Control" later in this chapter.

The key to adjusting memory size is to compare your system software's memory size before and after removing an item and weigh the potential memory savings against the benefit the item provides.

## Controlling program memory size

When you open a program, the system software gives it a chunk of the memory pie. You can change how much an application program gets by setting its memory size in its Info window, which the Finder's Get Info command displays (see Figure 13-3). You must quit an open program before changing its memory size.

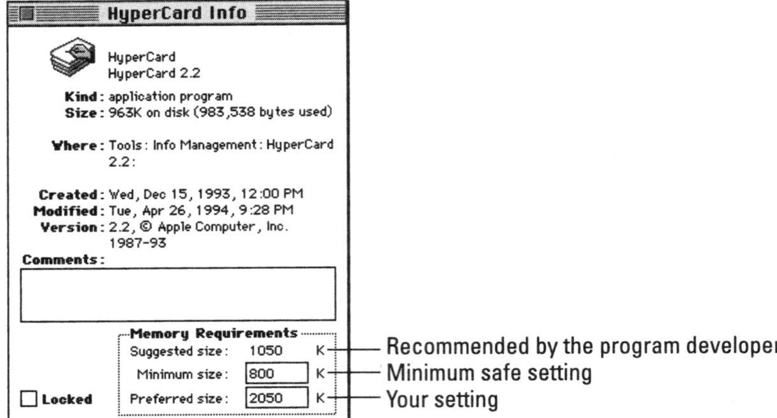


**Figure 13-3: Use the Get Info command to set memory sizes for an application.**

In System 7.1 and newer, Info windows show three memory sizes: Minimum, Preferred, and Suggested. The system won't open a program unless there is a block of available memory at least as large as the Minimum size. The system allocates more memory, if available, but never more than the Preferred size. The Suggested size, which you can't change, is the amount of memory the program's developer recommends for standard program performance. In versions of System 7 older than 7.1, the Preferred size is called the Current size and the Minimum size is not shown.

Setting the Preferred size higher than the Suggested size may improve performance or enable you to open more documents or larger documents. Setting the Preferred size below the suggested size usually has the opposite effect. For example, setting HyperCard 2.2's Preferred size below the suggested 1050K reduces the number of stacks you can have open simultaneously, limits your access to painting tools and scripting, and prevents opening some stacks altogether.

On a Macintosh with a PowerPC processor, a special note at the bottom of some Info windows advises you that turning on virtual memory changes the memory requirements (see Figure 13-4). This note only appears in the Info windows of programs that are optimized for the PowerPC processor. These programs require less memory when virtual memory is turned on, as described in the section "Using virtual memory" later in this chapter. Instead of turning on virtual memory, you can get the same benefit by installing RAM Doubler version 1.5.1 or later from Connectix (800-950-5880 or 415-571-5100). RAM Doubler uses far less disk space and causes less slowdown than virtual memory. The relationship described above still holds among the various memory sizes in the Info window — Suggested, Minimum, and Preferred.

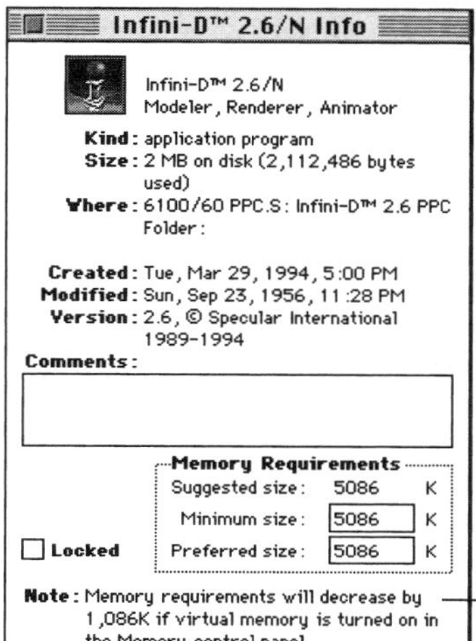


This advice appears only for programs optimized for PowerPC processors

**Figure 13-4: Some Info windows on Power Macs have special advice about memory sizes.**

## Don't Shortchange the Minimum Size

Every application has a memory size that's not listed in its Info window. This fourth memory size, which is set by the program developer, specifies the least amount of memory in which a program will work without crashing. Most programs use this safe minimum size for the initial setting of the Minimum size in the Info window. You can also see the safe minimum size with a resource editing program such as Apple's ResEdit (available from APDA, 800-282-2732 in the U.S., 800-637-0029 in Canada, and 716-871-6555 internationally). Use the resource editor to open the application's SIZE -1 resource. The minimum size listed there is the application's safe minimum size in bytes; divide by 1024 for the size in K (kilobytes).

Setting the Minimum size lower than the safe minimum may cause the program to crash. For example, HyperCard 2.2 does not work properly if you set its Minimum size below Apple's recommended minimum of 800K. The Finder (in System 7.1 and newer) warns you when you close an Info window if you have set the Minimum size lower than the safe minimum recommended by the developer.

QUICK TIPS

### When RAM is Scarce, Cut Memory to the Bone

If your Macintosh has just the minimum amount of RAM required for your version of System 7, you should pare program memory sizes to the bone. (The minimum is 2MB for version 7.1 and earlier and 4MB for System 7.1.1 (System 7 Pro). For System 7.5 on a Mac with a 680X0 processor, the minimum is 4MB without PowerTalk or QuickDraw GX, and 8MB with PowerTalk and QuickDraw GX. For System 7.5 on a Mac with a PowerPC processor, the minimum is 8MB without PowerTalk or QuickDraw GX, and 16MB with PowerTalk and QuickDraw GX.)

For example, giving your favorite word processing program the full amount of memory available after the system software takes its chunk leaves no room to use a desk accessory, let alone another application program. Also, there wouldn't be any memory left for background printing (which is described in Chapter 12).

You can't change the memory size of a desk accessory. Each desk accessory gets 20K and it generally increases the system software memory size by a good deal more.

## Avoiding memory fragmentation

As you open and quit a series of programs, the unused portion of the memory pie tends to become fragmented into multiple small chunks, as shown in Figure 13-5. You may find yourself unable to open a program because it needs a chunk of memory bigger than the biggest unused chunk (the Largest Unused Block amount in the About This Macintosh window). The total of all unused chunks may be large enough to open the program, but System 7 cannot consolidate fragmented memory nor open a program in multiple chunks of memory.

To consolidate fragmented memory, quit all open programs and then open them again. Restarting your Macintosh fixes fragmentation and may reduce the amount of memory used by system software as well.

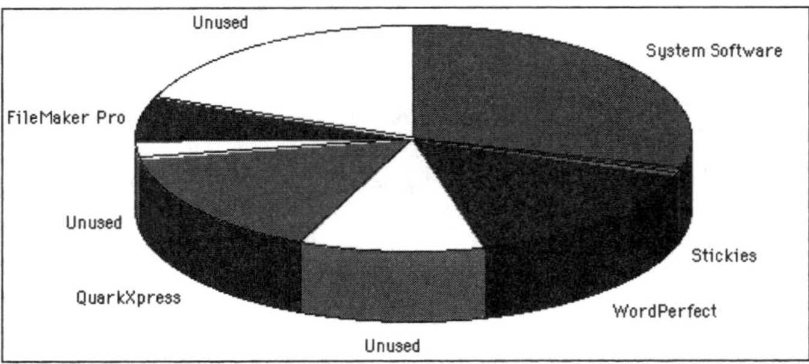


**Figure 13-5: Opening and closing programs may eventually fragment memory.**

### Is Your Mac Fragmented?

To check for memory fragmentation, add up the memory sizes of all the open programs and the system software as listed in the About This Macintosh window. If you have a Power Mac 6100, 7100, or 8100 with a monitor connected to its AV monitor port, add another 600K (or less if you have limited the number of colors as described in "Monitors" in Chapter 8 ). If you have a Macintosh IIsi or IIci with a monitor connected to its back-panel video port, add another 320K (or less if you have limited the number of colors to less than 256 as described in "Monitors" in Chapter 8 ). If the total exceeds the Largest Unused Block amount by more than 50K or so, the unused memory is fragmented into two or more chunks.

You can avoid memory fragmentation by planning the order in which you open and quit programs. First open the programs you're least likely to quit, and then open the programs that are the most expendable in your work session, starting with the most important of them and finishing with the least important. When you need more memory to open another program, quit the most recently opened program. If that doesn't free enough memory, quit the next most recently opened program, and so on. This method frees up a contiguous chunk of memory. Quitting programs helter-skelter leads to memory fragmentation.

All versions of System 7 (except Systems 7.0 and 7.0.1 without Apple's Tune-Up installed) sometimes hasten memory fragmentation in low-memory situations. If you try to open an application that needs more memory than is available, System 7 (except 7.0 or 7.0.1 without Tune-Up) suggests quitting all programs with no open windows — or the largest open program, if all have open windows. Accepting the Finder's suggestion can fragment memory. To avoid memory fragmentation, you must quit programs in the reverse of the order in which they were opened. (For more information on the System 7 Tune-Up, see Chapter 3.)

## Making a standing memory reservation

Do you sometimes have trouble opening a program after quitting another to free up memory? Background printing may be fragmenting your Mac's memory. This can happen unless you have QuickDraw GX printer icons on your desktop, because without QuickDraw GX installed, System 7 automatically opens the PrintMonitor application to handle background printing as needed. PrintMonitor may be opening right after you quit a program, thereby using part of the memory you just freed by quitting a program. The largest unused block of memory may be too small for the next program you need to open, and so may the block that would be available if you quit another open program. But both unused blocks together would be enough if you could consolidate them by quitting PrintMonitor.

To prevent this problem, have the Finder automatically reserve 100K for PrintMonitor during startup, before any other programs are opened. Follow the steps described in the Step-by-Step box "Reserving Memory for the PrintMonitor."

### Reserving Memory for the PrintMonitor

The instructions in this box show how to reserve memory for the PrintMonitor during startup. Doing so prevents the PrintMonitor's background printing from fragmenting your memory.

1. Put a copy of PrintMonitor in the Startup Items folder along with an alias of the program you will least want to quit.
2. Add a blank space to the beginning of the name of the PrintMonitor copy so it comes first alphabetically in the Startup Items folder.
3. Set the Minimum memory size of the PrintMonitor copy to 100K with the Finder's Get Info command.

Now the renamed PrintMonitor copy opens first during startup, followed by the program you will least want to quit. Then the PrintMonitor copy closes because there is nothing to print. The block of memory freed in this process remains available for the original PrintMonitor (in the Extensions folder). The original PrintMonitor's Minimum memory size is set to 96K so it fits in the 100K space even if that space shrinks by 1K or 2K as sometimes happens. Because PrintMonitor no longer fragments memory, you can quit and open programs without postponing background printing.

The memory reservation technique described in the preceding Step-by-Step box does not work if you open small programs such as desk accessories, which take 20K each, while PrintMonitor is not open, and leave them open. The technique also does not work if you quit the other program that opened during startup and open another program while PrintMonitor is not open. In that case, the newly opened program takes the space reserved for PrintMonitor and part of the space used by the now closed application.

# Memory Control

Although the memory management tactics described so far help you make the most efficient use of your Mac's memory pie, the settings in the Memory control panel affect the overall size of the memory pie. The settings available in the Memory control panel vary according to the capabilities of your Macintosh model. Figure 13-6 shows nearly all the settings that can appear in the Memory control panel: Disk Cache, Virtual Memory, 32-Bit Addressing, and RAM Disk. If your Memory control panel shows fewer settings, then your Macintosh cannot take advantage of the missing settings. These settings are discussed in the following sections.

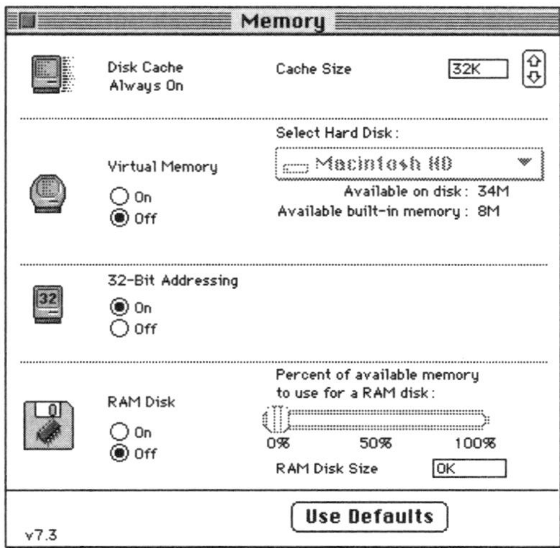


**Figure 13-6: A Memory control panel with nearly all possible settings.**

# Resizing the Disk Cache

A portion of the system software's slice of the memory pie always goes to the Disk Cache, which improves system performance by storing recently used information from disk in memory. When the information is needed again, it can be copied from memory instead of from disk. Copying from memory is much faster than copying from disk.

## Disk Cache and Video Performance

If you have a Mac IIsi and you set the number of colors or grays for a monitor attached to the back-panel video port to four or more colors or grays, you can improve system performance by setting the Disk Cache to 768K. Then the Disk Cache and the built-in video circuitry together use up all the memory that's soldered to the main circuit board. This forces the system software and your programs into the part of memory in the four SIMM sockets, which may help the programs run much faster than they would if they shared the soldered-on memory with the built-in video circuitry. The same trick works on a Mac IIci with 5MB, 9MB, or 17MB of RAM. To get the performance boost, the 256K SIMMs must be installed in the four sockets nearest the disk drive. Realizing a performance increase on a IIci with other RAM capacities is not feasible because you would have to set the Disk Cache so high that it would waste a large amount of memory.

You can use the Memory control panel to adjust the amount of memory allocated for the Disk Cache, as shown in Figure 13-7. The Memory control panel shows the Disk Cache settings on every Macintosh model. Even though you can turn off the equivalent of the Disk Cache in system software older than System 7, you *cannot* turn off the Disk Cache in System 7.

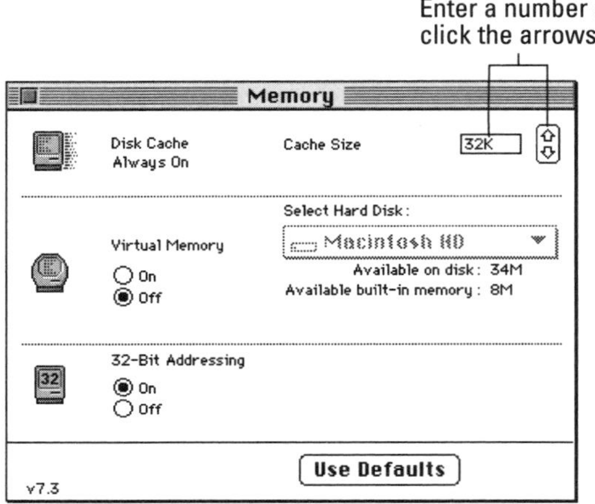


**Figure 13-7: Setting the Disk Cache size.**

# Employing 32-Bit Addressing

Some Macintosh models can access a larger memory pie by using System 7's 32-Bit Addressing capability. To turn it on and off, you use the Memory control panel, as shown in Figure 13-8. These controls are not available on late-model Macs such as the Quadra 630, LC 630, Performa 630, and all Power Macs, because those models all have 32-Bit Addressing turned on permanently.

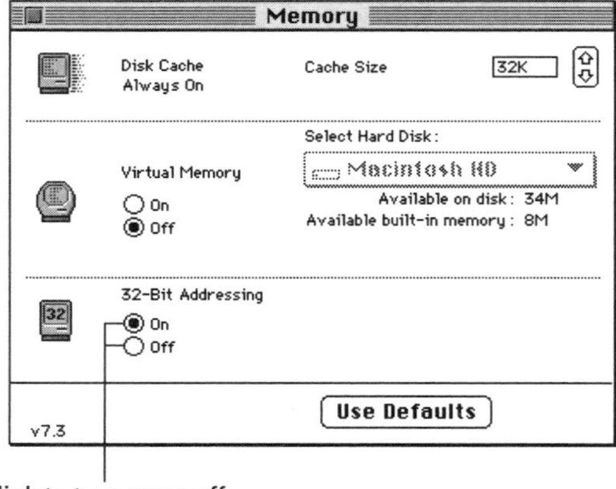


**Figure 13-8 Setting 32-Bit Addressing.**

Turning on 32-Bit Addressing lets you use all the RAM installed in your Mac. If 32-Bit Addressing is off (as it always is with older system software), you can only use 8MB of RAM regardless of the amount installed. If your Mac has more than 8MB installed and you turn off 32-Bit Addressing, the About This Macintosh command adds the unusable amount to the system software size. On a 20MB Quadra 605, for example, turning off 32-Bit Addressing adds 12,000K (12MB) to the system software size.

Mac Classic, SE, Plus, Portable, and PowerBook 100 models can't use 32-Bit Addressing because their 68000 central processing units can't access more than 8MB. The PowerBook 140, 145, and 170 models can use 32-Bit Addressing, but it is not useful because only 8MB can be installed in those models.

The 68020 and 68030 central processing units in Mac SE/30, II, IIx, and IIcx models can access more than 8MB, but the ROMs (permanent read-only memory) in those models are not *32-Bit Clean.* With System 7 versions 7.1.1 and earlier, you can get around the ROM problem and use 32-Bit Addressing on a Mac SE/30, II, IIx, or IIcx by installing one of two system extensions, either Apple's 32-Bit System Enabler or Connectix's MODE 32. Apple distributes 32-Bit System Enabler free through dealers; both are also available from user groups and on-line information services that cater to Mac users. Do not install MODE32 version 1.2 or earlier, or Apple's 32-Bit System Enabler, with System 7.5. Using that old software with System 7.5 may cause serious file corruption. If you have already installed MODE32 version 1.2 or the 32-Bit Enabler with System 7.5, you must re-install a clean copy of System 7.5 (as described under "Performing a Clean Installation" in Chapter 22). After installing a clean version of System 7.5, you can install MODE32 version 7.5 to use 32-Bit Addressing on a Mac II, IIx, IIcx, or SE/30.

## Are You 32-Bit Clean?

If you upgrade to System 7 from an older version of system software, some of your programs may not be compatible with 32-Bit Addressing. Apple began exhorting developers to make their products *32-Bit Clean* in 1987, but not all have complied. For help in determining whether your programs are 32-Bit Clean, see Chapter 21.

If you need to use programs that are not 32-Bit Clean, you can open programs and documents in up to 14MB of RAM by installing the MAXIMA utility software from Connectix. If your Mac has more than 14MB and you want to go further, MAXIMA enables you to use the amount beyond 14MB as a RAM disk.

## Using virtual memory

You may be able to increase the size of your memory pie without buying and installing more RAM modules. System 7 can transparently use part of a hard disk as additional memory. This extra memory, called *virtual memory*, enables you to get by with less RAM. You buy only as much as you need for average use, not for peak use.

Virtual memory has other benefits on Power Macs and on other Macs with PowerPC upgrade cards installed. Turning on virtual memory may help you avoid running out of memory when you use programs that are optimized for the

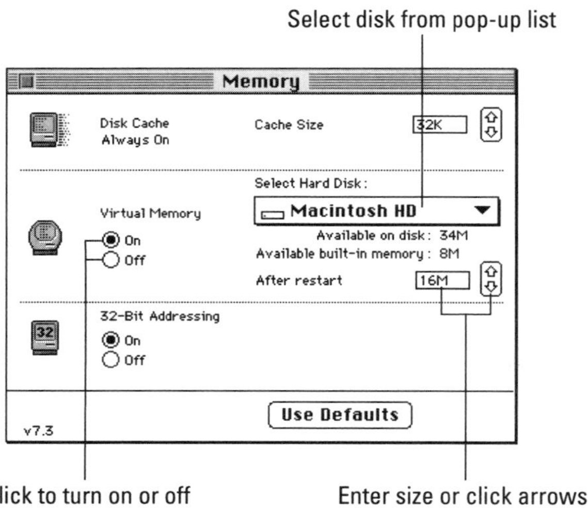


**Figure 13-9: Setting virtual memory.**

PowerPC processor (programs that use only native PowerPC instructions). Native PowerPC programs need less memory with virtual memory on than off.

To turn virtual memory on and off, you use the Memory control panel, as shown in Figure 13-9. You also set the size of total memory and select a hard disk that has a block of available space as large as the total amount of memory you want available (RAM plus virtual memory). The hard disk space cannot be on a removable hard disk.

Virtual memory controls are available on all Macs equipped with an MMU (memory-management unit). The Classic II, LC II, SE/30, IIcx, IIx, IIsi, IIci, IIvx, IIvi, and IIfx models all have MMUs, and so do all Performas, all Centrises, all Quadras, all Power Macs, and all PowerBooks except the 100.

A Mac II can be retrofitted with an MMU that's compatible with virtual memory, and an LC can be upgraded with an accelerator card containing an MMU. How-

## Reducing Virtual Memory Fragmentation

If you use System 7's virtual memory with 32-Bit Addressing turned off, memory is fragmented at the 8MB point, where memory space is reserved for the ROM. As a result, the largest possible unused block is 8MB (8192K) minus the memory size of the part of the system software that can't be swapped to the virtual memory storage file on disk. There's nothing you can do about this fragmentation.

You can do something about potential fragmentation between 9MB and 14 MB (the maximum for virtual memory without 32-Bit Addressing). Memory beyond 8MB is a contiguous block unless you place NuBus cards haphazardly or use built-in video on a IIci. You can avoid fragmenting memory above 8MB on most Mac models with multiple slots by placing all NuBus cards consecutively in the rightmost slots. Place NuBus boards at the opposite end — filling the leftmost slots first — on a Quadra 700 or 800, Centris 650, IIvx, IIvi, or IIci. You can't avoid fragmentation if you use the built-in video on a Mac IIci because it uses a middle NuBus slot space. Built-in video is not a problem on other models because they don't use a middle NuBus slot space for it.

With 32-Bit Addressing off, System 7's virtual memory extends memory beyond 8MB by reclaiming memory space reserved for NuBus slots. All Macs that can use System 7's virtual memory have memory space reserved for six NuBus slots even if they actually have fewer than six slots. Each unused NuBus slot space yields 1MB of virtual memory, up to a maximum of 6MB. Thus with no slots in use, virtual memory can extend total memory to 14MB.

To eliminate fragmentation of extended memory on all models, turn on 32-Bit Addressing. Then the ROM and the NuBus slots use memory space above 1 gigabyte (1024MB), and virtual memory doesn't use NuBus slot space to extend memory.

ever, a Mac Plus, SE, Classic, or Portable with such an accelerator can't use System 7's virtual memory because the ROMs in those models are missing some information System 7 needs to implement virtual memory. To use virtual memory on those models, install Connectix's utility software Virtual.

With virtual memory on, the About This Macintosh window reports the total amount of memory and the amount of built-in memory (RAM). It also tells you how much disk space is used for virtual memory storage and on which disk the storage file is located (see Figure 13-10).

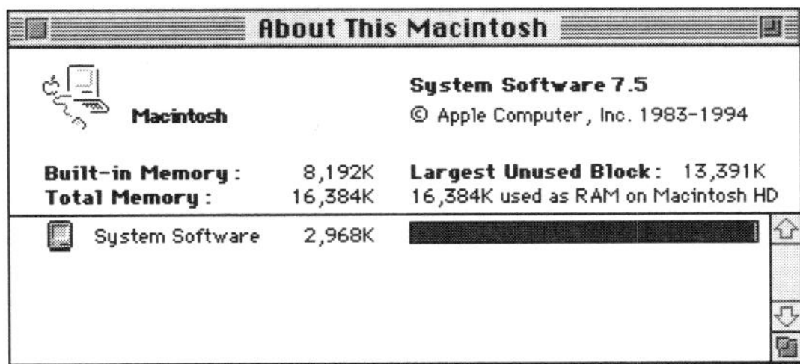


Figure 13-10: Virtual memory statistics.

The limit on total memory (virtual memory plus RAM) depends on whether 32-Bit Addressing is on or off. With 32-Bit Addressing on, the limit on total memory is one gigabyte (1024MB). With 32-Bit Addressing off, total memory cannot exceed 14MB. On Macintosh models with NuBus boards installed, the limit is 1MB lower than 14MB for each installed board. Subtract 1MB if you use built-in video on your Mac (for example, on a Classic II, SE/30, LC II, IIsi, IIci, Ivx, IIvi, Quadra, Performa, or PowerBook). Think of built-in video as a fake NuBus slot with a video adapter card in it.

Virtual memory works by keeping the most active program and document segments in RAM. Less-used segments of open programs and documents are kept in an invisible file named VM Storage on the hard disk. (The VM Storage file becomes visible if you start up with system software older than System 7.) An additional scheme makes virtual memory more efficient on Power Macs and Macs with PowerPC upgrade cards. Less-used segments of native PowerPC programs are kept in their original place on disk, the program file, instead of the VM Storage file. (Non-native programs use the VM Storage file on a Power Mac as they do on any other Mac.)

When a program needs a segment not currently in physical memory, System 7 automatically swaps the least-used segment in RAM with the needed segment on disk. For example, a swap often occurs when you switch programs.

Because a hard disk is much slower than RAM, using virtual memory can degrade system performance. The performance penalty is barely noticeable if a swap happens when you switch programs. The slowdown may be severe if you use virtual memory to open a program that's bigger than the amount of RAM left after system software gets its share. The disk may thrash for several minutes as it tries to swap segments back and forth. For best results, set virtual memory no higher than double the installed RAM and use it for opening multiple small programs.

***Tip:*** You can often improve system performance by using the Hide Others command in the Application menu. Hidden windows don't require updating, which may require disk access when virtual memory is on. Some programs continue working in the background even with their windows hidden. For example, a database program might generate a report in the background. But the Hide Others command usually reduces the amount of background work going on.

## Using the RAM disk

In contrast to virtual memory, which uses part of a hard disk as if it were RAM, a RAM disk uses part of RAM as if it were a hard disk. The RAM disk has an icon that appears on the desktop, and you manipulate folders and files on a RAM disk the same as any other disk. A RAM disk works much faster than a hard disk, but only stores items temporarily. The RAM disk feature is not available on all Macintosh models. If it is available on your Macintosh, your Memory control panel will have settings for it, as shown in Figure 13-11.

## Trouble with Old Drivers

Some driver software for hard disks made before 1992 does not work with System 7's virtual memory or 32-Bit Addressing options turned on. Every hard disk contains driver software, which the Mac copies to its RAM while starting up. The software acts as an intermediary between the system software and the hard disk. You install or update the driver software with hard disk utility software from the maker of your drive. Usually, you can do this without any loss of data.

Several companies sell disk utility programs whose driver software works with a wide variety of hard disks. Some companies claim their driver software is faster than the competition. In reality, you won't notice any performance difference when using most application programs on popular-sized drives.

To pick a driver, consider other features of the disk utility program that installs the driver. You want a program that's easy to use and can partition a hard disk into volumes. Optional features include password protection, encryption, security erase, and disk defragmentation.

Important: Be sure you install driver software that complies fully with SCSI Manager 4.3 if you have a 660AV, 840AV, or any Power Mac. The same standard applies if you use System 7.5 on any Quadra or Centris model.

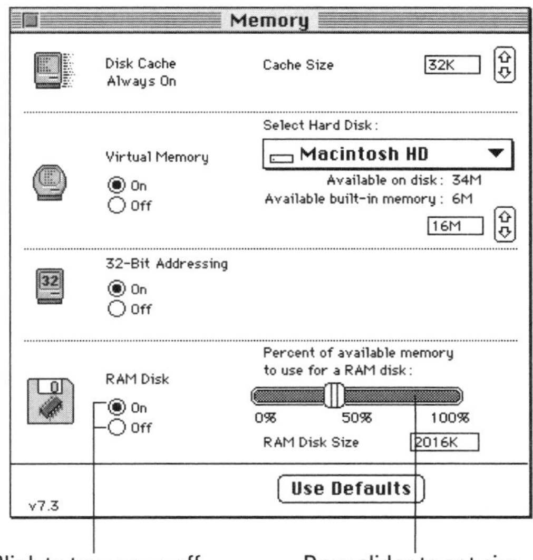


**Figure 13-11: Setting a RAM disk.**

***Warning:*** With versions of System 7 prior to 7.5, the Finder's Shut Down command removes the RAM disk, and all its contents are lost. A power failure or system crash also removes the RAM disk.

Because a RAM disk only stores items temporarily, you should observe these precautions:

- ❖ Don't store a file exclusively on a RAM disk. Copy documents from RAM disk to another disk frequently.
- ❖ Copy files from the RAM disk to another disk before shutting down.
- ❖ Don't use a program for the first time on a RAM disk. Test it on another disk first.

To resize or remove a RAM disk, first copy the files you want to save from it to another disk. Then drag everything from the RAM disk to the Trash and empty the Trash. Finally use the Memory control panel to turn the RAM disk off or change its size, and restart your Mac.

To create a RAM disk that survives shutdowns and works on any Mac, use Connectix's utility software Maxima.

# Memory Optimizers

You can get twice as much out of the RAM installed in your Mac with very little performance penalty by using one or two software products — RAM Doubler and OptiMem. You can use either product alone or use them together.

RAM Doubler from Connectix (800-950-5880 or 415-571-5100) actually doubles the amount of total memory as reported by the About This Macintosh command. RAM Doubler accomplishes its magic by reallocating RAM automatically behind the scenes while you continue working.

It takes over the RAM reserved but not used by open applications (the lighter portion of the bars graphed by the About This Macintosh command) and temporarily reallocates the unused RAM to applications that need it. RAM Doubler also compresses parts of programs in RAM that probably won't be used again, such as parts that initialize a program when you open it. Also, RAM Doubler may store infrequently used areas of RAM to disk, just like conventional virtual memory, but only on Macs with 6MB or less of physical RAM. RAM Doubler reduces overall system performance five to ten percent, but you probably won't notice the slight slowdown in normal operations.

Like virtual memory, RAM Doubler requires an MMU, so it doesn't work on a Mac with a 68000 processor, or on a Mac with a 68020 processor unless it's been upgraded with a 68030 accelerator, a 68040 accelerator, or a 68851 PMMU chip. Your Mac must have at least 4MB of physical RAM installed but not more than 128MB. In addition 32-Bit Addressing must be on, and the programs you use must work with 32-Bit Addressing.

You can't use RAM Doubler in combination with virtual memory (including Connectix's Virtual). You can't set the memory size of any application higher than the amount of physical RAM installed in your Mac; Connectix recommends leaving your programs set at their usual memory sizes.

The benefits of OptiMem from Jump Development (412-681-2692) can't be stated precisely. OptiMem doesn't literally double the total available memory, but it does allow you to keep more programs open at the same time. In addition, it allows open programs to use more memory than the Preferred sizes set in their Info windows.

OptiMem takes a different approach to memory optimization and has fewer restrictions than RAM Doubler. OptiMem opens a program in its Minimum memory size, not its Preferred memory size, as specified in the program's Info window. If a program needs more memory, OptiMem gives it more from the unused portion of RAM on your Mac. When the program no longer needs the extra memory, OptiMem reclaims it for future reallocation. You probably won't notice any performance degradation in normal operations.

You can use OptiMem on a Mac with less than 4MB of RAM installed, and there is no RAM maximum. OptiMem does not require 32-Bit Addressing or an MMU. OptiMem works with virtual memory on or off.

## Power Mac Virtual Memory

Turning on virtual memory changes how a Power Mac organizes its memory. With virtual memory on, an application's native Power Mac code (if any) does not go into the portion of memory whose size is determined by the application's Get Info memory settings. That portion of memory, called an application partition, contains an application's 680X0 code (if any), resources such as menu and dialog box definitions, and data. With virtual memory on, an application's native code goes into another part of memory alongside native code from other open applications. (An application's native Power Mac code does go into the application partition if virtual memory is off.)

Virtual memory performance is somewhat better with native Power Mac applications than with 680X0 applications. When you open a 680X0 application, its code is loaded into the application partition (in RAM) but may be immediately written out to a monolithic virtual-memory swap file, whose size equals the total amount of memory (RAM plus virtual memory). This thrashing doesn't happen with native Power Mac applications because the operating system only loads native code into RAM as it's needed. When an application needs native code that's not in RAM, the operating system automatically replaces an expendable fragment of native code in RAM with the needed fragment of native code from the application's disk file. Thus each native Power Mac application's disk file acts as a virtual-memory swap file. Furthermore the operating system assumes native code is read-only and never writes native code back to disk. The operating system can't make any such assumptions about the amorphous contents of an application partition.

Virtual memory is worth trying with Power Mac applications, although you may still find its performance unacceptable with applications that manipulate large amounts of data, such as Photoshop.

# CHAPTER 13 CONCEPTS AND TERMS

- Monitoring the use of memory gives you more control over your Mac's performance and prevents unexpected software failures.
- Selecting About This Macintosh in the Finder brings up a window that shows how the Mac currently divvies up its memory among the system software and application programs.
- The Memory control panel contains switches for the Disk Cache, 32-Bit Addressing, virtual memory, and the RAM disk. (Some options are not available on all Mac models.)
- Virtual memory enables you to use disk space as memory, and 32-Bit Addressing increases the amount of memory most Macintosh models can use.
- Managing memory becomes more important as you use more of it, and as you keep more programs open at the same time.

**32-Bit Addressing**
A System 7 capability that increases the amount of RAM that most Mac-intosh models can use. Without 32-Bit Addressing, a Mac can only take advantage of 8MB of RAM, even if more is installed, and virtual memory is limited to 14MB. With 32-Bit Addressing, a Mac can make use of RAM beyond 8MB.

**32-Bit Clean**
Describes software that works with the 32-Bit Addressing option turned on (in the Memory control panel). Using software that is not 32-Bit Clean restricts the amount of memory a Mac can use to 8MB.

**Disk Cache**
Improves system performance by storing recently used information from disk in a dedicated part of memory. Accessing information in memory is much faster than accessing information on disk.

**Memory control panel**
Contains settings that affect memory use and availability, including Disk Cache, 32-Bit Addressing, Virtual Memory, and RAM Disk. The settings available in the Memory control panel vary according to the capabilities of your Macintosh model.

**memory fragmentation**
The condition wherein available memory has become divided into multiple disjointed blocks, with each block separated by an open program. System 7 cannot automatically consolidate fragmented memory nor open a program in multiple blocks. You can fix memory fragmentation by quitting all open programs.

**memory-management unit (MMU)**
A part of the 68030, 68040, or PowerPC processor chip, the MMU is required for virtual memory.

**memory optimizer**
Software that lets you get twice as much from the RAM installed in your Mac. For example, you can keep more programs open with OptiMem installed than without, and it allows open programs to use more memory than the Preferred sizes set in their Info windows. Another product, RAM Doubler, actually doubles the amount of total memory available.

**Minimum memory size**
The smallest amount of memory in which the system will open a program. System 7 versions 7.1 and later display and let you change a program's Minimum size in its Info window, and warn you if you try to set it below the minimum safe size determined by the program's developer.

**NuBus slots**
With 32-Bit Addressing off, System 7 increases the maximum amount of virtual memory available by 1MB for each empty NuBus slot. Macs with no slots or fewer than six slots gain 1MB of virtual memory capacity for each slot fewer than six. Built-in video counts as a filled slot.

**Preferred memory size**
The maximum amount of memory the system allocates to a program. A program's Info window displays and lets you change the Preferred size. (In versions of System 7 older than 7.1, the Preferred size is called the Current size.)

**RAM disk**
You can use the Memory control panel to set aside RAM to be used as if it were a very fast hard disk. A RAM disk only stores items until the next restart, shut down, or power outage.

**Suggested memory size**
The amount of memory the program's developer recommends for standard program performance. A program's Info window displays, but does not let you change, the Suggested size.

**virtual memory**
Additional memory made available by System 7 treating part of a hard disk as if it were RAM.

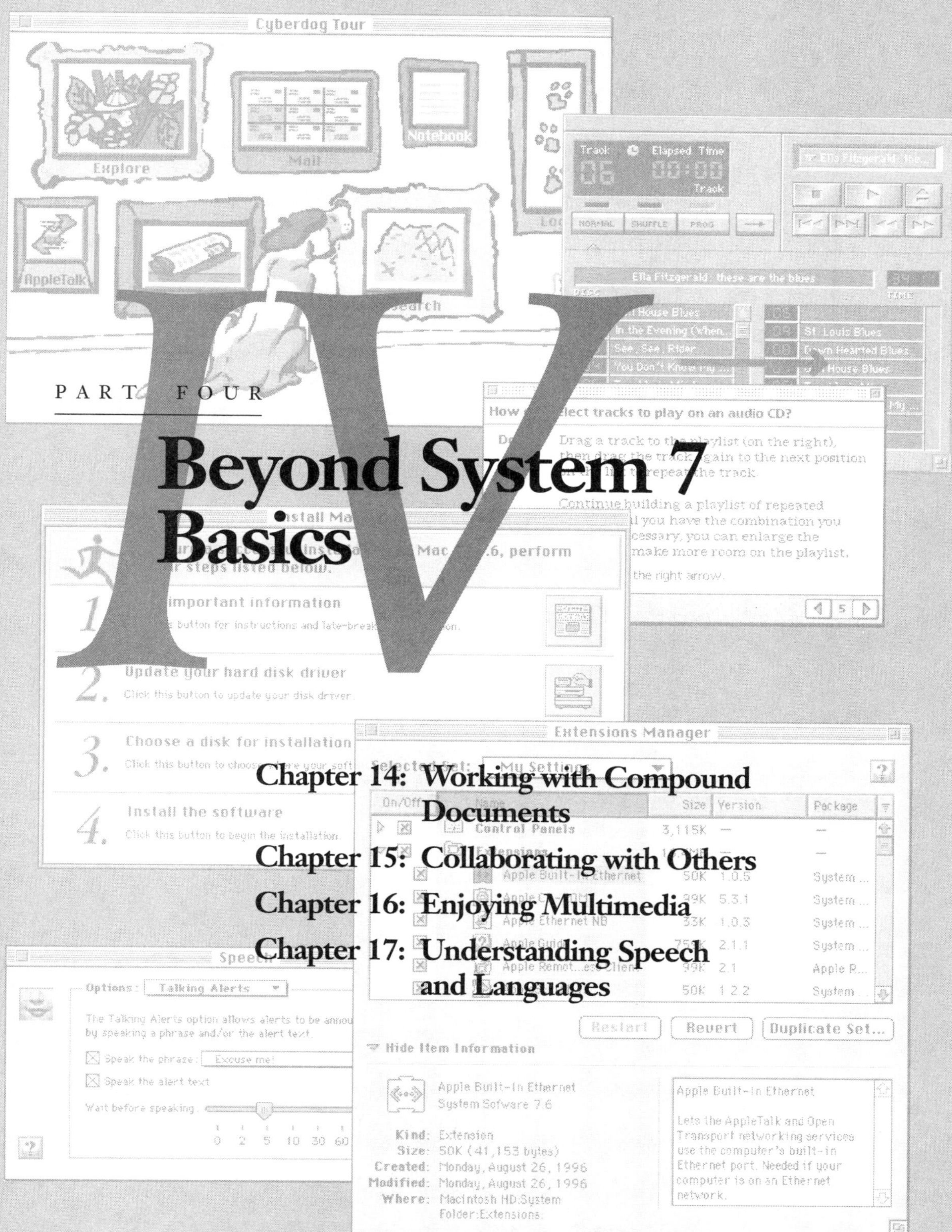

PART FOUR

# IV

# Beyond System 7 Basics

CHAPTER FOURTEEN

# Working with Compound Documents

- Creating publishers: saving live copies of material from your documents as edition files
- Subscribing to editions: including live copies of material in your document from other documents
- Updating a subscriber automatically or manually when you change a publisher
- Copying and moving text and graphics by dragging them within and between participating applications
- Taking stock of OpenDoc

The United States Constitution is often referred to as being a living document because it has the capability to change with the times. Application programs that support System 7's publish and subscribe capabilities enable you to create your own living documents. The Create Publisher and Subscribe To commands enable you to share information between documents dynamically.

Think of the Create Publisher and Subscribe To commands as being live Copy and Paste commands. You can use these commands to copy a group of cells or a chart from a spreadsheet and paste it into a word processing report. Anytime the selected information in the spreadsheet changes, the report is updated automatically.

In this chapter, you'll learn how to breathe life into your documents by using the Create Publisher, Subscribe To, and other related commands.

## Understanding Publishers, Editions, and Subscribers

System 7 borrows concepts and terminology from the publishing industry for its publish and subscribe technology. A selected area of a document becomes a *publisher* when you make a live copy of it available to other documents. The publisher can include any information that you can select within a document.

Publishing material from a document creates a live copy of the material in a separate file, which is called an *edition* (see Figure 14-1). You include a copy of an edition in another document by subscribing to the edition. The area of the document that contains a copy of an edition is called a *subscriber*. A document can contain any number and combination of publishers and subscribers.

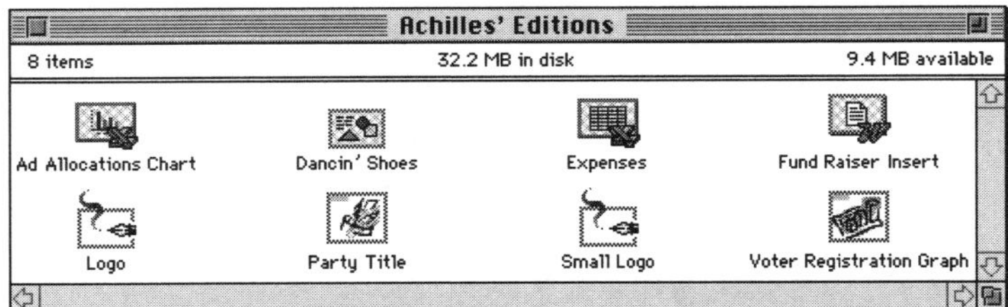


**Figure 14-1: Some edition files.**

Saving a document after changing a publisher in it can update the publisher's edition automatically (or you can update the edition manually). When an edition is updated, System 7 notifies all subscribers to that edition that a new edition is available. The subscriber can automatically reflect the latest information from the edition, or you can update it manually.

Documents containing subscribers do not have to be open for the subscribers to receive edition updates. System 7 stores notices of edition updates destined for closed subscribers; it forwards each stored notice when you open the document that contains the subscriber. Information always flows from the publisher to an edition and then to the edition's subscribers, as shown in Figure 14-2.

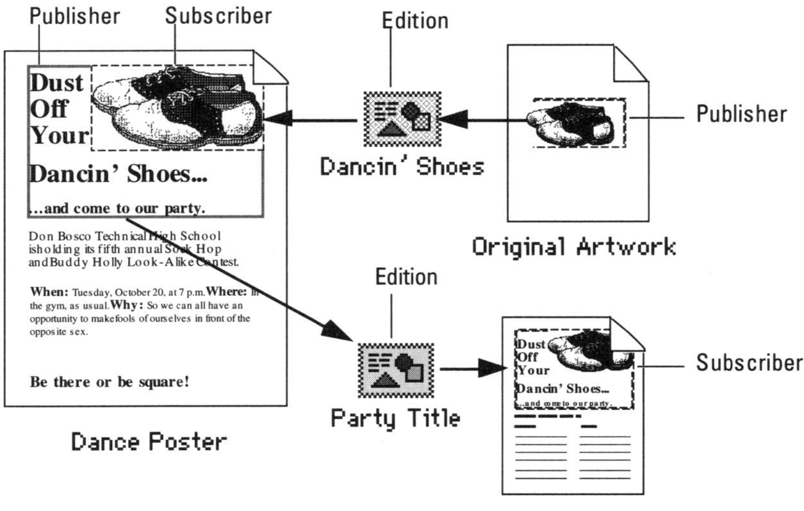


**Figure 14-2: The relationship between publisher, edition, and subscriber.**

Publishing and subscribing work across a network just as well as they work locally on your Macintosh. You can subscribe and get updates to editions that are on any disk or folder that you are sharing from someone else. Likewise, other people can subscribe and get updates to editions on disks or folders that those people are sharing from you. If you are not sharing a disk or folder when an edition on it is updated, System 7 stores the update notice and forwards it to the subscribers on your local disks the next time you share the disk or folder. (For more information on file sharing, see Chapter 9.)

The publishing-and-subscribing process works only in programs that are designed to take advantage of it. Such programs contain publishing commands in the Edit menu or in a submenu of the Edit menu. If you have a program that lacks those commands, check with the program's developer to see whether an upgraded version is available.

# Creating a Publisher

You create a publisher by selecting the information that you want to share and then choosing Create Publisher from the Edit menu of your program (see Figure 14-3). Many programs put the Create Publisher command in a Publishing submenu or an Editions submenu of the Edit menu.

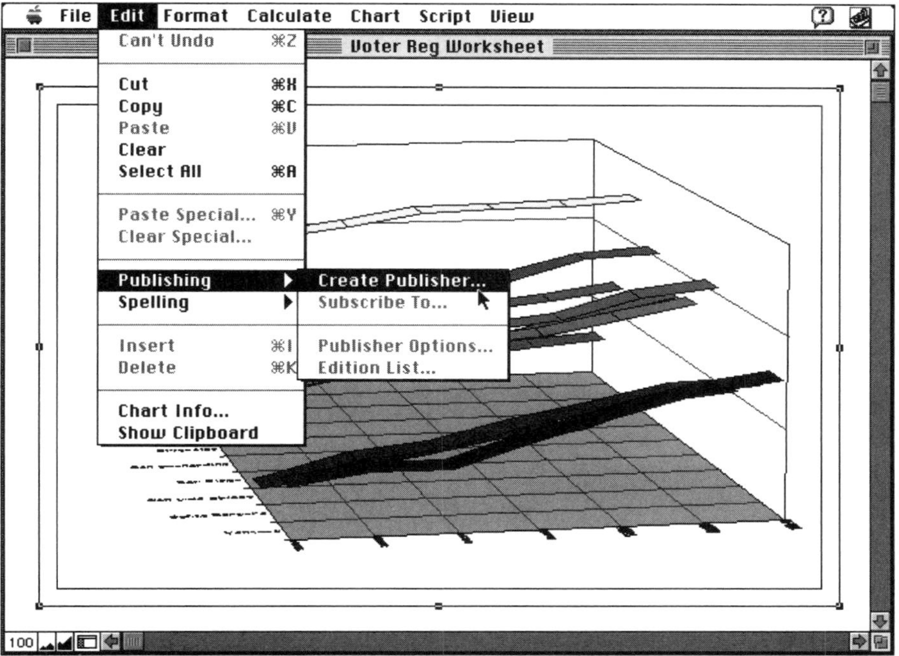


**Figure 14-3: Creating a publisher.**

In most programs, you need to select text or graphics in your document to create a publisher. If you haven't selected anything, the Create Publisher command is dimmed. In a few programs, such as Adobe Photoshop, you can publish an entire document by choosing Create Publisher without selecting anything.

After you choose the Create Publisher command, the Publisher dialog box appears, as shown in Figure 14-4. A thumbnail view of the material that you selected appears in the Preview area of the dialog box.

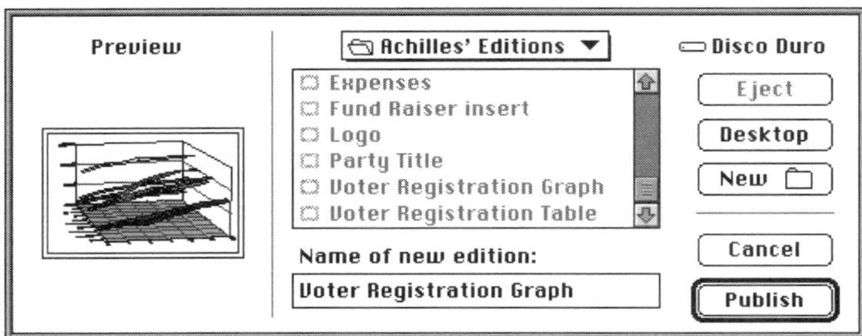


**Figure 14-4: Saving an edition.**

Usually, the folder in which you saved the last edition is open in the dialog box. System 7 knows which folder to open because it keeps an alias of the most recently saved edition in the Preferences folder inside the System Folder. You can go to a different folder by using the same methods you would use with the Save As command. If you want to make the edition available to other users on your network, be sure to save the edition in a folder or disk that you allow those users to share.

To keep a new publisher, you must save the document that contains it. If you close the document without saving, the program asks whether you want to save changes. You lose the publisher if you decline to save.

You can create as many independent publishers in a document as you want. Some programs permit publishers to overlap partially or completely; one publisher can include all or part of the information contained in another publisher. Apple's guidelines suggest that word processing programs permit nested publishers but not overlapping publishers. Spreadsheet programs and graphics programs should permit both nesting and overlapping publishers. A program that does not allow overlapped or nested publishers dims the Create Publisher command when you select any part of a document that already is part of an existing publisher.

### Smart Multiformat Editions

An edition's format — plain text, styled text, paint-type picture, object-type graphic, and so on — is determined by the program that created the document containing the publisher. Some programs save information in several formats in an edition file. When you subscribe to a multiformat edition, the program that created the subscribing document uses the most appropriate format. Microsoft Excel, for example, saves spreadsheet cells as a picture, as a text table, and as a range of formatted Excel cells. A graphics document subscribing to an Excel edition uses the picture format; a word processor probably uses the text table (although Microsoft Word uses the formatted cells to create a formatted Word table); and another Excel worksheet uses the formatted cells.

# Subscribing to an Edition

You subscribe to an edition to incorporate live information from another document into the document on which you're working. To subscribe to an edition, select a place in your document for the edition and then choose Subscribe To from the Edit menu, as shown in Figure 14-5. Some programs put the Subscribe To command in a Publishing submenu of the Edit menu.

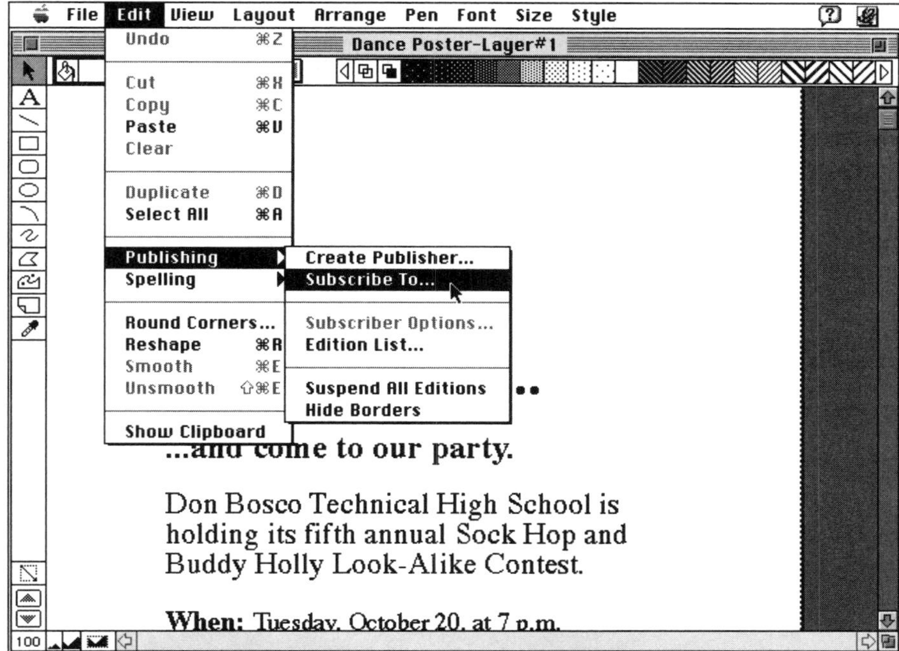


**Figure 14-5: Subscribing to an edition.**

The place you select for the edition depends on the type of document that's subscribing to it. In a word processing document, you click an insertion point. In a spreadsheet document, you select a cell or range of cells. You do not have to select a place in most graphics documents, because you can move the subscriber after placing it in the document.

Choosing Subscribe To from the Edit menu displays the Subscribe To dialog box, shown in Figure 14-6. The dialog box displays the highlighted name of the last edition that you published or subscribed to, and you can select a different edition as though you were using an Open command. When you select an edition, a thumbnail view of its contents appears in the Preview area of the dialog box. Clicking the Subscribe button places a copy of the selected edition in your document.

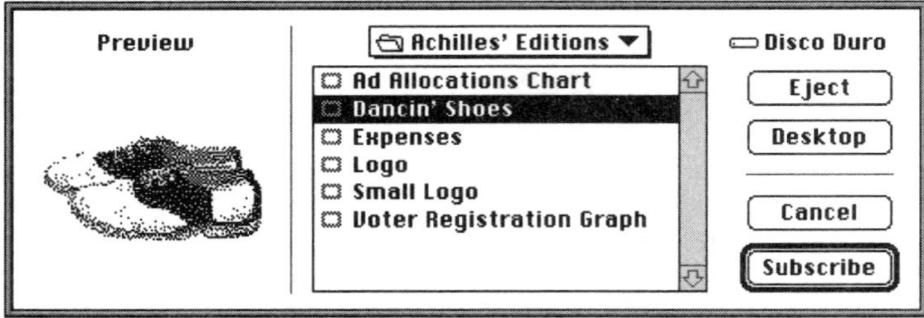


**Figure 14-6: Selecting an edition to subscribe to.**

A document can subscribe to any number of editions. The editions can be on a disk directly connected to your Macintosh, or on a disk or folder that you're sharing from another Macintosh on the same network.

# Controlling Publisher and Subscriber Borders

Most programs display a gray border around a publisher or subscriber when you click or select something inside the publisher or subscriber. The border also appears if you select part of a document that contains a publisher or subscriber, as shown in Figure 14-7. The standard border lines, which are three pixels thick, are medium gray (50 percent gray) for publishers and dark gray (75 percent gray) for subscribers. Clicking outside the publisher or subscriber makes the border disappear.

An optional Edit menu command, Show Borders, displays borders around all publishers and subscribers in the active document. After you choose the Show Borders command, it becomes the Hide borders command, which (surprise!) hides all borders except the one for the subscriber or publisher that you clicked.

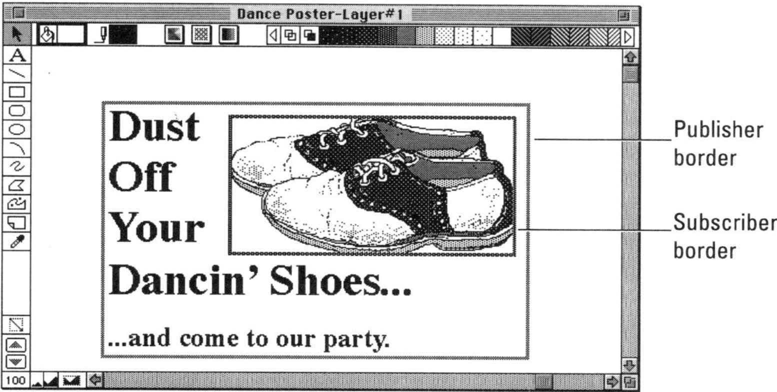


**Figure 14-7: Borders around publishers and subscribers.**

Some programs, including Microsoft Excel 4, don't show publisher or subscriber borders. Excel's Links command can select a publisher's range of cells (but not a chart, another type of publisher, or a subscriber). You select the name of the publisher that you want from a list of publishers in the document, and then you click a Select button. Excel selects the range of cells and scrolls the document window so that you can see it.

# Setting Publisher and Subscriber Options

System 7 provides several options for working with publishers and subscribers. You can *adorn* a subscriber (change its formatting), locate and open a subscriber's publisher, control edition updates, and cancel or suspend a publisher or subscriber.

Application programs use different methods to make publisher and subscriber options available. Some programs place a Publisher Options command in the Edit menu when a publisher is selected in the active window, and they place a Subscriber Options command in the menu when a subscriber is selected. Choosing one of those commands brings up a dialog box in which you set the publisher or subscriber options (see Figures 14-8 and 14-9).

Publisher to: Dance Poster

Send Editions:
On Save
Manually
Send Edition Now
Latest Edition: Monday, April 22, 1991 8:01:02 PM

Cancel Publisher
Cancel
OK

**Figure 14-8: A Publisher Options dialog box.**

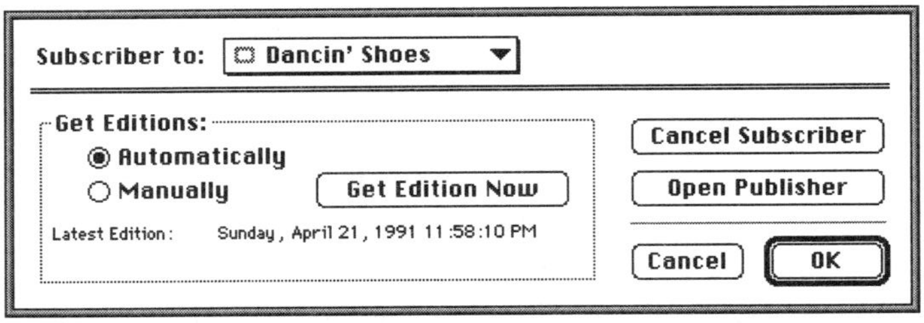

**Figure 14-9: A Subscriber Options dialog box.**

Other programs put the Publisher Options and Subscriber Options commands in a Publishing submenu or an Editions submenu of the Edit menu. As a shortcut, many programs bring up the appropriate options dialog box when you double-click a publisher or subscriber while pressing Option.

Microsoft Excel 4 has its own eccentric methods. In Excel, you choose the Links command from the File menu to display the Links dialog box. In that dialog box, you choose Publisher or Subscriber from the Link Type pop-up menu to see a list of the publishers or subscribers that are in the document. Then you select the one whose options you want to see, and click an Options button. As a shortcut, you can double-click any part of a publisher or subscriber on a worksheet. (The double-click trick doesn't work for chart publishers, however.) Excel's eccentric methods for publish and subscribe have their origins in Microsoft's own data sharing technology called OLE (Object Linking and Embedding). Excel has a hybrid of OLE and publish and subscribe.

## Adorning a subscriber

Most programs do not permit you to change the contents of a subscriber directly, because your changes would disappear the next time the subscriber was updated. Many programs, however, permit you to adorn a subscriber in ways that the program can reapply to a new edition. For example, you may be able to resize or crop an entire subscriber as you would resize or crop a graphic in a word processing document. You may be able to change all the text in a subscriber to a different font, style, or size.

Programs that allow adornment generally have an option in the Subscriber Options dialog box that you can set to maintain or cancel adornments (see Figure 14-10). When this option is on, the program reapplies the changes that you made to the subscriber the next time the subscriber is updated.

## Opening a subscriber's publisher

Generally, you make changes to a subscriber by opening its publisher and changing the publisher. To help you open a publisher, the Subscriber Options dialog box includes an Open Publisher button. Clicking this button is supposed to open the document that contains the subscriber's publisher (and the program that created the publisher's document, if it's not already open), scroll the publisher into view, and

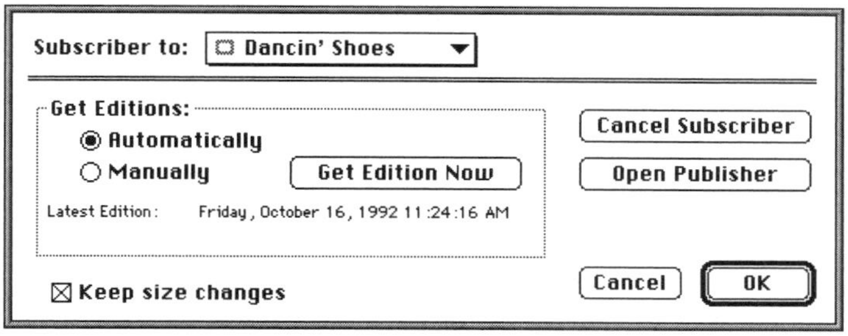

Subscriber to:
Dancin' Shoes
Get Editions:
Automatically
Manually
Get Edition Now
Latest Edition: Friday, October 16, 1992 11:24:16 AM
Cancel Subscriber
Open Publisher
Keep size changes
Cancel
OK

**Figure 14-10: The Subscriber Options may include an option such as that maintains subscriber adornment.**

select the publisher. Some programs also open a publisher when you press Option while double-clicking a subscriber. In practice, however, clicking the Open Publisher button and Option-clicking the subscriber do not always open the publisher.

Sometimes you can open a publisher by opening its edition icon in the Finder. When you do, an edition window appears, as shown in Figure 14-11. The window contains a miniature view of the publisher and an Open Publisher button. Clicking this button is supposed to open the publisher's original document, just as the Open Publisher button does in the Subscriber Options dialog box, but the Open Publisher button doesn't always work.

Dancin' Shoes
PICT
Open Publisher

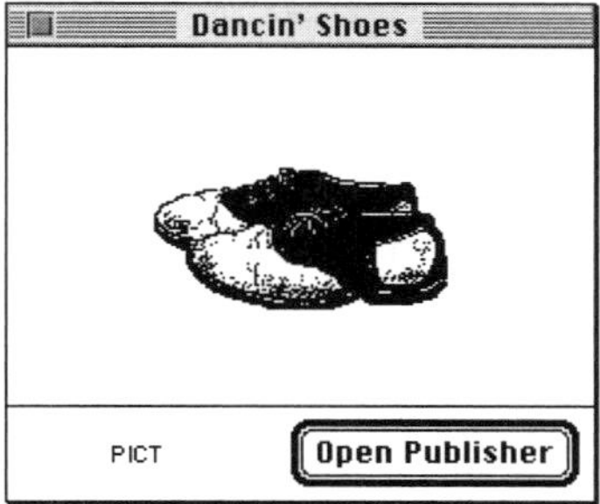

**Figure 14-11: An edition window.**

You can see the last edition that you used by opening the Preferences folder in the System Folder. Opening the alias named Last Edition Used displayed the edition window of the last edition you saved.

**Suspend Before You Amend**

In programs that permit you to modify a subscriber, you should suspend or cancel automatic edition updating before you begin editing the subscriber (as explained in "Updating Editions" in this chapter). This action preserves your changes until you update the subscriber manually by clicking the Get Edition Now button in the Subscriber Options dialog box. When a subscriber is updated, changes you have made directly to it (not to the corresponding publisher) may be lost. Some programs warn you before automatically updating a subscriber that you have modified, but many automatically update without warning.

# Making Changes to a Publisher

You can modify a publisher within a document the way you would any other part of a document. You can add material to a publisher or delete material from it, making the publisher larger or smaller. You can cut an entire publisher and paste it in a different place in the document. Copying and pasting or otherwise duplicating a publisher, however, isn't a good idea. If you do, all duplicates of the publisher share one edition, making the contents of subscribers to that edition seem to be unpredictable. (The edition reflects the contents of the most recently updated duplicate publisher.)

Each time you save a document that contains a revised publisher, the application program automatically updates the publisher's edition. You can turn off automatic updating and update only manually, however, as described in the following section.

# Updating Editions

The Subscriber and Publisher Options dialog boxes enable you to control whether edition updates are sent or received automatically or manually. Various programs label these dialog-box options differently. You can set update options individually for each publisher and subscriber. For example, you may want one subscriber in a document (such as a logo) to be updated on request and another subscriber (such as daily sales figures) to be updated automatically.

A publisher's Publisher Options dialog box (refer to Figure 14-8) controls when new editions of the publisher are sent. When you activate the standard setting, On Save, the program automatically sends a new edition the next time you save the document (if you modified the publisher). Setting the Manually option suspends sending new editions of the publisher until you click the Send Edition Now button in the Publisher Options dialog box.

The subscriber can receive new editions automatically or manually. If the Automatically option is set in the subscriber's Subscriber Options dialog box (refer to Figure 14-9), the subscriber gets updated as soon as the program receives a new edition. You can suspend automatic subscriber updating by setting the Manually option in the subscriber's Subscriber Options dialog box. To get a manual update, click the Get Edition Now button in the Subscriber Options dialog box.

You can cancel a publisher or subscriber by clicking the Cancel Subscriber or Cancel Publisher button in the Publisher Options or Subscriber Options dialog box. Canceling a publisher or subscriber permanently breaks the link between the publisher and the subscriber.

Some programs enable you to suspend all updating activity temporarily by providing a Suspend All Editions command (or its equivalent) in the Edit menu. When this command is activated, a check mark appears next to it in the menu, and the program blocks all publishers from sending new editions and all subscribers from receiving new editions. Turning off the command removes the check mark from the menu and updates, with any new editions, all subscribers that are set to receive new editions automatically. The Stop All Editions command affects only publishers and subscribers in documents created by the program in which you use the command.

# Editing the Drag-and-Drop Way

If you don't need live links between editions, you can create compound documents by copying and pasting parts from documents that you created in different programs. System 7.5 and later provides a more direct way to copy text, graphics, and other material within a document, between documents, and between applications. This capability, called *drag-and-drop editing*, works only with applications that are designed to take advantage of it. The versions of SimpleText, Stickies, the Note Pad, the Scrapbook, Desktop Patterns, and the Finder that are included with System 7.5 and later all work with drag-and-drop editing.

To copy material within a document, open the document and select the text, graphic, or other material that you want to copy; then hold down the Option key and drag the selected material to the place where you want the copy. As you drag, an outline of the selected material follows the mouse pointer, and an insertion point shows where the copy will appear when you stop dragging (see Figure 14-12). If you want to move selected material within a document rather than copy it, drag the selected material without pressing the Option key.

To copy material between documents, first open both documents and position them so that you can see the source material and the place where you want to drop a copy of it. Select the text, graphic, or other source material and then drag the selected material to the place in the second document where you want the copy. As you drag, an outline of the selected material follows the mouse pointer. When the pointer enters the destination window, a border appears around the content area of the window, and an insertion point shows where the copy will appear when you stop dragging (see Figure 14-13). You can use the same method to copy between documents in a single application or between two applications.

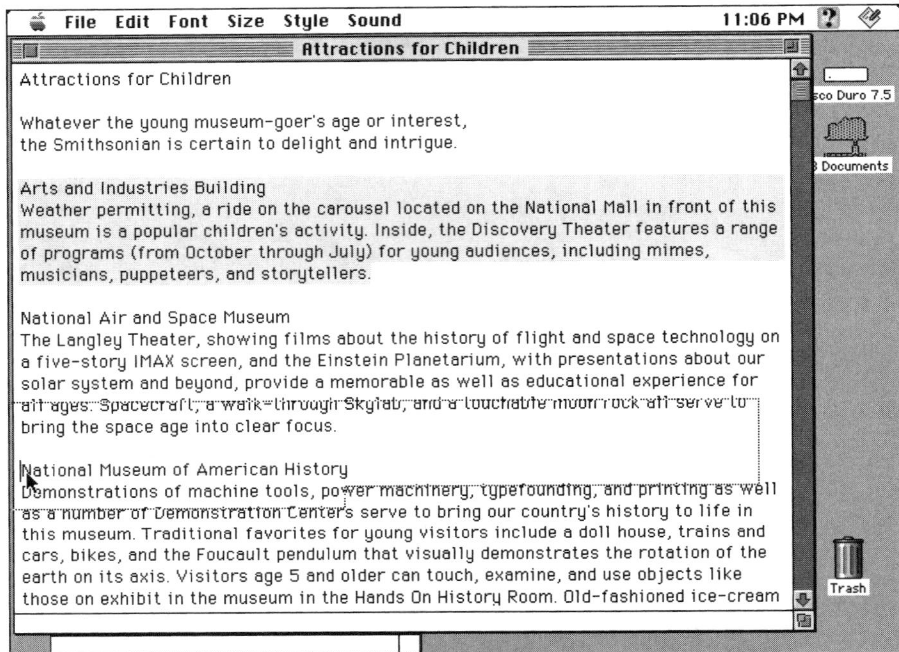


**Figure 14-12: Drag-and-drop editing within a document.**

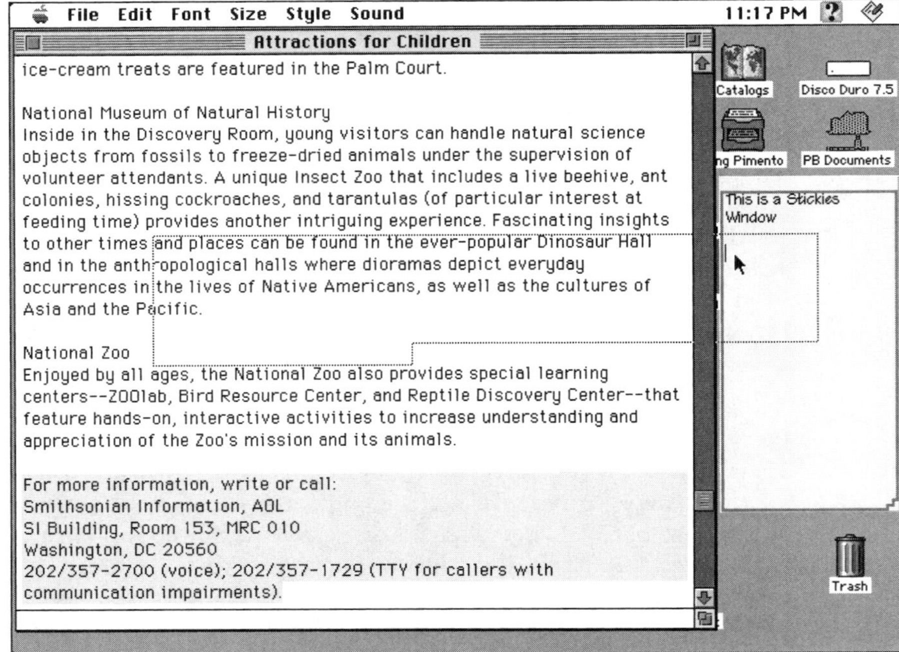


**Figure 14-13: Drag-and-drop editing between documents.**

You also can drag selected material from a document to the Desktop or a folder window, where the Finder creates a clipping file that contains a copy of the dragged material. You can open the copied material to inspect it. To copy the contents of a clipping file to a document, drag the clipping-file icon to the open document's window.

You can use a clipping file over and over. For example, you can keep handy clippings that contain your letterhead, the company logo, a list of your e-mail addresses, and any other element that you use frequently.

Some people prefer drag-and-drop to cut-and-paste editing because they find it easier to use. Drag-and-drop has one clear advantage: It doesn't wipe out the contents of the Clipboard, so it's a good method to use when the Clipboard contains important material that you're not ready to replace.

# OpenDoc Overview

No matter which way you choose to use content from one document in another — copy and paste, publish and subscribe, or in some cases drag-and-drop — you are constrained by the types of content allowed in the destination document. You can incorporate plain text and pictures in most kinds of documents, but many kinds of documents can't accept spreadsheets, graphs, database records, QuickTime movies, sounds, styled text, and so forth. Ideally, you'd like to be able to put any kind of content into any document. That's the basic idea behind Apple's OpenDoc infrastructure.

In an OpenDoc document, you're not limited to the kinds of content that any particular application can handle. You're free to choose any kind of content for which an appropriate OpenDoc plug-in software component, called a part, is installed on your computer. In general, each OpenDoc part lets you work on one type of document content — text, graphics, spreadsheets, charts, database information, sound, movies, Web pages, e-mail, and so on. You can drag any combination of OpenDoc parts into an OpenDoc document. Mix and match OpenDoc parts to create any document you can think of. If you want to use a new kind of content, you simply plug in an OpenDoc part that can handle it. Figure 14-14 shows an OpenDoc document with several parts.

OpenDoc changes how you think about working with documents. Instead of thinking in terms of applications, you think in terms of content. Instead of switching applications to work on a different kind of content, you just select the content you want to work on and the appropriate menus appear automatically in the menu bar. You can use the menu commands to view or edit the content.

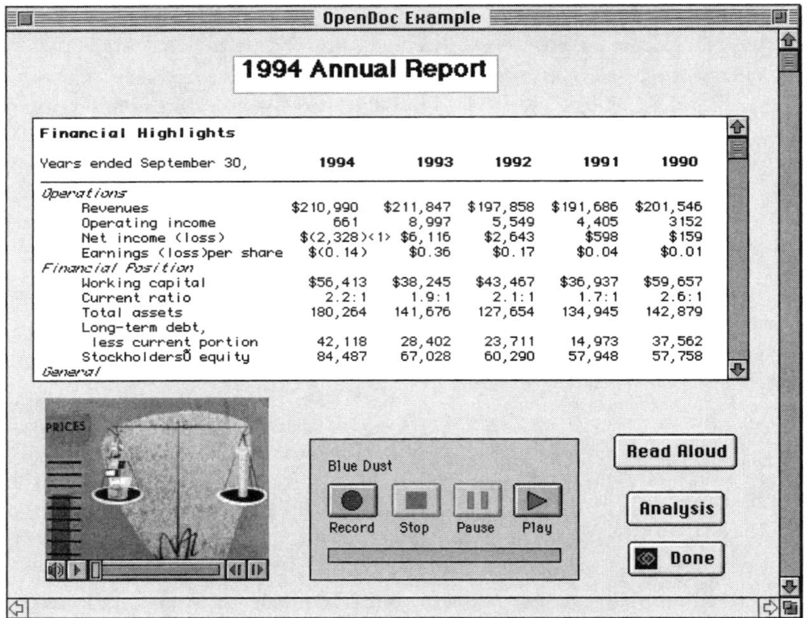


**Figure 14-14: OpenDoc documents can include all kinds of content.**

When you give your OpenDoc documents to other people, they need OpenDoc parts that handle the kinds of content in your document. That doesn't mean another person's OpenDoc parts have to be exactly the same as yours. For example, you might use the Brand X graphics part while someone else uses the Brand Y graphics part. As long as other people have OpenDoc graphics parts with the same basic capabilities as yours, those people will be able to view graphics in OpenDoc documents you send them. If you don't have the necessary OpenDoc part for a kind of content in an OpenDoc document you receive, OpenDoc displays a gray box in place of the content and tells you the name of the missing part.

OpenDoc and OpenDoc parts, which are also known as Live Objects, first became available in 1996 for Mac OS, Windows 95, AIX (IBM's variant of Unix), and OS/2 computers. Apple includes OpenDoc, a starter set of OpenDoc parts, and the Cyberdog suite of Internet-related OpenDoc parts with Mac OS 7.6. Those pieces are also available separately from Apple's software archive on the Internet or a commercial online service (see "Obtaining Installation Software" in Chapter 22).

For a more detailed description of how you work with OpenDoc documents, see "OpenDoc Plug-in Software Update" in Chapter 21.

# CHAPTER 14 CONCEPTS AND TERMS

- The Create Publisher command saves a live copy of selected material in an edition file, and the Subscribe To command puts a copy of an edition in the document on which you're working.
- You can publish editions to your shared folders and disks, and you can subscribe to editions from folders and disks that you're sharing with other computers on your network.
- In most programs, you can recognize publishers and subscribers by their gray borders.
- Although you usually can't change a subscriber directly, you may be able adorn it. To change the content of a subscriber, open its publisher by clicking the Open Publisher button in the Subscriber Options dialog box or the edition window.
- The Publisher Options and Subscriber Options dialog boxes control whether an individual publisher or subscriber is updated automatically or manually.
- Publishing and subscribing methods differ somewhat from one program to the next.
- With some programs, if you have the Macintosh Drag-and-Drop extension installed, you can copy items across window borders by selecting them and then dragging.
- OpenDoc plug-in software makes it easy to work on many kinds of content in a single document without switching applications.

**adorn**
To *adorn* a subscriber means to change its formatting.

**drag-and-drop editing**
To copy text, graphics, and other material within a document, between documents, and between applications. This capability works only with applications that are designed to take advantage of it. The versions of SimpleText, Sticky Memos, the Note Pad, the Scrapbook, and the Finder that are included with System 7.5 all work with drag-and-drop editing.

**edition**
A file that contains a live copy of the material in a publisher. When the publisher changes, the edition is updated. Subscribers contain copies of editions.

**Live Object**
An OpenDoc plug-in that's been through a certification process to ensure that it works and plays well with others.

**part**
An OpenDoc plug-in component that lets you work on a particular kind of content, which could be text, graphics, sound, movies, spreadsheets, charts, databases, Web pages, e-mail, or something else.

**publisher**
A section of a document, a copy of which has been saved as an edition for other documents to subcribe to.

**subscriber**
A copy of an edition that has been placed in a document and can be updated automatically when the edition is updated by its publisher.

CHAPTER FIFTEEN

# Collaborating with Others

- Apple Open Collaboration Environment (AOCE) offers communications between workgroup members directly on the desktop
- PowerTalk, Apple's first product based on AOCE, provides catalogs, messages, mail, and privacy support, letting you send and receive electronic mail from any compatible application or the desktop
- PowerShare server software enhances the security, catalog support, and messaging services of PowerTalk

The nature of personal and business communication is changing. On a personal level, people need to exchange messages and information quickly with people nearby and far away. They need to send and receive messages and documents even when all parties are not available at the same time. In business, more and more companies are forming flexible teams that come together quickly to accomplish a task and then break up. Communication among members of these ad hoc workgroups is becoming a crucial part of everyone's working world. In addition, decisions made lower down in organizations require the flow of information among a broader range of people. These changes in organizational structures and personal communication needs are driving an increasing demand for collaborative software.

System 7 Pro and System 7.5 (but not Mac OS 7.6 and later) provide collaboration services through PowerTalk system software and PowerShare collaboration server software. PowerTalk and PowerShare are based on Apple's collaboration technology called Apple Open Collaboration Environment (AOCE). This chapter describes AOCE, PowerTalk, and PowerShare.

## Apple Open Collaboration Environment (AOCE)

AOCE is not software; it's an operating system framework for the following communication services:

❖ **Mail and messaging** allow applications and people to send and receive messages and documents over a network whether or not the sender and receiver are available at the same time. Messages and documents can be stored until the recipient is ready to receive them.

- **Catalogs** store information about people and network services needed for effective collaboration.
- **Authentication and privacy** verify the identity of the sender and receiver, protect messages against snooping while en route, and simplify access to multiple file servers and network services.
- **Digital Signature** allows you to add a unique electronic signature to electronic documents, guaranteeing that a document has not been altered since you "signed" it and that you are who you say you are.

Some AOCE services, such as catalog and mailbox management, are based in the Finder. Many AOCE services are available to all applications, much like printing and file access. It's up to the application to include menu commands and other means of accessing the AOCE services, just as applications must include Print and Page Setup commands to access printing and Open and Save commands for file access. For example, a spreadsheet program that has a Send command in its File menu can send any spreadsheet as e-mail — no need to attach the spreadsheet file to an e-mail message created in an e-mail program. The Send command attaches a *mailer*, which like a paper envelope lists the address of the sender and recipient, to the spreadsheet. Your address is added to the mailer automatically. Even better, you can place the recipient on the mailer by dragging the recipient's icon from an open catalog on your desktop to the mailer at the top of the open spreadsheet. As another example, you can get a file from an on-line service such as CompuServe or eWorld, open the file in your word processing program, add comments, and send the amended file by e-mail to someone else. If you have the appropriate software installed, you can send a fax or e-mail message from within any application.

## Mail and messaging services

Just as System 7's file sharing (described in Chapter 9) enables you to share files with anyone on your network, AOCE enables you to exchange e-mail with anyone on the network. Prior to AOCE, exchanging e-mail required that everyone on the network have a special e-mail application. In addition, one Mac on the network had to run a program called an e-mail server, which managed e-mail exchanges like the post office manages paper mail. AOCE makes the e-mail server optional and does more than provide the mail transport infrastructure (analogous to the trucks, planes, and postal clerks of the U.S. Mail service).

The mail and messaging services of AOCE also provide a consistent interface so that you have to learn only one method for sending mail. Every application that takes advantage of AOCE's mail and messaging services can attach a standard mailer to a document (see Figure 15-1), causing the document to be sent as e-mail. Sending documents by e-mail becomes as easy and consistent as printing.

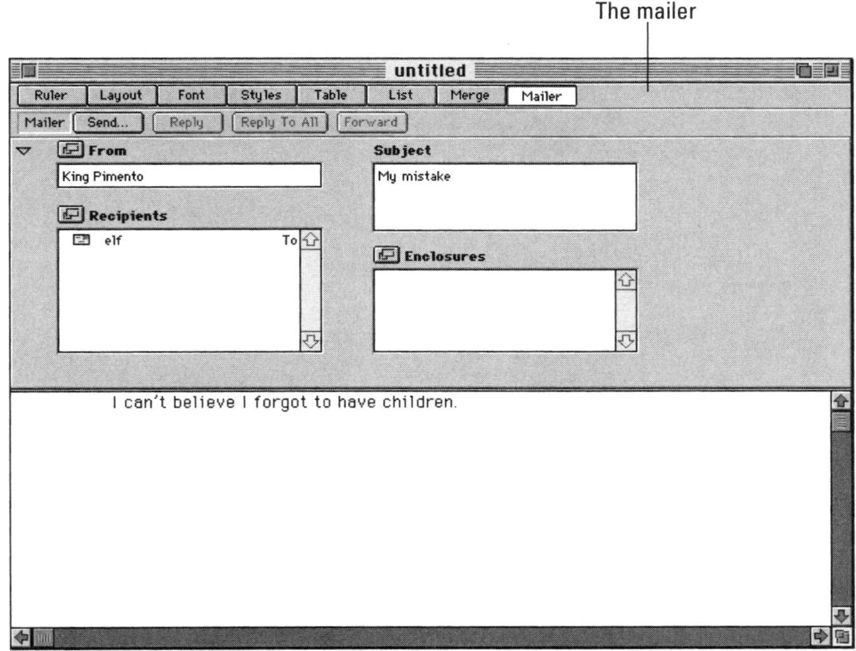


**Figure 15-1: The universal mailer attachment in an AOCE-compliant application.**

The mailer isn't the only standard interface item that AOCE provides. It also puts a universal mailbox for receiving or sending mail on your desktop.

Although AOCE doesn't require an e-mail server on the network, there are advantages to having one. An AOCE e-mail server can store messages sent to you while your Mac was not connected to the network (perhaps it was turned off) and forward them to you the next time you connect to the network. Likewise, the AOCE server can store and forward messages you send to other people. It makes sure that the message gets through, even when the recipient resides on a remote network.

In addition, you can send messages at stated times by using an *agent.* Agents are software entities that manage the flow of messages between computers. You can write your own agents with AppleScript (described in Chapter 18) serving as your front-end for message management. Your agent filters incoming messages and prioritizes them according to criteria that you set. Because Apple events are heavily involved with agents, you can send messages to perform work in your applications if these programs respond to Apple events.

## Catalog services

AOCE organizes your personal and network addresses into *catalogs*. You can move and copy items from one catalog to another by dragging, just as you move items between folders in the Finder. You can also drag items from catalogs to open documents of applications that include a Send command in the File menu or are otherwise designed to take advantage of AOCE services. For example, you can easily send e-mail to a team member by dragging that person's icon from your open catalog to the open e-mail. (The e-mail must be created by an AOCE-compliant program such as AppleMail, the AOCE mail program that Apple includes with System 7 Pro and System 7.5.)

Catalogs can hold other information, such as phone numbers, Internet addresses, and CompuServe numbers. Thus catalogs act like contact management programs, creating electronic business cards that can be enclosed in other messages or sent by themselves over the network. Workgroups can share catalogs to maintain common contact information, joint calendars, and so on.

Catalogs also manage AppleTalk network devices and network zones more efficiently than the Chooser.

## Authentication and privacy services

Today, when so many messages are flying through the ether, collaboration services must be able to ensure that communications remain private while in transit. An AOCE server encrypts and decrypts messages, making them unrecognizable to someone who manages to tap your network. The AOCE server also uses an encryption method to authenticate the identities of a message's sender and receiver. These authentication and privacy services are not provided unless your network has an AOCE server.

An AOCE server does not require AOCE to supply the correct passwords automatically when you access file servers or other network services. Instead of entering passwords individually for each file server or network service you use, you enter a single access code once. The access code verifies that you are who you say you are. After the verification process, AOCE automatically supplies passwords as needed so file servers and network services no longer interrupt you with password requests.

## Digital signatures

Digital signatures serve the same function as handwritten signatures, namely identifying the person who vouches for the accuracy of the signed document. Signatures make documents legally binding and trustworthy. Anyone can compare the document's signature with a sample signature and verify that the so-signed document is authentic. Digital signatures perform exactly the same function, providing a way to verify the authenticity of an electronic document.

# PowerTalk

PowerTalk software is the first Apple product based on AOCE technology. It runs on individual Macs to provide a consistent interface to AOCE services — mail and messaging, catalogs, authentication and privacy, and digital signature. In other words, PowerTalk provides the icons, windows, menu commands, and other means to manipulate AOCE services. It consists of several system extensions, as well as the AppleMail and DigiSign Utility applications, and requires the Finder that comes with System 7.1.1 (System 7 Pro) through System 7.5.5.

Installing PowerTalk inserts two new commands in the Finder's Special menu and places several new icons on your desktop as well as inside the PowerTalk folder and the Mail and Catalogs folder, as shown in Figure 15-2. These icons provide access to the following PowerTalk services:

- **Key Chain** keeps track of the passwords and other information (the "keys") you must supply to gain access to file servers and other network services. It automatically provides the correct password and other necessary information when you begin using a file server or network service.
- **Catalogs** keep track of information about individual people, groups, file servers and other network devices, and so on. This information simplifies sending e-mail, connecting to file servers, and using other cataloged items.
- **Mailbox** accumulates incoming and outgoing messages, faxes, e-mail, and voice mail.
- **AppleMail** creates and manages e-mail messages and files attached to them.
- **Digital Signature** applies an electronic signature to a document so that anyone with PowerTalk can verify who signed the document and can confirm that it has not been changed since that person signed it.

Installing PowerTalk adds AOCE services to the Finder and enables you to create e-mail with the AppleMail application, but it does not add AOCE services to other applications. It's up to the developers of other applications to add the menu commands necessary to take advantage of the AOCE services that PowerTalk enables. Developers must upgrade old applications to work with PowerTalk, and you must obtain and install the upgraded applications if you want to create e-mail and use other PowerTalk services from within your applications.

To gain any value from these PowerTalk collaboration services, you must network your Macintosh with other Macs that have PowerTalk installed. PowerTalk works on all types of AppleTalk networks — LocalTalk (using either Apple cabling or phone-type cabling), EtherTalk (using any type of Ethernet cabling), Apple Remote Access (using modems and telephone lines), and TokenTalk (using Token Ring cabling).

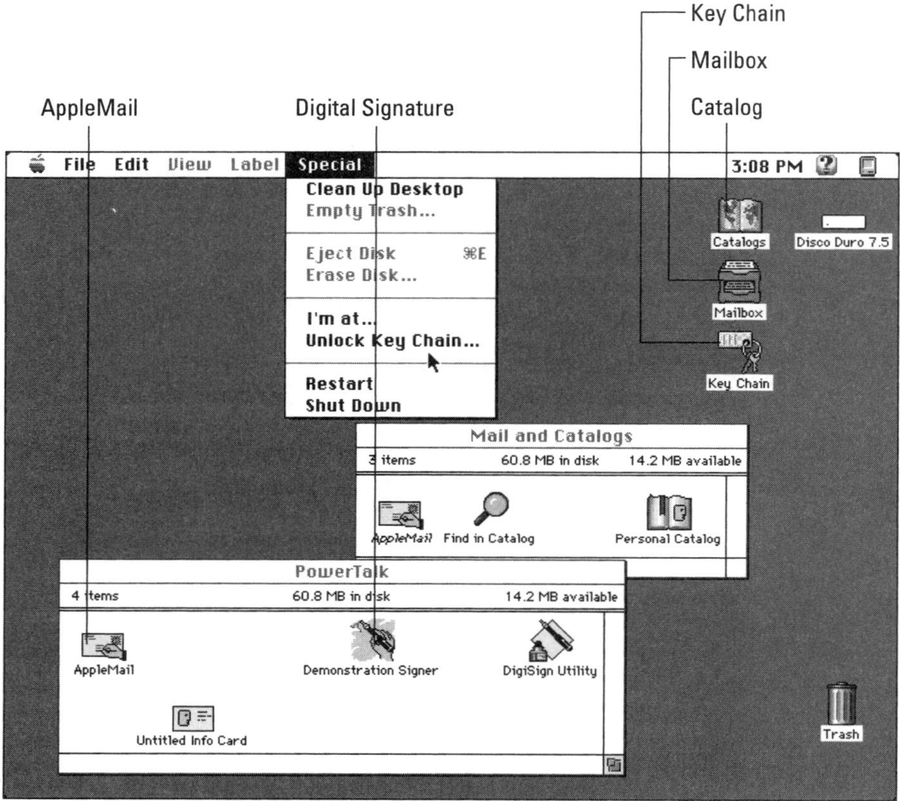


**Figure 15-2: PowerTalk at a glance.**

The following sections describe the PowerTalk collaboration services in more detail.

## Key Chain

Some of the most visible symbols of PowerTalk's presence on your desktop are its three new desktop icons that sit on the right side of your Mac's screen. The Key Chain is a powerful mechanism for automatic access to file servers and other network services that require a password to connect. In System 7.5, you can also have the Key Chain prevent unauthorized startup of your Mac. Using the Key Chain requires entering an *access code* (also called your Key Chain password or key). This access code protects your correspondences, because without knowledge of your password, no one can open your desktop mailbox.

## Setting up your Key Chain

You set up the Key Chain access code by choosing Unlock Key Chain from the Finder's Special menu. A dialog box appears and welcomes you to PowerTalk. When you click the Proceed button, another dialog box appears asking whether you have a PowerShare account. If you click the Yes button, the Mac searches the network for all available PowerShare services and displays a list of them in yet another dialog box, asking you to select your PowerShare service from the list. The Mac does not search for PowerShare services if you click the No button.

Next, another dialog box appears in which you must enter the Key Chain owner's name and access code (see Figure 15-3). You do not have to enter your real name or the Owner name entered in the Sharing Setup control panel (see "Identifying Your Macintosh" in Chapter 9). Your access code must be at least six characters long and should be easy for you to remember but hard for others to guess. Don't use your name or the name of a close relative. Longer access codes are harder to guess, as are access codes that combine two unrelated words, include punctuation and numbers, and mix uppercase and lowercase letters, such as "D1G+b0z0." When you finish setting up your access code, PowerTalk gives your Mailbox the name you entered.

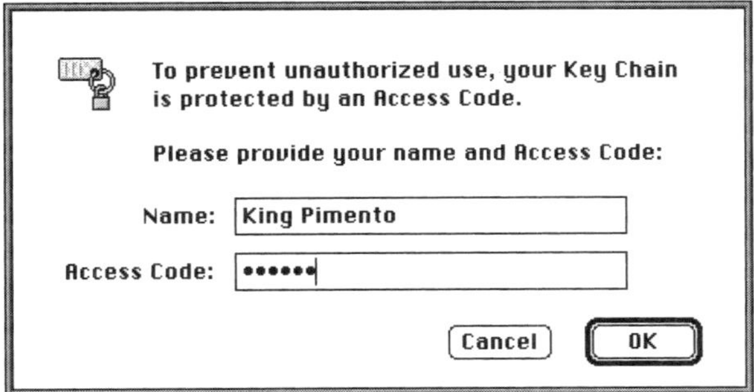


**Figure 15-3: Setup information for the Key Chain.**

## Changing Key Chain services

Your Key Chain always includes at least one service, the AppleTalk network mail service. You can add or remove file servers and other network services at any time. To see the network services that your Key Chain offers, double-click its icon. A list of services appears in the Key Chain window, as shown in Figure 15-4.

QUICK TIPS

## Setting Your Clock and Computer Name

When setting up PowerTalk, it's a good idea to check the accuracy of your system clock. PowerTalk uses the system clock to stamp your outgoing correspondence with the time and date. To check the clock and adjust it if necessary, you can use the Date & Time control panel. If you have not already done so, use the Sharing Setup control panel to set your computer's name (see "Identifying Your Macintosh" in Chapter 9). The name you set is the "address" to which other PowerTalk users can send you mail. Give your computer a name that makes it easy for others to find you. Consider including your name in the name of your computer: for example, "Biff's Power Mac."

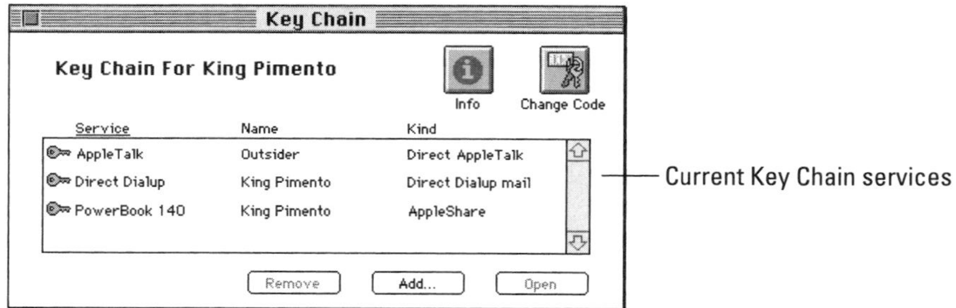


**Figure 15-4: The Key Chain window lists network services.**

To add the file server, simply connect to it as you usually do. Immediately after you enter the server's correct name and password, PowerTalk displays a dialog box asking whether you want to add the file server to your Key Chain. Click the Yes button to connect to the file server and add it to your Key Chain, click the No button to connect to the server without adding it to your Key Chain, or click the Cancel button to neither connect to the file server nor add it to your Key Chain. For details about connecting to a file server, see "Connecting as a registered user or guest" in Chapter 9.

To add another type of service, open your Key Chain icon and click the Add button in the Key Chain window.

To remove a service from your Key Chain, select the service in the Key Chain window and click the Remove button there. You cannot remove your AppleTalk network mail service.

### Changing the Key Chain name or access code

You can change the Key Chain owner's name or Key Chain access code at any time. Simply open the Key Chain icon on your desktop and click the Change Code button in the Key Chain window, as shown in Figure 15-5. If you try to open your Key Chain while it's locked, PowerTalk asks you to enter the correct Key Chain access code.

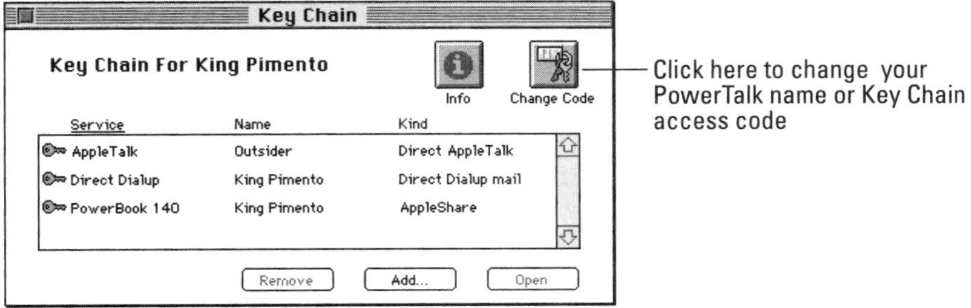


**Figure 15-5: Change your access code in the Key Chain window.**

When you change the name in the Key Chain window, PowerTalk changes the name of the desktop Mailbox icon to match. You cannot change the name of the Mailbox icon by using normal methods for editing icon names in the Finder (as described in "Renaming Icons" in Chapter 4). You can change the name of the Key Chain icon by using normal icon name-editing methods, however.

## Locking your Key Chain

The Key Chain access code provides the first line of defense against snooping eyes. You can lock your catalog and mailbox information by choosing Lock Key Chain from the Finder's Special menu. Choosing this command lets you walk away from your computer while restricting access to your data until you re-enter your access code. You can also set PowerTalk to lock your Key Chain after a certain period of inactivity. Use the PowerTalk Setup control panel, shown in Figure 15-6.

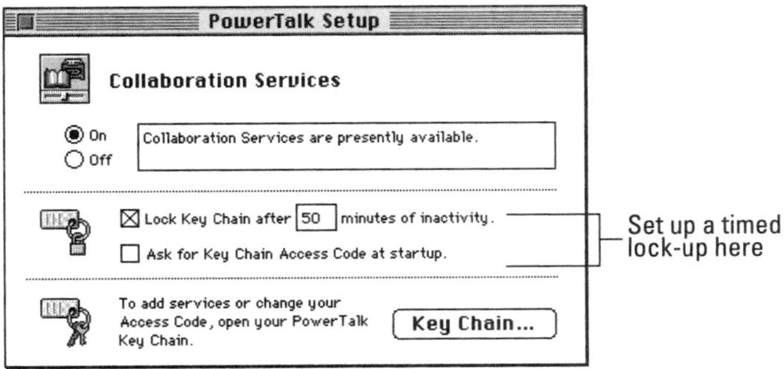


**Figure 15-6: The PowerTalk Setup control panel.**

You can also use draconian methods and turn off your collaboration services by clicking the Off option in the PowerTalk Setup control panel. When you restart your computer, no mailbox or catalog appears on the desktop. Your Key Chain icon appears when PowerTalk is off, but you can't open it. To regain access to your collaboration services, you have to go back into the PowerTalk Setup control panel, click On, and restart your Mac.

## Catalogs and information cards

PowerTalk organizes information about people, shared network devices, and services such as file servers. You can use catalogs to access these people and things quickly and find information about them. All Macs with PowerTalk have at least two catalogs, one shared and one personal.

### Shared catalogs

Every Mac with PowerTalk has an AppleTalk catalog, which contains information about each PowerTalk computer and file server on the network. To see the AppleTalk catalog, open the Catalogs icon on the desktop and then open the AppleTalk icon, as shown in Figure 15-7.

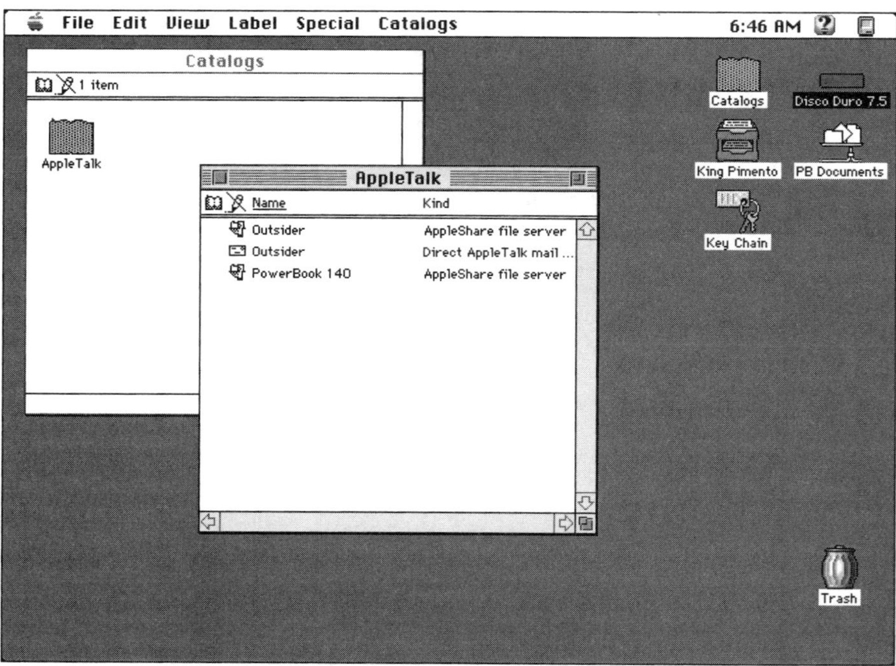


**Figure 15-7: Access the AppleTalk catalog via the Catalogs icon.**

The Catalogs icon contains shared catalogs. If you have other shared catalogs on your network, you see their icons when you open the Catalogs icon. You cannot actually move catalogs out of the Catalogs window, but you can make aliases of icons in the Catalogs window and place them anywhere you like. To make an alias of a catalog in the Catalogs window, simply drag the catalog's icon to the desktop or any folder window. The Finder automatically makes an alias; you don't have to use the Make Alias command.

## Personal catalogs

The other catalog on every Mac with PowerTalk is called the Personal Catalog. It resides on your Mac, so you can use your personal catalog even when you are not connected to a network. Initially, your personal catalog is in the Apple Menu Items folder or in the Mail and Catalogs folder inside the Apple Menu Items folder. Either way it is easy to open from the Apple menu, as shown in Figure 15-8. You can move your personal catalog anyplace you like and make aliases of it as needed.

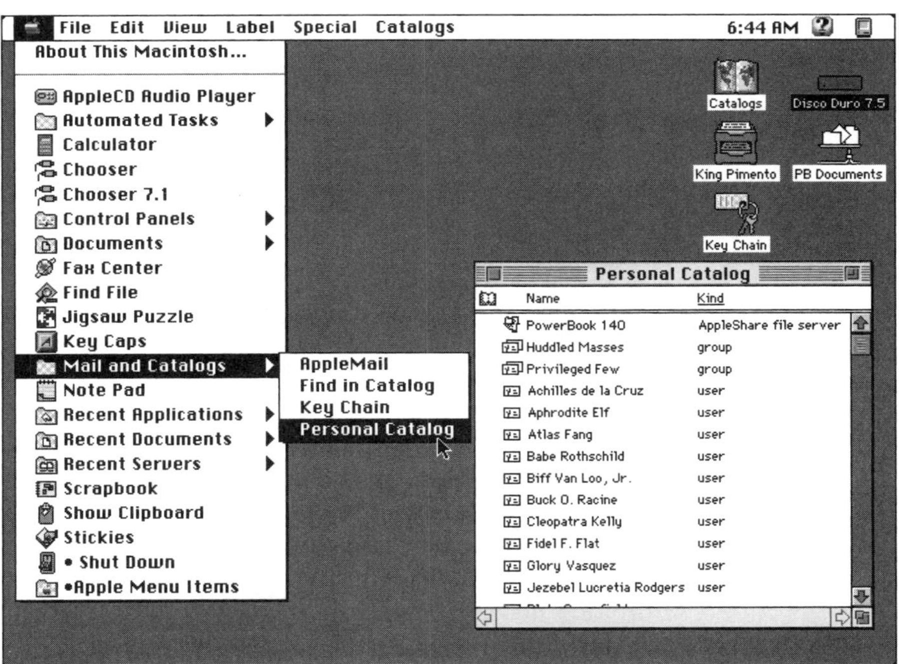


**Figure 15-8: Open your Personal Catalog from the Apple menu.**

Your personal catalog starts out empty. You add information about the individuals and groups with whom you work and about the file servers and network services you use. You can use your personal catalog to create a personal information management system, recording business or pleasure contact information that you can use to contact people by e-mail, fax, telephone, or postal mail.

If one personal catalog is not enough, you can create more. You can name them anything you want and place them anywhere on your hard disk for easy access. To create a new personal catalog, first open your main Personal Catalog (in the Apple menu) or open the Catalogs icon (on the desktop). A Catalogs menu appears next to the Finder's Special menu. Choosing New Personal Catalog from the Catalog menu creates a new personal catalog on the desktop, as shown in Figure 15-9. You can change its name by using normal icon-editing methods (see "Renaming Icons" in Chapter 4).

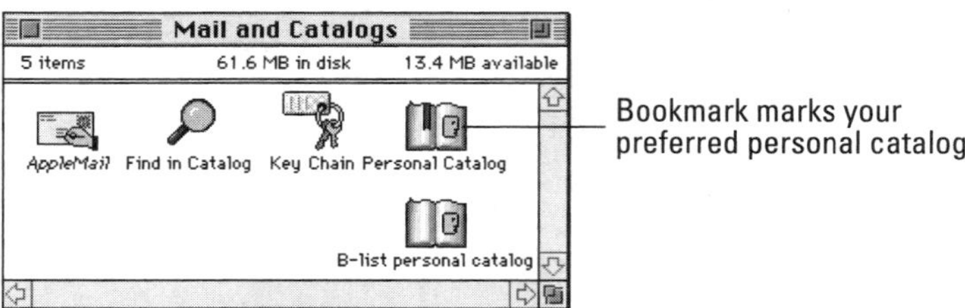


**Figure 15-9: Personal catalog icons.**

When you have more than one personal catalog, you can designate one as your preferred catalog. Applications that take advantage of PowerTalk services can always find items in your preferred personal catalog, no matter where it is on your hard disk. PowerTalk marks the icon of your preferred personal catalog with a bookmark (see Figure 15-9). Initially, your preferred personal catalog is the one in the Apple menu.

To designate a preferred personal catalog, select its icon and choose Get Info from the Finder's File menu to bring up the catalog's Info window (see Figure 15-10). In the Info window, click the Set Preferred button, and then close the Info window.

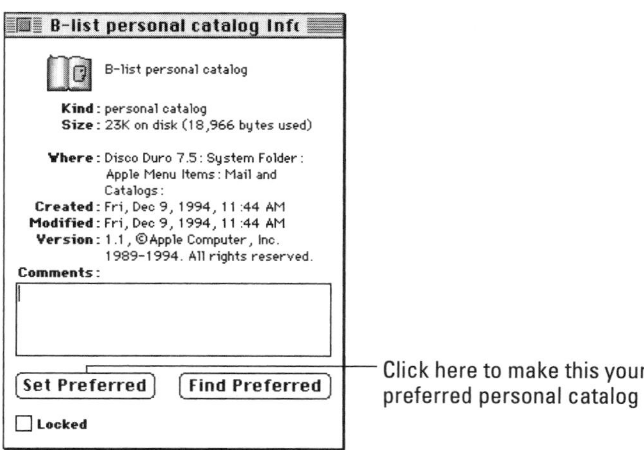


**Figure 15-10: A personal catalog's Info window.**

## Catalog items

PowerTalk represents each person, group, file server, network service, or other catalog item with an information card. Opening an information card (for example, by double-clicking it) brings up a window that contains information about the catalog item in a window. The content and appearance of an information card window depend on the kind of item the card represents.

- **User information cards** include a person's name, postal addresses, electronic addresses, telephone numbers, and any other pertinent details you want to record, such as hobbies and spouse's name (Figure 15-11 provides an example). Cards that contain electronic addresses simplify addressing e-mail to individuals, as described in the section "AppleMail and the Mailer" later in this chapter. To create a new user information card, open a personal catalog and choose New User from the Finder's Catalog menu.

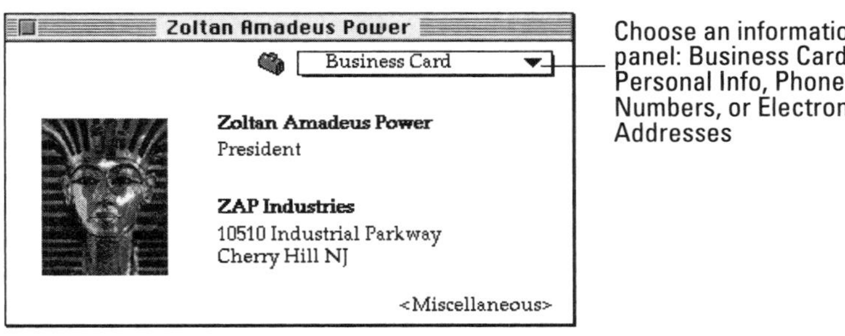


**Figure 15-11: The window of a user information card.**

- **Group information cards** contain aliases that point to user information cards (see Figure 15-12). You can use group information cards to address e-mail to groups, as described in the section "AppleMail and the Mailer" later in this chapter. To create a new group information card, open a personal catalog and choose New Group from the Finder's Catalog menu. To add a user to a group, drag the user's card from a personal catalog to the group's card. To add one group to another group, drag the first group's card to the second group's card.
- **File server information cards** contain the information you need to connect to the file servers (usually a registered user name and password) and a list of volumes that are available on the server (see Figure 15-13). Opening a volume listed in a server information card connects you to the server, puts the volume icon on your desktop, and opens the volume. Your AppleTalk catalog (in the Catalogs icon) automatically lists each file server to which you have access. You can copy a file server from the AppleTalk catalog to a personal catalog by dragging the server's card.

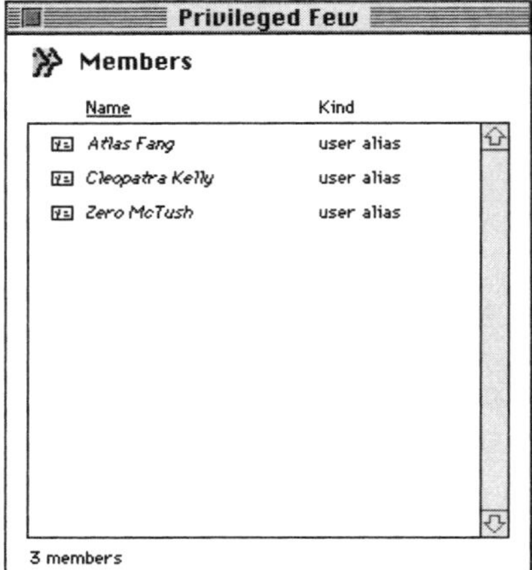


**Figure 15-12: The window of a group information card.**

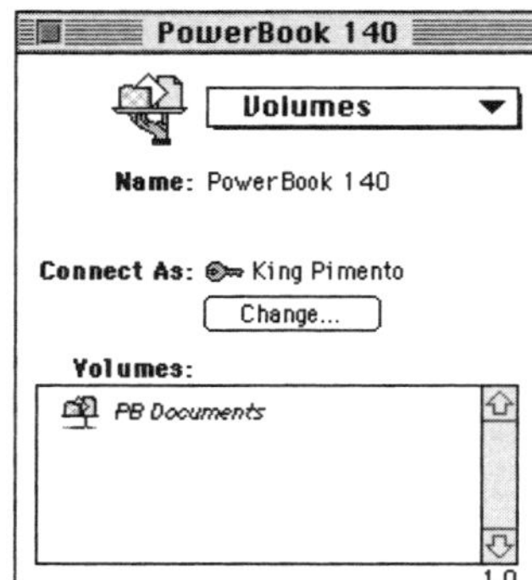


**Figure 15-13: The window of a file server information card.**

## Browsing and searching catalogs

While browsing a catalog, you can use the Finder's View menu to choose the order in which the catalog window lists items — by name or by kind. Alternatively, you can sort catalog items by clicking a column heading in the catalog window. The Finder underlines the heading of the column by which catalog items are currently sorted.

You can also use the View menu to list only file servers, only users (including groups), or only miscellaneous items in the catalog.

You use the Catalogs icon on the desktop to search for network catalogs and copy addresses from network-based catalogs to your information cards and catalogs. You can also locate shared catalogs over the network by using the Find in Catalog command from the Apple menu. This utility lets you search specific servers as well as search by type of information (for example, file servers or user information cards) and then copy found items to the location you choose.

If you're not sure which catalog contains an item you need, choose Find in Catalog from the Apple menu, as shown in Figure 15-14. (With System 7.5, Find in Catalog is in the Mail and Catalogs submenu of the Apple menu.) Use the pop-up menus in that window to tell the Finder which kind of item you are looking for and where to look. Type at least the first part of the item's name and click the Find button to begin the search. A list of matching items appears in the Find in Catalog window. You open a found item by double-clicking it, or you can drag a copy to the desktop or a personal catalog.

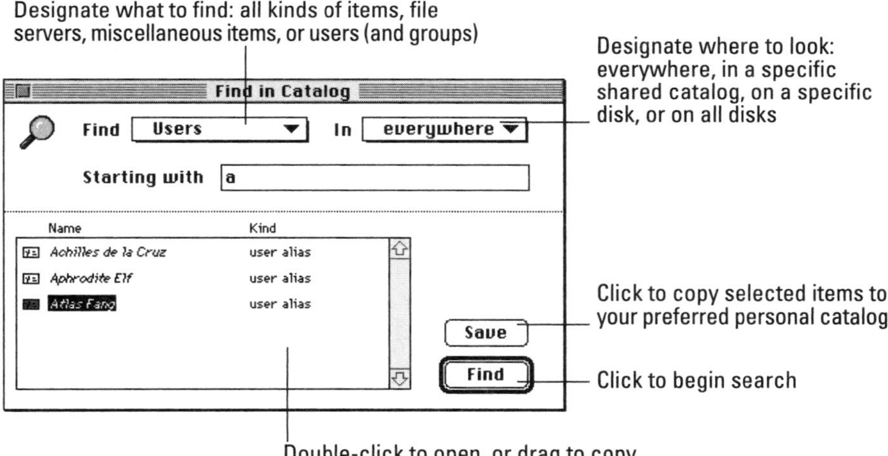


**Figure 15-14: Choose Find in Catalog from the Apple menu to search for a forgotten catalog item.**

# Messaging and mail

One exciting thing about PowerTalk is that it brings consistent e-mail services to both your desktop and to applications designed (or upgraded) to take advantage of PowerTalk. E-mail services, such as sending and receiving messages, enclosing documents, and sending carbon copies, are included with System 7 Pro and System 7.5, extending the reach of your Mac. PowerTalk's mail services are compatible with third-party e-mail systems, existing beside these stand-alone products to provide a standard interface throughout all applications.

With PowerTalk, you can perform the following mail activities:

❖ Send documents, applications, and folders by dragging them onto a user or group information card containing the recipient's electronic address.

- Centralize all your incoming and outgoing e-mail in one place in your desktop mailbox. It has an In Tray that lists all incoming mail, regardless of its origin, and an Out Tray showing mail that has been sent, regardless of its destination.
- With a PowerShare server on your network, you can send mail to workgroup members who are not logged onto the network. Likewise, you can receive mail even if your Mac was not connected to the network when the e-mail was sent. You can also check for PowerShare mail from another computer on the network.

By purchasing and installing additional software called a *personal gateway*, you can extend PowerTalk to handle other communications. You may install personal gateways to handle e-mail from other sources such as QuickMail, Microsoft Mail, the Internet, CompuServe, eWorld, America Online, and Prodigy. Other personal gateways can send and receive faxes and take phone messages.

## Checking your mailbox In Tray

The mailbox icon that appears on your desktop after you install PowerTalk is your file cabinet for incoming and outgoing mail. Your mailbox contains PowerTalk e-mail, which may include many different types of materials, such as documents, information cards, letters, application programs, fonts, and movies. Your mailbox may also contain e-mail from other sources, faxes, voice mail, and other communications if you have installed the appropriate personal gateway software.

When you open your mailbox, the first thing you see is your In Tray window, as shown in Figure 15-15. As you can probably guess, your In Tray lists mail that you have received. You can also gain access by selecting the In Tray from the Mailbox menu that appears in the menu bar when you open the mailbox.

### Sending Files and Folders as E-Mail

To send files, folders, or information cards as e-mail, drag them to a user or group information card icon. You can drag one item at a time or select several items and drag them together. After you drag items to a user or group information card, PowerTalk asks you to confirm or cancel the sending operation. Usually, you keep information cards in your personal catalogs, but you can also keep information cards or their aliases on the desktop or in a folder.

Note that you cannot send user information cards to a group by dragging the user information cards directly to a group information card icon. When you do so, the Finder assumes that you want to add the users to the group. To work around this situation, put the user information cards in a folder and drag the folder to the group information card icon.

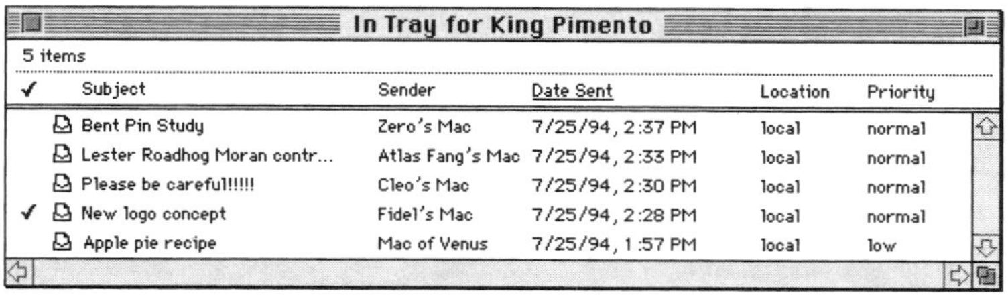

In Tray for King Pimento

5 items

| ✓ | Subject | Sender | Date Sent | Location | Priority |
|---|---|---|---|---|---|
| | Bent Pin Study | Zero's Mac | 7/25/94, 2:37 PM | local | normal |
| | Lester Roadhog Moran contr... | Atlas Fang's Mac | 7/25/94, 2:33 PM | local | normal |
| | Please be careful!!!!! | Cleo's Mac | 7/25/94, 2:30 PM | local | normal |
| ✓ | New logo concept | Fidel's Mac | 7/25/94, 2:28 PM | local | normal |
| | Apple pie recipe | Mac of Venus | 7/25/94, 1:57 PM | local | low |

**Figure 15-15: The In Tray lists your incoming mail.**

Opening your mail is as easy as double-clicking. You can also select a piece of mail and use the Open command to perform the same function. Delete mail by dragging its icon from the In Tray to the Trash. To copy a piece of mail, select and drag it to the desktop or a folder. The In Tray operates exactly like any window in the Finder, providing all the Finder's file management tools for your use with mail items.

You can categorize items in your In Tray by attaching tags to them. Select one or more items and choose Tags from the Finder's Mailbox menu (which appears to the right of the Special menu when the In Tray is the active window). The Tags window appears, in which you can either type a tag or choose one from the pop-up menu that lists previously used tags. To attach multiple tags to an item, use the Tags command repeatedly, specifying a different tag each time. To remove tags from the list that appears in the pop-up menu, use the Preferences command in the Mailbox menu.

The In Tray is designed for easy viewing of your mail from many vantage points. The View menu provides six views: by whether or not you have read your mail (indicated by a check mark next to the item), by subject, by sender, by date sent, by location, and by priority, as demonstrated in Figure 15-16. You can also use the View menu to filter your mail to show only those items you have read or not read. Alternately, you can click a column heading in the In Tray to sort the window's contents by that heading. The View menu also lets you filter your mail by tags you have previously attached to mail items, showing only those pieces of mail labeled with specific tags. You can edit tags in the Preferences dialog box, as well as add to or delete them as needed.

## Checking your mailbox Out Tray

After opening your desktop mailbox, you can choose Out Tray from the Mailbox menu to see a list of items you have sent recently, as shown in Figure 15-17. The Out Tray window shows you the status of any message that you have sent. The status possibilities are as follows:

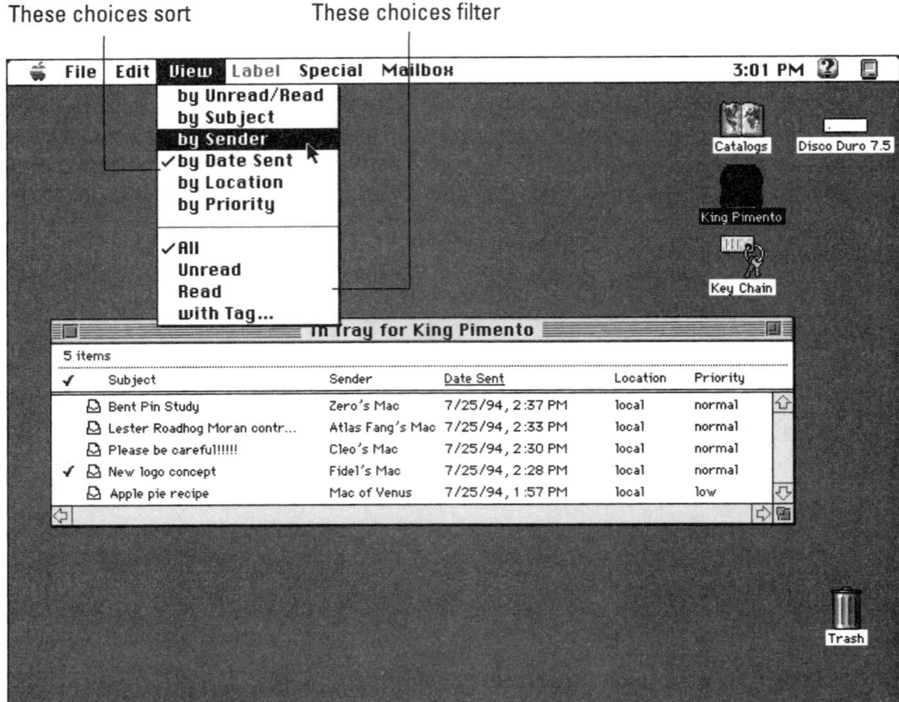


**Figure 15-16: Use the View menu to organize incoming mail.**

- **Sending** means that PowerTalk is in the process of sending out this mail.
- **Waiting** means that PowerTalk has not yet sent the mail.
- **Done** means that PowerTalk has delivered the mail from your Mac to its next destination (or has given up after repeated attempts).

Out Tray for King Pimento

3 items

| Subject | Date Sent | Status | Mail Connection |
|---|---|---|---|
| Steering Committee Meeting | 7/25/94, 3:40 PM | sending | Direct AppleTalk |
| Vasquez Promotion | 7/25/94, 3:37 PM | waiting | Direct AppleTalk |
| New Executive Assistant | 7/25/94, 3:35 PM | waiting | Direct AppleTalk |

**Figure 15-17: Review outgoing mail in the Out Tray.**

You can't tell by looking in your Out Tray if a recipient has read or even received mail you sent. All you know is that PowerTalk has sent mail marked Done over the network. If your network has a PowerShare server, you know that mail marked Done arrived at the server for forwarding.

Items marked Done are complete copies of the sent items. By default, PowerTalk stores Done items on your hard disk for 14 days. You can change how long PowerTalk retains sent mail by using the Preferences command in the Mailbox menu.

You can sort the Out Tray contents by various criteria. Use the View menu or click the column headings in the Out Tray window.

## AppleMail and the Mailer

You probably don't want to send all your mail from the Finder (by dragging documents to user and group information cards) any more than you want to print all your documents from the Finder. You want to be able to send documents as e-mail from the applications in which you create the documents. You can do so in applications that incorporate the PowerTalk Mailer (see Figure 15-18). The Mailer is like an address label for a document. It specifies the sender, lists the recipients, states the subject, and lists enclosed files. You use the Mailer the same way in every application that includes it.

The AppleMail application, which Apple includes with System 7 Pro and System 7.5, incorporates the Mailer. You can use AppleMail to write, send, read, reply to, and forward electronic letters and memos. AppleMail includes a pretty powerful text editor that lets you use multiple fonts, styles, and formats in your e-mail. You can also paste pictures, sounds, and QuickTime movies into e-mail that you create with AppleMail.

AppleMail is not the only application that incorporates the Mailer. QuickMail AOCE, for example, is an alternative e-mail application with the same basic capabilities as AppleMail. ClarisWorks 2.1 through 4.0, an integrated productivity application, lets you attach a mailer to any ClarisWorks document.

The Mailer is linked to your preferred personal catalog, your shared catalogs, and your Key Chain, making addressing as easy as clicking or dragging. You can also search catalogs from the Mailer and type addresses directly if necessary. If you want to enclose files or folders with a message, you can select them from a directory dialog box (like the one you get with an Open command) and drag their icons from folder windows or the desktop to the Mailer.

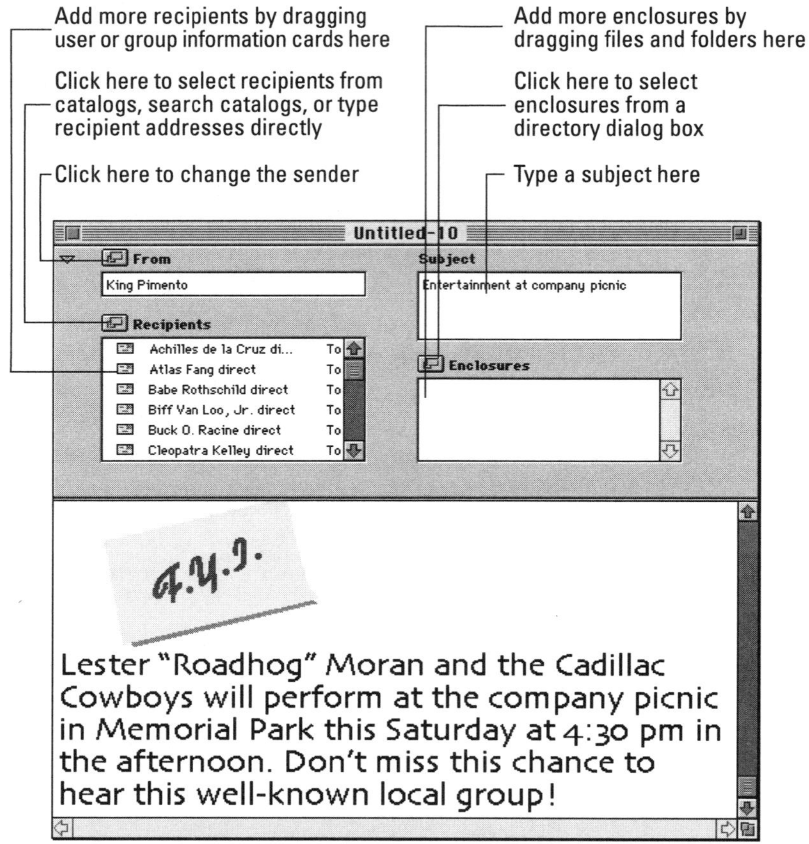


**Figure 15-18: The PowerTalk Mailer on an AppleMail letter.**

## Sending e-mail

After filling out a mailer, you send it and its contents with the Send command, whose menu location varies from one application to the next. In AppleMail, the Send command is in the Mail menu. In ClarisWorks 2.1, the Send command is in the Mail submenu of the File menu. Choosing the Send command brings up a Send dialog box, as shown in Figure 15-19.

In the Send dialog box, you can use the pop-up menu to choose a format for e-mail to which the Mailer is attached. The choice of formats is not the same in every application. In AppleMail, you can choose the AppleMail format or the Snapshot format. When you choose the AppleMail format, the recipient is able to read and edit the e-mail by using AppleMail or an application that understands the

## Typing Addresses Directly

To type an address directly in a mailer, click the Recipient button to bring up the Mailer's panel for locating and adding recipients, as shown in the following figure. In the Recipients panel, click the button labeled with a picture of a pencil to display the panel for typing an address. As you type, keep the following guidelines in mind:

- ❖ Pay strict attention to capitalization, spelling, and punctuation. Type the address correctly or the mail will not reach the addressee.
- ❖ If your network does not have a PowerShare server, PowerTalk assumes that you are sending the mail to a recipient located in your zone. If the recipient is not located in your zone, specify the zone in the following format: *name@zone* (where *name* is the recipient's name and *zone* is the recipient's zone). For example, if the recipient's name is Zoltan Amadeus Power and his zone is Pellucidar, then the complete address is Zoltan Amadeus Power@Pellucidar.
- ❖ Be as complete as possible when typing PowerShare addresses to speed up sending. Enter zones and folder names where appropriate. Use the @ symbol between the recipient's name and the catalog name, and put colons between folder names, as in Aphrodite Elf@Laconia:Sparta.
- ❖ When you finish typing an address, you can add it to the list of recipients by clicking the To button or the CC button in the Type-In Addressing panel. You can also designate this address to receive a blind copy by pressing Option, which changes the CC button to a BCC button, and clicking that button. Other recipients don't see addresses that receive blind copies.

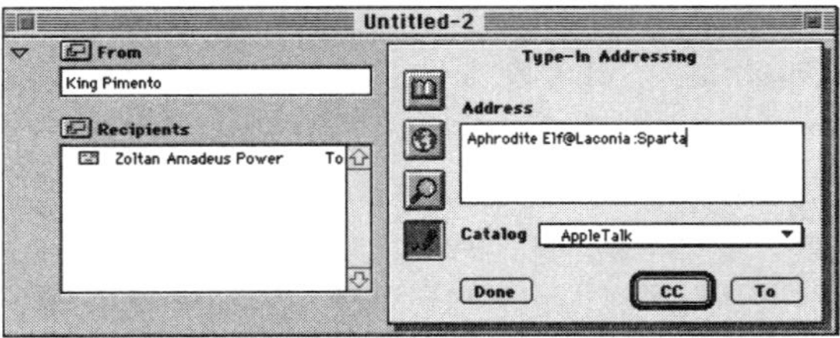


AppleMail format. The recipient can copy text, pictures, sounds, and movies that you included in the e-mail. When you choose the Snapshot format, the recipient gets a picture of the e-mail and cannot copy individual parts of it. The Snapshot format creates a PICT file that many applications can read, including SimpleText. In applications other than AppleMail, you may not be able to choose the AppleMail format, but you probably can choose a proprietary format that works with the application you're using. ClarisWorks 2.1, for example, gives you a choice of ClarisWorks, AppleMail, and Snapshot formats (and offers other formats if you have translators installed in the Claris folder in your System Folder). You can also

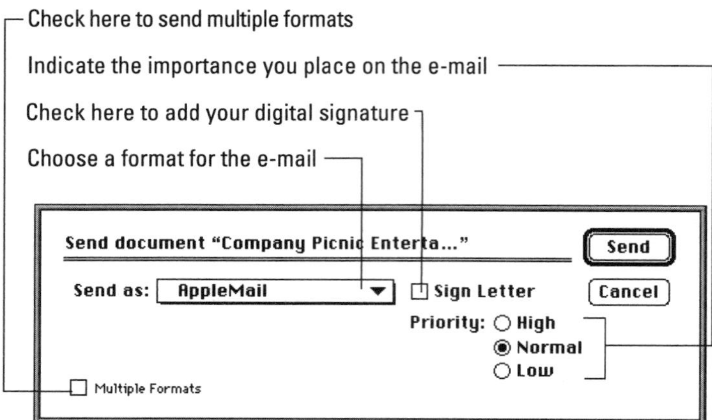


**Figure 15-19: Set options for sending e-mail in the Send dialog box.**

elect to use multiple formats to ensure that the recipients can open the letter even if they do not have AppleMail installed. Click the Multiple Formats checkbox to turn on this option. Note that sending e-mail in multiple formats takes up more disk space, but it is good insurance if you do not know which applications the recipients have. Your choice of format does not affect enclosed files, whose formats were established when they were created.

You can set a priority in the Send dialog box, but it has no effect on how PowerTalk handles e-mail. The priority you set only indicates to recipients of the e-mail how important you consider it to be.

Setting the Sign Letter option in the Send dialog box puts your digital signature on the e-mail item to ensure its authenticity. To use this option, you must have a DigiSign Signer file, which is described in the section "Digital Signatures" later in this chapter. You do not need to sign a letter digitally to ensure its authenticity if you have a PowerShare account. PowerShare guarantees that the source of every piece of e-mail its servers handle is genuine.

## Reading e-mail

E-mail sent to you by someone using AppleMail, QuickMail AOCE, ClarisWorks 2.1, or another application that incorporates the PowerTalk Mailer appears in your In Tray. To read e-mail, double-click its icon. The e-mail opens in the application that created it. If the e-mail has enclosures, you can open them by double-clicking them or by dragging them to the desktop or a folder.

### Using PowerTalk with a PowerBook

PowerTalk provides special tools just for PowerBook users. Installing PowerTalk adds the I'm At command to the Finder's Special menu. This command lets you activate and deactivate individual electronic addresses based on your location. For example, you can directly connect your PowerBook to an AppleTalk network when you're at work, but you can use Apple Remote Access to connect to the network by modem and phone lines from home.

Choosing the I'm At command brings up the dialog box shown in the figure. In that dialog box, you choose your location from a pop-up menu, and then you select the PowerTalk services available at that location. Your service options depend on what you have installed, such as the following:

- **Direct AppleTalk Mail**, which uses the AppleTalk catalog to send mail.
- **PowerShare Server Mail,** which uses the shared catalogs and PowerShare to manage mail.
- **Direct Dialup Mail,** which uses Apple Remote Access to connect to a network by modem and phone lines.

If you choose Off-Line as your location, PowerTalk disconnects you from all service options. You can still create and send e-mail and read e-mail in your In Tray. Items you send while off-line go into your Out Tray, and PowerTalk delivers them later when you connect with the appropriate service.

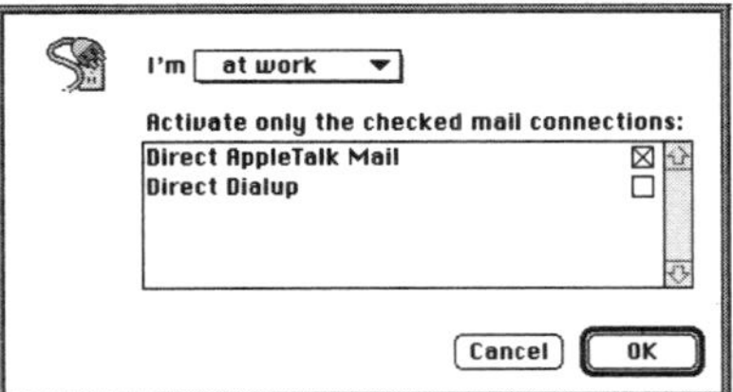


You can reply to received e-mail by using the Reply command, and you can forward e-mail by using the Forward command. The menu location of these two commands varies from one application to the next. In AppleMail, they are in the Mailer menu. In ClarisWorks 2.1, the Reply and Forward commands are in the Mail submenu of the File menu.

## Digital signatures

With a PowerTalk digital signature, you can vouch for the content of an electronic document just as you vouch for the content of paper mail by signing your name to it. Anyone can use a Mac with PowerTalk installed to verify a digital signature. You don't have to apply a digital signature to items you send electronically with PowerTalk software. A document sent without your digital signature is like a memo or letter sent without your handwritten signature — the recipient can't verify that it truly came from you. A digital signature goes a step further than a handwritten signature, guaranteeing that the document has not been altered since you applied the digital signature.

Before you can apply a digital signature to any document, you must obtain a special file called a Signer. You create an unapproved Signer with the DigiSign utility program that comes with System 7 Pro and System 7.5. When DigiSign creates an unapproved Signer, it also creates an approval request form that you submit to an agency or person authorized to issue you an approval file. The approval file contains the information the DigiSign program needs to change your unapproved Signer into an approved Signer. Once you have an approved Signer, you can apply digital signatures in the Finder, AppleMail, and other applications that incorporate the PowerTalk mailer.

To apply your digital signature to a file in the Finder, drag the file to your Signer. PowerTalk asks you to enter your DigiSign identification code, as shown in Figure 15-20. (You specify your code when you create your unapproved Signer, and you can change your code with the DigiSign program.) To apply your digital signature in AppleMail or another application that incorporates PowerTalk Mailers, set the Sign Letter option in the Send dialog box (as described in the section "Sending E-mail" earlier in this chapter).

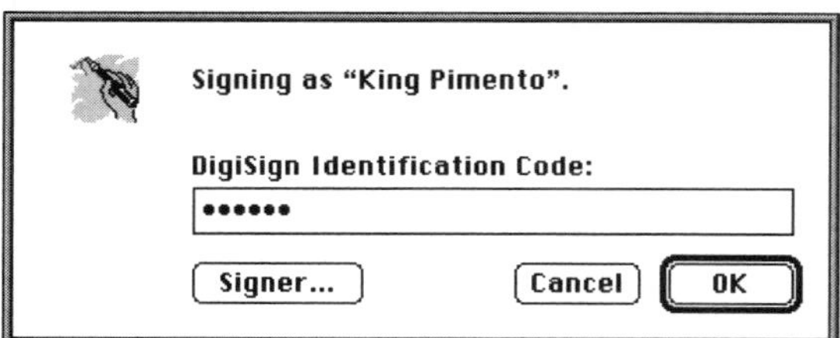


**Figure 15-20: Use your secret Signer code to set up a digital signature for a document.**

Don't tell anyone your DigiSign identification code. Anyone who knows your code can use your Signer to forge your digital signature. PowerTalk cannot prevent this type of forgery or other intentional misuse (such as obtaining a Signer with false ID).

When you apply a digital signature to a document, it does not show up on the document like a handwritten signature does. The digital signature appears as a button in the document's Info window, as shown in Figure 15-21 (you display a document's Info window with the Finder's Get Info command). Clicking this verification button brings up a dialog box that asks whether you want to verify or remove the signature. After you click Verify, a dialog box appears, displaying information about the signature and either verifying or not verifying the digital signature. PowerTalk is unable to verify a digital signature if it has been tampered with or if the document has been altered since it was signed.

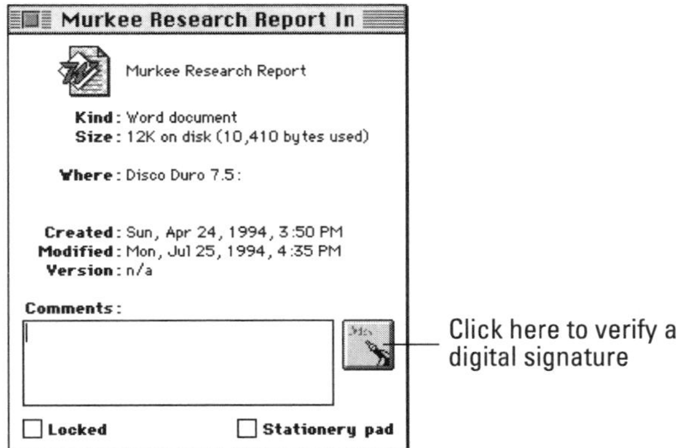


**Figure 15-21: Verify a digital signature in the signed document's Info window.**

# PowerShare Servers

PowerShare servers augment the collaboration services provided by PowerTalk. Installing PowerShare software on a Mac being used as a server on the local network adds the following collaboration services to every PowerTalk user on the network:

- **Shared catalogs** let network users share a common pool of information cards.
- **Authentication and privacy** automatically authenticate the addresses of a message's sender and receiver and guarantee the security of e-mail.
- **Store-and-forward messaging** lets you send mail to people who are not currently connected to the network and lets other people send you e-mail when you are not connected to the network.

In addition, PowerShare servers can provide central access to collaboration services outside the local network — external e-mail, file servers, and so on.

These additional services are managed by two PowerShare servers, the Catalog server and the Mail server. They can reside on one Mac or two and can reside on the same Mac as an AppleShare server (described in Chapter 9) or not.

## PowerShare catalogs

As with PowerTalk, the basic foundation of PowerShare is the catalog. On PowerShare, catalogs store information about the different members of a network, be they approved users, groups, file servers, other shared devices, administrative materials such as forms, or planning materials such as calendars and project management tools. PowerShare catalogs help locate shared items on the network and assist in managing information about these networked items.

A person acting as system administrator sets up PowerShare's Catalog server, making its catalogs available through the Catalogs icon located on each networked Mac. The administrator decides which catalogs can be shared and who can share them. The Catalogs icon is the doorway to PowerShare resources, such as AppleShare file servers, shared printers, fax modems, and data modems. In addition, PowerShare catalogs list user and group information in the same fashion as Personal catalogs, letting users share addresses and data about network members.

## Authentication and privacy

The Catalog server acts as a trusted third party, vouching for the authenticity of users who share information over the network. Authentication of users prevents unauthorized access to catalogs and files. Each user or group recorded in a catalog has an authentication key. These keys, managed on individual Macs by the PowerTalk Key Chain, serve to verify approved use of collaborative services located on the PowerShare system, such as the sending of e-mail to workgroup members. When an authenticated session is established, data transmitted across the network is encrypted to thwart network crackers.

## PowerShare e-mail

PowerShare Mail servers route and store e-mail sent between network users. The Mail server stores e-mail and forwards it when its destination becomes available. Mail sent to users who are not currently connected is not lost, but is held and delivered as soon as they connect.

# CHAPTER 15 CONCEPTS AND TERMS

- AOCE provides extensive enhancements to Macintosh communications and security by bringing Mac standards to the world of electronic mail.
- PowerTalk lets you organize your information flow, providing centralized storage areas for personal contact information, network addresses, and so forth via catalogs, as well as a central repository for all incoming and outgoing information via the Mailbox. The Mailer utility lets you use the Mac's intuitive interface to send e-mail from any compatible application or the Finder. Digital signature technology lets you send tamper-proof documents over the network, bringing you closer to a paperless office. In addition, the Key Chain secures all communications. Altogether, PowerTalk is the first step toward true data sharing and collaboration among workgroup members.
- PowerShare server software enhances the power of PowerTalk's desktop communications environment by providing authentication services, store-and-forward messaging services, and shared catalog services that let workgroup members safely share proprietary information.

**access code**
A password that you enter to verify that you are who you say you are.

**agent**
A software entity that manages the flow of messages between computers. Filters incoming messages and prioritizes them according to criteria you set.

**AOCE (Apple Open Collaboration Environment)**
An operating system framework that provides mail and messaging, catalogs, authentication and privacy, and digital signature services, many of which are available in all applications. Enables you to send e-mail to anyone on your network, making the formerly required e-mail server optional.

**bookmark**
Marks your preferred personal catalog.

**catalog**
Holds information such as phone numbers, Internet and postal addresses, and CompuServe numbers. Acts like a contact management program, creating electronic business cards that you can enclose in other messages or send them alone over the network.

**digital signature**
Functions as a handwritten signature, identifying the person who vouches for the accuracy and authenticity of the signed document.

**encryption**
The process of making messages unrecognizable to someone who taps into your network without authorization and authenticating the identities of a message's sender and receiver.

**file server**
A hardware or software mechanism that makes files centrally available for other Macs on a network.

**In Tray**
The folder in your Mailbox that lists mail that you have received. You can categorize items in your In Tray by attaching tags to them.

**Key Chain**
A master key that simplifies access to file servers and other network services that require a password to connect.

**mailer**
The electronic equivalent of an address label and envelope. Specifies the sender, recipients, subject, and enclosed files for a piece of e-mail.

**Out Tray**
The folder in your Mailbox that lists the mail you have sent recently, showing you the status of each message: Sending, Waiting, or Done.

**personal gateway software**
Additional software that you can purchase and install to extend PowerTalk to handle other communications, such as e-mail from CompuServe, Microsoft Mail, the Internet, and America Online.

**PowerShare server**
Augments the collaboration services provided by PowerTalk, adding shared catalogs, authentication and privacy, and store-and-forward messaging services. Also provides central access to collaboration services outside the local network.

**PowerTalk**
The first Apple software product based on AOCE technology. Provides a consistent interface to AOCE services, such as mail and messaging, catalogs, authentication and privacy, and digital signature. Consists of the AppleMail and DigiSign Utility applications as well as several system extensions.

**tag**
Attach one or more of these items to an e-mail message to categorize it. You can sort and filter your mail by using these tags.

CHAPTER SIXTEEN

# Enjoying Multimedia

- The tricks that QuickTime uses to play back movies on a Macintosh
- How QuickTime extends the system software
- What's in a QuickTime movie
- What's new in QuickTime 2
- Comparing the standard compression methods
- How you control movie playback
- Finding and filming movie content
- Coming to grips with data in motion

With System 7.1 and later, you get QuickTime, Apple's multimedia technology. Quick-Time is a large system extension that gives your Mac the capability of playing movies, animation, sound, and other time-related data.

Don't throw away your TV set yet, though, because today's QuickTime movies are a bit jerky on all but the fastest Macs. What's more, movies take up lots of disk space, so you'll want a big hard disk and a CD-ROM drive.

QuickTime can display movies on a monochrome monitor, but it requires a color-capable Mac (one originally equipped with a 68020, 68030, 68040, or PowerPC processor) with at least 5MB of RAM. If you want to make movies, not just watch other people's work, you'll need more RAM and special equipment costing $500 to $8,000 to set up a movie-making studio on your Mac.

Why would anyone want to give up a lot of disk space to watch inferior movies? For one thing, they're fun. Beyond its entertainment value, however, QuickTime is being used for training, entertainment, communications, presentations, and other purposes. The QuickTime pioneers who worked with version 1 in 1991 knew that QuickTime's limitations, burdens, and costs will decrease over time as its technology improves and storage costs inexorably come down. Case in point: With the delivery of QuickTime version 1.5 in October 1992 — less than a year after delivery of version 1 — Apple improved picture quality fourfold and improved playback rates of movies stored on CD-ROM, movies stored on network file servers, and all movies played on black-and-white Macs. QuickTime 2, which shipped in June 1994, provides even faster playback of bigger movies.

QuickTime 1.5 and later versions also work with Kodak's Photo CD technology, which enables you to have your photographs digitized onto a CD-ROM. With a compatible CD-ROM drive and a recent version of QuickTime, you can view thumbnail miniatures of your digitized photos, see a slide show of the photo images, and paste the images as standard Mac PICT graphics into almost all applications.

In addition, QuickTime 1.6.1 and later versions can open audio tracks on a CD. With an Apple CD 300 or 300i CD-ROM drive, you can convert an audio CD to a QuickTime movie.

# The Magic behind QuickTime

A Mac shouldn't be able to play movies any more than a bumblebee should be able to fly. A single full-screen color picture on a 14-inch monitor takes a megabyte of disk space. To get 30 pictures per second, which is what you see on TV, the Mac would have to store, retrieve, and display 30MB per second. Dream on.

QuickTime pulls every trick in the book to play movies. Most movies are considerably smaller than the full 640 by 480 pixels available on a 14-inch color monitor. Although QuickTime 2 can play back full-screen movies from a hard drive on many recent Mac models, quarter-screen movies (320 by 240 pixels) are the largest that play back well from double-speed CD-ROM drives, such as the Apple CD 300. With older versions of QuickTime, the optimum movie size is smaller.

Furthermore, many QuickTime movies play back fewer frames per second than TV or movies. Whereas TV shows 30 *fps* (frames per second) in the United States and other countries that use the NTSC standard (25 in Europe and other places that use the PAL or SECAM standards), QuickTime movies generally play at 15 fps. QuickTime 2 is the first version that can achieve 30 fps at a useful movie size (320 by 240) without special hardware, and it can achieve that playback rate only from a hard disk on a Mac that has a 68040 or PowerPC processor.

Showing smaller pictures at slow frame rates reduces the amount of data to be stored, retrieved, and displayed, but not nearly enough. So QuickTime compresses movies, throwing out the redundant parts.

# QuickTime Technology

QuickTime extends the standard Macintosh system software so that you can incorporate time-based data, such as video and animation, into documents that you create with mainstream application programs. After installing QuickTime, you can copy and paste movies as easily as you copy and paste graphic images. You also can use QuickTime to compress individual graphics. When you open the compressed graphic, QuickTime decompresses it automatically.

Installing QuickTime puts two new pieces of system software into your System Folder. The QuickTime extension goes into System 7's special Extensions folder. A new version of the Scrapbook desk accessory, which can play QuickTime movies,

goes into System 7's Apple Menu Items folder. If the Apple Menu Items folder contains an old desk accessory named Scrapbook, the new Scrapbook desk accessory replaces it.

There is more to QuickTime than software, as Figure 16-1 shows. Video, sound, animation, and other time-related data, which Apple collectively calls QuickTime movies, are a new type of data. To represent this data in the computer's memory and on disk, QuickTime establishes a standard format called MooV. Time-based data tends to be very bulky, so QuickTime provides a mechanism for compressing and automatically decompressing it. QuickTime also extends the standard PICT graphics format to include individual compressed images. Furthermore, QuickTime establishes standard methods for you to recognize movies and control movie playback.

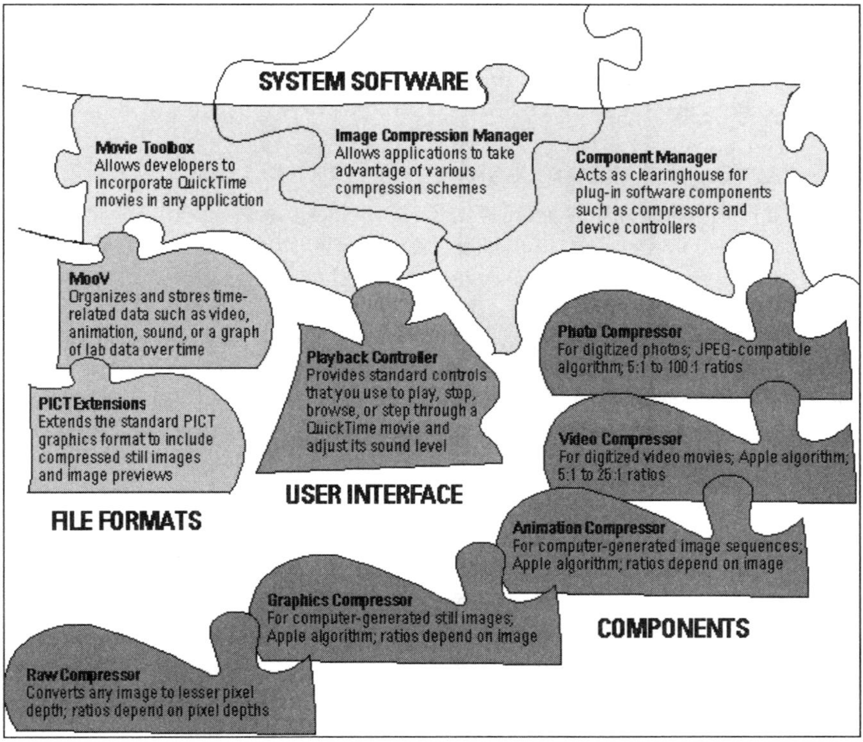


**Figure 16-1: QuickTime at a glance.**

# System Software

The QuickTime extension provides three major pieces of system software: the Movie Toolbox, the Image Compression Manager, and the Component Manager. Application programs take advantage of these software modules to play back or record QuickTime movies.

## Movie Toolbox

The Movie Toolbox includes software tools with which application developers can give old and new programs the capability of copying, pasting, and playing back movies. You then can use the Cut, Copy, and Paste commands with a QuickTime movie as though it were an ordinary graphic; the application program has the Movie Toolbox do the work.

When you play a movie, the Movie Toolbox takes care of synchronizing audio, video, animation, and other time-related data, regardless of system speed. An application doesn't have to do anything to make a QuickTime movie run at the same speed on a stripped Mac LC as on a loaded Power Mac 8100/80.

## Image Compression Manager

The Image Compression Manager provides software tools for image compression and decompression. Application developers incorporate these tools, called *codecs* (for compressor-decompressor), into applications so that you can compress movies when you record them and graphic images when you save them. You choose a compression method from a pop-up menu, which lists the compression methods available on your system that are relevant to the type of image or movie that you are compressing (see Figure 16-2). The Image Compression Manager controls the compression.

**Figure 16-2: Choosing a compressor (also known as a codec).**

When you open a compressed graphic image or play back a QuickTime movie, the Image Compression Manager automatically applies the correct codec to decompress the image or the movie. You can add or remove codecs by dragging icons in or out of the System Folder; the Image Compression Manager automatically revises the pop-up menu for the application program.

## Component Manager

The Component Manager handles modular software tools called *components*. These components are to Macintosh systems what stereo components are to music systems. Some people want the simplicity of a preconfigured stereo system; others prefer to mix and match pre-amps, amps, equalizers, tuners, CD players, tape drives, and speakers. The Component Manager brings similar flexibility to application programs.

The QuickTime extension has several types of built-in components, including the following:

- ❖ Movie controller components that provide a standard interface for playing back QuickTime movies
- ❖ Clock components that provide timing signals
- ❖ Media handler components that access data and interpret it as a movie or other time-based data
- ❖ Image compressor components that compress and decompress video, animation, and individual graphics
- ❖ Sequence grabber components that enable applications to obtain video and sound from sources outside the Macintosh and to save the video and sound as a QuickTime movie
- ❖ Video digitizer components that obtain and digitize video from an analog source, such as a VCR or camcorder
- ❖ Movie data exchange components that import nonmovie data into a QuickTime movie — for example, converting still pictures to frames in a movie
- ❖ Preview components that create and display previews of QuickTime movies

You can add more components by dragging icons into the System Folder. For example, some add-on components compress and decompress graphics faster than QuickTime's built-in graphics compressor. Some components are entirely unrelated to QuickTime.

# What's in a MooV?

Although Apple's QuickTime file format is dubbed MooV, it encompasses more than just visual data. In fact, MooV is designed to organize, store, and exchange any time-related data.

Each QuickTime movie contains one or more tracks; a simple movie might consist of one video track and one sound track. A more complex movie may have several video tracks, several audio tracks, and closed-caption tracks for text subtitles. Each video track could be designed specially for playback with a certain number of available colors (black and white, 256 grays, 256 colors, thousands of colors, or millions of colors). Each audio track could provide dialog in a different language (English, Spanish, Japanese, and so on). Each closed-caption track could provide subtitles in a different language.

Each track specifies one type of data, but it doesn't actually contain any data. Instead, the track identifies where the data segments are stored, the order in which the data segments are played, a playback speed, spatial properties such as image size, and a loudness level (see Figure 16-3). The data may be stored in a disk file that contains digitized video, digitized audio, an animation sequence, or a graphic image (PICT). The data also may be on a videodisc or on an audio CD.

The movie, its tracks, and the actual data may have different time scales. QuickTime correlates the different time scales and synchronizes the tracks.

The MooV format also specifies a *poster*, which is a single image that represents the movie, and a *preview*, which is a brief excerpt of the movie (like the trailers that you see in a theater).

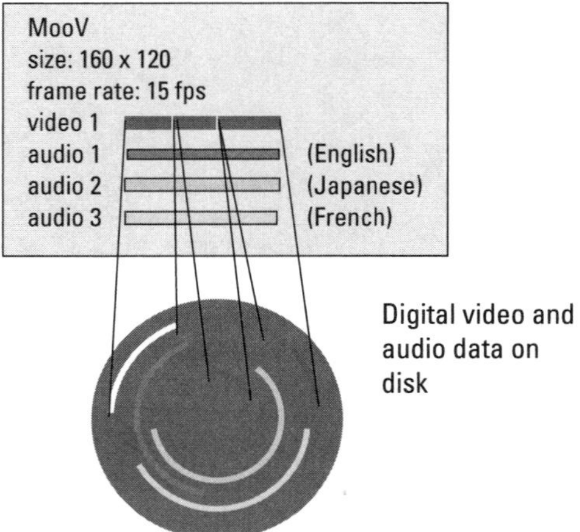


**Figure 16-3: Storing MooV data.**

Storing data segments in separate modules rather than with the movie description keeps the MooV small. The data required to play a QuickTime movie easily can occupy several megabytes, whereas the complete MooV specification takes up only a few kilobytes. This approach makes it practical to copy and paste (or to publish and subscribe) QuickTime movies between documents. The modular approach also makes it easy and efficient to use one data segment several times in a single movie or in several movies. Additionally, modularity makes it easy to use data from different sources — such as disk files, videodisc, and videotape — in a single movie.

On the down side, having a MooV file doesn't mean that you can play the QuickTime movie it specifies. You may copy a MooV file to a floppy disk on your Mac at work, take the floppy home, and open the movie on another Mac there, but you wouldn't be able to play the QuickTime movie at home because its data would be at work. And even at work, some data segments may be in files on an unavailable file server on your office's network.

You can throw away data files that a movie uses without any word of warning or caution from the system. Eventually, the Finder and the file system probably will get smart about such linked files, but in the meantime, expect to see alerts from the system when it can't find a movie file that you forgot to copy or accidentally deleted.

# PICT Extensions

QuickTime not only defines the new MooV format, but also extends the standard graphics format, PICT, to handle compressed still images and image previews. An application that knows about these extensions can compress a graphic image with any software or hardware compressor available on your computer. Any application that currently can open a PICT-format image needs no changes to be capable of opening a compressed PICT; QuickTime automatically decompresses a compressed PICT image without requiring changes to the application program.

Updated application programs can save a small (4K to 5K) thumbnail version of a PICT image along with the image itself. An application's Open command can display these thumbnails in its dialog box to assist you in deciding which file to open, as described in the following section.

# User Interface

With QuickTime, Apple is addressing not only the issue of how application programs include movies and compressed PICTs, but also how people use them. Applications can use two methods for controlling movie playback, as described in the following sections.

## Playback with controllers

Applications may display a standard VCR-like controller just below the movie, as shown in Figure 16-4. You use this playbar to play, stop, browse, or step through the movie and to adjust its sound level. Some applications have variants of the standard controller and may put the controller in a palette that floats above the document window.

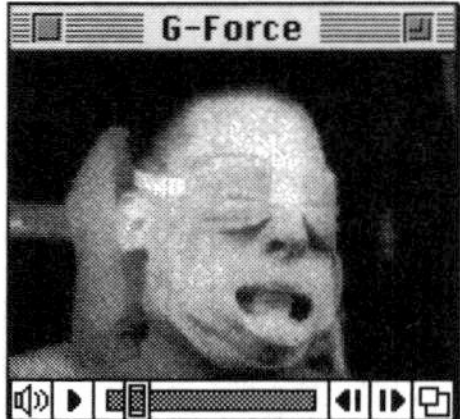


**Figure 16-4: Controlling movie playback.**

Clicking the volume control (labeled with a speaker) in the movie controller pops up a slider that you can use to adjust the volume. Clicking the play button (labeled with a right-pointing triangle) next to the volume control plays the movie. While the movie is playing, the play button becomes a pause button. The gray play bar in the middle of the movie controller shows the position of the currently playing frame relative to the beginning and end of the movie. You can drag the frame marker in the play bar, or simply click the play bar, to go to a different place in the movie. The two step buttons at the right of the play bar step backward and forward one frame per click. You can change the size of the movie window by dragging the size box at the left end of the movie controller.

In addition, the standard movie controller has several hidden capabilities. You can turn the sound off and on by Option-clicking the speaker button. You can select part of a movie by pressing the Shift key while dragging or clicking in the play bar, and then using the Cut, Copy, or Clear command in the Edit menu. After cutting or copying part of a movie, you can paste it anywhere in the same movie or another movie. To deselect, Command-click anywhere in the gray bar. Command-click the reverse-step button to play the movie backward. Control-click either step button to reveal a slider that controls the direction and playback rate. Option-click a step button to jump to the beginning or end of the movie, as indicated by the direction of the step button. (If part of the movie is selected, Option-clicking the step button also jumps to the end of the selection.) To make the movie an optimal size, press the Option key while dragging or clicking the size box.

## Playback without controllers

Applications also may display movies without controllers. In this case, a badge in the lower-left corner of the movie distinguishes it from a still graphic, as shown in Figure 16-5. To play a movie that has a badge and no controller, you double-click the movie. Clicking a playing movie stops it.

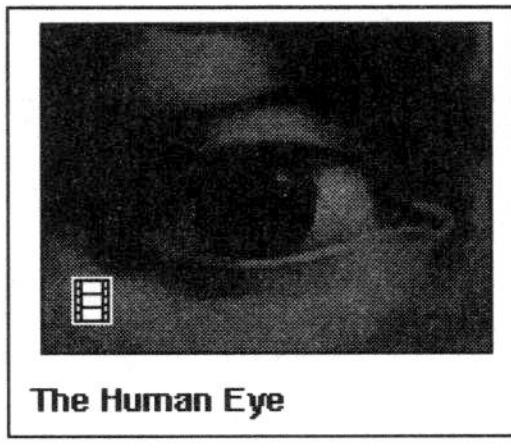


**Figure 16-5: Identifying a movie without a controller.**

QuickTime also extends the directory dialog box that appears when you use the Open command (and similar disk-related commands) to show what a movie or PICT contains before you open it (see Figure 16-6).

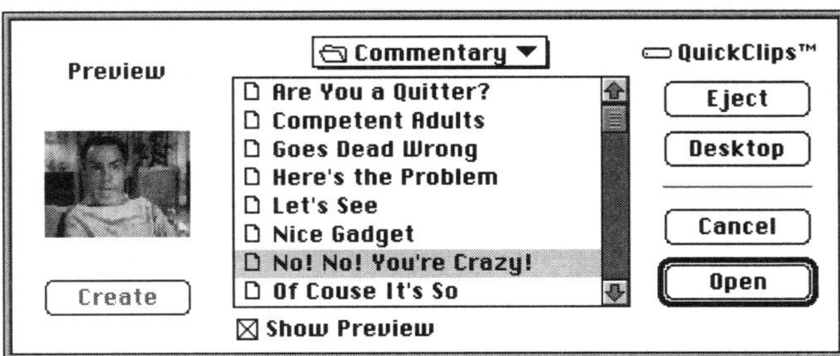


**Figure 16-6: Previewing movies with the Open command.**

# Image Compression

It's possible, if not practical, to digitize video on the Mac without QuickTime. The problem is that digitized video involves so much data that it overwhelms disk-drive capacity and may even exceed the data-transfer rates of the fastest Mac. The solution is universal image compression.

QuickTime includes six standard image compressors: two for video, one for animation, one for graphics, one for photos, and one for raw compression of any image. Each compressor applies a particular method, called a *compression algorithm*, that's especially suited to one type of image. Three characteristics of a compression algorithm determine how effectively it compresses: compression ratio, image fidelity, and speed.

## Compression ratio

The compression ratio measures how much the algorithm reduces the size of an image. A compression ratio of 2:1 means that an average image compresses to half its original size; at 20:1, the compressed image is 1/20 of its original size. No algorithm compresses every image by exactly the same amount, because image content affects the compression ratio. For example, many compression algorithms can't compress a patterned area as much as a solid block of color.

All compression algorithms remove data from an image by analyzing the data within the image — a technique called *spatial compression.* Algorithms for compressing sequences of images may also use temporal compression, also called *frame differencing*, to remove part of a frame that's unchanged from the preceding frame.

## Compression fidelity

The compression ratio directly affects the fidelity of the decompressed image. *Lossless compressors*, which decompress images identical to their originals, have compression ratios between 2:1 and 4:1. *Lossy compressors*, which lose some image fidelity during compression, generally achieve satisfactory results at compression ratios between 20:1 and 30:1. Lossy image compression relies on your mind's tendency to blend adjacent tiny bits of color into one color. For example, you tend to see a pattern of black and white dots on your screen as a medium gray.

## Compression speed

A complex compression algorithm that tries to achieve the utmost image fidelity and greatest compression ratio will be slower than a simple algorithm. Efficient software (or hardware) that implements the algorithm and a fast computer will accelerate any compression algorithm. Decompression speed is especially important in video and animation, because it affects the frame rate, frame size, and color depth. Faster decompression means that you can increase one or more of those factors.

## Compressors

The six software compressors that Apple supplies with QuickTime are meant for pixel-map (*pixmap*) images created by scanners, digitizers, painting programs, or animation programs. None of these compressors can reduce the size of object-oriented graphics created by CAD, drawing, or 3-D-modeling programs; neither can these compressors reduce the size of EPS (Encapsulated PostScript) graphics.

## Photo compressor

The Photo compressor uses the international standard JPEG (Joint Photographic Experts Group) algorithm. This compressor is best suited for compressing digitized photographs and other natural images, which vary smoothly and have few edges or other sharp details.

The JPEG algorithm spatially compresses an image by removing data that is redundant or imperceptible to the human eye. Compression ratios range from 5:1 to 50:1 at 24 bits per pixel (millions of colors), depending on image content and size. Compression ratios ranging from 10:1 to 20:1 yield good picture quality.

## Video compressor

The Video compressor uses a compression algorithm that Apple developed specifically for fast decompression of digitized video movies. This compressor spatially compresses each image in the movie and also can perform frame differencing. You can adjust the degree of frame differencing to get different levels of image quality. Color depth can be 8-, 16-, or 24-bit (256, thousands, or millions).

With QuickTime 1, the video compressor achieves compression ratios ranging from 5:1 to 25:1 (5:1 to 8:1 without frame differencing); you can expect to store 10 to 20 seconds of compressed video per megabyte. With QuickTime 1.5 and later versions, the video compressor achieves higher compression ratios.

Decompression rates permit playing back small frames (160 by 120 pixels, or 1/16 of a 13-inch monitor with QuickTime 1; and 320 by 240 pixels, or 1/4 of a 13-inch monitor with QuickTime 1.5 and later versions) at ten frames per second on a Macintosh LC or Color Classic. Smaller frame sizes play back proportionally faster. Faster Macintosh models can play back at higher frame rates, larger frame sizes, or both. Compressing a movie (while recording it) takes about five times longer than playing it back.

## Cinepak compressor

The Cinepak compressor (formerly the Compact Video compressor) is another video compressor. Using a different Apple compression algorithm from the Video compressor, the Cinepak compressor achieves better compression ratios, better image quality, and faster playback speeds.

This compressor can be set to compress video so that during playback, the data transfer will not exceed a specified rate — for example, the relatively slow rate of a CD-ROM drive.

### Animation compressor

The Animation compressor uses a compression algorithm that Apple developed for animation and other computer-generated images, at any color depth (2, 4, 16, 256, thousands, or millions of colors). The compressor uses a lossless run-length encoding (RLE) technique to spatially compress each image in an animation sequence. The animation compressor also can perform lossy frame differencing to achieve full-size, real-time playback (640 by 480 at up to 30 frames per second). Actual performance and compression ratios depend greatly on the content of images in the animation sequence.

The animation compressor works best with synthetically created images. Natural images, such as those captured from videotape, generally have too little edge definition and too much visual noise, making it difficult for the animation compressor to achieve a good compression ratio.

### Graphics compressor

The Graphics compressor uses an algorithm that Apple developed especially for 8-bit (256 color) still images for which compression ratio matters more than compression speed. Generally, the graphics compressor reduces an image to half the size of the animation compressor but takes twice as long to do it. The slow speed of the graphics compressor is less noticeable when it is decompressing images stored on relatively slow devices, such as a CD-ROM.

### Raw compressor

The Apple Raw compressor reduces storage requirements by converting an image to a lesser *pixel depth* (number of available colors). For example, converting from 32-bit to 16-bit compresses by a 2:1 ratio. Converting from 32-bit to 24-bit achieves a 4:3 compression ratio with no loss of image quality, because the extra eight bits do not store picture information.

Some of the other compressors implicitly use the Raw compressor. The Photo compressor, for example, works directly only with 32-bit images, so it uses the Raw compressor when it needs to work with an image at a different pixel depth. Reducing the pixel depth reduces image fidelity. Converting to a higher pixel depth usually does not affect image fidelity, but converting from 8-bit to 16-bit sometimes loses information.

## Content, Content, Content

Having the option to play QuickTime movies is great, but if you want to record them, where will your video content come from, and how will you get the rights to use it? Apple's QuickTime Startup Kit contains quite a bit of video on CD-ROM, and other publishers also are publishing clip video on CD-ROM.

You can record your own QuickTime movies directly onto your hard drive. You need video digitizing hardware, which is built into the Centris and Quadra 660AV; Quadra 840AV; and Power Mac 6100/60AV, 7100/66AV, and 8100/80AV models. To digitize video with another Mac model, you need a video-capture card such as RasterOps MoviePak or SuperMac VideoSpigot. In addition, you need a video source: a VCR, camcorder, videodisc player, or professional video-playback equipment.

You also can create QuickTime movies entirely on the computer. The Movie Converter program that comes with the QuickTime Starter Kit enables you to create QuickTime movies from PICT graphics files, PICT images in the Scrapbook, PICS animation files, and AIFF sound files. (PICT, PICS, and AIFF are standard types of Macintosh files.) Also, MacroMedia Director 3.1 can save its animations as QuickTime movies. If you have System 7.5 with QuickDraw GX installed, you can use animated fonts to create simple animated sequences, such as a person riding a bicycle or a bird flapping its wings.

Unless you film your own video with a camcorder or your own animation with animation software, you also must wrestle with copyright issues. Video, being a form of expression, has international copyright protection unless it has been placed in the public domain. Legally, you must get permission from the copyright holder before you record any copyrighted video as a QuickTime movie.

After you have QuickTime movies on disk, you can slice, dice, chop, mix, combine, and bake them with video editing and composing programs such as Adobe Premiere and Diva's VideoShop. And now that a version of QuickTime exists for Windows, it's possible to make QuickTime movies that play on both Macintosh and Windows computers. (The Windows computer must have an 80386SX or better processor, a processor speed of at least 20MHz, 4MB or more of conventional and extended memory, a hard disk with 4MB free for basic QuickTime for Windows software, a graphics adapter, and a mouse. The Windows computer probably also should have a CD-ROM drive, a sound card, and additional hard-disk space to store movies.)

# QuickTime in Your Life

Apple wants you to be able to copy, paste, resize, move, and play movies in any document where you now can put PICT graphics. QuickTime's Movie Toolbox makes it easy for developers to add those capabilities to their applications. By comparison, it's harder to figure out what to do with movies in an application such as a word processing program, which seems to exist for creating static printed documents.

WordPerfect was one of the first general productivity applications to include QuickTime movie capabilities. It's not immediately obvious how you can use movies in a word processing document, but WordPerfect has demonstrated several ideas. One idea is an interactive newspaper whose static illustrations of movie reviews become movie trailers when you double-click them. Imagine seeing an interactive newspaper in a kiosk at the front of a movie-theater complex.

In another example, a business letter describes a new helmet design and includes an animated 360-degree view of the helmet (see Figure 16-7). You can use the movie controller to look at the helmet from any angle. The letter and the animation fit onto a 50-cent floppy disk and can be read by anyone who has a QuickTime-equipped Macintosh. Larger documents — such as a student's report about travel to the moon, illustrated with movies of NASA space missions — could be delivered by network.

Storing movies uses a great deal of disk space, but some documents are short-lived. For example, a TV news director could review several clips pasted into a memo and make comments on them in the same document, as shown in Figure 16-8. The alternative is to hand the director a stack of videotapes and scrawled notes. This document probably would exist (and occupy disk space) only for a day.

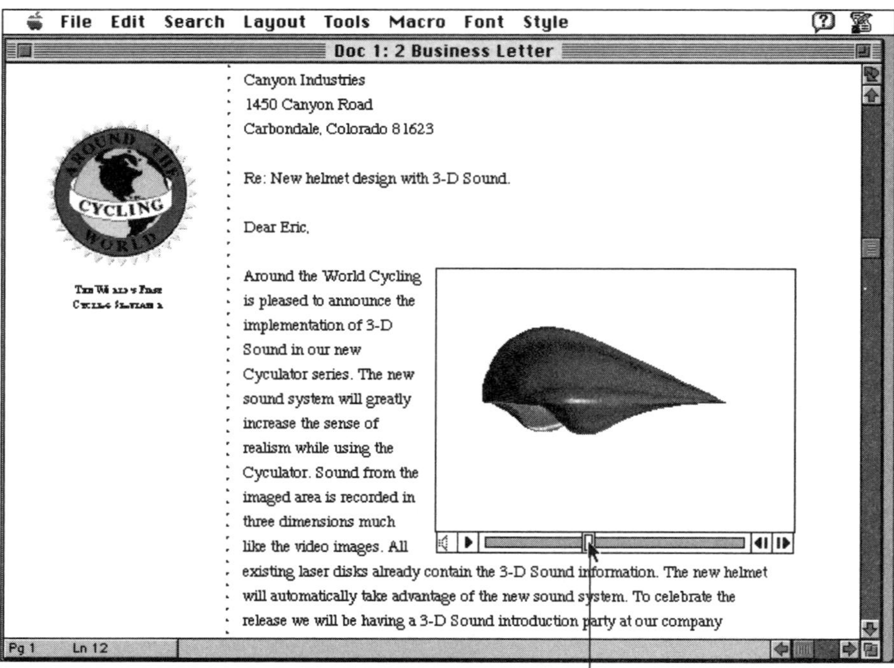


**Figure 16-7: An interactive letter using QuickTime.**

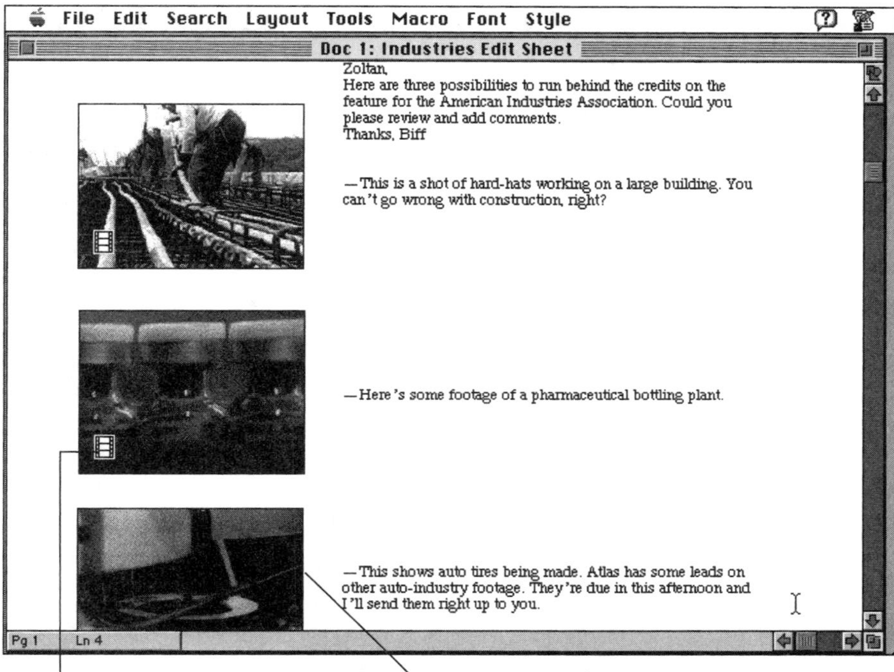


**Figure 16-8: A document containing temporarily stored QuickTime movie clips and accompanying commentary.**

QuickTime makes including video, sound, and animation in your documents as easy as including graphics. Movies are a new type of data on the computer, however, and don't lend themselves to traditional, paper-oriented ways of thinking about computer documents. Suddenly, you have a dynamic new way to communicate. You have to change how you think about using your computer. It's not just for preparing messages, but for delivering the messages as well.

# CHAPTER 16 CONCEPTS AND TERMS

- QuickTime uses several tricks to enable playback of movies on a Macintosh: reduced picture size, slower playback speed, and image compression.
- The QuickTime extension provides three major pieces of system software: the Movie Toolbox, the Image Compression Manager, and the Component Manager. Application programs take advantage of these software modules to play back or record QuickTime movies.
- To represent video, sound, animation, and other time-related data in the computer's memory and on disk, QuickTime establishes a standard format called MooV.
- Time-based data tends to be bulky, so QuickTime provides a mechanism for compressing and automatically decompressing it. QuickTime comes with six standard compressors: Video, Cinepak, Animation, Graphics, Photo, and Raw (none).
- QuickTime extends the standard PICT graphics format to include individual compressed images.
- QuickTime establishes standard methods for you to recognize movies and control movie playback: the movie controller and the movie badge.
- You can film your own movies and convert them to QuickTime movies with a digitizer card. You also can use existing footage (be sure to get permission from the copyright holder) or even QuickDraw GX animated fonts.

**components**
A software module that provides a service to or extends the capabilities of one or more application programs — for example, by compressing and decompressing data or controlling an external device such as a scanner, VCR, or digitizer card.

**compression algorithm**
A method for compressing and decompressing data. Each compression algorithm generally works best with one type of data, such as sound, photographs, video or motion pictures, and computer-generated animation. Three characteristics of a compression algorithm determine how effectively it compresses: compression ratio, image fidelity, and speed.

**compression ratio**
Indicates the amount of compression and is calculated by dividing the size of the original image by the size of the compressed image. Larger compression ratios mean greater compression and generally mean poorer image quality.

**compressor**
Something that compresses data so that it takes less space to store, and decompresses compressed data back to its original form for playing or changing. A compressor may consist of software, hardware, or both. Sometimes also called **codec,** a shortened form of "compressor-decompressor."

**fps (frames per second)**
Measures how smoothly a motion picture plays. More frames per second means smoother play back.

**frame**
One still image that is part of a series of still images, which, when shown in sequence, produce the illusion of movement.

**frame rate**
The number of frames displayed in one second. The TV frame rate is 30 fps in the U.S. and other countries that use the NTSC broadcasting standard; 25 fps in countries that use the PAL or SEACAM standard. The standard movie frame rate is 24 fps.

**full motion**
Video displayed at frame rates of 24 to 30 fps. The human eye perceives fairly smooth motion at frame rates of 12 to 18 fps.

**lossless**
A type of compression algorithm that regenerates exactly the same data as the uncompressed original and has a relatively low compression ratio.

**movie**
1. Any time-related data, such as video, sound, animation, and graphs that change over time. 2. Apple's format for organizing, storing, and exchanging time-related data.

**multimedia**
A presentation combining text or graphics with video, animation, or sound, and presented on a computer.

**pixel**
Short for picture element. The smallest dot that the computer and monitor can display.

**pixel depth**
The number of colors available for each pixel of a displayed image. Also, the number of memory bits used to store each pixel's color. The number of colors available depends on the number of bits. For example, 256 colors require 8-bits per pixel, and 32,768 colors require 16 bits per pixel.

**track**
One channel of a QuickTime movie, containing video, sound, closed-captioned text, MIDI data, time codes, or other time-related data.

CHAPTER SEVENTEEN

# Understanding Speech and Languages

- Speaking to AV Macs, which can use Apple's PlainTalk software to recognize (without special training) what most North Americans say
- Creating speech-activated commands
- Hearing ordinary text read aloud by any Mac that has the MacInTalk 2 or MacInTalk Pro components of PlainTalk software
- Working in multiple languages on a Mac with WorldScript software, foreign-language software kits, and compatible application programs

One compelling aspect of Macintosh system software is the ease with which it can incorporate new technologies seamlessly and deeply into its guts, providing new ways to perform work. Apple's PlainTalk extensions to System 7 together with the powerful processing capabilities of some Mac models confirm Apple's dedication to innovation.

This chapter discusses how PlainTalk enables several Macintosh models — the Centris and Quadra 660AV; the Quadra 840AV; and the various Power Mac models — to recognize and act on North American speech. The chapter also describes how part of PlainTalk enables almost all Macs to speak ordinary typed text.

Last, this chapter describes the software pieces that make it possible to work in multiple languages on a Mac. This *globalization* of the Macintosh, as Apple puts it, is made possible by the WorldScript system extensions, the language kits for Japanese and Chinese, and other foreign-language applications.

## PlainTalk Speech Technologies

Keyboarding and mousing are not particularly natural ways to communicate. For years, computer designers have looked for a more natural way to operate computers. One of the most compelling ways to work with a computer is simply to talk to it. Present-day Macs are on the forefront of progress toward achieving the science fiction of *Star Trek*, when people of the future speak naturally and conversationally with their computers. When the crew of the space ship *Enterprise* traveled back in time to a mid-1980s San Francisco in the movie *Star Trek IV*, chief engineer Scotty tried to use a Mac SE by speaking into the mouse. Of course it was a big joke. If he had returned to 1993 and tried the same trick with the microphone of a Quadra 660AV or 840AV, he would have met with limited success. These same speech recognition capabilities are available on most Power Mac models.

Recognizing speech requires extra computing power. Power Macs, with their PowerPC central processors, have the power to recognize speech while you do other work. Apple bundles the necessary software with the Power Mac AV models and with Power Macs that have a built-in CD-ROM drive. Among the Macs that use other central processors, only the Centris and Quadra 660AV and the Quadra 840AV have sufficient processing power to recognize speech while you continue working. The 660AV and 840AV have a special coprocessor, an AT&T 3210 digital signal processor (DSP), that handles speech recognition; therefore, speech recognition does not burden the 68040 central processor in the 660AVs and 840AVs. The DSP handles speech recognition while the 68040 does other work.

Listening is harder than talking, both for people and for computers. The high-powered hardware required for recognizing speech is not needed to synthesize speech from text; all Macs from the Plus on up are capable of basic speech. Macs from the LC on up are capable of more sophisticated speech.

PlainTalk Speech Technologies require a great deal of memory. Speech recognition uses about 2.4MB on a 660AV or 840AV, and text-to-speech uses 2.6MB to generate its best-quality male voice on these models.

## PlainTalk speech recognition

Apple made headlines in 1992 when it began touting its speech recognition technology, then called Casper. Now called PlainTalk Automatic Speech Recognition, the technology enables Macs that have enough processing power and can input high-quality sound to take commands from any type of human voice at any time without the need for training on coded words, intense pauses, unnatural diction, or special voice sounds.

PlainTalk speech recognition works by digitizing sounds into individual phonemes that are compared to a dictionary of such sounds. When the PlainTalk software recognizes a spoken menu command, it sends an Apple event message for the current application to carry out the command. The application must be designed to accept Apple event messages that are the equivalents of menu commands. If the application does not act on Apple events, the spoken command will not be carried out. (For more information on Apple events, see Chapter 18.)

One drawback is that PlainTalk recognizes only North American English speech as of version 1.5; therefore, British, Australian, and other English dialects confuse the software.

The PlainTalk speech recognition software consists of a control panel, several system extensions, and other items that go in the Extensions folder. This software enables the Finder to obey spoken commands.

In addition, if you want applications to recognize speech, you must write scripts using Apple events to invoke speech recognition. Therefore, programs that do not work with AppleScript or Apple events will not naturally obey speech. In this case, CE Software's QuicKeys 3.0 comes into play. The developers of QuicKeys worked closely with Apple during the development of PlainTalk speech recognition. Consequently QuicKeys includes a speech recognition option.

## Control of speech recognition

You control speech recognition with the Speech Setup control panel (see Figure 17-1). This control panel enables you to turn speech recognition on and off, and it contains a slider you can use to adjust the sensitivity of recognition. Move the slider to the left to accept a wider range of accents, grammatical rules, and vocabulary words. When the slider is at its most tolerant setting, speech recognition is very sensitive to ambient noise; in fact, it sometimes mistakenly interprets room sounds as commands.

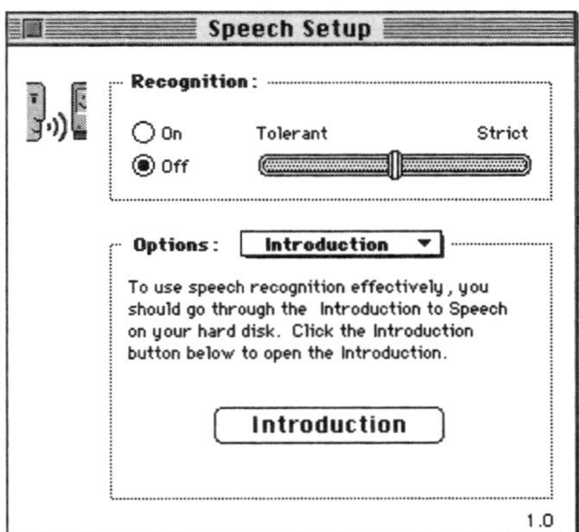


**Figure 17-1: Turning speech recognition on and off and adjusting its sensitivity.**

Turning on speech recognition brings up a feedback window. This window displays the text of the voice commands that PlainTalk recognized, along with the computer's response. If PlainTalk doesn't recognize something it heard, it displays "Pardon me?" in the feedback window.

## Speech recognition code name

PlainTalk speech recognition normally is set up to recognize commands preceded by a code name that you specify, such as "Computer" (which is the word that *Star Trek's* characters use to address a computer) or the name of your Mac. You specify the code name in the Speech Setup control panel (see Figure 17-2). After choosing Name from the Options pop-up menu, you can edit the name to which speech recognition responds, and you can designate the context in which the computer should respond to that name.

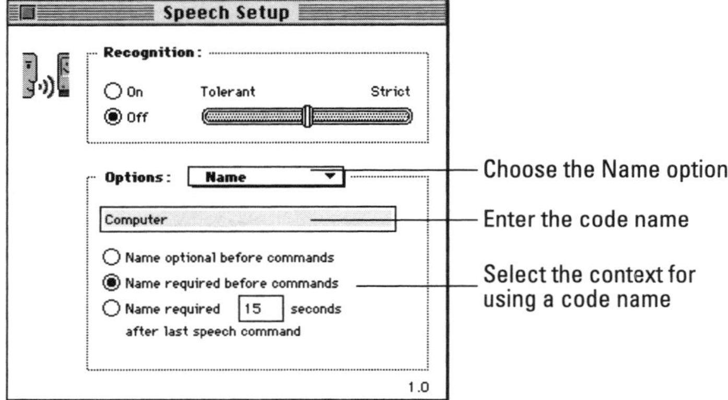


**Figure 17-2: Setting the speech recognition code name.**

You can make the code name optional, but not without risk: the Mac could interpret something you say in conversation as a voice command.

The option that requires the code name within 15 seconds (or another interval that you specify) after the last command is based on the idea that when you have the computer's attention, you shouldn't have to get its attention all the time. You can tell whether you need to speak the code name by looking at the speech recognition feedback window.

## Speech recognition feedback sounds

The Speech Setup control panel also has options for sounds that speech recognition uses to provide feedback on your spoken commands. You can set the voice to be used in spoken messages, the sound that speech recognition makes when it responds to a spoken command, and the sound that speech recognition makes when it completes a command. To display these options, choose Feedback from the Options pop-up menu (see Figure 17-3).

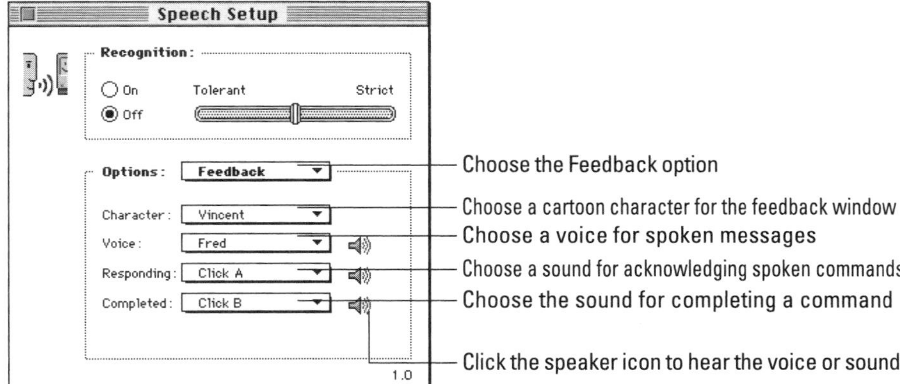


**Figure 17-3: Setting the sounds that speech recognition makes.**

## Speech recognition on-off key

You use an option in the Speech Setup control panel to designate a key or combination of keys that, when pressed, makes speech recognition alternately listen and *not* listen to spoken commands. To display this option, choose Attention from the Options pop-up menu (see Figure 17-4). Select the text box and then press the key or keys you want to use to switch listening on and off. (Keys in the numeric keypad are considered to be separate from the number keys in the main keyboard.) You can construct combination keystrokes with the Shift and Option keys, but not with the Control and ⌘ keys.

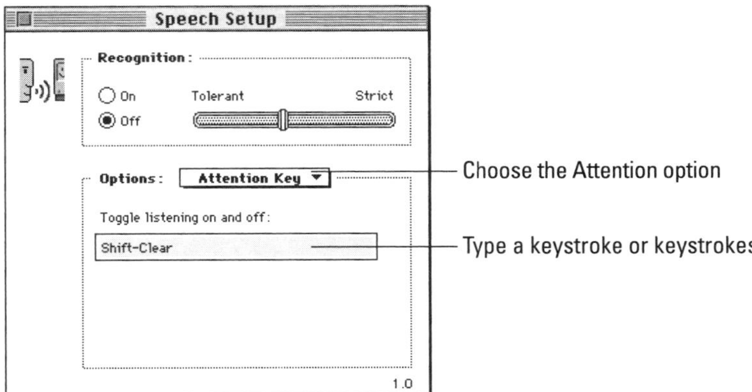


**Figure 17-4: Setting a key that makes speech recognition listen or not listen.**

### What speech recognition understands

After using the Speech Setup control panel to set up and turn on speech recognition, you are ready to speak commands (such as "Computer, open Chooser"), expecting the Mac to carry out your order. But what commands will the Mac obey?

Macs equipped with PlainTalk speech recognition come with utility programs for creating voice-activated macros that scroll windows, operate dialog boxes, choose tools from palettes, and so forth. Speech recognition can choose menu items in any application that creates its menus with standard Mac programming practices. (Technical note: a program must use MENU resources to define its menus.) In programs that use proprietary menu schemes, such as Microsoft Word, you can create voice-activated QuicKeys macros to choose menu items (as described under "QuicKeys and speech recognition" later in this chapter).

Your voice also can open specific files, folders, and disks that have aliases in the special Speakable Items folder, which is in the Apple Menu Items folder. This folder has aliases preinstalled for common items such as control panels and the Chooser. You can add your own aliases for items that you want to open, close, save, or print by spoken command. Although you can add as many items as you want, the performance of the Mac degrades as you add items.

The phrases you can use in spoken commands are defined by a file of speech rules in the Extensions folder. The speech rules cover common commands used in all applications, such as opening, closing, saving, and printing. Like rules of English grammar, these speech rules define recognizable word order. You could use any of the following voice commands to open the Chooser:

"Open Chooser"

"Open the Chooser"

"Open menu item Chooser"

Speech recognition cannot understand commands unless you speak them in an order defined by the speech rules. "Chooser open," for example, means nothing under the standard speech rules. Software developers may add rules to cover actions that aren't covered by the standard rules.

## Speech Macro Editor

To make a voice command do more than perform simple commands, you must have voice-activated macros or scripts. You can use macros or scripts that other people created, or you can create your own by using a macro editing or script editing program. Macs equipped with PlainTalk speech recognition come with a macro editing program called the Speech Macro Editor. You use this program to record or write a new speech macro or to change an existing speech macro.

The Speech Macro Editor has two windows (see Figure 17-5). One window lists the defined speech macros. Double-clicking one of the listed macros brings up an editing window in which you can display and change the macro.

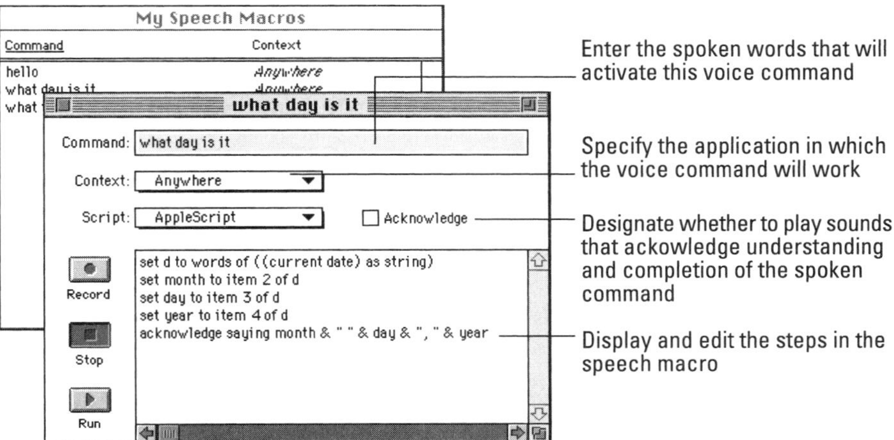


**Figure 17-5: Use the Speech Macro Editor to write AppleScript scripts for speech recognition.**

At the top of the editing window, you enter or edit the spoken words that will activate the macro. Use the Context pop-up menu to specify where the voice command will work; your choices are Anywhere or one of the applications that you currently have open. The Script pop-up menu designates the scripting system on which the macro is based (usually, AppleScript). If you turn on the Acknowledge option, speech recognition plays sounds to acknowledge hearing and completing the voice command. You use the Speech Setup control panel to specify particular sounds for these situations (as described in "Speech recognition feedback sounds" earlier in this chapter).

The editing window also contains buttons that enable you to record a new speech macro, run a macro, and stop the recording or execution of a macro. You see, and can edit, the steps of the speech macro in a scrollable text area.

The Speech Macro Editor enables you to create speech macros only to control applications that work with AppleScript scripts (described in Chapter 18). Speech macros work like AppleScript scripts, sending Apple event messages that cause the receiving application to perform specific tasks. Furthermore, you can record speech macros only to control applications that permit the recording of AppleScript scripts.

## QuicKeys and speech recognition

CE Software's QuicKeys 3.0 enables you to use voice commands to trigger QuicKeys shortcuts or AppleScript macros. In the QuicKeys world, *shortcuts* are small programs that perform complex tasks such as opening specific files, sending data from one program to another, and changing control-panel configurations. The benefit of using a QuicKeys shortcut rather than a Speech Macro Editor macro is that you can apply the QuicKeys shortcut to any application, not just to those that are designed to work with AppleScript. QuicKeys works as an extension of PlainTalk on Macs with PlainTalk speech recognition installed.

To add voice activation to any QuicKeys shortcut, choose QuicKeys from the Apple menu to open the QuicKeys Main Editor window (see Figure 17-6) and click the microphone column for the shortcut you want to trigger. Marks in this column denote speakable shortcuts. After closing the Main Editor window, you can speak the command as you would any other voice command — for example, you could say, "Computer, run *shortcut name*" (if "Computer" was the name you designated in the Speech Setup control panel). You also can make any QuicKeys shortcut that has a Finder icon speakable by placing its alias in the Speakable Items folder.

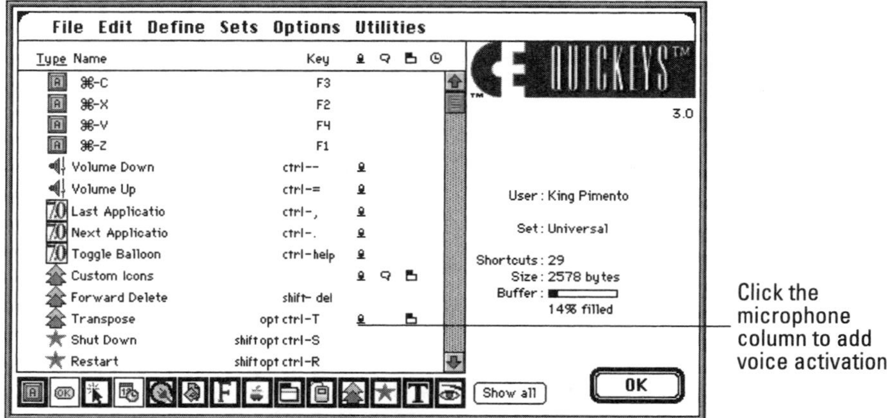


**Figure 17-6: Adding voice activation to a QuicKeys 3.0 shortcut.**

QuicKeys 3.0 includes QuicKeys Script, an alternative language for creating speech macros or scripts. You can use this language instead of AppleScript to build complex sequences and activate each sequence with a voice command. For example, a voice command could trigger a sequence that looks up a phone number and dials the phone.

The QuicKeys Script language is based on the QuicKeys commands that you use to edit QuicKeys shortcuts. If you already know how to edit QuicKeys sequences, you will be familiar with QuicKeys Script. Further, you can use QuicKeys Script to record, write, and edit scripts that work with any program. By contrast, macros based on AppleScript only work with certain applications.

When QuicKeys Script is installed on your startup disk, you can use this language, instead of AppleScript, with Apple's Speech Macro Editor. To make the switch, choose QuicKeys from the Script pop-up menu in the Speech Macro Editor's editing window. As an alternative to the Speech Macro Editor, you can use the confusingly named AppleScript Editor program, which comes with QuicKeys 3.0. Despite its name, the QuicKeys AppleScript Editor works with the QuicKeys Script language as well as the AppleScript language. The QuicKeys AppleScript Editor looks and works much like Apple's Speech Macro Editor (described in "Speech Macro Editor" earlier in this chapter).

If you use QuicKeys Script instead of AppleScript, floating control palettes appear while you record or run scripts. The Recording palette, for example, appears when you click the Record button in the macro editing window. The tools in this palette allow you to pause, continue, stop, cancel, or insert a QuicKeys shortcut while you record a macro. The Playback palette appears when you run a script that includes a pause command or a wait command. The tools in the Playback palette enable you to pause, continue, or stop a macro.

## PlainTalk text-to-speech

PlainTalk has a second component — speech synthesis — that has been available to Macs since 1985. Apple beefed up its venerable MacInTalk text-to-speech software, producing a powerful tool that allows the Mac to speak clearly almost any text that you specify.

PlainTalk text-to-speech enables the Mac to speak, providing verbal feedback for your actions. This feature also provides capabilities that previously were available only on minicomputers and mainframes. Text-to-speech makes it theoretically possible to telephone a Macintosh and have the computer play back voice mail or electronic-mail messages, or perform any other telephone-controlled data access or manipulation action.

### The Two Versions of MacInTalk

PlainTalk text-to-speech converts typed text to speech. Text-to-speech is based on the MacInTalk speech synthesizers, which contain grammar, syntax, and contextual rules that tell the PlainTalk software how to pronounce the words. Two versions of this speech synthesizer exist: MacInTalk 2, which can run on any Macintosh under System 6 or System 7, and MacInTalk Pro, which requires more RAM and System 7 to operate properly. Both versions are included with AV Mac models: Power Mac 6100/60AV, 7100/70AV, 8100/80AV; Centris and Quadra 660AV, and Quadra 840AV. In addition, some developers are distributing PlainTalk text-to-speech with their products. MacInTalk Pro is the more robust product, enabling the Mac to speak in relatively human fashion. Compared with MacInTalk 2, MacInTalk Pro recognizes more unique words. The software also recognizes the differences between abbreviations (such as "Dr." for "doctor" or "dr." for "drive"), depending on context, as well as numbers, proper names, and nonstandard English.

Text-to-speech also opens computing to handicapped people. A Macintosh can speak to visually impaired users or serve as a voice for users who have trouble speaking.

Text-to-speech someday may be useful for proofreading documents and performing other editorial tasks. The capability of this feature to perform such tasks today is limited by the software's unsophisticated syntax rules.

## How text-to-speech works

You do not use PlainTalk text-to-speech directly. You use an application designed to speak text, and the application uses software in the MacInTalk system extension to convert the text to speech. The SimpleText application that comes with System 7.5 (and with the AV Mac models, which have PlainTalk installed at the factory) can speak text if PlainTalk text-to-speech is installed. In addition, software developers are building speech synthesis into both existing and new specialized applications, using one of the two versions of PlainTalk text-to-speech.

The engine that drives PlainTalk text-to-speech is a system extension called Speech Manager, which resides in the Extensions folder. Speech Manager converts character strings to speech, which then is dispatched to the MacInTalk speech synthesizer for actual speech output.

Speech Manager calls on MacInTalk to perform the actual speech work, based on its dictionaries, rules, and libraries of digitized voices. MacInTalk is also a system extension, residing in the Extensions folder along with its voice files.

Apple includes several male and female voices with MacInTalk. The application can select a voice, or the application can allow the person using it to select a voice. For example, SimpleText has a Voices submenu from which you can choose one of the available voices (see Figure 17-7).

## QuicKeys and text-to-speech

Text-to-speech basically is a developer's tool because nowhere does it provide a window in which you can type text you want spoken. CE Software provides a solution to this problem with QuicKeys 3.0. The Speak Ease shortcut speaks text you enter in its text window (see Figure 17-8) or text you copy from a document (up to 32K) to the Clipboard. Whenever you type the shortcut's keystroke, the Mac speaks the text that you entered or copied. You also can set up a timer so that the Mac speaks the text at specified intervals.

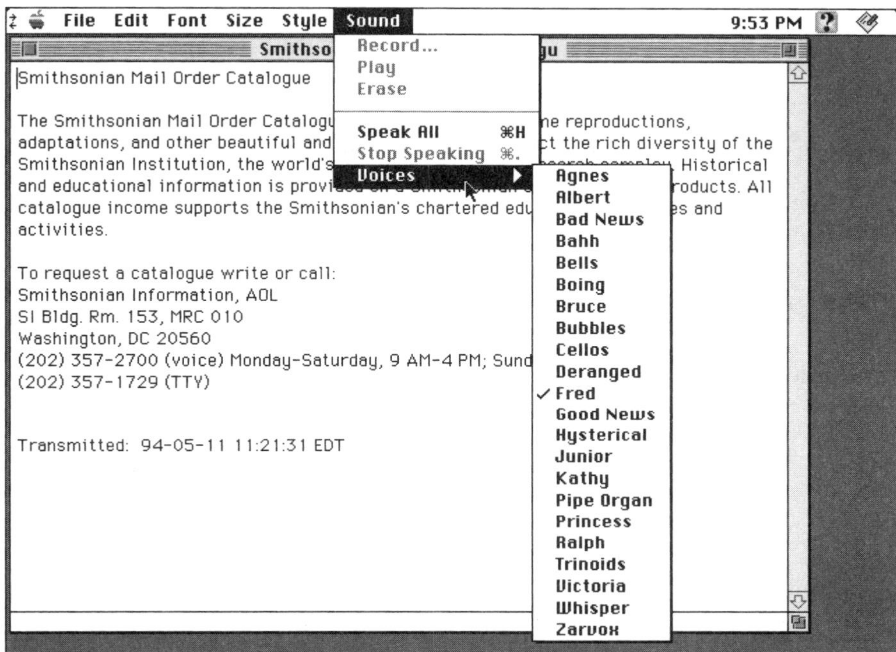


**Figure 17-7: Choosing a speaking voice in SimpleText.**



**Figure 17-8: The QuicKeys Speak Ease shortcut allows you to enter text-to-speech text.**

# WorldScript

Systems 7.0, 7.0.1, and earlier system software work with multiple keyboard layouts and European languages that use Roman and Cyrillic alphabets. Those versions of system software also have been translated into Japanese, Chinese, Hebrew, Arabic, and other languages that use bidirectional, contextual, and large alphabets.

System 7.1 is the first Macintosh System software capable of handling all these multiple languages without modification. Two system extensions give System 7.1 this international capability: WorldScript I handles bidirectional and contextual languages, and WorldScript II handles languages with large alphabets.

The Macintosh enhanced its position as an international computer with its introduction of WorldScript with System 7.1. WorldScript I and II enable developers to write software that supports languages that require more than single-byte characters, including Japanese, Chinese, Korean, Hebrew, and Arabic. WorldScript also enables developers to write software that uses language-specific terms for dialog-box messages, screens, menus, and other screen elements. This capability, called *localization*, is important for users who want to cross cultural borders through computing.

Nisus and WordPerfect, for example, have been localized for Japanese; both word processing programs use correct Japanese for menus, dialog boxes, and toolbars. Other vendors, such as Claris and Aldus, offer versions of some of their products in several languages.

Apple offers two language kits that allow you to write in Japanese or Chinese alongside English in any application that works with WorldScript. Apple intends to introduce other WorldScript II-based language kits, such as Korean and Arabic.

## Language script systems

When WorldScript is activated, the Mac works with multiple languages and methods of writing (vertical or horizontal, left to right, or right to left). The software defines a method of writing a *language script system*, or simply a script. Do not confuse this kind of script with the kind of script you create with AppleScript (as described in Chapter 18).

A language script system tells System 7 which character in the specified language every keystroke produces, as well as how the characters should behave — for example, the direction in which text flows. The script also specifies sort order, number and currency formats, and date and time formats.

One language script system can be used by multiple languages. For example, the Roman script is used in most Western languages, such as English, French, Italian, Spanish, and German.

Each language has its own rules of behavior, even though it may use the same script as another language. You teach the Mac the rules to use by selecting the language behavior in the Text control panel included in the language kit (see Figure 17-9). The options in this control panel tell the Mac how to produce text from characters. For languages that flow right to left, the control panel provides additional controls. You can split the caret insertion point so that you can see insertion points for left-to-right writing as well as for right-to-left.

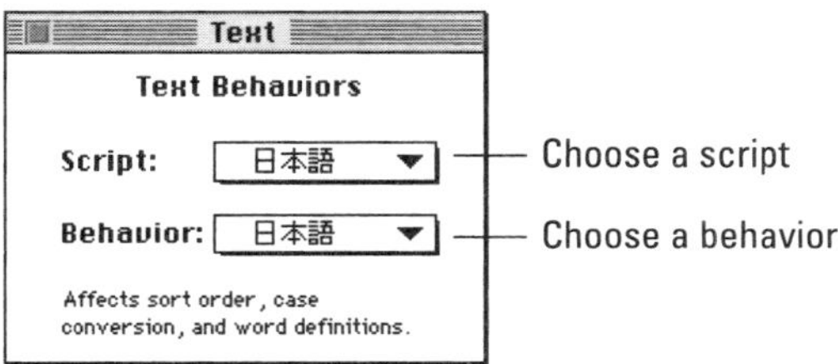


**Figure 17-9: The Text control panel controls language behavior for each installed script.**

The Mac can handle more than one language script system at a time. The system-level script is called the *primary script*. If you are working on a Mac that is set up for English, Roman is your primary script; your secondary script can be any other installed language kit's script, such as Japanese.

# Keyboard menu

If your system software contains more than one language script system, a Keyboard menu appears between the Help menu and the Application menu near the right end of the menu bar, as shown in Figure 17-10. You choose a keyboard layout and language from the Keyboard menu.

**Figure 17-10: The Keyboard menu.**

You use the Keyboard menu to switch between the keyboards you use to enter text because each language requires a specific text-entry method. Each keyboard layout is associated with one language script system, so choosing a keyboard effectively chooses a script.

English and other Western languages typically provide only one way to enter text, and U.S. keyboards are based on that text input method. But in languages that are based on ideograms, such as Japanese and Chinese, text can be input in multiple ways. The Japanese language kit comes with an input method called Kotoeri that enables entering Kanji, Katakana, Hiragana, and Romaji. Other input methods are available. (Input methods are listed in the Keyboard menu.) The Chinese language kit comes equipped with Pinyin, Zhuyin, Cangjie, and Wubi input-method software, as well as two character sets: simplified and traditional.

## Registering languages

Each language kit includes a language register utility. You use this utility to designate a language script system to be used with each individual application (see Figure 17-11). Registered applications use the correct fonts for menus, dialog boxes, buttons, and so on. You can store two copies of the registered applications so that one application can open in the primary script and the other in a secondary script.

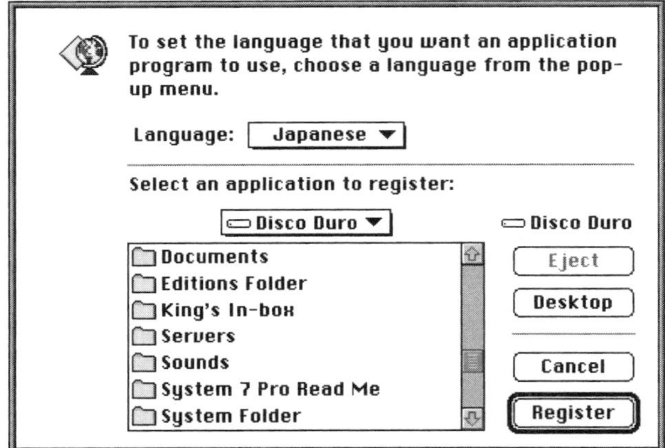


**Figure 17-11: Registering an application tells the Mac which language the application uses.**

## Foreign-language applications

After installing a language kit (such as the Japanese language kit), you can use applications that have been localized for use in that language (such as TeachText Japanese). In localized programs, the menus, dialog boxes, help messages, and other elements appear in the localized language. Using a localized application, you can enter English and the foreign language in a single document. You also can use multiple languages in a document created by an application that takes advantage of WorldScript (including WorldScript I or II, if needed for the language kit).

# CHAPTER 17 CONCEPTS AND TERMS

- PlainTalk includes both speech recognition and text-to-speech capabilities.
- PlainTalk speech recognition requires the processing power of the Power Macs' PowerPC processor or the 3210 DSP coprocessor in the 660AV and 840AV Macs plus the ability to input high-quality sound.
- PlainTalk speech recognition allows most North American speakers to give spoken commands to a Mac. You use the Speech Setup control panel to tell the Mac how to interpret and provide feedback on spoken commands. The Speakable Items folder makes spoken commands easy to use by teaching the Mac to understand up to 30 macros or file/folder aliases contained in the folder. With the Speech Macro Editor you can create voice-command macros to control applications that work with AppleScript.
- You can use spoken commands to activate QuicKeys macros, which can control any application (including applications that do not work with AppleScript).
- PlainTalk text-to-speech works with a Mac Plus or better, but high quality speech requires at least a Mac LC. PlainTalk text-to-speech does not include a window for entering text you want spoken, but any application can take advantage of text-to-speech to speak ordinary text.
- The QuicKeys shortcut Speak Ease provides a window in which you can type text that you want spoken. Speak Ease can also speak text copied to the Clipboard.
- System 7.1 introduced WorldScript to support character sets for languages that have larger alphabets than English. Apple has published language kits for Japanese and Chinese; these kits take advantage of WorldScript II to provide bilingual menus, dialog boxes, and text-entry capabilities for the Mac. You can type multiple languages in a single document of an application that takes advantage of WorldScript.

**globalization**
The incorporation of foreign languages into Macintosh systems through a software technology called WorldScript.

**localization**
The development of software whose dialog-box messages, screens, menus, and other screen elements use the language spoken in the region in which the software is sold.

**primary script**
The language script system used by system dialog boxes and menus. If you are working on a Mac that is set up for English, Roman is your primary script; your secondary script can be any other installed language kit's script, such as Japanese.

**script**
Short for language script system, which is software that defines a method of writing (vertical or horizontal, left to right, or right to left). A script also provides rules for text sorting, word breaks, and the formats of dates, times, and numbers. Do not confuse this kind of script with the kind of script you create with AppleScript.

**shortcuts**
A sequence of QuickKey steps that perform complex tasks such as opening specific files, sending data from one program to another, and changing control-panel configurations. A QuicKeys shortcut can be voice-activated and works any application, not just to those that are designed to work with AppleScript.

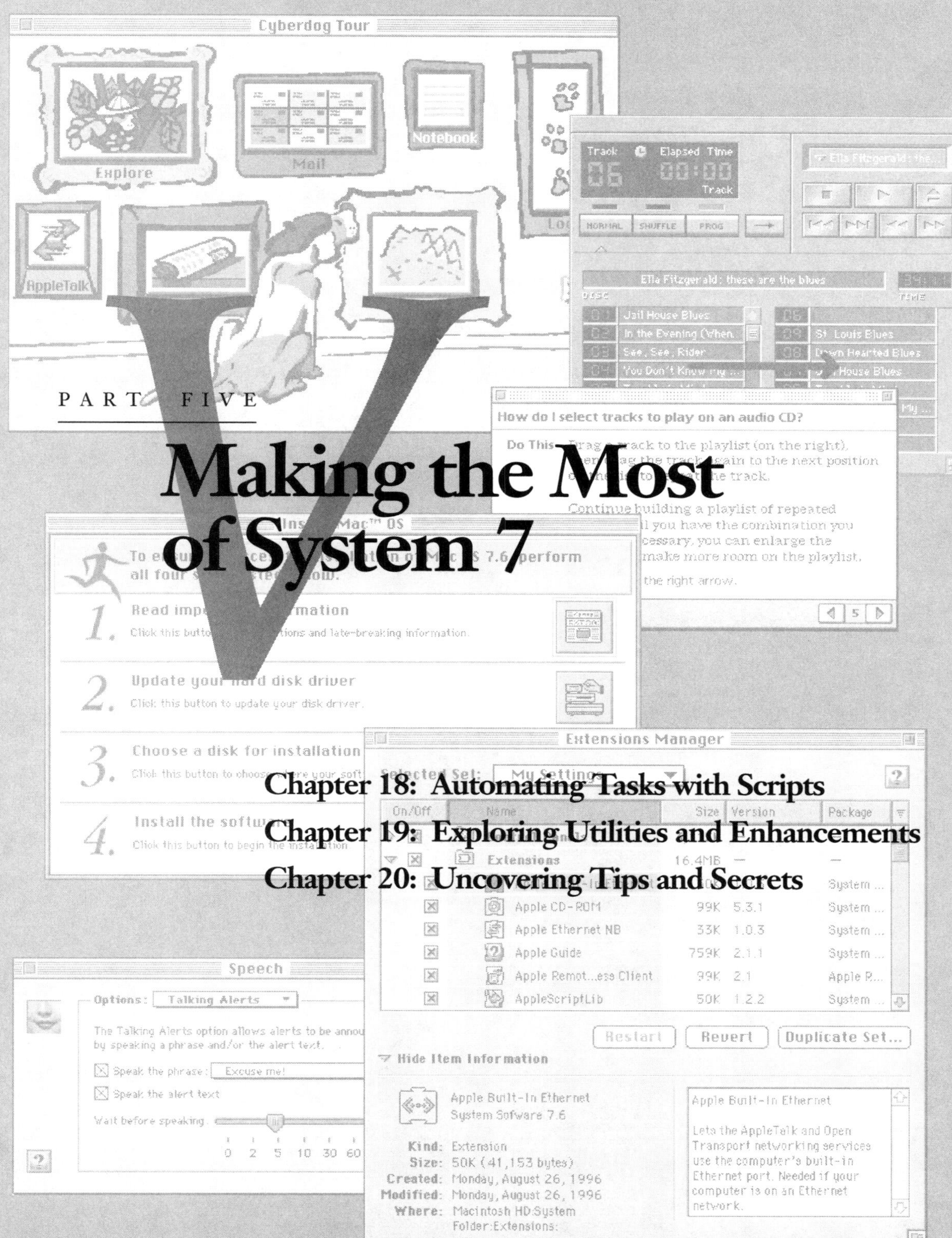


PART FIVE

# V

# Making the Most of System 7

CHAPTER EIGHTEEN

# Automating Tasks with Scripts

- Programs can share services behind the scenes by sending and receiving messages called Apple events
- AppleScript is a user-oriented programming language that allows end users to send Apple events to programs
- A sample script demonstrates AppleScript's usefulness
- You can use AppleScript to control applications on other people's machines; sharing programs by sending and receiving Apple events across a network is called program linking

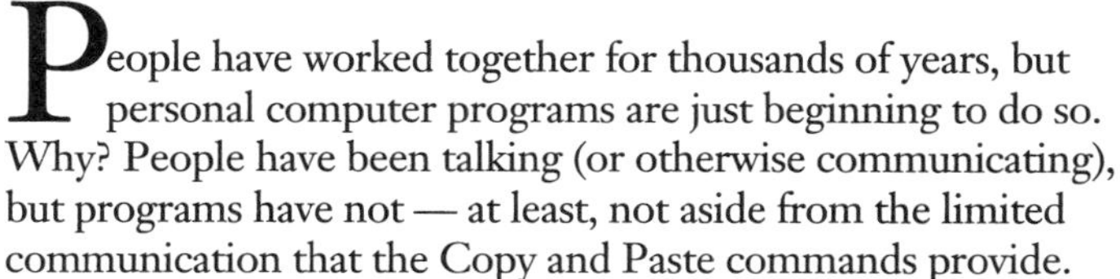

People have worked together for thousands of years, but personal computer programs are just beginning to do so. Why? People have been talking (or otherwise communicating), but programs have not — at least, not aside from the limited communication that the Copy and Paste commands provide.

The technology that enables programs to work together, which Apple calls *interapplication communication* (IAC), was not implemented system-wide before System 7. The publish and subscribe capabilities described in Chapter 14, together with the Copy and Paste commands, are one part of IAC. The other part of IAC enables programs to share services.

## Apple Events

Unlike publish and subscribe, in which you actively participate, programs can share services behind the scenes by sending and receiving messages called *Apple events*. When an application receives Apple event messages sent by another program, the receiving application, also known as the *server application*, does something. The action that the server application takes depends on the contents of the Apple event messages. This action can be anything from executing a particular command to taking some data, working with it, and then returning a result to the program that sent the Apple events, known as the *client application*.

When you choose Shut Down or Restart from the Special menu, for example, the Finder sends the Apple event Quit to every running program. When you drag and drop icons into an application, the Finder sends the Apple event Open Documents, which includes a list of all the items that you dragged into the icon. You may have seen programs that make aliases or shut down your machine for you. These programs accomplish these tasks by sending Apple events to the Finder.

A program, however, does not automatically send or receive Apple events; the developer must build in the capability to receive and act on Apple events. More and more developers are putting Apple-event capability in their applications. Most applications introduced or revised since the middle of 1991 can receive and act on at least the four basic Apple events: Open Application, Open Documents, Print Documents, and Quit Application, all of which are defined in Table 18-1.

The System 7 Finder uses the basic Apple events messages to open programs, open documents, print documents, and quit programs. When you double-click a program icon, the Finder sends the program an Open Application message. When you double-click a document, the Finder sends the program that created the document an Open Application message and an Open Documents message with the name of the document you double-clicked. When you select one or more documents and choose Print from the Finder's menu, the Finder sends the application an Open Application message, a Print Documents message with the names of the documents you selected, and a Quit Application message. When you choose the Shut Down or Restart command, the Finder sends a Quit Application message to each open program. For programs that don't understand the basic Apple events, the Finder uses its traditional means of opening, printing, and quitting.

Programs that go beyond the four basic Apple events messages understand another two dozen messages. These messages encompass actions and objects that almost all programs have in common, such as the close, save, undo, redo, cut, copy, and paste commands. Programs with related capabilities recognize additional sets of Apple events messages. Word processing programs understand messages about text manipulation, for example, and drawing programs understand messages about graphics manipulation. Program developers also can define personal messages that only their own programs know.

System 7 provides the means of communicating Apple events messages between programs. The programs can be on the same computer or on different computers connected to the same network. A program doesn't have to be open or even accessible to receive messages; System 7 stores messages and forwards them when

Table 18-1
**Basic Apple Events Messages**

| ***Message*** | ***Meaning*** |
|---|---|
| Open Application | Open the selected program |
| Open Documents | Open the selected documents |
| Print Documents | Print the selected documents without displaying them |
| Quit Application | Same as choosing Quit from the program's File menu |

the program becomes available. Only application programs can send and receive Apple events; desk accessories cannot. A desk accessory can work around this limitation by sending and receiving through a small surrogate application program that always is open in the background. This background application does not have to appear in the Application menu, and the Macintosh user does not have to know that the application is open.

To understand how Apple events work, think of them as a telephone system. System 7 software furnishes a telephone and answering machine for each program, as well as the wires that connect them. For messages sent across a network, System 7 uses the built-in AppleTalk networking software and LocalTalk or other networking connectors and cables (described in Chapter 8). Application programs talk on the telephones and leave Apple events messages for each other. Desk accessories aren't capable of talking on the phone, but some of them have agents that forward incoming and outgoing messages.

Apple events offer many intriguing possibilities for the world of personal computing. No longer does an application need to handle every possible function; instead, it can send messages to smaller, more specialized, applications and use the information that those applications provide. Your word processing program, for example, may be able to communicate with a small, very good spell checker. The developer doesn't have to spend time working on a spell checker, and you don't have to worry about the poor performance of the spell checker that the developer may introduce.

Apple events do more than provide professional software engineers a means by which their programs can communicate and share services — Apple events also enable ordinary people to automate tasks that involve several programs. For example, Aladdin's StuffIt program can have files that it decompresses checked for viruses by sending Apple events to a virus-checking program. But you may need to decompress only the files that begin with the word *Acme*. Unless you can find an application that performs this kind of task via Apple events, you're stuck. You can use AppleScript to perform this kind of task.

# Understanding AppleScript?

*AppleScript* is a user-oriented programming language that allows end users to send Apple events to programs. Now you can write your own programs, called *scripts*, to perform complex tasks easily. You can use AppleScript to move data between many applications. You can develop your own tools to accomplish exactly what you need.

Because AppleScript is aimed at users, Apple has made the scripting language as easy as possible to understand and use. The language is very natural and English-like. You can look at scripts and know right away what they're supposed to do. Also, AppleScript removes the need for you to decipher the four-letter codes that make up Apple events. Instead, you get information from the application itself about what words to use to represent the Apple events that the program understands. Inside an application, a Get Data event is represented by codes like "core" and "getd," but you may see only "get." This way, even novice users can understand AppleScript. Finally, AppleScript can actually watch you as you work with an application and write a script for you behind the scenes.

Although AppleScript is designed for end users, it offers all the capabilities of a traditional programming language and won't frustrate programmers and more advanced users. You can store information in variables for later use; write if…then statements to execute different commands, depending on some criteria; or repeat a set of commands as many times as you want. AppleScript also offers error checking and even enables you to do object-oriented programming.

# Setting up AppleScript

Several pieces make up a complete AppleScript setup. Most noticeable are the two extensions that are installed as part of AppleScript. One of these extensions, called Apple Event Manager, manipulates Apple events. Although System 7 has a built-in Apple Event Manager, this extension replaces the built-in extension with one that has special capabilities that AppleScript needs.

The other extension is the AppleScript extension, which actually contains the AppleScript language. AppleScript adds new capabilities to the System software for applications to use.

Another important piece of the AppleScript installation is a folder called Scripting Additions, which resides in the System Folder. This folder contains special files, called *scripting additions*, that add commands to the AppleScript language, much as plug-in filters add menu commands to Photoshop or the contents of the Word Commands folder add various features to Microsoft Word.

In addition to these pieces, you should have two applications. One of these applications, Script Editor, is a simple application for writing scripts. The other application, Scriptable Text Editor, is an example of an application that works with AppleScript. Any program that is compatible with the open scripting architecture (OSA) works with AppleScript.

In addition to the AppleScript setup, you need the Finder Scripting Extension, which allows AppleScript to manipulate the Finder. This extension is part of System 7.5 and later; you should make sure that it is installed for this chapter.

# Introducing the Script Editor

The program that you probably will use the most when you use AppleScript is Script Editor. This simple program allows you to write and run scripts. Find the Script Editor icon on your hard drive and open it.

When you open Script Editor, a new window appears (see Figure 18-1). This window, called the *script window*, represents one script. The bottom pane of the script window is the *script editing area*, where you type the text of the script. The top pane of the window is the *script description area*. You use this area to type a description of what the script does.

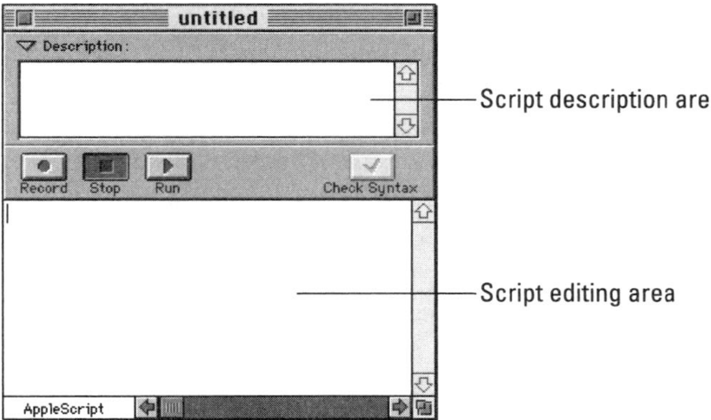


**Figure 18-1: A new script window.**

The middle area of the window contains four buttons. The first button puts you in Record mode. When you click this button, AppleScript begins watching you as you work with applications. If you are working in an application that accepts recording, AppleScript writes out the script commands that correlate to the things you do with that application. Pressing Command-D also starts recording.

Clicking the Stop button takes you out of recording mode or stops a script that is running, depending on which action is relevant at the time. Pressing Command-period (.) is the same as clicking the Stop button.

The Run button starts running the script in the script editing area. You also can press Command-R to run the script.

Finally, the script window contains a Check Syntax button. Clicking this button compiles the script. *Compiling* a script means putting it in a format that AppleScript recognizes as a script. While AppleScript compiles your script, it checks your script for things that it doesn't understand. If you forget a parentheses where AppleScript expects to find one, it lets you know. After you fix any syntax errors, AppleScript compiles the script.

# Recording a Script

One of the easiest ways to see how AppleScript looks is to record your actions and let AppleScript write a script for you. You cannot record scripts for every scriptable program because software developers must do more work to make an application recordable than to make it scriptable. One recordable application is Scriptable Text Editor, which is installed when you install AppleScript. You can use this program to see how recording works.

Go to the Finder, and find the Scriptable Text Editor icon. The icon probably is in the same folder as Script Editor, but you may need to hunt around if you moved either application. Open Scriptable Text Editor; a blank document appears.

Switch back to Script Editor and click the Record button. Notice that the apple icon in the menu bar starts alternating with a small picture of a tape cassette. This display is AppleScript's signal that it is recording your actions.

Switch back to Scriptable Text Editor and start doing things — type some text, move the window, change the font and style, whatever you want. When you finish, switch back to Script Editor and click the Stop button. AppleScript displays a script that mimics all your actions, similar to the script shown in Figure 18-2.

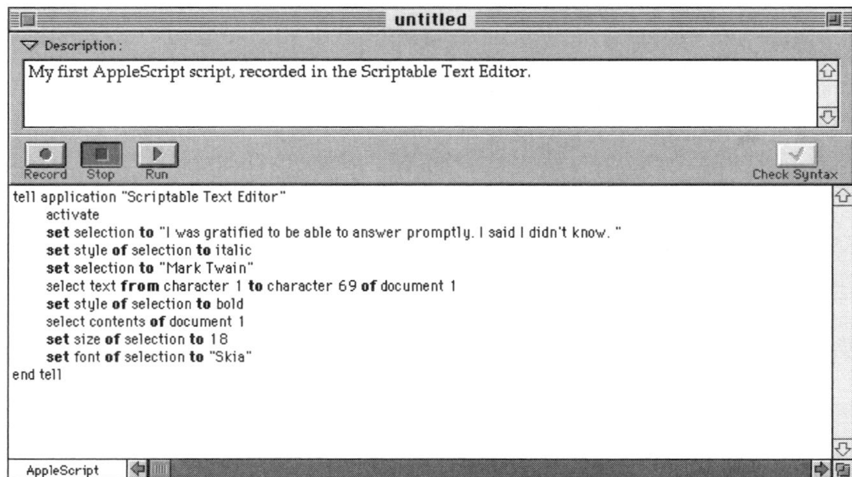


**Figure 18-2: A sample script recorded with the Scriptable Text Editor program.**

Go back to Scriptable Text Editor, close all the windows that are open, and create a new document by choosing New from the File menu. This procedure ensures that Scriptable Text Editor starts out the same way as when you started recording your script.

You can quit Scriptable Text Editor if you wish. When you run the recorded script that uses Scriptable Text Editor, AppleScript opens it automatically. AppleScript always opens applications needed by a script it is running.

Now switch back to Script Editor and click the Run button. AppleScript plays back everything you did. If you make a typing error while recording and correct the mistake, AppleScript repeats the mistake. When the script finishes running, the window will look the same as it did when you finished recording.

Switch to Script Editor again, and examine the script. You'll find the script to be fairly understandable. The text isn't exactly fluent, perfect English, but many of the commands will make sense as you read them.

# Analyzing a Script

Having looked through the script that AppleScript wrote, you may be surprised to learn that AppleScript doesn't know anything about word processing. The program doesn't know how to make words bold, or how to move windows, or how to do any of the things that your script did in Scriptable Text Editor. In fact, AppleScript knows how to perform only five commands: Get, Set, Count, Copy, and Run. AppleScript learns how to perform other commands in a script from the application controlled by the script. Each scriptable application contains a dictionary that defines procedures for performing additional AppleScript commands that work with it.

Look at the script you recorded. The first line says "tell application 'Scriptable Text Editor'." To AppleScript, this means "start working with the application named Scriptable Text Editor." When a script is compiled, AppleScript looks at the application you specified. By looking at the program's dictionary, AppleScript figures out what Apple events the program understands. AppleScript learns, for example, that Scriptable Text Editor understands the Get Data Apple event. The dictionary also tells AppleScript what kind of information, or *objects*, the application knows how to work with, such as words, paragraphs, and characters. Finally, the dictionary tells AppleScript what words to use as AppleScript commands instead of the four-letter codes that the application understands.

When you run your sample script and AppleScript reaches the line "tell application 'Scriptable Text Editor'," AppleScript starts sending Apple events to the application program named in that line. AppleScript translates every command it encounters in your script into a four-letter Apple event code based on the program's dictionary, and it sends that code to the application. The application receives the Apple event and takes the appropriate action.

When AppleScript hits "end tell," which appears at the bottom of the script you recorded, it stops sending messages to Scriptable Text Editor. If you are working with several applications, you may have another "tell" statement; AppleScript starts talking to that application, translating the commands into their four-letter equivalents.

You can look at the dictionary of an application to see what commands the application understands. In Script Editor, choose Open Dictionary from the File menu. A standard directory dialog box appears. Select Scriptable Text Editor, and click the Open button. Scriptable Text Editor's dictionary appears (see Figure 18-3).

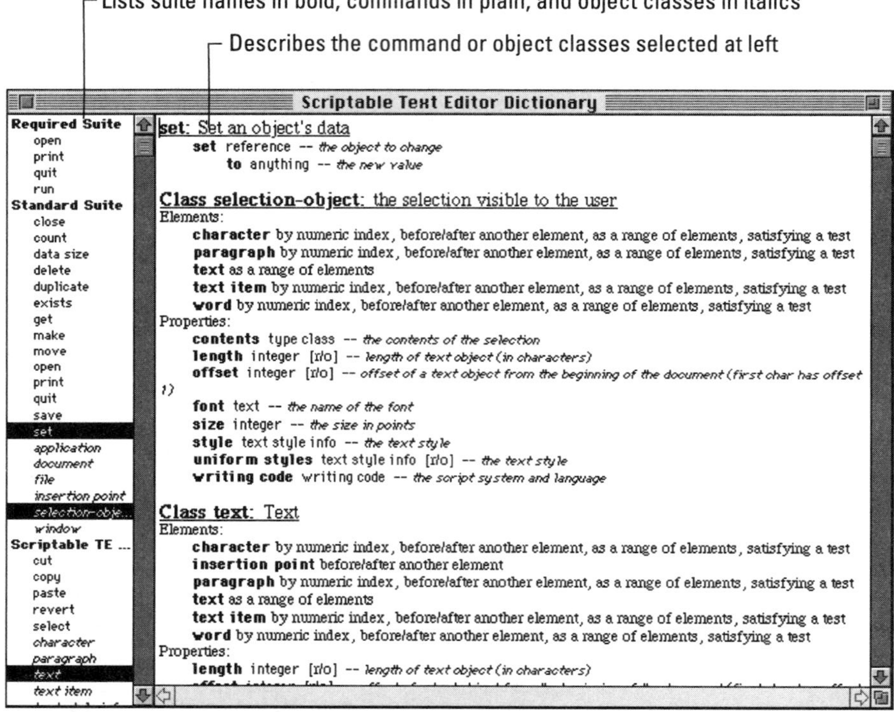


**Figure 18-3: A scriptable application's AppleScript dictionary.**

The left side of the dictionary window displays a list of commands, classes of objects, and suites that the application recognizes. A *suite* is a group of commands and other items for a related activity, but you don't have to worry about them when you're scripting.

You can select one or more terms listed on the left side of a dictionary window to see detailed descriptions on the right. Just as you can get more information about a command from a program's dictionary, so can AppleScript.

Because AppleScript gets all the relevant information from the application itself, you never have to worry about controlling a new application. As long as the application has a dictionary, AppleScript can work with it.

***Tip:*** Scripting additions also have dictionaries, which you can open the same way as you open applications' dictionaries. In fact, in the Open Dictionary dialog box, Script Editor provides a button that takes you directly to the Scripting Additions folder.

# Saving Your Script

The Script Editor allows you to save your scripts in three distinct forms. You choose the form from a pop-up menu in the Script Editor's Save dialog box, as shown in Figure 18-4.

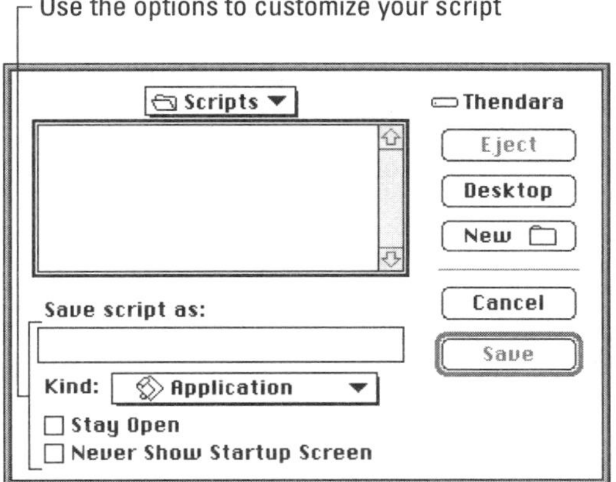


**Figure 18-4: Options for saving an AppleScript script.**

The pop-up menu contains three options:

❖ **Application** saves the script as an application, complete with icon. Opening the icon (by double-clicking it, for example) runs the script. You must have AppleScript installed to open a script application.

❖ **Compiled Script** saves the script in a compiled form that you can open with the Script Editor and run or change from there.

❖ **Text** saves the script as a plain text document, which you can open in Script Editor, any word processing program, and many other applications.

If you choose Application from the pop-up menu in the Save dialog box, two checkboxes appear in the dialog box. The Stay Open checkbox, if checked, causes the script application to stay open after its script finishes running. If the Stay Open checkbox is not checked, the script application quits automatically after running its script. Checking the Never Show Startup Screen checkbox suppresses the display of an identifying "about" window when the script application is opened.

# Creating a Script from Scratch

You know how to use Script Editor to record your actions and write an AppleScript script for you. This type of script, however, has limited value. A recorded script is not much more intelligent than a simple macro, because the script doesn't take advantage of the fact that AppleScript is a full programming language. Furthermore, not all applications that work with AppleScript permit recording, so you can't always rely on being able to record.

More frequently, you'll use AppleScript to create complex scripts from scratch.

The following sections show that you can create a full-blown script quickly and use your own custom utilities to augment a program's capabilities.

## Making a Finder utility

One of the nice features of System 7 enables you to drag files into the System Folder and have the Finder figure out where those files should go. Control panels are stored in the Control Panels folder, Fonts go in the Fonts folder, Desk Accessories are placed in the Apple Menu Items folder, and so on.

This capability, however, is limited to whatever the people at Apple provide. If you drag an After Dark module into the System Folder, for example, the Finder won't put the module in the After Dark Files folder. If you drag a scripting addition into the System Folder, the Finder won't put it in the Scripting Additions folder. You must dig your way through the System Folder hierarchy to get to the relevant folders.

You can, however, write a simple script that uses the Finder and mimic the System Folder's behavior, but moves the files you want to move to the folders in which you want those files to go. As you'll see, the script is more powerful than the System Folder, because the target folder can be anywhere. For example, you can make your QuickTime movies find their way into a folder that's nowhere near your System Folder.

## Beginning the script

Open Script Editor, or create a new window if Script Editor already is open. This blank window is where you'll write your script.

***Tip:*** You can change the default size of a new script window. Make the script window the size you want and then choose Set Default Window Size from the File menu in Script Editor.

The first thing this script must do is provide a way to select the file you want to move. One of the scripting additions that comes with AppleScript, Choose File, allows you to bring up a dialog box for selecting a file from within the script.

In the script editing area of the window, type

```
choose file
```

Then click the Check Syntax button. AppleScript changes the text fonts as it compiles the script, using different type styles to show different kinds of words. Geneva 10 Bold, for example, represents words that are native to AppleScript, whereas Plain Geneva 9 represents words that come from another application.

***Tip:*** You can change these if you prefer, using the AppleScript Formatting command in Script Editor's Edit menu.

Click the Run button to run the script you wrote, selecting any type of file and clicking the Open button. AppleScript shows you the result of the script in a window named, appropriately enough, "the result." (If this window isn't open, choose Show Result from the Controls menu.) The window contains the word *alias* and the path through your folders to the file you selected (see Figure 18-5). Notice that this word does not mean that the file is an alias, however; in the context of a script, *alias* means the same thing as *file path*.

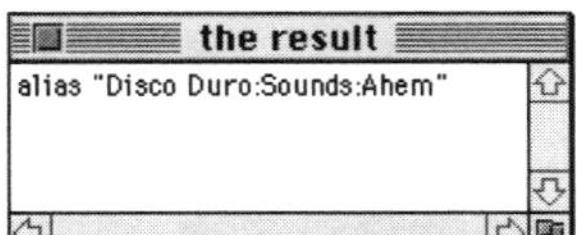


**Figure 18-5: Checking a file specification in Script Editor's "the result" window.**

The result of the Choose File command is called a *file specification*, or *file spec*. A file spec tells the system software exactly where to find a file or folder.

You will need the file spec later in the script, so you must put it in a *variable*, which is a container for information. You can place data in a variable and then retrieve it whenever you want before the script finishes running. You also can place new data in a variable during the course of the script.

On the next line of the script, type the following:

```
copy the result to filePath
```

This line takes the result of the choose file command and places that result in a variable named filePath. To access the information, type the name of the variable in your script; AppleScript understands this name to represent the file spec you got from the first command.

When you run the script, you'll see that the result of the script is the same. The result of copying information to a variable is the information itself.

Before you go further, you need to make a change in your script. Although some parts of the system software understand file specs, the Finder does not. The Finder does recognize the path of a file, but not when that information is contained in a file spec. You need to take the file spec and turn it into an ordinary piece of text, called a *string*, so that the Finder can see the path of the file.

Change the second line of your script to read as follows (enter everything as plain text; the Script Editor changes words to bold as appropriate):

```
copy (the result as string) to filePath
```

This line tells AppleScript to take the result of the Choose File command, turn it into a string, and put *that* information in the variable named filePath. Now run the script again. The result is the same, except the text is plain text and does not include the word *alias*.

## Working with the Finder

Ultimately, the script you are creating decides where to move a file you select, based on the file's four-letter file type. That means you have to get the file type of the file you selected. You can use the Finder to get this information. Enter the following commands in the script, starting on the third line of the script:

```
tell application "Finder"
copy the file type of file filePath to fileType
end tell
```

The first of these lines tells AppleScript to start using the Finder. Remember that after encountering this tell command, AppleScript knows all the commands and objects from the Finder's AppleScript dictionary.

The second line asks the Finder for the file type of the file you selected and then copies that information into the variable named fileType. Even though the word *Finder* doesn't appear in this line, the tell command in the preceding line tells AppleScript to direct these requests to the Finder.

Finally, End Tell tells AppleScript to stop working with the Finder for now.

Run the script, select a file, and look at the result. The result window contains the four-letter file type of the file you selected, displayed as a piece of text.

## Executing Script commands conditionally

For the next part of the script, you have to provide the information; you can't get it from the Finder. You need to write the commands that will move the file to the folder you want, based on the file type of the file (stored in the variable fileType).

To accomplish this task, you write a series of conditional statements, or *conditionals* for short. A *conditional* is a command or set of commands that AppleScript runs only when a certain condition is met. AppleScript evaluates the condition you set forth, and if the condition is true, AppleScript runs the specified commands.

The condition you will set up for each conditional is whether the information in the variable fileType is equal to a four-letter string that you will provide. You attach to the conditional a command that moves the file to a designated folder. In other words, if the information in the variable fileType is equal to a particular four-letter string, AppleScript moves the file to a certain folder. In AppleScript, the conditional looks like this:

```
if fileType is "sfil" then move file filePath to folder "Disco
Duro:Sounds:"
```

In this example, the condition is whether the information in fileType is "sfil," which is the four-letter type of sound files. If it is, AppleScript moves the file specified by the variable filePath to the folder named Sounds on the hard drive named Disco Duro.

Include as many of these conditionals as you want. In each conditional, use a different four-character file type for the type of file you want to move, and specify the path of the folder to which you want AppleScript to move files of that type.

The following is one example of what your final script may look like. This script moves sounds into a Sounds folder at the root level of the hard drive, moves scripting additions into the Scripting Additions folder in the Extensions folder, and moves After Dark modules into the After Dark Files folder in the Control Panels folder.

```
choose file
copy (the result as string) to filePath
tell application "Finder"
    copy the file type of file filePath to fileType
    if fileType is "sfil" then move file filePath to folder
"Disco Duro:Sounds:"
    if fileType is "osax" then move file filePath to folder
"Disco Duro:System Folder:Extensions:Scripting Additions:"
    if fileType is "ADgm" then move file filePath to folder
"Disco Duro:System Folder:Control Panels:After Dark Files:"
end tell
```

## Trying out your script

After creating a new script, you must run it and test it thoroughly. To test the script that moves files according to their type, run the script. When the dialog box appears, select a file that is of a type your script should recognize but that is not in the destination folder, and click the Open button. Switch to the Finder, and make sure that the file you selected moved from the source folder to the destination folder. Then repeat the test, selecting a different file type that your script should recognize.

## Some Tips To Speed You Along

A quick way to enter several conditionals is to select one conditional, copy it, and paste it into the script. Thereafter, you can simply change the relevant pieces of information and paste the next conditional.

You may not know the file type of the files that you want to move. You may know that you want to put After Dark modules in the After Dark Files folder, for example, but you may not know that the four-letter file type of After Dark modules is "ADgm." To make the process easy, copy the first five lines of the script, open a new window in Script Editor, and paste the copied five lines into that window. Run this five-line script, and select a file whose four-character file type you need to learn. If the result window is not visible, choose Show Result from the Controls menu. The result of the script is the file type of the file you selected. You can copy and paste the result into a conditional in your longer script.

If you don't know the full path of the folder to which you want to move the files, you can use a script to get this information. Open a new window in Script Editor and type the following script in the script editing area:

```
choose folder
```

Run the script, and select a folder. The result is a file spec for the folder you selected. You can copy only the text (don't include the word *alias,* because the Finder doesn't know about file specs), and paste it in a conditional in your longer script.

When you finish, close these extra scripts. You don't have to save them, but you can if you want.

## Creating a drag-and-drop script application

Although this sample script is useful, it would be more useful as an icon on your desktop to which you could drag files and have them move to their appropriate spots, just as you can with the System Folder. You wouldn't have to run Script Editor every time you want to move files, and you could move more than one file at a time. AppleScript gives you this capability.

You know that AppleScript can make stand-alone applications from your scripts. With a little extra work, you can make an application with drag-and-drop capability so that you can simply drag files to it.

Remember that when you drag and drop a set of icons into an application on the desktop, the Finder sends that application an Open Documents message that includes a list of the files that you dragged to the icon. This message is sent to all applications, even ones that you make with AppleScript.

You need to tell your script to intercept that Apple event and run the appropriate commands. Place the following line at the beginning of your script:

```
on open (docList)
```

Now enter the following line at the end of your script:

```
end open
```

The first line tells the script to intercept the Open Documents message and to put the list of files in a variable named docList. The End Open command helps AppleScript know which commands to run when the open message is received. Any lines between the first and second lines are run when the script receives an Apple event Open Documents.

Save this script by choosing the Save As command from the File menu. From the pop-up menu in the Save As dialog box, choose the Application option. If you switch to the Finder and look at the icon of the application you just created, you notice that the icon contains an arrow on it, showing you that this application is a drag-and-drop application. Script Editor knows how to use this kind of icon, because it sees that the application's script intercepts the Apple event Open Documents. (You can give the application a custom icon, as described in Chapter 4.)

The script won't be fully operational until you make a couple more changes. As the script stands, it places the list of files in a variable, but it doesn't do anything with that information. If you dragged several files to the application now, the script would merely bring up a dialog box asking you to pick a file, and then quit, having accomplished nothing.

First, delete what now are the second and third lines of the script (the ones beginning with the words *choose* and *copy*), and replace them with the following:

```
repeat with x from 1 to the number of items in docList
copy (item x of docList) as string to filePath
```

Between the End Tell and End Open commands, enter the following:

```
end repeat
```

Your script now should look like this:

```
on open (docList)
     repeat with x from 1 to the number of items in docList
          copy (item x of docList as string) to filePath
          tell application "Finder"
               copy the file type of file filePath to
fileType
               if fileType is "sfil" then move file filePath
to folder "Disco Duro:Sounds:"
               if fileType is "osax" then move file filePath
to folder "Disco Duro:System Folder:Extensions:Scripting Addi-
tions:"
               if fileType is "ADgm" then move file filePath
to folder "Disco Duro:System Folder:Control Panels:After Dark
Files:"
          end tell
     end repeat
end open
```

In this modified script, AppleScript repeatedly executes the commands between the Repeat and End Repeat commands for the number of times specified in the Repeat command. This arrangement is called a *repeat loop*. The first time AppleScript executes the Repeat command, it sets variable x to 1, as specified by "from 1." When AppleScript encounters the End Repeat command, it loops back to the Repeat command, increments the variable x by 1, and compares the new value of x to the number of items that were dragged to the icon ("the number of items in docList"). If the two values are not equal, AppleScript sequentially executes the command following the Repeat command. If the two values are equal, AppleScript goes to the command immediately following ΔEnd Repeat. The End Open command ends the script.

The first command in the repeat loop that you just created takes item x (remember that x is a number ranging from 1 to the number of items in the variable docList) of the variable docList, converts it to a string, and then copies that information to the filePath variable. (The list that comes with the Open Documents message is a list of file specs, so you need to convert each item to a string before the Finder can use it.)

Save the script, and switch back to the Finder. You now have a drag-and-drop application that you can use to move certain types of files to specific folders. Any time you want to add a file type, use Script Editor to open the script, add a conditional that covers that file type, and save the script. You can place several different files in a single folder, if you want, but you can't place files of the same type in different folders.

***Tip:*** You can drag and drop a script application to the Script Editor icon, and Script Editor will open the script for you.

# Using AppleScript with Applications

The Finder is only one application that you can use with AppleScript; more and more vendors are including AppleScript capability in their applications. This section provides a few examples of scripts that use some popular scriptable programs. These scripts are reasonably small, so you can type them quickly. The scripts also give you an idea of other things that AppleScript can do.

## FileMaker Pro 2.0 and later

When Claris released FileMaker Pro 2.0, it added extensive scriptability. You can retrieve data from a database, set the values in fields, find data, and even run native FileMaker scripts from AppleScript.

Most people, however, will want to retrieve data via AppleScript so that they can use that data later. The small script in this section shows how you can use FileMaker to fill in information in Scriptable Text Editor.

To use this script reliably, you need to do a little preparation. In FileMaker, create a new database named Address Book. When the Add Fields dialog box appears, add the following fields:

Name

Street

City

State

Zip

Phone #

Fill in a few records with the relevant information for friends and family.

Type the following script in Script Editor:

```
tell application "Scriptable Text Editor"
    copy the contents of the selection to theText
end tell

tell application "FileMaker Pro"
    Show every Record of Database "Address Book"
    Show (every Record of Database "Address Book" where Cell
"Name" = theText)
    copy Cell "Street" to street
    copy Cell "City" to city
    copy Cell "State" to state
    copy Cell "Zip" to zip
end tell

tell application "Scriptable Text Editor"
    set the selection to theText & return & street & return &
city & ", " & state & return & zip
end tell
```

Compile the script by clicking the Check Syntax button. Now launch Scriptable Text Editor and type the name of one of the people you entered in the database, exactly as you entered it. Select the name. Switch back to Script Editor and run the script.

When the script finishes running, go back to Scriptable Text Editor. You see that AppleScript took the address of the specified person from the database, stored the various components of the address in variables, and then put that information in Scriptable Text Editor. In effect, you have created a useful shortcut for filling in a person's address.

*Tip:* Wish that you could just run this script from within Scriptable Text Editor, almost like a new menu command? A piece of freeware called OSA Menu, by Leonard Rosenthal, creates a system-wide Scripts menu. OSA Menu is available from on-line information services and from user groups.

This script also shows how you can work with different applications in a single script. Although this script uses only two different applications, you can use as many as you want.

## StuffIt Deluxe

StuffIt Deluxe, from Aladdin, is not only scriptable and recordable but also attachable. This means that you can execute AppleScript scripts directly from the application itself; you don't have to switch to Script Editor. With StuffIt, you can place an AppleScript script in the Scripts menu. This feature is very handy for small utility scripts that augment StuffIt's capabilities. StuffIt Deluxe comes with several sample scripts you can inspect with the Script Editor.

## MacWrite Pro 1.5

MacWrite Pro 1.5, from Claris, provides several useful text-manipulation commands. You can use these commands to find data, select text, insert new text, apply styles, and perform other tasks. The script in this section shows how you can set up a script to number each paragraph in MacWrite Pro's document window (the frontmost document window if there are more than one).

You may wonder why you wouldn't use Scriptable Text Editor, which is heavily scriptable and comes as part of AppleScript. The main reason is that Scriptable Text Editor cannot handle documents larger than 32K. In addition, MacWrite Pro is notably faster than Scriptable Text Editor.

This script demonstrates some other capabilities of AppleScript. For example, you can create *handlers*, which allow you to group a set of commands under one command that you call from the script. If you have to repeat a set of commands several times in different parts of the script, you could use one command to which that set of repeated commands is attached. You saw a handler earlier in this chapter, in the script that moves files according to their file type. In that script, the Open Documents Apple event was handled by commands in an open handler.

The handler in this script demonstrates another powerful capability of AppleScript: you actually can try a command and then make changes if an error occurs. No error dialog box appears, and you get a chance to perform some relevant action when an error happens. In this case, the script returns a false value to the main script, so that you can check to see whether a paragraph exists.

```
copy 1 to x
tell application "MacWrite Pro"
    tell me to paraExists(1)
    copy the result to paragraphExists
```

```
    repeat while paragraphExists is true
           select paragraph x
           copy (get chars) to paraText
           copy (x as string) & ". " & paraText to newText
           put chars newText
           tell me to paraExists(x + 1)
           copy the result to paragraphExists
           copy x + 1 to x
    end repeat
end tell

on paraExists(whichPar)
    tell application "MacWrite Pro"
           try
                  select paragraph whichPar
                  return true
           on error
                  return false
           end try
    end tell
end paraExists
```

# Linking Programs

You have seen how AppleScript can automate tasks on your own machine. You also can send Apple events to open applications on other machines in a network. As a result, you can use AppleScript to control applications on other people's machines. Sharing programs by sending and receiving Apple events across a network is called *program linking*.

Program linking adds tremendous potential to AppleScript. If you are in charge of a network, you can use AppleScript to perform network installations or backups. If you have a script that uses many applications, you can speed the script by sending a command to a remote application and retrieving the data later. You send only a blip across the network; the other program does the work while other parts of your script are running, and you get the results later. In addition, this capability can help you get around possible memory problems that might arise from opening several applications from a script.

## Setting up program linking

Program linking can be controlled much like file sharing. The person using a Macintosh can turn program linking on and off, can control who on the network is allowed access to the shared programs, and can deny access to specific programs.

## Starting and stopping program linking

Before other users in your network can share your programs, you must activate program linking on your Macintosh. To activate program linking, click the Start button in the Program Linking section of the Sharing Setup control panel, as shown in Figure 18-6.

Sharing Setup
Network Identity
Owner Name: Buck O. Racine
Owner Password: ••
Macintosh Name: Buck's Mac IIci
File Sharing
Stop
Status
File sharing is on. Click Stop to prevent other users from accessing shared folders.
Program Linking
Start
Status
Program linking is off. Click Start to allow other users to link to your shared programs.

**Figure 18-6: Starting program linking with the Sharing Setup control panel.**

After you click the Start button, it changes to a Stop button. Clicking the Stop button prevents all other computers in your network from sending Apple events to any of your programs.

## Authorizing access to shared programs

You use the Users & Groups control panel to control which computers in your network can share your programs. To give everyone on your network access to your programs, open the Guest icon in the Users & Groups control panel to display the Guest privileges window (see Figure 18-7) and turn on the "Allow guests to link to programs on this Macintosh" option. Turning off that option prevents unauthorized users from sharing your programs.

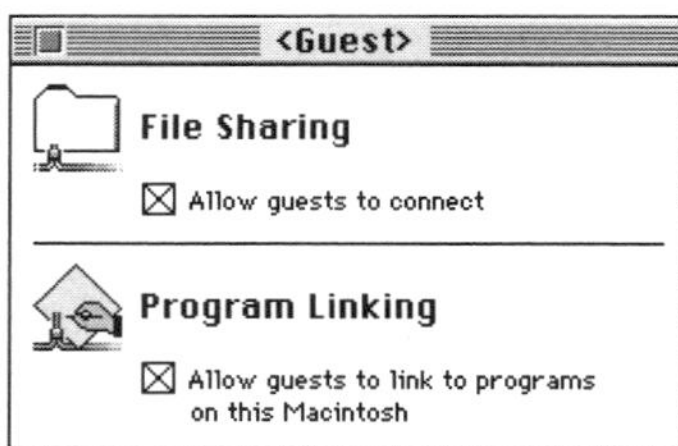


**Figure 18-7: Giving guests access to your shared programs.**

If you don't give guests program-linking privileges, you need to designate which registered users in your Users & Groups control panel can share your programs. To allow a registered user to link his or her programs to yours, open that user's icon in your Users & Groups control panel to display the user's access privileges window, as shown in Figure 18-8. In that window, turn on the "Allow user to link to programs on this Macintosh" option. (For information on registering users, see Chapter 9.)

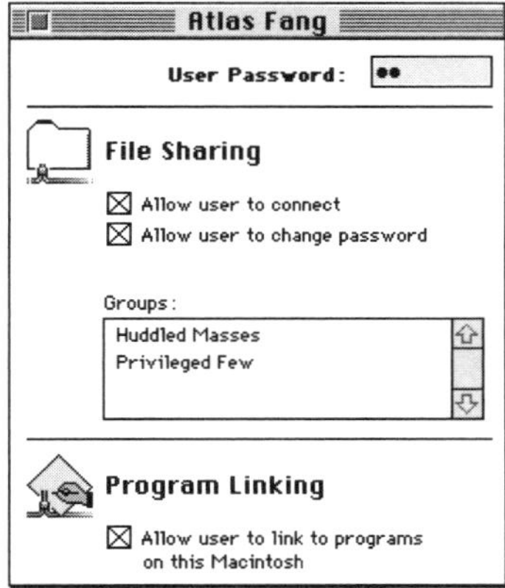


**Figure 18-8: Giving a registered user access to your shared programs.**

You can block any registered user from linking to your programs by turning off that user's "Allow user to link to programs on this Macintosh" option.

## Denying access to specific programs

Even though you may allow certain people to use your programs, you may want to specifically deny access to a particular application, just as you may want to prevent someone from seeing a particular folder when sharing your hard drive. To prevent others from sending Apple events to one of your programs, select the program and choose Sharing from the Finder's File menu. The Finder displays a program-linking information window, as shown in Figure 18-9. Turn off the "Allow remote program linking" option and close the window. Turning off that option prevents other users from linking to the program. If the option is dimmed, the program is open; you must quit a program before changing its program-linking option.

**Figure 18-9: Preventing other users from sharing a specific program.**

## Scripting across a network

Using AppleScript to run a program across the network doesn't take much more work than writing a script to use a program on the same Macintosh. Start program linking on a networked Mac. On the same Mac, open Scriptable Text Editor. This Mac doesn't have to have AppleScript installed. AppleScript will be installed on another Mac and will translate the commands into Apple events before they are sent across the network to the Scriptable Text Editor you just opened.

Now go to another Mac in the network. This computer must have AppleScript installed. Open the Script Editor, and type the following command:

```
choose application
```

This command brings up a dialog box in which you select an application on your own machine or on the network (see Figure 18-10). On the left side of this dialog box, select the machine you set up (you may need to select a zone if your network has zones and the machine is in a different zone); you see the applications that are running on that computer. One application is Scriptable Text Editor, which you left open on that machine. Select it and click OK.

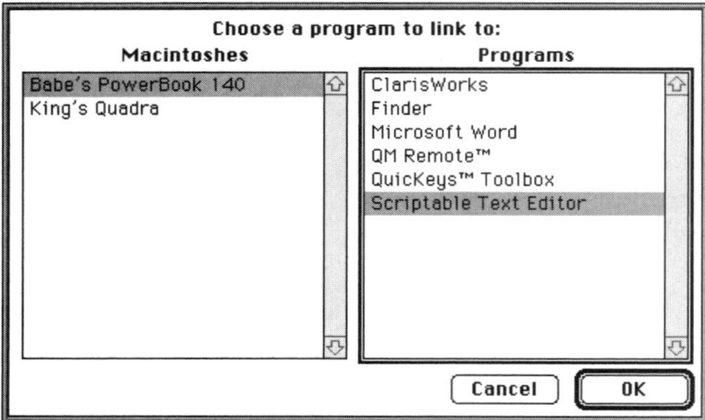


**Figure 18-10: Selecting a program to receive Apple events.**

Open the result window in Script Editor, if it's not open already. You see that the result of this short script is the network path of the application you selected: the name of the application, the name of the machine, and the name of the zone (if your network has more than one zone).

Enter the following line below the first one and then run the script, selecting the same application on the same machine:

```
copy the result to netpath
```

This script places the path to the application in a variable named netpath. To send Apple events to this application, you use a tell statement, as always. Now enter the next two lines in the script:

```
tell netpath
end tell
```

This tell command specifies the name of the application with the variable netpath instead of with the word *application* and the literal name of the application. The effect is the same: AppleScript starts sending Apple events to that application, which in this case happens to be on a different machine.

Enter the following command lines between the Tell and the End Tell command lines:

```
set the contents of window 1 to "This was sent from another
machine!"
set the style of word 1 of window 1 to bold
get word 2 of window 1
```

Run the script. As before, the script displays a dialog box in which you select the Scriptable Text Editor that is running on the other machine. Before the script can send Apple events to that program, however, the script must connect your Mac to the other machine. To do this, the script displays a connection dialog box like the ones you use to connect to other machines for file sharing, as shown in Figure 18-11.

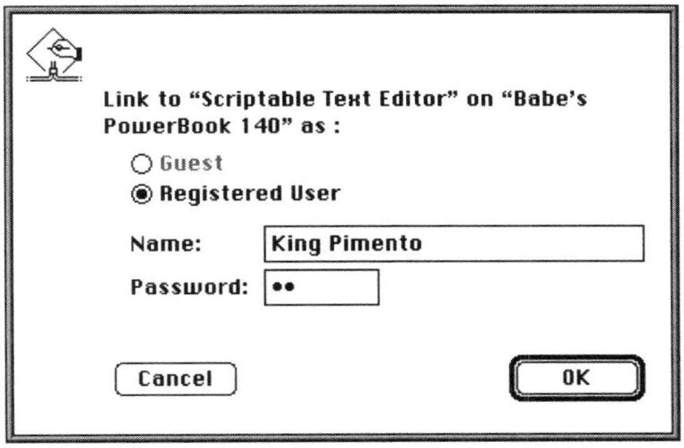

**Figure 18-11: Linking to another machine as a registered user.**

In the connection dialog box, you specify whether you want to connect as a guest (if the other machine allows guests) or as a registered user. To connect as a registered user, enter your name and password as they were set up in the other machine's Users & Groups control panel. A password dialog box appears. Enter the password you used when you set up your account on the other machine. When the script finishes running, open the result window. The window contains the word *was*, because the next-to-last line of your script gets the second word in window 1 from the copy of Scriptable Text Editor running on the remote machine.

Before you run over to the other machine, however, run the script again. This time, you don't get a password dialog box. After you connect to another Mac, you don't have to retype your password every time you want to send an Apple event. You have to re-enter your password only if you restart your machine or the other machine.

Now go over to the other Mac, and look at Scriptable Text Editor. You see the words that you sent from your script, with the first word boldfaced, as your script specified.

That's all the work you have to do if you want to script a remote application. You don't have to use the choose application command, either. You can simply write the network path of the application, as in this example:

```
tell application "Scriptable Text Editor" of machine "King's
Quadra"
...
end tell
```

Program linking offers many possibilities for scripters. For example, you could use a script to create a large catalog by farming out different sections of that catalog to several networked machines. Each machine could work on its section, and the script could pick up the resulting file via file sharing from the machines as they finish their individual sections. As another example, a network administrator could back up crucial documents from machines across the network onto a central tape drive and then shut down the individual machines.

## Working Around Program-Linking Barriers

One of the biggest problems with using Apple events over a network is the fact that some applications do not accept Apple events that come from a remote machine. You cannot send remote Apple events to the Finder, for example, because it simply won't accept them.

There is a way around this problem, however. *Script applications* — that is, scripts you save as applications from the Script Editor — accept Apple events from across a network. When a script application runs a script, the application acts as though the script is on the local machine. If you're trying to control a remote application that does not allow networked Apple events, you can send a message to a script application on the remote machine. The script application in turn executes a script to control other applications on the same machine.

To see how this process works, create the following simple script application on a networked machine that has AppleScript installed:

```
on netMessage()
tell application "Finder"
      open about box
end tell
end netMessage
```

This script has a handler for netMessage, just as the earlier drag-and-drop script had a handler for open. This netMessage handler tells the Finder to display the "About this Macintosh" window. This script has no problem sending Apple events to the Finder on the same machine, because no network is involved.

When you save this script as a script application, be sure to turn on the Stay Open option in the Save dialog box. With this option checked, the script stays open after you open it, rather than quitting after the script runs.

Save the script application, open it again, and go to another networked machine that has AppleScript installed. On that machine, write the following script:

```
choose application
copy the result to netPath
tell netPath to netMessage()
```

Run the script, and use the dialog box to select the name of the script application that you left open on the other machine. The script gets the result and tells the script application to netMessage. The script application on the other machine receives this message and runs the commands in the netMessage handler, showing the "About this Macintosh" window on that machine.

# CHAPTER 18 CONCEPTS AND TERMS

- Programs can share services behind the scenes by sending and receiving messages called Apple events. When an application receives Apple event messages sent by another program, the receiving application, also known as the server application, does something.
- AppleScript is a user-oriented programming language that allows end users to send Apple events to programs.
- One of the easiest ways to see how AppleScript looks is to record your actions and let AppleScript write a script for you.
- More and more vendors, such as Claris and Aladdin, are including AppleScript capability in their applications.
- You also can send Apple events to open applications on other machines in a network. As a result, you can use AppleScript to control applications on other people's machines. Sharing programs by sending and receiving Apple events across a network is called program linking.

**Apple events**
System 7's language for IAC. Applications can send messages to one another. When an application receives an Apple event, it takes an action according to the content of the Apple event. This action can be anything from executing a particular command to taking some data, working with it, and then returning a result to the program that sent the Apple event.

**AppleScript**
An English-like programming language that you can use to send Apple events to programs. With AppleScript you can write your own programs, called scripts, to perform complex tasks easily. For example, you can use AppleScript to move data between many applications.

**AppleTalk**
The networking protocol built into all Macintosh computers and most LaserWriter printers for passing messages and information to each other. The content that is passed back and forth could be Apple events, page images to be printed, e-mail, file contents, or any other kind of information. The content and the protocol can be transmitted through LocalTalk cabling, EtherNet cabling, or other media.

**client application**
The application that receives and act on Apple events from an Applescript script.

**compile**
To put a script in an internal format that AppleScript can run. Before compiling a script, AppleScript checks your script for things that it doesn't understand. If you forget a parentheses when AppleScript expects to find one, it lets you know. After you fix any syntax errors, AppleScript compiles the script.

**conditional**
A command that evaluates a condition (stated as part of the conditional) to determine whether another command or set of commands should be run.

**file specification (or file spec)**
Tells the system software exactly to find a file or folder.

**handler**
A named set of script commands that you can execute by naming the handler elsewhere in the same script. Instead of repeating a set of commands several times in different parts of a script, you can make the set of commands a handler and invoke the handler each place you would have repeated the set of commands.

**interapplication communication (IAC)**
The technology that enables programs to send each other messsages requesting action and receiving the results of requested actions. System 7's IAC is called Apple events, and is the basis of AppleScript.

**LocalTalk**
Apple's cabling system for connecting computers, printers, and other devices to create an AppleTalk network. LocalTalk uses the built-in printer ports of Macintosh computers and the LocalTalk ports of many LaserWriter printers.

**network**
A collection of interconnected, individually controlled computers, printers, and other devices together with the hardware, software, and protocols used to connect them. A network lets connected devices exchange messages and informtation.

**object**
A kind of information, such as words, paragraphs, and characters, that an application knows how to work with. An application's AppleScript dictionary lists the kind of objects it can work with under script control.

**program linking**
The process of sharing programs by sending and receiving Apple events across a network. You must turn on program linking in the Sharing Setup control panel, and you can use the Finder's Sharing command to prevent linking to individual programs.

**repeat loop**
An arrangement of AppleScript commands that begins with a Repeat command and ends with an End Repeat command. AppleScript executes the commands between the Repeat and End Repeat commands for the number of times specified in the Repeat command.

*(continued on next page)*

(continued from previous page)

**script description area**
The top pane of a Script Editor window, in which you type a description of what the script does.

**script editing area**
The bottom pane of the Script Editor window, in which you type the text of the script.

**scripting additions**
Files that add commands to the AppleScript language, much as plug-in filters add menu commands to Photoshop or the contents of the Word Commands folder add various features to Microsoft Word. Scripting additions reside in a folder called Scripting Additions, which is in the System Folder.

**script**
A collection of AppleScript commands that performs a specific task. (Do not confuse with a language system script, which enables the Mac to use an additional natural language such as Japanese, as described in Chapter 17.)

**variable**
A container for information in a script. You can place data in a variable and then retrieve it or change it whenever you want before the script finishes running.

CHAPTER NINETEEN

# Exploring Utilities and Enhancements

- Commercial software, Apple utilities, shareware, and freeware
- Alias-assistance shareware and freeware
- Disk- and file-utility shareware and freeware
- Finder-helper shareware and freeware
- System-management shareware and freeware
- Window and dialog-box shareware and freeware
- Font and sound shareware and freeware
- Menu, folder, and icon shareware and freeware
- Networking-enhancement shareware and freeware
- PowerBook-enhancement shareware and freeware
- Summary tables telling you where to find this software

## Enhancing System 7

Although System 7 offers significant enhancements in performance and ease of use over older Macintosh operating systems, even System 7 can stand some assistance in performing its disk and file management, alias management, networking, and other duties. Software that enhances System 7 is the subject of this chapter.

Many programmers have developed small accessory applications, control panels, and system extensions that enhance the performance of the Finder and other system software. Macintosh users are an idiosyncratic lot and like to personalize their systems. These shareware, freeware, and commercial software utilities personalize the activities of the Finder and other system software so that the Macintosh does exactly what you need it to do, when you need it to. With these programs, you can open specific files directly without having to know where they are located. You also can throw away files while using an application without going to the Finder, create aliases in new ways, and make your Mac much more fun.

Each section of the chapter describes commercial and noncommercial utility programs that provide specific assistance for one aspect of your work on the Macintosh. In each section, a table summarizes each program's cost, size, and type (for example, control panel, system extension, or application). Software is updated often, especially noncommercial software, and you may find that newer versions of programs have features not described here.

# Where to Get Utility Software

You can use several avenues to acquire the software listed in this chapter: Apple Computer, APDA, user groups, companies that sell collections of shareware (such as Educorp), Apple dealers, and companies that make commercial products. Each type of supplier has its pluses and minuses.

The software listed in this chapter is available from one or more of several sources, according to the type of software:

- ❖ **Apple Computer's Order Center** (800-293-6617), **Apple Developer Catalog** (800-282-2732, U.S.; 800-637-0029, Canada; and 716-871-6555, other countries), and **Apple dealers** (dealer referral, 800-538-9696) supply minor upgrades and bug fixes for System 7, upgrades of driver software for Apple printers, and basic utility programs.
- ❖ **User groups** such as **Berkeley Macintosh Users Group (BMUG)** (510-549-2684), and **on-line information services** such as America Online (800-827-6364), CompuServe (800-800-2222), and various Internet sites (try *http://www.info.apple.com*, *http://www.filez.com*, *http://www.shareware.com*, and *http://www.macworld.com*) have much of the Apple utility software, as well as thousands of programs from noncommercial sources. Some user groups distribute System 7.0.1 under license from Apple. BMUG has a collection of System 7 utilities, including many of the ones listed in this chapter, that you can order by phone (see the coupon in the back of this book). Apple will refer you to the user group nearest you (800-538-9696).
- ❖ **Software stores, computer stores, mail-order companies, and other software resellers** have commercial products from software and hardware development companies. These products include the latest version of System 7 and Apple's major enhancements of it, such as At Ease and AppleSearch.

## How to use utility software

This chapter describes utility software but does not include detailed operating instructions. Commercial software usually comes with a printed manual, and noncommercial software usually comes with a documentation file. With both types of software, you also should check for on-screen help and documentation. Look for on-screen help in the Help menu, the About command in the Apple menu, or in other program menus.

## About shareware and freeware

Much of the software described in this chapter is not available in any store. This noncommercial software is distributed through user groups and on-line information services. The money you pay the user groups or on-line services covers the cost of distribution; none of that money goes to the authors of this noncommercial software. Most software authors encourage you to try their software and to share copies with friends and coworkers. This doesn't mean, however, that noncommercial software is in the public domain — most authors of noncommercial software retain the copyrights to their works.

Noncommercial software falls into two categories: *shareware* and *freeware*. The authors of shareware ask you to send them modest fees if you decide to use the software, whereas the authors of freeware ask for no payment.

Shareware and freeware programs typically are written by enthusiasts who can't afford to provide technical support by telephone, as the developers of commercial programs can. Moreover, shareware and freeware authors can't afford to thoroughly test their software with many combinations of Mac models, System 7 versions, and other software. All the programs listed in this chapter worked on a Quadra 610 with System 7 Pro, but this does not mean that they will work on other Mac models, with other System 7 versions, or even on differently configured Quadra 610s

Noncommercial software, on the whole, is not as stable as commercial programs. Be sure to follow the instructions and discussions provided by the authors in their ReadMe or Help files before using any of these programs. You use shareware and freeware at your own risk.

## Supporting Shareware Authors

Shareware depends on the honor and honesty of the people who use it. If you decide to keep shareware installed on your disk, the *Honorable Society of Civilized People* politely insists that you immediately send payment to the author. The $5 to $30 that you pay for the shareware you use today helps fund development of more great shareware. For detailed information about the amount of payment requested for a particular shareware product and where to send payment, check the product's ReadMe file, About command (in the Apple menu), or on-screen help.

# System 7 Utilities by Category

Apple, commercial developers, and shareware and freeware sources offer thousands of utility programs. Many new programs become available each day. The software listed in this chapter has been culled from the pack based on its usefulness, ease of use, completeness, and reliability. This list is not meant to be all-inclusive, but rather to be an example of the types of software that are available to enhance the performance of your Macintosh with System 7.

## Alias assistance

Software in this category provides enhancements to System 7's alias-generation capability. You can use this software to generate aliases on the fly by using drag-and-drop icons, as well as to manage your aliases more efficiently.

### AKA

Creates aliases in the Finder when you press Control while dragging an item to another folder, a disk, or the desktop.

### Alias Assassin

Finds orphaned aliases and deletes them, or reunites them with their original files or folders.

### Alias Director

Written to make creating and deleting aliases as easy as using them. The program operates either automatically or interactively, creating aliases of your applications and placing those aliases where you want them, such as in the Apple menu or in any folder on your desktop. Figure 19-1 shows the dialog box used in Alias Director to create an alias and save it to the Apple menu.

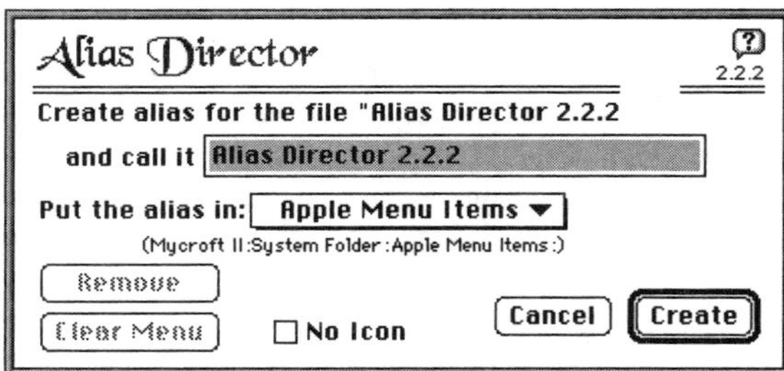


**Figure 19-1: Use Alias Director to create and place aliases anywhere in your system.**

### AliasBOSS

Creates, validates, moves, and deletes alias files. You drag any icon of a file into the program's drop box to create an alias. If you press Shift while dropping a volume or disk icon, you can scan for files of your selected file type. You also can scan a volume for aliases by pressing and holding the Option key while dragging.

### AliasZoo

Identifies aliases and their originating files, using hierarchical menus. The program also can reattach the alias to its rightful owner or to a new owner, or delete it from the disk if you decide that it is obsolete.

### Easy Alias

Makes it easy to create an alias with the same name as the original file and to save it in the location where it is needed.

### Power Alias

Groups your application aliases for easier access. The software opens up to five applications. You also can use the software to specify which word processing program should be used to open generic text files.

### ZMakeAlias

Adds to the Save As dialog box a bullet that enables you to create an alias within an application, rather than use the Make Alias command in the Finder.

## Summary of alias-assistance software

Table 19-1 summarizes the pertinent data about alias-assistance software. (EXT is a system extension, and APP is an application program.)

## Disk and file utilities

These programs help manage your files and desktop in order to customize your Macintosh for the way you want to work. The list includes some items that hackers (advanced users or programmers) can use to edit file types and creator information, as well as applications that maintain Desktop files and other useful housekeeping programs. You can purchase third-party software that restores deleted files and repairs hard disks. Symantec's Norton Utilities for the Mac 2, Central Point's MacTools 3, and many other disk-maintenance programs are available from any software store that sells Macintosh products.

**Table 19-1**
**Alias-Assistance Software**

| *Software* | *Type* | *Size* | *Cost* | *Author* |
|---|---|---|---|---|
| AKA | EXT | 8K | free | Fred Monroe |
| Alias Assassin | EXT | 12K | $5 | N/A |
| Alias Director | APP | 38K | $5 | Laurence Harris |
| AliasBOSS | APP | 98K | $15 | Scott Johnson |
| AliasZoo | APP | 110K | $20 | Optimize Information Control |
| Easy Alias | APP | 5K | free | Alan Simon |
| PowerAlias | APP | 25K | $5 | Andrew Anker |
| ZMakeAlias | EXT | N/A | N/A | N/A |

### AppDisk

Creates a RAM disk to use extra RAM memory as though it were a very fast hard disk. The disk appears on your desktop just like any other disk, and you can copy files to it as you would to a normal disk. The difference between this program and most other RAM disks is that AppDisk gets the memory for its disk from its application memory. Most RAM disks take memory away from your total System memory when you start up, so you can't get that memory back without restarting.

To get the memory back with AppDisk, all you have to do is quit the AppDisk program or remove the RAM disk from your desktop by dragging it to the Trash.

### Apple HD SC Setup

Apple provides this small utility program with System 7 for formatting Apple hard drives.

### BunchTyper

Changes the type or creator information of a file or group of files. The program provides detailed information on types and creators of Macintosh files (including extensive help balloons) to help you avert costly mistakes.

### CommentKeeper

Makes your Mac retain the comments that you enter in Get Info windows when you rebuild your desktop database (by pressing ⌘-Option while restarting).

## DART™

DART (Disk Archive/Retrieval Tool) is an application from Apple Computer that allows you to duplicate disks, archive hard disk contents to floppy disks, and restore their contents to your hard disk. DART can read Macintosh, Lisa, Apple II, and MS-DOS disks as well as disk images created by DiskMaker or Disk Copy.

## Discolour

Enables the Finder to display beautiful, full-color floppy-disk icons in place of black-and-white icons when your monitor is set for 16 colors or more.

## Disk First Aid

Apple's program can check disk-filing structures and repair damaged catalogs automatically. Disk First Aid is on the System 7 Disk Tools floppy disk; you may find a more recent version through an on-line service or user group.

## Locksmith

Enables you to lock or unlock files, folders, and disks quickly and easily without using the Finder's Get Info windows. You drop files or folders into the program's drop box to unlock or lock, as needed.

## MacCheck

Creates a profile of your Macintosh system for use by Apple technicians to diagnose possible problems when you call the support system. MacCheck surveys the processor, memory, expansion cards, SCSI drives, keyboard, and monitor, as well as all installed applications and system software on your startup drive, and generates a report for Apple. The software also runs several tests to ensure that your logic boards, file system, and system files are operating correctly and that no duplicate System Folders exist on your startup disk.

MacCheck comes with some (but not all) Mac models and versions of System 7; check your Disk Tools floppy disk.

## PickTURE

Adds a scrollable list of small previews of your files to every Open dialog box. You can see what is in a file and then open it by double-clicking its thumbnail.

## PowerScan

Looks for duplicate files across your hard disks and allows you to delete or save those files, as required.

## Put Away

A drag-and-drop utility that places files in folders based on their file types and creators — much as the System 7 Finder places System-specific files in special folder locations. You can configure the prograe to recognize unlimited types, creators, and folder locations. The application moves files to the destination folders unless you press Option to have them copied.

### Save-A-BNDL

Gets the Finder to recognize changes in a program's icon, which is linked to the program through its BNDL resource. You use Save-A-BNDL after upgrading an application to update its icon without rebuilding the desktop database or restarting your Macintosh. After Save-A-BNDL updates a BNDL resource, it can restart the Finder to update the desktop database without interfering with any other applications that are open.

### Scale

Counts the number of files and folders that you select (including files and folders within folders) and calculates the total logical and physical size of that group. The software enables you to determine the size of a selected group of files and folders without using the Get Info command on each and then breaking out the Calculator. This application is useful as a quality-control check when you are moving files around to ensure that you moved everything you wanted to, but no more.

### SparedDisk

Spots floppy disks that contain bad sectors that the system software spared (internally marked as unusable) when the disks were formatted. Such a floppy disk appears on the desktop as a disk with a Band-Aid.

### Stationer

Creates stationery files without you having to use the Get Info command.

## Summary of disk and file software

Table 19-2 summarizes the pertinent data about disk- and file-utility shareware. (EXT is a system extension, and APP is an application program.)

## Finder helpers

These packages assist the Finder in performing finding, opening, saving, printing, changing, copying, and moving operations. Commercial software is available to enhance the Finder's capability to locate folders and documents across the desktop. Programs such as Now's SuperBoomerang (part of Now's Now Utilities 4) and Symantec's Directory Assistance II (part of Symantec's Norton Utilities 2) add a menu to the directory dialog box that enables you to select your latest opened folders, files, and volumes in any application, bringing the Finder's power to your applications.

Table 19-2
**Disk- and File-Utility Software**

| *Software* | *Type* | *Size* | *Cost* | *Author* |
|---|---|---|---|---|
| AppDisk | APP | 39K | $15 | Mark Adams |
| Apple HD SC Setup | APP | 84K | free | Software Utility Update |
| BunchTyper | APP | 97K | $10 | Kwang Lee |
| Comment Keeper | EXT | 10K | free | Maurice Volaski |
| DART | APP | N/A | free | Apple Computer |
| Discolour | EXT | 11K | free | Andrew Welch |
| Disk First Aid | APP | 40K | free | Software Utility Update |
| Locksmith | APP | 20K | $2 | Robert Gibson |
| MacCheck | APP | 208K | free | Software Utility Update |
| PickTURE | EXT | 102K | demo | Boris Tsikanovsky |
| PowerScan | APP | 166K | $10 | Jonas Walladen |
| Put Away | APP | 27K | free | Pete Johnson |
| Save-A-BNDL | APP | 12K | free | Michael Engber |
| Scale | APP | 19K | $2 | Robert Gibson |
| SparedDisk | EXT | 2K | free | Martin Gannholm |
| Stationer | APP | 21K | $2 | Robert Gibson |

## Applicon

Provides an efficient way to access your frequently used applications. Applicon displays a small square window for each application you have open. Each window shows the icon and name of the application that the window represents. If you click a window, the corresponding application becomes active. Option-clicking hides the currently active application as the new application becomes active. If all Applicon's windows are hidden behind other programs' windows, moving the mouse to a previously designated corner of the screen will bring them forward.

## AppSizer

Enables you to change your application's memory size (the suggested size in the Get Info window) as you open it, rather than having to use the Get Info command before opening.

## Blindfold

Hides or displays icons in the Finder as you require. The program can add security to your desktop by hiding private folders or applications; it also enables you to restore these personal folders and applications to view when required.

## Carpetbag

Opens all the fonts, desk accessories, sounds, and function keys that you designate without having to install them in the System Folder.

## DTPrinter

Enables you to drop files that you want to print onto an icon that represents a particular printer, fax/modem, or other output device. You can create a separate icon for every printer you use. The program replaces using the Chooser with dragging an icon on your desktop.

## Find Pro II

Searches for multiple files at the same time. In addition, the program opens files and connects aliases with their originating files. The author claims that the program is 10 to 20 times faster than the Finder's Find command, because it searches for multiple files simultaneously.

## Finder Palette

Creates a series of 3-D tiles that represent your most frequently used programs, enabling you to open these applications by clicking their tiles. You can create palettes of tiles, each associated with a type of work you do, and save each palette. Figure 19-2 displays tiles created with Finder Palette's menu-based commands.

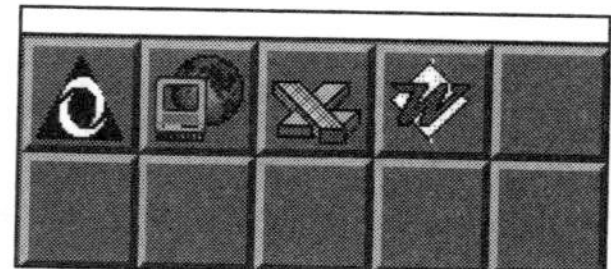

**Figure 19-2: Finder Palette creates full-color application tiles on your desktop to make opening your programs easy.**

## Finder 7 Menus!

Enables you to change the ⌘-key shortcuts in the Finder's menus.

## GetFolder

Enhances the performance of Symantec's Directory Assistance II utility to locate and open folders from all your available volumes. This application does not work with Now Utilities' SuperBoomerang.

## Just Click

This system extension modifies the Finder to let you simply click the application icon in the menu bar to switch between currently active applications without having to open the Application menu.

## Obliterate

Automatically deletes all files and folders dragged to its icon. The software also offers an optional shredding facility to make files totally unrecoverable. All folders dragged into this drop box are scanned, so that you can throw in sets of files, folders, or disks — or any combination of the three — for permanent or semipermanent erasure.

## Other Menu

This system extension creates a new menu in the Finder's menu bar. This hierarchical menu is loaded with the applications, documents, and function keys that you regularly use. Use the menu to launch applications, open or close documents, and generally manage your files.

## PowerBar

Gives you one-click access to your favorite files, folders, programs, control panels, and other icons, as well as one-click shortcuts for QuicKeys macros and Finder operations such as restarting, shutting down, dragging selected icons to the Trash, and emptying the Trash. PowerBar also creates and repairs aliases, and (optionally) hides windows automatically when you switch applications. Gauges show memory use, disk-space availability, and battery status (for PowerBooks). You install and rearrange icons in PowerBar by dragging.

## PrintChoice

This control-panel device lets you select regularly used printers or other Chooser devices without opening the Chooser. The printers, faxes, network volumes, and so on are placed in the Apple menu for easy access.

### PwrSwitcher

Enables you to switch to the next open program with your keyboard instead of the Application menu. You switch by pressing either Power-On or Esc plus one other key, which you designate in the PwrSwitcher control panel.

### Shutdown Delay

Interrupts the shutdown or restart process by displaying a dialog box that gives you several options. You can choose to wait for the completion of a specified command, cancel the shutdown or restart, continue as usual, or quit the program and return to the Finder. This dialog box appears whenever you choose Shutdown or Restart from the Special menu.

### Suitcaser

Creates suitcases for fonts, desk accessories, function keys, and sounds so that they can be used with System 6.

### SuperTools

SuperTools is a series of three applications that speed the launching, printing, and erasing of documents. SuperPrint is a drop-box desktop printer that prints a document on the currently selected printer when you drag and drop the document's icon onto SuperPrint. SuperLaunch lets you bundle a series of documents with their application to create workbooks by dragging the collection on top of the SuperLaunch icon. SuperTrash permanently erases a document by writing zeroes on top of its data before deletion.

### TattleTale

Presents information about your computer and its system-related software. The data provided includes the name and number of your Macintosh, volumes and drives, monitors, NuBus cards, SCSI devices, ADB devices, serial ports, general system attributes, startup environment, System-file contents, desk accessories, fonts, printer drivers, currently open files, currently active programs, available applications, and traps. In addition, the program can mount volumes and close files.

### Trash Chute

Automatically empties your Trash without displaying the cautionary dialog box associated with the Empty Trash command.

### Trash Selector

Replaces the Empty Trash command with a Trash Selector command. This command displays a dialog box that enables you to selectively delete files that you have placed in the Trash.

### TrashMan

Provides a timed deletion of items that you have thrown into your Trash. The program can age items in your Trash, making the action of emptying the Trash occur automatically at times that you specify in the control panel.

## Summary of Finder-helper software

Table 19-3 summarizes the pertinent data about Finder-helper software. (CP is a control panel, EXT is a system extension, APP is an application program, and DA is a desk accessory.)

Table 19-3
**Finder-Helper Software**

| ***Software*** | ***Type*** | ***Size*** | ***Cost*** | ***Author*** |
|---|---|---|---|---|
| Applicon | APP | 84K | free | Rick Holzgraf |
| AppSizer | CP | 63K | $19.95 | Peirce Software |
| Blindfold | APP | 20K | $2 | Robert Gibson |
| Carpetbag | CP | 45K | $5 | James Walker |
| DTPrinter | APP | 24K | free | Leonard Rosenthol |
| Find Pro II | APP | 91K | free | Ziffnet Mac |
| Finder Palette | APP | 169K | $20 | Anchor Beech Software |
| Finder 7 Menus! | APP | 12K | $10 | Adam Stein |
| GetFolder | APP | 24K | free | Michael Love |
| Just Click | EXT | 10K | free | Luis Bardi |
| Obliterate | APP | 24K | $2 | Robert Gibson |
| Other Menu | EXT | 55K | $10 | James Walker |
| PowerBar | CP | 291K | $25 | Scott Johnson |
| PrintChoice | CP | 60K | $14 | Kerry Clendinning |
| PwrSwitcher | CP | 16K | free | David Lamkins |
| Shutdown Delay | CP | 16K | $5 | Alessandro Montalcini |
| Suitcaser | APP | 20K | free | Troy Gaul |
| SuperTools | APP | 64K | $25 | Pascal Pochet |
| TattleTale | DA | 234K | free | John Mancino |
| Trash Chute | APP | 6K | free | Milissa Rogers |
| Trash Selector™ | CP | 38K | free | HCS Software |
| TrashMan | EXT | 12K | $10 | Dan Walkowski |

## System management

Some of the programs in this section help you make the transition from System 6 to System 7 by providing methods for switching between systems. Other software listed in this section modifies or enhances system-level functions. These programs handle such operations as selecting your startup disk, colorizing various parts of the interface, loading system extensions, editing resources, and managing memory.

Now Software markets a desktop-pattern program as part of its Now Fun package. In addition, Now Fun lets you colorize windows, buttons, and menus for a more aesthetic Macintosh environment. Logical Solutions offers the Chameleon program, which provides an extensive array of desktop graphics as well as the ability to create your own desktop patterns by using standard PICT files.

### Before Dark

Installs desktop patterns up to 128 by 128 pixels (the standard desktop pattern is 8 by 8 except on Performas and on Macs with System 7.5 and later, in which it is 64 by 64). The program includes several patterns and shows you how to build your own with commercial painting programs.

Figure 19-3 displays the dialog box used in Before Dark to import, apply, and install colored desktop background patterns.

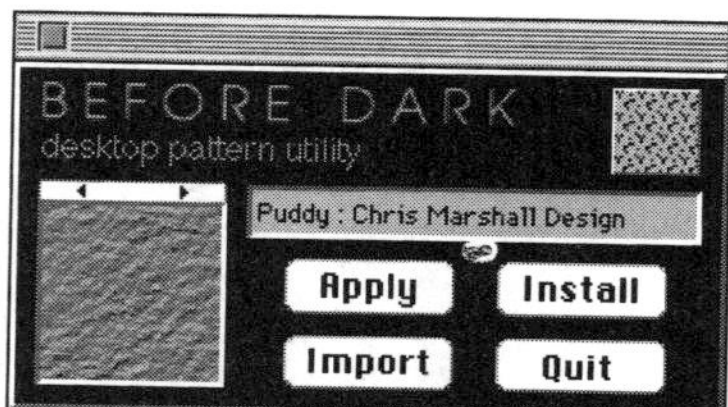


**Figure 19-3: Choose among several artistic computer-graphic patterns to decorate your Desktop with Before Dark.**

### CClock

Displays an analog clock in a window on the Mac. You can resize and reposition the window anywhere, and the program remembers where you put the window every time you open the program. You can set up to 50 alarms for any time up to the year 2079, and you can set a chime from among your system sounds to sound on the hour, half-hour, or both. You also can open other applications from this program and create a menu of applications to be opened at any time.

### Color Alias

Switches the color depth that you require for each program you are using without using the Monitors control panel. The program switches your main monitor to the color depth that you preset, sets the sound volume, and can turn off the 68040's cache, all before opening the original application.

### Dark Side of the Mac

This application is a screen-saver engine that provides access to a dozen moving pictures that prevent screen burn-in.

### DepthMaster

This control panel device monitors loaded applications and automatically sets your monitor's color bit depth and sound volume to fit each program's requirements.

### Desktop Remover

Removes the System 6 Desktop file from the hard disk. System 7 does not use this file. If you do switch from System 7 to System 6 after removing the Desktop file, your Mac simply rebuilds it.

### Extensions Manager

Selectively turns off or on system extensions, control panels that contain system extensions, and Chooser devices. You can define sets of extensions and enable or disable each set. You can designate the types and creators of items that Extensions Manager includes. Apple includes Extensions Manager 3 with System 7.5, but not with earlier versions of System 7.

### MenuChoice

This control panel device creates hierarchical menus in the Apple menu that display the contents of such folders as Control Panels, Chooser, and Apple Menu Items to let you select hidden items more readily.

### Monitor Energy Saver

This control panel device from Apple Computer enhances the energy efficiency of your Macintosh by giving you the option of setting your monitor to go into low-power mode after your Macintosh has been idle for a specified period (up to one hour). Monitor Energy Saver works only on Quadra, Centris, and LC III Macintoshes and on Apple Energy Star-compliant monitors that use the built-in video support of newer Macs.

### Overhead

Measures the overall performance of a Macintosh in terms that an engineer or advanced user can understand. Overhead analyzes the raw speed of the microprocessor (a measure of the computer's maximum potential speed), the effect of system overhead on the maximum speed of event processing, and the interference by system overhead on normal application-event processing.

### Reset DTDBs

Removes System 7's desktop database files from all hard disks whose icons are on the desktop, and then restarts the Mac, forcing complete recreation of the desktop database.

### SCSI Startup

Enables you to make a SCSI disk the startup disk by dragging that disk's icon to the SCSI Startup icon. Otherwise, you have to open the Startup Disk control panel to change the startup disk.

### Shutdown Items

Sets up your Macintosh to open selected items during the shutdown process, just as the Startup Items folder does at startup time. Any item placed in the Shutdown Items folder is opened (played, if it's a sound) during shutdown just as though you double-clicked the item in the Finder. PICT-type graphics are displayed, and QuickTime movies can be played as well.

### Sounder

This system extension lets you set the sound volume of your Macintosh by using hot keys.

### SuperClock!

Displays the time and date near the right end of the menu bar. (If you're using a battery-powered Mac, SuperClock! also displays the battery status there.) You can set the program to chime on the hour, quarter-hour, and half-hour. SuperClock! has a count-down and count-up timer. Apple includes most of the program's functions in the Date & Time control panel in System 7.5 and later, but not in earlier versions of System 7.

### System Picker

Enables you to specify which System Folder your Mac will use the next time you restart the computer. You can choose among multiple System Folders on a single hard disk, multiple hard disks, or multiple partitions of hard disks.

### Too Many Lawyers...

Teaches respect for an important Apple legal requirement.

### zapParam™

*Zaps* (resets to factory settings) the Parameter RAM while using System 7.

## Summary of system-management software

Table 19-4 summarizes the pertinent data about system-management software. (CP is a control panel, EXT is a system extension, and APP is an application program.)

Table 19-4
**System-Management Software**

| *Software* | *Type* | *Size* | *Cost* | *Author* |
|---|---|---|---|---|
| Before Dark | APP | 159K | $10 | Craig Marciniak |
| CClock | APP | 36K | $15 | Stephen Martin |
| Color Alias | APP | 18K | $10 | Mark Adams |
| Dark Side of the Mac | APP | 106K | $15 | Tom Dowdy |
| DepthMaster | CP | 46K | $20Aus | Victor Tan |
| Desktop Remover | APP | 6K | free | Adam Stein |
| Extensions Manager | CP | 29K | free | Ricardo Batista |
| MenuChoice | CP | 54K | $15 | Kerry Clendinning |
| Monitor Energy Saver | CP | N/A | free | Apple Computer |
| Overhead | APP | 10K | free | Anabolic Systems |
| Reset DTDBs | APP | 9K | free | Brian Gaeke |
| SCSI Startup | APP | 16K | $2 | Robert Gibson |
| Shutdown Items | APP | 69K | free | John Covele |
| Sounder | EXT | 7K | free ($10 custom) | Andy Barbolla |
| SuperClock! | CP | 30K | free | Steve Christensen |
| System Picker | APP | 30K | free | Kevin Aitken |
| Too Many Lawyers . . . | EXT | 5K | free | David Koziol |
| zapParam™ | CP | 27K | free | Reata Software |

## Windows and dialog boxes

These software packages enhance the visual effect and performance of the windows and dialog boxes in System 7.

### Aurora

Adds color to windows, menus, scroll bars, and buttons throughout your applications. Figure 19-4 displays the dialog boxes used to select colors for windows, title bars, text, and menus with Aurora.

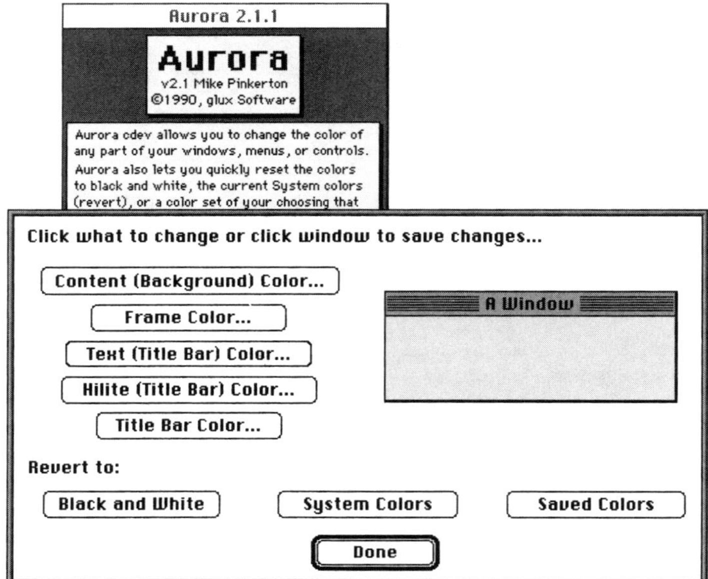


**Figure 19-4: Aurora can colorize your menus, dialog boxes, title bars, and buttons via its flexible control panel.**

## Color7

This control panel lets you create colored menu bars, windows, dialog boxes, and buttons. The control panel works with the Mac's color picker to customize colors and matches appropriate colors to prevent clashes (for example, orange and purple).

## Escapade

Enables you to use the keyboard to operate buttons in dialog boxes and to select commands from menus without using the mouse. This control panel can be customized to work with function keys and common Macintosh keyboard equivalents, as well as any other keyboard requirements you may specify.

## Greg's Buttons

This control-panel device lets you replace dialog-box buttons with 3-D versions and further customize your dialog boxes by replacing the default Chicago system font with a font of your choice (as long as it is Helvetica or Palatino). You also can colorize the background of dialog boxes.

## It's Your Default!

Changes the default application font. You can set the font for the current session (until you restart) or save the changes across restarts in Parameter RAM. Figure 19-5 displays the control panel of It's Your Default! that enables you to set the default font of your selected application.

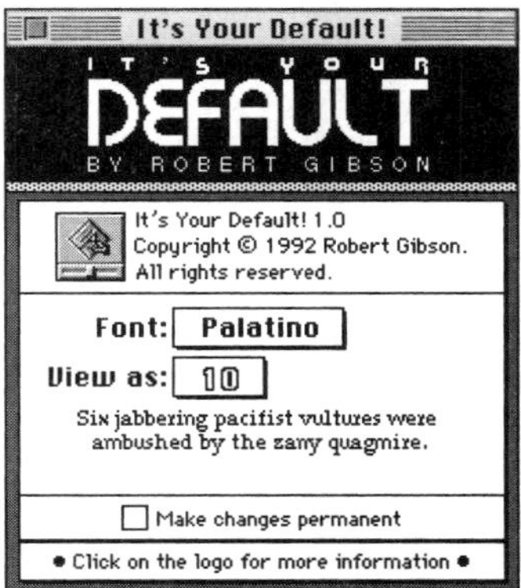


**Figure 19-5: It's Your Default! lets you change the font most applications use by default.**

## Kilroy

Makes your Macintosh historic (as in World War II). Install this control-panel device, which includes a system extension, and see what pops up in dialog boxes in the least expected places.

## Stretch

This control-panel device lets you resize your windows from any corner or side. The device also lets you iconize your windows (as in Microsoft Windows) and restore each window to its original size and location.

## WindowShade

Gets its name from the old window blinds that roll up when given a sturdy pull. This utility brings the same functionality to Macintosh windows. Apple includes WindowShade 1.3 with System 7.5 and later, but not with earlier versions of System 7.

## WindowWizard

Displays a menu that lists the currently active application's foreground and background windows. Using this tool enables you to go to other windows within the application without resorting to the Open command.

## WrapScreen

This control-panel device lets you wrap the screen vertically or horizontally onto itself so that your mouse can travel from right to left or up or down and never leave the screen.

### ZoomBar

Groups windows so that they appear either stacked or tiled, no matter what size you make any individual window. The utility resizes all the windows together to maintain the stacking order. This tool enables you to reach all windows you need without worrying about the size of the active window.

## Summary of window and dialog-box software

Table 19-5 summarizes the pertinent data about window and dialog-box software. (CP is a control panel, and EXT is a system extension.)

Table 19-5
**Window and Dialog-Box Software**

| *Software* | *Type* | *Size* | *Cost* | *Author* |
|---|---|---|---|---|
| Aurora | CP | 19K | free | Mike Pinkerton |
| Color7 | CP | 57K | $10 | Michael Landis |
| Escapade | CP | 50K | free | Christopher Wysocki |
| Greg's Buttons | CP | 102K | $15 | Gregory Landweber |
| It's Your Default! | CP | 18K | free | Robert Gibson |
| Kilroy | CP | 12K | free | Dave Koziol |
| Stretch | CP | 116K | $10 | Ross Tyler |
| WindowShade | CP | 27K | free | Rob Johnston |
| Window Wizard | EXT | 26K | $20 | Eric del la Musse |
| WrapScreen | CP | 11K | free | Eric Aubourg |
| ZoomBar | CP | 72K | $5 | Brian Westley |

## Sounds

This section includes sound utilities and a sample of the many shareware and freeware system sounds that have been recorded. Install sounds by dragging their icons to the System Folder icon, and select them with the Sound control panel.

### BeepSounds

An assortment of system sounds, ranging from the sublime (symphony) to the ridiculous (burps), for placement in your System file.

### CARP

Replaces Apple's CD Remote application for use in playing audio compact discs from your Macintosh. (*CARP* stands for *Craig's Audio ROM Player*.)

### sndConverter

Converts sounds from other Macintosh system versions to be compliant with System 7's *snd* (the system sound format) requirements.

### SoundExtractor

Extracts sounds from suitcases, applications, and HyperCard stacks and then plays them. The program also converts the sounds to System 7-compliant snd files and places them where you specify.

## Summary of sounds software

Table 19-6 summarizes the pertinent data about the sounds and sound utilities. (Note that CP is a control panel, EXT is a system extension, and APP is an application program.)

Table 19-6
**Sounds Software**

| *Software* | *Type* | *Size* | *Cost* | *Author* |
|---|---|---|---|---|
| Beep Sounds | N/A | N/A | free | N/A |
| CARP 1.0a | APP | 73K | $10 | Craig Marciniak |
| sndConverter 1.2.1 | APP | 29K | free | Joe Zobkiw |
| SoundExtractor | APP | 34K | $5 | Alberto Ricci |

## Menus, folders, and icons

This section covers software that enhances menus, folders, and icons. In addition, several little programs are included in this section because they reside in the menu bar. Now Utilities 4 offers several modules that provide enhanced menu management. Now Menus creates hierarchical menus under the Apple menu and creates a new launch menu to the left of the Apple menu for easy loading of any application on your hard disk. Now WYSIWYG Menus lets you see your fonts, sizes, and styles the way they appear in print in any application. You also can customize your menus to list items in other fonts and sizes than the standard Chicago used by the system software. Several other vendors also offer ways to display your fonts in their actual forms.

## Custom Killer

Removes custom icons from files, folders, and even disks. You drag an item, or multiple items, onto the Custom Killer icon for quicker response than using the Finder's Get Info command.

## Folder Icon Maker

Lets you customize the appearance of your folders by copying application icons without using the Get Info command. The program acts like a drop box, copying the icon that you drop onto it to a new folder.

## FolderPict

This application lets you create customized folder icons from any PICT-format graphics image.

## Assorted folders and icons

America Online, CompuServe, Berkeley Macintosh Users Group (BMUG), and other Macintosh user groups maintain extensive libraries of color icons, some of them 3-D, for use in replacing standard icons. These icons are stored in Scrapbook files that you place in your System Folder after removing your everyday Scrapbook file. Then you can copy the icons from the special Scrapbook file to the Info windows of your old, boring icons. Following are examples of these icon libraries:

- **AFC Helmet Icons:** a selection of American Football Conference helmets
- **Color Hard Disk Icons:** a Scrapbook containing landscapes, arrows, sunsets, comic-book characters, and business symbols for use as icons
- **Mo' Better Folders:** a series of abstract designs and business symbols on colored folders
- **Mo' Fun Icons:** a collection of icons that leans toward cute symbols and abstracts
- **New Color Icons for System 7:** more folder designs, including application icons attached to color folders

## Helium

Enables you to view and print help balloons without using the Help menu. Press a combination of keys (which you can select) to inflate the balloons as needed.

## Ikon VII

Provides a MacPaint- or SuperPaint-based tool kit for creating custom colored icons for folders and files on your Macintosh. The application includes sample icons, as well as software you can use to create and install your own icon designs.

### Visage™

Installs new, colored icons for your disks without using the Get Info command. The application contains a library of disk shapes and cartoon characters that you can use; you also can install your own icons in the library for customized use.

## Summary of menu, folder, and icon software

Table 19-7 summarizes the pertinent data about the menu, folder, and icon software. (CP is a control panel, and APP is an application program.)

Table 19-7
**Menu, Folder, and Icon Software**

| *Software* | *Type* | *Size* | *Cost* | *Author* |
|---|---|---|---|---|
| Custom Killer | APP | 20K | $2 | Robert Gibson |
| Folder Icon Maker | APP | 20K | free | Gregory Robbins |
| FolderPict | APP | 49K | $10 | Lawrence Harris |
| Helium | CP | 52K | $7 | Robert Mathews |
| Ikon VII | APP | 12K | free | Golden Eagle Software |
| Visage™ | APP | 84K | $25 | Scott Searle Network Enhancements |

## Network enhancements

This section describes software that enhances the performance of System 7's file-sharing features. The section also describes some software that enhances AppleShare and other network services.

### Anchor Stuff

Mounts a network or secondary hard disk without using the Chooser. The application operates as an alias on your startup disk and does not require any other copies on the network or server to perform its function.

### AppleSearch

AppleSearch consists of two parts — client software and server software — that work jointly to retrieve needed information from large network-based databases. To use the program, you must have your Macintosh connected to an AppleShare-based network server that has the AppleSearch server software installed. In addition, each local Macintosh volume requires a copy of the client software to create the necessary reporters to direct the searches.

The client software lets you create an AppleSearch reporter that will search for information on a specific topic based on a series of keywords that you provide. The Reporter returns a list of documents relevant to the query, ranked with one to five stars. You can view the text of each document or retrieve the full document in its original format.

The server software is the search engine that recognizes and processes the queries of the client software's reporters. The capability to rapidly search myriad sources of information is based on an index that the server software maintains. This index contains all potential query terms in a document and their relationships to one another. The server software can provide access to more than 20,000 document files per server volume.

The AppleSearch server software works with any Centris, Quadra, or Apple Workgroup Server.

### ARACommander

The ARACommander control-panel device is an adjunct to the Apple Remote Access software provided by Apple (described in Chapter 9). ARACommander automates dialing into remote networks by creating connectors that contain the telecommunications and network configuration information necessary to complete the transaction. The device requires less disk space and less RAM than Apple's ARA 1 or the ARA 2 client/server package.

### DownLine

A drop-box backup program that offers automatic archiving and de-archiving functions in the background while you work with another program. The software can read and write to other archiving formats, such as StuffIt and PackIt.

### MailSlot

Creates a small electronic-mail system for your network, based on System 7 file sharing. The software monitors a designated mail folder and informs you when mail is delivered to that folder from another node on the network.

### Mount Alias

Automatically creates aliases for AppleShare volumes when you connect to them.

### Remote Controller and Server Controller

Apple provides these applications to let you remotely start or stop a file server, such as AppleShare, running on a Macintosh.

### SpeedMessage

Transmits a message to another Macintosh connected to a tiny network. One copy of SpeedMessage can establish a link with another copy of a SpeedMessage open on another Mac on the network or with a copy open on the same computer as the original (or even with itself!), thus establishing a small electronic mail system. The software also transmits very short segments (five seconds) of voice mail between computers on a network.

### UnMountIt

This application lets you unmount and eject disks and disk partitions, even if they are being shared by file sharing. UnMountIt quickly turns off file sharing, puts away the disk of your choice (removing its icon from the desktop), and turns file sharing back on.

## Summary of network-enhancement software

Table 19-8 summarizes the pertinent data about network-enhancement software. (Note that CP is a control panel, EXT is a system extension, and APP is an application program.)

Table 19-8
**Network-Enhancement Software**

| ***Software*** | ***Type*** | ***Size*** | ***Cost*** | ***Author*** |
|---|---|---|---|---|
| Anchor Stuff | APP | 7K | free | Zerom |
| AppleSearch | APP | N/A | $1,799 for server and client packages | Apple Computer |
| ARACommander | CP | 65K | $149.95/10 users | Ron Duitsch, Trilobyte Software |
| DownLine | APP | 100K | $25 | Morpheus Systems |
| MailSlot | CP | 65K | $10 | AnalySYS Software |
| Mount Alias | CP | 16K | free | Jeff Miller |
| Remote Control and Server Controller | APP | 25K | free | Jim Luther, Apple Computer |
| SpeedMessage | APP | 86K | free | Scott Johnson |
| UnMountIt | APP | 13K | free | Jim Luther, Apple Computer |

## PowerBook enhancements

This section describes software that enhances the performance of Macintosh PowerBooks. You also can get most of the functions provided by the software listed in this section with commercial PowerBook utility packages such as Connectix PowerBook Utilities (CPU).

### BackLight Control

Dims the screen backlighting after a period of inactivity that you designate. You don't need this program if you have Apple's PowerBook control panel version 7.2 or later.

### CapsControl

Disables the Caps Lock key.

### Duo Extension Picker

Loads one set of extensions if you start your Duo while docked and a different set if you start when not docked.

### Fat Cursors

Improves visibility of the mouse pointer (the cursor) on PowerBooks with passive-matrix screens by enlarging the arrow and I-beam pointers.

### Find Cursor

Helps you spot the mouse pointer (the cursor) by temporarily changing it to a thick-bordered box when you Control-click.

### Keyboard Plus

Maps all the extra keys from an extended keyboard to a PowerBook keyboard. The program gives you access to the function keys (F1 to F15), Page Up, Page Down, Home, End, Insert, Help, and all keypad keys.

### MyBattery

Shows the voltage levels for three different batteries. The program also lets you enable and disable AppleTalk, and turn your modem on and off.

### PlugAlert

Displays very clear warnings if the AC adapter isn't getting power or if the plug is not fully inserted into the PowerBook.

### SafeSleep™

Provides enhanced security for PowerBooks. The program blanks the screen and requests a password whenever a sleeping PowerBook is awakened.

## Shhh!

Eliminates the annoying click that you hear when the PowerBook turns on its sound circuitry. Normally, the PowerBook saves power by shutting down its sound circuitry after about ten seconds of inactivity. Shhh! prevents this shutdown, thereby decreasing battery life slightly.

## Siesta

Puts your PowerBook into sleep mode when you press a function key. Sleep mode preserves the charge in your battery, enabling you to use the computer longer between recharges.

## Software FPU

Enables you to run software that requires a floating-point unit (FPU) on a PowerBook that lacks one. The program improves compatibility but operates slower than a hardware FPU.

## SpinD™

Spins down the hard disk inside your PowerBook when you press a preset function key. *Spinning down* (or putting to sleep) the hard drive saves battery power and enables you to use your PowerBook longer between recharges.

## Threshold

Changes the voltage levels at which the first and second low-power warnings occur and the level at which the automatic shutdown occurs as the battery runs out of power. Use this program to set the thresholds for external batteries or to get a little more time from a higher-capacity internal battery.

## ToggleAT

A function key that alternately enables and disables AppleTalk (assuming that AppleTalk was loaded during startup).

## Volts

An application that monitors battery power and can graph voltage levels over time, as shown in Figure 19-6.

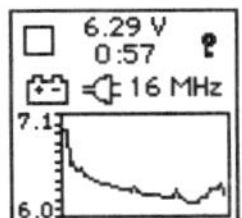


**Figure 19-6: Volts displays recent voltage history.**

### Zync

A file-synchronization system that copies files between your PowerBook and your desktop computer (or between any two hard disks).

## Summary of PowerBook-enhancement software

Table 19-9 summarizes the pertinent data about PowerBook-enhancement software. (CP is a control panel, EXT is a System extension, APP is an application program, and FKey is a function key.)

Table 19-9
**PowerBook-Enhancement Software**

| *Software* | *Type* | *Size* | *Cost* | *Author* |
|---|---|---|---|---|
| BackLight Control | CP | 12K | free | Ricardo Batista |
| CapsControl | N/A | N/A | free | S. Kevin Hester |
| Duo Extension Picker | CP | 12K | free | Alan Steremberg |
| Fat Cursors | CP | N/A | $5 | Robert Abetecola |
| Find Cursor | EXT | 3K | free | Mike Samuels |
| Keyboard Plus | CP | 45 | $15 | Berrie Kremers |
| MyBattery | APP | 48 | $10 | Jeremy Kezer |
| PlugAlert | EXT | 5K | free | Sean Hummel |
| Safe Sleep ™ | EXT | 3K | free | Bill Steinberg |
| Shhh! | EXT | 3K | free | Patrick C. Beard |
| Siesta | CP | 17K | $5 | Andrew Welch |
| Software FPU | CP | 45K | $10 | John Neil |
| SpinD™ | FKey | 1K | free | Bill Steinberg |
| Threshold | APP | 30K | $10 | Jeremy Kezer |
| ToggleAT | FKey | 2K | any | Jon Pugh |
| Volts | APP | 40K | $5 | Lawrence Anthony |
| Zync | APP | 19K | free | Ricardo Batista |

## CHAPTER  CONCEPTS AND TERMS

- You can check several sources for software that adds to the performance of your Macintosh. Apple Computer, third-party vendors, and independent programmers all write utility software that enhances your work with your Mac. These programs are available from Apple, APDA, AppleLink, commercial on-line services, Apple dealers, commercial shareware vendors, and user groups.
- Shareware carries some minimal costs, so be sure to read the ReadMe file that accompanies the software to find out how to register with the author.
- Alias-management shareware includes programs that create and track aliases throughout your system, system extensions that manage alias placement (including within the Apple menu), and control panels that enable you to delete aliases without using the Find command.
- Disk- and file-management software creates a RAM disk from application memory, tracks and enables you to edit creator and type information, helps you keep icons up to date, and more.
- Finder-management software performs such functions as substituting applications to open documents whose application is not on any disk, generating color desktop patterns, locating files better than System 7's Find command, switching between applications, creating alternative Application menus, and managing font and desk-accessory suitcases.
- System-management programs delete outmoded Desktop files, select startup disks, manage the orderly shutdown of your Macintosh, and zap the parameter RAM.
- Windows and dialog boxes are enhanced under System 7 through such software as Aurora, a program that colorizes windows and dialog boxes, and PickTURE, a demo package for an application that enables you to look at the contents of a file while you are in the Open dialog box.
- Additional sounds and color icons add to the creativity of your work on the Macintosh. Menu-related software adds submenus to the Apple menu and gives you more control of balloon help.
- File sharing and AppleShare server access is enhanced by software that mounts volumes, manages small electronic-mail services, and transfers messages across networks.
- PowerBooks can run longer when they use the available battery-saving software.

**BBS**
Acronym for bulletin board service. A noncommercial source that provides shareware, freeware, and information directly to your computer through telephone lines and modems. Some user groups have a BBS.

**download**
The process of receiving software or other computer files from another computer, generally through a modem and telephone lines.

**freeware**
Free software distributed through user groups and on-line information services. Most freeware is copyrighted by the person who created it; few programs are in the public domain.

**modem**
A device that connects a computer to telephone lines. It converts digital information from the computer into sounds for transmission over phone lines, and converts sounds from phone lines to digital information for the computer. Modem is a shortened form of modulator-demodulator.

**on-line information service**
A source that provides shareware and freeware directly to your computer through telephone lines and modems. Examples include America Online (800-827-6364), CompuServe (800-800-2222), and various Internet sites. Except for the Internet, on-line information services charge access fees and retrieval fees.

**shareware**
Low-cost software distributed through user groups and on-line information services, and written primarily by enthusiasts who don't have the resources to conduct exhaustive testing or to provide technical support. Shareware depends on the honor and honesty of people who use it. You're expected to pay the author a small fee if you plan to use the software.

**snd**
The technical name of the sound format that can be used as a system alert sound (installed in the System file), used as a startup sound (installed in the Startup Items folder), and opened by double-clicking it in the Finder.

**spin down**
To stop a hard drive from spinning. Spinning down the hard drive in a portable computer extends battery life.

**user group**
An organization that provides information to people who use computers. Many user groups, such as BMUG (510-549-2684), have extensive libraries of shareware and freeware, which they distribute on floppy disk for a nominal fee. Some user groups have a BBS from which you can obtain software by modem. For the names and phone numbers of user groups near you, call Apple's referral line (800-538-9696).

CHAPTER TWENTY

# Uncovering Tips and Secrets

- Finder tips: icons, aliases, the desktop, windows, folders, and the Trash
- The Apple menu, directory dialog box, and file-sharing tips
- System utility, control-panel, and application tips
- Memory use, performance, and more tips

Scattered throughout the first 11 chapters of this book are scores of tips and secret methods for getting more out of System 7. For your convenience, this chapter contains a digest of the most useful six dozen.

To use some of these tips, you need a copy of ResEdit, Apple's resource editor. You can get it from APDA, Apple Programmer's and Developer's Association (800-282-2732 in the United States, 800-637-0029 in Canada, and 716-871-6555 in other countries), on-line information services, and Macintosh user groups.

## Icons

In this section, you'll find ideas for saving time and effort while editing icon names, making and using aliases on the desktop, getting icons to look the way you want, and manipulating font icons.

### Spotting a name selected for editing

For a visual cue that you have selected the name of an icon on a color or grayscale monitor, use the Colors control panel to set the text-highlight color to something other than black and white. Then you'll know that a name highlighted in color (or gray) is ready for editing, whereas a name highlighted in black and white is not (see Figure 20-1).

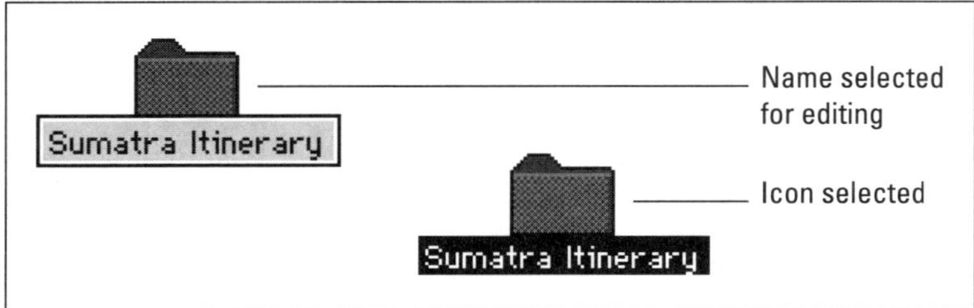


**Figure 20-1: Ready for editing, or not.**

## Edit, don't open

If you have trouble editing icon names without opening the item, try setting a briefer Double-Click Speed in the Mouse control panel, as shown in Figure 20-2. You must wait the duration of a double-click interval — about 1.9 seconds, 1.3 seconds, or 0.9 second, as set in the Mouse control panel — after selecting an icon name before selecting an insertion point, a word, or a range of text. If you click again too soon, the Finder thinks that you're double-clicking the icon and opens it.

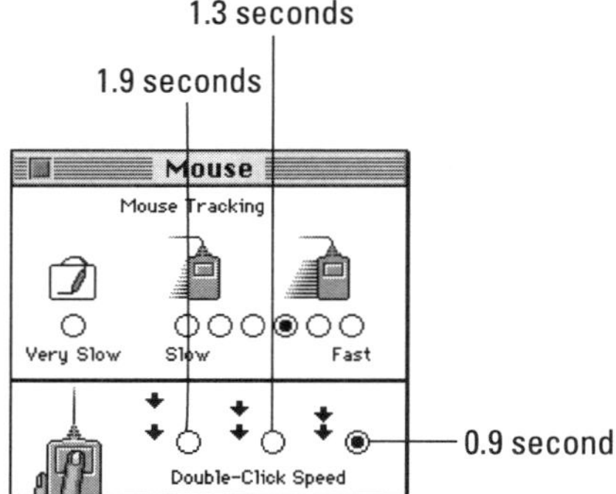


**Figure 20-2: After clicking an icon name to select it for editing, wait this long before clicking the name again.**

You don't have to wait if you move the mouse pointer slightly to the right after clicking the icon name. Click the name and then twitch the mouse, and the name is ready for editing. Another way to beat the wait is to click the name and then move the insertion point by pressing the arrow keys. Pressing the up-arrow key moves the insertion point to the beginning of the name; the down-arrow key moves it to the end; the left-arrow key moves it left; and the right-arrow key moves it right.

## Undoing accidental name change

If you rename an icon by mistake, choose Undo from the Edit menu (or press ⌘-Z) to restore the original name. Another way to restore the icon's original name is to press Backspace or Delete until the name is empty and then press Return or click outside the icon.

## Copy/Paste icon names

While editing a name, you can use the Undo, Cut, Copy, Paste, and Select All commands in the Edit menu. You cannot undo your changes to a name after you finish editing it, only while it is still selected for editing. You also can copy the entire name of any item by selecting its icon (or its whole name) and then choosing the Copy command from the Edit menu. This capability comes in handy when you're copying a disk and want to give the copy the same name as the original.

You can copy the name of a locked item — select the item and use the Copy command — but you can't change the name of a locked item. (Unlock an item by using the Get Info command or, if the item is a disk, by sliding its locking tab.)

System 7's Finder doesn't limit you to copying one icon name at a time. If you select several items and then use the Copy command, the names of all the items are put on the Clipboard (up to 256 characters in all), one name per line.

## Removing *alias*

The name that the Finder constructs for an alias can be so long that you can't see all of it in a list view, as shown in Figure 20-3. If you want to remove the word *alias* from the end, select the icon name for editing, press the right-arrow or down-arrow key to move the insertion point to the end of the name, and press Delete six times (or five times, if you want to leave a blank space at the end of the alias name to distinguish it from the original name).

Fizzz Operations

| Name | Size | Kind | Lab |
|---|---|---|---|
| Fizzz Customer Leads | 41K | FileMaker Pro docu... | |
| Fizzz Orders & Invoices | 41K | FileMaker Pro docu... | |
| *Fizzz Orders & Invoices al* | 1K | alias | |
| Fizzz Products & Services | 41K | FileMaker Pro docu... | |

**Figure 20-3: You can't see all of a long name in a list view.**

You also can drag the alias to the desktop, or switch the view to by Icon or by Small Icon, and then edit the name in icon view. In icon view, you can click the name one time to select it for editing, move the mouse slightly (or pause briefly), double-click the last word of the name, and press Delete twice (once if you want to retain a blank space at the end of the alias name). If you double-click too quickly after selecting the name, the Finder opens the alias instead of selecting the last word of the name.

## Permanently Removing *Alias*

If you always remove the word *alias* from the end of new alias names, you may prefer never to have the word appended to file names at all. You can make a change with ResEdit so that the Finder never appends the word *alias* to the names of new aliases. Follow these steps:

1. Open ResEdit, and use its Open command to open a copy of the Finder.

   You see a window full of icons, each icon representing a different type of resource in the Finder.

2. Double-click the STR# resource type, opening a window that lists all the Finder's string-list resources by number.

3. Locate STR# resource number 20500, and double-click it to open it.

4. Scroll to find the text *alias,* as shown in the figure. This is the text that the Finder appends to the original file name to make up the alias name.

5. Change the string to one blank space rather than making it completely empty, so that the names of original files and their aliases will be different.

6. To finish, close all the ResEdit windows or simply quit ResEdit. Answer Yes when you are asked whether you want to save changes.

To see the results of your work, you must restart your Macintosh.

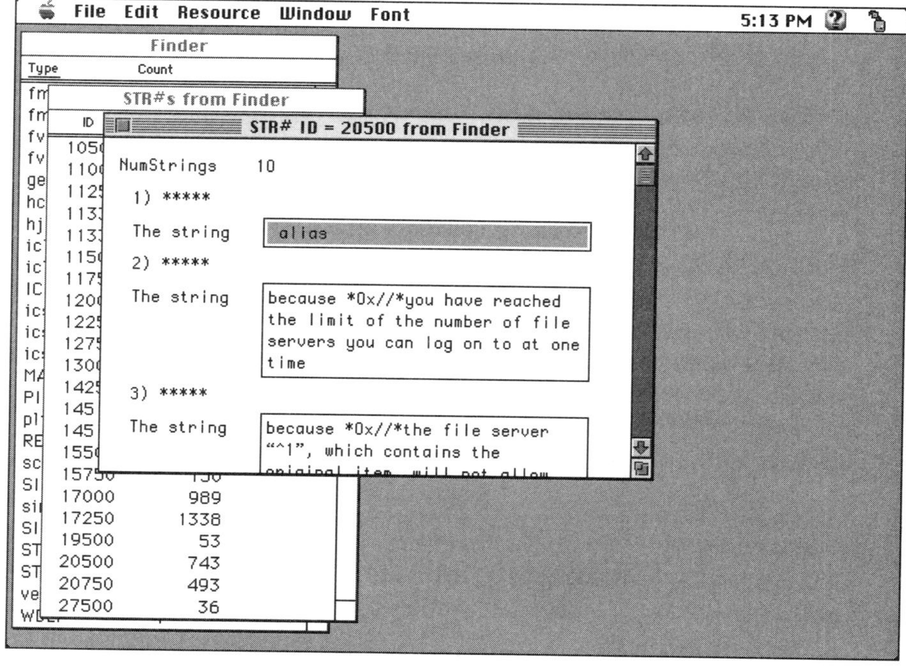

## Desktop aliases

Rather than drag frequently used programs, control panels, documents, and folders themselves onto the desktop, make aliases of those items and place the aliases on the desktop. You get quick access to the original items through their desktop aliases. Also, you can open several related items at the same time by opening aliases on the desktop, even if the original items happen to be in different folders or on different disks.

If your desktop becomes too cluttered with aliases, you can store related aliases together in a desktop folder.

## Trash everywhere

Are your Trash and hard-disk icons inevitably covered by the windows of other open programs? What a mess! Make aliases of the Trash and hard disk, put the aliases in a folder, and put the folder in your Apple menu for instant access. Leaving that folder open makes its window come to the front, along with the other Finder windows, whenever you switch to the Finder.

If you're lucky enough to have two monitors, put a Trash alias on the second monitor (beats dragging icons across two screens to throw them away).

### Copy fitting

When you copy batches of files from your hard drive to floppies, you must do some arithmetic beforehand so that the Finder won't tell you that there is not enough room on the disk. To have the Finder help you figure out how many files will fit on a floppy, follow these steps:

1. Create a new folder on the hard drive.

   The new folder must be in a window, not directly on the desktop.

2. Use the Finder's Get Info command to bring up the folder's Info window.
3. Begin dragging files into the folder.

   As you drag, the Finder updates the folder's size in its Info window.

4. When the size approaches 1400K for a high-density floppy or 800K for a double-density floppy, stop dragging files into the folder; the disk will be nearly full.

If the Trash is empty, you can collect items in it instead of a specially created folder. This method has two advantages: you can quickly return all items to their original places by choosing the Put Away command from the File menu, and you don't have to wait for the Finder to make copies of items that come from several disks. (The Finder doesn't copy items to the Trash, but it must copy items that you drag from one disk to a folder on another disk.)

The Get Info command reports the size of the Trash only to the nearest K, however, whereas it gives you the exact number of bytes in a folder.

## Express access to CD-ROM

Cut through the drudgery of wading through folders on a CD-ROM by making aliases of items inside the CD-ROM folders. Because CD-ROMs are permanently locked, you must put the aliases on your hard disk (or a floppy disk). Opening an alias makes a beeline to the original item on the CD-ROM.

## Cataloging items on floppy disks

You can use aliases to keep track of, and quickly open, items on floppy disks — even floppies that aren't inserted into your Macintosh. Make aliases of the items on a floppy disk, and copy the aliases to your startup disk. (You then can delete the aliases from the floppy disk.) When you need the item again, the system software tells you the name of the disk to insert so that it can open the alias's original item (see Figure 20-4). If you change your mind or can't find the needed disk, click the Cancel button.

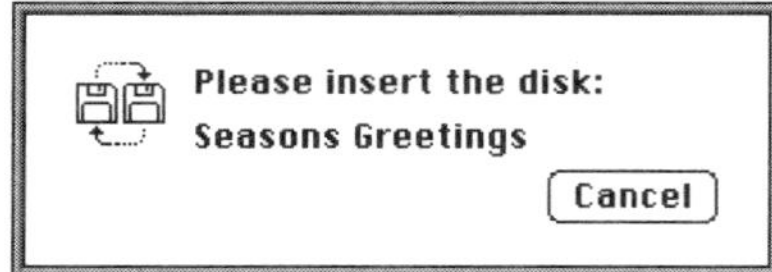


**Figure 20-4: The system software asks you to insert the disk that contains the original item for an alias you try to open.**

## Making many aliases

To make aliases for several items in the same window at the same time, select all the items and then use the Make Alias command. An alias appears for every item that you selected. All the new aliases are selected automatically so that you can drag them to another place without having to manually select them as a group. If you accidentally deselect the items, you can easily group them together for reselecting by changing the window's view to by Kind or by Date.

## Duplicating fonts

Because you can't rename individual fixed-size or TrueType fonts with the Finder, you can't duplicate them in the same folder. (You can rename or duplicate font suitcases and PostScript fonts, however.)

To duplicate a fixed-size or TrueType font, press Option and then drag the font to another folder or to the desktop. (Dragging to another disk automatically makes a copy of the font on the target disk.)

## Making a font suitcase

You can create a new, empty font-suitcase file in System 7 by duplicating an existing font suitcase file, opening the duplicate, and dragging its contents to the Trash, as shown in Figure 20-5.

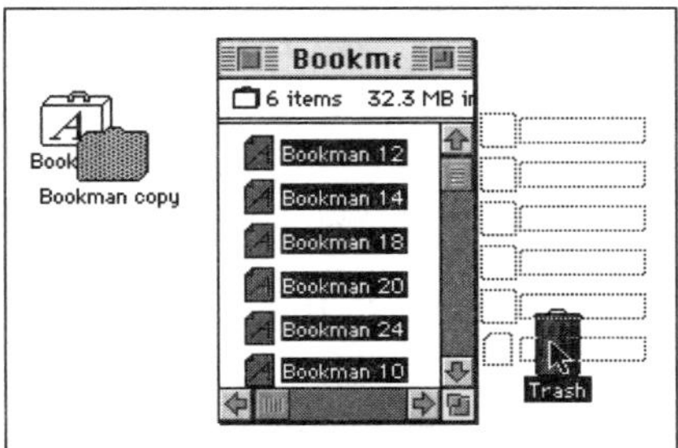


**Figure 20-5: Making a new font suitcase by emptying a copy of an existing suitcase.**

## Updating Icons

When you install an updated program that includes redesigned icons on your disk, you may not see the new icon until you rebuild the disk's desktop. To rebuild the desktop of any disk whose icon normally appears on the desktop after startup, press ⌘-Option while starting your Macintosh. For each disk in turn, the Finder asks whether you want the disk's desktop to be rebuilt (see Figure 20-6). To rebuild the desktop of a floppy disk or another removable disk whose icon is not on the desktop, press ⌘-Option while inserting the disk.

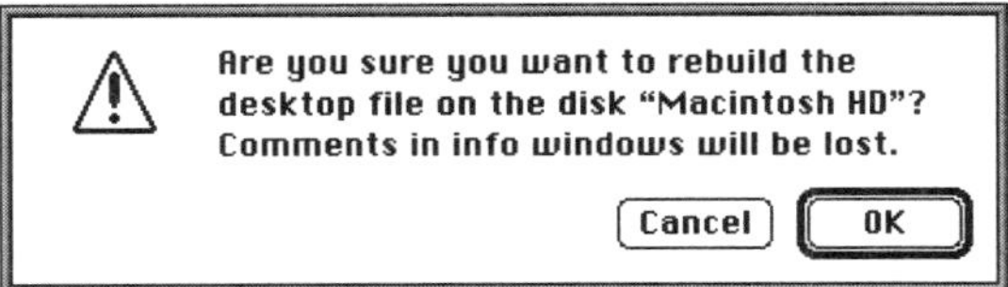


**Figure 20-6: The Finder asks you to confirm the rebuilding of a disk's desktop files.**

Rebuilding the desktop destroys all comments in Info windows. You can get software that preserves the comments through rebuilding and other software that resets the icon of any program that you designate (see Chapter 19).

## Fixing blank icons

Sometimes, a file that you copy onto your disk ends up with a generic (blank) icon. You really don't want to rebuild your desktop files just to fix one icon (especially if you have a large drive). Instead, open the icon's Info window and then click the icon. A box appears around the icon, indicating that you have selected the icon. Now copy, paste, and cut the icon — in that order. If you are lucky, the correct icon shows its face.

Here's how it works: copying the icon makes it possible to paste; pasting the icon causes the Finder to internally mark the file as one that has a custom icon; and cutting the icon causes the Finder to unmark the file and restore its standard icon. You can't do the cutting step unless you have done the pasting step, and you can't do the pasting step unless you have done the copying step.

## Making labels transparent

If you've avoided using System 7's labels because they discolor your beautiful color icons, wait no longer. You can label a color icon without changing its color if the label color is black, white, or any shade of gray. (On a color monitor, icons with white labels are invisible unless they are selected.) You still can view Finder windows by label, find items by label, and so on.

To change a label's color, open the Labels control panel, and click the color of the label you want to use. The standard color-picker dialog box appears, with its characteristic color wheel. Set Hue Angle and Saturation to 0; then set Brightness to 100 for white, 0 for black, or a number between 0.01 and 99.99 for a shade of gray. You can type the three values in the spaces provided, or you can click the center of the color wheel and adjust the slider. (Before System 7.5, you set Hue and Saturation to 65535 and then set Brightness to 65535 for white, 0 for black, or a number between 1 and 65534 for a shade of gray.)

## Customizing folder icons

If you use System 7 and you have too many boring, look-alike folders cluttering your desktop, you can enliven those folders by superimposing a relevant application icon, as shown in Figure 20-7.

First, copy a folder icon from its Info window (which you display by choosing the Finder's Get Info command), and paste the icon into a color paint program. Then open the folder that contains the application whose icon you want to use, view the folder window by Small Icon, and take a screen snapshot (press ⌘-Shift-3).

Next, open the screen-snapshot file (named Picture 1 on your startup disk) with the color paint program or with TeachText, copy the small application icon from the snapshot, and paste it over the pasted folder icon.

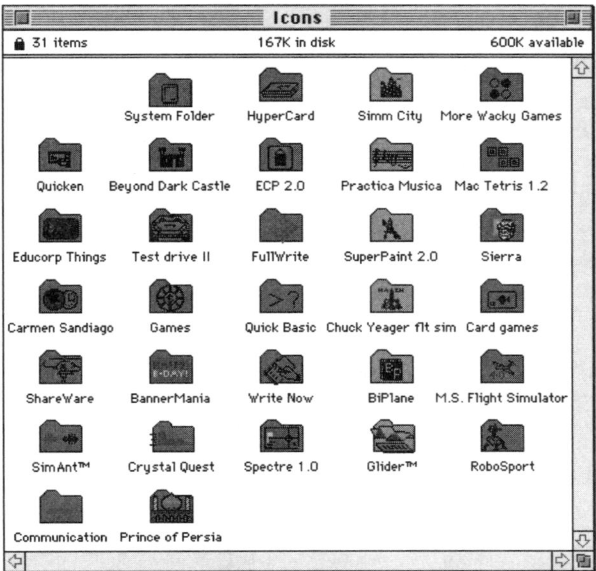


**Figure 20-7: Composite folder icons.**

Finally, copy the composite icon from the paint program, paste it into the folder's Info window, and close the Info window.

When you select the custom icon in the painting application, you must take care to select a rectangular area no larger than 32 by 32 pixels (the maximum size of an icon). If you select a larger area, including lots of white space around your custom icon, the Finder shrinks the selection to 32 by 32 when you paste it into the folder's Get Info window, and your custom icon ends up shrunken. If you select an area smaller than 32 by 32, the Finder centers the selection in the folder's icon space, and the custom icon will not line up horizontally with a plain folder icon, which is flush with the bottom of its icon space.

You can avoid this rigmarole by using the free utility Folder Icon Maker by Gregory M. Robbins. Just drag a great-looking application or document icon to Icon Maker, and presto — Icon Maker creates a new folder with a small version of that icon superimposed on it (see "Menus, folders, and icons" in Chapter 19).

The custom icons obscure any subsequent changes that you make to the folder's color (with the Finder's Labels menu) or to the folder's file-sharing status (with the Finder's Sharing command).

## Repairing broken icons

System 7 keeps the custom icon for a file in the file itself, but it keeps the custom icon for a folder or disk in an invisible file whose name is the word icon plus a return character. This file is created automaticallq in the folder or disk when you paste a custom icon in the Info window of a folder or disk. You cannot cut, clear, or paste the icon in the Info window of the folder or disk, if you manage to delete its invisible file. If you try, the Mac displays the obscure message "The command could not be completed because it cannot be found."

### Fixing Defective Icon Masks

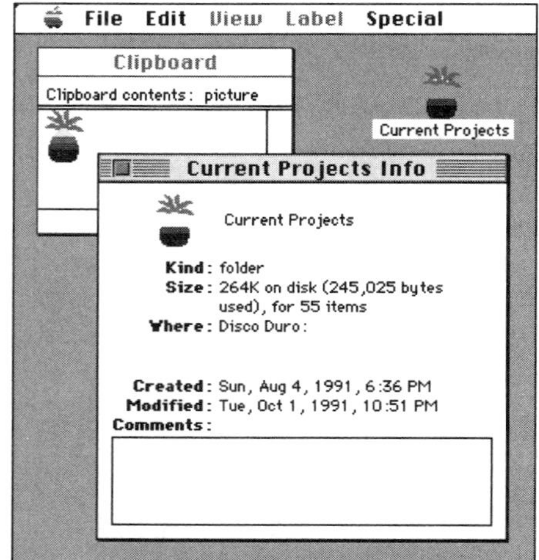


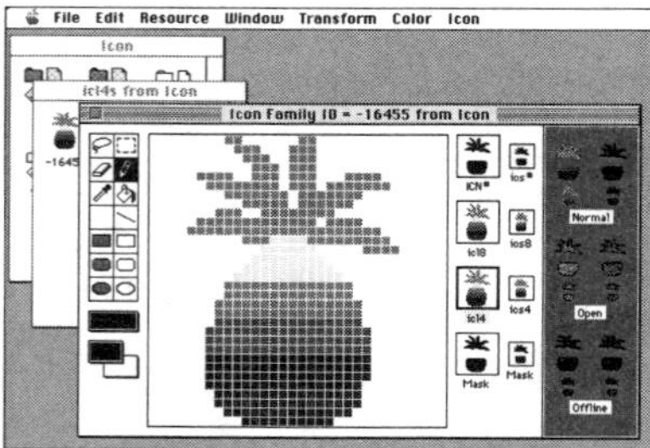


Steps 1 to 3

When you paste a color picture into an item's Info window, you don't always get the custom icon that you expect, because the Finder is partly color-blind. The Finder sees light colors (such as yellow and orange) at the picture's edge as being transparent parts of the icon, and it omits them from the mask that it makes for the custom icon. The defective mask punches an incomplete hole in the desktop for the icon, as shown in the figure.

You can fix a defective icon mask with ResEdit version 2.1 or later (see the beginning of this chapter for more sources of this program). Follow these steps:

1. Open ResEdit and use its Open command to open the item whose custom icon you want to fix.

   To get at the custom icon of a folder or disk, open the file named Icon inside the folder or disk (this file is invisible in the Finder). You can't fix the custom icon of an alias directly because you can't open the alias itself. Instead, make a new folder, paste the custom icon into that folder's Info window, fix the folder's icon as described here, and copy the fixed icon to the alias's Info window.

*(continued on next page)*

*(continued from previous page)*

2. After opening the item whose icon you want to fix, double-click the icl4 resource type.

   A window opens, containing the icon that you need to fix (and maybe some other icons).

3. Double-click the icon in that window to open an icon-editing window, as shown in the figure.

   This window contains a set of icon-editing tools and a panel in which you can edit the icon dot by dot. In addition, the window displays the icon mask and the six variations of the icon (large and small sizes in black-and-white, 16-color, and 256-color). The icon-editing window also shows what the icon looks like on the desktop in several conditions (not selected, selected, not open, open, and off-line).

4. To fix the large icon, drag the icl4 icon or the icl8 icon over the large mask, as shown in the following figure.

   This action creates a better mask based on the color icon. You may need to fine-tune the mask so that its black dots exactly correspond to the colored dots in the icl4 icon. To edit the mask, use the pencil tool or other tools. To check the correspondence of dots, alternately click the icl4 icon and the large mask.

5. Repeat step 4, using the ics4 icon to make a new small mask.

   You may want to touch up the ics4 and ics8 icons before making the small mask.

6. To finish, close all the ResEdit windows or simply quit ResEdit. Answer Yes when you are asked whether you want to save changes.

7. To see the results of your work (shown in the next figure), you must restart your Macintosh.

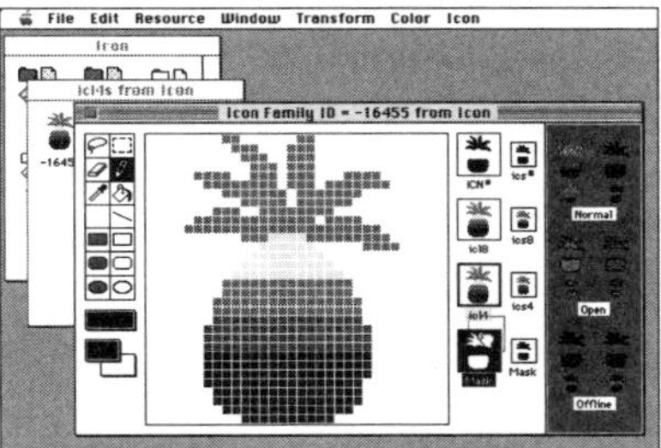


**Step 4**

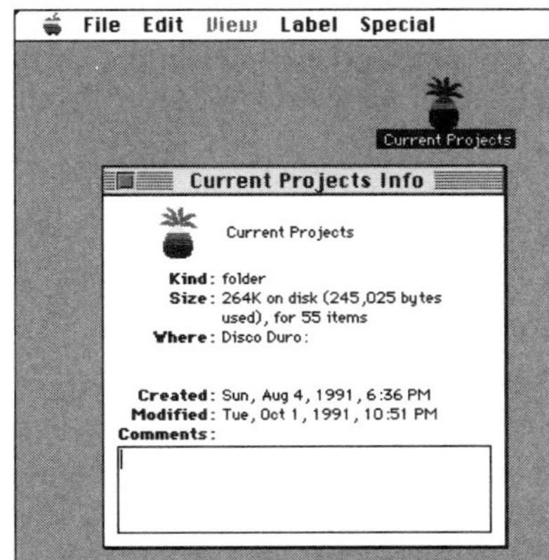


**Step 7**

Fortunately, working around a broken folder icon is relatively easy — move the contents of the broken folder to a new folder and discard the broken folder.

Note that this technique won't work for disks. You can fix these broken icons with the shareware utility Custom Killer by Robert Gibson (available from user groups and from on-line information services such as America Online). Custom Killer is designed to remove custom icons from files, folders, and disks; it also fixes screwed-up folder and disk icons like yours. You can remove custom icons faster by dragging them to the Custom Killer icon than by using the Finder's Get Info command.

### Reverting to standard icons

You can revert to an item's standard icon after replacing the icon with custom graphics. Just select the item, choose Get Info from the Finder's File menu, select the icon in the Info window, and choose Clear or Cut from the Edit menu.

## Desktop and Startup

In this section, you find tips for customizing your desktop, as well as the sights and sounds that you see and hear during startup.

### Desktop by name

If your desktop gets so cluttered that you can hardly find the icon for an inserted floppy disk, you may wish that you could use the View menu to arrange items on the desktop by name, as you can icons in windows. You can get this effect with System 7's custom-icon capabilities.

First, open a paint program, select some blank white space, and copy it. (If you don't have a paint program, open an empty folder in the Finder, and press ⌘-Shift-3 to make a screen shot of the empty folder. Open the screen shot in TeachText or SimpleText, and copy some white space there.)

After you copy some white space, use the Finder's Get Info command on each desktop item that you want to view by name, and paste the white space over the icon in each item's Info window. Pasting the white space leaves only the item names visible, and six items without icons fit into the space previously occupied by two items with icons, as shown in Figure 20-8.

### Custom startup screen

Instead of the plain old "Welcome to Macintosh" startup screen, your Mac can display a special picture like the one shown in Figure 20-9. If your System Folder contains a file named StartupScreen that contains a PICT resource with ID 0, the graphic image in that resource replaces the standard startup screen. You can use any of several programs to create such a startup screen for your Mac.

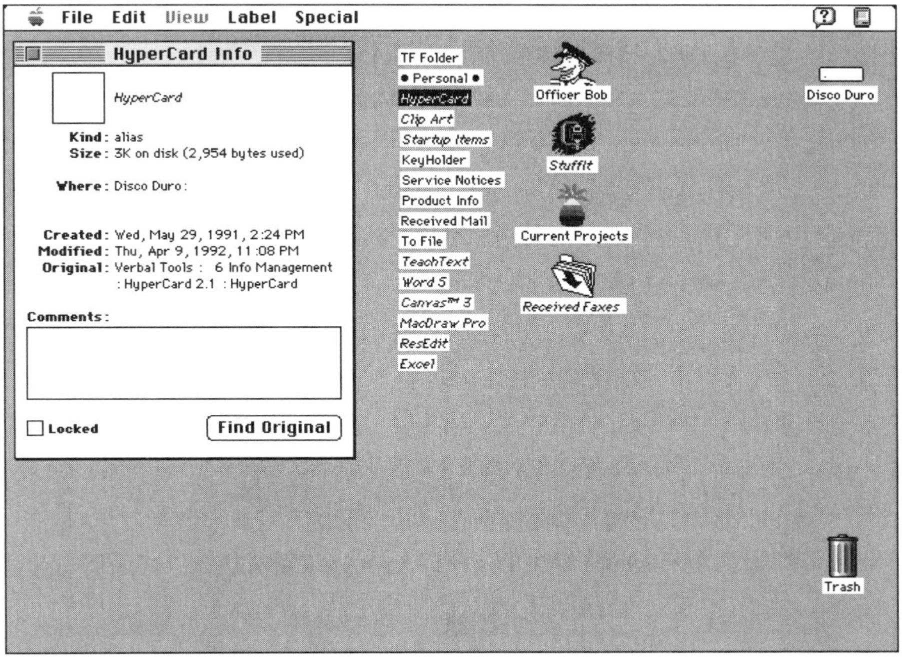

Figure 20-8: All you see of an item with a white icon is its name.

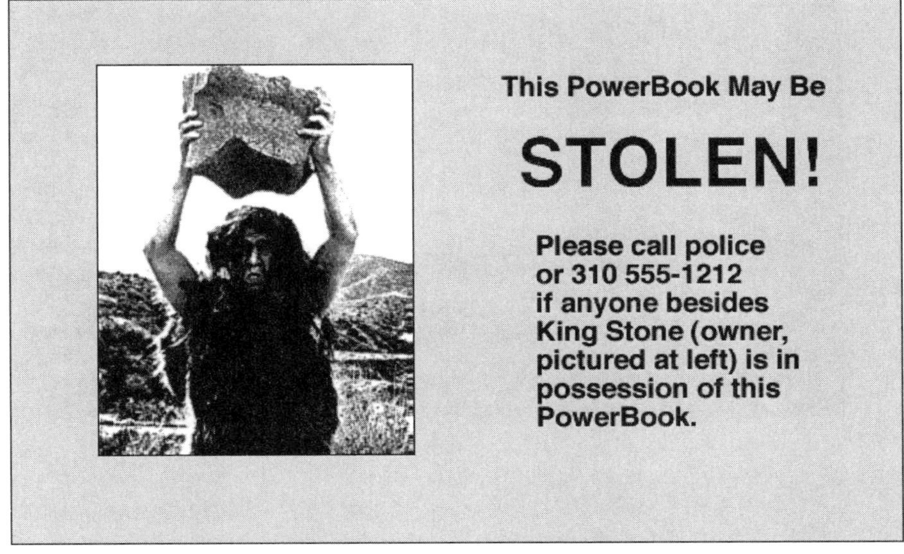
This PowerBook May Be
STOLEN!
Please call police
or 310 555-1212
if anyone besides
King Stone (owner,
pictured at left) is in
possession of this
PowerBook.

Figure 20-9: You can make a custom startup screen to replace the "Welcome to Macintosh" message.

## Colorful Desktop Patterns

System 7.5 and later and all Performa versions of System 7 have colorful desktop patterns composed of large pattern tiles. Other versions of System 7 have smaller pattern tiles (8 by 8 pixels), but you can use ResEdit to decorate your desktop with a large custom pattern based on a tile size up to 64 by 64 pixels. Unfortunately, designing 64-by-64-pixel patterns can be quite tedious.

The Terraform module of Berkeley Systems' More After Dark (which requires After Dark 2) can create striking patterns that repeat perfectly on the desktop, as shown in the figure.

To create desktop patterns, follow these steps:

1. In After Dark, select the Terraform module, and set the Repeat Size option to 64.
2. Activate After Dark by moving the mouse pointer to the sleep corner or by clicking the Demo button.
3. When you see a pattern that you like, press ⌘-Shift-3 to have System 7 capture the screen in a PICT file (at the root level of your startup disk).

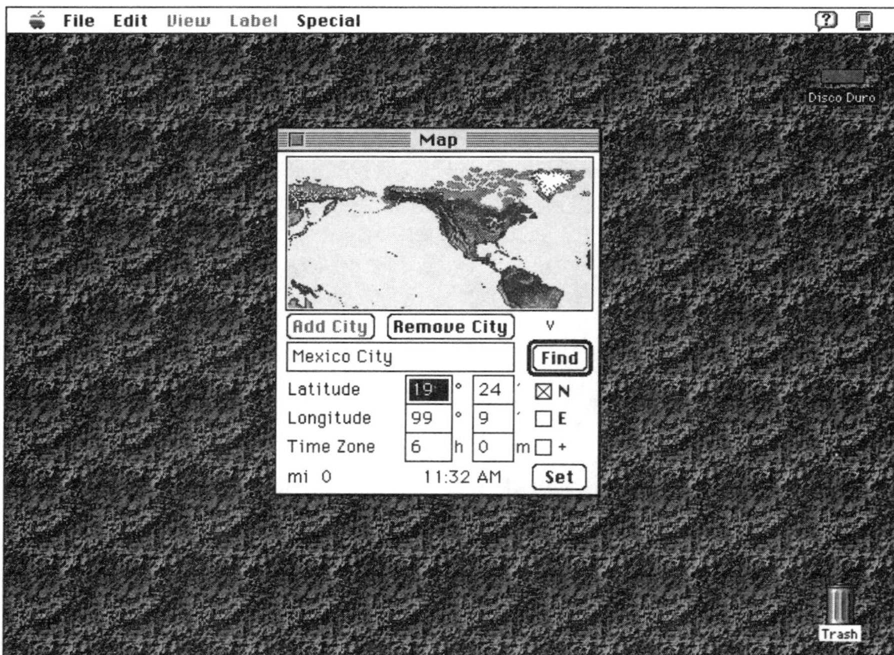


(continued on next page)

*(continued on next page)*

You can experiment with colors and textures by clicking the Terraform module's Terrain button and trying different settings in the dialog box that appears.

4. Open the screen capture, named Picture 1, with a program that enables you to select a 64-by-64-pixel piece of it.

   TeachText, which comes with System 7, will do, but drawing programs such as Canvas and SuperPaint 3 are more convenient because they show the size of the selection as you use the marquee tool (selection rectangle).

5. Select the 64-by-64 area that you want to become your desktop pattern, and copy it to the Clipboard (with the Edit menu's Copy command).
6. Make a copy of the System file by pressing Option while dragging it from the System Folder to the desktop and then open the copy with ResEdit 2.1 or a later version.
7. In ResEdit, scroll until you see the icon for the resource named ppat (pixel pattern), and double-click it to open it.
8. You should see one resource numbered 16; open it by double-clicking.

   A pattern-editing window appears, along with three new menus: Transform, Color, and ppat.

9. Choose Pattern Size from the ppat menu, and set the pattern size to 64 by 64, making the pattern-editing window larger.
10. Paste the pattern from the Clipboard to replace the standard gray pattern.
11. Quit ResEdit, and answer Yes when you are asked whether you want to save changes to the System file.
12. Drag the unedited System file out of the System Folder, drag the edited System file into that folder, and restart your Macintosh.

    When the Finder's menu bar appears, you should be rewarded with a very pleasing desktop pattern.

To take the next step in creating desktop patterns — multiple patterns in sizes up to 128 by 128 pixels — you can get the Wallpaper control panel from Thought I Could. This control panel works with System 6 (6.0.5 and later) as well as System 7 on any color-capable Mac (including an SE/30 or Classic II) and includes pattern-editing tools.

The following graphics programs can create startup screen files: Canvas 3, Capture Utilities (bundled with Capture 4), GIFConverter 2.2.10 ($40 shareware by Kevin A. Mitchell, P.O. Box 803066, Chicago, IL 60680-3066), ImageGrabber 3, Photoshop (all versions), SuperPaint 3, and UltraPaint 1.03. In all these programs except Image Grabber 3 and Photoshop, you specify Startup Screen or StartupScreen as the file type (generally by choosing it from a pop-up menu in the Save As dialog box). In Photoshop and Image Grabber, you choose Resource File as the type of file to save and then specify a resource ID of 0.

When you use a custom startup screen, your Mac takes longer and requires more memory to start. A small black-and-white image has the least effect; a large 24-bit color (millions of colors) image has the greatest effect.

If your Mac hangs during startup, the StartupScreen file is too large. You can reduce the size of the file by using a smaller image, reducing the color depth (with Canvas, Photoshop, or SuperPaint), or adding memory (if you have less than 4MB with System 7).

If you're using System 6, you may need to increase the size of the system heap portion of memory with utility software such as Bill Steinberg's free program Bootman! (available from on-line information services and from user groups). Upgrading to System 7, which dynamically adjusts system heap size as needed, also fixes System heap problems.

### Startup movie

If you have QuickTime installed, you can have a movie play during startup by naming it Startup Movie and placing it in the System Folder. (To halt the Startup Movie, press Command-period or any other key.)

### Startup sound

In System 7, you can put a sound file in the Startup Items folder (inside the System Folder), and that file will be played when you start your Mac.

If your Mac has a microphone, you can use the Sound control panel to record a message for the next person who uses the Mac, or just for fun. (To halt startup sounds, press ⌘-period.)

## Folders and Windows

The tips in this section involve Finder windows and folders.

### Locking folders

Everyone knows how to lock a file with the Finder's Get Info command, but how do you lock a folder? It's easy with System 7. Just select the folder that you want to lock, choose Sharing from the Finder's File menu to bring up the folder's file-sharing privileges window, and check the box labeled "Can't be moved, renamed or deleted." You don't have to actually share the folder or change any other settings in the privileges window.

For this trick to work, System 7's file sharing must be on; the Sharing command tells you to turn it on with the Sharing Setup control panel if necessary.

### Creating Your Own Startup Screen

If you don't have a graphics program that can save a startup screen but you do have ResEdit, you can use it and the Scrapbook to create your own Startup screen file.

1. Paste the image that you want to use as a startup screen into the Scrapbook.
2. Close the Scrapbook and use ResEdit to open a copy of the Scrapbook file (located in the System Folder).

   ResEdit displays a window containing icons that represent different types of resources in the Scrapbook file.
3. Open the Scrapbook file's PICT-resources icon and scroll through the images until you see the one that you want for your startup screen.
4. Copy the PICT resource that you want to use.
5. Create a new document in the System Folder and name it StartupScreen.
6. Paste the copied PICT resource into StartupScreen.
7. Open the PICT-resources icon again, select the image that you just pasted, and choose Get Resource Info from the Resources menu.
8. In the Resource Info window that appears, change the ID number to 0.
9. Quit ResEdit, clicking the Yes button when you are asked whether you want to save changes.
10. Restart your Mac to see the custom startup screen.

## Special folder replacement

Should you happen to discard one of the special folders inside the System Folder, you can make a replacement by using the Finder's New Folder command (File menu). After creating a new folder, change its name to that of the special folder you want: Apple Menu Items, Control Panels, Extensions, Fonts, Preferences, or Startup Items. Wait a few seconds, and you'll see its icon get the distinctive appearance of the special folder that you're creating.

## Special folder mistakes

The Finder sometimes makes mistakes when it puts items in the System Folder's special folders for you. The Finder may put some items in the correct places and incorrectly leave others in the System Folder itself. For example, it may put a control panel in the Control Panels folder but leave that control panel's auxiliary folder in the System Folder. That control panel won't work right thereafter, because it expects to find its auxiliary folder in the same folder that it occupies. To correct this problem, you must open the System Folder and drag the auxiliary folder to the Control Panels folder yourself.

## Abridged System Folder

Does finding the Apple Menu Items folder, Startup Items folder, or some other item in your System Folder take too long? Make aliases for the System Folder items that you access often — including an alias of the System Folder itself — and consolidate the aliases in a new folder. You can open and find an item in that folder faster than you can in the System Folder.

To make the new folder look like a System Folder, copy the icon from the System Folder's Info window and paste it into the new folder's Info window.

## Removing items from the System Folder

Before you can remove an item from the System Folder, you must know which inner folder it is stored in. If you're not sure, use the Finder's Find command to locate the item (see Chapter 6). Be sure to put items that you drag from the System Folder's special folders on the desktop or in an ordinary folder. Many items that you drag out of special folders still are effective if you merely drag them to the System Folder window.

## Easy startup items

If you want an item to open at startup time, put an alias of it in the Startup Items folder. Don't put original items there because returning them to their original locations when you no longer want them opened at startup time can be a drag.

When you finish using an alias, you can drag it to the Trash. Aliases in the Startup Items folder are opened alphabetically after any applications and before any documents that also are in that folder.

## Seeing desktop items

If the windows of open programs obscure desktop icons, you can hide those windows by choosing Hide Others from the Application menu while the Finder is active. If Finder windows cover desktop icons, you can close all those windows at the same time by pressing Option while clicking the close box of any Finder window.

## Narrow Finder windows

You can reduce the width of Finder windows to just the item names in list views without laboriously dragging the size boxes of each window. Use the Views control panel to temporarily set all List View options off. Then shrink each window to fit the new format by clicking its zoom box.

After shrinking all windows, you can turn on List View options in the Views control panel. You can scroll the contents of a narrow window horizontally to see columns that are out of view.

## Personalized Sample Text

You don't have to read about "razorback frogs and piqued gymnasts" when you open a TrueType or fixed-size font file with System 7's Finder. Use a resource-editing application such as Apple's ResEdit to change the sample text as follows:

1. Open your System Folder, and press Option as you drag a copy of the Finder to the desktop.
2. Open this duplicate Finder with ResEdit.
3. Open the Finder's STR# resource icon, and then open the STR# resource whose ID is 14516.

   You'll see a window that displays the sample text (see the figure).
4. Edit the text.
5. Quit ResEdit, answering Yes when you are asked whether you want to save your changes.
6. Drag the original Finder from your System Folder to the Trash, and drag the modified Finder from the desktop to the System Folder.
7. Restart your computer, and test the results of your modification.

If you have System 7.0 or 7.0.1, edit STR resource ID 14512. (Notice that STR# and STR are different types of resources.)

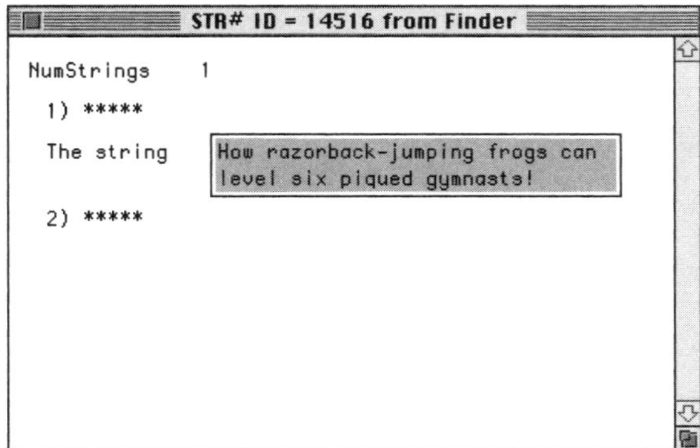


## Viewing by size

Items in Finder windows that are viewed by Size may be out of order right after you turn on the Calculate Folder Sizes option in the Views control panel. The Finder takes a while to calculate the sizes; in the meantime, it has displayed the window contents. You can force the Finder to re-sort a window's contents according to size by clicking another column heading (such as Name) and then clicking the Size column heading again.

## Folder-size slowdown

The Calculate Folder Sizes option in the Views control panel can slow your Mac when you're sharing someone else's files or accessing a file server. If you notice that the network-activity indicator is flashing in the left corner of the menu bar and you're not actively using a shared item, the Finder may be getting folder sizes from another Mac. (The Finder even does that in the background while you work with another program.) To end the slowdown, close the shared item's windows or turn off the Calculate Folder Sizes option.

### Find in next window

In System 7 versions older than 7.5, the Finder's Find Next command sometimes displays a window that contains many matches for what you specified in the Find command, but not the item that you want. To cancel searching in the active window and skip to the next folder that contains a match, close the window by clicking its close box or pressing ⌘-W.

### Drag to scroll

You can scroll a window in Finder 7 without using the scroll bars. Simply place the mouse pointer in the window, click the mouse button, and drag toward the area that you want to view. Drag the pointer up, down, left, or right past the window's active area, and scrolling begins. Dragging past a window corner scrolls diagonally.

To scroll slowly, drag just to the window's edge (and continue holding down the mouse button). Increase scrolling speed by dragging beyond the window's edge.

## Trash

This section provides tips on throwing stuff away and retrieving it from the Trash afterward.

### Skip the Trash warning

To skip the standard Trash warning the next time you empty the Trash, press Option while choosing the Empty Trash command. You also can reverse the Trash Personalized Sample Text

Warning setting by selecting the Trash, choosing Get Info, and reversing the setting of the Skip Trash Warnings option.

### Discarding locked items

When you use the Empty Trash command, the Finder normally doesn't discard locked items that you dragged to the Trash. Instead of unlocking each locked item with the Finder's Get Info command, you can simply press Option while choosing Empty Trash from the Special menu.

### Trashing Made Easy

QuicKeys users, are you tired of dragging things to the Trash with the mouse? A simple macro can do the job for you. The following procedure defines the macro. With the macro defined, you can put items in the Trash by selecting them wherever they may be, leaving the pointer on any of them, and pressing the keystroke that you designated to activate the macro.

To create the Trash pickup macro, follow these steps:

1. Open the QuicKeys editor and choose Click from QuicKeys' Define menu.

   The QuicKeys window disappears, and a microphone icon flashes over the Apple-menu icon.

2. Click the Trash.

   The Click editing window appears.

3. Click the Click button to display the Click Location editing window.

4. Choose Screen as the Drag Relative To option, and then choose Mouse as the Click Relative To option.

   These options instruct QuicKeys to click wherever the mouse pointer is and to drag from there to the coordinates of the Trash (which you recorded when you clicked it in step 2).

5. Click the OK button to return to the Click editing window.

6. Type a name for the macro and a keystroke for activating it (for example, ⌘-T).

7. Click OK to dismiss the Click editing window.

8. Click OK again to dismiss QuicKeys.

## Retrieving Trash

To put items that currently are in the Trash back where they came from, open the Trash, select the items, and choose Put Away from the Finder's File menu. The Finder returns each selected item to its previous folder, although not necessarily to the same place in the folder window.

## Discarding items from one disk

To remove items from only one disk, try putting away the icons of the disks whose trashed items you want to retain. To put away a disk icon, either select it and then choose Put Away from the Finder's File menu (or press ⌘-Y), or drag the disk icon to the Trash.

Alternatively, you can open the Trash, drag the items that you want to save to the desktop or to another folder and then use the Empty Trash command.

## Rescuing items

Sometimes, the Trash contains a folder named Rescued Items. This folder usually contains formerly invisible temporary files that were found when you started your Macintosh. The Rescued Items folder may appear after a system crash, and you may be able to recreate your work up to the time of the system crash from the contents of the Rescued Items folder.

# Apple Menu

Use the tips in this section to get more from the Apple menu and the Application menu.

## Apple-menu organization

After you add more than a few items to the Apple menu, it becomes a mess. You can group different types of items by prefixing different numbers of blank spaces to their names — the more blank spaces, the higher on the Apple menu. For example, you may prefix three blank spaces to control-panel names, two blanks to desk-accessory names, one blank to application-program names, and none to other items.

Prefixing a name with an Apple logo () or a solid diamond symbol (◆) makes the name appear below names that are prefixed with a space but above names that have no prefixes. Press Control-T to create the Apple logo or Control-S for the solid diamond. To make items appear at the bottom of the Apple menu, prefix them with a hollow diamond (◊) or a bullet (•). Press Shift-Option-V to create the hollow diamond or Option-8 for the bullet.

### The Non-ABCs Approach to Arranging Menu Items

Forcibly reordering items in the Apple menu by placing spaces or special symbols at the beginning of the items' names has side effects that you may not like. The spaces or symbols visibly alter the names, and they conspicuously shift the names to the right. To invisibly force the order you want, follow these steps:

1. Open the Note Pad or a new document in TeachText, SimpleText, or any word processing application.
2. Press Return to create a blank line, select the blank line, and copy it to the Clipboard.
3. Switch to the Finder.
4. In the Apple Menu Items folder, select the name of the item that you want to appear at the top of the Apple menu.
5. Press the up-arrow key to move the insertion point to the beginning of the selected name and then paste.
6. The entire name goes blank, but don't fret — just press Enter or click outside the name, and the name springs back into view.

   The renamed item jumps to the top of the window if you're viewing by name. To increase an item's alphabetic buoyancy, paste the blank line two or more times at the beginning of the item's name.

Caution: Some programs can't open documents whose names contain blank lines. If you have trouble opening a document whose name contains a blank line, rename the document without blank lines.

## Apple-menu separators

A long Apple menu — even one that's organized by type of item, as described in the preceding tip— can be hard to scan quickly. Visually separating the different types of items helps.

You can make separators by naming extra aliases with hyphens and prefixing the right number of blank spaces to the names so that each one appears between two different types of items. Aliases of the Finder work well as separators because accidentally opening one results in a message saying that the item can't be opened. You also can use ordinary folders instead of aliases to create separators in the Apple menu.

To further refine your Apple menu, you can hide the icons of the separators that you make. First, copy some white space in any paint program. Next, select a separator item's icon and use the Finder's Get Info command to display that item's Info window. Then select the icon in that window and paste the white space over it.

## Fast Apple-menu changes

To add or remove Apple-menu quickly, list the Apple Menu Items folder in the Apple menu. How? Make an alias of the Apple Menu Items folder and put the alias in that folder.

## Too-full Apple menu

If your Apple menu contains so many items that you must scroll to see them all, consider consolidating the less-used items in a folder or two within the Apple Menu Items folder.

In System 7.5 and later, the contents of folders in the Apple Menu Items folder appear as submenus of the Apple menu. If you are using a version of System 7 earlier than 7.5, you can get submenus in the Apple menu by installing a control panel such as Kiwi Power Menus (from Kiwi Software), HAM (from Microseeds), or Now Utilities (from Now Software).

## Universal Show Clipboard

Some application programs lack a Show Clipboard command; others that *do* have such a command use a private Clipboard whose contents may look different when pasted into another program. With System 7 installed, you can put a Show Clipboard command in your Apple menu and then use the command to review the standard Clipboard contents from any application program.

First, make an alias of the Clipboard file, which is in the System Folder. Then place the alias in the Apple Menu Items folder and rename the alias Show Clipboard. Now choose Show Clipboard from the Apple menu; System 7 switches to the Finder and opens the Clipboard.

## Hierarchical contact database

You can turn your Apple menu into a contact database. All you need is a utility that gives the Apple menu hierarchical submenus, such as System 7.5's Apple Menu Options control panel. By treating folder names as single-line entries in a database, you easily can create an elegant hierarchical database of often-used addresses, phone numbers, client contacts, and other information that you are tired of fumbling for on your crowded desktop.

You can access the data instantly from the Apple menu and its submenus, and view the data by traversing the menu structure without actually choosing any menu item, as shown in Figures 20-10 and 20-11. (When you finish viewing the data, just drag the mouse pointer away from the menus and release the mouse.) For a persistent display, choose the menu item whose submenu contains the data that you want to see; the Finder opens the folder that contains the data.

Adding, deleting, and modifying data is a snap. First, choose the menu item whose submenu you want to change and open the folder in which you need to make changes. To add a line of data, use the Finder's New Folder command and type the data as the new folder's name. To add a submenu, open a folder and add folders to it. Remove lines of data by dragging corresponding folders to the Trash and change data by editing folder names.

Because items appear alphabetically by name in the submenus, you may have to put extra spaces or other special characters at the beginning of folder names to arrange the names in the order you want. (You usually have to do this with a multiple-line address, for example.)

Another neat trick: use aliases to duplicate data if you want that data to appear in several places in the database. After making an alias of the folder that you want to clone, simply drag the alias to the folder that represents another location in the database where you want the information to appear. Cloned parts of your hierarchical database stay up to date, because aliases don't contain any duplicate data that can get out of sync; the aliases simply point to the folders that contain the actual data.

No matter how large your database of folders becomes, the Finder always calculates its size on disk as zero K! Yes, this *is* too good to be true. In fact, your data, consisting only of nested named folders, is kept in the startup disk's invisible catalog file, which contains information about the hierarchical organization of files and folders on that disk. The Finder reports only the sizes of aliases and other actual files that you may have in your hierarchical folders.

Keeping contact information in a hierarchical Apple menu has two advantages over using contact-database software such as TouchBase or InTouch: you can always locate your contacts without opening (or keeping open) another program, and you can find any contact quickly without typing or even remembering a name. Managing hundreds of contacts is easier with contact-database software, though.

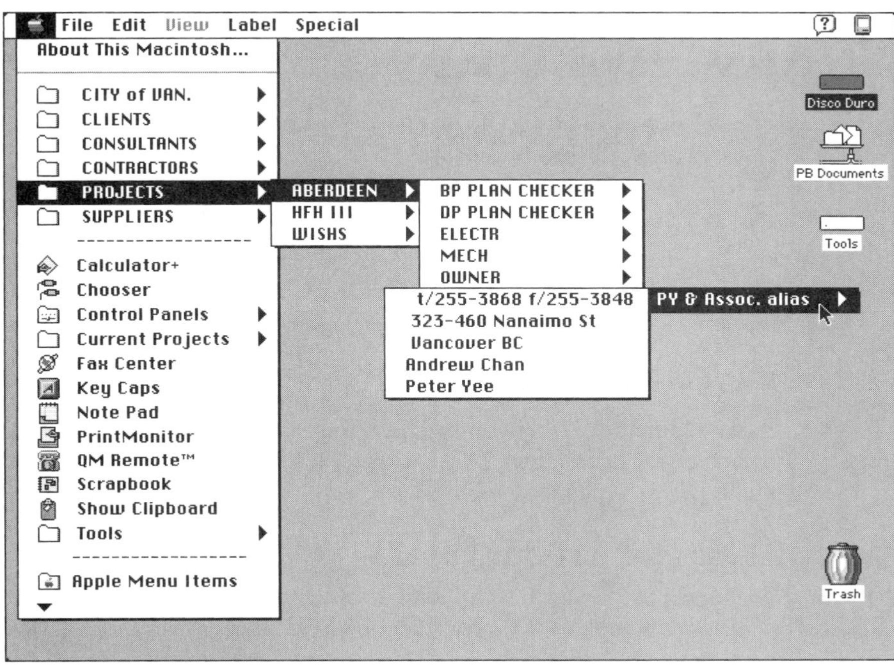


Figure 20-10: Viewing a contact database contained in submenus of the Apple menu.

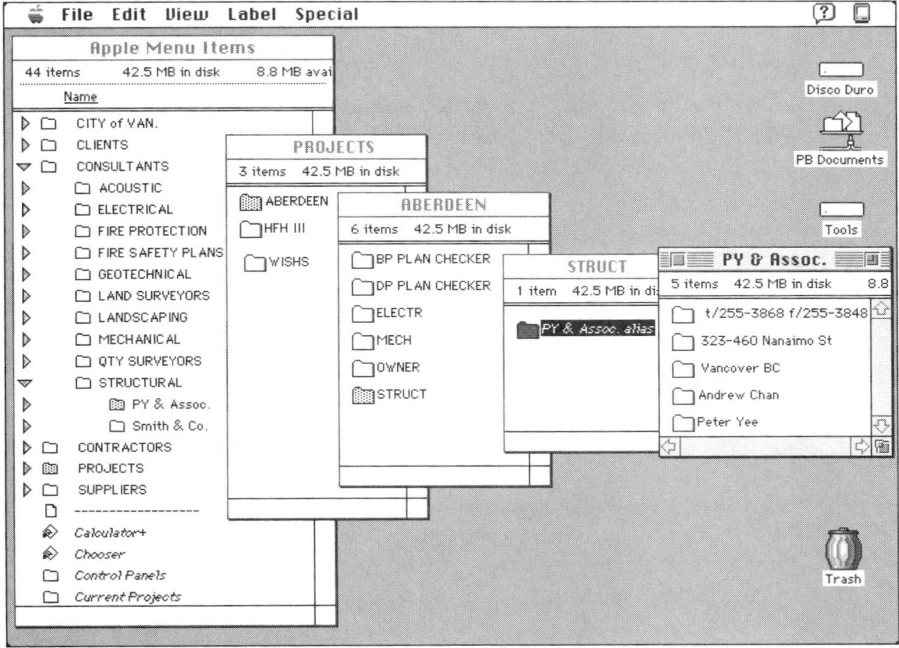


Figure 20-11: The folder structure behind the contact database shown in Figure 20-10.

# Directory Dialog Boxes

The tips in this section help you save time and effort in the directory dialog boxes that appear when you choose Open, Save As, and other disk-related commands.

## Find an alias's original item

You can go quickly to an alias's original item in a directory dialog box by pressing Option while opening the alias (by double-clicking it, for example). Alias names appear in italics in directory dialog boxes, just as they do in Finder windows.

## Folder switching

If you find that you frequently go back and forth between two folders, put an alias of each folder in the other. Whichever folder you are in, you can go to the other in one step by opening its alias.

## Aliases for favorite folders

Putting aliases of your favorite folders on the desktop or inside disk windows enables you to open a favorite folder quickly from a directory dialog box. Instead of working your way down through one branch of your folder structure and then working your way up another branch to the folder that you want, you zip to the desktop level or the disk level, and then open the alias of the folder that you want. This process is like jumping from one branch of a tree to the root level and then jumping to a spot on another branch without crawling up the trunk and along the other branch.

You can get to aliases of favorite folders on the desktop quickly by clicking the desktop button. Get to aliases at the disk-window level by choosing the disk from the directory dialog's pop-up menu.

## Copy and paste

You can copy and paste a document's name from the document to a Save or Save As dialog box, and vice versa. If the Cut, Copy, and Paste commands are not available from the Edit menu, you can use their keyboard equivalents (⌘-X, ⌘-C, and ⌘-V, respectively). When you paste, only the first 31 characters are used; any additional characters are omitted.

## Sidestepping a double click

As usual, you can open an item in the directory window by double-clicking it. If, before you release the mouse button, you realize that you double-clicked the wrong item, continue holding down the mouse button and drag the pointer to the item that you want to open. When you release the mouse button, the currently selected item opens.

### Canceling a double click

To cancel a double-click in a System 7 directory dialog box, hold down the mouse button on the second click and drag the pointer outside the dialog box before releasing the mouse button.

## File Sharing

Get more out of System 7's file sharing by using the tips in this section.

### Reducing network cabling costs

For a less expensive network, use Farallon's PhoneNet connectors (or the equivalent) and ordinary telephone cables instead of Apple's LocalTalk connectors and cables. Not only does PhoneNet cost less, but it also works with greater cable lengths than LocalTalk does.

### Picking a secure password

Pick a password that is easy for you to remember but difficult for other people to guess. For better security, mix letters with numbers; try replacing the letters *I* and *O* with the numbers 1 and 0.

### Allowing saving, not trashing

You can allow other users to save changes to a file that you're sharing but prevent them from throwing the file away. Simply share an alias to the file, and put the original item in a folder to which only you have privileges for making changes. If someone discards the alias, the original item isn't affected.

### Sharing disks or outer folders

When you share a folder, System 7 won't let you share the outer folder or the disk that contains it (see Figure 20-12). You have to drag the shared folder to another place or unshare it before you can share the outer folder or disk. To avoid this situation, share from the highest level of your disk and folder structure.

### Improving file-sharing performance

For best performance of your Macintosh, share as few of your folders as possible. The more items that others can access on your Macintosh, the greater the demands on your Macintosh's performance. Sharing too many folders can slow your system to a crawl. When you need to share numerous files or to share folders simultaneously with several users, consider setting up a dedicated Macintosh to act as a centralized file server for the shared information.

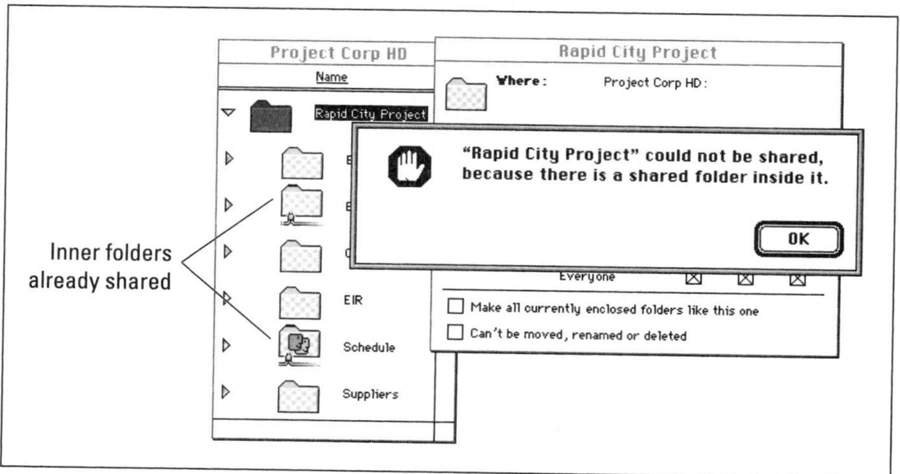


**Figure 20-12: You can't make a folder available for sharing if that folder contains shared folders.**

## Cutting file-sharing red tape

Getting access to shared items involves wading through a fair amount of bureaucracy. Aliases cut through the red tape.

First, access a shared disk or folder one time, using the Chooser desk accessory as described in Chapter 9. Next, select the shared item, or any folder or file in it; then choose Make Alias from the File menu. Finally, copy the alias to your desktop or hard disk. An alias keeps track of its original item even if the original item is on another networked Macintosh.

After you make an alias of a shared item, you can access the shared item by opening the alias either from the Finder or from an Open command's directory dialog box. Dragging something to the alias of a shared disk or folder also accesses that shared item automatically. You still must enter a password unless you initially accessed the original item as a guest. If the shared item is not available (when, for example, the Macintosh where it resides is turned off), a message tells you so.

## Office on a disk

Aliases can give you nearly automatic access to your Macintosh's hard disks by using a floppy disk in any other Macintosh on the same network. To access your disks easily from another Macintosh, open the Sharing Setup control panel, and check the status of File Sharing. If File Sharing is off, click the Start button and wait until it is on (the Start button becomes a Stop button).

Next, select all your hard-disk icons and choose Sharing from the File menu to open a Sharing Info window for each disk. In each window, turn on the Share this item and its contents option; also turn off the See Folders, See Files, and Make Changes options for the User/Group and Everyone categories. These settings restrict access to your disks so that only you can make changes or see files or folders. Make an alias of each disk and copy the aliases to a floppy disk.

As long as file sharing is active on your Macintosh, you can use that floppy disk to access your hard disk from any Macintosh on your network. Simply insert the disk, open the alias for the disk that you want to use, and enter your password when asked. Correctly entering your password gives you access to all applications, folders, and documents on your disk from any remote Macintosh. You don't have to bother with opening the Chooser, selecting AppleShare, selecting your computer, and typing your name as the registered user.

## The latest shared document

To make sure that others who share your documents have the latest version, share an alias of the original, and keep the original in an inaccessible folder. Other users can copy the alias to their disks and use the alias to open the original document. If you later replace the original document with a version that has the same name, the aliases that people copied will open the new version. People who share the alias always get the newest version of the original item that it represents, even if the original changes frequently.

## What people have trashed

Items from your shared disk or folder that someone has dragged to the Trash — but not yet permanently removed — on another Macintosh do not appear in your Trash. System 7 puts those items in folders whose names begin Trash Can #. You cannot see these folders with the Finder because they are in an invisible folder inside the shared folder or disk. To see the Trash Can # folders, use a utility program such as Norton Utilities for Macintosh.

## File sharing and removable disks

If you start file sharing (using the Sharing Setup control panel) with no CD-ROM inserted into your CD-ROM drive, you subsequently can insert and remove CD-ROMs as much as you want. Unfortunately, this procedure also prevents you from sharing any CD-ROMs. To share a CD-ROM, you must insert it before starting file sharing. But then, as you know, you can't remove the CD-ROM without stopping file sharing. This is a tough choice, and one that applies equally to all types of drives with removable media, such as SyQuest and magneto-optical.

The free utility program UnmountIt simplifies removing a cartridge that was inserted when file sharing was started. Simply drag the cartridge's icon to the UnmountIt icon instead of to the Trash. UnmountIt turns off file sharing (if it is on), removes the cartridge's icon from the desktop (also ejecting the cartridge with some types of drives), and then turns file sharing back on (if it was on to begin with). Before turning off file sharing, the program warns you if anyone is connected to your Mac; it also includes other common-sense safeguards. UnmountIt is available from user groups and on-line information services.

# System Utilities

In this section, you'll find ideas for getting more from the standard accessory programs that come with System 7.

## Scripted Calculator

You can copy the text of a calculation — for example, 69.95+26.98+14.99*.0725 — and paste it into the standard Calculator desk accessory. Be sure to use the asterisk (*) symbol for multiplication and the slash (/) symbol for division.

## Alternative Scrapbooks

After extensive use, your Scrapbook may become cluttered with old clippings. If you can't bear to throw them out, make a copy of the Scrapbook file in your System Folder (use the Finder's Duplicate command) before you start weeding. Later, you can use the old copy that you made by dragging the current Scrapbook file out of the System Folder, dragging the old copy in, and changing the copy's name to Scrapbook.

## Print later

If you travel with a PowerBook, you may wish that you could print a document as soon as you finish it. If you do not have QuickDraw GX installed on your PowerBook, turn on the Background Printing option in the Chooser and set preferences that tell the PrintMonitor program not to bother you if it can't find the printer (see Figure 20-13). Now you can print any number of documents at any time, and the printer-driver software saves the page images for each document as a spool file in the PrintMonitor Documents folder (inside the System Folder).

If PrintMonitor can't find the printer, it flashes its icon in the menu bar. Ignore the flashing icon until you have a printer connected and ready. Then open Print-Monitor. When it asks what you want to do about the printing problem, click the Try Again button to have all the waiting spool files printed.

## Printed Key Caps

You may want to print the Key Caps desk accessory as a handy reference, but it has no Print command. To work around this problem, take a picture of the screen and print that picture. Follow these steps:

1. Open Key Caps, choose the font that you want it to display, and press any modifier keys (Shift, Option, Control, or ⌘) that you want to be in effect.
2. Move the mouse pointer to an empty area of the menu bar, and hold down the mouse button.
3. Temporarily release the modifier keys, and press ⌘-Shift-3.
4. Again press the modifier keys that you released temporarily.
5. Release the mouse button.

   Your gyrations should be rewarded by the sound of a camera shutter as the System snaps a picture of the screen.
6. Open your startup disk, and look for a document named Picture 1.
7. Print this document, using TeachText or any graphics program.

Cut out the Key Caps window with scissors after printing, or crop it out with a graphics program before printing. If you take additional snapshots, they are numbered sequentially.

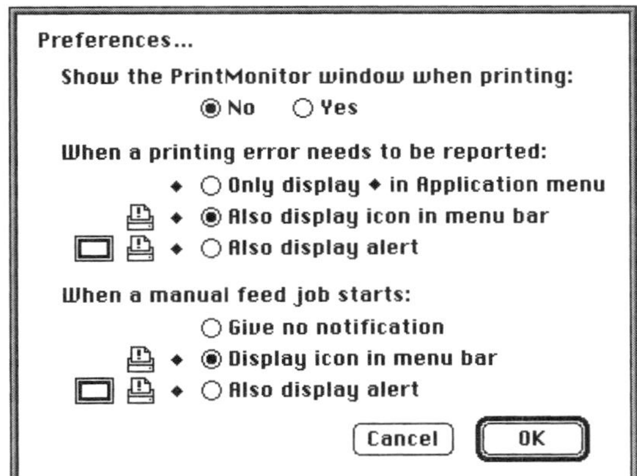


**Figure 20-13: These settings keep PrintMonitor from nagging you when you print.**

To shut down your Mac without deleting spool files that are waiting to be printed — without QuickDraw GX installed — you must respond correctly to two alert boxes that appear at the end of the shutdown process. The first alert box tells you that something is being printed and asks whether you want to finish printing or print later; you must click the Print Later button. Then the other alert box tells you that the printer can't be found; click the Cancel Printing button to conclude the shutdown process without losing any spool files. (If you click Try Again instead, you abort the shutdown process, and PrintMonitor tries again to find the missing printer.) This procedure is somewhat confusing, because clicking Cancel Printing except after clicking Print Later *does* delete the spool file that is being printed.

### LaserWriter test page

The LaserWriter Font Utility program, which comes with System 7, can turn a LaserWriter's test page on and off. The Installer does not put this utility program on your hard disk automatically when you install System 7.

## Control Panels

This section contains tips on using the standard control panels that come with System 7.

### Revert to standard labels

If you want to reset the Labels control panel to factory-standard colors and names, use the settings listed in Table 20-1.

Table 20-1
**Values for Standard Label Colors**

| | ***System 7.0, 7.0.1, 7.1, 7.1.1, 7.1.2*** | | | ***System 7.5*** | | |
|---|---|---|---|---|---|---|
| ***Label*** | ***Hue*** | ***Saturation*** | ***Brightness*** | ***Hue*** | ***Saturation*** | ***Brightness*** |
| Essential | 4223 | 64884 | 65535 | 23° | 100% | 50.5% |
| Hot | 108 | 63573 | 56683 | 1° | 94.18% | 44.54% |
| In Progress | 59733 | 63286 | 62167 | 328° | 93.36% | 49.06% |
| Cool | 35756 | 64907 | 60159 | 196° | 98.1% | 46.34% |
| Personal | 43690 | 65535 | 54272 | 240° | 100% | 41.41% |
| Project 1 | 23764 | 65535 | 25775 | 131° | 100% | 19.66% |
| Project 2 | 5332 | 61619 | 22016 | 29° | 88.72% | 17.8% |

## Easy Access shortcuts

Instead of using the Easy Access control panel to turn Mouse Keys or Sticky Keys on and off, you can use the keyboard. To turn on Mouse Keys, press ⌘-Shift-Clear; to turn it off, press Clear. (Mouse Keys requires a numeric keypad, so you can't use it from a PowerBook unless you install the Mouse Keys System extension, which is available from user groups and on-line information services.)

To turn on Sticky Keys, press Shift five times in succession; turn it off by pressing Shift five times again or by pressing any two modifier keys simultaneously.

To turn Slow Keys on or off, hold down the Return key for about 10 seconds. Listen for three short beeps about five seconds after you begin pressing Return, and listen for a whistle about five seconds later to confirm that Slow Keys is turning on or off.

## Big map

You can enlarge the world map in the Map control panel by pressing Option while opening the control panel. To magnify more, press Shift-Option while opening the map.

## Color map

If your Map control panel displays a black-and-white world map on your color or grayscale monitor, you can colorize the map. First, look through your Scrapbook for a color version of the world map used in the Map control panel. If you find one, copy it, open the Map control panel, and paste.

If you can't find a color version of the world map, you don't have the standard System 7 Scrapbook file. To get it, temporarily move the Scrapbook file from your System Folder to the desktop. Next, copy the Scrapbook file from the System 7 installation disk to your System Folder. Copy the color map as described in the preceding paragraph. Finally, select the Scrapbook file on the desktop, choose Put Away from the Finder's file menu, and click OK when the Finder asks whether it's OK to replace the Scrapbook file in the System Folder with the one that you're moving (putting away) from the desktop.

## What's your time?

If you regularly contact people in multiple time zones, you can use the Map control panel to keep track of local times for those people. Follow these steps:

1. Open the Map control panel.
2. Type the name of the city, and click the Find button.
3. Type the person's name over the city name, and click the Add City button.

Now you need only type a person's name in Map and click the Find button to find his or her time zone.

If you want Map to remember a person whose city isn't on the map, you can substitute a known city in the same time zone or add the unknown city. Whenever you add a new place or person to Map, verify the time zone and correct it, if necessary.

### Hidden free beep

The System 7 Scrapbook includes an extra system alert sound that you can paste into the Sound control panel. If your Scrapbook doesn't contain the sound, you don't have the standard System 7 Scrapbook file. This situation usually means that your System Folder had a Scrapbook file when the disk was upgraded to System 7. For instructions on getting the standard Scrapbook file, refer to the "Color Map" tip.

## Applications

In this section, you find tips for using System 7 features while working with application programs.

### Canceling an opening

If you have fast fingers, you can cancel the accidental opening of an application. You must press ⌘-period within a few seconds of opening the application.

### Hiding windows while switching

To hide the active program's windows as you switch to a particular program, press Option while choosing the other program from the Application menu, or press Option while clicking another program's window. You hide windows and switch to the Finder by pressing Option while clicking the desktop or a Finder icon.

### Hide windows to boost performance

When you have several programs open, you can spend a great deal of time waiting while inactive programs redraw portions of their windows as dialog boxes come and go. This delay is particularly protracted when you're using virtual memory, because the window redrawing may require disk access. Eliminate the delay by choosing Hide Others from the Application menu. Hidden windows don't require updating.

### Stationery workaround

You can work around the Finder's prompt to name and save a new document every time you open a particular stationery pad. Make an ordinary document, and lock it by using the Finder's Get Info command.

You may want to use this method with templates for printing single envelopes and mailing labels, for example. Then you can open the locked template, type or paste the recipient's address, print, and close without saving. (This method does not work with WriteNow 3 and other programs that do not permit changes in locked documents.)

## Dynamic references

Updating references to tables, figures, bibliographic entries, and so on can be a real chore in most Mac word processing programs, even when you use a Replace command. System 7's publish-and-subscribe capability can keep table numbers and other references current automatically. The references can be in the same documents as the referents or in different documents. You simply publish the number, name, title, or other identifier of each referent as a separate edition, and subscribe to the appropriate edition wherever you want to make a reference.

In Microsoft Word 5.1 and earlier versions, for example, you select a table number and use the Create Publisher command to save the table number as a new edition. Then, with the Subscribe To command, you subscribe to that edition wherever you want a reference to the table. If you subsequently change the table number (the publisher), System 7 propagates the change among all references to the table (subscribers).

System 7 normally doesn't notify subscribers (the references) about an update until you save the document that contains the publisher (the referent). In Word, you can make the update occur when you make changes by selecting the Publisher and then turning on the Send Edition When Edited option of the Publisher Options command.

## Changing the application font

By default, many application programs and desk accessories use the Mac's standard application font, which is Geneva. The Mac stores the identity of this font in its *parameter RAM*, which is a small amount of battery-powered memory that stores sundry system settings. You can override the application-font setting in parameter RAM by installing the free utility software DeFont or It's Your Default (available from user groups and on-line information services). DeFont and It's Your Default are control panels that allow you to choose any installed font as the application font.

Some programs (including MacWrite II, Microsoft Word, and WriteNow 3) do not use the application font, so DeFont and It's Your Default do not affect them. To change MacWrite II's standard font, create a new document, select the font that you want to use, and choose Save As from the File menu. In the Save As dialog box, choose MacWrite II Stationery from the pop-up menu, name the document MacWrite II Options, and save it in the Claris folder inside the System Folder. (Before saving, you can make other changes to the document's format and content; thereafter, MacWrite II applies the changes to all new documents that you create.)

You follow a similar procedure in WriteNow 3, using WriteNow's Save As Default Document command instead of its Save As command. In Word 5, the Preferences command has a Default Font option.

# Memory and Performance

The tips in this section help you make the most of your computer's memory and increase its performance.

## Disk Cache performance boost

If you have a Macintosh IIsi and you set the number of colors or grays for its built-in video to four or more, you can improve System performance by setting the Disk Cache to 768K in the Memory control panel. Then the Disk Cache and the built-in video together use all the memory that's soldered to the main circuit board, forcing the system software and your programs into the part of memory in the four SIMM sockets. Programs may work much slower if they are located in the soldered-on memory along with the built-in video.

The same trick works on a Macintosh IIci with 5MB, 9MB, or 17MB of RAM. To get the performance boost, you must install the 256K SIMMs in the four sockets nearest the disk drive. Realizing a performance increase on a IIci with other RAM capacities isn't feasible, because you would have to set the Disk Cache so high as to waste a large amount of memory.

## Quitting startup programs

If you have several programs opening during startup, you may have to quit some of them later to free memory for opening another program. Naturally, you want to quit the programs that are the least important to you. You'll get maximum benefit from quitting those programs if they were the last items opened during startup. To make that happen, rename the items in your Startup Items folder so that the most important item comes first alphabetically, the next most important comes second, and so on. You can avoid renaming original items by placing aliases in the Startup Items folder.

## Paring memory to the bone

If your Macintosh has just the minimum 4MB of RAM required to use System 7 (2MB for System 7.0, 7.0.1, or 7.1), you should pare program-memory sizes to the bone. For example, giving your favorite word processing program the full amount of memory available after the system software takes its chunk and leaves you no room to use the Chooser to select a printer or share someone's files. (You can, however, work around the file-sharing limitation by making aliases of the items that you most often share, as described in Chapter 9.) Also, you wouldn't have any memory left for background printing.

## Reducing system memory size

You can reduce the system software's memory size (as reported by the About This Macintosh command) to its minimum by pressing Shift while restarting your Macintosh. Look for the message "Extensions Off" during startup. This message confirms that you have suppressed loading of all items in the Extensions folder, the Control Panels folder, and the System Folder that would increase the system software's memory size. You also have bypassed opening items in the Startup Items folder, reduced the RAM cache to 16K, forced virtual memory off, and prevented file sharing from starting.

None of these changes persists when you restart without pressing Shift. To make persistent changes, you must drag items out of the special folders and then change settings in the Memory and File Sharing control panels.

For big memory savings, turn off file sharing and virtual memory if you're not using them. Reducing the RAM cache size reduces the system software's memory size K for K — and slows system performance.

## Fragmented memory

To check for fragmented memory, add up the memory sizes of all the open programs and the system software, as listed in the About This Macintosh window. If you have a Power Mac 6100, 7100, or 8100 with a monitor connected to its AV monitor port, add another 600K (or less, if you have limited the number of colors as described in "Monitors" in Chapter 8). If you have a monitor connected to the built-in video on a Macintosh IIsi or IIci, add another 320K (or less, if you have limited the number of colors to fewer than 256). If the total exceeds the Largest Unused Block amount by more than 50K or so, the unused memory is fragmented into two or more chunks.

To consolidate fragmented memory, quit all open programs and then open them again. Restarting your Macintosh also fixes fragmentation and may reduce the amount of memory used by system software as well.

You can avoid memory fragmentation by planning the order in which you open and quit programs. First, open the programs that you're least likely to quit first; and last, open the programs that you're most likely to quit last. When you need more memory to open another program, quit the most recently opened program. If that doesn't free enough memory, quit the next most recently opened program, and so on. This method frees a contiguous chunk of memory. Quitting programs helter-skelter leads to memory fragmentation.

## Standing memory reservation

If you sometimes have trouble opening a program after you quit another, background printing may be fragmenting your Mac's memory. Unless you are using QuickDraw GX's Desktop printers, the PrintMonitor application opens automatically to handle background printing as needed.

PrintMonitor may be opening after you quit a program, using part of the memory that you just freed by quitting a program. The largest unused block of memory may be too small for the program that you need to open, and so may the block that would be available if you quit another open program. Both unused blocks together, however, would be enough if you could consolidate them by quitting Print-Monitor.

To prevent this problem, have your Mac automatically reserve 100K for PrintMonitor during startup, before any other programs are opened. First, place a copy of PrintMonitor in the Startup Items folder, along with an alias of the program that you least want to quit. Next, put a blank space at the beginning of the name of the PrintMonitor copy so that it comes first alphabetically in the Startup Items folder. Finally, use the Finder's Get Info command to set the minimum memory size of the PrintMonitor copy to 100K.

Now the renamed PrintMonitor copy opens first during startup, followed by the other startup program. Then the PrintMonitor copy closes because there is nothing to print. The block of memory thus freed remains available for the original PrintMonitor (in the Extensions folder). The original PrintMonitor's minimum memory size is 96K, so it fits into the 100K space even if that space shrinks by 1K or 2K, as sometimes happens. Because PrintMonitor no longer fragments memory, you can quit and open programs without postponing background printing.

This technique does not work if you open desk accessories (which take 20K each) while PrintMonitor is not open and you leave those desk accessories open. The technique also does not work if you quit the other program that opened during startup and then open another program while PrintMonitor is not open. In that case, the newly opened program takes the space reserved for PrintMonitor and part of the space used by the now-closed application.

## Best partition sizes

If you work with many small files, you can save a significant amount of disk space by partitioning a large hard drive into several smaller volumes. The Mac file system allocates a minimum amount of disk space for each file, regardless of its actual contents. The minimum file size for a particular disk is set when it is formatted (or when it is partitioned, if it has multiple partitions) and increases incrementally as disk (or partition) capacity increases. For example, a short memo that takes 4K on a 230MB hard drive would take only 1K on a 60MB partition, saving 3K per small file.

Most formatting programs set a minimum file size of 1K on disks with capacities less than 64MB, 1.5K on disks with capacities between 64MB and 95MB, 2K on disks between 96MB and 127MB, and so on.

If you work mostly with large files, large volumes are more efficient.

# More Tips and Secrets

This section contains hidden treasures to help you with printing, typing symbols, saving startup time, and more.

## Easter-egg hunt

Apple's system-software engineers, true to their kind, have left a few Easter eggs in their work. In the Color control panel, for example, click the sample text a few times to see authorship credits. On a Mac whose Memory control panel has a virtual-memory section, try turning on virtual memory and pressing Option while clicking the Hard Disk pop-up menu. Instead of a list of disks, you see the names of virtual memory's creators.

If your Mac can use the Monitors control panel, click the version number in its upper-right corner to see a smiley face and the authors' names. Repeatedly press Option to mix up the first names and randomly replace them with the words *Blue Meanies.* (The Blue Meanies are Apple's system-software SWAT team.)

In the Finder, pressing Option changes the first command in the Apple menu to About the Finder. Choose this command, and instead of the usual memory-usage chart, you see the mountain-range picture that adorned Finder version 1.1 in 1984. Wait about ten seconds, and credits start scrolling from right to left across the bottom of the screen. Hold down ⌘-Option while choosing About the Finder, and the mouse pointer becomes a wacky smiley face. You may not see the smiley face, however, if you installed System 7 before its release date of May 13, 1991. If the Desktop folder on the startup disk was created before that date, the smiley face does not appear.

The Desktop folder normally is invisible in System 7 but is visible if you restart with a System 6 floppy disk or if you access your startup hard disk from another Mac, using file sharing.

## More Chicago symbols

In addition to the four special symbols that have always been part of the Chicago font — (⌘, ✓, ◆, and ) — the TrueType version of Chicago that ships with System 7 has many new special symbols. These symbols include ⌥ and ⇧, which Apple uses to represent the Option and Shift keys. You type the symbols by pressing Control-A and Control-D.

You can type other symbols by pressing Control with one of the letter keys, as shown in Figure 20-14. You probably won't see any of the new special symbols, however, if you set the font size to 12 points or any other size for which a fixed-size Chicago font is installed in your System file. (Chicago 12 is in the ROM of all Mac models except those older than a Plus.) Fixed-size versions of Chicago don't include the new symbols, and most programs use fixed-size fonts wherever possible.

**Figure 20-14: Press Control to type 21 extra symbols with the TrueType version of Chicago.**

If you have trouble typing the special symbols in a particular program, try typing them in the Key Caps desk accessory. Because Key Caps always displays 12-point text, you'll see a box instead of the special symbol. Copy it anyway, paste it where you want the special symbol to be, and change the font there to 13-point Chicago.

One other symbol — ⌫ — can't be typed in Key Caps or in most applications, but you can generate it by typing the following command in HyperCard's message box and then pressing Return: **put numToChar(8)**. HyperCard replaces the command with a box; copy it, paste it where you want the symbol to be, and change its font there to Chicago 13.

## Keyboard changes

In System 7, Apple changed the mapping of U.S. keyboards, largely to make the Caps Lock key more consistent with the Shift key. All versions of system software ignore the Shift key if you simultaneously press the ⌘ key, and System 7 likewise ignores the Caps Lock key when you simultaneously press the ⌘ key. System 7, unlike earlier system software versions, also ignores the Caps Lock key for Option-key combinations that produce these eight symbols: © (Option-G), ˚ (Option-K), ® (Option-R), † (Option-T), √ (Option-V), ∑ (Option-W), ≈ (Option-X), and Ω (Option-Z).

With System 7, you can directly type the accent produced by one of the dead-key combinations — ‘ (Option-‘), ´ (Option-E), ˆ (Option-I), ˜ (Option-N), or ¨ (Option-U) — by pressing the dead-key combination with Shift or with Caps Lock. Pressing Option-Shift-I produces a true circumflex (ˆ) in System 7 instead of the caret (^) of earlier system software, and pressing Option-Shift-N produces a true tilde (˜) instead of an equivalence sign (~). As always, pressing a dead-key combination without Shift or Caps Lock applies the accent to the next character that you type.

If you press a dead-key combination and then type a letter that doesn't take the accent, System 7 always produces the accent followed by the letter you typed. By contrast, System 6 substitutes a caret (^) for a circumflex (ˆ) and an equivalence symbol (~) for a tilde (˜); it produces the other accents correctly. The System 7 keyboard mapping enables you to directly type four additional accents — ˝ ˇ ˛ and ¸ — but you can't apply them to other characters as you can the four dead-key accents.

Table 20-2 shows the characters that are affected by the new keyboard map and the key combinations that produce them in System 7 and in System 6.

Table 20-2
**System 7 Keyboard Changes**

| *Character* | *System 6 Key Combination* | *System 7 Key Combination* |
|---|---|---|
| Â | Option-Shift-R<br>Option-Caps Lock-R | Option-Shift-M<br>Option-Caps Lock-M<br>Option-I; then Shift-A |
| È | Option-Shift-I<br>Option-Caps Lock-I | Option-‘; then Shift-E |
| Ê | Option-Shift-T<br>Option-Caps Lock-T | Option-I; then Shift-E |
| Ë | Option-Shift-U<br>Option-Caps Lock-U | Option-U; then Shift-E |
| Ì | Option-Shift-G<br>Option-Caps Lock-G | Option-‘; then Shift-I |
| Ù | Option-Shift-X<br>Option-Caps Lock-X | Option-‘; then Shift-U |
| Û | Option-Shift-Z<br>Option-Caps Lock-Z | Option-I; then Shift-U |
| Ÿ | Option-Shift-‘<br>Option-Caps Lock-‘ | Option-U; then Shift-Y |
| © | Option-G | Option-G<br>Option-Caps Lock-G |
| ° | Option-K | Option-K<br>Option-Caps Lock-K |
| ® | Option-R | Option-R<br>Option-Caps Lock-R |
| † | Option-T | Option-T<br>Option-Caps Lock-T |
| √ | Option-V | Option-V<br>Option–Caps Lock–V |
| Σ | Option-W | Option-W<br>Option-Caps Lock-W |
| ≈ | Option-X | Option-X<br>Option-Caps Lock-X |
| Ω | Option-Z<br>Option-Caps Lock-Z | Option-Z |

*(continued on next page)*

| Table 20-2 *(continued)* | | |
|---|---|---|
| ***Character*** | ***System 6 Key Combination*** | ***System 7 Key Combination*** |
| ‰ | Option-Shift-E<br>Option-Caps Lock-E | Option-Shift-R |
|  | Option-Shift-K<br>Option-Caps Lock-K | Option-Shift-K |
| ◊ | Option-Shift-V<br>Option-Caps Lock-V | Option-Shift-V |
| „ | Option-Shift-W<br>Option-Caps Lock-W | Option-Shift-W |
| ‚ | Option-Caps Lock-'<br>Caps Lock-'<br>' alone | Option-Shift-'<br>Option-Caps Lock-'<br>Caps Lock-'<br>' alone |
| ´ | Option-E, then Space | Option-Shift-E<br>Option-Caps Lock-E<br>Option-E, then Space |
| ˆ | Option-Shift-N<br>Option-Caps Lock-N | Option-Shift-I<br>Option-Caps Lock-I<br>Option-I; then Space |
| ^ | Option-I; then Space<br>Shift-6 | Shift-6 |
| ˜ | Option-Shift-M<br>Option-Caps Lock-M | Option-Shift-N<br>Option-Caps Lock-N<br>Option-N, then Space |
| ~ | Option-N; then Space<br>Shift-' | Shift-' |
| ¨ | Option-U; then Space | Option-Shift-U<br>Option-Caps Lock-U<br>Option-U; then Space |
| ¸ | None | Option-Shift-Z |
| ˝ | None | Option-Shift-G |

## Cancel startup items

At times, hearing David Letterman say "Hypnotized!" while your Mac starts up is not politically correct. You can suppress the playing of sounds and opening of all other items in System 7's Startup Items folder by pressing Shift when the Finder's menu bar appears. After the opening of startup items has begun, you can cancel it by pressing ⌘-period. The Mac immediately stops any sound that it was playing and skips all startup items that it has not already opened.

If you press ⌘-period while the Mac is opening an application, document, or desk accessory from the Startup Items folder, the Mac finishes opening that item and ignores all other startup items. Pressing ⌘-period also stops any sound that you started playing by opening its icon in the Finder.

## Confirm startup items

Here's a trick for System 7 users who sometimes want items in the Startup Items folder to be opened and sometimes don't. Make a duplicate of an application (such as SimpleText or TeachText), and make an alias of the duplicate. Then drag the duplicate application to the Trash, and empty the Trash. Place the alias of the application that you just deleted into the Startup Items folder, and give the alias a name that alphabetically precedes the other items in that folder. When the Finder encounters the alias, it displays an alert box, telling you that it could not find the alias's original item. Click Stop to cancel opening the startup items, or click Continue to finish opening them.

## Talk in your headphones

If you have no microphone for your Mac, try plugging the headphones from a portable tape recorder into your Mac's microphone jack and recording your voice with the Sound control panel. Headphones have a similar technology to microphones, but in reverse.

## Hide or sleep

The menu-bar clock, which you set with the Date & Time control panel in System 7.5 and later, has a couple of tricks that you may not have discovered. You can temporarily hide the clock (so that it doesn't show while you're doing a presentation, for example) by holding down the Option key and clicking the clock. Option-click the same spot again to reveal the clock. In addition, you can put a PowerBook to sleep quickly by pressing Control while clicking the battery indicator in the menu bar.

## Finder hacks

If you have itchy fingers and an idle copy of ResEdit, you can put a personal stamp on your Mac's Finder. Table 20-3 lists some interesting changes, or *hacks,* that you can make to the Finder. (Be sure to back up your Finder before attempting any of these hacks.)

Table 20-3
**Where to Modify the Finder**

| ***Effect*** | ***Resource Type*** | ***ID*** | ***Where*** | ***Change To*** |
|---|---|---|---|---|
| Add a ⌘-key equivalent for Make Alias | fmnu | 1252 | Offset 9E | M or any key not used for another Finder command |
| Add a ⌘-key equivalent for Empty Trash | fmnu | 1255 | Offset 2C | T or any key not used for another Finder command |
| Add a ⌘-key equivalent for Restart | fmnu | 1255 | Offset 7E | R or any key not used for another Finder command |
| Change the suffix for a new alias's name | STR# | 20500 | Item 1 | One blank space or any text up to 31 characters |
| Change the initial name of a new folder | STR# | 11250 | Item 3 | Any text up to 31 characters |
| Change the sample text displayed when you open a TrueType or fixed-size font | STR# | 14516 | Item 1 | Any text |
| Disable animated zooming when opening and closing windows | CODE | 2 (4 before Finder 7.1.3) | Offset 472 (Offset 78 before Finder 7.1.3) | 6000 00E6 (from 48E7 1F38) |

## A Hacker's Agenda

The basic procedure is the same for all the hacks listed in Table 20-3. As a model, here's how to disable the animated zooming that occurs when a window opens or closes:

1. Open your System Folder, and press Option as you drag a copy of the Finder to the desktop.
2. Open this duplicate Finder with ResEdit.
3. Open the Finder's CODE resource icon, and then open the CODE resource whose ID is 2 (ID 4 before Finder 7.1.3).

   You see a window that displays the contents of the CODE resource.
4. Find hexadecimal 48E7 1F38 at offset 472 (offset 78 before Finder 7.1.3), and replace it with 6000 00E6.
5. Quit ResEdit, answering Yes when you are asked whether you want to save changes.
6. Drag the original Finder from your System Folder to another folder, and drag the modified Finder from the desktop to the System Folder.
7. Restart your computer, and test the results of your modification by opening or closing a window.

   You should not see any zooming animation.

Successfully performing any of the hacks listed in Table 20-3 gains you membership in the Loyal Order of the DogCow, which entitles you to wear an extra-large T-shirt and sneakers to work and to litter your work space with candy-bar wrappers and empty cola cans!

# CHAPTER  CONCEPTS AND TERMS

- There are many ideas for saving time and effort while editing icon names, making and using aliases on the desktop, getting icons to look the way you want, and manipulating font icons.
- You can personalize the startup process with a startup picture, movie, and sound. You can also hide individual icons on your desktop and decorate your desktop with a custom pattern tile size up to 64 by 64 pixels.
- There are many ways to work smarter with folders and windows in the Finder, the Trash, the Apple menu, and directory dialog boxes.
- Applying the right tips helps you get the most from System 7's file sharing capability, accessory programs, and control panels.
- Some secret ways of using System 7 capabilities make your work with application programs more productive.
- You won't run out of memory or disk space so often if you pay attention to several key ideas for conserving these resources.
- If you have itchy fingers and an idle copy of ResEdit, you can put a personal stamp on your Finder by using some interesting hacks.

**DogCow**
The official mascot of Mac hackers, this beast is pictured in many Page Setup Options dialog boxes.

**hack**
An unauthorized change made to software, usually with the intent of altering its appearance or behavior to suit the whim of the person making the change.

**hacker**
A person who likes to tinker with computers, and especially with computer software. Some hackers create new software, but many hackers use programs such as ResEdit to make unauthorized changes to the system software or other software.

**parameter RAM**
A small amount of battery-powered memory that stores system settings such as time, date, mouse tracking speed, speaker volume, and choice of startup disk. Also known as PRAM.

**resources**
Information such as text, menus, icons, pictures, or patterns used by the system software, an application program, or other software. Resources are classified by type, and each type is identified by a four-character code, such as STR#, MENU, ICN#, PICT, or ppat. You can modify some resources in meaningful ways with Apple's ResEdit program.

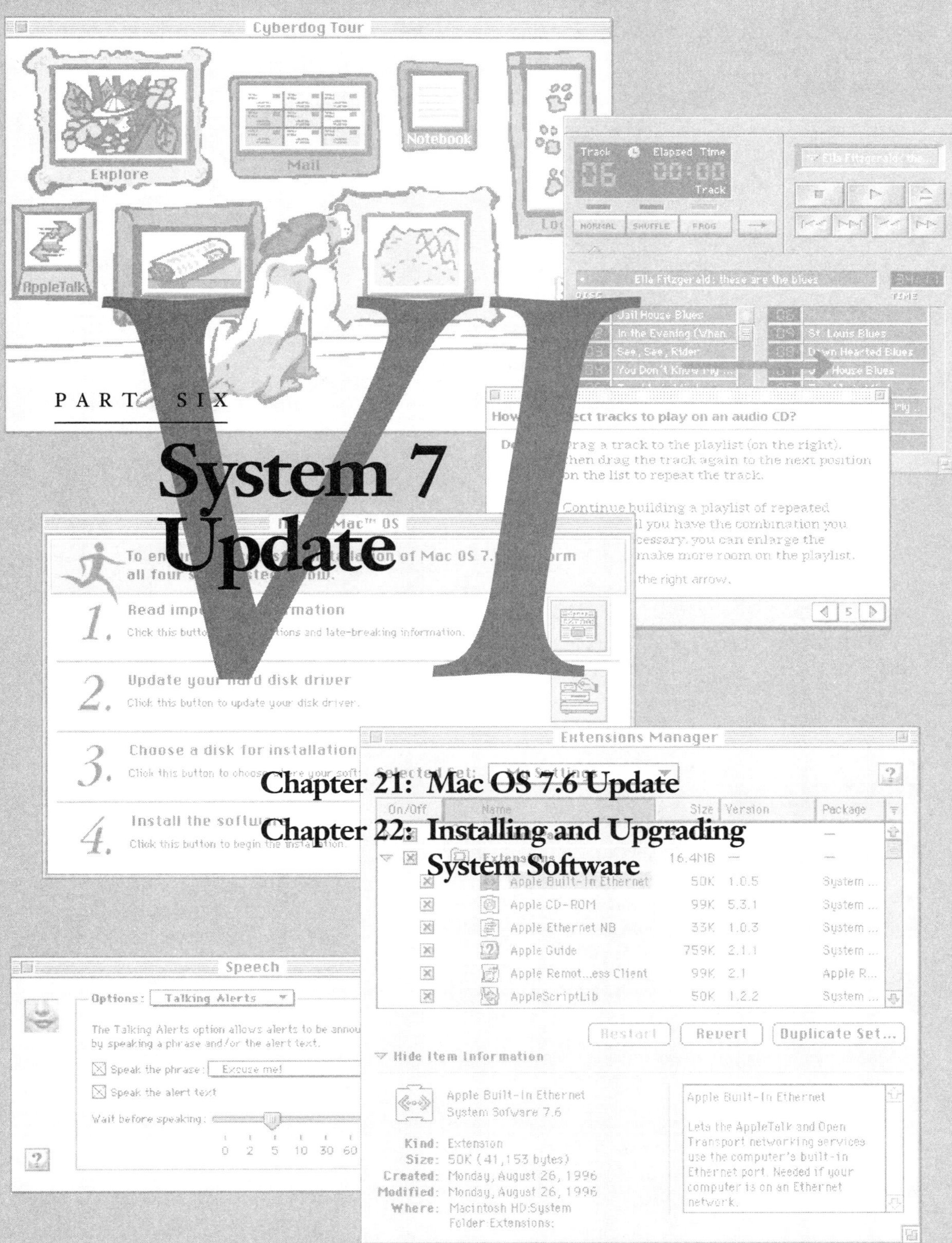


PART SIX

VI

# System 7 Update

CHAPTER 21

# Mac OS 7.6 Update

- Overview of new and improved features in system software 7.5.3 through 7.6
- New System Folder Items, Control Panels, and accessories in system software 7.5.3 through 7.6
- Improvements in screen captures, Finder operations, and file sharing.
- Changes to opening, saving, and printing documents in system software 7.5.3 through 7.6
- Internet and communications features of system software 7.5.3 through 7.6
- OpenDoc plug-in software in system software 7.5.3 through 7.6
- Changes to PowerTalk, QuickTime, QuickDraw 3D, QuickTime VR, ColorSync, and PlainTalk in system software 7.5.3 through 7.6

You may already be using a version of system software that is newer than System 7.5, or you may be considering upgrading from System 7.5 to a later version such as System 7.5.3, System 7.5.5, or Mac OS 7.6. In either case, this chapter explains how Mac OS 7.6 and the updates to System 7.5 differ from the original System 7.5.

The first three sections provide overviews of the three major system releases after System 7.5: System 7.5.3, System 7.5.5, and Mac OS 7.6. These sections do not detail the changes in system software versions 7.5.1 and 7.5.2 since they are effectively superseded by versions 7.5.3 and 7.5.5. These sections also do not detail System 7.5.4, which Apple distributed only to a small number of software developers before yanking it.

Following the overview of the major system releases, you'll find a list of files made obsolete by System 7.5.3 and System 7.5.5. The remainder of the chapter details the changes mentioned in the overview sections.

If you're not sure which version of the system software is currently installed on your computer, you can find our by choosing About This Macintosh or About This Computer from the Apple menu when the Finder is the active application. The About This Macintosh window or the About This Computer window reports the system software version number in the upper left corner, as shown in Figure 21-1.

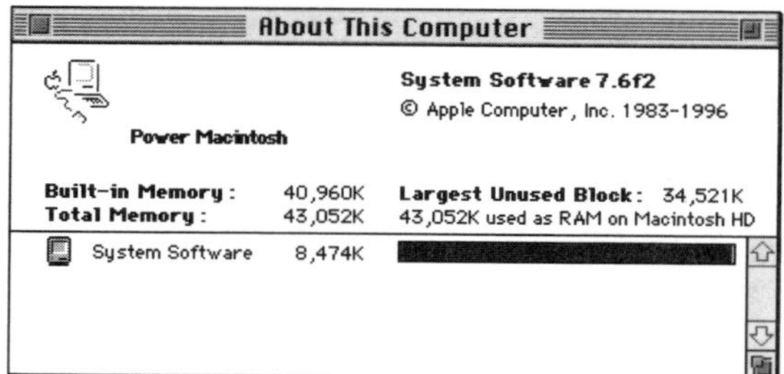


**Figure 21-1: Determining the system software version.**

# Overview of Mac OS 7.6

Mac OS 7.6 doesn't bring a whole lot of truly new features to your computer, not if you're the type who diligently grabs and installs every new or updated item from Apple's software archive on the Internet or a commercial online service (see "Obtaining Installation Software" and "Installing Additional System Software" in Chapter 22). What, you don't have everything? You're not sure if you have it all? The Mac OS 7.6 CD-ROM or floppy disks can bring you up to date as of January 1997 (well, almost).

## Mac OS 7.6 core features

The core Mac OS 7.6 software includes the following:

❖ **QuickTime 2.5**, like previous versions, lets you create, edit, and play movies, pictures, animations, sounds, music, and other time-based content right in a document (of a QuickTime-aware application), from a CD-ROM title, and over the Internet. New features in this version automatically start playing a CD-ROM or audio CD; play MIDI music with CD quality sound on Power Mac systems; route music to external MIDI devices; directly import diverse graphic formats such as GIF, MacPaint, Silicon Graphics, and Photoshop using SimpleText or any other QuickTime-aware application; and more (see "Multimedia Update" later in this chapter).

❖ **LaserWriter 8.4.2** makes it easier to select a printer and is faster than previous versions, especially when printing complex documents in the foreground and when printing on PowerPC computers. Unlike previous versions, this version doesn't require a spool file on disk (see "Printing Update" later in this chapter).

❖ **Open Transport 1.1.1** is Apple's modern networking software for AppleTalk and TCP/IP networking. Unlike previous versions of the system software, MacTCP and classic AppleTalk networking are not an option with Mac OS 7.6 (see "Internet and Communications Update" later in this chapter). A later version, Open Transport 1.1.2, became available too late to be included with Mac OS 7.6.

- ❖ **Multiprocessor support** can deliver blazing speed on a Mac OS computer with two or more PowerPC processors, but like multiprocessor environments on any operating system, applications must be designed to take advantage of multiple processors. Some Mac OS programs are designed for multiprocessing, including Adobe Photoshop, Adobe Premiere, QuickTime 2.5 (if MP Movie Pack from DayStar Digital is present), Kodak Color Processors, and Strata StudioPro Blitz.
- ❖ **Desktop Printing 2.0.2** enhances your control of background printing more elegantly than earlier versions and lets you print a document by dragging its icon to a desktop printer icon — all this without the overhead of QuickDraw GX (see "Printing Update" later in this chapter).
- ❖ **ColorSync 2.1.1** is a refinement of Apple's color management technology that delivers more predictable and accurate color across applications, scanners, digital cameras, displays, and printers (see "Multimedia Update" later in this chapter).
- ❖ **Extensions Manager 7.6** makes it easier than earlier versions to get your system extensions under control (see "Control Panel and Accessories Update" later in this chapter).
- ❖ **Screen capture options** let you take a picture of the whole screen as always or of a window or a selected area, and either save the picture on disk or copy it to the Clipboard (see "Windows, Icons, and Menus Update" later in this chapter).
- ❖ **Basic English Text-to-Speech 1.5** reads text aloud in your choice of voices — and in this version includes the ability to speak alert messages.
- ❖ **Performance and reliability improvements** include allocating more memory to the Finder so it doesn't complain so often about being out of memory; saving what's stored in the disk cache more often to reduce the chance of a system crash corrupting a disk; making the sound volume controls work on Mac 5200, 5300, 6200, and 6300 series computers; speeding up the Resource Manager, which system software and applications use extensively; making OpenDoc faster; increasing the maximum disk size to 2 terabytes on 68040 computers and PowerPC computers with NuBus slots (4MB maximum on 68040 computers for startup and virtual memory disks); and more.

You also get the performance increases and bug fixes first made in System 7.5.5, 7.5.3, and earlier versions of the system software. Be sure to read about the virtual memory speedups and the multitude of other improvements described in "Overview of System 7.5.5" and "Overview of System 7.5.3" later in this chapter.

## Mac OS 7.6 options

The Mac OS 7.6 installation software makes it easy to include any of the following items in a standard installation:

- **OpenDoc 1.1.2** is a new type of plug-in software that makes it easy to work on many types of data in a single document without switching applications (see "OpenDoc Plug-in Software Update" later in this chapter).
- **OpenDoc Essentials Kit 1.0.1** is a starter set of plug-in OpenDoc modules, which are called Live Object parts (see "OpenDoc Plug-in Software Update" later in this chapter).
- **QuickDraw 3D 1.0.6** brings a standard method for including and manipulating three-dimensional graphics to participating application, as easily as if the 3D images were ordinary pictures or QuickTime movies (see "Multimedia Update" later in this chapter). A later version, QuickDraw 3D 1.5, became available too late to be included with Mac OS 7.6.
- **MacLinkPlus 8.1** is file translation software that lets you easily use DOS and Windows files on your Mac, convert Mac files to DOS or Windows files, and convert files between different Mac formats (see "Control Panel and Accessories Update" later in this chapter).
- **Apple Remote Access Client 2.1** lets your computer connect to a remote AppleTalk network by telephone (and modem) at faster speeds than earlier versions — up to 112.5 Kbps on some computers (see "File Sharing Update" later in this chapter).
- **Cyberdog 1.2.1** is Apple's ground-breaking software for incorporating live Web pages and other Internet content into your documents as if they were static pictures, tables, or text paragraphs (see "Internet and Communications Update" later in this chapter).
- **Open Transport PPP 1.0** lets you connect your computer by telephone (and modem) to remote TCP/IP networks such as the Internet (see "Internet and Communications Update" later in this chapter).
- **Full English Text-to-Speech 1.5** provides best-quality speech on computers with a 68040 or PowerPC processor. In addition, you have the option of installing Mexican Spanish text-to-speech and English speech recognition (on computers with PowerPC processors) from the Mac OS 7.6 CD-ROM (see "Speech Update" later in this chapter).
- **QuickDraw GX 1.1.5** is a minor update that still promises the same extensive typography enhancements and simpler yet more flexible printing as GX 1.0 did in 1994, but few applications let you take advantage of the possibilities and Desktop Printing 2.02 plus LaserWriter 8.4 give you many of the printing services with less overhead (see "Printing Update" later in this chapter).

## Mac OS 7.6 caveats

Some Macs can't use everything that comes with Mac OS 7.6, and some can't use Mac OS 7.6 at all. You can only install QuickDraw 3D on a PowerPC computer. OpenDoc, OpenDoc Essentials, Cyberdog, and LaserWriter 8.4.2 also require a PowerPC processor until Apple fixes the CFM 68K Runtime Enabler problem, which prevents using them on computers with 68030 and 68040 processors (for details, see "Installing Mac OS 7.6 — Compatibility" in Chapter 22). The following Macs can't use Mac OS 7.6: Plus, SE, SE/30, II, IIx, IIcx, Portable, PowerBook 100, original Classic, and original LC.

There are also some technologies and capabilities that Mac OS 7.6 can't use. PowerTalk is incompatible with Mac OS 7.6. Classic AppleTalk networking is no longer an option with Mac OS 7.6; you must use Open Transport. Also, Mac OS 7.6 does not let you turn off the Modern Memory Manager feature in the Memory control panel.

# Overview of System 7.5.5

System 7.5.5 doesn't add any new features; it simply upgrades system software version 7.5.3 or 7.5.4 to improve reliability and performance. In particular, System 7.5.5 is faster than earlier versions of system software when virtual memory is turned on. With virtual memory turned on, the computer starts up faster, applications open faster on PowerPC computers, and QuickTime movies play more smoothly. Switching is faster between two big applications or between two big documents in the same application. Naturally, the performance you experience depends on how much RAM your computer has, on settings in the Memory control panel, and on which applications you are using. In addition, virtual memory is more stable under System 7.5.5.

Other updates in System 7.5.5 fix a variety of problems that can cause freezes and crashes; eliminate one cause of the dreaded Type 11 error on PowerPC computers; cure floppy disk problems on computers with 180MHz PowerPC 604 and 604e processors; improve networking reliability on the Mac 5400 and 6400 series; and make the buttons work right on remote controls for the Apple TV Tuner and Macintosh TV.

Caveats: System 7.5.5 causes some applications to require 23K more memory each — you must increase the Preferred size by 23 in their Get Info windows. System 7.5.5 is incompatible with the Sagem GeoPort ISDN Adapter 1.0. System 7.5.5 is also incompatible with the combination of the Motorola Math Library and Connectix Speed Copy 1.3.1 (part of Speed Doubler); either one can be installed, but not both. In addition, System 7.5.5 makes the Desktop Shortcut feature of Aladdin Desktop Tools unable to change folders in an Open or Save dialog box when you click a folder on the desktop.

You can upgrade to System 7.5.5 from any version of System 7.5.3 by installing the System 7.5.5 Update (see "Installing System 7.5.5" in Chapter 22). Before upgrading from System 7.5, 7.5.1, or 7.5.2, you must first upgrade to System 7.5.3 using either a System 7.5 Version 7.5.3 commercial product or the System 7.5 Update 2.0 package (see "Overview of System 7.5.3" in this chapter and "Installing System 7.5.3 or 7.5" in Chapter 22). To upgrade from a version of system software prior to 7.5, you must install System 7.5 Version 7.5.3 and then install System 7.5.5 Update.

# Overview of System 7.5.3

Apple released seven slightly different versions of System 7.5.3 in 1996. They served a variety of needs, including delivering new features, improving performance, fixing problems, and supporting new hardware. The following are the versions in a nutshell, listed chronologically from earliest to latest:

- **System 7.5 3** was first installed in February 1996 to fix problems on computers that initially required System 7.5.2, including the Power Mac and Performa 7200, 7500, 7600, 8500, and 9500 models. With this original version of System 7.5.3 installed, the About This Macintosh window reads simply "System Software 7.5.3."
- **System 7.5 Update 2.0**, released in March 1996, upgrades any computer that is running System 7.5, 7.5.1, or 7.5.2 to System 7.5.3. The update fixes problems that existed with the earlier system software versions and improves performance on computers with PowerPC processors. After installing the System 7.5 Update 2.0, the About This Macintosh window reads "System Software 7.5.3 System 7.5 Update 2.0."
- **System 7.5.3 Revision 2** was released in June 1996 to fix problems that affected PowerBooks and computers with PCI slots but were not addressed by the original (February 1996) System 7.5.3 or System 7.5 Update 2.0. System 7.5.3 Revision 2 also updates the original (February 1996) version of System 7.5.3 with most of the changes implemented by System 7.5 Update 2.0. After installing the System 7.5.3 Revision 2, the About This Macintosh window reads "System Software 7.5.3 Updated to Revision 2."
- **System 7.5 Version 7.5.3** (also known as System 7.5.3 Unity), released in July 1996, is a complete package of all software needed to install System 7.5.3 on almost all Mac OS computers from a Mac Plus through the Mac OS computers shipping at the end of 1996 (excluding the Power Mac 5400 series). It consolidates System 7.5, System 7.5 Update 2.0, and System 7.5.3 Revision 2. After installing System 7.5 Version 7.5.3, the About This Macintosh window reads "System Software 7.5.3. Revision 2" (note that it does not include the words *Updated to*).

❖ **System 7.5.3L** is a version that Apple licensed to other companies that make Mac OS computers (Mac clones). It may not include components such as the Energy Saver control panel and the AppleCD Audio Player accessory.

❖ **System 7.5.3 Revision 2.1** was factory installed on specific Macintosh models including the Performa 6400 series.

❖ **System 7.5.3 Revision 2.2** was factory installed on specific Macintosh models including the Power Mac 9500/200 and Performa 6360.

If you want to upgrade to the final version of System 7.5.3 from any earlier version of System 7, you can simply install the System 7.5 Version 7.5.3 commercial product. As an alternative if you're upgrading from System 7.5, 7.5.1, 7.5.2, or the first version of 7.5.3, you can install the combination of System 7.5 Update 2.0, System 7.5.3 Revision 2, LaserWriter 8.3.3, and CD Setup 5.1.7, all of which are available from Apple's online software archive (see "Obtaining Installation Software" in Chapter 22).

## System 7.5.3 core features

All versions of System 7.5.3 include the following improvements:

❖ **The Finder** turns an icon translucent when you drag it on a PowerPC computer; shows longer item names in windows that you view by name, size, kind, label, or date; takes less time to copy a large group of small files; and generally does not lose any comments in Get Info windows while rebuilding the desktop file (see "Finder Update" later in this chapter).

❖ **Apple Guide** lets you copy a picture of the current window by Option-clicking (see "Windows, Icons, and Menus Update" later in this chapter).

❖ **Control panels and accessory programs** include the following updates and additions (for details, see "Control Panel and Accessories Update" later in this chapter):

  ❖ **Automated Tasks** include a new task, Share a Folder (No Guest), and improved task, Synchronize Folders.

  ❖ **Close View** has new keyboard shortcuts.

  ❖ **Find File** has a new preference for displaying the kinds of found items.

  ❖ **General Controls** has a new option for saving documents, "Folder that is set by the application."

  ❖ **Launcher** lets you drag-and-drop to add, remove, and reorganize items.

  ❖ **Memory** has a larger standard Disk Cache size.

  ❖ **Monitors & Sound** replaces Sound & Displays on computers with PCI slots.

- ❖ **Power key** lets you turn off the computer by pressing the Power key on the keyboard.
- ❖ **SimpleText** shows QuickDraw 3D images, fixes printing problems, and more.

❖ **File sharing** lets you eject removable disks and CD-ROMs without turning off file sharing, and a removable disk or CD-ROM is shared automatically when you insert it. If a file server (including a shared disk or folder) disconnects unexpectedly and you have documents open from it, you can usually save them. For details, see "File Sharing Update" later in this chapter.

❖ **Open Transport 1.1**, the first reliable version of Apple's modern networking software, comes with System 7.5.3 but has been superseded by the even more reliable version 1.1.1 that comes with Mac OS 7.6, not to mention version 1.1.2 (available separately from Apple's on-line software archives). For those who use classic AppleTalk, System 7.5.3 includes MacTCP 2.0.6, which makes configuration easier and communications more reliable than earlier versions. You switch between Open Transport and classic AppleTalk networking with the Network Software Selector program located in the Apple Extras folder. MacTCP 2.0.6 was first included with System 7.5.1.For more information, see "Internet and Communications Update" later in this chapter.

❖ **QuickTime 2.1**, which is automatically installed with all versions of System 7.5.3, adds a slew of new capabilities but is superseded by QuickTime 2.5, which is included with Mac OS 7.6 (see "Multimedia Update" later in this chapter).

❖ **Text-to-speech software** reads English text aloud in your choice of voices. The System 7.5 Version 7.5.3 CD-ROM and the System 7.5 Update 2.0 CD-ROM include the complete PlainTalk 1.4.1, giving you the option of installing Mexican Spanish text-to-speech and English speech recognition (on computers with PowerPC processors). A later version, PlainTalk 1.5, comes with Mac OS 7.6. For more information, see "Speech Update" later in this chapter.

## System 7.5.3 options

You can add the following features to System 7.5.3:

❖ **Desktop Printing 1.0.3** greatly enhances your control of background printing and lets you print a document by dragging its icon to a desktop printer icon all without the overhead of QuickDraw GX 1.1.3, which is also included. Desktop Printing 2.0.2, included with Mac OS 7.6 and available separately is even better. For more information, see "Printing Update" later in this chapter.

❖ **Digital signatures** capability of PowerTalk can be installed separately, and PowerTalk 1.2.3 fixes some problems with previous versions (see "Collaboration Services Update" later in this chapter).

❖ **QuickDraw 3D 1.0.3** is a bonus item on CD-ROMs that brings 3D graphics to participating applications; Mac OS 7.6 has a newer version; and an even newer version is available from Apple's on-line software archive (see "Multimedia Update" later in this chapter).

❖ **OpenDoc 1.0.4**, another CD-ROM bonus, is the plug-in software that makes it easy to work on many types of data in a single document without switching applications; Mac OS 7.6. has a newer version as well as a starter kit of Live Object plug-in parts (see "OpenDoc Plug-in Software Update" later in this chapter).

You must install each of the items listed above individually (see "Installing Additional System Software" in Chapter 22). Note that Mac OS 7.6 comes with newer versions of QuickDraw GX, QuickDraw 3D, and OpenDoc, and includes the OpenDoc Essentials Kit (a starter set of OpenDoc plug-in parts) For more information, see "Printing Update," "OpenDoc Plug-in Software Update," and "Collaboration Services Update" later in this chapter.

## Performance and reliability improvements

System 7.5.3 improves performance and fixes countless problems. For example, it copies files faster; speeds up PowerPC computers in several ways; makes Apple Guide faster; reduces the occurrence of Type 11 errors on PowerPC computers; eliminates conflicts between the General Controls control panel and non-Apple software; and properly handles disabled control panels and extensions disabled during installation. This is only a small sample of the problems fixed by System 7.5.3. For a complete list, refer to the 27-page document contained in the three text files "Technical Details — Part 1," "Technical Details — Part 2," and "Technical Details — Part 3," which are in the Technical Information folder inside the Apple Extras folder on the startup disk after upgrading to System 7.5.3.

# Obsolete Files

This section lists individual files made obsolete by System 7.5.5 and 7.5.3.

## System 7.5.5

System 7.5.5 incorporates the Power Mac Format Patch extension, making that extension file obsolete.

# System 7.5.3

Installing any version of System 7.5.3 streamlines the System Folder by consolidating many individual files into a few existing files. The System 7.5 Update file supersedes the Enabler files on all computers capable of running system software versions 7.5. or 7.5.1. The System 7.5.2 Update file supersedes the Enabler files on all computers capable of using System 7.5.2. All computers using System 7.5.3 must have the System 7.5 Update file or the System 7.5.2 Update file because those update files contain most of the fixes that are part of System 7.5.3.

Upgrading to System 7.5.3 incorporates the following independent files into the System 7.5 Update file, System 7.5.2 Update file, or System file:

- 7.5.2 Printing Fix
- 040 VM Update
- 601 Processor Card Enabler
- 630 SCSI Update
- CFM Updater
- Color Classic Update
- Display Enabler 2.0
- EM Sound Update
- MathLib
- Mount IDE Drive
- Network Software Installer 1.5.1 and earlier
- PowerBook 150 Update
- PowerBook 2300c Update
- PowerBook 5300 Enabler
- PowerBook 5300/190 Enabler
- PowerBook 5300/2300/190 Enabler
- PowerPC Enabler
- SCSI Manager 4.3 and earlier
- Serial Update 406
- SerialDMA
- Sound Manager 3.2 and earlier
- System Enabler 406

- ❖ System Enabler 701
- ❖ ThreadsLib
- ❖ Workgroup Server Enabler

The following additional files are not needed after installing System 7.5.3:

- ❖ Apple Multimedia Tuner (rolled into QuickTime 2.1)
- ❖ Finder Update (rolled into the Finder)
- ❖ LaserWriter 8.0 (replaced by LaserWriter 8)
- ❖ PowerPC Finder Update (merged into the Finder)
- ❖ Sound & Displays (replaced by Monitors & Sound)

If you upgrade with a System 7.5 Version 7.5.3 CD-ROM or floppy disk set after previously installing System 7.5 Update 2.0 or System 7.5.3 Revision 2, then the Installer removes the System 7.5 Update 2.0 file or the System 7.5.3 Revision 2 file, since you no longer need them.

# Windows, Icons, and Menus Update

With Mac OS 7.6 you can take a picture of all or part of the screen by pressing the following keystrokes:

- ❖ ⌘-Shift-3 takes a picture of the whole screen (includes the pointer in the picture).
- ❖ ⌘-Shift-4 takes a picture of the rectangular region that you drag to select after pressing the key combination (omits the pointer from the picture).
- ❖ ⌘-Shift-4-Caps Lock takes a picture of the window that you click to select after pressing the key combination (omits the pointer from the picture).
- ❖ Press the Space bar to cancel a ⌘-Shift-4 combination.
- ❖ Add the Control key to any of the above key combinations to copy the picture to the Clipboard instead of saving it as a PICT file on the startup disk. With the ⌘-Shift-4 combinations, you can alternatively press the Control key while selecting the region or window you want to take a picture of.

When using Apple Guide with system software versions 7.5.3 and later, you can copy a picture of the Guide window to the Clipboard by pressing the Option key and clicking the panel. This ability does not apply to all topic windows, and it does not apply to items in the Guide menu that are not based on Apple Guide. For example, most application help screens are not based on Apple Guide.

# Opening and Saving Update

A standard installation of Mac OS 7.6 includes file translation software you don't get with earlier versions of the system software. When you try to open a document that was created by an application you don't have, the Mac OS Easy Open software (first included with System 7.5 as Macintosh Easy Open) displays a dialog box that lists available translation options, as described in "Macintosh Easy Open" in Chapter 5. The Easy Open dialog box lists more translation options with Mac OS 7.6 because it includes a package of MacLink Plus file translators that Apple licensed from DataViz, as shown in Figure 21-2.

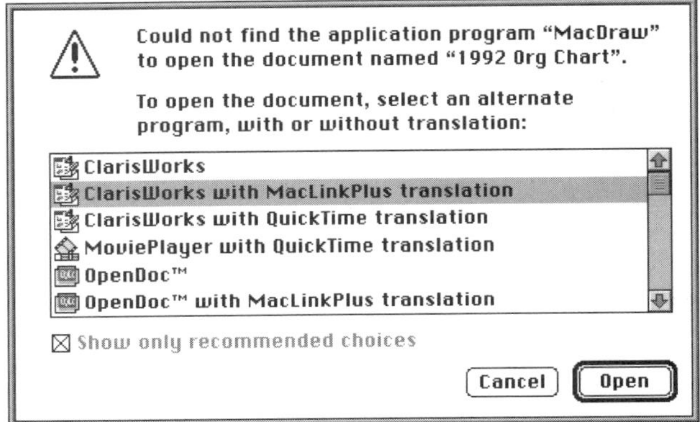


**Figure 21-2: The Easy Open dialog box lists appropriate MacLinkPlus translators included with Mac OS 7.6.**

In addition to a package of file translators, the MacLink Plus package includes Apple's Document Converter software, which you can use to convert a file's format without opening the file, as described in "Macintosh Easy Open" in Chapter 5. Prior versions of the system software included Easy Open but not Document Converter.

# Finder Update

When you drag an icon on a PowerPC computer using system software versions 7.5.3 and later, the icon becomes translucent so you can still identify the icon while you see through it to see where you're dragging. If you drag a group of icons, only the icon under the pointer is translucent; the others in the group are outlines. In system software prior to version 7.5.3, you always see icons' outlines when you drag them. Figure 21-3 illustrates translucent icon dragging.

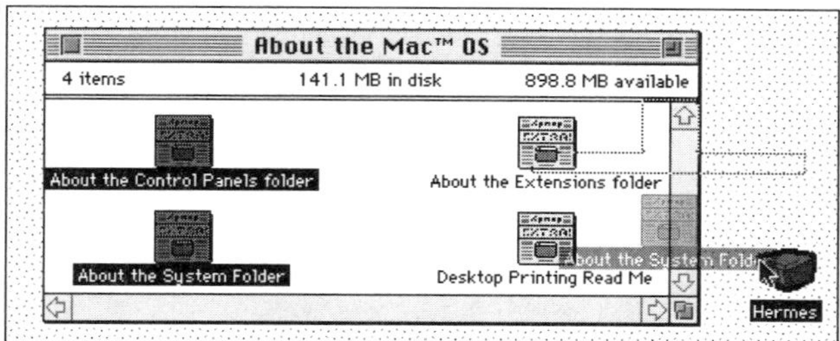


**Figure 21-3: An icon appears translucent when you drag it on a PowerPC computer with system software versions 7.5.3 and later.**

The Finder takes less time to copy a large group of small files. Prior to System 7.5.3 the Finder spent more time updating the progress gauge on screen and less time copying. Prior to System 7.5.1 copying of small files was even slower because the Finder copied more of the unused part of small files.

Rebuilding the desktop file with system software versions 7.5.3 and later does not lose any comments you have typed in the Get Info windows of files, folders, and disks (see "Cleaning Up Desktop Corruption" in Chapter 7). Get Info comments are still lost if you force the Finder to build a new brand new desktop file by deleting the existing one with a utility such as Reset DTDBs by Brian Gaeke or TechTool from MicroMat Computer Systems (707-837-8012, *http://micromat.com/mmcs/*).

You can have the Finder's Find command always invoke the bare-bones Find feature introduced in System 7.0 instead of the Find File utility introduced in System 7.5 simply by removing the Find File extension and the Find File application. This convenience was initially part of System 7.5.1.

# System Folder Update

Some of the software included with Mac OS 7.6 and System 7.5.3 puts additional items in the System Folder. These items include the following:

- **Control Strip Modules** folder contains modules used by the Control Strip (see "Control Panel and Accessories Update" later in this chapter and "Control Strip" in Chapter 8). Control strip is part of a standard installation on a PowerBook, but requires a custom installation on desktop computers.
- **Editors** folder contains OpenDoc part editors, which are programs that let you work with different types of content in an OpenDoc document. Each part editor has a corresponding stationery document in the Stationery folder on your hard disk. OpenDoc is part of a standard Mac OS 7.6 installation but is an add-on for system software 7.1.1 through 7.5.5.

- **Text Encodings** folder contains items used by Cyberdog, which is an optional module included with Mac OS 7.6 and is available separately for earlier system software.
- **DataViz** folder contains the MacLink Plus translators used with Easy Open. MacLink Plus is part of a standard installation of Mac OS 7.6 and is available separately for earlier system software.

# Control Panel and Accessories Update

A number of new control panels and accessory programs have been added to the system software since System 7.5, and some of the existing ones have changed. This section describes the new and modified control panels and accessory programs, which are listed here alphabetically.

## AppleTalk

With Open Transport networking active (mandatory with Mac OS 7.6 and on computers with PCI slots, optional on other computers with earlier system software), you specify your AppleTalk network connection in the AppleTalk control panel (see Figure 21-4). For information on specifying an AppleTalk network connection, see "File Sharing Update" later in this chapter.

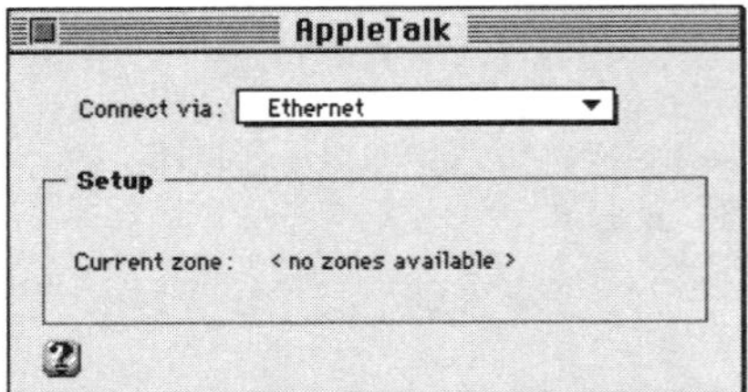


**Figure 21-4: The AppleTalk control panel used with Open Transport networking.**

## Automated Tasks

The automated task "Share a Folder (No Guest)" takes care of making a folder available for sharing with guest access disabled. Also, the "Synchronize Folders" automated task handles nested folders correctly. These changes first appeared in System 7.5.1. Automated tasks are AppleScript applications in the Automated Tasks folder inside the Apple Menu Items folder.

## CloseView

The keyboard shortcuts changed for the CloseView control panel beginning with System 7.5.3, since some of the former shortcuts were used by the Finder. Now pressing ⌘-Option-K turns Close View on and off; ⌘-Option-Plus increases magnification; and ⌘-Option-Minus (actually, ⌘-Option-Hyphen) decreases magnification.

## Editor Setup

The Editor Setup control panel specifies the preferred OpenDoc editors for kinds of content handled by OpenDoc parts. The preferred editor handles a part whose original editor you don't have. For more information on using OpenDoc, see "OpenDoc Plug-in Software Update" later in this chapter.

## Extensions Manager

Although the basic function and operation of the Extensions Manager control panel is the same in Mac OS 7.6 as in system software 7.5 through 7.5.5 — you use it to individually disable and enable control panels, extensions, and other software that's loaded during startup — the newer version has numerous improvements. For each listed item, the newer Extensions Manager displays its status (enabled or disabled), name, size, version, and the package it was installed with. You can also display each item's type and creator codes by selecting options with the Preferences command (in the Edit menu). Figure 21-5 shows the Extensions Manager that comes with Mac OS 7.6.

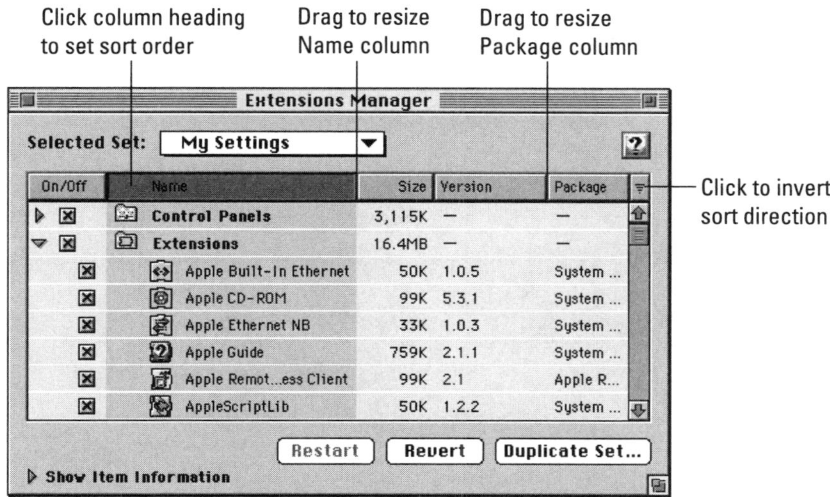


**Figure 21-5: The Extensions Manager that comes with Mac OS 7.6.**

You can reorganize the Extensions Manager list as follows:

- ❖ View items grouped by the folders they're in, grouped by the package they were installed with (but generally only for packages created by Apple), or ungrouped by choosing from the View menu.
- ❖ Collapse and expand a group by clicking the triangle next to the group name or by double-clicking the name.
- ❖ Sort the list within each group by clicking any column heading to set the sort order.
- ❖ Adjust the widths of the Name and Package columns by dragging the right boundary line of the Name column heading or the left boundary line of the Package column heading. You can't adjust the other column widths.

To see more information about a particular item, you click its name to select it and then click the triangle labeled Show Item Information at the bottom left corner of the Extensions Manager window. You can also select an item and choose Get Info from the Extensions Manager's File menu to open the item's Get Info window in the Finder, or choose Find Item to open the folder that contains the item and select the item. Figure 21-6 shows the Extensions Manager expanded to show item information.

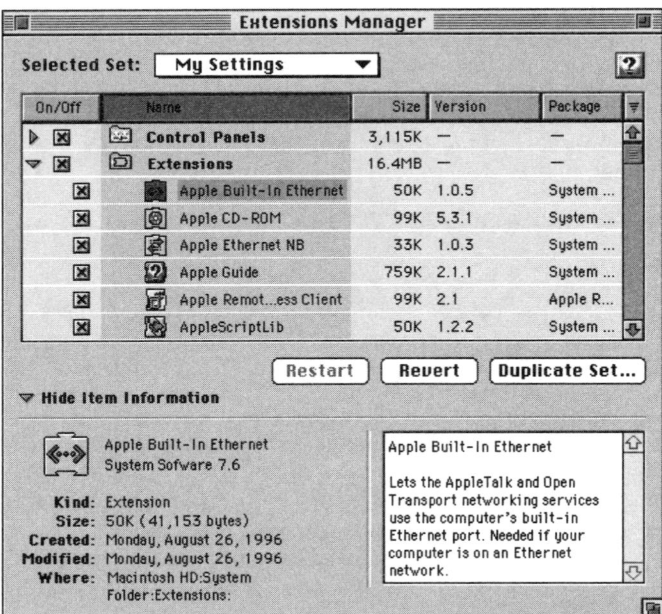


**Figure 21-6: The Extensions Manager expanded to show item information.**

You disable or enable an extension or other item by clicking the checkbox next to the item's name. Enabling or disabling a group affects all the items in the group. You can save the current configuration of the Extensions Manager as a named set by choosing New Set from the File menu. Your named sets appear in the Selected Set pop-up in alphabetical order, and choosing a set from that pop-up changes Extensions Manager to the configuration saved for that set. To enable or disable all items, use the All On or All Off commands in the Edit menu.

Changes you make to the status of any items take place when you restart. To restart immediately, click the Restart button. To restart later, quit Extensions Manager and use the Restart command in the Finder's Special menu when you are ready to restart. To cancel the changes you've made, click the Revert button in the Extensions Manager window.

# Find File

The Find File accessory program included with system software versions 7.5.3 and later lets you specify where you want to search by dragging an icon or a group of icons to the pop-up menu at the top of the Find File window. You can see a list of Find File shortcuts by choosing Find File Shortcuts from the Guide menu (the menu with the question-mark icon). And there's a new preference option, "Use full descriptions for found items." Selecting that option results in more specific Kind descriptions for found items, but slows sorting of the found-item list. Figure 21-7 shows the new option in the Preferences dialog box.

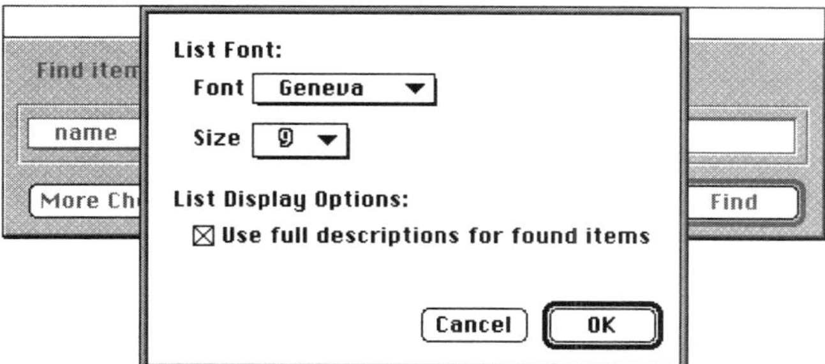


**Figure 21-7: Find File has an additional Preferences option in system software versions 7.5.3 and later.**

# General Controls

In the General Controls control panel included with system software versions 7.5.3 and later, you have an additional option for the folder location where documents are saved by default. The new option, "Folder that is set by the application," is the folder that contains the document you opened to launch the application (the application's folder, if you opened the application instead of one of it's documents).

## Launcher

In the Launcher that comes with system software versions 7.5.1 and later, you can choose one of three sizes for icons in the Launcher window. You can also drag icons to, from, and within the Launcher window (without opening the Launcher Items folder or its subfolders), including opening a document by dragging it to a compatible application in the Launcher. Specifically, you can do the following:

- ❖ Add an item by dragging its icon to the Launcher window, including to a category button in the Launcher window.
- ❖ Move an item in the Launcher by pressing the Option key and dragging the item.
- ❖ Open a document by dragging its icon to a compatible application's icon in the Launcher. (An application icon becomes highlighted when you drag a document icon over it in the Launcher if the application is able to open the document.)
- ❖ Move or copy an item to a folder by dragging the item's icon to the folder's icon in the Launcher.
- ❖ Remove an item from the Launcher by pressing the Option key and dragging the item to the Trash. Do not Option-drag an item from the Launcher over a desktop printer icon, or your computer may crash.
- ❖ Open the folder for a Launcher category by pressing the Option key while clicking the category button.
- ❖ Change the icon size for the visible Launcher category by pressing the ⌘ key, clicking inside the Launcher window, and choosing from the menu that pops up (see Figure 21-8).

## Map

Munich, Germany and Cork, Ireland were added to the Map control panel in Mac OS 7.6.

## Memory

To increase performance, the standard disk cache is larger in the Memory control panel. With system software versions 7.5.3 and later, the standard cache size is 32K per megabyte of RAM installed (not counting virtual memory). You can open the Memory control panel to change the disk cache size.

The Modern Memory Manager cannot be turned off in Mac OS 7.6.

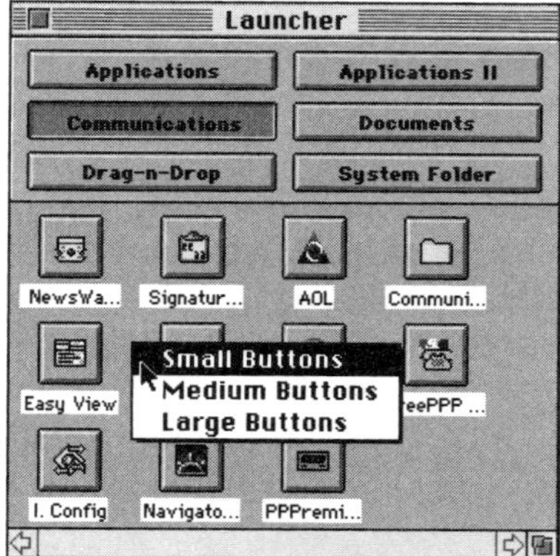


**Figure 21-8: ⌘-click to change icon size in the Launcher with System 7.5.1 and later.**

# Modem

Before using Open Transport PPP to make a telephone connection to the Internet (or other TCP/IP network), you set up your modem or ISDN terminal adapter with the Modem control panel. For more information, see "Open Transport" later in this chapter.

# Monitors

The Monitors control panel that comes with System 7.5.3 always displays gamma options, if there are any, when you click the Options button. With previous versions you had to press the Option key while clicking the Options button to see gamma options (see the sidebar "Gamma Options" in Chapter 8).

# Monitors & Sound

The Monitors & Sound control panel replaces the Sound & Displays control panel on computers with PCI slots that use system software versions 7.5.3 and later. You can also use the Sound control panel if you need it for older applications. The Sound control panel is in the Apple Extras folder on the startup disk of a computer with PCI slots.

# Power key

You can turn off a computer that's using system software versions 7.5.1 or later by pressing the Power key on the keyboard. Even a PowerBook whose keyboard lacks a Power key (one of the PowerBook 100 series) responds to the Power key of an attached external keyboard. Pressing the keyboard Power key brings up an alert that lets you choose to make the computer shut down, restart, or sleep (if it's capable of sleep), as shown in Figure 21-9.

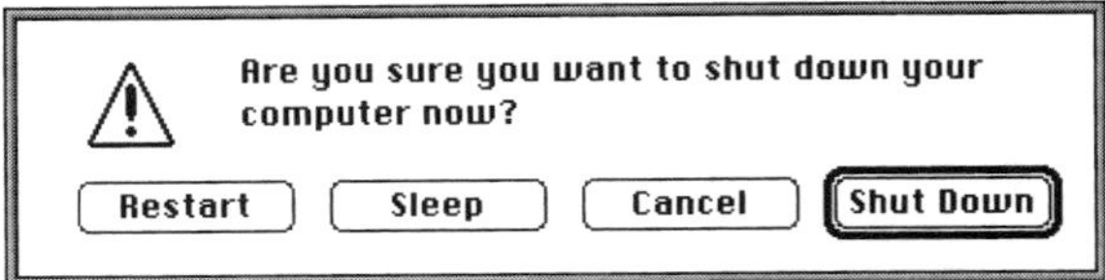


**Figure 21-9: After pressing the Power key in System 7.5.1 and later.**

It is possible for application programs to change the behavior of the Power key. Applications can disable or enable it, and can automatically dismiss the Power key's alert.

# PPP

You use the PPP control panel to make a telephone connection to the Internet (or other TCP/IP) network with Open Transport PPP. For more information, see "Open Transport" later in this chapter.

# QuickTime Settings

With the QuickTime Settings control panel, you specify whether to automatically play an audio CD when inserted, automatically start a CD-ROM when inserted, and route MIDI music through the computer's speaker or external MIDI devices.

# Scrapbook

Scrapbook 7.5.1, which you get when you install QuickDraw 3D, is enhanced to show QuickDraw 3D images and let you manipulate them.

# SimpleText

SimpleText 1.3.1 and later can show QuickDraw 3D images and let you manipulate them. It also inherits some improvements from SimpleText 1.2, the version that comes with System 7.5.1. They include printing large documents, pictures, and ranges of pages correctly; keyboard shortcuts for page up, page down, scrolling, cut, copy, forward delete, and other editing actions; and Program Linking enabled by default for controlling SimpleText with AppleScript from another computer. SimpleText 1.3.2 comes with Mac OS 7.6, and SimpleText 1.3.1 comes with System 7.5.3 as well as with QuickDraw 3D.

# Speech

You use the Speech control panel to choose the voice the computer uses to speak text aloud (although an application can choose a different voice for its use). You also use the Speech control panel to configure the Talking Alerts feature that's new with Mac OS 7.6. If you have installed speech recognition software on a computer capable of using it, you configure that with the Speech control panel as well. For information on configuring speech capabilities, see "Speech Update" later in this chapter. The Speech control panel comes with system software versions 7.5.2 and later, and replaces the Speech Setup control panel of earlier system software versions. Figure 21-10 shows the Speech control panel.

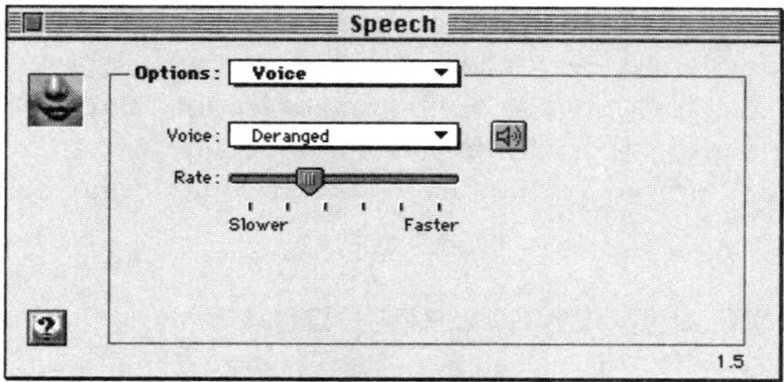


**Figure 21-10: The Speech control panel.**

# TCP/IP

With Open Transport networking active (mandatory with Mac OS 7.6, optional with earlier system software on computers without PCI slots), you specify your TCP/IP network connection in the TCP/IP control panel (see Figure 21-11). For information on specifying a TCP/IP network connection, see "Internet and Communications Update" later in this chapter.

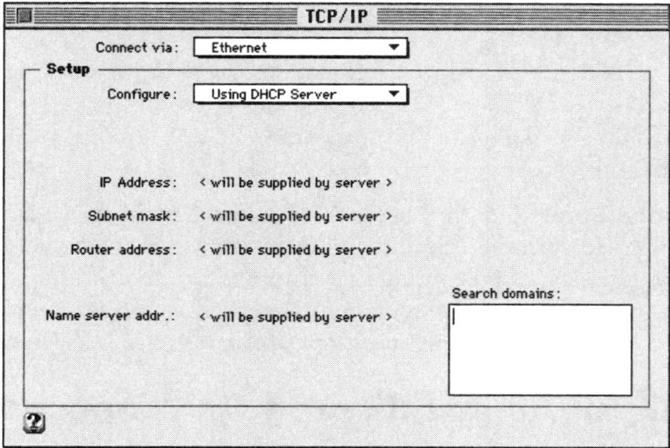


**Figure 21-11: The TCP/IP control panel used with Open Transport networking.**

# File Sharing Update

With system software versions 7.5.1 and later, file sharing does not exert the grip of death on removable disks and CD-ROMs. You can eject removable disks and CD-ROMs without first turning off file sharing. Also, a removable disk or CD-ROM is shared automatically if you insert it after turning on file sharing. (Audio CDs are not shared.)

If a server volume (such as a shared disk or folder) disconnects unexpectedly while you have some of its files open, system software versions 7.5.1 and later let you save most small open files on a local disk. You may lose some files that don't fit entirely in memory, but some applications let you copy the contents that are in memory and paste them into a new document. Prior to System 7.5.1, trying to save files from a disconnected server could lead to serious problems.

## Connecting to a network by phone

Apple Remote Access Client 2.1, included with Mac OS 7.6, lets your computer connect to a remote AppleTalk network by telephone (and modem or ISDN terminal adapter) at faster speeds than earlier versions. The maximum rate, which requires an ISDN or better telephone line, is 112.5 Kbps. The built-in serial ports are not capable of that speed on all Mac OS computers. The following Apple computers have built-in serial ports capable of 112.5 Kbps:

- Centris and Quadra 660AV and 840AV
- Performa 6100 series
- Power Mac 6100, 7100, 7200, 7500, 8100, 8500, and 9500 series
- Workgroup Server 6150, 7250, 8150, 8550, and 9150

If you choose a modem script in the Remote Access Setup control panel that specifies a speed of 112.5 Kbps (115200 bps) and your computer's serial port is not capable of that speed, Apple Remote Access 2.1 automatically falls back to 56 Kbps (57600 bps).

Other changes in Apple Remote Access 2.1: Modem scripts move from the Extensions folder to a Modem Scripts folder inside the Extensions folder. Compatibility with ARA 1.0 is automatic, eliminating the need for the Compatibility option in ARA Client documents. There is no longer a separate Remote Access Aliases extension. And some problems have been fixed.

## Specifying an AppleTalk network connection

If your computer uses Open Transport networking, you specify an AppleTalk network connection with the AppleTalk control panel instead of the Network control panel described in Chapter 9. All computers that use Mac OS 7.6 use Open Transport networking. Computers that use System 7.5.3 can use either Open Transport or classic AppleTalk networking, except that all computers with PCI slots must use Open Transport regardless of system software version. If your computer can use both types of networking, you use the Network Software Selector program in the Apple Extras folder to choose one type. Selecting Open Transport networking hides the Network control panel and reveals the AppleTalk control panel.

The AppleTalk control panel specifies the port through which your computer connects to an AppleTalk network. If your computer is connected to an AppleTalk network that's divided into multiple zones, the AppleTalk control panel also specifies the zone in which your computer resides. Depending on the characteristics of your computer and network, you may be able to change the network connection port, the zone, or both. If your computer has only one network connection port, you won't be able to change the port. If your computer is connected to a network with only one zone, there won't be any zones available to choose from. If someone else sets up your computer's AppleTalk network connection, the port and zone settings may be locked so you can't change them. Figure 21-12 shows an AppleTalk control panel with several port choices.

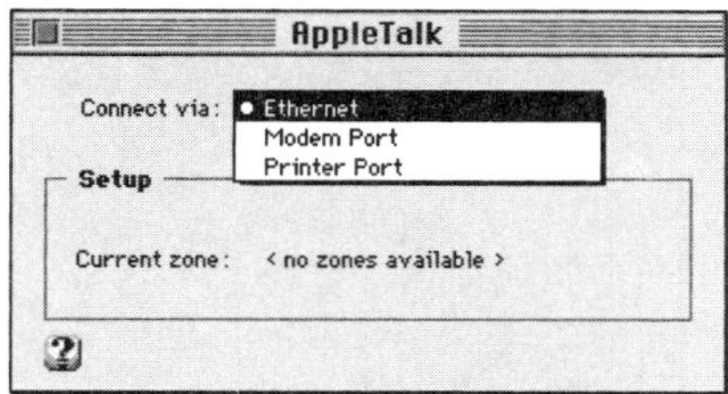


**Figure 21-12: Choosing a connection port for an AppleTalk network in the AppleTalk control panel.**

You can see and use three groups of settings, or user modes, in the AppleTalk control panel. The Basic mode shows the settings most people need. The Advanced mode shows additional settings for special situations. The Administration mode provides control over which settings can be changed. To change the user mode, choose User Mode from the Edit menu, and select the mode in the dialog box that appears. If you select Administration mode, you can set a password so that only people who know the password can access Administration mode. Figure 21-13 shows the User Mode dialog box.

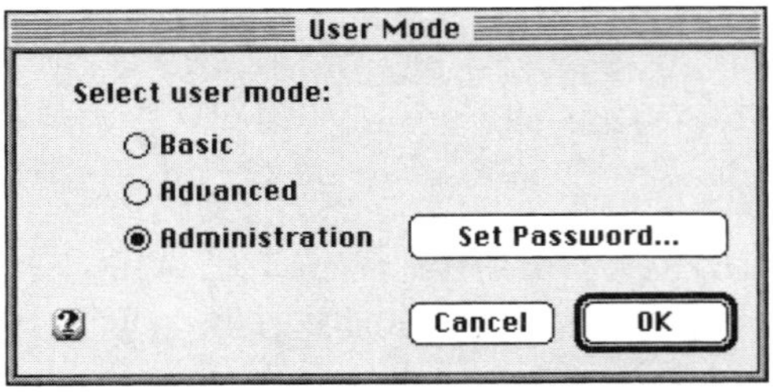

**Figure 21-13: Selecting a user mode for the AppleTalk control panel.**

In the Advanced mode, you see the network address that was dynamically assigned to your computer when it connected to the network. By selecting the "User defined" checkbox, you can assign a fixed address to your computer. If you assign a fixed address, you must be sure that no other Mac OS computer on the network has the same address. Figure 21-14 shows the AppleTalk control panel's Advanced mode.

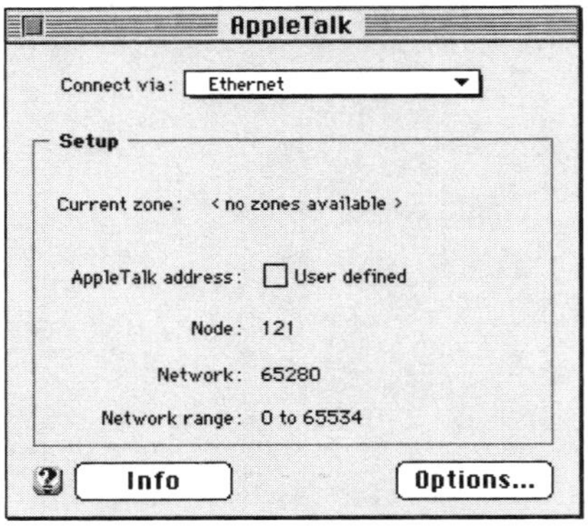

**Figure 21-14: The AppleTalk control panel's Advanced mode.**

In the Administration mode, you can assign a fixed network address as in the Advanced mode. In addition, you can lock each of the three settings independently — port, zone, and AppleTalk network address. Locked settings can't be changed in Basic or Advanced modes. Figure 21-15 shows the control panel's Administration mode.

You can save the current state of the AppleTalk control panel as a named configuration by choosing Configurations from the File menu to bring up the Configurations dialog box. Your saved configurations are listed in the dialog box, and you can make any one active, import or export them individually, and delete or rename one at a time.

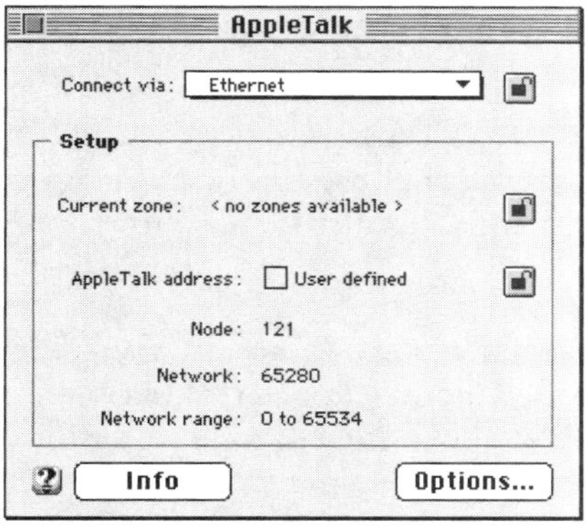

**Figure 21-15: The AppleTalk control panel's Administration mode.**

# Printing Update

Much of the convenience that QuickDraw GX brought to printing in 1994 as an option with System 7.5 is available without the overhead of QuickDraw GX in Mac OS 7.6 and to a lesser extent with System 7.5.3. Mac OS 7.6 and System 7.5.3 include desktop printing that works remarkably like GX desktop printing. The new breed of desktop printing works transparently with existing applications and printer driver software, unlike QuickDraw GX which requires applications to be modified to take advantage of it and requires special GX printer drivers. What's more, the version of desktop printing installed as part of Mac OS 7.6 has a more modern look and feel than GX desktop printing.

In addition to GX printing, Mac OS 7.6 includes the LaserWriter 8.4.2 driver software, which reorganizes and streamlines the Page Setup and Print dialog boxes although not as much as QuickDraw GX.

## Desktop printing without QuickDraw GX

You can get the convenience of desktop printing without the overhead of QuickDraw GX by installing Apple's Desktop Printing software. It works with all applications and printer drivers that previously worked with the original PrintMonitor, which is to say most applications and printer drivers. Mac OS 7.6 includes Desktop Printing 2.0.2 as part of a standard installation, and System 7.5.3 includes Desktop Printing 1.0.3 as a custom installation option. Desktop Printing is available separately as an add-on for system software versions 7.1 and later from Apple's online software archive (see "Obtaining Installation Software" in Chapter 22).

Desktop Printing 2.0.2 has several improvements over version 1.0.3. You can move desktop printer icons off the desktop. An optional printer menu located next to the Guide menu, and an optional Control Strip module, make it easy to switch printers. And you can easily turn off notification that the printer is waiting for you to manually feed paper.

The description that follows pertains to Desktop Printing 2.0 and later. Earlier versions have most of the same functions, but use text buttons and menu commands in place of Desktop Printing 2.0's picture buttons.

## Creating desktop printers

With Desktop Printing installed, you generally do not use the Chooser to choose a printer; instead, you use the Chooser to create desktop printer icons for each printer that you use. After creating the desktop printer icons, you use the Finder, not the Chooser, to choose and set up a printer.

Installing desktop printing creates a desktop printer icon for the printer that was selected in the Chooser before installation. If you use more than one printer, or if you had not selected a printer in the Chooser before installing desktop printing, you use the Chooser to create desktop printer icons. Each printer must have its own icon. If you use three LaserWriters, for example, you need three LaserWriter desktop icons. You cannot print to a printer until you create a desktop icon for it.

You do not create desktop icons for most fax modems, including Global Village fax modems and Apple's Express Modem. To send a fax, you either use the fax modem's keyboard shortcut or you choose the fax modem in the Chooser.

To create a desktop icon for any printer, open the Chooser. Each printer or other output device for which there is a printer driver in the Extensions folder appears as an icon in the Chooser. Select the type of printer on the left side of the Chooser and select the specific printer on the right side of the Chooser. To set up the selected printer, click the Setup button or the Create button. To place an icon on the desktop for the selected printer, switch to the Finder by closing the Chooser, clicking the desktop, or choosing Finder from the application menu. You may have to wait several seconds before the desktop printer icon appears. Figure 21-16 shows the Chooser being used to create a desktop printer.

You can handle desktop printer icons as you would other Finder icons. You can rename them, drag them to the Trash, and create aliases for them. With Desktop Printing 2.0 and later, you can move printer icons from the desktop to a folder.

## Choosing the default printer

After creating desktop printer icons for all the printers you use, you must designate which one you want to use by default. First, select the printer's desktop icon; a Printing menu appears next to the Finder's Special menu.

Choose Set Default Printer from that menu. The Finder indicates the default printer by drawing a heavy black border around its desktop icon. Figure 21-17 shows a couple of desktop printer icons and the Printing menu.

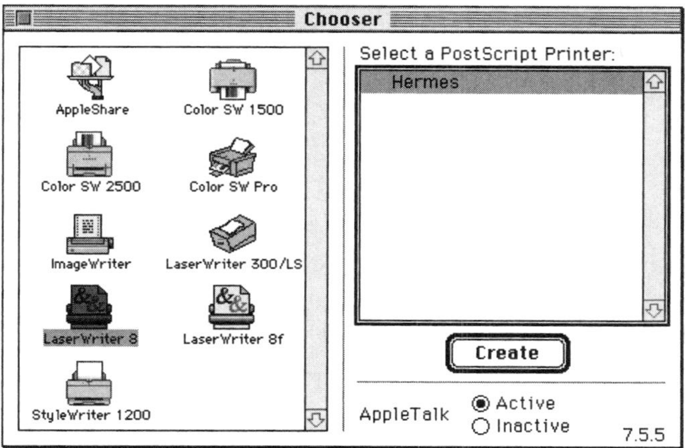


**Figure 21-16: Create desktop printer icons with the Chooser.**

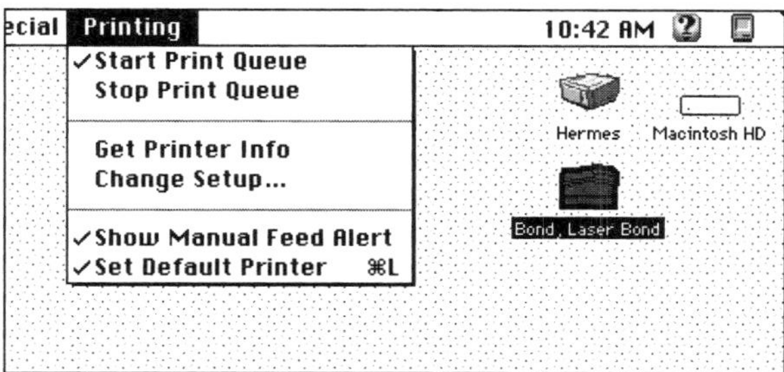


**Figure 21-17: Desktop printer icons and the Finder's Printing menu.**

The Printing menu is only available in the Finder. With Desktop Printing 2.0 and later, you can choose a printer from an optional Printer menu that's available in all applications. Alternatively, you can choose a printer from the Control Strip if it's installed on your computer. To get the Printer menu and control strip module, you can do a custom installation of the Mac OS 7.6 module's Desktop Printing component. To use the Control Strip on a desktop computer you must do a custom installation of the Mac OS 7.6 module's Control Strip component. The Printer menu and Printer control strip module are not part of a standard installation of Mac OS 7.6, although the rest of Desktop Printing 2.0.2 is.

## Printing to a desktop printer

You can print to any desktop printer by dragging icons of documents you want to print to the printer's icon. You can also print using classic methods: select icons of documents to print and choose Print from the Finder's File menu, or use the Print command in an application. Note that some documents cannot be printed, such as clipping files.

## Managing desktop printing

When you print a document to a desktop printer, the printer driver creates page descriptions for each page to be printed, saving the page images in a file for later printing. Normally, these files are printed in the background automatically, while you continue working. You can view and manage the queue of waiting print files for each printer individually by using the desktop printer icons and the Finder's Printing menu.

At any time, you can see the queue of files waiting to be printed on a particular printer by opening that printer's desktop icon in the Finder. Opening a desktop printer icon brings up its window. A desktop printer's window identifies the file that it is printing, reports the status of that print job, and lists the files that are waiting to be printed. You can sort the list of waiting print files by name, number of pages, number of copies, or print time. Choose a sort order from the View menu, or click the column heading in the desktop printer's window. Figure 21-18 shows a printer's window.

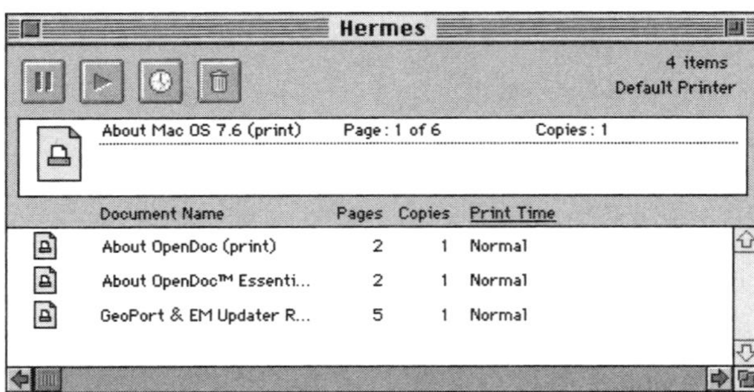


**Figure 21-18: A desktop printer's window lists files waiting to be printed.**

You can redirect a file waiting to be printed by dragging it from its current desktop printer window to the icon or window of a compatible desktop printer. In general, compatible printers have the same icon in the Chooser.

Files in a desktop printer's window print in listed order. You can change the order of files by dragging them up and down in the window. You can also change a file's place in line by setting its priority to urgent, normal, or scheduled a specific time and date. To set a file's priority, select it and click the Set

Print Time button (with the clock icon) in the desktop printer's window. A file's priority changes automatically if you drag it to a place among files of a different priority. For example, dragging a scheduled file above an urgent file makes the scheduled file urgent.

You can postpone printing a file indefinitely. Select a file in the desktop printer's window and click the Hold button (looks like a tape recorder's pause button). To resume printing a file that is on hold, select it and then click the Resume button (looks like a tape recorder's play button) in the desktop printer's window. Clicking this button displays the Resume Print Request window, in which you can specify the page at which you want printing to resume. You can also stop a file from printing by dragging it out of the desktop printer's window.

To print an additional copy of a file, select the file and choose Duplicate from the File menu. To make a copy of the file that you can use to print again later, press the Option key and drag a copy of the file out of the desktop printer's window. Drag the file back to the desktop printer icon or window when you want to resume printing.

To remove a file from a desktop printer's window, either drag it to the Trash or select it and click the Remove button (with the trash can icon).

You can apply all the actions described above on more than one file at a time in a desktop printer's window. To select multiple files, press the Shift key while clicking them or drag across them.

### Manual paper feed notification

With Desktop Printing 2.0, the Printing menu makes it easy to turn off notification that the printer is waiting for you to manually feed paper. Just choose Show Manual Feed Alert from the Printing menu so that there is no check mark next to it in the menu.

### Starting and stopping printing

To stop all printing on a particular printer, select its desktop icon and then choose Stop Print Queue from the Printing menu. A small stop sign appears on the printer's desktop icon.

To start printing again, select the printer's desktop icon and then choose Start Print Queue from the Printing menu.

## LaserWriter 8.4

The LaserWriter 8.4 driver makes several improvements to printing on PostScript printers. It's faster than earlier LaserWriter drivers, especially when you print medium to highly complex documents with background printing turned off (a new option of the Print command). With background printing turned off, LaserWriter 8.4 does not create a spool file on disk. As a result, the first page of a document prints more quickly than with earlier LaserWriter drivers. Moreover, you don't have to worry about running out of disk space when printing large documents.

LaserWriter 8.4's redesigned Page Setup and Print dialog boxes make it easier to switch desktop printers and to format the page for printing. The Page Setup dialog box has two groups of settings, one for page attributes and one for PostScript options, as shown in Figure 21-19.

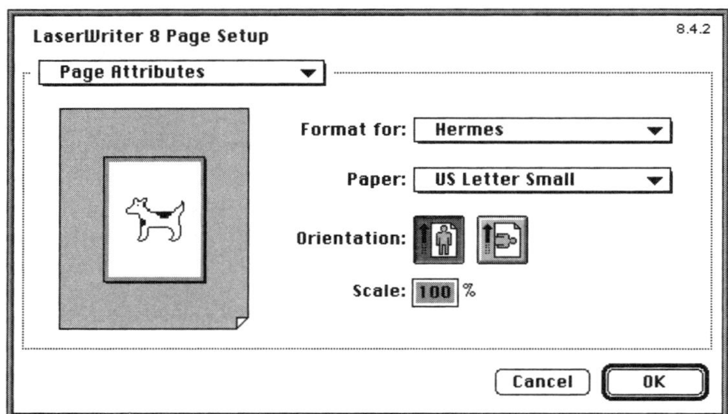


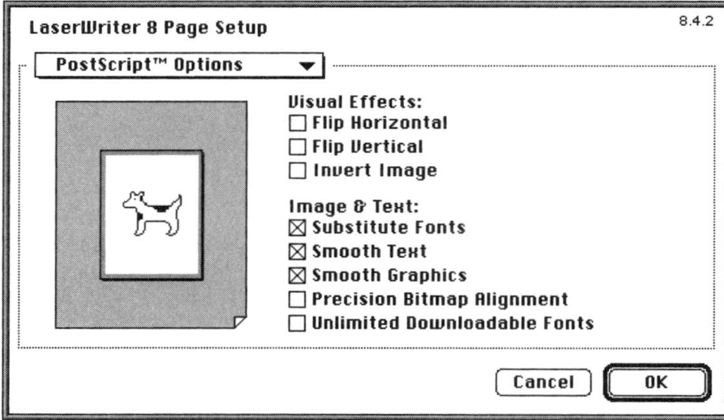


**Figure 21-19: LaserWriter 8.4 Page Setup dialog box.**

The Page Setup dialog box has several groups of settings depending on the capabilities of the selected printer. Figure 21-20 shows eight typical groups of settings.

8.4.2
Printer: Hermes
Destination: Printer
General
Copies: 1
Pages: All
From: To:
Paper Source: All pages from: Auto Select
First page from: Multipurpose Tray
Remaining from: Multipurpose Tray
Save Settings
Cancel
Print

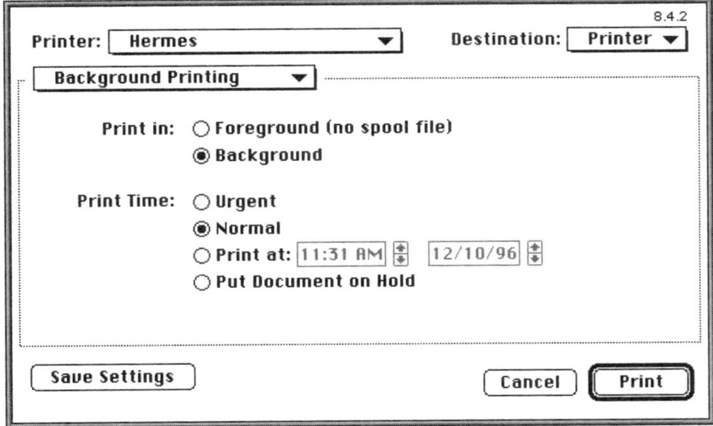


**Figure 21-20 (continues): LaserWriter 8.4 Print dialog box.**

8.4.2
Printer: Hermes
Destination: Printer
Cover Page
Print Cover Page: None
Before Document
After Document
Cover Page Paper Source: Same as document
Save Settings
Cancel
Print

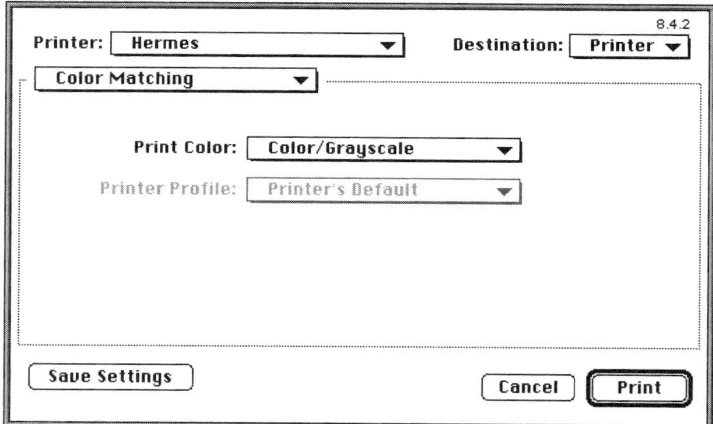


**Figure 21-20 (continues): LaserWriter 8.4 Print dialog box.**

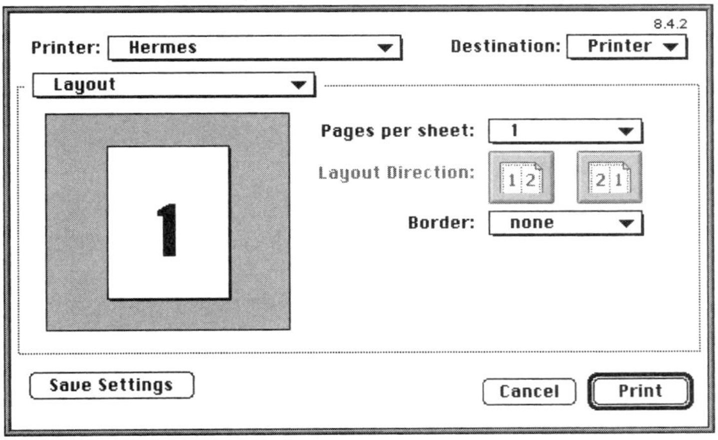

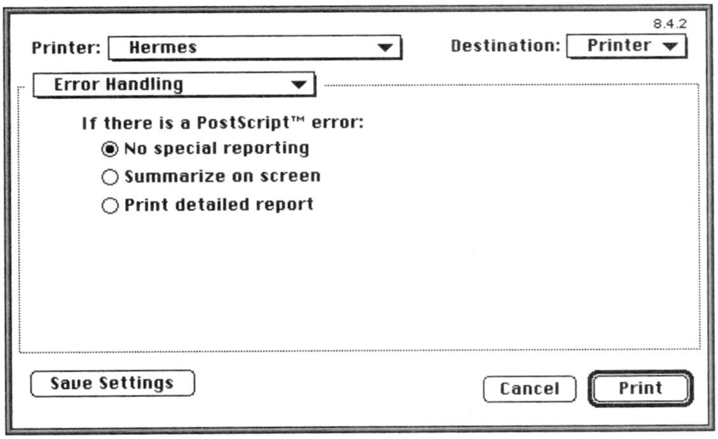

8.4.2
Printer: Hermes
Destination: Printer
Layout
Pages per sheet: 1
Layout Direction:
Border: none
Save Settings
Cancel
Print

8.4.2
Printer: Hermes
Destination: Printer
Error Handling
If there is a PostScript™ error:
No special reporting
Summarize on screen
Print detailed report
Save Settings
Cancel
Print

**Figure 21-20 (continues): LaserWriter 8.4 Print dialog box.**

8.4.2
Printer: Hermes
Destination: Printer
Save as File
Format: PostScript Job
PostScript Level: Level 1 Compatible
Level 2 Only
Data Format: ASCII
Binary
Font inclusion: None
Save Settings
Cancel
Print

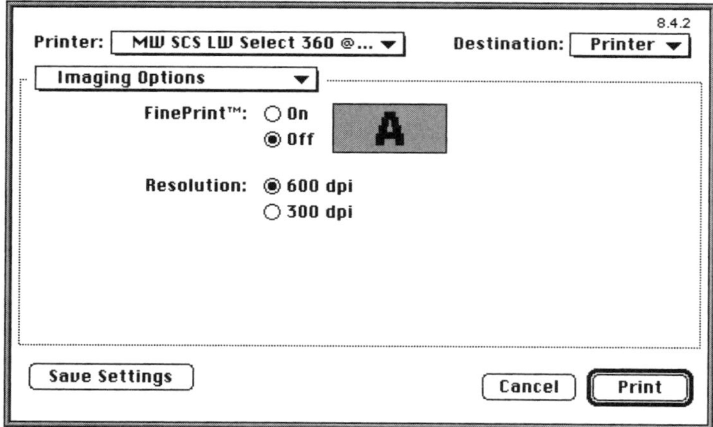


**Figure 21-20 (continued): LaserWriter 8.4 Print dialog box.**

Mac OS 7.6 includes LaserWriter 8.4.2 as part of a standard installation. LaserWriter 8.4 is also available separately from Apple's on-line software archive (see "Obtaining Installation Software" in Chapter 22), but it requires a PowerPC processor until Apple fixes the CFM 68K Runtime Enabler problem, which prevents using it on computers with 680x0 processors (for details, see "Installing Mac OS 7.6 — Compatibility" in Chapter 22).

# Internet and Communications Update

In response to the phenomenal popularity of the Internet, Apple modernized its networking software to make the Internet's TCP/IP networking protocol used on the Internet a full peer of the AppleTalk networking protocol used on Macintosh and other Apple computers. In addition, Apple started bundling several software packages for accessing the Internet. This section describes those developments. For a description of changes to AppleTalk networking, see "File Sharing Update" earlier in this chapter.

## AICK

The Mac OS 7.6 and System 7.5.3 CD-ROMs include the Apple Internet Connection Kit (AICK, pronounced "Ike"), a collection of software for accessing all kinds of Internet content. Apple also includes AICK with all Macintosh computers, and it is available separately from software resellers. AICK 1.2 includes the following items:

- **Netscape Navigator** for exploring the multimedia content of the World Wide Web
- **Plug-in software** for viewing and hearing various types of media with Netscape Navigator, including the following:
  - **QuickTime VR** for viewing 360-degree scenes
  - **LiveAudio** for hearing music and sounds embedded in a Web page
  - **Shockwave** for viewing animations, presentations, and graphics
  - **RealAudio** for hearing audio without delay
- **Claris Emailer Lite** for sending and receiving electronic mail over the Internet
- **NewsWatcher** for reading and participating in newsgroup (electronic bulletin board) discussions
- **Fetch** for transferring (downloading and uploading) files to and from FTP file servers on the Internet
- **Aladdin Stuffit Expander** for automatically decompressing and decoding files obtained on the Internet
- **Farallon Look@Me** for viewing the screen of another computer on the Internet
- **NCSA Telnet** for connecting as a terminal to remote computers on the Internet and accessing their resources such as library catalogs and databases
- **SLIP and PPP** for connecting to the Internet through the telephone system
- **Internet Config** for specifying preference settings used by many Internet applications
- **OnBase DragNet** for organizing stuff you find on the Internet

- **Apple Internet Dialer** for signing up with your choice of companies that provide Internet access and for subsequent one-button connection to the Internet
- **Apple Guides** for on-screen, interactive assistance in the diverse methods of accessing the many types of Internet content

To use AICK 1.2, you need a computer with a 68030, 68040, or PowerPC processor, 12MB of memory (16MB strongly recommended), 25MB of disk space, and a 9600 bps or faster modem (28800 bps recommended for multimedia Web access). The computer must use system software version 7.5.1 or later, and if it uses Open Transport it should have version 1.1.1 or later.

# Cyberdog

Taking advantage of high interest in the Internet, Apple created a unique software package called Cyberdog as a demonstration of the company's OpenDoc plug-in software system. Cyberdog has acquired a strong cult following among savvy Internet users who appreciate how easy it makes customizing their use of the Internet. Cyberdog is a suite of software components (OpenDoc Live Object parts) for accessing the Web, sending and receiving e-mail, following discussions in Usenet newsgroups (electronic bulletin boards), exchanging files with FTP file servers, and connecting as a Telnet terminal to computers on the Internet. Cyberdog lets you view text, pictures, audio, movies, and QuickTime VR panoramas on the Internet without helper applications. In addition, Cyberdog can take the place of the Chooser in connecting to AppleShare file servers, including computers with file sharing turned on. Figure 21-21 shows one starting point for accessing the Web, e-mail, newsgroup discussions, your AppleTalk network, and more through Cyberdog 1.2.

To keep track of Web sites plus individual pictures, movies, text, and sounds that you find on the Web, you can use Cyberdog's Notebook. That's not all the Notebook can help you organize. It can also store e-mail addresses, newsgroups, FTP sites, Telnet sessions, and more. In addition, a Cyberdog log gives you three ways to view a history of your Internet and AppleTalk activities: chronologically, alphabetically, and hierarchically. Figure 21-22 shows the Cyberdog Notebook.

Cyberdog 1.2.1 comes with Mac OS 7.6 as an optional module that you can include in a standard installation. Cyberdog is also available separately from Apple's Cyberdog site on the Web (*http://cyberdog.apple.com*).

Cyberdog 1.2.1 requires a PowerPC computer with 16MB of memory (8MB of actual RAM and virtual memory set to 16MB are OK). The computer must use system software version 7.5.3 or later, OpenDoc 1.1 or later, and MacTCP 2.0.4 or later or Open Transport 1.1 or later with the TCP/IP control panel installed and configured. OpenDoc must be installed before installing Cyberdog.

**Figure 21-21: Cyberdog's standard starting point for accessing the Internet and your AppleTalk network.**

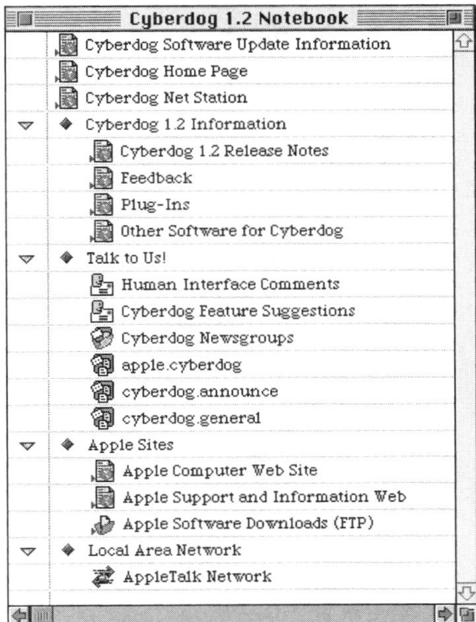


**Figure 21-22: Cyberdog's Notebook organizes your favorite Internet stuff.**

Cyberdog also requires a connection to the Internet either through a telephone connection to an Internet service provider (ISP) or through local area network (LAN) that has an Internet connection. If your computer does not have an Internet connection, you can use the Apple Internet Connection Kit to register and configure a connection with an ISP. You can also contact an ISP directly; the woods are full of them. If your computer is connected to a LAN, ask your network administrator about Internet access.

You can't use Cyberdog with Mac OS 7.6 on a computer with a 68030 or 68040 processor until Apple fixes the problem with the CFM 68K Runtime Enabler software. Apple discovered the problem in the last part of 1996 and could not fix it in time to include the fix in Mac OS 7.6. Although it's possible to use Cyberdog on a 68030 or 68040 computer with System 7.5.3 and 7.5.5, the problem with the CFM 68K Runtime Enabler may cause system crashes.

# Open Transport

Macs have long been able to connect to different types of networks, but until Apple developed Open Transport, AppleTalk was the chief networking protocol and other types of networks such as the Internet's TCP/IP were subordinate. (A networking protocol is a set of rules for exchanging data.) Open Transport puts AppleTalk and TCP/IP on an equal footing, and enables Apple and other companies to put other networking protocols on that same equal footing.

## Specifying a TCP/IP network connection

If your computer uses Open Transport networking, you specify a TCP/IP network connection with the TCP/IP control panel instead of the MacTCP control panel described in Chapter 8. All computers that use Mac OS 7.6 use Open Transport networking. Computers that use System 7.5.3 can use either Open Transport or classic AppleTalk networking, except that all computers with PCI slots must use Open Transport regardless of system software version. If your computer can use both types of networking, you use the Network Software Selector program in the Apple Extras folder to choose one type. Selecting Open Transport networking hides the MacTCP control panel and reveals the TCP/IP control panel.

The TCP/IP control panel specifies how your computer connects to a TCP/IP network. To properly specify a TCP/IP connection, you need to get specific configuration information from your Internet service provider or network administrator. Then you can enter that information in the TCP/IP control panel. If someone else sets up your computer's TCP/IP network connection, the connection and configuration settings may be locked so you can't change them. Figure 21-23 shows a TCP/IP control panel configured for a typical dial-up (telephone) connection.

You can see and use three groups of settings, or user modes, in the TCP/IP control panel. The Basic mode shows the settings most people need. The

Advanced mode shows additional settings for special situations. The Administration mode provides control over which settings can be changed. To change the user mode, choose User Mode from the Edit menu, and select the mode in the dialog box that appears. If you select Administration mode, you can set a password so that only people who know the password can access Administration mode. In the Administration mode, you can lock several settings independently. Locked settings can't be changed in Basic or Advanced modes.

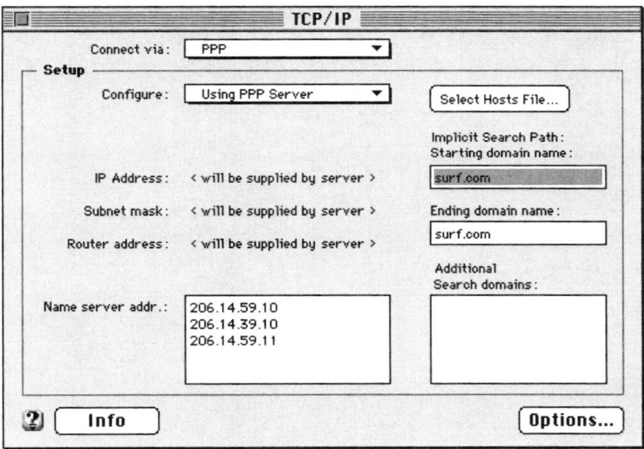


**Figure 21-23: Specifying a PPP dial-up connection in the TCP/IP control panel.**

You can save the current state of the TCP/IP control panel as a named configuration by choosing Configurations from the File menu to bring up the Configurations dialog box. Your saved configurations are listed in the dialog box, and you can make any one active, import or export them individually, and delete or rename one at a time.

## Open Transport sources and requirements

Mac OS 7.6 includes Open Transport 1.1.1 and cannot use classic AppleTalk networking. If you need to use classic AppleTalk, stick with System 7.5.5 or 7.5.3, which can use either type of networking.

You can upgrade to the latest Open Transport version by getting it from Apple's online software archives (see "Obtaining Installation Software" in Chapter 22). Open Transport 1.1 works on computers with 68030, 68040, and PowerPC processors except the Power Mac and Performa 5200, 5300, 6200, and 6300 series. Open Transport 1.1.1 works on all 68030, 68040, and PowerPC computers, although some computers in the Power Mac and Performa 5200, 5300, 6200, and 6300 series require hardware repairs first (see "Installing Mac OS 7.6 — Compatibility" in Chapter 22). Note that the special considerations just described do not apply to the PowerBook 5300 models.

# Open Transport PPP

To take full advantage of Open Transport networking for dial-up connections to the Internet (or any TCP/IP network), Apple developed Open Transport PPP and included it with Mac OS 7.6.

## Setup for Open Transport PPP

Before making a connection with Open Transport PPP, you must set up your modem or ISDN terminal adapter with the Modem control panel. You specify the port to which your modem is connected, the type of modem, and other settings as shown in Figure 21-24.

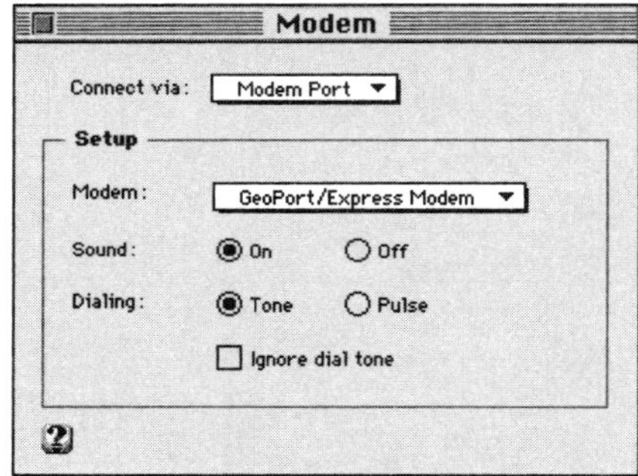


**Figure 21-24: The Modem control panel sets up your modem for making an Open Transport PPP connection to the Internet.**

The Modem control panel has two modes, Basic and Administration. The Basic mode shows the settings most people need. The Administration mode provides control over which settings can be changed. To change the user mode, choose User Mode from the Edit menu, and select the mode in the dialog box that appears. If you select Administration mode, you can set a password so that only people who know the password can access Administration mode. In the Administration mode, you can lock several settings independently. Locked settings can't be changed in Basic mode.

You can save the current state of the Modem control panel as a named configuration by choosing Configurations from the File menu to bring up the Configurations dialog box. Your saved configurations are listed in the dialog box, and you can make any one active, import or export them individually, and delete or rename one at a time.

## Making an Open Transport PPP connection

To connect to the Internet or other TCP/IP network with Open Transport PPP, you use the PPP control panel. In the control panel you indicate whether you're connecting as a registered user (with a user name or user ID and a password) or as a guest (anonymously). If you're connecting as a registered user, you type your name or ID, your password, and the phone number provided by your Internet service provider in the spaces provided. Click the Connect button to make the connection. Figure 21-25 shows the PPP control panel.

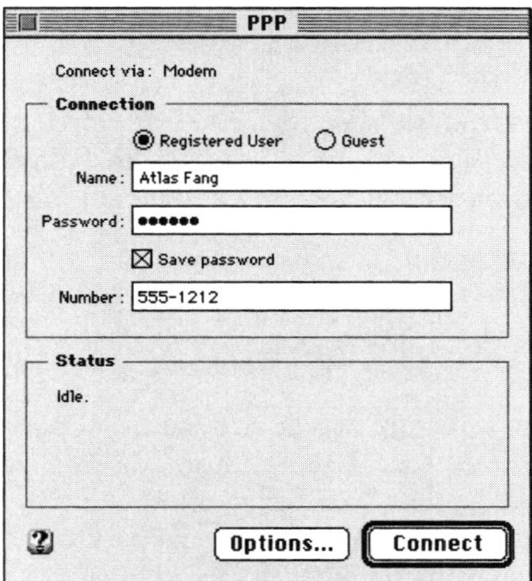


**Figure 21-25: The PPP control panel makes an Open Transport PPP connection to the Internet.**

Clicking the Options button in the PPP control panel brings up a dialog box in which you can set the following options:

- **Redialing.** No redialing when busy; redial main number only, or redial main and alternate numbers.
- **Connection.** Connect automatically when starting TCP/IP applications; use verbose logging.
- **Reminders.** Flash icon in menu bar while connected; prompt every *x* minutes to maintain connection; disconnect if idle for *y* minutes (you set values for *x* and *y*).
- **Protocol.** Allow error correction and compression in modem; use TCP header compression; connect to a command-line host either in a terminal window or with a connect script you specify.

If you're calling from a place where you must dial the number yourself (such as making an operator-assisted call), don't click the Connect button in the PPP control panel. Instead, choose Dial Manually from PPP's PPP menu and follow the instructions on the screen.

The PPP control panel has two modes, Basic and Administration. The Basic mode shows the settings most people need. The Administration mode provides control over which settings can be changed. To change the user mode, choose User Mode from the Edit menu, and select the mode in the dialog box that appears. If you select Administration mode, you can set a password so that only people who know the password can access Administration mode. In the Administration mode, you can lock several settings independently. Locked settings can't be changed in Basic mode.

You can save the current state of the PPP control panel as a named configuration by choosing Configurations from the File menu to bring up the Configurations dialog box. Your saved configurations are listed in the dialog box, and you can make any one active, import or export them individually, and delete or rename one at a time.

# OpenDoc Plug-in Software Update

OpenDoc creates an infrastructure for a new type of general purpose plug-in software that's not designed for one particular application or even one category of applications. In fact, OpenDoc kind of does away with the notion of applications altogether because each plug-in component, called a part, can conceivably do anything an application can do. In general, each OpenDoc part lets you work on one type of document content — text, graphics, sound, movies, spreadsheets, charts, databases, Web pages, e-mail, you name it. Here's the great part: You can drag any combination of OpenDoc parts into an OpenDoc document. Mix and match OpenDoc parts to create any document you can think of. You aren't restricted by the types of data any particular application can handle. The only limitation is the availability of OpenDoc parts on your computer.

Apple includes some basic OpenDoc parts along with OpenDoc itself in Mac OS 7.6. This collection of parts is called the OpenDoc Essentials kit, and it contains the following:

- **Apple Draw** for creating and editing basic graphics
- **Apple 3DMF Viewer** for viewing and manipulating 3D shapes created with QuickDraw 3D
- **Apple Audio** for recording and playing back sound or playing a sound file saved in a variety of formats
- **Apple Button** for adding buttons that can play sounds, start AppleScripts, or take you to an Internet location
- **Apple Image Viewer** for viewing pictures saved in the GIF, TIFF, JPEG, or PICT formats

The Apple QuickTime Viewer for playing QuickTime movies and manipulating QuickTime VR scenes is available separately from Apple's on-line software archive (see "Obtaining Installation Software" in Chapter 22).

You can also add any of the parts included with Cyberdog, which is based on OpenDoc, into your own OpenDoc documents. In addition, Apple and many other companies have developed and are developing more OpenDoc parts.

## What OpenDoc comprises

Installing OpenDoc adds the OpenDoc system software in the Extensions folder, an Editors folder in the System Folder, and a Stationery folder at the root level of the startup disk. Installing the OpenDoc Essentials Kit or other OpenDoc parts puts items in the Editors folder and the Stationery folder. For each OpenDoc part, there is a part editor in the Editors folder and part stationery in the Stationery folder.

### Part editors

You can think of an OpenDoc editor as a small, focused application that specializes in a particular kind of data. Editors are like the items in the Extensions folder in that you don't open or use an editor directly. You get access to a part editor's functionality through the corresponding part stationery.

Some editors, called viewers, allow you to see, hear, or otherwise experience a type of content, but do not allow you to change the content. For example, the Apple 3DMF Viewer lets you see a 3D image and adjust your view of it, but does not let you change the image.

Officially, all OpenDoc editors, including viewers, must remain in the Editors folder inside the System Folder. Some editors exist as separate files, and other editors exist together in a conjoint file. Editor files do not have to be directly in the Editors folder; they can be in folders within the Editors folder. But Apple warns that if you move an editor file so that it is no longer contained within the Editors folder, OpenDoc will not be able to find it. Despite Apple's admonitions, OpenDoc seems to work properly when the Editors folder contains aliases of part editors that actually reside in other folders. There is no guarantee aliases will always work, but they seem to work with OpenDoc 1.1.2 and earlier. The Editors folder contains other items that OpenDoc uses in addition to part editors (and part viewers). Figure 21-26 shows the contents of the Editors folder after installing Mac OS 7.6.

### Part stationery

Part stationery serves a dual purpose. You can open stationery to create a new OpenDoc document, or you can drag stationery to an OpenDoc document to add a part to the document. You can keep stationery in the Stationery folder or you can move it to another folder or disk. Figure 21-27 shows the contents of the Stationery folder after installing Mac OS 7.6.

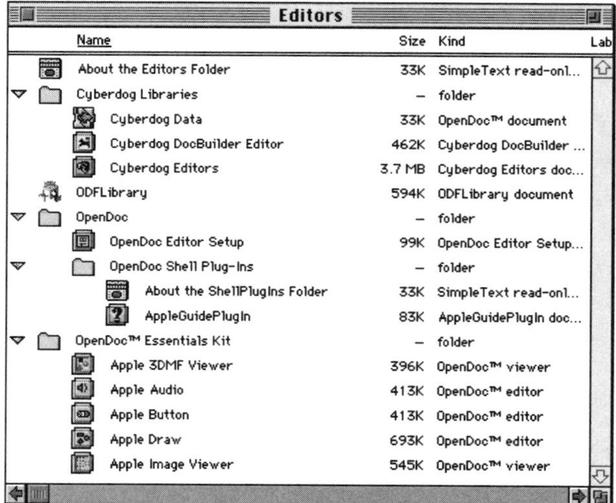


**Figure 21-26: Some part editors, part viewers, and other OpenDoc items in an Editors folder.**

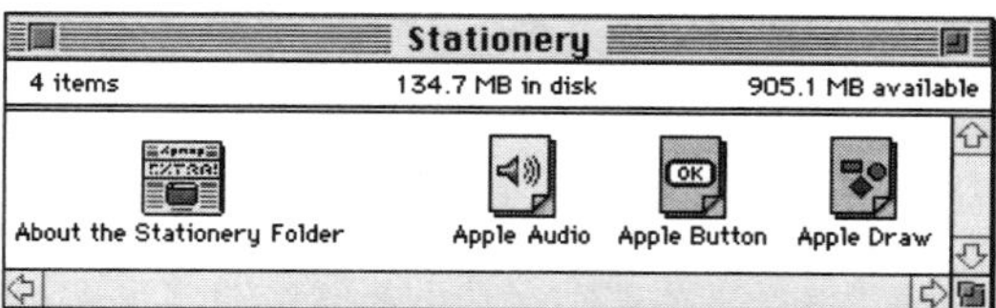


**Figure 21-27: Some part stationery in a Stationery folder.**

# Creating an OpenDoc document

You can create an OpenDoc document from stationery or from another OpenDoc document. To create a document from stationery, find the stationery for the part that you want to use as your document's root part and open the stationery.

There are several ways to create a new document from an existing OpenDoc document. You can create a new document based on the root part of the existing document or on parts in the existing document. To create a new document based on the root part of an existing document, open the document and choose New from the Document menu. To create a new document based on a part in an existing document, first select the part and then choose New from the Document menu. You can create a new document by dragging a part from an existing document to the desktop, a folder, or a disk. You can also create a new document by selecting multiple parts, content from a part, or content that includes one or more parts and dragging the selection to the desktop, a folder, or a disk.

Regardless of the method you use, when you create an OpenDoc document, a window opens with a name based on the part name and the document is listed in the Applications menu at the right end of the menu bar.

## Adding parts to OpenDoc documents

You can add parts to some OpenDoc documents and to some parts inside OpenDoc documents. To add a part to an OpenDoc document, you can drag the part's stationery icon into the document window, or you can drag a part from one OpenDoc document to another. Either way, a copy of the part you dragged is placed in the destination window. To add a part to another part that's inside an OpenDoc document, drag the part you want to add to the part inside the document window. Figure 21-28 shows part stationery being dragging into an OpenDoc document.

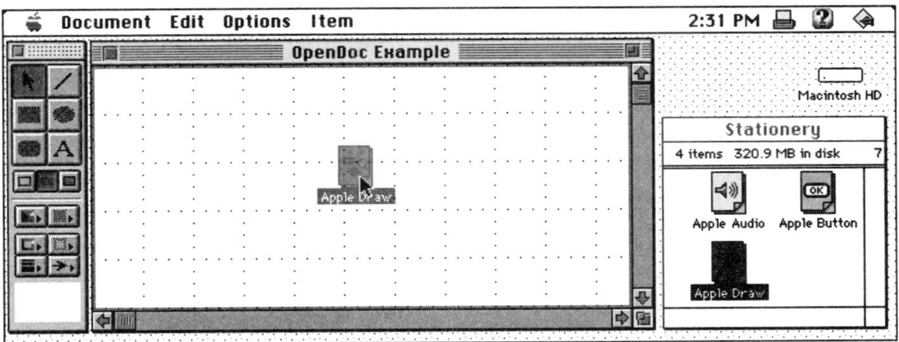


**Figure 21-28: Dragging a part into an OpenDoc document.**

You can also add a part to a document or to a part in a document with the Insert command in the Document menu. First you make the document active (bring its window to the front). If you want to add a part to a part that's already in the document, select the part you want to add to. Then choose Insert from the Document window. In the Open dialog that appears, select the stationery for the part you want to add. For example, to add a drawing part, you could select the Apple Draw stationery.

Instead of adding a part directly, you can add a part indirectly by adding a file whose content the part handles. Either drag the file to the OpenDoc document window, or use the Insert command and select the file. For example, you could add an Apple Audio part to an OpenDoc document by dragging a sound file to the document window or by choosing the Insert command and selecting a sound file.

Not all OpenDoc documents and parts can contain other parts. A part that can contain other parts is called a container. An OpenDoc document can contain other parts only if its root part (the part you used to create the document) is a container. You don't do anything to make a part a container or not. Engineers determine whether a part is a container when they design it. For example, Apple engineers made the Apple Draw part a container but did not make the Apple Button part a container.

## Working with parts

Once a part is in an OpenDoc document, you can edit its content, move it, resize it, copy it, delete it, or get information about it. Before moving, resizing, copying, deleting, or getting information about a part, you must select it.

### Editing a part

You can add content to a part in an OpenDoc document by dragging a file onto the part. The file must contain something the part can handle. For example, you can drag a sound file or a QuickTime movie but not a text file to an Apple Audio part because a sound file and a QuickTime movie contain sound but a text file does not. If a file's content is compatible with a part, the part becomes highlighted when you drag the file to the part. Some parts can handle more than one type of content. For example, Figure 21-29 shows a sound file being added to an Apple Audio part.

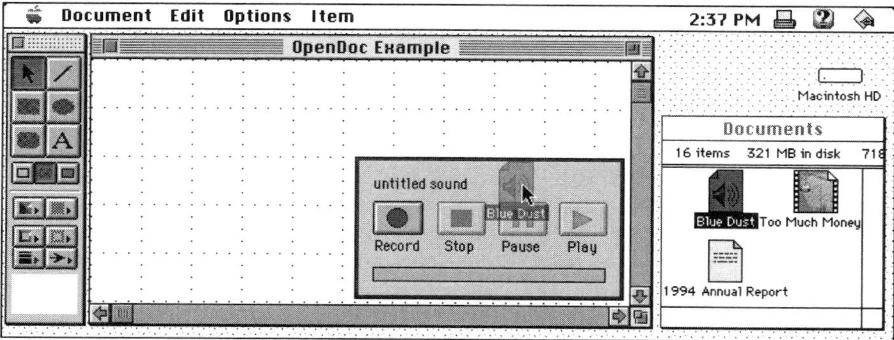


**Figure 21-29: Adding content to an OpenDoc part by dragging a compatible file to it.**

If a part has content, you can edit the content by making the part active and making your changes. To make a part active, you click anywhere inside it. There can be only one active part, and it has a distinctive border made of two dotted lines. (No border appears around a document's root part when it is the active part.) Figure 21-30 shows the border around an active part.

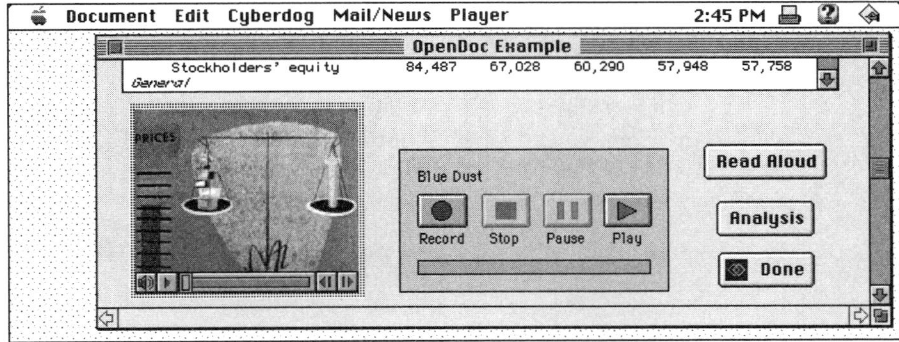


**Figure 21-30: The active part (here, the QuickTime movie on the left) usually has a distinctive border.**

When you activate a part, the part editor's menus appear in the menu bar. You can use the menu commands to edit the part.

## Selecting a part

Before you can move, resize, copy, delete, or get information about a part, you must select it. To select the active part, click its dotted-line border. To select an inactive part, press the Shift key or the ⌘ key and click the part. To select more than one part in the same container, make the container active and press the Shift key while you click each part. You can also select one or more parts by dragging a selection rectangle around the part or parts. A selected part has small black square handles at its corners. Figure 21-31 shows a selected part.

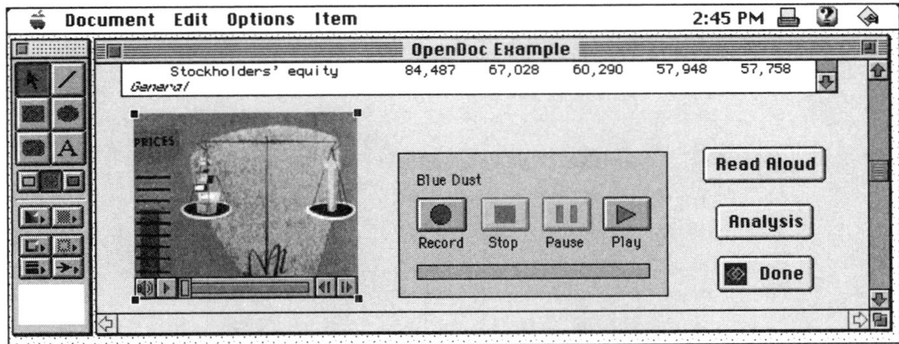


**Figure 21-31: A selected part has small black handles.**

Some parts can only be selected by making the part's container active and pressing the Shift key or the ⌘ key while clicking the part. For example, an Apple Button part might play a sound when clicked unless you shift-click or ⌘-click it to select it for editing.

### Moving a part

You can move a part by selecting it and dragging it to a new location in the document. To move the selected part to another OpenDoc document, press the Control key and drag. (If you drag to another document without pressing the Control key, you add a copy of the selected part to the other document.) You can also use the Cut and Paste commands to move the selected part to another document.

In some types of OpenDoc documents you can move the selected part by pressing the arrow keys. The characteristics of the document's root part determine whether the arrow keys work. For instance, the arrow keys work in a document whose root part is an Apple Draw part.

### Resizing a part

You change the size or shape of a part by selecting it and dragging one of its small black handles.

### Copying a part

You can make a copy of a part in the same document by selecting the part and pressing the Option key while dragging the part. To copy the selected part to another OpenDoc document, simply drag it without pressing any keys. You can also use the Copy and Paste commands to copy the selected part.

### Deleting a part

You delete a part by selecting it and dragging it to the Trash, choosing Clear from the Edit menu, or pressing the Delete key.

### Getting part information

You can get information about a part by selecting it and choosing Part Info from the Edit menu. You can change some of the items in the Part Info dialog box; the type of part and the part editor determine which items you can change. Figure 21-32 shows a Part Info dialog box.

## Setting document memory size

Each OpenDoc document has a memory size, much the way conventional applications have memory sizes. If you get a message saying memory is running low, you can increase the document's memory size. To change the active (frontmost) document's memory size, you choose Document Info from the Document window. The Document Info dialog box appears, and in it you click the Size button to bring up the Memory Requirements dialog box. In that dialog box you select the option Use Document Preferred Size and click the nearby up arrow or down arrow to increase or decrease the amount of memory the document uses. Then click OK to dismiss the Memory Requirements dialog box, click OK again to dismiss the Document Info dialog box, close the document, and reopen it. The new memory size takes effect when you reopen the document. Figure 21-33 shows the Memory Requirements and Document Info dialog boxes.

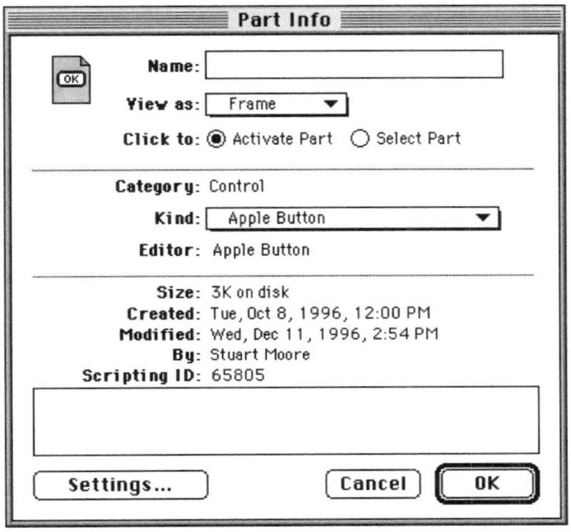

**Figure 21-32: Getting information about an OpenDoc part.**

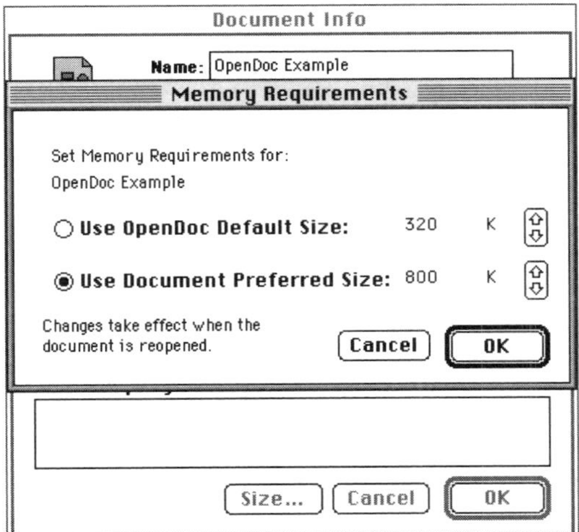


**Figure 21-33: Adjusting an OpenDoc document's memory size.**

## Setting up part editors

It's very likely you have two or more OpenDoc part editors that handle a particular kind of content, yet it's possible you may receive an OpenDoc document that someone else created with a different part editor for the same kind of content. To cope with those situations, you use the Editors Setup control panel to specify a preferred editor for each kind of content. If you open a document that contains a part created by an editor you don't have, OpenDoc uses the preferred editor for the kind of content in that part.

To specify a preferred editor for a kind of content, open the Editor Setup control panel. In its list select a kind of content and click the Choose Editor button (or double-click the kind) to see a list of editors available on your computer for that kind of content. Select an editor to be the preferred editor for that kind of content and click OK (or simply double-click the editor). Figure 21-34 shows the Editor Setup control panel with the Choose Editor dialog box open.

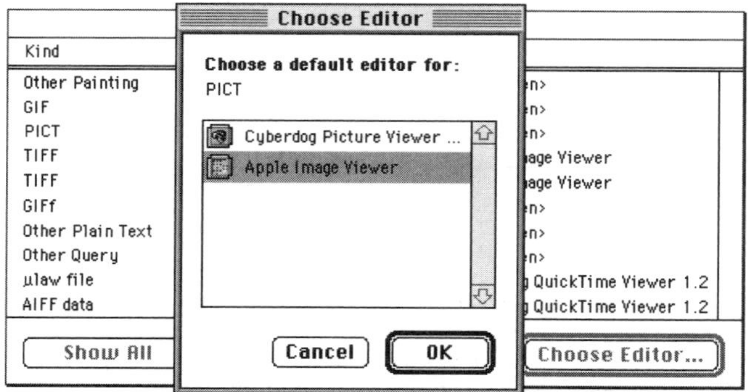


**Figure 21-34: Use the Editor Setup control panel to set your preferred editor for a kind of content.**

# Collaboration Services Update

The big news in the version of PowerTalk that comes with System 7.5.3 is that you don't have to install all of it just to use digital signatures (see "Digital signatures" in Chapter 15). Use the PowerTalk 1.2.3 Installer's Custom Install option and select the Digital Signatures component (see "Installing Additional System Software" in Chapter 22).

With Mac OS 7.6, the big news with PowerTalk is that you can't install any of it. PowerTalk is not compatible with Mac OS 7.6. Apple intends to add similar services to future versions of the Mac OS, and plans to base the future services on any Internet standards that apply. In the meantime, you can get digital signatures and privacy for e-mail and files by using ViaCrypt PGP from PGP, Inc. (602-944-0773, *http://www.pgp.com*).

# Multimedia Update

Since releasing the System 7.5, Apple has improved QuickTime twice, released and improved QuickTime 3D, released QuickTime VR, and improved ColorSync. This section describes the changes.

## QuickTime

Mac OS 7.6 includes QuickTime 2.5 as part of the core Mac OS, and System 7.5.3 includes QuickTime 2.1 as part of a standard installation. You can get the latest version of QuickTime separately from Apple's on-line software archive (see "Obtaining Installation Software" in Chapter 22).

Here's what's new in QuickTime 2.5:

- **Speed boosts** affect not only on PowerPC computers but computers that use 68040 and 68030 processors, and amounts to at least a 25 percent improvement.
- **More graphics formats** let you open GIF, MacPaint, Silicon Graphics, and Adobe Photoshop documents in any QuickTime-enabled application; for instance, you can open a Photoshop document in SimpleText.
- **Premium MIDI** lets you hear MIDI soundtracks in CD-quality sound (44.1 KHz, 16 bit, stereo) on PowerPC computers.
- **MIDI routing** benefits professional musicians and music enthusiasts who can choose between playing MIDI music through the computer's speaker or routing it to external MIDI devices using Apple's MIDI Manager, Opcode's Open Music System, or Mark Of The Unicorn's FreeMIDI system; you specify routing with the QuickTime Settings control panel.
- **Karaoke playback** shows you the lyrics of a song synchronized with playing the MIDI accompaniment (look out, Ed McMahon); karaoke movies are commonly available on the Internet.
- **Autoplay** automatically starts playing an audio CD when you insert it, and automatically starts a CD-ROM when you insert it; you can disable either type of autoplay with the QuickTime Settings control panel.
- **QuickDraw 3D** can render 3D objects in real time within a QuickTime movie, setting the stage for 3D modeling applications to create resolution-independent 3D movies.
- **Multiprocessor support** accelerates compressors and other components designed to take advantage of the presence of two or more PowerPC processors.
- **Universal M-JPEG**, a video format, will enable video professionals to exchange their work more easily if it's widely adopted.

In addition, QuickTime 2.5 inherits the improvements first introduced in QuickTime 2.1, including sprites; significantly enhanced sound on PowerPC computers; better looking large-frame movies; improved playback on a monitor set for 256 colors; playback of sound files in the WAV and AU formats (commonly embedded in Web pages); movie control of full-screen mode; QuickTime Teleconferencing support; expanded MPEG support; and better acceleration with some add-on video compression cards.

## QuickDraw 3D

There they go again, putting another type of media at your disposal. First the Macintosh popularized pictures, then QuickTime made digital movies commonplace, and now QuickDraw 3D makes it just as easy to view three-dimensional images in any application designed to take advantage of it, such as SimpleText 1.3.1 and Scrapbook 7.5.1. QuickDraw 3D provides a common file format for 3D documents, called 3DMF (for "3D metafile"), and a viewer with four buttons for changing the view of the 3D image. Figure 21-35 shows a 3D viewer with a sample 3D image.

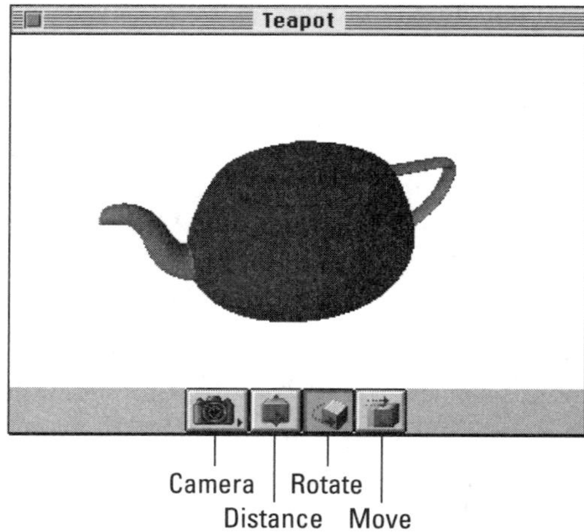


**Figure 21-35: A QuickDraw 3D viewer has four buttons for changing the view.**

A 3D viewer's four buttons let you move the image closer or farther away, rotate and tilt the image, move the image in the viewer frame, and restore the original view. Here's how the buttons work:

- **Camera.** Choose a view from the menu that pops up when you click the Camera button. Choosing Camera #1 restores the original view.

- **Distance.** Click in the frame and drag toward the bottom of the frame to move the image closer, or drag toward the top of the frame to move the image farther away.
- **Rotate.** Click the image and drag to rotate it, or click outside the image and drag to tilt it.
- **Move.** Drag the image to move it vertically or horizontally in the frame.

Mac OS 7.6 includes QuickDraw 3D 1.0.6 as an optional part of a standard installation. System 7.5.3 CD-ROMs include QuickDraw 3D as a bonus. The latest version of QuickDraw 3D is available from Apple's on-line software archive (see "Obtaining Installation Software" in Chapter 22).

# QuickTime VR

QuickTime VR lets you view panoramas and objects in 360 degrees. When you view a panorama you can look up, look down, turn around, zoom in to see detail, and zoom out for a broader view. When you view an object you can turn it around to examine it from all sides (some objects can only be turned on one axis, vertical or horizontal). Figure 21-36 shows a QuickTime VR panorama and a QuickTime VR object.

**Figure 21-36: A QuickTime VR panorama (left) and a QuickTime VR object (right).**

You change the view in a panorama by clicking the picture and dragging left, right, up, or down. When viewing a panorama, press the Option key to zoom in, or press the Control key to zoom out. When viewing an object, you can place the pointer near an inside edge of the viewer frame and press the mouse button to rotate the object continuously. The pointer shape changes when you use it to change the view of a QuickTime VR scene, and the shape suggests the effect of dragging.

To view QuickTime VR scenes you need the QuickTime VR Player application. If you want to view QuickTime VR scenes embedded in Web pages with Netscape Navigator 3.0 or later, you can use the QuickTime VR plug-in component. The latest versions of all that software plus links to sample QuickTime VR scenes are available at Apple's QuickTime VR Web site on the Internet (*http://qtvr.quicktime.apple.com*). The QuickTime VR Player and the plug-in are not included with any system software packages, but you can view QuickTime VR scenes with Cyberdog's QuickTime part, which is included with Mac OS 7.6.

## ColorSync 2.1.1

A standard Mac OS 7.6 installation includes Apple's color management technology, ColorSync 2.1.1, to give you more predictable and accurate color from your applications, scanners, digital cameras, displays, and printers. Each device has a color profile, and ColorSync quickly adjusts colors in an image as it goes from scanner or camera to display screen and then to print. Features added with ColorSync 2.1 include the following:

- ❖ **Named color profiles**, which let ColorSync work in a color space represented as a list of colors, such as the popular Pantone and Toyo color spaces.
- ❖ **Hi-Fi color** makes it possible to separate images into five to eight color channels, not just the traditional four CMYK channels.
- ❖ **Speed** is 15 to 20 percent faster than versions prior to 2.1.
- ❖ **Saves space** by embedding a profile identifier in a document instead of embedding an entire profile.

ColorSync is also available separately from Apple's on-line software archive (see "Obtaining Installation Software" in Chapter 22). Earlier versions of ColorSync are included with System 7.5 and 7.5.3 as part of QuickDraw GX.

# Speech Update

The versions of PlainTalk speech software that comes with Mac OS 7.6 and System 7.5.3 have a Speech control panel instead of the Speech Setup control panel used by earlier versions of PlainTalk. This section tells you how to use the Speech control panel to configure and text-to-speech and speech recognition.

## Text-to-speech

You can choose your computer's voice and set a speaking rate with the Speech control panel that's included with text-to-speech software versions 1.4 and later. A pop-up menu lists the available voices, a slider adjusts the speaking

rate, and a button lets you hear a sample using the current settings. Figure 21-37 shows the Speech control panel's Voice settings.

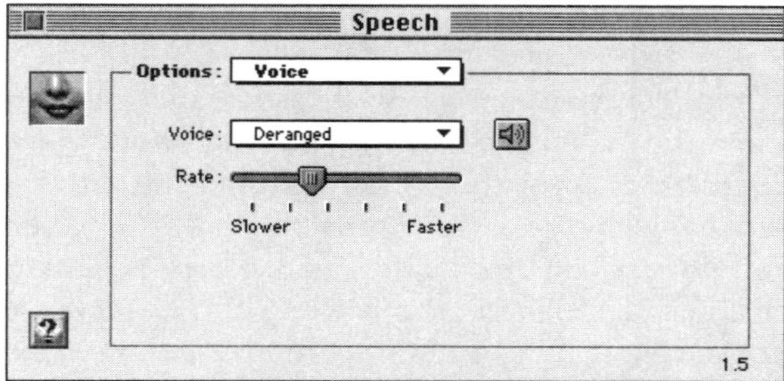


**Figure 21-37: The Speech control panel's Voice settings.**

With text-to-speech software versions 1.5 and later, you can also use the Speech control panel to set up the manner in which the computer announces its alert messages. There's an option for having the computer read the text of alert messages aloud, a slider for adjusting how long the computer waits after it displays an alert message before it speaks, and an option for having the computer speak a phrase such as "Excuse me!" when it displays an alert. There's also a button that lets you hear a sample alert using the current settings. Figure 21-38 shows the Speech control panel's Talking Alert settings.

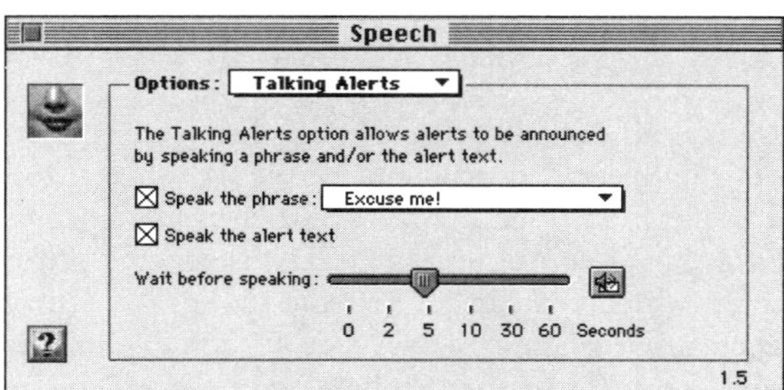


**Figure 21-38: The Speech control panel's Talking Alert settings.**

If you select the option to have the computer speak a phrase when it displays an alert, you choose the phrase you want from a pop-up menu. The pop-up menu includes a choice that tells the computer to use the next phrase listed in the menu each time it speaks an alert. The pop-up also includes a choice that tells the computer to pick a phrase at random from the list each time it speaks an alert. There's also a choice that lets you edit (change, add, or delete) phrases.

If you set the time the computer waits before speaking an alert to more than two seconds, the computer plays the alert sound as soon as it displays an alert and then waits to speak. If you set the time to wait before speaking to less than two seconds, the computer does not play the alert sound when it displays an alert message.

There are three qualities of text-to-speech. Standard quality is provided by the standard voice files and the Macintalk 2 extension, which works on any Mac OS computer. Better quality is provided by the standard voice files and the Macintalk 3 extension, which works on computers with a 33 MHz or faster 68030, a 68040, or a PowerPC processor. Best quality is provided by the Macintalk Pro extension and Macintalk Pro voices, which require a 68040 or PowerPC processor. Macintalk 3 increases the system memory size (as reported by the About This Macintosh or About This Computer command) more than Macintalk 2, and Macintalk Pro increases the system memory size even more.

A standard installation of the core Mac OS 7.6 always includes Macintalk 2 or Macintalk 3 (depending on the computer's processor). A standard Mac OS 7.6 installation includes Macintalk Pro if you select the English Text-To-Speech 1.5 installation option and the computer has a 68040 or PowerPC processor.

System 7.5.3 includes version 1.4.1 of the English text-to-speech software as part of a standard installation. The Mac OS 7.6 and System 7.5.3 CD-ROMs also include Mexican Spanish text-to-speech for optional installation. The text-to-speech software is available separately from the Apple on-line software archive (see "Obtaining Installation Software" in Chapter 22).

## Speech recognition

If you install speech recognition software version 1.4 or later, you configure it with three sections of the Speech control panel. You turn speech recognition on or off in the Speakable Items section of the Speech control panel. When you click the On button, your computer recognizes the names of items in the Speakable Items folder (which you can access from the Apple menu) as commands. You make the computer understand more spoken commands by adding items to the Speakable Items folder. For example, you can add aliases of documents, applications, and folders that you want it to open; if you give each alias a name that begins with "open" and ends with the name of the original item, then you can open an alias's original item by saying "Open" followed by the original item's name. Figure 21-39 shows the Speakable Items section of the Speech control panel.

In the Listening section of the Speech control panel, you specify how you want to signal the computer that you are speaking a command. The "push-to-talk" method is most reliable. With that method, the computer only listens for commands while you are holding down the key or key combination specified at the top of the Listening section of the Speech control panel. To select the push-to-talk method, click the option labeled "Listen only while key(s) are pressed." If you don't like that method, you can speak the computer's name to get it to pay attention. To select that method, click the option labeled "Key(s) toggle listening on and off." Then you can type a name for the computer in the space provided, and you can choose from the nearby pop-up menu to specify if and when you must speak the name. Figure 21-40 shows the Listening section of the Speech control panel.

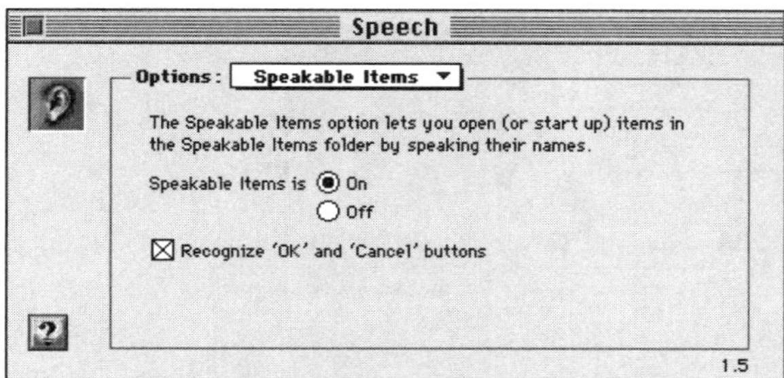


**Figure 21-39: The Speakable Items section of the Speech control panel.**

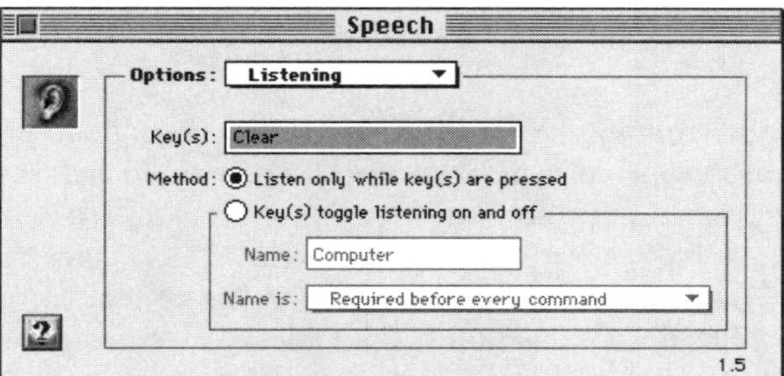


**Figure 21-40: The Listening section of the Speech control panel.**

The settings in the Feedback section of the Speech control panel determine how the computer lets you know whether it heard and recognized your spoken commands. You can choose a cartoon character from a pop-up menu that lists nine alternatives. The cartoon character is animated and appears in the speech recognition feedback window. You can have the computer speak its response to your commands (using the settings in the Voices section of the Speech control panel) as well as displaying them in writing in the speech recognition feedback window. To have the computer respond vocally, select the "Speak text feedback" option. You can also choose a sound from a pop-up menu that lists the sounds in the System file and the computer will play that sound when it recognizes what you said. Figure 21-41 shows the Feedback section of the Speech control panel and the speech recognition feedback window.

With speech recognition versions 1.4 and later you do not use the Speech Macro Editor program, which came with earlier versions of speech recognition software, to compose multi-step speakable commands. Instead you use the Script Editor program or equivalent to create AppleScript applications and you put them, or aliases of them, in the Speakable Items folder.

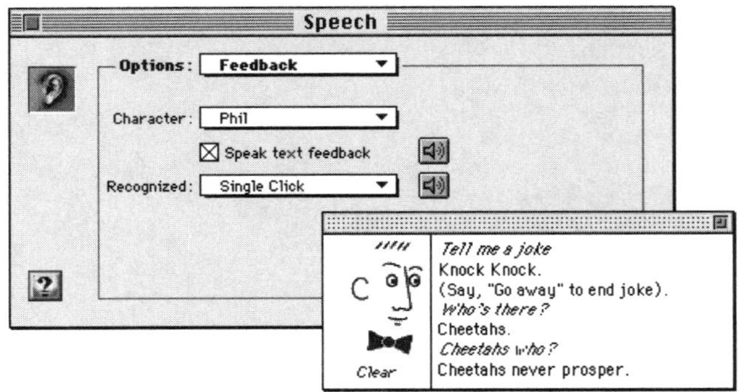


**Figure 21-41: The Feedback section of the Speech control panel and the speech recognition feedback window.**

The Mac OS 7.6 and System 7.5.3 CD-ROMs include PlainTalk speech recognition software for optional installation. The text-to-speech software is available separately from the Apple on-line software archive (see "Obtaining Installation Software" in Chapter 22). English text-to-speech speech recognition software works on most PowerPC computers using system software version 7.5 or later. The computer must be capable of 16-bit sound input and must be equipped with a PlainTalk microphone or the microphone built into Apple audiovisual displays. The Centris and Quadra 660AV and 840AV computers can use PlainTalk 1.3's speech recognition, but not later versions. The Performa 5200, 5300, 6200, and 6300 series require PlainTalk 1.5 or later for speech recognition. Early production models of the Performa 5200 and 5200 LC have 8-bit sound input and can't use speech recognition software. You can determine whether a 5200 has 16-bit sound input by looking at the Sound Out settings in the Sound control panel. If the 16-bit option is grayed out, the 5200 has 8-bit sound and speech recognition won't work.

## CHAPTER  CONCEPTS AND TERMS

- The core Mac OS 7.6 software QuickTime 2.5, LaserWriter 8.4.2, Open Transport 1.1.1, multiprocessor support, Desktop PrintMonitor 2.0.2, ColorSync 2.1.1, Extensions Manager 7.6, basic English Text-to-Speech 1.5 new screen capture options, and improved performance and reliability.
- As part of a standard Mac OS 7.6 installation, you can also include OpenDoc 1.1.2, OpenDoc Essentials Kit 1.0.1, QuickDraw 3D 1.0.6, MacLinkPlus 8.1, Apple Remote Access Client 2.1, Cyberdog 1.2.1, Open Transport PPP 1.0, full English Text-to-Speech 1.5, and QuickDraw GX 1.1.5.
- System 7.5.5 speeds up virtual memory and fixes a variety of problems.
- System 7.5.3 includes Finder enhancements, several new and revised control panels and accessories, file sharing improvements, Open Transport 1.1, MacTCP 2.0.6, QuickTime 2.1, English text-to-speech 1.4.1, and numerous performance and reliability enhancements.
- System 7.5.3 options include Desktop PrintMonitor 1.0.3, separate installation of PowerTalk's digital signatures capability, and as CD-ROM bonuses, QuickDraw 3D 1.0.3 and OpenDoc 1.0.4.

**category**
A type of information handled by an OpenDoc part, such as text, sound, video, or AppleScript.

**container**
An OpenDoc part that allows you to place other OpenDoc parts inside it.

**classic AppleTalk**
The chief networking protocol of the Mac OS prior to Open Transport.

**Live Object**
An OpenDoc plug-in part that's been through a certification process to ensure that it works and plays well with others.

**OpenDoc**
An infrastructure for a type of plug-in software that makes it easy to work on many types of data in a single document without switching applications.

**Open Transport**
A modern networking subsystem that makes AppleTalk, TCP/IP, and other types of networks equals.

**part**
An OpenDoc plug-in component that lets you work on a particular kind of content, which could be text, graphics, sound, movies, spreadsheets, charts, databases, Web pages, e-mail, or something else.

**part editor**
The item that provides the functionality of an OpenDoc part.

**part stationery**
The item that gives you access to an OpenDoc part's functionality.

**port**
The place a cable or wire connects to your computer.

**PPP**
A protocol for connecting to a TCP/IP network over dial-up telephone lines (with a modem or an ISDN terminal adapter).

**protocol**
A set of rules for computers exchanging data on a network.

**QuickDraw 3D**
System software that lets you see and interact with three-dimensional graphics in any application designed to take advantage of it.

**root part**
The part (or the part whose stationery) you used to create an OpenDoc document.

**TCP/IP**
The networking protocol used by the Internet.

**zone**
One segment of an AppleTalk network that has been subdivided for more convenient access.

CHAPTER 22

# Installing and Upgrading System Software

- Obtaining installation software
- Preparing for installation
- Deciding whether to upgrade or install a new system
- Installing some or all Mac OS 7.6 modules including the core Mac OS, OpenDoc, QuickDraw 3D, MacLinkPlus, Apple Remote Access, Cyberdog, Open Transport PPP, English Text-to-Speech, and QuickDraw GX
- Installing all or part of the basic System 7.5.3 or 7.5 software, adding QuickDraw GX, PowerTalk, or OpenDoc, and upgrading to System 7.5.3 with System 7.5 Update 2.0
- Installing additional system software
- Upgrading System 7 on an old Mac Performa
- Installing System 7.1.2 and earlier
- Troubleshooting installation problems

As the Mac OS has become more complex over the years, the process of installing and upgrading it has become increasingly automated. Where once you dragged a handful of icons from an installation disk to your startup disk, you now run an installer program named the Installer. Its actions are directed by a script that Apple engineers carefully wrote to copy the pieces of system software you're installing from the installation disk or disks to the correct places on your startup disk, and remove outdated software from your startup disk as necessary. The installer script typically offers you a few simple choices, such as whether to install all of the system software or just the pieces you select from a list, and then the Installer takes care of the nitty-gritty.

This chapter explains how to use the installation software for the following versions of System 7:

- ❖ Mac OS 7.6
- ❖ System 7.5.5
- ❖ System 7.5.3 or 7.5
- ❖ System 7.5 on old Mac Performas
- ❖ System 7.1.2 and earlier

In addition, this chapter explains how to install add-on system software such as QuickTime, OpenDoc, and QuickDraw GX. Most add-on system software can be installed over any of several versions of the Mac OS.

First, this chapter discusses the sources of installation software and explains some measures you can take to reduce compatibility problems no matter which Mac OS software you install.

# Obtaining Installation Software

Installation software — the Installer program, installer script, and pieces of software to be installed — comes on several forms of media. You may install from a set of floppy disks, in which case the Installer asks by name for each disk it needs and ejects the disk it no longer needs. As an alternative to floppy disks, you can put the installation software on a hard disk or removable hard disk as described in the sidebar "Net Install."

## Net Install

Installing software from a set of floppy disks is considerably slower than installing from a hard disk or CD-ROM, and you have to pay attention so you know when the Installer needs the next floppy disk. Moreover, installing from floppies is a huge inconvenience if you have to install the same software repeatedly (for example, on a number of networked computers). Rather than installing from floppy disks, you can use them to create an installation folder on a hard disk and install from there. Here's the simplest method:

1. Create a new folder on the hard disk that you want to use for installation. If you need to install the same software on several networked computers, create the new folder on a network file server or a shared hard disk.
2. Copy each floppy disk to the new folder. To copy a floppy, insert it and drag its icon to the new folder's icon.
3. For convenience, make an alias of the Installer in the first installation folder and put the alias in the same folder as the set of installation folders.

You end up with a set of installation folders having the same names as the installation floppy disks. It's important to keep all of the installation folders in the same folder on the hard disk and not to change their names. The Installer won't work if you relocate or rename any folders.

To install from the set of installation folders, you simply start the Installer program in the first installation folder by double-clicking its icon or an alias of it. If you have trouble installing from a set of installation folders — for example, the Installer asks you to insert a floppy disk when it should use the next installation folder — try putting a copy of the Installer program and the Installer script file into the same folder as the set of installation folders, and start the installation with that copy of the Installer. (To copy the Installer and the script file, open the first installation folder and press the Option key while dragging the Installer and the script file to the folder that contains the set of installation folders.)

An alternative method of putting installation software on a hard disk involves creating a disk image file for each floppy disk. This method requires more effort, but it works in cases when the simpler method described above fails. You create the disk image files with a utility program such as Apple's Disk Copy or Aladdin's ShrinkWrap (originally distributed as shareware by its author, Chad Magendanz). For more information on disk image files, see the sidebar "Disk Image Files."

### Disk Image Files

Software you obtain from the Internet, America Online, CompuServe, or other online sources may come in the form of disk image files. These are files from certain utility programs that you can use to create a set of installation floppy disks. Two such utilities are Apple's free Disk Copy (available from Apple's software archive as described below in "Installation Software On-line") and ShrinkWrap (408-761-6200, *http://www.aladdinsys.com*). With ShrinkWrap, you don't have to make floppy disks to install from the disk image files. ShrinkWrap can mount any number of disk image files directly onto your desktop. It's as if you had inserted a whole bunch of floppy disks simultaneously. Because you can mount all of the "disks" needed for installation, you don't have to sit in front of your computer to swap floppies. Once you start the installation process, it proceeds without further attention from you.

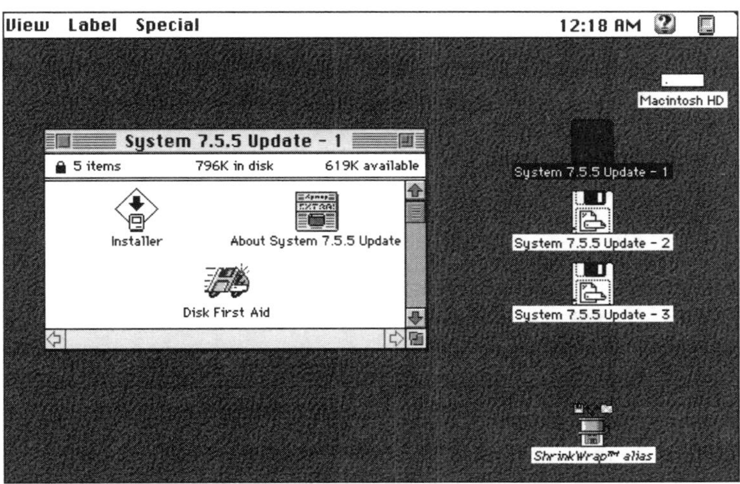


# Installation CD-ROMs

When more than a few floppy disks are involved in the installation process, Apple generally makes a CD-ROM equivalent. It's not unusual for an installation CD-ROM to include extra software that won't fit on the equivalent installation floppy disks. Major releases of the Mac OS, such as System 7.5 and 7.6, are sold in stores and catalogs. Apple usually makes upgrades to the latest major release available at lower cost to System 7 owners through the Apple Order Center (800-293-6617). The Apple Order Center also distributes minor releases of the Mac OS and some updates to individual Mac OS pieces for a shipping fee.

You may use an installation CD-ROM in your computer directly, or you may access it over a network. Using installation software over a network is pretty much the same as using it from a CD-ROM in your computer's CD-ROM drive.

## Installation software on-line

Apple maintains an archive of system software on America Online, CompuServe, and the Internet, and you can copy software from those sources to your hard disk. New versions of individual Mac OS pieces show up in Apple's on-line software archive before they're available on CD-ROM or floppy disk. The archive also contains older versions of many Mac OS pieces, including System 7.0.1 complete (other versions of System 7 are not available in the archive). Here's how to access Apple's software:

- On the Internet, point your Web browser to *http://www.info.apple.com* and follow the links to the software archive or a featured item. For premium access, check out Apple Club at *http://www.club.apple.com*.
- On America Online, use the keyword **applecomputer** to go directly to the Apple Computer window. All software is located in the software area of that window.
- On CompuServe, use the Go word APLSUP to take you to the Apple Computer Support forum, where you can find Apple USA SW Updates, or use the Go word APLWW to access the Apple Worldwide Software Updates Forum.

# Preparing for Installation

Before installing new Mac OS software — whether that means upgrading to a newer version of System 7, installing a new Mac OS technology, or installing System 7 to replace System 6 (or something even older) — you need to determine whether the new software will work with the software you already have. Ideally you would make a list of every piece of software that's not part of the Mac OS and check with the software publishers or distributors to make sure the versions you have are compatible with what you're about to install. If you have the time and patience to do that — great. If not, at least do the following to minimize the risk of incompatibilities:

- Make a backup of your hard disk and of any RAM disk you have
- Verify the directories of all your hard disk volumes
- Update hard disk driver software
- Turn off any security, virus protection, and screen saver software
- Turn on standard extensions

- ❖ Look in the SimpleText installation file for known incompatibilities and disable, remove, or upgrade any incompatible software that you have
- ❖ Optionally label all items in your System Folder with the Labels menu (after installation, the new items will be the unlabeled ones)
- ❖ If you are installing on a PowerBook, make sure it's plugged in
- ❖ If you're installing on a computer that can go to sleep, make sure it won't go to sleep during installation

The remainder of this section discusses these tasks in more detail.

## Backing up disks

If you use more than one hard disk, or if your hard disk is partitioned into multiple volumes, make backups of all of them. Making backups is like buying car insurance — it's a terrific imposition and you hope it's a total waste of effort. Do it anyway.

If you have a RAM disk, copy its contents to another disk before upgrading or installing any version of System 7. The RAM disk may be turned off and its contents lost during the installation process.

Backing up today's large hard disks onto floppy disks is impractical. You need some type of high-capacity backup storage device, either another hard disk of equal or greater capacity, a tape drive, or a hard disk with removable cartridges. If you have a second hard disk, you can back up your main hard disk by simply dragging its icon to the backup disk's icon. That method isn't very efficient if you want to keep your backup up-to-date on a regular basis, but it's adequate for pre-installation purposes.

You could back up onto removable hard disk cartridges by dragging folder icons, but it's simpler to use a special backup utility such as DiskFit from Dantz Development (510-253-3000, *http://www.dantz.com*). It automates the process of backing up a large hard disk onto several smaller disk cartridges. DiskFit also makes it easy to keep your backup files current. Each time you back up, it copies only the files and folders that have changed since the last backup. That minimizes the amount of time and number of disk cartridges you need for backup.

If you have a tape drive, you must use backup software such as Dantz's Retrospect. You can't backup folders to a tape by dragging icons in the Finder.

## Verifying disk directories

It's important to check the condition of a disk before installing new system software on it. You can do that with Apple's Disk First Aid utility, which comes with System 7. Disk First Aid checks the condition of a disk's directory, which keeps track of where files are stored on the disk, and can often repair any problem it finds. The Mac OS maintains each disk directory automatically, updating it every time you save changes to a file or create a new file. The directory can become damaged when the Mac freezes or crashes, when an application quits unexpectedly, and so on. The damage may be so slight that you don't notice a problem, but over time the damage can grow and become irreparable. Disk First Aid is easy to use: you simply select one or more disks in its window and click the Verify or Repair button (see Figure 22-1).

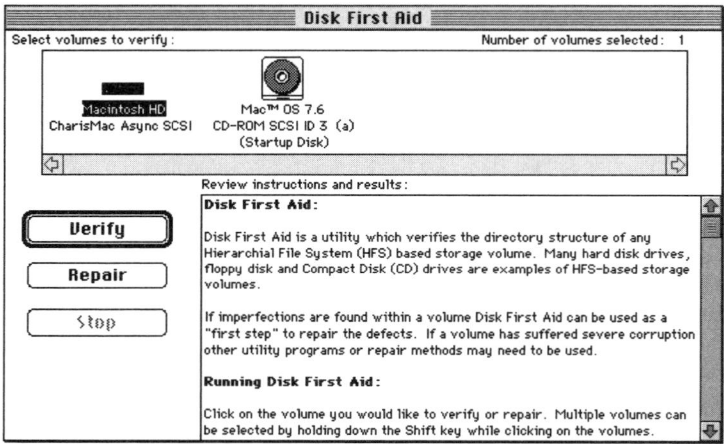


**Figure 22-1: Disk First Aid verifies and repairs disk directories.**

Disk First Aid has a limitation that you can avoid by starting up your computer from a Disk Tools floppy disk or a System 7 CD-ROM and opening the copy of Disk First Aid from there. You see, Disk First Aid can't repair problems it finds on the current startup disk or on the disk that contains the running Disk First Aid program. This limitation doesn't get in your way if you start up from a Disk Tools disk or a CD-ROM and run Disk First Aid from it. A Disk Tools floppy disk comes with every set of installation floppy disks for a major release of System 7, including Mac OS 7.6, System 7.5.3, and System 7.5, but not with installation floppy disks for minor System 7 releases such as 7.5.5. The Disk Tools floppy may come as a disk image file on CD; use Apple's Disk Copy utility or Aladdin's ShrinkWrap to make a real floppy. Similarly, you can start up a Mac and run Disk First Aid from any CD-ROM that contains a major release of System 7 as well as from the CD-ROM that comes with a Macintosh. You cannot start up from a CD-ROM that contains a System 7 update or minor release, such as System 7.5 Update 2.0.

Some disk problems are beyond Disk First Aid's restorative powers. If Disk First Aid says it can't fix a problem, put the problematic disk through the repair process several more times anyway. The problem may be one that Disk First Aid can fix bit by bit. If after several repair attempts Disk First Aid doesn't tell you the disk appears to be okay, you need to bring in a high-priced disk mechanic — Norton Utilities from Symantec (408-253-9600, *http://www.symantec.com*). Norton Utilities can detect and fix significantly more problems than Disk First Aid. If it can't repair the disk, it may be able to recover individual files that the Finder can no longer access. After recovering lost files and copying them to another disk together with other files that haven't been backed up, you can resurrect the disk by formatting it.

## Updating hard disk driver software

The driver software that resides on every hard disk and removable hard disk cartridge must be compatible with the Mac OS version in use or problems can result. For example, old driver software made by Transoft (805-897-3350, *http://www.transnet.net/transoft/*) causes a problem with System 7.5. The old Transoft driver considers the startup disk to be ejectable, and this causes System 7.5 to display a message asking you to insert the startup disk when you shut down the computer, although the startup disk was never ejected. To check whether your startup disk has a Transoft driver, select the disk's desktop icon and choose Get Info from the Finder's File menu. If the Get Info window's Where information contains "NS-SCSI" or "NS-ACAM" then the disk contains a Transoft driver. Transoft drivers were distributed with various brands of hard disks, notably APS Technologies, as well as with Transoft's SCSI Director formatting utility. The problem does not affect APS hard disks with Power Tools software versions 3.0 and later, nor does it affect Transoft SCSI Director version 3.0.9 and later.

Updating disk driver software takes just a minute and in most cases doesn't affect disk contents in any way. (To update the driver on an old hard disk formatted with Apple's HD SC Setup version 2.0, you must reformat the hard disk, erasing the disk contents in the process.) To update a disk's driver software, use the most recent version of the formatting utility program that came with the disk. There are three formatting utility programs from Apple, and the one to use depends on the model of Mac you have and the version of System 7 you're installing. The three formatting utilities include:

- ❖ **Drive Setup.** Use this utility to update the hard disk driver before installing System 7.5.3 or Mac OS 7.6 on any Apple Power Macintosh or any Apple Macintosh computer that has an IDE (not SCSI) internal hard disk, except a PowerBook 150. Apple Macintosh computers with IDE hard disks include the PowerBook 190, 1400, 2300, and 5300; the Performa and LC 580 series; the Performa, LC, and Quadra 630 series; and the Performa 5200, 5300, 5400, 6200, and 6300 series.
- ❖ **Apple HD SC Setup.** Use this utility to update the hard disk driver before installing any version of System 7 on a Quadra (except 630 series), Centris, LC (except 580 and 630 series), Mac II, Classic, SE, or PowerBook with a SCSI internal hard disk. Also, use this utility to update the hard disk driver before installing System 7.5.2, 7.5.1, 7.5, or 7.1.2 on a Power Macintosh

that can use those versions of the Mac OS. This utility does not work with any IDE hard disks.

- **Internal HD Format.** This utility is for formatting the internal IDE hard disk on an Apple Macintosh that originally shipped with System 7.5.1 or earlier. To update the hard disk driver on any of those computers except a PowerBook 150, use the Drive Setup utility. You do not need to (and in fact cannot) update the driver of a PowerBook 150's internal hard disk, because the driver is in the PowerBook 150's ROM.

The above utilities work on most Apple-brand hard disks. If you have an internal or external hard disk from another company, contact the company for the latest version of its hard disk formatting utility. If that version is more recent than the one you have, use the more recent version to update your non-Apple hard disk's driver.

You can also switch to a different brand of driver software, such as Hard Disk Toolkit from FWB Software (415-463-3500, *http://www.fwb.com*). However, once you switch from an Apple driver to another brand, you generally can't switch back. Before switching to another brand of driver software, keep in mind that Apple always updates its hard disk driver software to be compatible with the latest Mac OS. Other companies sometimes take longer than Apple to update their hard disk drivers for the latest Mac OS. The startup disk is particularly susceptible to incompatibilities between disk driver software and the Mac OS, so don't switch the startup disk from an Apple driver to another brand without good reason.

## Configuring extensions

Some system extensions and control panels can interfere with installing or upgrading System 7. To avoid problems caused by anti-virus, security, screen-saver, or energy-saver software, be sure to do the following before you begin the installation process:

- Disable At Ease or other security software that locks or restricts access to files, folders, or disks.
- Disable software that protects against viruses.
- Turn off screen-saver software.
- Deactivate all but the standard set of extensions and control panels for your version of System 7, plus any other extensions and control panels required for installation, as follows:
    - If you're upgrading from System 7.5 through 7.5.5, open the Extensions Manager control panel and from its pop-up menu, choose the extensions set named System 7.5 Only, System 7.5.2, System 7.5.3, or System 7.5.5 (see Figure 22-2).

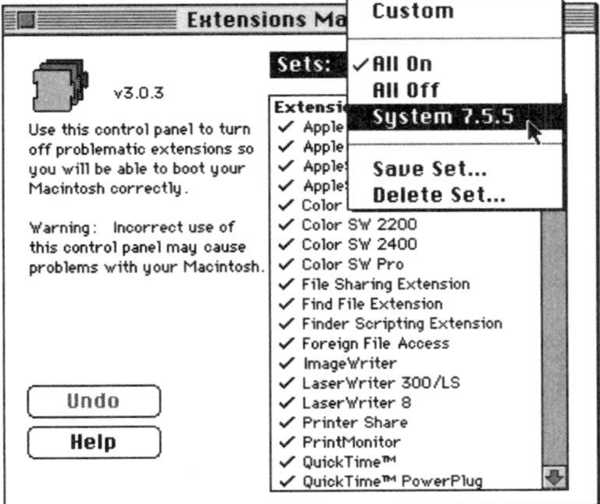


**Figure 22-2: Activate only the standard extensions and control panels.**

- ❖ If you're reinstalling Mac OS 7.6, choose Mac OS 7.6 All, Mac OS 7.6 Base, or Mac OS 7.6 Minimum from the Extensions Manager's pop-up menu.
- ❖ If you have special equipment that requires extensions or control panels to start up, turn them back on in the Extensions Manager.
- ❖ If you are upgrading from System 7.0 through 7.1.4, turn off all extensions by holding down the Shift key while restarting your computer.

❖ Make sure the computer is not set to go to sleep or shut down automatically.

# Tracking Installer actions

When you update System 7 or reinstall it, the Installer program not only adds entirely new items, it also removes existing items from the startup disk (for which the installation software includes replacements), and then copies the replacements into the correct places on the startup disk. But the Installer gives you no record of what it has done. You can use the Labels menu to keep tabs on the changes by following these steps:

1. Print a report of the System Folder contents before running the Installer. To do that, open the System Folder, choose By Name from the View menu, choose Select All from the Edit menu, and press ⌘-Option-Right Arrow to expand all folders within the System Folder. Then choose Print Window from the File menu to print the hierarchical list of System Folder contents.

If you have System 7.5 or later installed, you can use its Find File utility to make a document containing an alphabetical list of the System Folder contents. Start by opening the startup disk icon and selecting the System Folder icon. Next open Find File and set it to find items in the current Finder selection whose name is not "????" (or any other name you know doesn't exist). When Find File displays its list of found items you can select all, copy, and paste into the Scrapbook, the Note Pad, or any text document for later reference (see Figure 22-3).

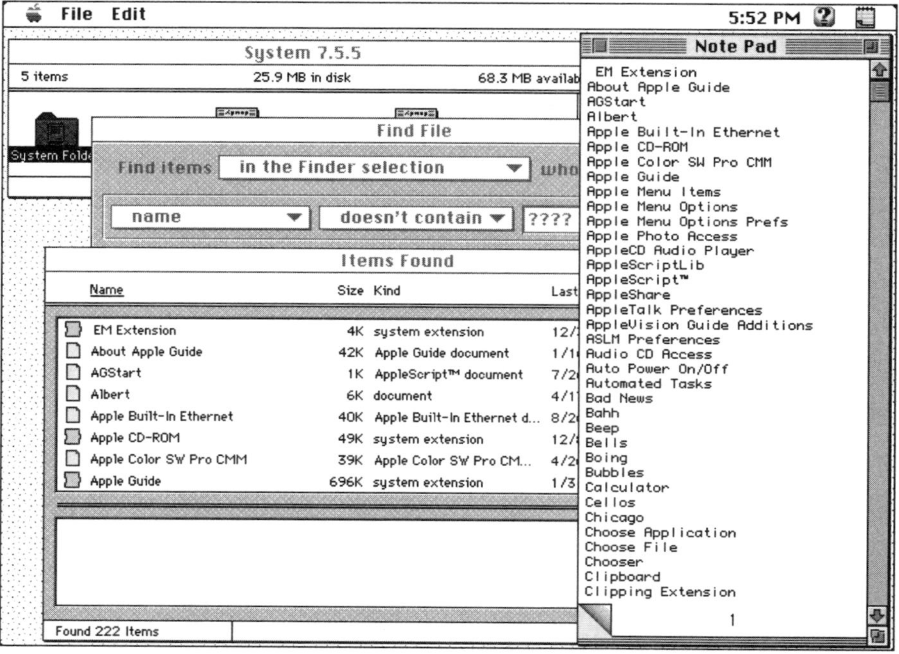


**Figure 22-3: Making a list of all System folder items.**

2. Use the Label menu to label every item you want to keep track of in the System Folder. The simplest method is this: after expanding all folders as described in Step 1, choose Select All from the Edit menu and choose one of the labels from the Label menu. Alternatively, you can use multiple labels to categorize items. For example, you could label all items that are part of the Mac OS with one label and all items you have added with a different label. Use the Labels control panel if you want to change label names or colors (see "Labeling Items" in Chapter 6).

3. Install or upgrade System 7 as described later in this chapter. The installation process removes some of the items you labeled and adds other items, which are all unlabeled.

4. To see which items are new or replacements, look in the System Folder for unlabeled items. You can search for unlabeled items in the System Folder using the Find File feature in System 7.5 and later. Start by selecting the System Folder icon or folders inside it if you want to look for new items only in them. Next open Find File and set it to search for items in the Finder selection whose label is None (or is not the label you applied in Step 2). You can label items listed in the Found Items window by selecting any number of them and using Find File's Label menu.

   To determine which items are completely new and which have been deleted, print another report or make another alphabetical list of the System Folder contents following the procedures described in Step 1. Compare the newer and older reports or the newer and older alphabetical lists. Brand new items appear in the newer list but not in the older list. Deleted items appear in the older list but not in the newer list.

   The one thing this procedure does not tell you is which unlabeled replacement items are newer versions of the items they replaced and which replacements are the same versions as the items they replaced. Since there's a rough correlation between an item's version and its modification date, you can get a rough idea of which items are new versions by using Find File to find the unlabeled items and then viewing the found items by date. Items at the top of the list are more likely to be new versions than items at the bottom of the list.

# Installing on a PowerBook

Although you can install or upgrade System 7 on a PowerBook under battery power, it's better to have the PowerBook plugged in, especially if you're installing from a set of floppy disks. If you are called away during installation, the PowerBook could go to sleep if it's operating on batteries.

You cannot install or upgrade System 7 correctly on a PowerBook's hard disk when it is in SCSI disk mode. A PowerBook is in SCSI disk mode when it is connected with a SCSI Disk Adapter cable to another computer, and that computer is using the PowerBook as an external hard disk. In this scenario, you would be running the Installer on the other computer, not on the PowerBook, and the Installer would not install the pieces of the Mac OS specifically designed for PowerBooks.

To install or update System 7 correctly on a PowerBook, you must run the System 7 Installer on the PowerBook. You can use a set of floppy disks, a CD-ROM (in a drive connected to the PowerBook or in a shared drive you access over a network), and so on.

# Performing a Clean Installation

Ordinarily, Apple's installation software upgrades the Mac OS that already exists on a computer, merging the new with the old. You get some entirely new items and some replacements for existing items that haven't changed, but preference files and files that contain your data are not replaced. For example, installing Mac OS 7.6 replaces the Scrapbook program but not items you have added to the Scrapbook file. That is the right thing to do unless your system has become unreliable and you can't seem to resolve its problems. You can usually eliminate nagging system problems by installing a pristine copy of the Mac OS. This is known as a clean install or a clean installation, and it's a favorite tonic of telephone technical support personnel because it's so effective. The trouble is, a clean installation of the Mac OS forces you to laboriously re-install all of the control panels, extensions, fonts, Apple menu items, Startup items, and anything else that you have added to your System Folder since you started using your computer. You'll also have to reconfigure your control panels and reset options in most of your application programs since all of their settings are kept in preference files in the System Folder. And that's not all. You'll also need to reinstall application programs that keep auxiliary files and folders in the System Folder, such as most Claris and Adobe applications. Sure, you could simply copy files from the old System Folder to the new one, but that defeats the purpose of a clean installation, which is to stop using old, possibly damaged files. Performing a clean installation of the Mac OS is like moving to a new apartment because your old one smells bad. It might be easier to figure out what's causing the stink and fix it. See "Troubleshooting Installation Problems" at the end of this chapter.

Still, there are times when a clean slate is the simplest cure, or at any rate a useful diagnostic tool, since a computer clearly doesn't have a hardware malfunction if it works reliably with a cleanly installed System Folder. Apple's installation software makes it easy to do a clean installation of Mac OS 7.6, System 7.5.3, or System 7.5. For specific instructions, see "Installing Mac OS 7.6 — Standard," "Installing Mac OS 7.6 — Custom," or "Installing System 7.5.3 or 7.5 — Standard" later in this chapter.

# Installing Mac OS 7.6

Mac OS 7.6 debuts a simplified installation program called Install Mac OS. You can use this program to install some or all Mac OS 7.6 modules, and you have the option of performing a clean installation (see "Performing a Clean Installation" above). The Install Mac OS program will help you update the disk driver software on most Apple-brand hard disks you have, and you can have it check the condition of the hard disk on which the Mac OS 7.6 modules will be installed (see "Verifying Disk Directories" and "Updating Hard Disk Driver

Software" earlier in this chapter). The modules you can install include the following:

- Mac OS 7.6 core software
- OpenDoc 1.1.2
- OpenDoc Essentials Kit 1.0.1
- QuickDraw 3D 1.0.6
- MacLinkPlus 8.1
- Apple Remote Access Client 2.1
- Cyberdog 1.2.1
- Open Transport PPP 1.0
- English Text-to-Speech 1.5
- QuickDraw GX 1.1.5

The remainder of this section tells you how to use the Install Mac OS program to prepare for installation and then to install standard or custom Mac OS modules for one computer, or to install a universal Mac OS for starting up any computer capable of running Mac OS 7.6.

# Installing Mac OS 7.6 — compatibility

Several of the Mac OS 7.6 modules are not compatible with every Mac model and with all Mac software, as detailed in the following paragraphs.

## Core requirements

The Mac OS 7.6 core software requires a Mac that was originally equipped with a 68030, 68040, or PowerPC processor and has a 32-bit clean ROM. The following models can't use Mac OS 7.6: Plus, SE, SE/30, II, IIx, IIcx, Portable, PowerBook 100, original Classic, and original LC. System 7.5.5 is the latest version those models can use. Those models cannot be made eligible for Mac OS 7.6 by installing software for 32-bit addressing (see "Employing 32-Bit Addressing" in Chapter 13) or by installing hardware accelerators. (Models older than a Plus can't use any version of System 7.)

## QuickDraw 3D

QuickDraw 3D requires a PowerPC processor. You can't install it on a computer with a 68030 or 68040 processor.

## OpenDoc, Cyberdog, and LaserWriter 8.4

OpenDoc, Cyberdog, and the LaserWriter 8.4 printer driver use a common piece of software that has a problem on computers without PowerPC processors. The software, called the CFM 68K Runtime Enabler, is not included with

Mac OS 7.6. You cannot use Install Mac OS to install OpenDoc, OpenDoc Essentials, Cyberdog, or LaserWriter 8.4 on a computer with a 68030 or 68040 processor. (You can install those items on a computer with a PowerPC processor.) A few application programs also require the CFM 68K Runtime Enabler, including Apple Telecom 3.0, Apple Games Sprockets, and the Apple Media Tool. Apple is working on a solution to the problem and will release a replacement for the CFM 68K Runtime Enabler as soon as possible.

### Mac 5200, 5300, 6200, and 6300 series

Some Performa and Power Macintosh computers in the 5200, 5300, 6200, and 6300 series can't use Mac OS 7.6 until a hardware problem is fixed, except that the problem does not affect the Performa 6360 model. You can test for the problem by using the 5xxx/6xxx Tester utility in the Utilities folder on the CD-ROM. In addition, the Mac OS 7.6 installation software checks for the problem and alerts you if repairs are needed. The repairs are covered under an Apple warranty extension program that's in effect until 2003.

### Open Transport

If you have installed Open Transport 1.1.2 or newer, it will be replaced with an older version when you install Mac OS 7.6. After installing Mac OS 7.6 you must reinstall your newer version of Open Transport.

### AppleShare Workstation software

If your computer has AppleShare Workstation software installed, you must make sure it is version 3.6.3 or later before installing Mac OS 7.6 over a network. Apple Workstation 3.6.3 is included in the Utilities folder of the Mac OS 7.6 CD-ROM. To install it, drag its icon to the System Folder icon of the startup disk.

### QuickDraw GX drivers

If you have a printer that doesn't use Apple printer driver software, such as LaserWriter 8, and you want to install QuickDraw GX, you need to get a QuickDraw GX driver for your printer. Once QuickDraw GX is installed, you will not be able to print without a GX driver. Mac OS 7.6 includes GX printer drivers for Apple printers. Contact the maker of your printer for assistance.

### Adobe Acrobat

If your computer has Adobe Acrobat installed and you use the Mac OS 7.6 installation software to install or remove QuickDraw GX, Acrobat will display a message about missing fonts each time you start up the computer. Reinstall Acrobat to stop the message — simply disabling QuickDraw GX with the Extensions Manager control panel does not stop the message.

### Apple Remote Access

If you install Apple Remote Access Client software after installing Open Transport PPP, an Installer tells you that a more recent version of Open Transport PPP is already installed. Respond that you want to use the newer version of Open Transport PPP.

### System 6

You can't install Mac OS 7.6 directly over System 6. You must either install an older version of System 7 first, or do a clean installation of Mac OS 7.6.

## Installing Mac OS 7.6 — setup

The Install Mac OS program begins by leading you through some of the preparatory tasks that ensure a successful installation of Mac OS 7.6. To prepare for installing some or all Mac OS 7.6 modules, be sure to read "Preparing for Installation" earlier in this chapter, and then follow these steps:

1. Insert the Mac OS 7.6 CD-ROM disc or the Mac OS 7.6 Install Me First floppy disk and find the Install Mac OS program.
2. Start the Install Mac OS program by double-clicking its icon. After a few seconds, the Install Mac OS window appears, as shown in Figure 22-4.

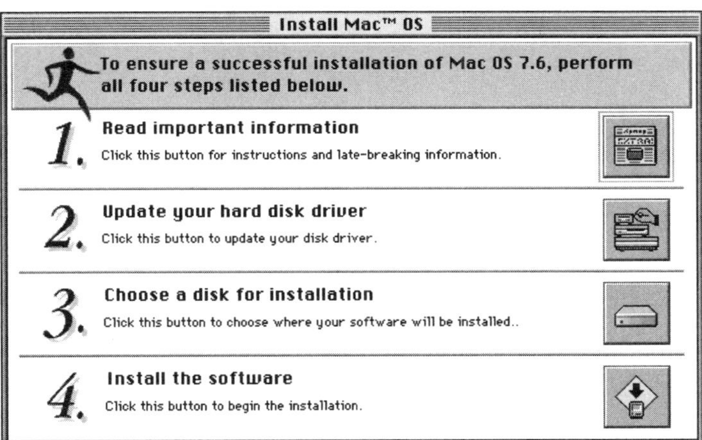


**Figure 22-4: The Install Mac OS window.**

3. Click the button for task 1 in the Install Mac OS window. The SimpleText program displays a document containing last-minute installation information for Mac OS 7.6. After reading, attending to, and optionally printing that document, close its window and switch back to the main Install Mac OS window.

You can skip Step 3 if you have already read the last-minute installation information.

4. Click the button for task 2 in the Install Mac OS window. An alert gives you the opportunity to skip this task if none of your hard disks have Apple drivers. If you click the Continue button, the Drive Setup or HD SC Setup program opens, whichever is appropriate for your computer. Select each Apple hard disk and click the Update Driver button or the Update button to update its driver software. Then quit the Drive Setup or HD SC Setup program and switch back to the main Install Mac OS window.

   To update the driver software of hard disks that have non-Apple driver software, see "Updating Hard Disk Driver Software" earlier in this chapter. You can skip this step if you have already updated the driver software on your hard disks.

5. Click the button for task 3 in the Install Mac OS window. A dialog box appears in which you choose the disk on which you want to install the Mac OS 7.6 modules. Choose the disk by name and click the Select button. If you skip this task, then in task 4 the Install Mac OS program will display a dialog box that asks you to specify the disk on which to install Mac OS 7.6.

6. Click the button for task 4 in the Install Mac OS window when you are ready to select the Mac OS 7.6 modules you want installed.

   Continue at "Installing Mac OS 7.6 — Standard" below if you want to install the basic Mac OS 7.6 modules plus some or all additional modules, each in its entirety.

   Continue at "Installing Mac OS 7.6 — Custom" below if you want to install any of the Mac OS 7.6 modules partially or completely.

   Continue at "Installing Mac OS 7.6 — Universal" below if you want to install a Mac OS that can start up any computer capable of running Mac OS 7.6.

## Installing Mac OS 7.6 — standard

A standard installation of Mac OS 7.6 always includes the Mac OS core module and the OpenDoc and OpenDoc Essentials modules if they will work on your computer. Other modules you can optionally install are QuickDraw 3D, MacLinkPlus, Apple Remote Access Client, Cyberdog, Open Transport PPP, English Text-To-Speech, and QuickDraw GX. Use the Install Mac OS program to select the optional modules you want to install, and under the control of the Install Mac OS program, each selected module is installed by a separate Installer program. The individual Installer programs do not require any response from you unless you are installing from floppy disks or a problem occurs.

The following steps explain how to do a standard installation of Mac OS 7.6, optionally doing a clean standard installation:

1. Start the Install Mac OS program and go through its four numbered tasks as described in Steps 1 through 6 in "Installing Mac OS 7.6 — Setup" above. After you complete all of the numbered tasks, a dialog box appears in which you can select the Mac OS 7.6 modules you want installed, as shown in Figure 22-5.

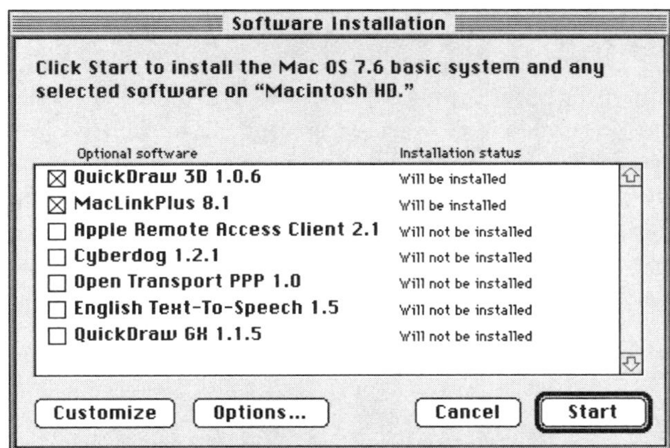


**Figure 22-5: The standard Software Installation dialog box in the Install Mac OS program.**

2. Select the modules of Mac OS 7.6 that you want installed by clicking the appropriate checkboxes. The Install Mac OS program may select some modules by default, depending on the type of computer you're installing on. The three basic modules — Mac OS, OpenDoc, and OpenDoc Essentials — are not shown because they are always included in a standard Mac OS 7.6 installation. (OpenDoc and OpenDoc Essentials are included only if they will work on your computer.)

3. To perform a clean installation, click the Options button in the standard Software Installation dialog box. A dialog box appears in which you select the option "Create new System Folder (clean installation)" and then click OK.

4. Verify that the disk named at the top of the standard Software Installation dialog box is where you want the software installed (click the Cancel button and go back to Step 1 if it isn't), and click the Start button in the standard Software Installation dialog box to begin installation.

   The Install Mac OS program checks the condition of the disk on which it's going to install the software, and tries to fix any problems it finds. While checking, it displays a progress gauge. If you want to stop the installation at this point, click the Stop button and go back to Step 2.

5. The Install Mac OS program gives control to a succession of Installer programs, one for each Mac OS 7.6 module to be installed. The first Installer program displays an Apple license agreement for you to read and optionally print. If you agree to its terms, click the Agree button and installation begins.

   Each Installer program briefly displays the message "Preparing to install." If you are installing onto the startup disk and other programs are open (such as SimpleText), the Installer displays an alert message advising you that it can't continue while other applications are open. You can click a Cancel button to cancel installation or click a Continue button to have the Installer quit the other open applications. (The Installer also turns off file sharing if it is on.) As each application quits, it may come to the front and ask whether you want to save any changes that you haven't yet saved. After quitting the other open applications, the Installer displays the folders (or disks) it will need and begins installation, as shown in Figure 22-6.

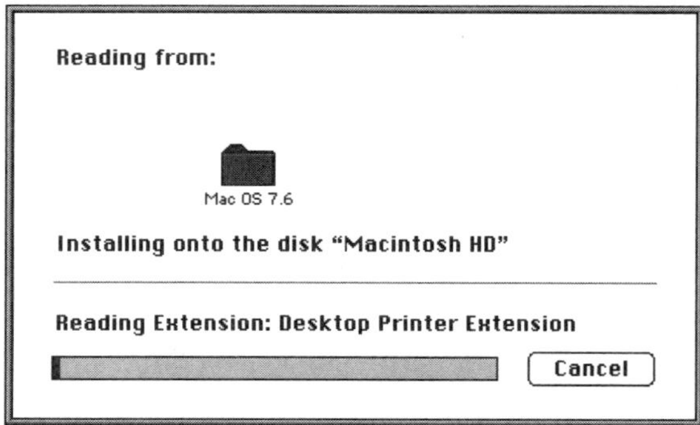


**Figure 22-6: Installation is underway.**

A standard installation proceeds automatically unless you are installing from floppy disks or a problem occurs. The individual Installer programs do not display welcome messages or offer installation options. If you are installing from a CD-ROM, a standard installation doesn't require more of your attention until it finishes. If you are installing from floppy disks and the Installer needs a different disk, the Installer ejects the disk that it is using and asks you to insert the disk it needs. You can always cancel an installation by clicking the Cancel button.

If you cancel an installation in progress, the Install Mac OS program displays an alert asking how you want to proceed. To stop installation, click the alert's Stop button and go back to Step 2. To skip installation of the module currently being installed, click the alert's Skip button. To try installing the current module again, click the alert's Try Again button.

6. When the last Installer finishes, the Install Mac OS program asks whether you want to continue to install additional Mac OS 7.6 modules. If your answer is yes, click the Continue button to repeat Steps 2 through 5 to install the modules. Otherwise quit the Install Mac OS program and restart the computer to use the new system software. As the startup disk and any other hard disks appear on the desktop during the first restart after installation (or later, in the case of removable hard disk cartridges), the Finder may automatically rebuild the desktop database files (see "Desktop Database" in Chapter 7).

## Installing Mac OS 7.6 — custom

A custom installation of Mac OS 7.6 gives you the choice of installing any of the following modules: Mac OS, OpenDoc, OpenDoc Essentials, QuickDraw 3D, MacLinkPlus, Apple Remote Access Client, Cyberdog, Open Transport PPP, English Text-To-Speech, and QuickDraw GX. In addition to installing complete modules, you can selectively install portions of each module. For example, the following are some of the components you can selectively install from the Mac OS module:

❖ Printer driver software for a kind of printer you haven't used before

❖ Control Strip, which provides quick access to various control panel settings

❖ Easy Access, which lets you move the pointer with the numeric keypad, type a key combination one stroke at a time, and so on

❖ Close View, which can magnify the entire display image

Do a custom installation only if you are sure that you know which individual items must be present for a module to work properly. If you're not sure, do a standard installation as described at "Installing Mac OS 7.6 — Standard" above.

In a custom installation, you use the Install Mac OS program to select the modules you want installed, and the Install Mac OS program has individual Installer programs install the modules you select. You must interact with each Installer program to specify whether you want it to install all or part of its module.

The following steps tell you how to custom install Mac OS 7.6, optionally doing a clean custom installation:

1. Start the Install Mac OS program and go through its four numbered tasks as explained in Steps 1 through 6 in "Installing Mac OS 7.6 — Setup" above.

After you complete all of the numbered tasks, the standard Software Installation dialog box appears, in which you can select modules to be installed and indicate that you want to do a custom installation (review Figure 22-5 above).

2. Click the Customize button in the standard Software Installation dialog box to change to the Custom Software Installation dialog box, as shown in Figure 22-7.

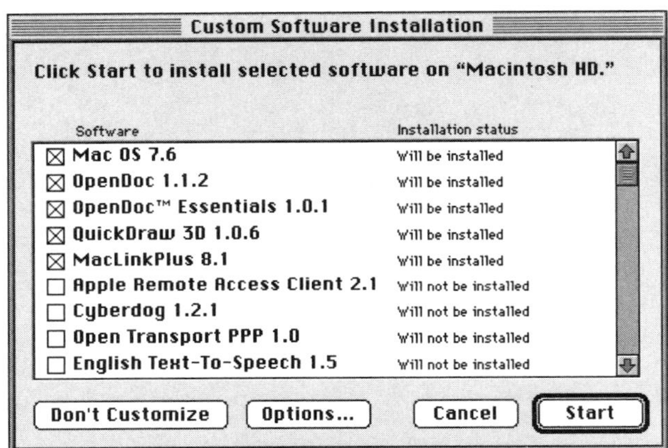


**Figure 22-7: The Custom Software Installation dialog box in the Install Mac OS program.**

3. Select the modules of Mac OS 7.6 that you want installed by clicking the appropriate checkboxes. Only the selected modules will be installed. You will have an opportunity later to selectively install portions of each module you select in this step.

4. Click the Options button in the Custom Software Installation dialog box if you want to do a clean installation or disable checking of the destination disk's condition. A dialog box appears in which you can turn on or off the options "Create new System Folder (clean installation)" and "Check Destination Disk." If the disk checking option is absent then you are doing a standard installation, which always includes the disk check.

5. Verify that the disk named at the top of the Custom Software Installation dialog box is where you want the software installed (click the Cancel button and go back to Step 1 if it isn't), and click the Start button in the Custom Software Installation dialog box to begin installation.

   Unless you disabled the Check Destination Disk option in Step 4, the Install Mac OS program checks the condition of the disk on which it's going to install the software, and tries to fix any problems it finds. While checking, it displays a progress gauge so you can monitor its progress. If you want to stop the installation at this point, click the Stop button and go back to Step 3.

6. The Install Mac OS program gives control to a succession of Installer programs, one for each Mac OS 7.6 module you selected in Step 3.

   Before displaying its main window, each Installer except the one for the OpenDoc Essentials module first displays a welcome message. After you dismiss that, some Installers display an Apple license agreement for you to read and optionally print. You must agree to its terms to continue installation. The Installer displays its main window, which describes what will be installed (see Figure 22-8).

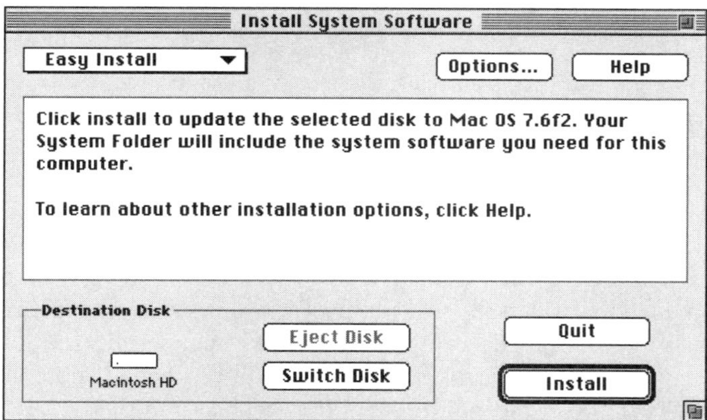


**Figure 22-8: Ready to install one complete Mac OS 7.6 module.**

   To install a complete module, choose Easy Install from the pop-up menu in the Installer's main window and click the Install button in that window. (For the OpenDoc Essentials module, simply click the Install button, since its Installer has no pop-up menu.)

   To selectively install portions of the module, choose Custom Install from the pop-up menu in the Installer window. The Installer lists components, and in some cases groups of components that you can install. To expand a component group, click the triangle next to it. You can get information about a component by clicking its information button at the right side of the Installer window. Select the components that you want to install by clicking the appropriate checkboxes, and then click the Install button (see Figure 22-9).

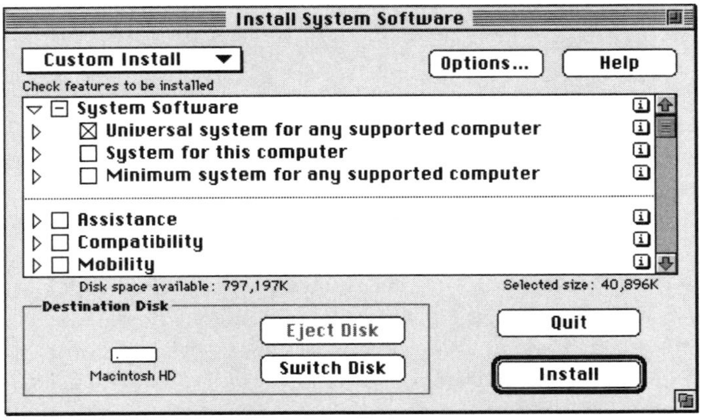

**Figure 22-9: Select components to be installed from one Mac OS 7.6 module.**

After you click the Install button, the Installer briefly displays the message "Preparing to install." If you are installing onto the startup disk and other programs are open (such as SimpleText), the Installer displays an alert message advising you that it can't continue while other applications are open. You can click a Cancel button to cancel installation or click a Continue button to have the Installer quit the other open applications. (The Installer also turns off file sharing if it is on.) As each application quits, it may come to the front and ask whether you want to save any changes that you haven't yet saved. After quitting the other open applications, the Installer displays the folders (or disks) that will be needed and commences installation. If you are installing from floppy disks and the Installer needs a different disk, the Installer ejects the disk that it is using and asks you to insert the disk it needs. You can always cancel an installation by clicking the Cancel button and quitting the Installer program.

If you cancel an installation in progress, the Install Mac OS program displays an alert asking how you want to proceed. To stop installation, click the alert's Stop button and go back to Step 3. To skip installation of the module currently being installed, click the alert's Skip button. To try installing the current module again, click the alert's Try Again button.

7. When the last Installer finishes, the Install Mac OS program asks whether you want to install additional Mac OS 7.6 modules. Click the Continue button if you want to repeat Steps 3 through 6 to install additional modules, otherwise quit the Install Mac OS program and restart the computer to use the new system software.

## Installing Mac OS 7.6 — universal

Normally the Install Mac OS program installs only the Mac OS software for the type of computer it's running on. For example, Install Mac OS installs mobility software only on portable Mac OS computers such as Apple's PowerBooks. If you want to install the Mac OS software needed to start up any type of Mac OS computer — a universal Mac OS — you must do a distinct type of custom installation. Perform Steps 1 through 8 as outlined in "Installing Mac OS 7.6 — Custom" above, with the following particulars:

- ❖ In Step 3, be sure to select the Mac OS module.
- ❖ In Step 6, as each Installer program takes its turn, specify the following conditions:
  - ❖ Mac OS 7.6 Installer — choose Custom Install from the Installer's pop-up menu and select either "Universal system for any supported computer" or "Minimum system for any supported computer." You may also select other listed components that you want installed by clicking their checkboxes.
  - ❖ OpenDoc — choose Easy Install from the Installer's pop-up menu.
  - ❖ OpenDoc Essentials — nothing to specify.
  - ❖ QuickDraw 3D — choose Easy Install.
  - ❖ MacLinkPlus — choose Easy Install.
  - ❖ Remote Access Client Install — choose Easy Install.
  - ❖ Cyberdog Installer — choose Easy Install.
  - ❖ Open Transport PPP — choose Custom Install and select all components if the universal Mac OS is to be used with PowerPC processors and 68030 or 68040 processors. Easy Install is OK if it is to be used with only one type of processor.
  - ❖ English TTS Installer — choose Easy Install.
  - ❖ QuickDraw GX Installer — choose Custom Install and preferably select all components; at least select the "Base QuickDraw GX Software for any Macintosh" component.

# Installing System 7.5.5

System 7.5.5 can only be installed as an upgrade to System 7.5.3 or 7.5.4. It works on all Mac OS computers from the Mac Plus to the latest models shipping at the end of 1996, except the PowerBook 1400, all Motorola computers, all APS Technologies computers, and all Apple Workgroup Server computers. System 7.5.5 is the latest version of the Mac OS you can install on the following models: Plus, SE, SE/30, II, IIx, IIcx, Portable, PowerBook 100, original Classic, and original LC.

Problems can occur when installing System 7.5.5 on a computer that has the Energy Saver control panel version 1.2 and earlier. Look in the Control Panels folder for Energy Saver. If you find it, use the Finder's Get Info command to determine its version number. If the version number is 1.2 or lower, drag the Energy Saver from the Control Panels folder to the desktop before installing System 7.5.5. After installing System 7.5.5, you can drag the Energy Saver back to the Control Panels folder.

To upgrade to System 7.5.5, follow these steps:

1. If your Mac has System 7.5.2 or earlier, upgrade it to System 7.5.3 by following the instructions at "Installing System 7.5.3 or 7.5 — Standard" or "Upgrading with System 7.5 Update 2.0" in the next section.
2. Insert the first System 7.5.5 floppy disk or open the first System 7.5.5 installation folder and start the Installer program by double-clicking its icon.
3. The Installer program displays an Apple license agreement for you to read and optionally print. Click the Agree button to continue. The Installer's main window appears. This window identifies the disk on which the software will be installed and describes what will be installed, as shown in Figure 22-10.

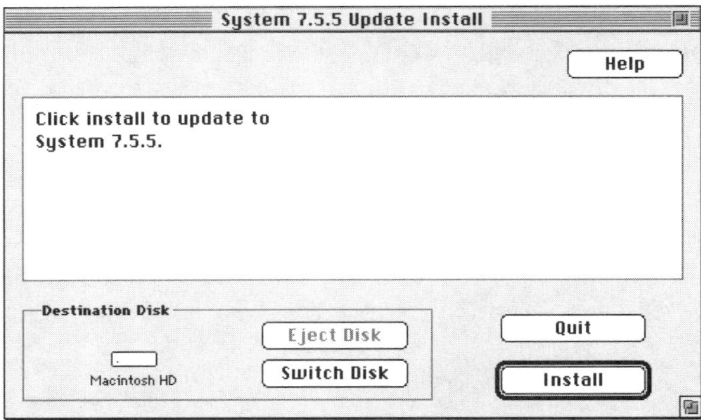


**Figure 22-10: The main window for the System 7.5.5 Installer.**

4. Make sure the destination-disk name is the one on which you want to install the software. If you have more than one hard disk, you can switch disks by clicking the Switch Disk button.

5. Click the Install button in the main Installer window to begin installation. The Installer briefly displays the message "Preparing to install." If you are installing onto the startup disk and other programs are open (such as SimpleText), the Installer displays an alert message advising you that it can't continue while other applications are open. You can click a Cancel button to cancel installation or click a Continue button to have the Installer quit the other open applications. (The Installer also turns off file sharing if it is on.) As each application quits, it may come to the front and ask whether you want to save any changes that you haven't yet saved. After quitting the other open applications, the Installer displays the folders (or disks) it will need and commences installation, as shown in Figure 22-11.

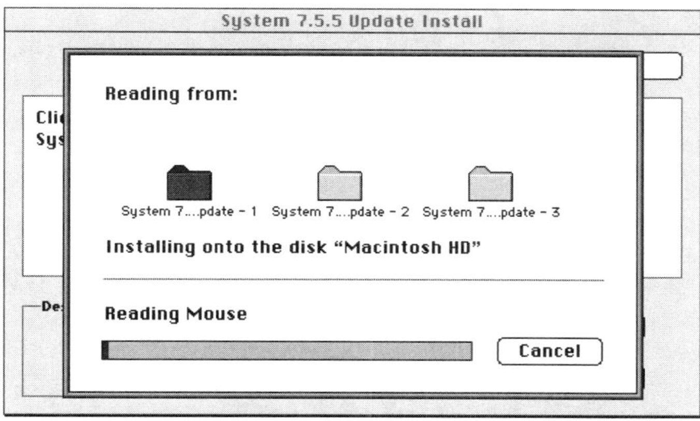


**Figure 22-11: Installation of the System 7.5.5 upgrade is underway.**

If you are installing from floppy disks and the Installer needs a different disk, the Installer ejects the disk it used and asks you to insert the next disk it needs. You can always cancel an installation by clicking the Cancel button.

6. When the Installer finishes upgrading to System 7.5.5, it tells you to restart the computer to use the new system software.

After upgrading to System 7.5.5, you can still install individual components of System 7.5.3 such as desktop printing or the Control Strip. You can use the System 7.5 Version 7.5.3 installation CD-ROM or floppy disks as described in "Installing System 7.5.3 or 7.5 — Custom" below. You can also use System 7.5 Update 2.0 to install individual components of System 7.5.3 onto System 7.5.5, but only if you obtain a special installer script from Apple. The regular installer script that comes with System 7.5 Update 2.0 will not allow you to install individual components into System 7.5.5. The special installer script, named Sys 7.5 Upd 2.0 Custom Install, is available from the Unsupported folder of Apple's on-line software archives, whose locations are described in "Obtaining

Installation Software" at the beginning of this chapter. Apple does not provide any support for the special installer script, so you can't call 800-SOS-APPLE if you have trouble with it.

# Installing System 7.5.3 or 7.5

Installing all of the software that comes with System 7.5.3 or its predecessor System 7.5 involves using several Installer programs. There is one Installer for the basic system software, a second Installer for the optional QuickDraw GX software, and a third Installer for the optional PowerTalk software. System 7.5.3 on CD-ROM includes Installers for additional optional software including QuickDraw 3D and PlainTalk.

The following section tells you how to install all or part of the basic System 7.5.3 or System 7.5 software. To install additional system software such as QuickDraw GX, PowerTalk, or OpenDoc, follow the instructions in "Installing Additional System Software" later in this chapter.

Before installing or upgrading to a new version of system software, be sure to back up the startup disk, verify the disk directories, update the hard disk driver software, and turn off all but the necessary extensions and control panels (see "Preparing for Installation" earlier in this chapter). If you have a RAM disk smaller than 416K, you must move its contents to another disk prior to installing or upgrading to System 7.5.3. Effective with System 7.5.3, the minimum RAM disk size is 416K. A smaller RAM disk will be turned off and its contents lost when you restart your computer after installing System 7.5.3.

## Installing System 7.5.3 or 7.5 — standard

The following steps tell you how to install all the basic components of System 7.5.3 or 7.5, optionally doing a clean installation:

1. Locate the Installer program for the basic system software. On a System 7.5 Version 7.5.3 CD-ROM, the Installer has an alias in the System Software Installers folder. On a System 7.5 CD-ROM, the Installer is in the System Install folder inside the Installation folder. On a set of floppy disks for System 7.5.3 or 7.5, the Installer is on the disk labeled Install Disk 1.
2. Start the Installer program. After a few seconds, the Installer displays a welcome message. When you dismiss the welcome message, the Installer's main window appears. This window identifies the disk on which the software will be installed and describes what will be installed, as shown in Figure 22-12.
3. Make sure that the destination disk name is the one on which you want to install the software. If you have more than one hard disk, you can switch disks by clicking the Switch Disk button.

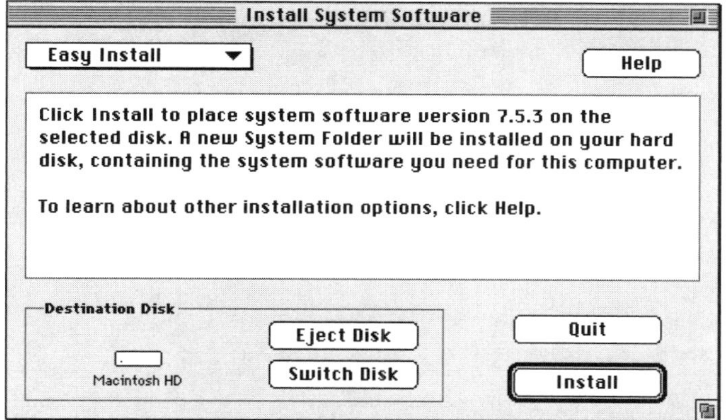


**Figure 22-12: The main window of the System 7.5.3 Installer.**

4. Click the Install button in the main Installer window to begin installation.

   If you want to perform a clean installation, press ⌘-Shift-K. This brings up a dialog box in which you indicate the type of installation you want. Select the Install New System Folder option, and then click OK. In the main Installer window, click the Clean Install button to begin installation.

5. The Installer briefly displays the message "Preparing to install." If you are installing onto the startup disk and other programs are open (such as SimpleText), the Installer displays an alert message advising you that it can't continue while other applications are open. You can click a Cancel button to cancel installation or click a Continue button to have the Installer quit the other open applications. (The Installer also turns off file sharing if it is on.) As each application quits, it may come to the front and ask whether you want to save any changes that you haven't yet saved. After quitting the other open applications, the Installer displays the folders (or disks) that will be needed and commences installation, as shown in Figure 22-13.

   If you are installing from floppy disks and the Installer needs a different disk, the Installer ejects the disk that it used and asks you to insert the next disk it needs. You can always cancel an installation by clicking the Cancel button.

6. When the Installer finishes, it asks whether you want to continue doing installations. Click the Continue button if you want to repeat Steps 3 through 5 to install on other disks. Otherwise quit the Installer and restart the computer to use the new system software.

Installing System 7.5.3 resets the Apple Menu Options and Views control panels to their original factory settings. If you had changed settings in either of those control panels, you will need to reset them after installing System 7.5.3.

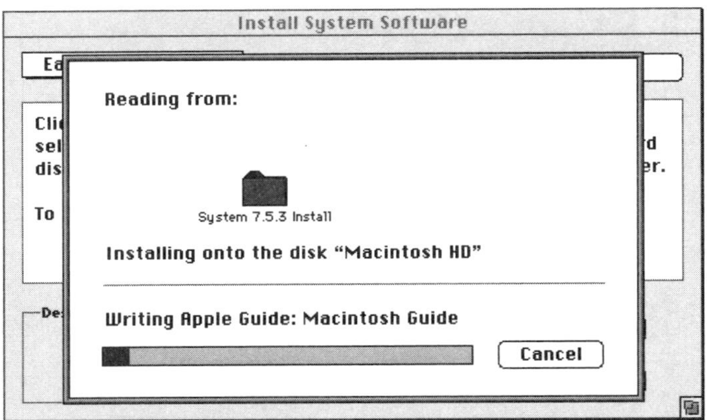


**Figure 22-13: Installation of System 7.5.3 is underway.**

After performing a clean installation of System 7.5.3 on a Mac OS computer with PCI slots, virtual memory will be turned on. You can turn off virtual memory in the Memory control panel.

After performing a clean installation of System 7.5, the About This Macintosh command (in the Apple menu when the Finder is active) no longer reports a specific Macintosh model name. Instead it displays a generic name such as Macintosh, Macintosh PowerBook, or Power Macintosh. If you upgrade to System 7.5 without doing a clean installation, the About This Macintosh command continues reporting the specific model name.

## Installing System 7.5.3 or 7.5 — custom

In a custom installation of System 7.5.3 or 7.5, you can select the individual components you want installed. The following are some of the components you may need to install using the Custom Install option:

- Printer driver software for a kind of printer you haven't used before
- Control Strip, which provides quick access to various control panel settings
- Easy Access, which lets you move the pointer with the numeric keypad, type a key combination one stroke at a time, and so on
- Close View, which can magnify the entire display image

Do a custom installation only if you are sure that you know which individual items must be present for the software to work properly. If you're not sure, do a standard installation as described in "Installing System 7.5.3 or 7.5 — Standard" above.

To perform a custom installation, and optionally do a clean custom installation, follow these steps:

1. Locate the Installer program for the basic system software. On a System 7.5.3 CD-ROM, it has an alias in the System Software Installers folder. On a System 7.5 CD-ROM, the Installer is in the System Install folder inside the Installation folder. On a set of floppy disks for System 7.5.3 or 7.5, the Installer is on the disk labeled Install Disk 1.
2. Start the Installer program. After a few seconds, the Installer displays a welcome message. When you dismiss the welcome message, the Installer's main window appears. This window identifies the disk on which the software will be installed and describes what will be installed.
3. Choose Custom Install from the pop-up menu. The Installer lists groups of components that you can install, as shown in Figure 22-14.

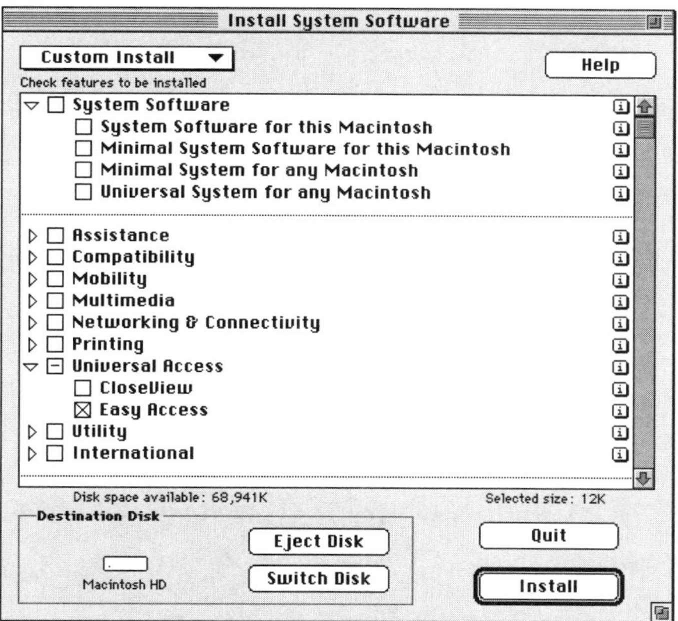


**Figure 22-14: Selecting components of System 7.5.3 to be installed.**

4. Select the components that you want to install by clicking the appropriate checkboxes. To expand a component group, click the triangle next to it. You can get information about a component by clicking its information button at the right side of the Installer window.

5. When you finish making your selections, click the Install button to begin the installation process.

   If you want to perform a clean installation, press ⌘-Shift-K. This brings up a dialog box in which you indicate the type of installation you want. Select the Install New System Folder option, and then click OK. In the main Installer window, click the Clean Install button to begin installation.

6. The Installer briefly displays the message "Preparing to install." If you are installing onto the startup disk and other programs are open (such as SimpleText), the Installer displays an alert message advising you that it can't continue while other applications are open. You can click a Cancel button to cancel installation or click a Continue button to have the Installer quit the other open applications. (The Installer also turns off file sharing if it is on.) As each application quits, it may come to the front and ask whether you want to save any changes that you haven't yet saved. After quitting the other open applications, the Installer displays the folders (or disks) that will be needed and commences installation. If you are installing from floppy disks and the Installer needs a different disk, the Installer ejects the disk that it used and asks you to insert the next disk it needs. You can always cancel an installation by clicking the Cancel button.

7. When the Installer finishes, it tells you to restart the computer to use the new system software.

After performing a clean installation of the Custom Install component "Minimal System for any Macintosh" or "Universal System for any Macintosh" for System 7.5.3, virtual memory will be turned on. You can turn off virtual memory in the Memory control panel.

Installing System 7.5.3 resets the Apple Menu Options and Views control panels to their original factory settings. If you had changed settings in either of those control panels, you will need to reset them after installing System 7.5.3.

## Upgrading with System 7.5 Update 2

You can use System 7.5 Update 2.0 to upgrade to System 7.5.3 from System 7.5, 7.5.1, or 7.5.2. To upgrade from an earlier version of System 7, use the System 7.5 Version 7.5 CD-ROM or disks, as described in "Installing System 7.5.3 or 7.5 — Standard" above.

To use System 7.5 Update 2.0, follow these steps:

1. Insert the System 7.5 Update 2.0 CD-ROM or the first floppy disk, and start the Installer program by double-clicking its icon.

2. The Installer program displays a welcome message. When you dismiss the welcome message, the Installer's main window appears. This window identifies the disk on which the software will be installed and describes what will be installed, as shown in Figure 22-15.

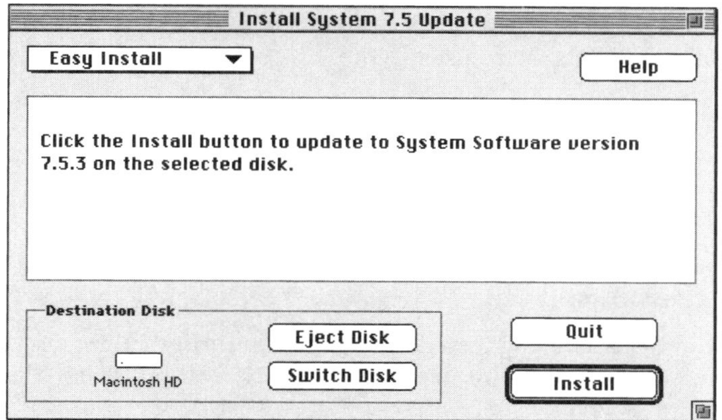


**Figure 22-15: The main window for the System 7.5 Update 2.0 Installer.**

3. Make sure that the destination disk name is the one on which you want to install the software. If you have more than one hard disk, you can switch disks by clicking the Switch Disk button.

4. Click the Install button in the main Installer window to begin installation. The Installer briefly displays the message "Preparing to install." If you are installing onto the startup disk and other programs are open (such as SimpleText), the Installer displays an alert message advising you that it can't continue while other applications are open. You can click a Cancel button to cancel installation or click a Continue button to have the Installer quit the other open applications. (The Installer also turns off file sharing if it is on.) As each application quits, it may come to the front and ask whether you want to save any changes that you haven't yet saved. After quitting the other open applications, the Installer displays the folders (or disks) it will need and commences installation.

   If you are installing from floppy disks and the Installer needs a different disk, the Installer ejects the disk that it used and asks you to insert the next disk it needs. You can always cancel an installation by clicking the Cancel button.

5. When the Installer finishes upgrading to System 7.5.3, it tells you to restart the computer to use the new system software.

# Installing Additional System Software

Apple periodically releases new or upgraded system software modules that you can add to existing versions of System 7. Examples from the past include QuickTime, QuickDraw GX, QuickDraw 3D, AppleScript, PlainTalk, and

PowerTalk. You install most add-on system software with an Installer program, and the following steps usually apply:

1. Locate the Installer program for the add-on software, and start the Installer by double-clicking its icon.
2. If the Installer displays a welcome message, dismiss it to proceed with the installation.
3. If the Installer displays a license agreement, you must agree to its terms to continue installation.
4. When the Installer's main window appears, confirm that the destination disk is correct. If you have more than one hard disk, you can switch disks by clicking the Switch Disk button (see Figure 22-16).

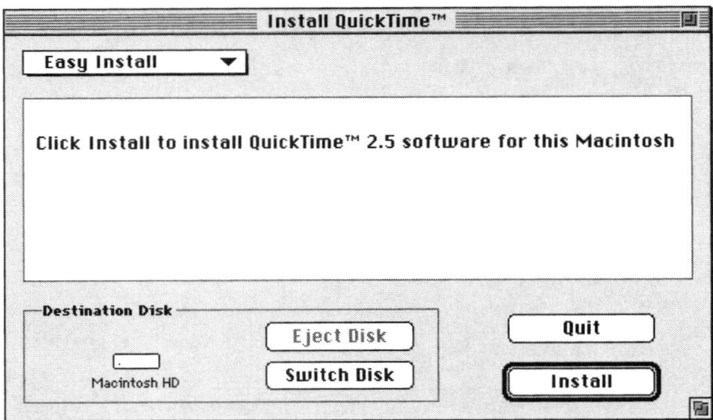


**Figure 22-16: An Installer's main window.**

5. To install the complete add-on software module, choose Easy Install from the pop-up menu in the Installer's main window and click the Install button in that window. If there is no pop-up menu in the Installer window, simply click the Install button.

   To selectively install portions of the add-on software module, choose Custom Install from the pop-up menu in the Installer window. The Installer lists components, and in some cases groups of components that you can install. To expand a component group, click the triangle next to it. You can get information about a component by clicking its information button at the right side of the Installer window. Select the components that you want to install by clicking their checkboxes, and then click the Install button (see Figure 22-17).

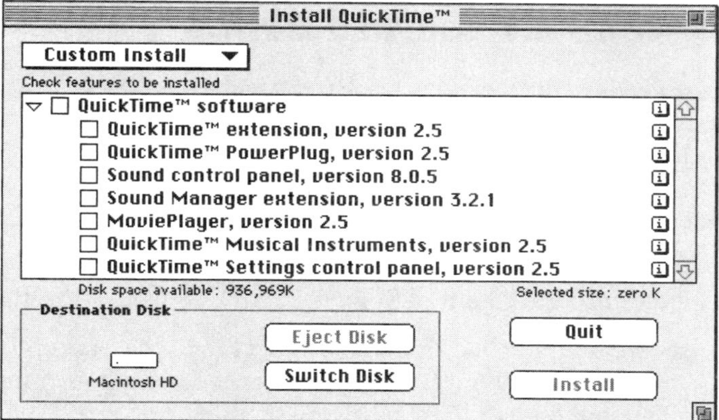


**Figure 22-17: Selecting components to be installed from an add-on software module.**

6. The Installer briefly displays the message "Preparing to install" and then commences installation. If you are installing from floppy disks and the Installer needs a different disk, the Installer ejects the disk that it used and asks you to insert the next disk it needs. You can always cancel an installation by clicking the Cancel button.

7. When the Installer finishes, it may ask if you want to quit or continue doing installations; quit unless you want to repeat Steps 4 through 6 to install the module on other disks. Alternatively, the Installer may tell you to restart the computer to use the new system software.

# Upgrading System 7 on Old Mac Performas

Some Macintosh Performa models came with System 7.0.1P, 7.1P, or 7.1.2P installed, and those versions had special features to make them more appealing to people who use computers at home. Those Performas work perfectly well with regular System 7 software. You can purchase a newer version of System 7 from a software reseller and install it on a Performa as described in the preceding sections. System 7.5 and later have all the special features that were unique to the Performa versions of System 7.1 and 7.0.1. The affected Performa models are the 200, 250, 400, 405, 410, 430, 450, 460, 465, 467, 475, 476, 550, 560, 575, 577, 578, 600, 600CD, 630, 630CD, 635CD, 636, 636CD, 637CD, and 638CD.

# Installing System 7.1.2 and Earlier

The Installer for System 7 versions prior to System 7.5 gives you the option of a standard installation or a custom installation, but does not have a built-in option for clean installation. To perform a clean installation of System 7.1.2 or earlier, you must start by deactivating the current System Folder while preserving all of the desk accessories, system extensions, sounds, and control panels that you have added to the System Folder over time.

To set up for a clean installation of System 7.1.2 or earlier, follow these steps:

1. Open the System Folder and drag the System file to the Startup Items folder. If you are upgrading from System 6, create a new folder inside the System Folder and drag the System file to that new folder.
2. Close the System Folder window and change the name of the System Folder to Previous System Folder.

To install System 7.1.2 or earlier from floppy disks or CD-ROM, follow these steps:

1. Insert the floppy disk named Install 1, and open it if necessary. If you are using a CD-ROM, insert it and open the Install 1 folder.
2. Start the Installer program by double-clicking its icon in the Install 1 window.
3. When the "Welcome to the Installer" notice appears, click the OK button to proceed. The Easy Install dialog box appears.
4. Make sure the hard disk named is the one on which you want to install the software. If you have more than one hard disk, you can switch disks by clicking the Switch Disk button.
5. If you want to install only portions of the system software, click the Customize button. This brings up the Custom Installation dialog box, which lists all available modules of the system software.

   Scroll through the list and select the items you want to install. If you select one item, the Installer displays a detailed description of it. If you select multiple items, the Installer lists the first few by name. To select multiple items, press Shift while clicking each item.
6. Click the Install button. During installation, the Installer displays the name of the file that it currently is installing. If you are installing from floppy disks, the Installer periodically ejects the disk that it used and asks you to insert the next disk.
7. When the Installer finishes, it asks you if you want to quit or restart the Macintosh. Restart to begin using the new system software.

# Troubleshooting Installation Problems

If your computer will not restart after you install new Mac OS software, try restarting while holding down the Shift key until you see the message "Extensions Disabled." Then follow the instructions in the sidebar "Resolving a Conflict" to resolve a possible conflict among your system extensions. When you find an incompatible extension, disable it and contact its publisher about an upgrade.

If you don't want to troubleshoot an extension conflict, you can try doing a clean installation of the system software versions 7.6, 7.5.3, or 7.5 (see "Installing Mac OS 7.6 — Standard," "Installing Mac OS 7.6 — Custom," or "Installing System 7.5.3 or 7.5 — Standard" earlier in this chapter). If a clean installation clears up the problem, you can begin adding other items such as fonts, sounds, control panels, and extensions to the new System Folder. To keep the System Folder as clean as possible, you should install the additional items from their original installation disks. If you don't have the installation disks, you can move items from your old System Folder, which was renamed Previous System Folder. Look for items to move from the old Fonts folder, Apple Menu Items folder, Preferences folder, Extensions folder, Control Panels folder, System File, Startup Items folder, and the Previous System Folder itself. Move only a few items at a time, and make sure they do not cause a problem before moving more. You can use the Labels menu to categorize old items before you move them into the new System Folder. While moving items from the Previous System Folder or from folders inside it you may get a message asking if you want to replace items that already exist in the new System Folder. If you get a message like that, click Cancel unless you are very sure you want to replace items in the new System Folder with items from the Previous System Folder.

Sometimes problems occur after a clean installation that don't occur after upgrading the existing system software. For example, a PowerBook or other computer with an internal Express Modem and a Power Macintosh with a GeoPort Telecom Adapter will lose modem services after a clean installation because the Apple Telecom software that's required for modem services with those devices is not included in a clean installation. To troubleshoot problems with a clean installation, try moving items from the old System Folder (now named Previous System Folder) into equivalent places in the new System Folder as described in the previous paragraph. Alternatively, you can deactivate the new System Folder by opening it and dragging the System file into the Startup Items folder. Then activate the old System Folder, now named Previous System Folder, and restart the computer. Make a backup copy of the old System Folder, and then install the new system software without doing a clean installation.

If problems arise after installing new Mac OS software and they only affect a few application programs, contact the affected applications' publishers or developers for assistance. They may know about incompatibilities between their software and the new system software you just installed.

## Resolving a Conflict

If items you add to the System Folder, Extensions folder, or Control Panels folder don't work, if your computer refuses to start up, or if you start experiencing system crashes or freezes, then some of the system extensions in those places may be in conflict during startup. The easiest way to resolve an extension conflict is with Conflict Catcher from Casady & Greene, Inc. (408-484-9228, *http://www.casadyg.com*), or the Now Startup Manager from Now Software (503-274-2810, *http://www.nowsoft.com*). Those utilities take the place of the Extensions Manager control panel that comes with System 7.5 and later. Conflict Catcher and Now Startup Manager walk you through a diagnostic procedure that finds incompatible System Folder items in the least possible amount of time.

You can also troubleshoot a conflict between system extensions and control panels with the Extensions Manager control panel that comes with System 7.5 and later (see "Extensions Manager" in Chapter 19), but it is not nearly as convenient or foolproof as Conflict Catcher or Now Startup Manager. Start by disabling half of the extensions and control panels and restart. If this solves the problem, the offending item is among the disabled half of the extensions, so write down all of their names and enable half of them. If disabling half of the items did not cure the problem, the offending item is among the half you did not disable, so write down all of their names and disable half of them. In either case, you leave only half the group containing the offending item (one quarter of all extensions and control panels) enabled, and then restart. If the problem occurs again, the offender is among the group still enabled; if not, it is among the group you just disabled. Continue halving the offending group until you reduce it to a single item (the trouble-maker).

Sometimes changing the order in which the Mac OS loads system extensions during startup resolves a conflict. You can make an extension load before others by adding one or more blank spaces to the beginning of its name. You can make an extension load after others by adding a tilde (~) or diamond (◊) to the beginning of its name.

Regardless of their names, all items in the Extensions folder load before items in the Control Panels folder, and they load before items directly in the System Folder. To have a control panel whose name begins with blank spaces load before items in the Extensions folder, put that control panel in the Extensions folder. To have a control panel whose name starts with a tilde or diamond load last during startup, put that control panel in the System Folder. For convenient access to the control panels you move out of the Control Panels folder, make aliases of them and put the aliases in the Control Panels folder.

To have a system extension whose name begins with a tilde or diamond load last during startup,

*(continued on next page)*

(continued from previous page)

drag that extension from the Extensions folder to the System Folder. Leave system extensions whose names begin with blank spaces in the Extensions folder so they will be installed first during startup.

As a last resort, remove all system extensions and control panels to the desktop. Then put them in the System Folder (not the Extensions or Control Panels folder) one at a time, from most important to least. Restart your Macintosh each time you add another item to the System Folder. When you find an item that causes a conflict, discard it and try the next item you previously moved to the desktop. You may be able to resume using the items you discarded when they are next upgraded.

(If a conflict prevents starting up from your hard disk, start from a floppy disk with any version of system software. Make a change to the System Folder on the hard disk and try restarting from it.)

# CHAPTER 22 CONCEPTS AND TERMS

- Before installing a new version of System 7, you should back up your disks, verify disk directories, update hard disk driver software, and turn off all but the essential extensions and control panels.
- You can track installation activity with the Labels menu.
- A clean installation prevents the carrying over of damaged files from the previous system software, but a normal installation is quite effective and not nearly as much work.
- You can install any or all of the Mac OS 7.6 modules, each in its entirety, or you can selectively install portions of any module.
- You can install all or part of the basic System 7.5.3 or 7.5 software and optionally add QuickDraw GX and PowerTalk.
- To troubleshoot installation problems, check for extension conflicts with Conflict Catcher, Now Startup Utility, or Extensions Manager.

**installation**
Places a new or updated version of software on your disk.

**clean installation**
Deactivates your old System Folder and installs a new one with new copies of Mac OS software. You must then reconfigure control panels, reinstall application programs, and reset preferences in them.

**custom installation**
You can selectively install portions of the Mac OS 7.6 modules (or just parts of System 7.5 and QuickDraw GX). Do this only if you are sure that you know which individual items must be present for the software to work properly.

**easy installation**
Installs all of a module's components that are software recommended for your Mac model.

**standard installation**
For Mac OS 7.6, installs the basic modules — Mac OS, OpenDoc, and OpenDoc essentials — plus any additional modules you select. Each module is installed in its entirety.

For System 7.5.3 or 7.5, installs the basic system software components appropriate for your computer.

# Index

## — Symbols/ Numbers —



## — A —

## — D —

## — E —

## — F —

## — G —



## — H —

## —I—

## — J —



## — K —

## — L —



## — M —

## — O —



## — P —

## — Q —



## — R —

## — S —

## — T —



## — U —

## — V —



## — W —

## — Z —

# About the Author

**Lon Poole**, based in Kensington, California, is a contributing editor to *Macworld* magazine who answers readers' questions every month in his "Quick Tips" column. Lon helped create *Macworld* magazine in 1983, and writes feature articles for the publication regularly. His 1988 article entitled "Installing Memory" won a Maggie Award for Best How-To Article in a Consumer Publication. His feature article, "Here Comes System 7" was a finalist in the 1990 Excellence in Technology Communications competition. His three-part series, "How It Works" won First Place, Best In-Depth Technical Feature Article 1993 from the American Society of Business Press Editors.

In addition, Lon Poole has authored five Macintosh books, including the best-selling *Macworld Guide to System 7*. He also wrote the now-classic *Apple II User's Guide*, which sold over a half million copies worldwide. He has been writing books about personal computers and their practical applications since 1976. He has a BA in Computer Science from the University of California, Berkeley.

# Credits

**Senior Vice President and Group Publisher**
Brenda McLaughlin

**Director of Publishing**
Walt Bruce

**Acquisitions Editor**
Nancy E. Dunn

**Marketing Manager**
Melisa M. Duffy

**Executive Managing Editor**
Terry Somerson

**Editorial Assistant**
Sharon Eames

**Development Editor**
Amy Thomas

**Copy Editor**
Katharine Dvorak

**Technical Editor**
Dennis Cohen

**Production Director**
Andrew Walker

**Project Coordinator**
Katy German

**Layout and Graphics**
Renée Dunn
Andreas F. Schueller

**Quality Control Specialist**
Mick Arellano

**Proofreader**
Christine Langin-Faris

**Indexer**
Sherry Massey

**Production Administration**
Tony Augsburger
Todd Klemme
Jason Marcuson
Christopher Pimentel
Leslie Popplewell
Theresa Sánchez-Baker
Melissa Stauffer

# IDG BOOKS WORLDWIDE REGISTRATION CARD

RETURN THIS REGISTRATION CARD FOR FREE CATALOG

**Title of this book:** Macworld® System 7.6 Bible

**My overall rating of this book:** ❑ Very good [1] ❑ Good [2] ❑ Satisfactory [3] ❑ Fair [4] ❑ Poor [5]

**How I first heard about this book:**

❑ Found in bookstore; name: [6] ❑ Book review: [7]

❑ Advertisement: [8] ❑ Catalog: [9]

❑ Word of mouth; heard about book from friend, co-worker, etc.: [10] ❑ Other: [11]

**What I liked most about this book:**

**What I would change, add, delete, etc., in future editions of this book:**

**Other comments:**

**Number of computer books I purchase in a year:** ❑ 1 [12] ❑ 2-5 [13] ❑ 6-10 [14] ❑ More than 10 [15]

**I would characterize my computer skills as:** ❑ Beginner [16] ❑ Intermediate [17] ❑ Advanced [18] ❑ Professional [19]

**I use** ❑ DOS [20] ❑ Windows [21] ❑ OS/2 [22] ❑ Unix [23] ❑ Macintosh [24] ❑ Other: [25] ________ (please specify)

**I would be interested in new books on the following subjects:**
(please check all that apply, and use the spaces provided to identify specific software)

❑ Word processing: [26] ❑ Spreadsheets: [27]

❑ Data bases: [28] ❑ Desktop publishing: [29]

❑ File Utilities: [30] ❑ Money management: [31]

❑ Networking: [32] ❑ Programming languages: [33]

❑ Other: [34]

**I use a PC at** (please check all that apply): ❑ home [35] ❑ work [36] ❑ school [37] ❑ other: [38] ________

**The disks I prefer to use are** ❑ 5.25 [39] ❑ 3.5 [40] ❑ other: [41] ________

**I have a CD ROM:** ❑ yes [42] ❑ no [43]

**I plan to buy or upgrade computer hardware this year:** ❑ yes [44] ❑ no [45]

**I plan to buy or upgrade computer software this year:** ❑ yes [46] ❑ no [47]

Name: Business title: [48] Type of Business: [49]

Address (❑ home [50] ❑ work [51]/Company name: )

Street/Suite#

City [52]/State [53]/Zipcode [54]: Country [55]

❑ **I liked this book!** You may quote me by name in future IDG Books Worldwide promotional materials.

My daytime phone number is ________

IDG BOOKS®

THE WORLD OF COMPUTER KNOWLEDGE

# YES!

Please keep me informed about IDG's World of Computer Knowledge. Send me the latest IDG Books catalog.

NO POSTAGE NECESSARY IF MAILED IN THE UNITED STATES

**BUSINESS REPLY MAIL**

FIRST CLASS MAIL PERMIT NO. 2605 FOSTER CITY, CALIFORNIA

**IDG Books Worldwide**
**919 E Hillsdale Blvd, STE 400**
**Foster City, CA 94404-9691**